PROGRESS

INTO THE PAST

PROGRESS

INTO THE PAST

THE REDISCOVERY OF MYCENAEAN CIVILIZATION

SECOND EDITION

WILLIAM A. McDONALD
CAROL G. THOMAS

INDIANA UNIVERSITY PRESS
Bloomington and Indianapolis

The Indiana University Press gratefully acknowledges the support of the Archaeological Institute of America in the preparation of the second edition of this work.

Manufactured in the United States of America

Library of Congress Cataloging-in-Publication Data

McDonald, William A. (William Andrew)
Progress into the past: the rediscovery of Mycenaean civilization
William A. McDonald, Carol G. Thomas.—2nd ed.
p.cm.
Bibliography: p.
Includes index.
ISBN 0-253-33627-9.—ISBN 0-253-20553-0 (pbk.)
1. Civilization, Mycenaean. 2. Greece—Antiquities. I. Thomas, Carol G. II. Title.
DF220.5.M37 1990
938—dc20   89-45196
                                                                                      CIP

1 2 3 4 5 94 93 92 91 90

TO

Elizabeth, Sue and Betsy

for faith, hope and charity

in the busy months when these chapters

were being written

CONTENTS

ILLUSTRATIONS

Following page 494

Maps

Part Title Illustrations

PREFACE TO THE
SECOND EDITION

I N 1983, I ORDERED *Progress into the Past* for use in a course on early Greece and learned that it was out of print with no plans for reprinting. My disappointment with the book's unavailability was the first step in the process that has led to this second edition.

The next step was taken at a conference in New York in May of 1984. William McDonald and I were participants in a symposium entitled "Pylos Comes Alive," planned by Bronze Age specialists Thomas Palaima and Cynthia Shelmerdine. It was obviously a propitious occasion to discuss the possibility of reviving an account that explains exactly how Pylos and other Mycenaean sites were brought to light in the past century and a quarter.

Two advances toward this end result occurred almost simultaneously. Indiana University Press agreed to publish a revised edition, and the Publications Committee of the American Institute of Archaeology, then chaired by Robert Carter and more recently directed by Machteld Mellink, voted a subsidy to help defray expenses, particularly those costs associated with the illustrative material. As important as the illustrations are to the book, the subsidy was also a tribute to Professor McDonald whose work in the field, as well as in print, has carried research forward in creative, fundamental directions. Thus, not only the AIA grant but this volume are intended to do honor to the man and his achievements.

Professor McDonald has read the revised and new materials offering his advice, but he should bear none of the criticism that they may generate. The first seven chapters have not been altered. Chapter eight has been revised and renamed; chapter nine is a new chapter; and chapter ten, formerly nine, reflects the current state of opinion on the subjects discussed in the first edition and adds several topics that have generated theories.or raised problems in the last two decades. Bibliographic material has been expanded and updated; there is an additional map designating sites recently investigated; a new index reflects the additions. In adding to or revising the sections, every attempt has been made to conform to the original biographical and historical approach. Perhaps the most significant difference is due to the proliferation of important figures in the field. It has not been possible to study the most recent developments through two or three key figures; consequently, the bibliographic element has diminished.

The goal of the second edition also remains much the same: it is a study of the rediscovery of the Mycenaean civilization. The time dimensions have expanded: the one hundred years during which the discovery occurred up to the original publication of *Progress into the Past* has grown to 125 years. And it is necessary to lengthen the epoch known as Mycenaean; recent scholarship has demonstrated both its earlier roots and its later significance. The endurance of elements of Mycenaean culture carries the account further into the period known as the Dark Age. In fact, this portion of the story has enriched our understanding of the relationship between the world of Homer and the Heroic Age of the Mycenaeans.

This edition owes a debt to many people and publications. At the head of the list stands the name of William McDonald, who first told the story and whose advice was essential to presenting the sequel. For the plethora of detail in archaeological work in Greece, *Archaeological Reports* is an invaluable tool. Published annually by the Hellenic Society and the British School at Athens, the reports survey major activities in all phases of archaeological investigation, not simply Bronze Age. In many instances, there is a lengthy time lag between discovery and official publication. Especially in these cases, the accounts provide timely notices of finds or work in progress. The current editor is H. W. Catling, whose name occurs in several contexts in *Progress into the Past*. Other editors whose volumes guided me from 1965 to the present were A. H. S. Megaw until 1968 and P. M. Frazer, who edited the Reports between 1968 and 1971.

Another essential form of bibliographic assistance was provided by the editors of *Nestor,* published now by the Program in Classical Archaeology at Indiana University. Its scope is Bronze Age Aegean research and scholarship. Notices of conferences, meetings, published scholarship and reviews are worldwide in their compass.

This book is intended for students, that is, those who are adherents of Socrates' view that it is incumbent to always seek after new knowledge whether or not one is enrolled in formal classes. As a faculty member, I constantly hope to meet people who fit this definition. It is my great joy to have known several such individuals. Special acknowledgments are owed to Anne Lou Robkin, who has added new illustrations in the character of the original drawings, and to Lis Stubberfield for her assistance in the compilation of the new index.

Carol G. Thomas

PREFACE

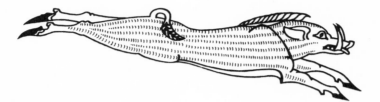

I N A VERY REAL SENSE all scholarship is motivated by curiosity and an urge to investigate mysteries. So this is going to be a kind of detective story, a historical whodunit. Yet the analogy is not exact or complete. For example, you will not find "the answer" by peeking at the last chapter. Ironically enough, if a scientist is fortunate in "solving" a minor puzzle, the solution usually involves new and deeper mysteries.

In a standard mystery novel we finally learn that the culprit was the imperturbable butler or the harmless old gardener. In our story, on the contrary, such neat and satisfying solutions are conspicuously lacking. If we may be pardoned for comparing the Dorians with the butler and the "gray Minyan people" with the gardener, both are suspected of certain crimes of violence; but they as well as their victims are no longer available for questioning. Some intriguing clues have been left at the scene, however, and it may eventually be possible to construct an airtight case against them or to exonerate them completely. Meanwhile, it is entertaining to follow what the experts have so far made of the developing evidence and even to have a try ourselves.

The chief source of information in our search will be the clues unearthed by three detectives—or excavators, as they are known in archaeological circles. Each of them has made crucial contributions toward the solution of a complicated series of historical puzzles that can be summed up under the term "Mycenaean civilization." We shall also be interested in learning what these three and other scholarly sleuths have been able to discover about the relationship between this Mycenaean civilization and Homer's famous epic poems, the *Iliad* and the *Odyssey*.

Our three guides are giants and pioneers in their profession. This book is intended as a tribute to them, but it is not (we hope) an uncritical eulogy. Heinrich Schliemann laid the foundations of Greek prehistoric archaeology between 1870 and 1890; Arthur Evans in the next generation established its reputation as an exact field of research; Carl Blegen, still

vigorous in the waning years of the third generation, guided the developing science into responsible and flexible maturity.

The usual way to organize an account of any early civilization is to compose a synthesis of solid knowledge and responsible inference as it exists
at the moment of writing. Scholars who made major contributions at various earlier stages of the reconstruction will of course be mentioned; but
the approach will be *contemporary* and *encyclopedic*. The author will sum
up as fairly as he can the verdict of his own day on the available information. Fortunately, several dependable handbooks of this sort have recently
been produced by competent scholars in our field.

In contrast, however, we intend to use the *biographical* and *historical*
approach to our subject. That is, we shall review the evidence on Mycenaean civilization as it has been gradually accumulating over the past
ninety-five years. The successive discoveries and reactions to discoveries
will be seen, as far as possible, through the eyes of the protagonists themselves. Our method has unavoidable drawbacks and may at times tax the
reader's patience and powers of recall and concentration. This approach
is bound to take up more space, which means that we must be drastically
selective to keep the account within reasonable bounds. Crucial conclusions and hypotheses have to be fully presented, even though some of them
were subsequently disproved or modified. The discussion of a particular
problem must be interrupted and then resumed when later evidence produced new light on its solution. Yet, if followed faithfully and judiciously,
the historical approach ought to result in a sounder appreciation of the
process by which present-day evaluations have been reached. The reader
can be drawn into a kind of active re-creation and partnership as the successive stages of discovery and interpretation are reviewed, rather than
simply being informed about the end product.

On the biographical side, personal anecdotes about Schliemann, Evans
and Blegen will be kept to a minimum. No connected account of extra-
professional aspects of their careers will be attempted. We shall come to
know these unusually able and fortunate men almost entirely in terms of
their archaeological work—or, perhaps better, to see their professional
accomplishments through their own developing experience. A valuable
means to this end is to quote often and at length from their publications.
Sometimes the way in which an idea is expressed reveals more about the
speaker or writer than does the idea itself. Style and diction offer fascinating
insights into the personality of eras as well as individuals.

We may as well attempt at this point to face a perfectly natural question: "Why single out only three protagonists? Aren't you slighting other
pioneers of equal or nearly equal stature?" Very possibly we are, although

we have tried not to. A separate chapter on Michael Ventris was at one time projected. His brilliant achievement, announced in 1952, would so far have to be ranked first among the claims of several contenders for primacy in the present (fourth) generation. As for contemporaries of the three we have chosen, other historians of the science might feel compelled to assign an equally prominent place to such great figures as Christos Tsountas, Wilhelm Dörpfeld and Alan Wace. And in a real sense, apart from such distinctions as chapter headings, these men do occupy a comparable position in our narrative.

The names and contributions of dozens of other talented scholars will of course be found on nearly every page. In a sense, every innovator who makes an independent discovery or sees a new and meaningful relationship in previous discoveries is a pioneer; and it may be unrealistic as well as risky to attempt to single out *the* outstanding figure in each generation of a science. Yet no one who has studied the record would deny that Schliemann, Evans and Blegen were authentic pacesetters. There is something mysterious about such individuals. They seem to possess a special blend of brilliance, self-assurance, intuition and luck. Scholars of this caliber do not appear very often in any field of study.

A colleague who generously consented to read these chapters in manuscript suggested that a fair number of important excavations and excavators find no place in the narrative. He appended a list of such items, which incidentally could easily be quadrupled. The only rejoinder is that this was intended from the start to be a selective, not a complete historical account. As such, it is sure to incur the criticism of some specialists, particularly those who may rightly feel that their own work has been slighted.

Perhaps a valid objection may also be made to the concentration on excavations and research published in English. Again, to attempt to justify the basis for selection may only make matters worse. It may or may not be a fair judgment that our German, French and Italian colleagues have been more interested in earlier or later horizons, or in Crete rather than the Greek mainland. Nevertheless, omissions of vital contributions by scholars of any nationality to the subject *as we have defined it* are to be attributed solely to ignorance; and sincere apologies are hereby offered.

Our story has two dimensions in time. One is the comparatively short span of slightly less than 100 years before the present. In it our pioneers and their colleagues lived their lives and made their contributions to Greek prehistory. The second is a much longer epoch, extending from about 1600 to 1100 years before the birth of Christ. In the Aegean area this period is technically known as the Late Bronze Age. Those far-off days when Mycenaean civilization grew and flourished and died became almost

as real to Schliemann, Evans and Blegen as the time into which they themselves were actually born. Indeed, every dedicated archaeologist and historian, as he gains familiarity with his chosen period of time, does begin to
lead a double life. If the following pages should succeed in producing something of the same effect on a few impressionable readers even for a matter
of hours, they will have more than fulfilled the author's hopes.

There are, of course, a great many interesting prehistoric cultures that
archaeologists all over the world are bringing to light. But our particular
chapter of man's kaleidoscopic past can perhaps claim a special place for
at least three reasons. The Mycenaean age is in a material sense better
documented than most of its fellows; it has the immense advantage of
contact (however complex and controversial) with the earliest known
European mythology and literature; and it left a rather impressive cultural
legacy to the classical Greek civilization that flourished roughly a thousand
years later.

Our geographical focus is the Greek mainland; but contemporary phases
at Troy and in Crete and some of the smaller islands form such an integral
part of the story that they have to be included. The contemporary situation
in the Near East is taken into account only so far as is necessary to understand Mycenaean contacts there or vice versa. For the same reason, the
whole of Europe is involved to some degree.

The criteria for material to be included in the following chapters were
originally based on relevance either to the work of our three pioneers or
to the illumination of the Homeric poems. Yet in practice such distinctions are extremely slippery. The story is really indivisible and cumulative.
An obviously relevant problem has a frustrating tendency to require the
inclusion of a less vital item, and so on. This eventually seemed to require
what might be called "synopses of syntheses" to link the three main chapters. That is, at three junctures (about 1900, 1920 and 1939) highlights
are excerpted from one or two publications that best sum up the state of
knowledge in their respective epochs. This method has the advantage of
ensuring the historical continuity; and it does not seem to obscure seriously the biographical context. It also became clear during the writing that
a somewhat comparable account was needed for the years since World
War II. And, finally, some kind of overview had to be attempted. These
subjects constitute the bases for the last two chapters.

A word now about Homeric parallels and comparisons. To Schliemann,
the connection was simple enough. Archaeology was the means of au-
thenticating and illustrating the poems, much as biblical archaeology is
still regarded in some quarters nowadays. Later excavators in our field
have usually been more cautious; but parallels in Homeric epic and tradi-

tional mythology are almost inevitably in the back of their minds as they handle new material and review former discoveries. We shall therefore pay particular attention to the way in which successive generations have assessed the connections and realized the discrepancies. Selected references (arabic numerals in the text, correlated with Homeric References) are supplied in particular contexts; but they should be regarded as samples only. A thorough correlation would have been tedious for the general reader; and a detailed account of the technical problems in each case would have been intolerably complicated. The reader whose interest is sufficiently piqued may browse among the specialized studies that are recommended in the list of Suggested Reading.

Those already familiar with the *Iliad* and the *Odyssey* will no doubt be at a considerable advantage as they follow our story. Homer-less readers might be well advised to spend a few hours with a good translation of the poems before plunging into this narrative. They will certainly not regret the experience. But the process can be reversed. A quick mind innocent of Homer should have little trouble in following the narrative; and this book will have truly accomplished its purpose if a few of its "graduates" decide that the next items on their reading list will be the Homeric epics themselves.

A few words may be required to draw attention to additional features of the book that are meant to be of assistance to the reader. The Glossary contains definitions and explanations of certain technical terms. They have been purposely kept to the minimum but a fair number are needed for clarity and brevity. Also included are identifications of ancient proper names that occur in the narrative. An asterisk (*) is printed with the first occurrence of each item to remind the reader of the existence of the *Glossary*. Also, throughout the book dimensions and distances, which are regularly indicated by the metric system in scientific publications, have been converted (even within quotes) to fairly close equivalents in English feet and miles.

The spelling of proper names and the use and formulation of technical terms may cause some unavoidable confusion because of the individual preferences of the various authorities whose direct words are quoted. Apart from quotations, however, it is hoped that the terminology is simple and consistent and that the spelling system is also as consistent and accurate as the complicated problems of transcription and usage allow. In the Index the stressed syllable in all unusual Greek proper names has been indicated, as in Zygouriés.

Geographical locations are essential to follow the narrative, and the reader is directed to a brief atlas at the back of the book. Most locations are indicated in the general map of the Aegean area. Other sites may be found on the general map of the Mediterranean. There are also detailed maps of the immediate area of the major sites of Troy, Mycenae, Knossos and Pylos.

The list of Suggested Reading is provided for those who become interested in following up the general subject or specific topics in more detail. The arrangement is alphabetical by author. The list is rather rigorously selective and is meant particularly for the reader whose only language is English. For the occasional reader who may want to check the source of specific quotations, detailed Chapter Bibliographies have been provided. Here again, however, there has been no attempt to supply a comprehensive bibliography on the whole subject.

Finally, some well-earned acknowledgments are due various persons. The original idea for the book evolved in 1962 during a canoe trip with two of my friends, Professors Walter Pattison and Reginald Allen. In the following year a College Honors Seminar provided the opportunity to develop it with a group of talented undergraduates majoring in a variety of departments. More of the content of Chapters II, IV and VI than I can now identify is owed to the stimulation and rapport of those pleasant weekly meetings.

As the book began to take shape, I discussed its progress (or lack of same) with a neighbor, Stanley Aschenbrenner, manager of Product Design and Coordination, Control Data Corporation. He most generously offered to read and criticize preliminary drafts of each chapter and to provide in advance the typical reactions of the kind of reader for whom the book is primarily intended. My wife, Elizabeth McDonald, skillfully typed and retyped the manuscript, showing no other reaction than an eye occasionally raised heavenward when presented with another draft.

My colleagues Professor Erle Leichty and James Muhly of the Department of History at Minnesota gave me generous help—particularly on problems where the Aegean and Near Eastern evidence overlaps. Probably the deepest debt of all is owed to my friends John Chadwick, Lecturer in Greek in Downing College, Cambridge University, and Vincent Desborough, Lecturer in History, University of Manchester. They took time from busy schedules of teaching and research to read the next-to-final draft of the whole text and to send me detailed comments. Their control of the material in general as well as in their specialities has prevented many infelicities, inaccuracies and outright errors. If, as is very likely, others remain, they must not share the blame. The explanation would probably be either that they were too polite to pile Ossa on Pelion or else that the errors occur in passages added after the stage of the work that they saw.

A word must be said, too, about the relationship of the book to one of its "heroes." Professor Blegen has been my mentor and senior colleague and friend for twenty-seven years. At various times in that lengthy span we have talked over most of the problems here outlined, and a good many of the ideas that do not appear within quotes may stem from those discussions. But, again, he should not be charged with the shortcomings, and there are undoubtedly positions taken or theories suggested in the final chapter with which he will not agree. He was invited to read the manuscript, but since he had a general idea of his own prominent position in the text, he declined with characteristic modesty. His brother, Theodore Blegen, dean emeritus of the graduate school, University of Minnesota, who has always followed Carl's career with the closest interest, kindly consented to act as family arbiter on the Blegen chapter.

The illustrations were drawn by John Harris and William Williams. In general, Mr. Williams undertook the work connected with architecture and the vignettes, while Mr. Harris was responsible for the rest. The illustrations in books on Mycenaean civilization seem to me to have become largely standardized, with the chief variety consisting in the quality of the photographs. Since we could not hope to rival such photographs as Alison Frantz's, we have concentrated entirely on line drawings. It was my original intention to try to avoid the kind of illustration that is thoroughly familiar—and indeed hackneyed—to the veteran of many such books. But Mr. Aschenbrenner and others convinced me that some readers may never have seen the standard reproductions. Hence, our selection represents an attempt to combine these with some new material. It will be obvious to the experts that Mr. Harris and Mr. Williams have not attempted an absolutely faithful and literal reproduction but have instead sought to portray the "atmosphere" that they as artists feel in this material. I believe their results are both attractive and instructive; and the association with these gifted young artists has been an education to me at least.

The portrait of Schliemann is reproduced from Carl Schuchhardt's *Schliemann's Excavations;* that of Evans is a print of the painting done by Sir William Richmond and now in the Ashmolean Museum at Oxford. Miss Joan Evans very kindly arranged for the museum authorities to allow us to reproduce it. The photograph of Blegen was loaned by his brother. The photographs of Tsountas, Dörpfeld, Wace and Ventris are reproduced respectively from *Epitoumbion Christou Tsounta* (published by the Society for Thracian Folklore and Linguistics); Peter Goessler's *Wilhelm Dörpfeld. Ein Leben im Dienst der Antike; Annual of the British School of Archaeology at Athens,* Vol. 46 (1951); and John Chadwick's *The Decipherment of Linear B.*

I am indebted to various publishers for permission to quote extensively from books and journal articles written by our major authorities in Chapters IV through VII. The following specific arrangements are hereby acknowledged: Society of Antiquaries of London for *Archaeologia,* Vol. 59; Methuen and Co., Ltd., for Pendlebury, *Archaeology of Crete* and Nilsson, *Homer and Mycenae;* Biblo and Tannen, Inc., and Agathon Press, Inc., for Evans, *Palace of Minos;* Williams and James, Gray's Inn, London, for *Scripta Minoa* and *Shaft Graves and Bee-hive Tombs;* Society for the Promotion of Hellenic Studies for *Journal of Hellenic Studies,* Vol. 32; Routledge and Kegan Paul, Ltd., for Glotz, *Aegean Civilization;* B. G. Teubner, Stuttgart, for Fimmen, *Die Kretisch-Mykenische Kultur.*

Finally, I wish to express my gratitude for three rather special acts of gener-osity: to the Managing Committee of the British School of Archaeology at Athens for the reproduction of numerous passages from the *Annual;* to Miss Joan Evans for full leave to quote from *Time and Chance;* and to Carl W. Blegen for permission to reproduce excerpts from a considerable number of his own publications.

La Pointe, Wisconsin

August 1966

I

Before Schliemann: Homer and the Philologists

BEFORE SCHLIEMANN'S EXCAVATIONS BEGAN IN 1870, what were the prevailing attitudes of professional scholars on the historical background of the earliest masterpieces of European literature? A brief review of the status of certain aspects of the so-called Homeric Question in the late nineteenth century may provide us with a useful starting point.

When Schliemann turned the first sod at Troy, debate concerning the composition, date and authorship of the *Iliad* and the *Odyssey* had been going on practically continuously for at least 2,500 years. Even now, almost a century later, most of the basic problems are unsolved; and some of them are probably insoluble in absolute terms. That is, we may never know exactly when (or even if) "Homer" lived, whether he was responsible for both of the great epics attributed to him, in what form the chronicles and legends and folk tales circulated before genius transformed and embedded them in monumental works of art, or what happened to the unified epics between Homer's time and the establishment of our text. With us, as with the ancient Greeks, belief in a historical Homer must to some extent constitute an "act of faith."

Yet in the past century much real progress has been made. In addition to the illumination of archaeological discoveries (which will be our major concern), the scholarly disciplines of philology, linguistics and comparative literature have made important contributions. The list of Suggested Reading contains readable descriptions of the fascinating discoveries being made about epic language and form, about the techniques still in use in out-of-the-way places for composing and perpetuating oral heroic poetry, and about comparable themes and thought patterns in the literature of the ancient Near East and elsewhere. Although satisfactory answers to many of the complex problems grouped under the Homeric Question still elude us, we now have far more evidence that bears on them than was available in any generation since the poems were composed.

In 1870 very little archaeological evidence from preclassical times was available or recognized. A considerable amount of Greek sculpture, architecture, coins and other material remains of the fifth century B.C. and later had, of course, long been known. Many classical art objects reflect Homeric reminiscences, since the education of the artist—like that of all his contemporaries—was in a real sense based on Homer. But the archaeological artefacts told no clearer story about the background and origin of the epics than did classical literature. The later Greek artists and writers and scholars did not, in fact, have dependable information about Homer and the composition of the poems. Or, to put it more formally, they did not receive from their distant ancestors, and so could not pass on to the modern world, solid and incontestable *external* evidence. The critics of Schliemann's day, therefore, had to base judgments on these unsatisfactory ancient sources, plus their own analysis of the *internal* evidence preserved in the poems themselves.

Some scholars of the nineteenth century were thorough skeptics. They believed that the *Iliad* and the *Odyssey* contain no historical truth, that Agamemnon and Pylos and the Trojan War had had no more real existence than Polyphemos or Lotus Land or the Council of the Gods on Mount Olympus. Homer's poetic imagination, they said, soars far above dull facts and has created a fiction truer than history. This attitude is typified by the reaction of a famous scholar after reading Schliemann's first account of his excavations at Troy. "I know as yet," he wrote, "of one Ilion [Troy] only, that is, the Ilion as sung by Homer, which is not likely to be found in the trenches of Hissarlik, but rather among the Muses who dwell on Olympus."

At the other end of the spectrum were the readers who might be described as literalists or fundamentalists. Like the ancient Greeks, they assumed that all of Homer's people had really lived and that every action had taken place exactly as narrated. Even the geographical descriptions, they thought, were accurately recalled from the poet's own memory, or at the very least were passed on to him by a fully dependable and unbroken tradition. Schliemann, for instance, refers to his boyhood trust in the *Iliad,* "the exactness of which I used to believe in as in the Gospel itself."

Between the two extremes there was—and still is to some extent—a bewildering variety of views. The major point at issue can perhaps be phrased as follows: If we assume a long evolution in epic technique with the present text of the poems as the end product, how can the history of their composition be reconstructed? The critical methods applied to the Homeric Question in the nineteenth century were very largely identical with those brought to bear on the biblical narrative. In the broadest terms there were two basically different and mutually exclusive theories. Both depended on *internal* evidence, that is on analysis of the content of the poems themselves. One theory held that an original genius fashioned the poems out of already traditional and widely disparate materials, but that in the long process of transmission thereafter many major and minor changes were made by poets of varying merit, all of them far inferior to the master poet. The second reconstruction in effect eliminated Homer completely. Its adherents sought to prove that our *Iliad* and *Odyssey* are the result of a rather late, haphazard and awkward job of stitching together a large number of separate songs or "lays" of varying quality and age.

One can immediately see that to prove or disprove either viewpoint dependable criteria are needed for assigning an approximate date to the various units or episodes or lays (assuming their existence and correct identification). The evidence on which the critics formed their judgments was based mainly on details of style and language. But one serious drawback was that the specialists' opinions varied widely, not only on what constituted significant differences but on the implications of such differences for the history of the poems. The fields of linguistics and form analysis had not reached a point where reliable objective standards existed.

If form and language could not provide conclusive evidence, some scholars saw another possibility. The date of a given unit or story might be inferred from detailed descriptions of material objects or of political, social or religious institutions or customs that it embodied. If the time was even approximately known when a given type of political organization or a specially distinctive weapon or implement or item of jewelry was in use, then one might conclude that the section of the poems containing the relevant description was composed within those limits. At the very least, it could not have been composed *before* the institution or object was created.

But this method also had serious limitations. Very few such "dating brackets" were known with sufficient precision. And the late-nineteenth-century scholars saw no way to improve the situation. They did not believe that much progress could be made in chronological accuracy for such early periods by restudying the ancient texts. And most of them were unconvinced that excavation might uncover the towns where the stories were alleged to have originated or might find in the heroes' palaces and tombs material objects closely similar to those described by Homer. This was, of course, a shortsighted attitude in view of the archaeological discoveries already being made in western Europe, Egypt and other parts of the Near East. But they can hardly be blamed for failing to foresee the day when some of the places and objects described by Homer not only would be found but could be quite closely dated by rigorous techniques that are based only indirectly on written records.

The chapters to follow trace this progress into the past. But before we leave the prearchaeological era, we might at least try to reconstruct the viewpoint of the general reader of the poems in the nineteenth century and before. What was his attitude, whether or not he had ever heard of the Homeric Question? He probably looked on Priam and Odysseus and their heroic companions very much as on King Arthur or Alexander the Great. The "tale of Troy divine" had a tremendous romantic appeal to a wide circle of readers and listeners; and this vogue had in turn stimulated a long tradition of purely fictional elaboration and expansion. The unsophisticated reader of Schliemann's time, as before and since, would have been serenely unaware of any argument over fact versus fancy. Probably he would not have been much interested even if he had heard something of scholarly analyses and dissections. Fiction, legend, myth or history —does it matter if all these elements and more are combined in a good story? And, if they are, who could ever disentangle them after all these centuries?

To such natural questions the Homeric scholar must have a reasonable answer if he is concerned to justify his existence. He will certainly agree that Homer's poems may be enjoyed simply as absorbing stories and superb literary achievements. But he cannot stop there. The very fact of their literary and technical perfection, standing as they do in the early mists of European civilization, forces him to ask questions. Could this perfection have been achieved suddenly and intuitively by one man? Could the author have imagined his heroic civilization in all the splendid and vital detail revealed in his elaborate word pictures? Is it possible that in the poems precious evidence is embalmed about a real historical stage of Greek civilization far earlier than classical times? How can we go about definitely proving or disproving such conflicting hypotheses?

As a matter of fact, these questions need not be confined to scholars. They could occur quite naturally to any intelligent lover of Homer and of history. Western man has for so long located most of his intellectual and cultural roots in classical Greece that simple curiosity about what preceded *that* epoch is almost inevitable. It is only in the last century that some fairly reliable answers are beginning to emerge and to win the adherence of most serious students of Homer.

II

Schliemann,
Priam and Agamemnon:
1870-1890

"And now the treasure-digger has become a scholar"

HEINRICH SCHLIEMANN, in his younger years, might be called an unsophisticated reader of Homer; and in his maturity he aspired to the status of professional scholar. But he was never really either the one or the other. He was a unique genius, and such a man can never be neatly labeled and confined to a single category.

This account is meant neither as another study of Schliemann's life nor as a detailed description of his excavations. Instead, as explained in the Preface, we want to review some of the highlights of his discoveries and to examine his theories of their relation to the civilization mirrored in the Homeric poems. Schliemann was the pioneer who made the decisive breakthrough into Greek prehistory. Knowledge about this tiny but important segment of human experience took a tremendous leap forward in his lifetime.

A few observations about the man and his methods are perhaps called for at the start. Psychologists and biographers have seen in his personality a strong element of psychotic compulsion. One can cite his devotion to his father and the shock following the breakup of his home in early boyhood, the long lonely search for the comfort of a wife and family of his own and the compensatory absorption in learning languages and making a fortune in business. Certainly he was egotistical, sensitive, volatile and hypochondriacal. His life was one continuous demonic drive to prove himself and his ideas to the world. But, again, he does not easily conform to a type. Some have maligned him as an avaricious megalomaniac, and others have flattered him as the more or less self-conscious founder of the science of archaeology. The variety of judgments during his lifetime and the continued interest of writers and readers are in themselves proof of the complexity of the man and the mystery of such prodigies.

Schliemann has for so long been associated in the public imagination with buried gold that nonspecialists are often unaware of the solid and lasting aspects of his work. The image of the "gold-seeker" was set early in his archaeological career, and clearly with his own encouragement. This was the line taken—as nearly always since in journalistic accounts of archaeology—in newspaper stories about his discoveries; and it is a very important element in the fascination that books by and about him have always had for their many readers. Archaeologists today profess impatience with the association of their profession and treasure trove. But the discovery of intrinsically valuable objects *was* clearly a major motivation for excavation all through the nineteenth century and earlier. It can probably be regarded as a more powerful stimulus to dig than is simple curiosity about one's predecessors. The search for buried treasure preceded scientific motivation by thousands of years. No present-day archaeologist has gotten completely beyond its lure, no matter how firmly he insists that he regards the commonest potsherd on the same terms as a golden diadem. Schliemann was quite frank about wanting to find treasure and supremely fortunate in fulfilling that wish.

But the truly significant result of his excavations was to show that there had been a brilliant and very distinctive civilization around the Aegean Sea *before the classical*. This fact, when eventually accepted by the experts, went a long way to "prove Homer right." And that was the hope, as Schliemann insists in his autobiography, that inspired the "great projects I formed when I was a poor little boy." The discovery of a prehistoric culture with firm Homeric connections was difficult for many contemporary scholars to accept, and the controversy provoked a "new War of Troy." They might with some justice criticize the rough-and-ready methods of his earlier excavations and his passion for making rash identifications of his finds with heroic people and places and things; but what upset them even more was the prospect of having to revise comfortable theories. Above all, Schliemann's work doomed the dogma that the Golden Age of classical Greek civilization had been created "out of nothing" by a few generations of supermen. Yet, for a doomed belief, it died hard; and its vestiges are with us even yet.

Schliemann was not usually overawed by learned authority and sometimes reacted to criticism in a not very tactful way. He apparently relished lengthy debates in newspapers and journals, enumerating for page after page the errors of fact committed by this or that "learned friend." In such situations, many authorities of our own day are inclined to sympathize with the experts. They feel that laymen do a disservice to science when they point out how "the scholars" were corrected by a courageous and gifted amateur. They fear that these irreverent disclosures may encourage the public to develop a skeptical attitude toward scholarly accomplishments. But a healthy skepticism is one of the qualities that education is supposed to plant and nourish. We all know that unquestioning public acceptance of the judgment of "the expert" can be dangerous. A "closed" science is on the way to becoming a mystery. The criticisms of crackpots will usually sputter out before long, as happened in the case of several of Schliemann's most malicious detractors. And the open-minded scholar will usually listen, as Schliemann did, when his mistakes are tactfully pointed out. The way should always be open for the gifted amateur to make himself heard. And Heinrich Schliemann is a prime example of the amateur of genius who became a scholar.

He not only had the originality to conceive the idea of testing an unpopular belief by excavation, but was persistent enough not to be discouraged by criticism and suspicion and lethargy. His successful earlier career in business was a useful background in this sense, for it was built on taking risks, outwitting his opponents and playing the brilliant hunch. The large fortune he had amassed gave him confidence and prestige in dealing with political authorities; and it freed him from the worry of finding funds to carry on his work. This brash amateur would probably have found it impossible to interest private donors or government agencies in financing his ambitious plans.

Schliemann's self-assertiveness irritated many, but without it he could never have forced himself to the attention of the learned world. And he was far from scornful of education and scholarly competence. His decision in 1866 to resume his own formal education at age forty-four, after a lapse of thirty years, shows clearly that he wanted to prepare himself to meet the experts on their own ground. And, when his own learning and fertile imagination failed to provide a satisfactory explanation for a problem, he did not hesitate to appeal for help. Reporting on his first campaign, he writes: "I find much in this stone period that is quite inexplicable to me, and I therefore consider it necessary to describe everything as minutely as possible, in the hope that one or other of my honoured colleagues will be able to give an explanation of the points which are obscure to me." In fact, there runs through his life a thread of insecurity that forms a striking complement to his more obvious egotism.

As the complexity of the job and the variety of the evidence gradually became clear to him, Schliemann tended more and more to associate various specialists in his work. In a very real sense, he anticipated by almost a century the "team approach" that is only recently gaining recognition in Greek archaeology. The only precedent then was the great French *Expédition Scientifique de Morée* (Peloponnese) more than a generation earlier; and it had the support of a government and the resources of a national treasury.

Of course, Schliemann hoped the opinion of the consultants would support his own and thereby strengthen his case against his critics; but the

passionate desire to get at the truth from every possible angle shines out
clearly. In the excavations at Troy in 1872 his staff included a professional
surveyor and a professional photographer. The following year there was
also a professional artist. Engineers and architects made elaborate and
accurate plans of the structures uncovered and the sites examined. The
"celebrated surgeon, Aretaeos of Athens" undertook a study of human
skeletal material, the specialty we now call physical anthropology. Laboratory analyses and opinions by chemists, metallurgists, geologists and
practicing goldsmiths are frequently quoted in the later publications.

Schliemann also realized the unique importance of the remains of the
ancient highways that were still to be seen in the vicinity of Mycenae. He
secured the services of Major Steffen, an army engineer, to measure and
record this evidence in the course of his detailed survey of Mycenae and
its environs. Steffen's report is still the only professional survey ever published on the evidence for land communications in the Aegean Bronze Age.

Emil Bournouf, director of the French School of Archaeology, provided assistance with the ceramic materials, and especially with the various
decorative motifs on the pottery and other terra-cotta objects. At that
time, however, no one knew much about the pottery of prehistoric periods.
An indication of the fluidity of the situation is the varying opinion of
eminent critics that the material Schliemann was unearthing should be
dated as early as the Stone Age, as late as the third century A.D. or even
the Middle Ages, or to assorted intermediate periods.

Schliemann gradually came to realize something of the crucial role that
pottery must play in serious archaeological work. "Pottery . . . is the
cornucopia of archaeological wisdom for those dark ages, which we,
vaguely groping in the twilight of an unrecorded past, are wont to call
pre-historic." He set out to learn all he could about it. On technical details such as clays, colors and glazes he consulted a professional chemist.
He took increasing pains in recording the exact position, type and condition of the pottery uncovered. He compared his finds with other pottery
from all over the world, sometimes suggesting reckless and misleading
parallels. Yet before his death he had made himself a serious scholar of
prehistoric ceramics.

The most valuable members of Schliemann's "team" were Rudolph
Virchow and Wilhelm Dörpfeld. These two, especially Virchow, probably
became the nearest equivalent of close friends that Schliemann ever had.
His genuine respect for their ability seems to have acted as a brake on
the violent outbursts of temper that made him a difficult colleague. Virchow was a fabulous polymath—a famous pathologist and member of a
university faculty, as well as politician, social organizer, geologist, eth-

nographer and general scientist. Extremely generous with his time and learning both in correspondence and in the field, he carried out painstaking investigations of the geographical, botanical and meteorological features of the Trojan plain. We shall hear a great deal more about Dörpfeld, who became the acknowledged authority on Greek architecture in the following generation. His excavation technique and meticulous plans did much to inspire confidence in Schliemann's later campaigns at Troy and Tiryns.

As Schliemann's archaeological career unfolds over two decades, one can see the fiercely self-assertive egotist gradually becoming more mellow and cautious. Perhaps the change was due in part to the growing respect and recognition shown him by the public and by many scholars. Certainly, his happy second marriage in 1869 to the seventeen-year-old Sophia Engastromenou brightened his last twenty years. The tact and sympathy of the beautiful Sophia cushioned many a crisis. In a typical outburst of mingled love, pride and scholarly obsession, he speaks of "My dear wife, an Athenian lady, who is an enthusiastic admirer of Homer, and knows almost the whole of the 'Iliad' by heart . . ."

Before his death he had the satisfaction of knowing that he had won his main point. The scholarly world was reluctantly coming around to the admission that there *had* really been a Troy and a Mycenae before Homer, and that some features of their material culture *are* reflected in Homer's account so faithfully that coincidence is ruled out.

ITHAKA

It is natural that Troy and Ithaka should have particularly attracted Schliemann since they are the chief locale of action in the *Iliad* and the *Odyssey*. In the first flush of leisure to take up his Greek studies, he briefly visited the island now called Ithaki or Thiaki and confidently identified various landmarks in the Ithakan countryside with Homer's topographical and geographical references. These observations are set forth in his first serious archaeological essay, *Ithâque, le Peloponnèse et Troie* (1869).

He returned to Ithaka ten years later for a more thorough survey. At that time he dug a few test trenches that showed that there had been a fair-sized town high up on Mount Aetos in the center of the island, at a spot that tradition called the Castle of Ulysses. But apart from emphasizing the "Cyclopean"* nature of its fortifications and house walls, he is vague

---

* Technical terms not explained in the text will be marked with an asterisk (*) and defined in the Glossary (pp. 443–53).

about its date or claim to be really Odysseus' town. Soundings elsewhere on the island proved negative in the main, and his final verdict was that "systematic excavations for archaeological purposes are altogether out of the question here."

Yet Schliemann apparently never doubted that modern Ithaki had been Odysseus' home nor that Homer actually knew this particular island at first hand. It was left to Dörpfeld and others to carry on a lengthy and largely inconclusive controversy about which of the western (Ionian) islands was Odysseus' Ithaka. And, in spite of extensive search and excavation on both the island of Leukas and Ithaki, no recognizable trace of Odysseus' home has yet been discovered.

T R O Y

Troy, on the other hand, occupied a major share of Schliemann's attention right up to his death. It was probably his favorite among all the sites he excavated or hoped to explore. After long and intricate negotiations with the Turkish authorities, he managed to carry out four major campaigns, in 1870–73, 1878–79, 1882 and 1890. Within an amazingly short time after all but the last season of digging he published a bulky book. Each report appeared in German, French and English, a gesture typical of the author's lavish scale of operations and of his well-founded expectation that the books would be widely read. The English edition of *Troy and Its Remains* appeared in 1875; of *Ilios: The City and Country of the Trojans,* in 1880; and of *Troja: Results of the Latest Researches,* in 1884. As in all his published reports, Schliemann combines in these absorbing volumes both day by day excavation notes and the results of at least a couple of years of over-all reflection and comparative study.

The Troy publications, along with his accounts of excavations at Mycenae and Tiryns, are the truest index to Schliemann's scientific accomplishments. They also provide at least as good a basis for understanding the man himself as all the books that have been written about him. The autobiography that forms the Introduction to *Ilios* is a fascinating example of the rags-to-riches story so dear to that epoch. For an outside evaluation of Schliemann's scientific accomplishments, Carl Schuchhardt's *Schliemann's Excavations* (1889; Eng. ed., 1891) is by far the most satisfactory. Written just at the end of Schliemann's life, it is a clear and sympathetic assessment that time has justified in the main.

Before Schliemann began his excavations some scholars would concede that a town called Troy (or Ilion) may have really existed before Homer in the northwest corner of Asia Minor (modern Turkey). But nearly all of them believed that its site was a high hill called Balli Dagh, near the village of Burnarbashi (see Map IV). They based their arguments almost entirely on its supposed correspondence with topographical descriptions in the *Iliad*. Now, there can be no objection to this "philological" or text-based kind of archaeological research if it is carried out with common sense. But the armchair archaeologists have too often tended to be so concerned with the traditions and opinions preserved by the ancient authorities that they neglect other types of evidence that may turn out to be more directly applicable. A case in point is that of the great English philologist R. C. Jebb. One of Schliemann's persistent critics, he tried to show that the majority of the finds from Troy were postclassical. Schliemann generally showed restraint in answering him, but on one occasion he was goaded into writing: "No courtesy on my part can save Professor Jebb from the fate on which an eminent classical scholar rushes when he mingles in an archaeological debate in ignorance of the first principles of archaeology."

Schliemann himself cannot wholly escape the criticism of putting too much trust in "book archaeology." He leaned on Homer and Pausanias* with a simple faith that few today would consider justified. And in his case, it must be admitted, the method proved its worth more than once. But he at least checked the ancient evidence on the ground. He used his own eyes and judgment in the modern countryside, which has not changed a great deal in its broader aspects since antiquity. Perhaps we should be charitable to the pre-twentieth-century scholars poring over the texts in their studies with the aid of bad maps. For them a trip to Greece or Turkey was usually out of the question or extremely difficult. But our contemporaries who shun field work and yet write learnedly on geographical and topographical problems can scarcely plead the same excuse.

The Burnarbashi theory shows how dangerous it is to place implicit and literal trust in Homer's geographical descriptions. One can point to a long series of attempts from antiquity to the present to prove geographical points by appealing solely to Homer's authority. It is not that these references are necessarily useless or misleading, or that the poet or his sources were demonstrably unfamiliar with the local topography; but most poetry is meant for readers or hearers who either already know the locale in question or do not care about precise geographical details. It is foolish to expect a singer in the court of a prehistoric king or an artist like Homer to supply, consciously or unconsciously, what would amount to an ancient traveler's handbook. In fact, not a single prehistoric site has ever been certainly identified solely by following descriptions in the poems, though learned treatises over the past 2,500 years are filled (not to say cluttered) with interminable attempts to do just that.

In any case, Schliemann looked carefully and with fresh eyes at the

Scamander plain, even though he kept a dog-eared copy of the *Iliad* in his pocket. He made brief and unproductive excavations at Burnarbashi in 1868 and 1871. His allusion to previous theorizing is rather amusing. "It [Burnarbashi] had been almost universally considered to be the site of the Homeric Ilium [Troy]; the springs at the bottom of that village having been regarded as the two springs mentioned by Homer,[1] one of which sent forth warm, the other cold water. But, instead of two springs, I found thirty-four . . . moreover, I found in all the springs a uniform temperature of . . . 62.6° Fahrenheit."

Schliemann, however, soon turned his full attention to a smaller hill called Hissarlik (see Map IV). The name means "fortress" or "acropolis" in Turkish, originally from the Arabic. Hissarlik lies about four miles south of the Dardanelles (ancient Hellespont) and rises some 100 feet above the plain. Its top surface is only about 225 by 175 yards, which had been a factor in causing searchers to look elsewhere for a bigger and more imposing site conforming better to the heroic account.

Schliemann describes the panorama from Hissarlik in rather picturesque language.

> The view from the hill . . . is extremely magnificent. Before me lies the glorious Plain of Troy, which, since the recent rain, is again covered with grass and yellow buttercups; on the north-north-west, at about an hour's distance, it is bounded by the Hellespont. The peninsula of Gallipoli here runs out to a point, upon which stands a lighthouse. To the left of it is the island of Imbros, above which rises Mount Ida of the island of Samothrace, at present covered with snow; a little more to the west, on the Macedonian peninsula, lies the celebrated Mount Athos, or Monte Santo, with its monasteries. . . . Between the . . . mounds [in the plain to the west—traditionally associated with the burial places of Homeric heroes] we see projecting above the high shores of the Aegean Sea the island of Tenedos. To the south, we see the Plain of Troy, extending again to a distance of two hours, as far as the heights of Burnarbashi, above which rises majestically the snow-capped Gargarus of Mount Ida, from which Jupiter witnessed the battles between the Trojans and the Greeks.

Hissarlik had been the focus of a large Greek and Roman town called Ilion and was almost universally believed in classical antiquity to be the site of Priam's Troy. The major voice raised against it in those days was that of the geographer Strabo*, who lived about the time of Christ. The adoption of his skeptical view by the majority of scholars in Schliemann's day has a curious parallel, as we shall see, in the case of Nestor's Pylos. But Hissarlik had at least a few modern champions. Several earlier scholars had declared in its favor; and Frank Calvert, the American vice-consul at the Dardanelles, had dug a small trial trench on the part of the hill that he owned. Calvert took Schliemann to see the site and helped him in many ways during his early negotiations and excavations. But it was his own reading of the ancient evidence (especially the *Iliad*) and an uncanny intuition that made Schliemann decide to excavate at Hissarlik. "Ever since my first visit," he wrote later, "I never doubted that I should find the Pergamus [citadel] of Priam in the depths of this hill."

THE CAMPAIGN OF 1870–1873

The first seasons at Troy were admittedly more of a rape than a scientific examination. But nearly all archaeological excavations were rough-and-ready affairs in those days; and Schliemann was inexperienced and without expert assistance. A horde of untrained workmen averaging 150 in number hacked great rents through the hill. Schliemann was determined to get to the bottom of the mound, since he had no doubt that Homer's Troy was the first settlement on the site and so the deepest. His great north-south trench bisected the mound, and nothing was allowed to stand in its path. With good reason the workmen named it "the grandmother of the trenches." Schliemann and Sophia were utterly unable to supervise the work properly and to decide what foundations should be preserved and where the digging could proceed deeper without too much damage. Remains of relatively well-preserved buildings were lost for all time when the foundations were wrenched out with no thought of exact measurement or detailed photography before their removal. Schliemann candidly admits that, "Unfortunately, owing to the great extent of my excavations, the hurry in which they were carried on, and the hardness of the *débris,* by far the greater portion of the terra-cotta vessels . . . were brought out more or less broken." Of course, much of the pottery recovered in the most careful excavation is found in crushed condition; but Schliemann's material would surely have shown too many fresh breaks. And there are ominous references to the use of battering rams and great iron levers to remove house walls and fortifications that impeded the impetuous downward thrust.

But in all fairness, if Schliemann's own naïve reports on his early methods are used to discredit him, as they were so often by his critics, other remarks such as the following should not be forgotten. "As every object belonging to the dark night of the pre-Hellenic times, and bearing traces of human skill in art, is to me a page of history, I am, above all things, obliged to take care that nothing escapes me." Elsewhere he says: "Archaeology shall on no account lose any one of my discoveries; every article which can have any interest for the learned world shall be photographed, or copied by a skilful draughtsman, and published in the Appendix to this work; and by the side of every article I shall state the depth in which I discovered it." And in still another place, "I have therefore thought it in the interest of science to fill the excavation up again, in order to preserve the house for future times." These are remarkable statements of principle in the 1870s, even if they were not always observed in practice. If all of his successors in hundreds of excavations had imposed on themselves as conscientious a code in excavation and publication, much valuable evidence would not have been lost forever.

In the reports of those first seasons one can sense that difficulties and perplexities were the chief reward. He had envisioned the rapid uncovering of the "city of Priam"; and his rationalizations for the lack of immediate and striking results are not entirely convincing.

> My expectations are extremely modest; I have no hope of finding plastic works of art [*i.e.,* monumental sculpture, the main motivation of excavations at that time]. The single object of my excavations from the beginning was only to find Troy, whose site has been discussed by a hundred scholars in a hundred books, but which as yet no one has ever sought to bring to light by excavations. If I should not succeed in this, still I shall be perfectly contented, if by my labours I succeed only in penetrating to the deepest darkness of pre-historic times, and enriching archaeology by the discovery of a few interesting features from the most ancient history of the great Hellenic race.

For Schliemann as for anyone else in his day, the proof that he had found Homeric Troy would have to be the remains of great fortification walls, monumental buildings and above all portable wealth in the form of precious metals. So the workmen were urged, in imminent peril of their own and their directors' lives, to burrow ever deeper. They penetrated in places more than 50 feet before reaching what he calls "primary soil."

Schliemann gradually came to believe that he could recognize four major levels of ruins below those of the Greek town of Ilion, which he thought had been founded about 700 B.C. He felt sure that these four pre-historic "nations" had all belonged to a related culture, because he could see a continuity in the artefacts. And he thought that the lower strata contained the artefacts of finer quality; that is, the level of culture had deteriorated as time went on. Furthermore, these people were all "Aryan" in race (a mania with nineteenth-century European students of early cultures), because designs such as the swastika inscribed on various small objects,

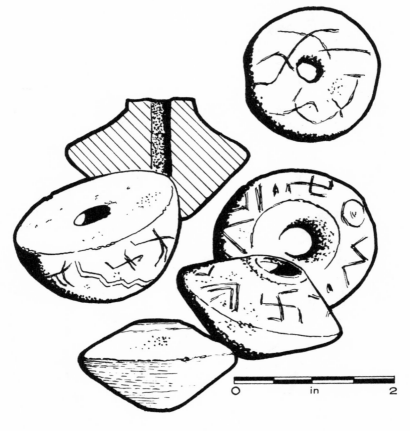

Figure 1

particularly on whorls*, reminded him and others he consulted of religious motifs found in India (Fig. 1).

Perhaps the most striking find extending through all four levels of the ruins was a series of large globular "owl vases," with handles like upraised arms or wings rising from the shoulder (Fig. 2). Eyes and nose (and later ears, too) were modeled on the neck or sometimes on a separate lid; and female breasts, navel and vulva were often shown on the body of the vessel. Schliemann regarded these interesting objects as representations of Athena, the protecting goddess of Homer's Troy. He was sure the scholars were wrong in translating *glaukōpis* (Homer's favorite epithet for Athena) as "gray-eyed" or "bright-eyed"; it must rather mean "owl-eyed," since *glaux* is the classical Greek word for "owl" and the owl was Athena's bird.

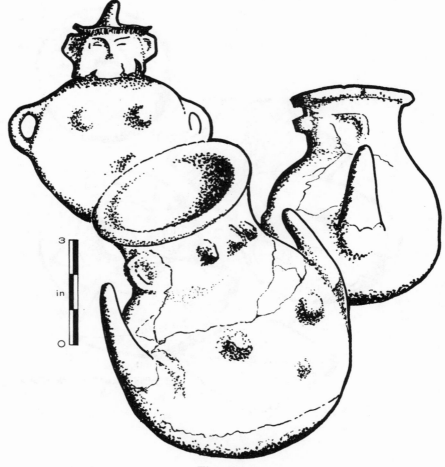

Figure 2

For some time Schliemann continued to believe that the lowest of his four prehistoric levels must be Homer's Troy. This conviction was shaken toward the end of the campaign by the appearance in the second level from the bottom of well-preserved foundations of a "Great Tower" (Fig. 13). Beside it there had been a "double gateway" with a paved ramp leading out through the fortification wall and dipping steeply toward the southwest edge of the hill. The gateway soon became the Scaean Gate, where Homer locates the famous recognition scene. "Here . . . sat Priam, the seven elders of the city, and Helen; and this is the scene of the most splendid passage in the Iliad. From this spot the company surveyed the whole Plain, and saw at the foot of the Pergamus the Trojan and the

Achaean armies face to face about to settle their agreement to let the war be decided by a single combat between Paris and Menelaus."[2]

It followed in Schliemann's reconstruction that the ruins of a large structure built on an artificial elevation immediately inside the Scaean Gate ought to mark the "palace of Priam." He could only partially uncover its ground plan since it extended under the temporary buildings where the staff lived. But prospects were getting brighter. The terra-cotta vases found within the "palace" were especially fine, and in or near it a silver vase and a cup made of electrum* were discovered.

So the stage was set for the high point of the first series of excavations. In the spring of 1873, while work was proceeding at the base of the fortification wall slightly west of the Scaean Gate, Schliemann reports that he detected through the dust and rubble "a large copper article of the most remarkable form, which attracted my attention all the more as I thought I saw gold behind it." He immediately told Sophia to announce a recess for the workmen.

> While the men were eating and resting, I cut out the Treasure with a large knife, which it was impossible to do without the very greatest exertion and the most fearful risk of my life, for the great fortification-

O　in　4

Figure 3

wall, beneath which I had to dig, threatened every moment to fall down upon me. But the sight of so many objects, every one of which is of inestimable value to archaeology, made me foolhardy, and I never thought of any danger. It would, however, have been impossible for me to have removed the Treasure without the help of my dear wife, who stood by me ready to pack the things which I cut out in her shawl and to carry them away.

One may observe parenthetically that his dear wife was apparently in equal peril of her life and also that, as will be seen, she must have had an extremely capacious shawl.

Below a copper "shield" (really a very large basin) lay a copper cauldron with horizontal handles, a silver jug (Fig. 3), a globular gold bottle and two gold cups (Fig. 4). One of the cups has two handles and two unusual spouts (Fig. 5). The form is very distinctive, and we now call it a sauce-boat*. It regularly has but a single longer spout and is the most typical vase shape on the Greek mainland in the mid-*third* millennium. Schliemann, of course, could not know this and immediately saw in the cup an example of Homer's *depas amphikypellon*.[3] Since the double-sauceboat shape

O in 2

Figure 4

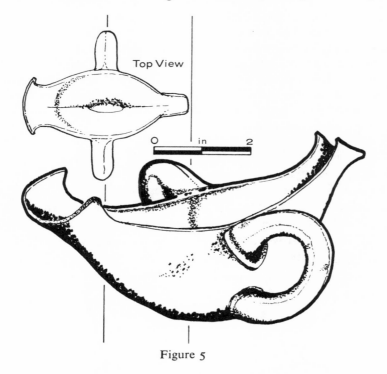

Top View

Figure 5

turned out to be unique, Schliemann later extended the equation to include another very common and distinctive two-handled conical goblet (Fig. 6).

In a transport of delight, Schliemann goes on and on with the inventory of "the Treasure"—more cups and vases of precious metals, lances, daggers, axes, knives. Many of the objects were fused and deformed by intense heat. Packed into the largest silver vase, he records "two splendid gold diadems . . . a fillet*, and four beautiful gold ear-rings of most exquisite workmanship: upon these lay 56 gold ear-rings of exceedingly curious form and 8750 small gold rings, perforated prisms and dice, gold buttons, and similar jewels, which obviously belonged to other ornaments; then followed six gold bracelets, and on the top of all the two small gold goblets."

Schliemann's reconstruction of the way the treasure reached this spot is typical of his vivid imagination.

As I found all these articles together, forming a rectangular mass, or packed into one another, it seems to be certain that they were placed on the city wall in a wooden chest, . . . such as those mentioned by Homer as being in the palace of king Priam.[4] This appears to be the

more certain, as close by the side of these articles I found a copper key
[it later proved to be a chisel]. . . . It is probable that some member of
the family of king Priam hurriedly packed the Treasure into the chest
and carried it off without having time to pull out the key; that when he
reached the wall, however, the hand of an enemy or the fire overtook
him, and he was obliged to abandon the chest, which was immediately
covered to a height of from 5 to 6 feet with the red ashes and the stones
of the adjoining royal palace.

This fabulous discovery finally convinced Schliemann that he must
change his view about which stratum represented Homer's Troy. "I formerly believed," he writes, "that the most ancient people who inhabited
this site were the Trojans [of Homer] . . . but I now perceive that Priam's
people were the succeeding nation. . . . In consequence of my former mistaken idea, that Troy was to be found on the primary soil or close above
it, I unfortunately, in 1871 and 1872, destroyed a large portion of the

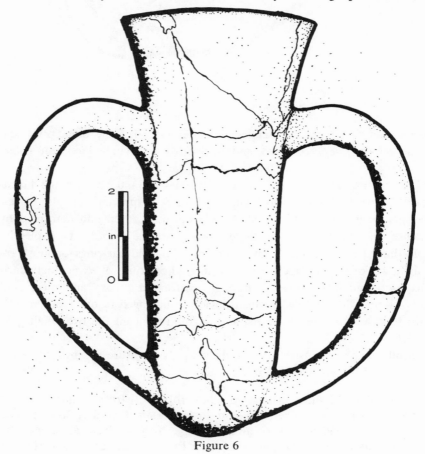

Figure 6

[second] city, for I at that time broke down all the house-walls in the higher strata which obstructed my way." One can hardly condone the impetuosity, but the frank admission of the mistake is courageous.

In another important respect, too, Schliemann had to change his thinking. All through the first three years he carefully datelined his field reports "Pergamus of Troy." Now Pergamus is the name Homer gives to the citadel as distinct from the lower town surrounding it. But Schliemann's soundings outside the fortified acropolis showed no signs of prehistoric habitation, and he finally came to the reluctant conclusion that the area within the walls must represent the total extent of the town. "I now most emphatically declare that the city of Priam cannot have extended on any one side beyond the primeval plateau of this fortress. . . . I am extremely disappointed at being obliged to give so small a plan of Troy; nay, I had wished to be able to make it a thousand times larger, but I value truth above everything, and I rejoice that my three years' excavations have laid open the Homeric Troy, even though on a diminished scale."

The higher stratum that we now believe to represent Homeric Troy was, as it later turned out, considerably larger than Schliemann's "second city" (Fig. 13); but it is still a characteristic failing of classical enthusiasts to form an inflated impression of the monumental size of ancient Greek "cities." Schliemann continues his apology:

> I venture to hope that the civilized world will not only not be disap-
> pointed that the city of Priam has shown itself to be scarcely a twentieth
> part as large as was to be expected from the statements of the Iliad, but
> that, on the contrary, it will accept with delight and enthusiasm the cer-
> tainty that Ilium did really exist, that a large portion of it has now been
> brought to light, and that Homer, even although he exaggerates, never-
> theless sings of events that actually happened. . . . But this little Troy
> was immensely rich for the circumstances of those times, since I find
> here a treasure of gold and silver articles, such as is now scarcely to be
> found in an emperor's palace; and as the town was wealthy, so was it
> also powerful, and ruled over a large territory.

As he finished the 1873 season, Schliemann had no idea of returning to "this little Troy" but was impatient to start work at Mycenae.

> I have excavated two-thirds of the entire city; and, as I have brought to
> light the Great Tower, the Scaean Gate, the city wall of Troy, the royal
> palace . . . I have also made an exceedingly copious collection of all
> the articles of the domestic life and the religion of the Trojans; and
> therefore it is not to be expected that science would gain anything more
> by further excavations. If, however, my excavations should at any time
> be continued, I urgently entreat those who do so to throw the *débris*

of their diggings from the declivity of the hill, and *not* to fill up the colossal cuttings which I have made with such infinite trouble and at such great expense, for they are of great value to archaeology, inasmuch as in these cuttings all the strata of *débris,* from the primary soil up to the surface of the hill, can be examined with little trouble.

We note here the first faint gropings toward scientific stratigraphy*, so vital to modern archaeology, already forming in his agile brain.

The stealthy removal of the treasure and nearly all of the other finds from Turkey to Athens is not a happy story. But, apart from charges and countercharges about broken agreements, one can point out that Schliemann was simply following accepted practice. In those days the fortunate discoverer of archaeological riches in the soil of "underdeveloped" countries took it for granted that he would carry home the loot. Sometimes he smuggled it out; but more often that was unnecessary, particularly if he had diplomatic immunity or powerful friends. And we are hardly entitled nowadays to pass moral judgment on such practices of the past when we know that rare antiquities illegally removed from the country of their origin (and probably discovered in illegal excavations) still appear in the museums and private collections of "overdeveloped" countries.

The publication of his first series of excavations did not have the positive effect that Schliemann had hoped. It was admitted that he had unearthed important evidence for early civilization in the Troad*, but most experts were critical of the methods by which he had gathered his material and of the conclusions he had drawn from it. One prominent scholar suggested that the funds might have been put to much better use by more experienced excavators. There were even slanderous insinuations that Schliemann had "planted" the more striking finds in advance of excavation. Few scholars saw any close connection between the antiquities he had unearthed and the Trojan buildings and artefacts described in the *Iliad*. In fact, Schliemann's confident association of various discoveries with Homer's people and places became something of a laughing stock in the public press as well as in scholarly circles, particularly in his native Germany. The Burnarbashi site still remained the favorite location for Homer's Troy, if it had ever actually existed.

THE CAMPAIGN OF 1878–1879

We have gained enough insight into Schliemann's character to guess that he would not give up the struggle at this point. He quickly changed his earlier attitude that no further excavation at Hissarlik was necessary and began the extremely difficult negotiations with the Turkish Government for a new permit. A lengthy lawsuit over the ownership of the treasure resulted in an order for him to pay the Turks an indemnity of 10,000 francs. He promptly paid five times the amount assessed and brought the precious objects out of their hiding places in the homes and farms of Sophia's numerous Greek relatives. With the support of many powerful friends, including Sir Austen Henry Layard, British Ambassador to Turkey and himself a renowned excavator in the Near East, permission to continue the work was finally obtained. Although the exciting excavation of the Shaft Graves* at Mycenae intervened, we shall defer that episode until we have reviewed the remaining campaigns at Troy. But it should be noted that Schliemann returned to Troy in 1878 with considerably more excavation experience than when he had left.

Unfair though some of the criticisms had been, their total effect was beneficial. Schliemann now refers more cautiously to the "city chieftain's house" and the "great Treasure" rather than to Priam's Palace and Priam's Treasure. Bournouf and Virchow were now associated with him in the field. The latter says, in his Preface to the publication of this second series of excavations: "I recognize the duty of bearing my testimony against the host of doubters, who, with good or ill intentions, have never tired of carping alike at the trustworthiness and significance of his discoveries." Virchow does indeed stake his own impeccable scholarly reputation, insisting, "This excavation has opened for the studies of the archaeologist a completely new theatre—like a world by itself. Here begins an entirely new science." Virchow's verdict is indeed a responsible statement of fact. Mistakes and vacillations would still occur, but from now on one senses that Schliemann and his staff are in control of the situation and are investigating specific and manageable problems.

Schliemann even found the patience to submit to the presence of armed soldiers and a Turkish commissioner, who held the keys to the building where the finds were stored. "The ten gensdarmes . . . were of great use to me, for they not only served as a guard against the brigands by whom the Troad was infested, but they also carefully watched my labourers whilst they were excavating, and thus forced them to be honest." We shall soon see the special point of this last remark.

The second campaign had two principal purposes, both of them responses to the previous adverse criticism. The first was to clear the ruins of the fortifications and of the large building of the second level near which the treasure had been discovered. The expedition succeeded in uncovering almost the whole western half of the mound down to this "Homeric" level. The second project was a very thorough and wide-ranging study of the whole Trojan plain—its topography, geology, flora, fauna and economic basis, as well as the antiquities of all periods. This, of course, was a reaction to the charge that Homer had no firsthand acquaintance with the area, or at least that Hissarlik did not correspond with ancient literary references to Troy.

The very title of the second book, *Ilios: The City and Country of the Trojans,* suggests the wider scope. Schliemann discusses in detail all the ancient literary evidence, the history and mythology of Troy and the ethnology of the Trojans and their allies. He and Virchow outline their research on the mountains, rivers, climate, zoology and botany of the area. They stress its strategic location, with command of the easiest land and sea routes between Europe and Asia. Virchow insists on Homer's "surprising knowledge of the meteorology of the district, of the flora and fauna, and the social peculiarities of its population. Three thousand years have not sufficed to produce any noteworthy alteration in these things. . . . The truth of this warrants us in assuming that the poet did visit the country, though perhaps he may not have stayed there long, and it does not exclude the hypothesis that a body of legend, though disjointed and incongruous, already existed before his time."

We see here that the possibility of a long gap between the Trojan War and Homer's lifetime is coming into focus. Virchow, in fact, frankly admits, "It is very questionable whether he [Homer] ever saw with his eyes even the ruins of the fallen city." This must have been a bitter blow to Schliemann's naïve credulity. But, to his credit, he does not dispute it; and, of course, his major thesis is still untouched.

Schliemann continues his bulky book with a full review of the controversy over the exact site of Homer's "city" and argues as strong a case as has ever been made since for Hissarlik. Then he begins at the bottom and describes, layer by layer, the *seven* successive settlements that they had by then succeeded in distinguishing. The introductory diagram makes it all appear deceptively simple. Stratum I occupies 52½ feet to 45 feet below the modern surface; Stratum II, 45 to 33 feet; Stratum III, 33 feet to 23 feet; Stratum IV, 23 feet to 13 feet; Stratum V, 13 feet to 6½ feet; Stratum VI, 6½ feet to 6 feet; Stratum VII, 6 feet and up. But even this schematic representation indicates tremendous progress in precision compared to the "four nations" discussed so vaguely only a few years before. In fact, the later work of Dörpfeld and Blegen in large part authenticated Schliemann's seven occupation levels, although two major phases were added; and with modern stratigraphical techniques Blegen was able to demonstrate a far more complex pattern of subphases in the long story of Trojan prehistory.

Schliemann was trying hard to improve on his past methods, but we shall see that not every change from earlier conclusions was a correction of error. What had previously been called the lowest level is now divided into the First and the Second City. He notes that the house walls (and possibly the fortifications) at the lower level were made of much smaller stones; but it is particularly the pottery types that are now recognized as being "so vastly, so entirely different."

With a new caution he says of the so-called Aryan motifs on the spindle whorls, "I abstain from discussing whether this ornamentation may be symbolical or not . . ." Similarly, in describing some little bird-faced statuettes, he hedges slightly compared with his previous confident identification of the owl vases with Athena. "As all these rude figures represent the same form, there can be no doubt that they are idols of a female goddess, the patron deity of the place, whether she may have been called Até* or Athené, or have had any other name . . ." But he still cannot resist the urge to tie in his finds with mythology and adds: "There appears to be the highest probability that all of them are copies of the celebrated primeval Palladium* [image of Pallas Athene], to which was attached the fate of Troy, and which was fabled to have fallen from heaven."

Laboratory analyses of thirteen stone axes, or celts*, from the lowest level showed that they were of jade (nephrite)—one of them a rare white variety—which must have been imported in rough or finished form from very distant eastern sources. Pure copper, not bronze, was the basic metal, and the art of gilding was known. "We, therefore, find in use among these primitive inhabitants of the most ancient city on Hissarlik, together with very numerous stone implements and stone weapons, the following metals: gold, silver, lead, copper, but no iron; in fact, no trace of this latter metal was ever found by me either in any of the pre-historic cities of Troy, or at Mycenae. Nothing, I think, could better testify to the great antiquity of the pre-historic ruins at Hissarlik and at Mycenae, than the total absence of iron."

The *new* Level II represents the occupation of a "different people." Since there are no signs of fire between this and the first "city," there may have been an intervening period when the hill was unoccupied. The house walls were more solidly built of large white limestone blocks, which presumably reached right up to the roofs, and the fortifications were in the monumental Cyclopean style. The Scaean Gate and its street paved with white slabs was built then; so perhaps were some house walls found *below* the foundations of the "house of the town chieftain" (*now* assigned to Level III), which might point to the existence of a "palace" belonging to Level II on the same spot.

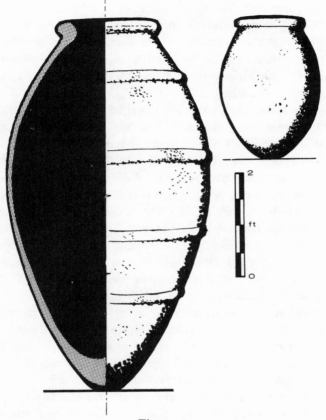

Figure 7

One of the ceramic innovations in Level II was the presence of many large clay storage jars, or pithoi*, some of them over 6 feet in height and as much as 5 feet in diameter (Fig. 7). In a characteristic example of his incorrigible habit of name-dropping, Schliemann records: "As his Highness Prince Otto Bismarck, the Chancellor of the German Empire, ingeniously remarked to me . . . the manufacture of these large jars proves already a high degree of civilization, for to make them is just as difficult as to bake them . . ." Also, the owl vases begin in Level II and continue in the following three strata; so do the equally distinctive conical goblets (Fig. 6). The connection of the one with "owl-eyed" Athena and of the other with Homer's double-handled drinking cup is reaffirmed. Carl Schuchhardt, the first scholar to review Schliemann's over-all achievement, remarks that this "Trojan cup would be exactly suited for guests sitting in a circle at their meal. It cannot stand, and it must therefore be emptied at one draught, or else be passed round, and this would be much facilitated by the two big handles . . ."

The settlement now called "the third, the burnt city" was built on the leveled ruins of its predecessor, probably after the hill had been abandoned for a long time. Schliemann continues to identify these ruins with the fabled Troy that the Greeks captured, but it has lost its earlier designation as the Second City because of the additional stratum recognized below it. The new people built the lower part of their walls of reddish stones laid in clay mortar; and "they, and they alone of all the prehistoric people who lived here, used bricks." Brick and timber superstructures crowned their fortifications and buildings, and the final conflagration left a layer of brick and ashes 6 to 10 feet deep.

Schliemann reasons that the Scaean Gate had been reused in this phase and that a new paving of reddish slabs was laid over the white ones of the earlier roadway. Several houses were excavated. "By far the most remarkable . . . is undoubtedly the mansion immediately to the north-west of the gate, which I attribute to the town-chief or king: first, because this is by far the largest house of all; and secondly, because . . . I found in or close to it nine out of the ten treasures which were discovered, as well as a very large quantity of pottery, which, though without painting and of the same forms as that found elsewhere, was distinguished, generally speaking, by its fabric." The exterior dimensions were approximately 24 by 49 feet. The surviving ground plan is peculiar, but Schliemann argued on the analogy of modern houses in the area that the surviving first level was simply a storage cellar. It would have been reached by wooden stairs from the floor above, and the deep layer of burned debris might indicate that there had been as many as five or six stories!

Now we can follow up the discovery of the *ten* treasures just mentioned. It will be remembered that Schliemann thought that someone had been trying to carry off the great treasure from this very building. "This was certainly my opinion at the time of the discovery; but since then I have found, in the presence of Professor Virchow and M. Bournouf [note the careful reference to reliable eyewitnesses], on the very same wall, and only a few yards to the north of the spot where the large treasure was discovered, another smaller treasure, and three more treasures on and near the walls of the adjoining royal house. I, therefore, now rather believe that all these treasures have fallen in the conflagration from the upper storeys of the royal house." The remaining hoards of precious objects came from spots in the same general area and level.

Although Schliemann never suspected it at the time, the great treasure was not the only precious find of the 1873 campaign. Again, we can best get the flavor by quoting his own version of what happened.

> I now come to the three smaller treasures, found . . . at a depth of 30 feet on the east side of the royal house and very close to it, by two of my workmen. . . . [They] had stolen and divided the three treasures between themselves, and probably I should never have had any knowledge of it, had it not been for the lucky circumstance that the wife of [one] . . . had the boldness to parade one Sunday with the ear-rings and pendants. . . . This excited the envy of her companions; she was denounced to the Turkish authorities . . . who put her and her husband in prison; and, having been threatened that her husband would be hanged if they did not give up the jewels, she betrayed the hiding-place, and thus this part of the treasure was at once recovered. . . . The pair also denounced their accomplice . . . but here the authorities came too late, because he had already had his part of the spoil melted down. . . . Thus this part of the treasure is for ever lost to science.

Schliemann then describes the gold earrings, bracelets, pendants and necklaces that were recovered, and he continues: "Both thieves concur in their statement that the other part of the treasures . . . contained, amongst other jewels . . . a very large round plate of gold with most curious signs engraved on it. The loss of this latter object grieves me more than anything else." Here we can detect the scientist winning out over the gold-seeker. Schliemann desperately wanted to find written records in the earlier levels but was doomed to disappointment—as are all prehistoric archaeologists *by definition.*

No wonder a determined effort was made to supervise the later work more closely! And fortunately this change came before the complete excavation of the "house of the chieftain," because the list of separate hoards of precious objects, usually enclosed in a terra-cotta vase, becomes almost monotonous. Hundreds of articles of gold, silver and electrum jewelry, as well as various bronze weapons, were recovered in and around the ruins of the building. This time most of them were turned over to the museum in Constantinople, but Schliemann retained the rights of publication. Among the most striking objects were heavy gold bracelets and brooches with applied decoration of spirals and rosettes, a fine gold eagle, an elegant silver spoon and a ceremonial dagger of silver (Fig. 8). Clearly the occupants of the "palace" had been exceedingly wealthy; and equally clearly the fire had left no time to rescue or pillage valuables, and their later recovery had for some reason been impracticable.

Schliemann was wise enough to consult an expert about the techniques of manufacturing shown by his unique collection of delicate jewelry. Carlo

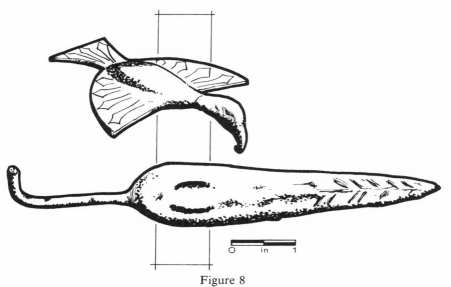

Figure 8

Giuliano, a famous London goldsmith and connoisseur of antiques, found that the gold was in general very pure (up to 23 carats fine) and that the craftsmen had been expert in making thin wire, punching complicated patterns from gold leaf and soldering microscopic beads (granulation). But "how the primitive goldsmith could do all this fine work . . . without the aid of a lens . . . is an enigma even to Mr. Giuliano." Schliemann draws a few vague parallels in details of design (especially the spirals and rosettes) with his recent finds from Mycenae, but he is not very optimistic about what the future might provide in the way of comparative material. "As nothing similar to any one of these various articles of gold has been ever found elsewhere, it will for ever remain a riddle to us whether they were home-made or imported; but if we compare them with the rude works of terra-cotta or the implements and weapons of stone or bronze found in the third city, we certainly feel inclined to think that they were imported."

Schliemann's "for ever" is somewhat of an overstatement. We now know that fortified settlements with comparable riches amassed in the chief's treasure rooms were fairly common in the same general period in the northern Aegean islands and in Anatolia. They testify to widespread trade and probably to piracy as well. But it is still difficult to define the sources of metals and other precious materials, as well as the precise centers of manufacture.

Implements and weapons of unalloyed or almost pure copper were common. But two different experts analyzed drillings from several axes and found that they were copper with between 5 per cent and 10 per cent tin; that is, the metal is proper bronze. Schliemann speculates on the source of the tin, which is not known to have occurred in any quantity in the east Mediterranean area and which he regards as a sure sign of long-distance commerce.

Among the terra-cotta vases, the big pithoi, or storage jars, interest him particularly.

> The number of large jars which I brought to light in the burnt stratum of the third city certainly exceeds 600. By far the larger number of them were empty, the mouth being covered by a large flag of schist or limestone. This leads me to the conclusion that the jars were filled with wine or water at the time of the catastrophe, for there appears to have been hardly any reason for covering them if they had been empty. Had they been used to contain anything else but liquids, I should have found traces of the fact; but only in a very few cases did I find some carbonized grain in the jars . . .

He is bothered by the continuing crudeness of the "monstrous representations of the tutelary deity" on the very numerous owl vases, when there is at least some evidence that the Trojans could model fair representations of normal human features. A possible explanation occurs in the well-known phenomenon of religious conservatism. A great many of the vases have tripod bases, but Schliemann is disappointed by the complete lack of proper tripods in metal, which are such a prominent article of exchange and value in the Homeric poems. Numerous globular jugs have a peculiar bent-back neck (Fig. 9), and there are a fair number of joined multiple vases. Both types show similarities to vases found in Cyprus. There are also some terra-cotta containers in the form of animals—hedgehogs, pigs and even a hippopotamus.

We can follow here, too, the infancy of the science of physical anthropology. Although very few burials were found in any of the prehistoric strata, several human skeletons were recovered in this level. Two of them were apparently warriors; they were wearing helmets and a bronze lance was beside one. Virchow studied the skulls carefully and found that the warriors were young males, long-headed (dolichocephalic*), with cranial indexes (the proportion of width to length) of 68.6 and 73.8. Another well-preserved skull was that of a young female, round-headed (brachycephalic*), with an index of 82.5. The considerable disparity perplexes him. "Thus we are led naturally to the question, whether we have not here before us the remains of a mixed race. . . . The temptation is very great to make further suppositions regarding the extraction of the individual persons and their social position." His good sense gets the upper

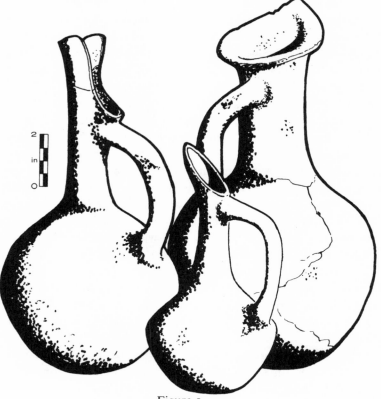

Figure 9

hand, as he adds, "This temptation, I believe, I must resist, because our real knowledge of the craniology of ancient peoples is still on a very small scale." Yet the urge to see early evidence for the master race is, after all, too much and a few lines later he confides, "But if besides the skull index we take into consideration the entire formation of the head and the face of the dolichocephalic skulls, the idea that those men were members of the Aryan race is highly pleasing."

Schliemann naturally gives a particularly careful description of the material remains recovered in his Level III, since he is still as sure as ever that it must be Homer's Troy. Yet he practically admits that the correspondences with the *Iliad* are not nearly so close as he had once believed, and he now echoes Virchow in accounting for the discrepancy. "I wish I could have proved Homer to have been an eye-witness of the Trojan war! Alas, I cannot do it! At his time swords were in universal use and iron was known, whereas they were totally unknown at Troy. . . . Homer gives us the legend of Ilium's tragic fate, as it was handed down to him by preceding bards, clothing the traditional facts of the war and destruction of Troy in the garb of his own day." Such a far-reaching hypothesis has a strangely modern ring and no doubt was in part the result of reading (in German) E. Buchholz's *The Homeric Artefacts*, which had appeared since Schliemann's first campaign.

We can be quite brief about the upper strata. Schliemann finds hints in legend that Troy was not permanently and completely destroyed by the Greeks, and he insists that archaeology has proved this true. In fact, he says, "We find among the successors of the burnt city the very same singular idols; the very same primitive bronze battle-axes; the very same terra-cotta vases, with or without tripod feet. . . . The only difference is that, in general, the pottery . . . is coarser and of a ruder fabric; and that we find . . . many new forms of vases and goblets." He complains particularly about the slovenliness of the housewives in Level IV. "The masses of shells and cockles accumulated in the *débris* of the houses are so stupendous, that they baffle all description. . . . A people which left all their kitchen-refuse on the floors of their rooms must have lived in a very low social condition." Present-day archaeologists, on the other hand, are more likely to complain when ancient housewives have been so tidy that their house floors are found swept clean.

No monumental fortification walls could be clearly associated with Levels IV and V. In the latter there was considerably more wheel-made pottery, and metal largely replaces stone for implements and weapons. Schliemann, noting the elements of both innovation and continuity, theorizes that the old stock continued to live alongside newcomers.

Between the fifth and "the seventh, the Greek Ilium," Schliemann found a thin deposit that definitely puzzled him. He calls it "the Sixth city, most probably a Lydian settlement." He could associate with it no fortifications and scarcely any house walls. He correctly suggests that the reason is a drastic leveling of the hilltop for the later Greek town. Some pottery shapes like the pithos continue; and we are reminded of the legendary Diogenes by the reference to one great jar, which "was lying . . . before my house at Hissarlik, and was always used as a lodging by one of my workmen; it even lodged two of them in rainy weather."

Most of the "Lydian" pottery in this sixth level is quite unparalleled in the lower strata, and it will prove to have a mighty importance for prehistoric archaeology (Fig. 10). "I found a vast quantity of very curious pottery, partly hand-made, partly wheel-made, which in shape and fabric, in colour and in the clay, is so utterly different from all the pottery of the preceding pre-historic cities, as well as from the pottery of the upper

Figure 10

Aeolic* Ilium, that I hesitate whether to refer it to pre-historic or to historic times." The color is black or gray, occasionally yellow or brown. Favorite shapes include cups and bowls with one or (more commonly) two high-swung handles. Many have sharp ridges, parallel grooves and abrupt surface transitions.

Schliemann, as usual, looked around the museums of Western Europe for parallels and concluded: "From the great resemblance this pottery has to . . . vases . . . found in Italy . . . held to be either archaic Etruscan or prae-Etruscan pottery, we think it likely that there may have been a Lydian settlement on Hissarlik contemporary with the colonization of Etruria by the Lydians, asserted by Herodotus, and that the Lydian dominion may have been established over the whole Troad at the same epoch." The fabulously wealthy Lydian kingdom, located in the coastal area of west central Turkey, was absorbed by the Persians in the sixth century B.C. Herodotus reports the story—still very controversial—that the mysterious Etruscan civilization in western Italy north of Rome owed its origin to a band of Lydians who were forced by famine to emigrate.[5]

When he feels that he has to suggest even an approximate date for Troy VI, Schliemann is naturally uncomfortable and vague. "Now, regarding the chronology of this Lydian city, I think every archaeologist will admit that all the articles which we have passed in review . . . denote an early state of civilization. . . . It is pretty certain that the immigration of the Etruscans into Italy took place before the Dorian invasion of the Peloponnesus [traditionally dated about 1104 B.C.] . . ." Such remarks are a commentary on the dense fog in which the pioneer was groping his way toward some kind of firm link between his own discoveries and the chaotic and vague prehistoric time scale of his day. We now know that his "Lydian" pottery is far earlier, and the earliest evidence for Etruscan culture considerably later than 1100.

THE CAMPAIGN OF 1882

The publication called *Troja,* which reports the results of the third campaign, is dedicated to "Her Imperial and Royal Highness Victoria . . . Princess Royal of Great Britain . . . illustrious patron of art and science." At the beginning Schliemann confesses that he had become increasingly unhappy about his identification of "the small town, the third in succession from the virgin soil" with the mighty Troy of legend. He finally felt compelled once more to recheck the evidence in the field. This time he was assisted by the architects Dörpfeld and Joseph Höfler. They were responsible for a completely new survey of the excavations. Time after time in the course of his last major Trojan publication Schliemann frankly and courageously admits that "my excellent architects have proved to me" that this or that previous theory was wrong.

One perceives throughout this book a more relaxed and mellow tone. The site and equipment were in good shape when they returned. The weather was good. Their quarters were larger and more comfortable. And, even more important, the commissary had improved. "My honoured friends, Messrs. J. Henry Schröder & Co., of London, had kindly sent me a large supply of tins of Chicago corned beef, peaches, the best English cheese, and ox-tongues, as well as 240 bottles of the best English pale ale." A footnote on this page probably represents the most personal remark ever made by the author of a serious archaeological publication. "I was the sole consumer," Schliemann confesses, "of these 240 bottles of pale ale, which lasted me for five months, and which I used as a medicine to cure constipation, from which I had been suffering for more than thirty years . . ." The only real irritant was that the Turkish authorities, still mindful of the disappearance of the treasure in 1873, had posted as overseer a certain suspicious and malicious Beder Eddin Effendi. "A wretch like him," comments Schliemann, "is an unmitigated plague in archaeological pursuits."

The results of the third campaign required no major revision in the previous conclusions about Level I. It was a small fortified citadel with relatively few buildings. But we are startled to see references to "the *second,* the burnt city." What, we wonder, has happened to "the *third,* the burnt city"? Schliemann apologizes quite candidly: "My architects have proved to me that, together with M. Bournouf, my collaborator in 1879, I had not rightly distinguished and separated the ruins of the two following settlements, namely, the Second and Third . . ." His explanation of this serious mistake is long and involved; but it amounts to the fact that the deep layer of burned debris (especially bricks) really marks the destruction of the buildings of the *second* level, and that the buildings of the next level were set immediately on this debris, sometimes sunk down into it and resting directly on earlier fortifications and house walls that had not been too much ruined. So, all references in the 1880 publication to the "*third,* the burnt city" must be erased from our minds, and we are back to the earlier equation of 1875: Level II=burned city=Homer's Troy.

To those who wonder why we bother to record such wavering, one may point out that it is often by means of a series of corrected hypotheses that archaeology or any other science reaches or approaches the truth. The usual statement that Schliemann believed that Level II was Homer's Troy is an oversimplification and in a sense a falsification of the record. The conclusion was not reached nearly as directly as that. In fact, as we have seen, his identification of Homeric Troy varied over those early years from Level I to Level II to Level III and back to II. And to anticipate for a moment, in his very last year of life he was apparently convinced that he would have to change his pronouncement once again—to Level VI. And even that equation did not stand the test of time, for we now believe that Homeric Troy was Level VIIa! Schliemann no doubt had an embarrassing habit of rushing into print; but no apology is needed in any scholarly field for a change of mind necessitated by new evidence. The unpardonable sin, indeed, is for a scholar to refuse to consider the possibility that a cherished theory may be mistaken. And archaeological annals, as we shall see, contain notable examples of such failings.

But to return to 1882, for the first time the foundations of buildings in the center of the fortified area of Level II were systematically cleared. Especially noteworthy were two large structures with heavy brick walls (Fig. 13). They "are most probably temples: we infer this in the first place from their ground plan, because they have only one hall in the breadth; secondly, from the proportionately considerable thickness of the walls; thirdly, from the circumstance, that they stand parallel and near each other, being only separated by a corridor about 20 inches broad; for if they had been dwelling-houses they would probably have had one common wall—a thing never found yet in ancient temples."

The larger structure (A) had an almost square porch at the front and a main room about 33 feet by 66 feet. The two rooms are called pronaos* (porch) and naos* (sanctuary) in the technical terms of classical temple architecture.

> Precisely in the middle of the naos is a circular elevation. . . . It consists, like the floor, of beaten clay, and seems to have served as the substruction to an altar or as a base for the idol; but we cannot say this with certainty, the greater part of the circle having been cut away by the great north trench. . . . Like all edifices in the prehistoric cities of Troy, this temple had a horizontal roofing, which was made of large wooden beams, smaller rafters, and clay. This is evident from the entire absence of any tiles, as well as from the existence in the interior of the edifice of a layer of clay 12 inches thick, mixed with calcined rafters and some large well-preserved pieces of wood. . . . This kind of roofing is still in general use in the Troad.

The smaller edifice (B) was built later than A, since there was no clay coating over the bricks of the exterior wall next to A. Its ground plan consisted of three rooms about 15 feet wide and one behind the other: pronaos; naos, about 24 feet long; and a rear room, about 30 feet long. "Although the division of the temple B into three rooms answers in a striking manner to the division of the house of Paris, according to Homer's description[6] . . . nevertheless the reasons given above seem to prove, with the greatest probability, that both the edifices, B as well as A, were temples." One can read between the lines that Schliemann would have very much preferred to call these buildings houses or even palaces; but he was over-awed by Dörpfeld, who was fresh from the exciting German discovery of classical temples at Olympia.

Only one new cache of metal objects was discovered in Level II, and Schliemann's description of the fate of one item suggests the satisfaction he took in outwitting the obnoxious Beder Eddin Effendi. "By far the most interesting object of the little treasure was a copper or bronze idol of the most primitive form. . . . I think it probable that it is a copy or imitation of the famous Palladium. . . . Fortunately . . . it had broken into three fragments; I am indebted to this lucky circumstance for having obtained it in the division with the Turkish Government; for the three pieces were covered with carbonate of copper and dirt, and altogether undiscernible to an inexperienced eye" (Fig. 11).

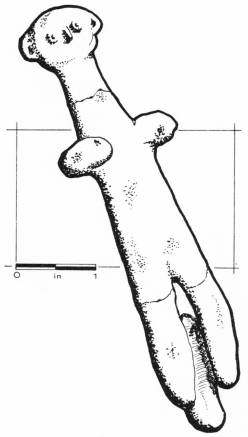

Figure 11

No significant changes are made in the brief discussion of Levels IV, V and VI. The latter is still called Lydian. He describes the results of his research in the uppermost level of Greek and Roman times and reviews the latest explorations in the plain of Troy. Then, with uncharacteristic detachment, which perhaps suggests that he was tiring, he sums up the whole series of campaigns: "My work at Troy is now ended for ever, after extending over more than the period of *ten years,* which has a fated connection with the legend of the city. How many tens of years a new controversy may rage around it, I leave to the critics: *that* is their work; *mine* is done."

THE CAMPAIGN OF 1890

The controversy that Schliemann predicted has indeed continued to the present day, though perhaps not along the lines he foresaw; but his own work at Troy was not quite done. The fabulous discovery of the royal Shaft Graves just inside the Lion Gate at Mycenae had kindled the hope that their counterparts might still exist undetected at Troy. The belief seems to have taken increasing hold of Schliemann that excavation around the main gate in the southwest section of wealthy Troy II would "pay off." And so in 1890, the last year of his eventful life, the old man was once more back at Hissarlik with Dörpfeld; and a new field railroad system

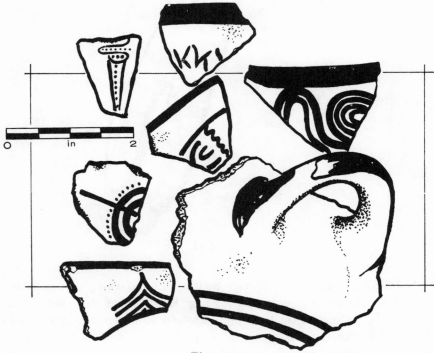

Figure 12

with metal track and dump cars was installed to dispose more quickly of the earth.

They found no gold-filled tombs associated with Troy II, but they made a discovery of far greater importance for the true understanding of the site. For Schliemann it must have been a tragically unwelcome realization. Troy II was apparently not "Homer's Troy" and the wonderful treasures had no connection with Priam. For on the slope outside the circuit of its walls they discovered the ruins of two buildings of excellent construction that had belonged to Troy VI, the "Lydian city"; and on the floors, mixed with the gray pottery that Schliemann still called Lydian, were a fair number of vase fragments clearly identical with those they already knew well from the most prosperous phases of Mycenae and Tiryns on the Greek mainland (Fig. 12).

The conclusion was inevitable. It was Level VI and not Level II that

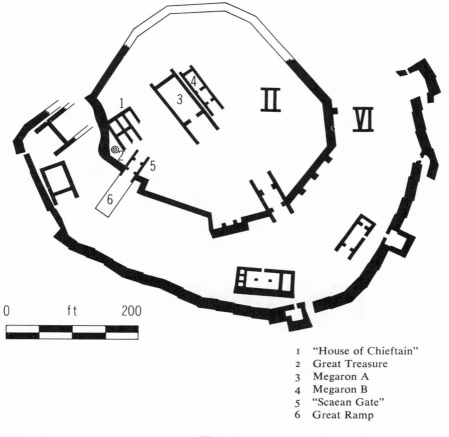

0   ft   200

1	"House of Chieftain"
2	Great Treasure
3	Megaron A
4	Megaron B
5	"Scaean Gate"
6	Great Ramp

Figure 13

was contemporary with the period of Mycenae's greatness; and it therefore would have been Troy VI that was attacked by the Greek armada. Between Levels II and VI lay the remains of three distinct phases of occupation, which showed that Troy II must be far older than the epoch of the Trojan War. With characteristic honesty and energy Schliemann saw that the shattering new evidence had to be followed up. His earlier excavations had largely missed or misinterpreted any monumental remains of the Lydian level. He had believed that segments of its marvelously constructed walls, encountered more than once in earlier campaigns, belonged to classical Greek times. They had enclosed a much larger area than had the walls of Troy II. Peripheral areas would probably yield a good deal of information about Troy VI, even though its higher central section had been destroyed when later Greeks and Romans leveled off the site (Fig. 13).

We can hardly pass over one discovery from Level II during this last excavation. Near the center of the citadel a "treasure" of stone objects was uncovered. The finest of the contents are four magnificent, highly polished artefacts that truly deserve the name "battle-axes" (Fig. 14). Three are of greenish stone said to be nephrite, and one bluish one resembles lapis

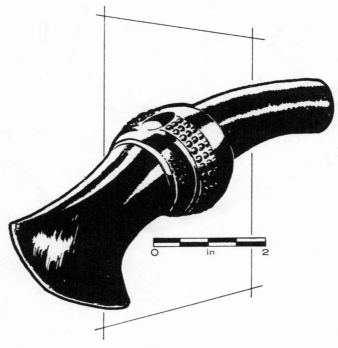

Figure 14

lazuli. Both the exotic materials and the elegant craftsmanship suggest that these, like the smaller objects of jade, probably come from much farther east—perhaps from Bessarabia.

Schliemann immediately began planning for a major campaign in the spring of 1891. But in December, when he was in Naples en route to be with his family for Christmas after an ear operation in Germany, death intervened. Perhaps it was just as well. Adjustment to the new evidence and explanations of all his earlier confident claims would have been a difficult ordeal. Now he could finally find a well-deserved resting place, as Dörpfeld writes, "in Athens, his second home, in sight of the acropolis."

POSTHUMOUS REVISIONS

For Schliemann's last word on the Trojan excavations, however, it is proper to add the modifications published by Schuchhardt. He had repeatedly conferred with Schliemann during the preparation of his German edition, which appeared in 1889; and Schliemann had given permission for his own summary of the 1890 campaign to be printed in the English edition (1891).

One important change was the realization that buildings A and B in Level II were indeed the remains of a "palace," and not temples at all. This had been made clear by the discovery of much later buildings of similar plan on the acropolises of Tiryns and Mycenae in mainland Greece. The central unit of the mainland palaces had been given the name "megaron*," which is Homer's own word to denominate the palace—or at least the throne room—of a king. The fragmentary circular structure about 13 feet in diameter in the center of the main room of the Trojan megaron A is recognized as the hearth "which Homer tells us is situated in the innermost part of the house and marks its most sacred spot."[7]

Confusion between the ground plan of prehistoric megaron and classical temple was a natural error, since the royal palace of the Bronze Age was apparently in a real sense a shrine as well as a dwelling, and there seems to have been a straight line of development from it to the stately building that sheltered deity in later times. The later connection of still another architectural feature first discovered at Troy is also more fully recognized. Schuchhardt points out that the monumental plan of the city gates and propylaea* (entranceway) of Level II is "not only found again at Tiryns and Mycenae, but it became the model for all subsequent Greek gate construction."

The "owl vases" were finally recognized as nothing more than primitive attempts to model the main features of the female body. The similarity to an owl—and therefore the connection with an "owl-eyed" Athena—was purely accidental. On another issue, Schliemann, as well as several eminent philologists, had at first professed to see writing symbols in the complicated patterns inscribed on some of the clay spindle whorls, balls and seals. In particular, several equations had been proposed between certain of these signs and the early writing systems of Cyprus and Hittite Asia Minor. Schuchhardt, however, states flatly: "On none of them . . . can anything beyond mere decoration be made out."

In his summary of Schliemann's work at Troy, Schuchhardt apparently makes just one rather awkward and oblique reference to the chronological revelations of the last campaign. We can accept, he asserts, "one fact as incontestable: there existed on the site of Hissarlik, at a period far anterior to any we know of on Greek soil, a proud and royal city [presumably Level II], mistress of sea and land; and the singers of the Trojan War, just as they were familiar with Ida and Skamander, with the Hellespont and the Isle of Tenedos, knew also of this city, knew of its golden age and of its mighty downfall." He seems here to be aware of the contemporaneity of Mycenae with Troy VI and yet still to link Troy II with the epic.

So it remained for Dörpfeld and Blegen to try in their turn to set the Homeric story in its proper archaeological context at Troy. As we shall see, they worked in a later epoch with new knowledge and new techniques— and yet always in the shadow of the pioneer.

MYCENAE

In his first archaeological book, Schliemann not only had insisted that modern Ithaki is Odysseus' island and that Hissarlik is Priam's Troy, but also had proposed a new theory about Agamemnon's Mycenae. In the case of Mycenae, there could be no question about the identification of the site. A strong and reverent tradition had apparently clung to the citadel, probably without a serious break, for fifteen centuries or more when its ruins were visited and described in the second century A.D. by the famous traveler Pausanias. And since then the Lion Gate (Fig. 15) itself was enough to keep the record clear. Indeed, the very massiveness of the remains continued to protect them, so that practically everything that Pausanias saw has been visible ever since. Naturally, a good many treasure hunters and archaeological dilettantes had probed among the monuments of "golden Mycenae" before Schliemann saw the site.

Figure 15

Pausanias was a conscientious antiquarian who took the grand tour of Greece in the heyday of the highly civilized *Pax Romana* when Hadrian and the later Antonine emperors had set the fashion of interest in "ancient" Greek history and archaeology. Local guides, who then as now mixed true traditions and solid fact with legend and personal imagination, gave him "the pitch." His notes on Mycenae, published in the monumental *Description of Greece,* are worth quoting at some length.

Among other remains of the wall is the gate, on which stand lions. They [the walls and the gate] are said to be the work of the Cyclopes, who built the wall for Proteus at Tiryns. In the ruins of Mycenae is the fountain called Perseia and the subterranean buildings of Atreus and his children, in which they stored their treasures. There is the sepulchre of Atreus, and the tombs of the companions of Agamemnon, who on their return from Ilium were killed at a banquet by Aegisthus. . . . There is the tomb of Agamemnon and that of his charioteer Eurymedon, and of Electra. Teledamus and Pelos were buried in the same sepulchre, for it is said that Cassandra bore these twins, and that, while as yet infants, they were slaughtered by Aegisthus together with their parents. . . . Clytemnestra and Aegisthus were buried at a little distance from the wall because they were thought unworthy to have their tombs inside of it, where Agamemnon reposed and those who were killed with him.[8]

To Schliemann, as he first stood on the acropolis with his copy of Pausanias in hand, almost everything seemed right (see Fig. 16). He had only to follow Pausanias' directions and to "get digging." He could see the massive Cyclopean fortification walls surrounding the acropolis, the famous Lion Gate at its northwest angle, and the Perseia fountain. To the west, outside the fortifications, the great domed underground structure, long recognized as Pausanias' "Treasury of Atreus," was accessible; and five other partially collapsed examples of the same type of monumental construction had been discovered in the vicinity.

On the other hand, the *tomb* of Atreus, those of Agamemnon and his companions, and of their murderers, Aegisthus and Clytemnestra, who "were buried at a little distance from the wall," were not so easy to identify. Modern scholars who had visited Mycenae before Schliemann understood Pausanias' "wall" to refer to the slight traces of a line of fortifications northwest of the citadel. This outer line (actually of Hellenistic* date) had presumably enclosed the lower town. So they expected the tombs of Agamemnon and the rest to lie *outside* the great fortified citadel and those of Clytemnestra and Aegisthus to be still farther on the periphery, beyond the city limits.

But Schliemann thought otherwise:

Pausanias could only speak of such walls as he *saw,* and not of those which he did *not see.* He saw the huge walls of the citadel, because they were at his time exactly as they are now; but he could not see the wall of the lower city, because it had been originally only very thin, and it had been demolished 638 years before his time [when Argos destroyed the little classical town of Mycenae in 468 B.C.]; nor was he an archaeologist, to search for its traces or still less to make excavations to find them. . . . For these decisive reasons, I have always interpreted the famous passage in Pausanias in the sense that the five tombs [Atreus; Agamemnon; Eurymedon; Cassandra and twins; Electra] were in the Acropolis.

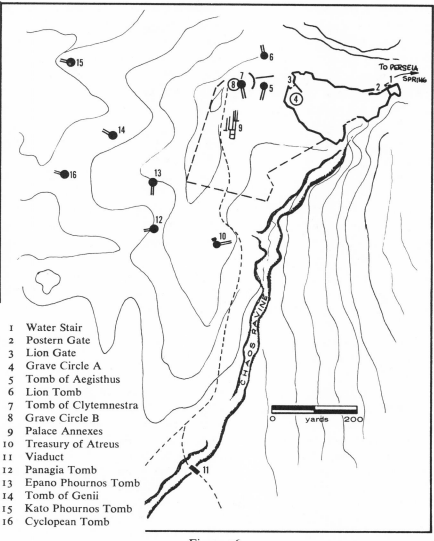

1   Water Stair
2   Postern Gate
3   Lion Gate
4   Grave Circle A
5   Tomb of Aegisthus
6   Lion Tomb
7   Tomb of Clytemnestra
8   Grave Circle B
9   Palace Annexes
10 Treasury of Atreus
11 Viaduct
12 Panagia Tomb
13 Epano Phournos Tomb
14 Tomb of Genii
15 Kato Phournos Tomb
16 Cyclopean Tomb

Figure 16

And it was *inside* the monumental fortifications of the acropolis that
Schliemann had made up his mind to search for Agamemnon's mortal
remains.

Negotiations for a permit from the Greek authorities were complicated
by the controversy with the Turks over the ownership of the Trojan treasure
and by widespread criticism of Schliemann's lack of care in the first campaign at Hissarlik. He was allowed to sink some experimental shafts at

Mycenae in 1874, but it was only in late summer of 1876 that the Greek government authorized a full-scale excavation. Even then, he had to give assurances that digging would be concentrated at only one spot at a time, that no damage would be done to structures uncovered and that a manageable number of workmen would be hired. Most galling of all, "a government clerk by the name of Stamatakes" (in fact a trusted and senior member of the Archaeological Service) was sent to see that the stipulations were followed.

Schliemann's motivation for the excavations at Mycenae was exactly the same as at Troy. In the dedication of his book titled *Mycenae* (1878) he speaks of "this account of discoveries made at Mycenae and Tiryns, tending to illustrate the POEMS OF HOMER." Incidentally, the book was dedicated to "The Right Honourable William Ewart Gladstone, M.P.," who had been prevailed upon to write a Preface. The great Gladstone maintained throughout his busy political life continuing research and reading in classical literature. Only two years earlier he had published the third of his book-length studies of Greek epic, *Homeric Synchronisms: An Enquiry into the Time and Place of Homer.* Gladstone was one of Schliemann's earliest and staunchest supporters; and Schliemann was almost pathetically grateful.

Schliemann's description of the site (see Map V), while perhaps not as lyrical as what he wrote at Troy, is still worth quoting.

The situation of Mycenae is beautifully described by Homer, "in the depths of the horse-feeding Argos,"[9] because it lies in the north corner of the plain of Argos, . . . whence it commanded the upper part of the great plain and the important narrow pass, by which the roads lead to Phlius, Cleonae, and Corinth. The Acropolis occupied a strong rocky height, which projects from the foot of the mountain behind it [the lofty Prophitis Elias] in the form of an irregular triangle sloping to the west. This cliff overhangs a deep gorge, which protects the whole south flank of the citadel. . . . The cliff also falls off precipitously on the north side. . . . Between these two gorges extended the lower city. The cliff of the citadel is also more or less steep on the east and west side, where it forms six natural or artificial terraces.

Excavation was concentrated just inside the Lion Gate. "I began the great work," writes Schliemann, "on the 7th August, 1876, with sixty-three workmen, whom I divided into three parties. I put twelve men at the Lions' Gate, to open the passage into the Acropolis; I set forty-three to dig, at a distance of 40 feet from [inside] that gate, a trench 113 feet long and 113 feet broad; and the remaining eight men I ordered to dig a trench on the south side of the Treasury [later called the tomb of Clytemnestra] in the lower city, near the Lions' Gate, in search of the entrance." The third area was under his wife's supervision.

It soon became clear that the accepted belief that the final destruction of the little classical town occurred in 468 B.C. was in error. Schliemann showed definitely that the upper three feet or so of fill contained potsherds, terra-cotta statuettes and coins that belong to Hellenistic times. "I presume that the new colony may have been founded in the beginning of the fourth, and may have been abandoned in the beginning of the second century B.C." One is immediately struck by the comparative precision with which the chronology of the historic material could even then be fixed.

Everywhere below this level, however, he found "fragments of those splendidly-painted archaic vases" (Fig. 12) whose shapes and decorative motifs he illustrates in the publication. He knew, of course, that comparable pottery had been known for some time from Attica, Rhodes, Cyprus, and even Egypt. In an Egyptian tomb, along with fragments of this distinctive pottery, was a scarab* with a "cartouche* of Amunoph III, who is thought by Egyptologists to have reigned not later than B.C. 1400." Here already is a strong contrast to the groping for parallels and the lack of any hint at absolute* chronology for the Trojan material. Almost from the beginning this "Mycenaean" culture could be placed in at least an approximate historical context because of Egyptian synchronisms.*

He also notes the discovery of many terra-cotta "idols of Hera, more or less broken, in the form of a woman or in that of a cow" (Fig. 17). As with the Trojan "owl-eyed Athena," he immediately recognizes in these little figures a connection with a Homeric deity, in this case Hera *bo-ōpis* ("ox-eyed").

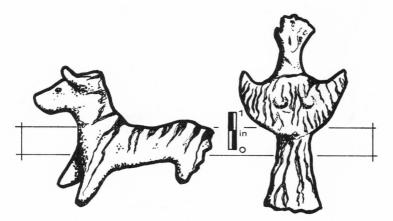

Figure 17

But more exciting finds soon began to appear in the big trench inside the Lion Gate. "I have brought to light two tombstones, which stand in a direct line from north to south, and are ornamented with bas-reliefs of the highest interest." Both showed chariot scenes. There is a single charioteer, and the horse (he uses the singular) is at full gallop. Underneath the horse portrayed on the slab, or stela*, that he identifies as #1, a dog and deer are running; while on stela #2 (Fig. 18) a man with a raised sword is shown just in front of the chariot group. Framing the figured scenes, particularly in the second example, is a careful border of parallel straight lines and elaborate spirals.

Schliemann immediately notices an odd feature in the sculpture. "I find such a marvellous accuracy and symmetry in all the spiral ornamentation, that I feel almost tempted to think such work can only have been produced by a school of sculptors which had worked for ages in a similar style. On the other hand, the men and the animals are made as rudely and in as puerile a manner as if they were the primitive artist's first essay to represent living beings." Above all, he is pleased with the new evidence on chariotry,

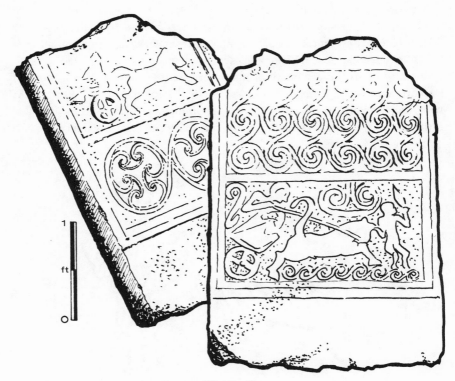

Figure 18

the first archaeological proof that the institution so typical in Homer was at home in prehistoric Greece. "The chariot gives us a unique and most precious specimen of the Homeric chariot, of which we had before but a confused idea."

Soon they uncovered two parallel rows of plain stone slabs, which "appear to form, with the part in the adjoining field, a full circle." The circular structure proved to be a low barrier formed by laying horizontal slabs on top of the two parallel lines of vertical ones (Fig. 19). The barrier was interrupted by an entrance, which faced the Lion Gate, and Schliemann long believed (with others) that he had found an example of the "sacred circle" of the Homeric agora, or assembly place.[10] Two more sculptured stelae were found within the circle. They were in the same line and farther south than the previous two. The third has in an upper register a chariot scene very similar to #2; and the lower part is adorned with running spirals within two circles linked in a horizontal figure-eight design. Stela #4 has no figured scene but simply three vertical panels, the middle plain, the others sculptured in a wave pattern. Several additional complete or fragmentary stelae were encountered at the same depth of 10 to 13 feet below the surface.

With serene confidence Schliemann states in the day-to-day diary his conviction that the "four sculptured and five unsculptured sepulchral slabs undoubtedly mark the sites of tombs cut deep in the rock. . . . I also found at the feet of most of the tombstones grey ashes of burnt animal matter, which I at first thought was from human bodies; but as I found together with them bones which on closer investigation turn out to be those of animals, I now think the ashes must be from sacrifices."

Furthermore, he has no doubts about the identity of the tombs he has not yet located. "Who have the great personages been, and what immense services did they render to Mycenae, to have received the signal honour of such a burial place? I do not for a moment hesitate to proclaim that I have found here the sepulchres which Pausanias, following the tradition, attributes to Atreus, to the 'king of men' Agamemnon. . . . But it is utterly impossible that Pausanias should have seen these tombstones. . . . He could only have known of the existence of these sepulchres by tradition."

Work was also proceeding beyond (south of) the circle of slabs in a "vast Cyclopean house." Later it was called the House of the Warrior Vase because it contained, among other finds, "fragments of a large vase, with two or three handles, the ends of which have been modelled into the shape of cowheads. . . . Some of the fragments . . . represent six full-armed warriors, painted with a dark red colour on a light yellow dead [dull monotone] ground; they are evidently setting out on a military expedition,

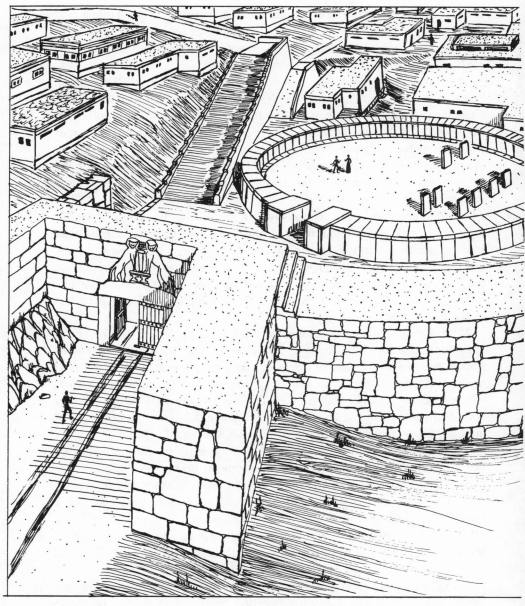

Figure 19

and all wear coats of mail which reach from the neck down to below the hips. . . . The shape of the lances is such as we were led to expect from the Homeric *'dolichoskion enchos'* [long-shadowing spear], for they are very long . . ."

He proceeds as follows with the description of the scene on the Warrior Vase, which is still the best-known and perhaps the most informative of all Mycenaean paintings (Fig. 20):

Figure 20

Now, with regard to the physiognomy of the six warriors, it is most decidedly not Assyrian or Egyptian. All have exactly the same type— very long noses, large eyes, small ears, and a long well-dressed beard. . . . Five of the warriors are followed by a woman, seemingly a priestess, who is dressed in a long gown fastened at the waist by a girdle. . . . Only her right arm remains, which is uplifted, and by the curve it forms it appears that the woman has lifted her joined hands and is praying to the gods to be propitious to the departing warriors, and to grant them a safe return. This custom of lifting both hands when praying is continually found in Homer.[11] On other fragments of the same vase are represented two warriors. . . . The armour . . . is perfectly identical . . . except for the head-dress, which, instead of bronze helmets, consists here seemingly of a low helmet of boarskin, with the bristles outside. In fact, these helmets vividly remind us of the low helm of oxskin which Ulysses put on his head when he and Diomede went in the night as spies to the Trojan camp.[12]

Back inside the circular agora the workmen were probing deeper, and the most spectacular find in the history of Greek archaeology was about to be made. Schliemann tells of the discovery of the first grave under dateline of December 6. His prose is curiously restrained when compared with the description of the great Trojan treasure found only three years before. "I excavated on the site of the three [tombstones] with the bas-reliefs representing the warriors and the hunting scene, and found a quadrangular tomb, 21 ft. 5 in. long and 10 ft. 4 in. broad, cut out in the slope of the rock." Before he could reach its bottom, however, a heavy rain occurred and he shifted operations about 20 feet away where the two unsculptured tombstones had been found.

> At a depth of 15 ft. below the level of the rock, or of 25 ft. below the former surface of the ground . . . I reached a layer of pebbles, below which I found, at a distance of three feet from each other, the remains of three human bodies, all with the head turned to the east and the feet to the west. . . . They had evidently been burned simultaneously. . . . There were the most unmistakable marks of three distinct funeral pyres. . . . These could not have been large, and had evidently been intended to consume merely the clothes and partly or entirely the flesh of the deceased; but *no more,* because the bones and even the skulls had been preserved . . .

He then records the offerings buried with the dead—gold diadems, small gold "crosses," badly decomposed objects of glass, terra-cotta figurines, obsidian* knives, a large silver vase, and "most remarkable wheel-made terracottas [vases]" (Fig. 21).

This grave he labeled II, and we shall retain the original numbering. It is worth remarking here that, although one would never guess the fact from his continual use of the first person singular, the hands that delicately cleared each of the precious objects in all of these graves were not Heinrich's, but Sophia Schliemann's. For those twenty-five days of continuous and incredibly painstaking work his excitable temperament simply would not have held up. We can imagine the scene—workmen dismissed, armed soldiers ringing the grave, Schliemann busily taking notes and counting the treasure, Stamatakes and officials watching and recounting, but Sophia down in the deep hole for hours on end in cramped and uncomfortable positions doing the real work.

The report resumes.

> Encouraged by the success obtained in the second tomb, I took out the two large unsculptured tombstones of the third line, which stood almost due south of the former. . . . In digging deeper I found . . . two sepulchres, of which I shall describe the smaller one. . . . I call [it] the Third Tomb. . . . [It measures] 16 ft. 8 in. long and 10 ft. 2 in. broad. . . . I found in this sepulchre the mortal remains of three persons who, to

Figure 21

judge by the smallness of the bones and particularly of the teeth, and by the masses of female ornaments found here, must have been women. . . . The bodies were literally laden with jewels, all of which bore evident signs of the fire and smoke. . . . The ornaments of which the greatest number was found were the large, thick, round plates of gold, with a very pretty decoration of *repoussé** work, of which I collected 701 [Fig. 22].

Grave III also contained masses of other gold objects in the form of seals, griffins*, lions, nude female figurines with doves perched on head and arms, octopus, butterflies, eagles. Many of them showed holes for attachment, and Schliemann concluded that they had been sewn on the dresses of the dead women. Near one cranium was a magnificent gold crown decorated in repoussé with intricate designs within circles, and a smaller gold diadem was still in place on another skull. There were seven simpler and smaller diadems, six crosses, a jewelbox with lid, a brooch, pendants, numerous earrings, pins, wheels, combs and various other gold objects for which he could not immediately determine the purpose. The grave also contained masses of amber beads of various sizes, objects of

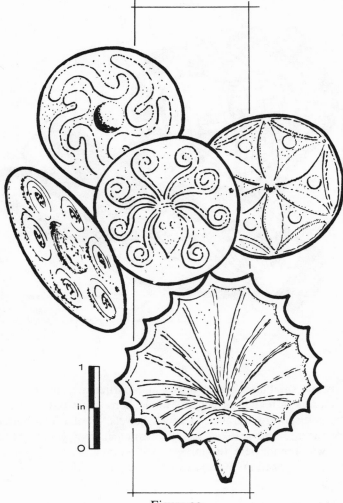

Figure 22

rock crystal, ivory, engraved gems. In addition to jewelry he inventories
several vases of gold (Fig. 23), two of silver and a number of terra-cotta.

Less than 5 feet from III lay Grave IV. Exactly over its center they
found an "almost circular mass of Cyclopean masonry with a large opening in the form of a well," which Schliemann identified as a "funeral altar—
erected in honour of those whose mortal remains reposed" in the grave
below. Grave IV contained the skeletons of five men, three lying with
head to the east and the other two with head to the north. The type of
tomb and the method of burial were exactly similar to that in Graves II

and III; that is, the tomb had been hollowed in the rock of the hillside, the walls lined with rubble and the floor covered with pebbles "intended to procure ventilation for the pyres." Schliemann adds some details that later proved significant: "Here, as well as in the first and third tombs, I have noticed that, for a reason unknown to me, the burned bodies, with their golden ornaments, had been covered, after the cremation, with a layer . . . of . . . white clay. . . . On this layer of clay was put the second layer of pebbles."

He was apparently becoming somewhat uneasy about his diagnosis of cremation, and perhaps for this reason he insisted on it all the more. "The cremation . . . has been officially authenticated by the three government clerks, whom the Director-General of Antiquities at Athens . . . has sent here to assist me in guarding the treasures . . . and by the thousands of people who flock hither from all parts of the Argolid to see these wonders; and, therefore, anyone who doubts the exactness of my statements as to the cremation is requested to apply to the said Director-General or to the

Figure 23

Ministry of Public Instruction at Athens." Naturally, he wanted the burial rite in these Mycenae graves to correspond with the cremations described in the *Iliad*.

Apropos of the intense public interest, Schliemann adds one of his characteristic and imaginative historical gambits:

> For the first time since its capture by the Argives in 468 B.C., and so for the first time during 2,344 years, the Acropolis of Mycenae has a garrison, whose watch-fires seen by night throughout the whole Plain of Argos carry back the mind to the watch kept for Agamemnon's return from Troy, and the signal which warned Clytemnestra and her paramour of his approach.[13] But this time the object of the occupation by soldiery is of a more peaceful character, for it is merely intended to inspire awe among the country-people, and to prevent them from making clandestine excavations in the tombs . . .

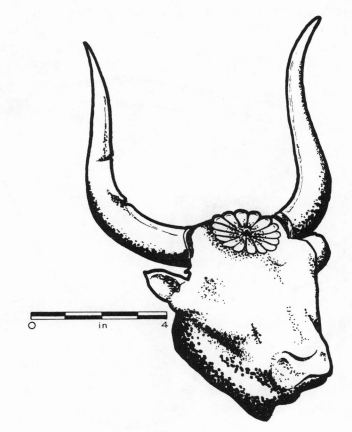

Figure 24

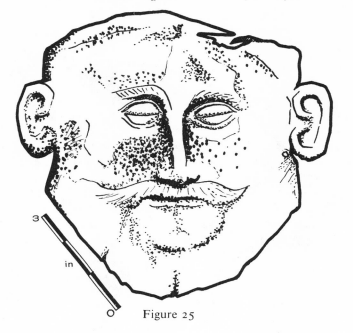

Figure 25

The five bodies in Grave IV had been literally smothered in costly burial offerings. In view of the previous warning, the following sentence will provoke a tolerant smile. "We have to do the work ourselves; the task is exceedingly difficult and painful to us, particularly in the present rainy weather, for we cannot dig otherwise than on our knees, and by cutting the earth and stones carefully away with our knives, so as not to injure or lose any of the gold ornaments." Among the finds were many objects that are still the finest examples known for their class and time. Schliemann's descriptions are really quite brief; yet they and the illustrations occupy more than twenty pages in the original publication. We can mention only a few of the most outstanding: a silver vase in the form of a bull's head (called a rhyton*) with golden horns (Fig. 24); three remarkable and awe-inspiring gold face masks (Fig. 25), apparently modeled on the actual features of the deceased; two large gold signet rings showing chariot scenes of battle and hunting; a massive gold bracelet; gold breastplates, diadems and a "shoulder-belt"; nine golden goblets and vases, including the famous "cup of Nestor" (Fig. 26); three "models of a temple" in gold; a number of fragments of silver vessels and one silver pitcher; more than 400 beads of amber; a large three-handled vase of alabaster; thirty-two copper cauldrons; a copper tripod; various adornments for armor and weapons; obsidian arrowheads; perforated boar's tusks; forty-six bronze

Figure 26

swords and daggers; four lances; three knives; numerous terra-cotta vases.

At least a few of Schliemann's observations on these discoveries must be recorded. Analysis of the bronze showed an alloy consisting of copper with 10 to 13 per cent tin. He notes that the Mycenaean goldsmiths, unlike those of Troy, did not practice soldering but made connections with "pins" (rivets). Also, they apparently could not plate gold over silver, except by using an intervening layer of copper. He also observes that the spiral decoration on some of the objects in the graves is "perfectly similar" to that on the grave stelae.

As for the representational art, he is sure that the long, rectangular shield portrayed in the battle scene on a gold ring (Fig. 27) is "one of the large Homeric shields, which were so enormous that the poet compares them to towers."[14] And after describing the scenes on the bezels of the two gold rings, he adds, "When I brought to light these wonderful signets, I involuntarily exclaimed: 'The author of the *Iliad* and the *Odyssey* cannot

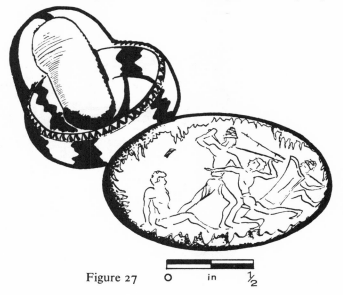

Figure 27

but have been born and educated amidst a civilisation which was able to produce such works as these. Only a poet who had objects of art like these continually before his eyes could compose those divine poems.' "

In discussing the golden goblet that "vividly reminds us of Nestor's cup,"[15] Schliemann comes to the conclusion that "the shape of the Nestorian goblet may be imagined as perfectly similar to the goblet before us, because this really has four handles; namely, the two horizontal ones, on which the pigeons lie, and the two lower ones which are produced by the thick vertical straps, which join them at the foot. If so, the only difference would be that Nestor's goblet had one more pigeon on each of these double handles." The three so-called temple models of gold, "perhaps the most curious objects of all," show a tripartite building, open at the front, with a column like those in the sculpture of the Lion Gate in the center of each opening. Motifs such as pairs of horns are shown at the base of each column, as well as above the roof of the higher central part. And birds perch above each of the outer parts (Fig. 28).

He notes that the swords are very long and narrow and that there is evidence from particles still attached to them that many had had sheaths of linen. The human bones in Grave IV were better preserved and "all which are not too much decayed will be displayed in the National Museum at Athens together with the treasures."

A fifth grave was discovered immediately to the northwest of the fourth and directly under four tombstones. It is important to note that two of

Figure 28

the stelae were found about 12 feet below the surface and two more, "evidently much older" and unsculptured, were about 10 feet below the others and only 3 feet above the grave itself. Grave V contained only one skeleton. The skull had a golden diadem around it, and the offerings included a lance, two small bronze swords and two long bronze knives, a golden goblet, a broken vase of "light green Egyptian porcelain" and many terra-cotta vases. One of the latter was "light red . . . ornamented with black spiral lines, and with two female breasts surrounded by circles of black strokes." Schliemann refers in this connection to the Trojan owl vases but sees an even closer parallel in vases found in 1866 on the island of Thera (Santorin) "in the ruins of the prehistoric cities which . . . were covered by an eruption of that great central volcano which is believed by competent geologists to have sunk and disappeared about 1700 to 1800 B.C." Geological dating, although sporadically attempted from that time to the present in archaeological contexts, is necessarily less exact than synchronisms with literate cultures.

When the mud in Grave I had dried sufficiently, its excavation was continued. There were three skeletons here. One had no offerings around it nor clay coating over it, which made Schliemann suspect that there had been later tampering. The bones indicated that the three men had been unusually large, while their position suggested to Schliemann that the bodies had been "forcibly squeezed into the small space of only 5 feet 6 inches which was left for them between the inner walls."

But the climax of the whole series of discoveries was still to come. Here, at least, is what Schliemann writes:

> Of the third body, which lay at the north end of the tomb, the round face, with all its flesh, had been wonderfully preserved under its ponderous golden mask; there was no vestige of hair, but both eyes were perfectly visible, also the mouth, which, owing to the enormous weight that had pressed upon it, was wide open, and showed thirty-two beautiful teeth. From these, all the physicians who came to see the body were led to believe that the man must have died at the early age of thirty-five. The nose was entirely gone. . . . The colour of the body resembled very much that of an Egyptian mummy. . . . A druggist from Argos, Spiridon Nicolaou by name, rendered it hard and solid by pouring on it alcohol, in which he had dissolved gum-sandarac.

An artist was also called in to make an oil painting, which is reproduced in the publication. Then, after being carefully undercut and boxed, the mysterious semimummy was transported to Athens.

The richness of the offerings in Grave I was surpassed only by those in IV and the types are comparable. It is indeed completely understandable that Schliemann unhesitatingly associated these graves with the acme of power and prosperity of Homer's "golden Mycenae." There were a great many swords, usually in fragments. Among the unusual finds were considerable fragments of wood in recognizable shape—three lids of boxes, and two sides of a small box on each of which are carved in relief a lion and a dog. "Food seems also to have been deposited . . . for I gathered in it a large quantity of oyster-shells, and among them several unopened oysters."

In the interval between the clearing of the tombs and the publication, Schliemann obviously thought a great deal about the significance of his finds; and the first scholarly reactions to the discovery were already known to him. He writes:

> I now proceed to discuss the question, whether it is possible to identify these sepulchres with the tombs which Pausanias, following the tradition, attributes to Agamemnon, to Cassandra, to Eurymedon, and to their companions. . . . For my part, I have always firmly believed in the Trojan war; my full faith in Homer and in the tradition has never been shaken by modern criticism, and to this faith of mine I am indebted for the discovery of Troy and its Treasure. . . . I never doubted that a king of Mycenae, by name Agamemnon, . . . had been treacherously murdered . . . and I firmly believed in the statement of Pausanias, that the murdered persons had been interred in the Acropolis. . . . My firm faith in the traditions . . . led to the discovery of the five tombs, with their immense treasures . . .

He proceeds to insist that these really are the graves of Agamemnon and his friends, foully murdered, although he is silent as to why their bodies would have been loaded with rich funeral offerings.

> The identity of the mode of burial, the perfect similarity of all the tombs, their very close proximity, the impossibility of admitting that three or even five royal personages of immeasurable wealth, who had died a natural death at long intervals of time, should have been huddled together in the same tomb, and, finally, the great resemblance of all the ornaments, which show exactly the same style of art and the same epoch—all these facts are so many proofs that all the twelve men, three women, and perhaps two or three children, had been murdered simultaneously and burned at the same time. . . . The site of each tomb was marked by tombstones, and when these had been covered by the dust of ages and had disappeared, fresh tombstones were erected on the new level, but precisely over the spot where the ancient memorials lay buried. . . . I think it therefore highly probable that the erection of the Agora coincides with the renewal of the tombstones . . .

On the chronological question he is on particularly slippery ground. "The period of the kings of Mycenae belongs to a very remote antiquity. Royalty ceased there at the Dorian invasion, the date of which has always been fixed at 1104 B.C. . . . But, in agreement with all archaeologists, I hold to the conclusion that, on the evidence of the monuments of Troy, the capture and the destruction of that city, and consequently also the Dorian invasion [which traditionally occurred eighty years later], must have occurred at a much earlier date." His early groping for a firm chronological link between Troy II and the monumental fortified sites on the Greek mainland was, of course, superseded by the results of the last Trojan campaign. But he already seems to have sensed correctly that the Egyptian evidence of a date around 1400 for the developed phases at Mycenae was too late for Troy II. Incidentally, he must have been in a particularly euphoric state when he refers to his "agreement with all archaeologists" about the chronological implications of the Trojan excavations.

Before we discuss the modified views on the graves in the agora that had developed by the time of Schliemann's death, we should very briefly summarize his opinions about the "treasuries" outside the acropolis walls. The largest and only uncollapsed structure was apparently the one attributed to Atreus by Pausanias (Fig. 38). Since it had been partially cleared in the early nineteenth century, Mrs. Schliemann was put in charge of excavating the most impressive of the others that lay just outside the Lion Gate. Describing the type, Schliemann says, "These conical buildings, 50 feet high, were constructed under the slope of a hill, and were destined to remain subterranean: for . . . the outside surface of the stones is quite irregular, and the whole building is covered all round with a thick layer of stones, the weight of which holds the masonry fast together. I feel certain that the tradition is correct which says that these mysterious buildings served as the store-houses of the wealth of the early kings. . . ." This, we remember, is how Pausanias explained their purpose.

The long horizontal entrance passage, or dromos*, of Mrs. Schliemann's "treasury" was nearly as monumental as that of the uncollapsed example attributed to King Atreus. Here too, at the inner end of the dromos, mighty doors had been flanked by half-columns, and above the great lintel was a triangular space, which Schliemann reasoned had once held a sculptured block comparable to that over the Lion Gate. He found no evidence of holes in the underside of the blocks of the great domed tomb chamber like those in the Atreus building, which were supposed to indicate that the curved surface had originally been decorated with bronze rosettes.

In commenting on the relative dating of the "treasuries" and the newly discovered graves within the citadel, Schliemann says, "I perfectly share Mr. Newton's opinion, that all the five immense and magnificent Treasuries in the lower city and in the suburb must necessarily be more ancient than the five royal tombs in the Acropolis; and if we reflect that princes, who used such magnificent underground palaces as storehouses of their wealth, should have been huddled away like impure animals into miserable holes, we find in this ignominious burial alone a powerful argument in favour of the veracity of the tradition which points to these sepulchres as those of the king of men, Agamemnon, and his companions . . ." Professor C. T. Newton, as we shall see, had a dominant voice in English classical circles and, to Arthur Evans at least, he typified the "old guard" who felt themselves threatened by the phenomenal growth of interest in Greek prehistory.

Schuchhardt in 1891 emphasizes three new sources of evidence on Mycenae. The first was the excavation we have been reviewing of "the pit graves filled with gold." The second, also carried out under Schliemann's auspices, was "Steffen's map of Mycenae in 1881." Lastly, Schuchhardt points to the importance of the "excavations of the Greek Archaeological Society in 1886 to 1888, when the palace was discovered on the summit of the citadel." We shall review this development in the next chapter.

In Schuchhardt's account we can readily see the major changes that had already been made in Schliemann's first impressions and theories. The so-called treasuries were shown to be real tombs, because at Menidi, near Athens, a similar structure had been found with six undisturbed skeletons lying on the floor and their funeral offerings around them. In any case, as Schuchhardt drily points out, "No prince would ever have kept his treasures outside the walls of his citadel." So before 1900 the great domed "tholos*," or "beehive" tombs are recognized as one of the most striking characteristics of Mycenaean civilization. At that time only five examples were known outside of Mycenae. But the older discredited theory of their use that goes back to Pausanias still persists to our own day in the common designation of the finest example, the magnificent intact tholos tomb at Mycenae, as the Treasury of Atreus.

The five graves within the circle of slabs were soon augmented by a sixth found by Stamatakes. It is typical of Schliemann's blind faith in the ancient authors that he stopped digging when he had found the five graves memorialized by Pausanias. In Schuchhardt's book the six graves within the circle are called "Shaft Graves*," by which designation they have been known ever since. Schuchhardt rejects the idea that the ring of slabs represents a Homeric agora. He insists that the construction was a later feature to mark the position of the Shaft Graves when the great existing fortification wall was built. At that time the sloping area inside the new walls was filled to such a height that the Shaft Graves were deeply buried. The stelae found near the modern surface would have been set up at the higher level within the circle, while the deeper stelae and the altar above Grave IV would mark an earlier stage of veneration of the buried royalty.

Most scholars had also hesitated to accept Schliemann's theory of the burial of all the bodies in the Shaft Graves on one single occasion. But, since the graves had apparently been immediately filled up and there seemed to be practically no sign of later disturbance, it was difficult to see how successive new burials could have been made. Dörpfeld, however, reviewed the chronicle of their excavation (he was not present himself) and realized that there was proof that the graves had been roofed. Schliemann had thought that slabs of schist that were found scattered just above the skeletons had lined the vertical walls; but Dörpfeld saw that they had really been laid horizontally over big wooden beams that in turn rested on the rubble walls that lined the graves. Four enigmatic copper "boxes" with long copper nails still holding rotted wood, found in Grave III, were now recognized as ornamental coverings over the ends of two great beams. And the layer of clay regularly found just above the skeletons and tomb furniture had clearly been spread over the stone slabs to make the grave coverings watertight. So, as long as the beams held firm, it would have been relatively simple to remove the overlying earth and reopen a grave for a new burial (Fig. 29).

Also, there was increasing doubt about Schliemann's insistence that

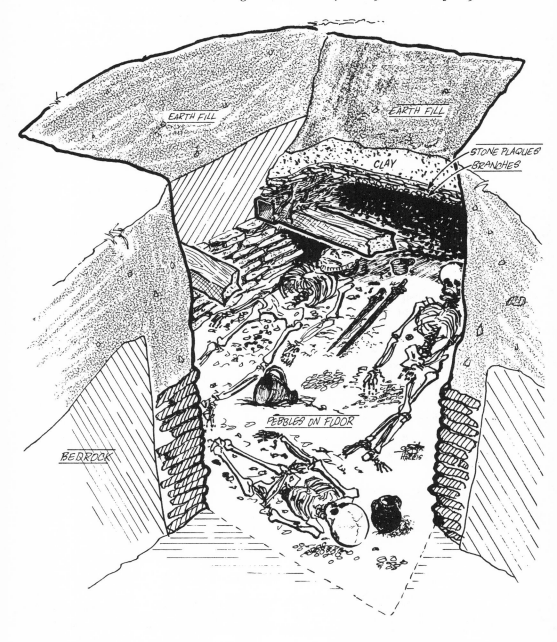

EARTH FILL

EARTH FILL

CLAY

STONE PLAQUES
BRANCHES

PEBBLES ON FLOOR

BEDROCK

Figure 29

the bodies had been at least partially cremated. A great funeral pyre is of course the universal method of burial for Homer's heroes, and Schliemann was always overanxious to point parallels between his finds and the poems. But it appeared from his own account that both the bodies and the fabulous funeral offerings had been largely untouched by fire. The graves did contain ashes and traces of the effects of fire, but this could be explained as the remains of sacrifices or purificatory rites or simply fumigation.

On the crucial matter of the identification of the Shaft Graves with those of "Agamemnon and his friends" pointed out to Pausanias, there was almost universal skepticism. The burials had certainly extended over a considerable length of time, perhaps a century. Stamatakes' sixth grave showed simpler and poorer offerings. It seemed to suggest a grouping with Schliemann's II and V; while Graves I, III and IV were much richer and presumably later.

Schuchhardt reviews the contents of the Shaft Graves in the light of the first careful examination by numerous authorities. They confirm Schliemann's insight that there is a curious dichotomy between two distinct artistic traditions, the one specializing in conventional geometric motifs such as spirals and linear patterns, the other preferring naturalistic scenes with plant, animal and human representations. And even in the second tradition, there is an astonishing gap between the immaturity and crudity of workmanship exhibited in scenes such as those on the stelae and the mastery of naturalistic representations on many other objects. Of all the magnificent examples in the latter category, the inlaid scenes on several of the newly cleaned daggers were especially striking (Fig. 30). These decorative friezes had completely escaped Schliemann's eagle eye at the time of discovery. Schuchhardt is impressed both by the technical skill required for this complicated "metal painting" and by the apparent historical implications of the representation of fighting and hunting in the light of Homeric descriptions.

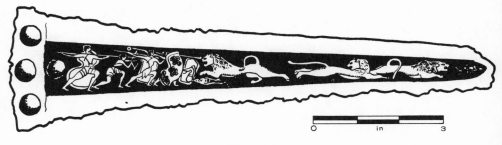

Figure 30

TIRYNS

Schliemann's discovery of the Shaft Graves was the most spectacular, and in many ways the most far-reaching in its historical implications, of any archaeological find ever made in Greece. With eyes dazzled by the gold of Mycenae, one has to think again about Herodotus' famous assertion that "Poverty is always a companion to Greece."[16] Yet only some eight miles to the south, another great fortified citadel was soon to produce new evidence that, in its way, was equally novel and important.

Apparently the Homeric name "Tiryns" has clung to it with equal tenacity through later ages. Its mighty walls rise around the edges of an isolated outcropping of rock dominating the plain of Argos only a little over a mile inland from the Gulf of Nauplia. Both here and at Mycenae the relatively complete state of the fortifications is probably to be explained by the huge size of the individual blocks, which made it too dangerous and laborious for conquerors to dismantle them or peasants to reuse them.

Pausanias speaks only of the impressive fortifications, with scarcely a word at this point on Tiryns' important mythological connections: "Nothing is left of the ruins of Tiryns except the wall, which is a work of the Cyclopes, and is made of unwrought stones, each stone so large that a pair of mules could not even stir the smallest of them. In ancient times small stones have been fitted in so as to bind together the large stones."[17] This is a useful description of the typical wall construction at that time, except that large and small stones were further solidified with a strong clay mortar in the interstices.

Perhaps it was the great fortifications of these prehistoric sites, even more than the pottery and other artefacts associated with them, that puzzled so many scholars of the late nineteenth century. As we have seen, they found it difficult to believe that "the Greeks" could have succeeded many centuries before classical times in developing a civilization so technically and artistically advanced. So they searched the literature for mention of an intrusive people to whom the wonders could be attributed; and many were convinced that they had found the explanation in a persistent tradition—noticeable as early as the *Odyssey* and popular with the later Greeks —that "Phoinikes" ("Red Men," "Phoenicians") had once occupied parts of the peninsula and introduced the civilizing arts to Greece. Schliemann long and stoutly resisted their theories and never adopted them in his official publications. But it was a lonely struggle for a self-made scholar against prestigious and plausible experts. We should not, therefore, be too surprised or disappointed to learn that in his later years he wavered and perhaps actually capitulated. In a letter to Virchow, dated 1885, he even appears to play down his earlier courageous attitude. "I have been at pains," he writes, "to demonstrate that Tiryns and Mycenae must have been built and inhabited by the *Phoenicians,* who in a remote prehistoric age flooded Greece and the islands of the Ionian and Aegean seas with colonies, and who were only finally expelled, around 1100 B.C., by the so-called Dorian Invasion." Fortunately, as we shall see, this aberration was firmly rejected by the leading scholars actually working in Greece.

As he first stood on the Tiryns acropolis and looked up inland toward Mycenae, Schliemann must have wondered about the relationship of these two contemporary sites separated by so short a distance. In fact, he never suggests a theory to explain the existence of a second fortress almost alongside "golden Mycenae." Nor has any later scholar proposed a wholly satisfactory solution for this contiguous pair of citadels, to say nothing of others that have been discovered on the mainland at Orchomenos-Gla, on Crete at Phaistos-Haghia Triada and (most recently) at Knossos-Arkhanes. Tiryns seems to belong to an older cycle of heroic stories than those that figure prominently in Homer's poems. It was reputed to be the home of the mighty Herakles, and in the time of the Trojan War it may have been the capital of Diomedes.[18] But, apart from its less striking heroic connections, excavation at Tiryns must have seemed almost as attractive as at Mycenae or Troy, and Schliemann was not the kind of man to leave any beckoning stone unturned.

Eight years separated the first trial trenches on the acropolis of Tiryns from the two excavation seasons of 1884 and 1885. Dörpfeld, who had proved his worth at Troy, was with him the first year and assumed sole charge during the second, while Schliemann was being lionized in London. Dörpfeld also wrote over his own name the section on the architectural remains in the publication *Tiryns.* This major concession to his assistant shows clearly that the old egotist Schliemann was mellowing and tiring.

Like Troy and unlike Mycenae, Tiryns produced no spectacular tombs. Nor have "royal" tombs like the Shaft Graves or tholoi (except for one possible unexcavated example) been since discovered in the vicinity. But at Tiryns for the first time reasonably well-preserved ruins of a Mycenaean palace were uncovered. "The dwelling-house of a ruler in the Heroic age," says Dörpfeld, "was until now only known to us by the descriptions of Homer. Nothing remained of the palaces of Menelaus, of Odysseus, or the other heroes [a rather premature assertion]. . . . How clearly, on the other hand, rises before us from these discoveries at Tiryns the image of the home of the prehistoric king!" Dörpfeld then conducts the reader on a tour of the main features of the inner citadel. Keeping an eye on the plan (Fig. 31), we may profitably follow along.

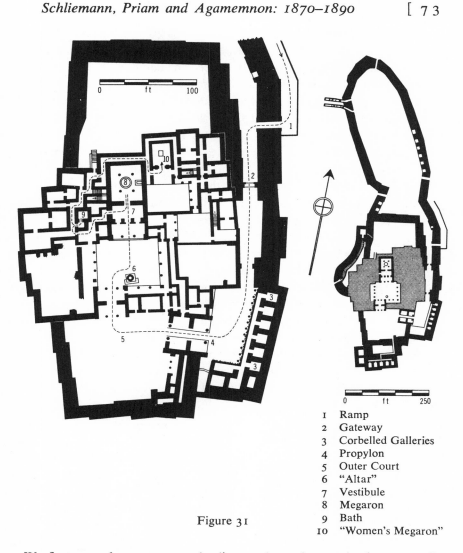

Figure 31

1　Ramp
2　Gateway
3　Corbelled Galleries
4　Propylon
5　Outer Court
6　"Altar"
7　Vestibule
8　Megaron
9　Bath
10　"Women's Megaron"

We first ascend a great ramp leading to the main gate in the east wall. The approach was so arranged that the right side of attacking warriors, unprotected by their shield, would be exposed to arrows and spears from the wall. Turning left inside the gate, we follow a wide corridor, pass through a second massive gateway (#2) and on to the southeast corner of the citadel where the false-vaulted (or corbeled*) galleries (#3) within the thickness of the wall are best preserved. Turning to the right through a stately propylon* (#4) with columned porches on both sides, we enter a large outer court (#5) from which another turn to the right through a similar propylon brings us to the main inner courtyard. Columned porches lined the south, west and east sides, while the two columns between the end walls of the main megaron on the north side completed the effect of a shaded peristyle*. In the court just to the right of the propylon and on the main axis of the megaron we see a rectangular stone curb surrounding a shallow circular depression (#6). Dörpfeld identified this structure as an altar or sacrificial pit, and we immediately think of the circular structure found over the fourth Shaft Grave at Mycenae. But it has been since shown that the curb (if not the pit) dates from much later times when a large building, perhaps an early temple, was apparently built over part of the Tiryns megaron.

We enter between the columns of the megaron porch and notice along the base of the short wall on our left a low frieze made up of seven alabaster blocks, alternating in width from narrow to square. Although badly damaged, these blocks retained traces of an elaborate inset design in blue glass paste (Fig. 32). The scheme consists of elongated half-rosettes on the square blocks and on the narrow blocks two vertical rows of small rosettes separated by a vertical space. Virtually the same intricate design was already known from better-preserved carved stone blocks at Mycenae and from small pieces of glass paste (no doubt from inlays) found in the tholos at Menidi in Attica. Dörpfeld feels confident that this kind of architectural decoration is reflected in Homer's description of the blue (*kyanos*) frieze around the walls of the palace of Alkinoos.[19] The resemblance to the triglyph-metope frieze* over the columns in classical Doric architecture is striking and scarcely accidental.

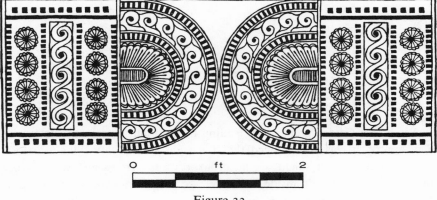

O   ft   2

Figure 32

From the porch we pass through the central of three doors into an antechamber or vestibule (#7). Beyond the vestibule lies the main throne room (#8), which perhaps alone deserves the Homeric name "megaron." The stucco floor of this main room was divided into a pattern of squares, each with painted decoration; and a slightly raised circular curb on the floor at the center of the room indicates the position of what Dörpfeld took to be a great ceremonial hearth. A rectangular interruption in the floor pattern toward the east wall opposite the hearth testified to the original location of a wooden construction, probably the king's throne (Fig. 36).

Placed symmetrically around the hearth were the stone bases of four columns. Dörpfeld reasoned that the columns must have supported a higher roof (clerestory*) over the central part of the building, thus providing for the escape of smoke and admission of light. After thoroughly reviewing the Homeric descriptions of royal palaces, particularly that of King Alkinoos,[20] Dörpfeld concludes: "This [Homeric] description agrees very well with the arrangement of the megaron of Tiryns. . . . Most probably the ground-plan . . . was a typical one, occurring in an identical manner in many heroic palaces." It now became clear that the so-called temple A in Level II at Troy, though it had no anteroom, was an essentially similar and much earlier megaron, with the hearth still partially preserved in the center of the main room. And we may add that Dörpfeld's inference of a standard plan for Mycenaean palaces proved remarkably accurate.

Retracing our steps to the anteroom, we pass through a door in its west wall and enter a winding passage leading to a small room paved with a single huge flat stone and with a drain carefully let into the east wall (#9). "I think it certain," says Dörpfeld, "that we have here found the bath-room, which must have existed in every Homeric palace. In the room there must have stood a *tub,* to be filled with water for the bather. . . . When washed and anointed, . . . [a visitor] went through the . . . corridor to the anteroom, and thence into the megaron."

We then circle around to the east behind the megaron and enter a smaller structure (#10) constructed parallel to the main building. It too has its own little court as well as the megaron plan, though it lacks the anteroom. In the center of the main room there is a rectangular gap in the floor, where again a hearth was presumably located. Dörpfeld confidently identified this as the "women's hall," which is said to have been a regular feature of important houses in classical times. Scholars have disputed whether the Homeric descriptions of palaces take for granted a separate hall for women. Dörpfeld feels that the Tiryns plan provides the needed confirmation. But the identification has never really been settled; and, as we shall see, the plan of the Pylos palace raises the question again.

Dörpfeld believed that all Mycenaean buildings, as well as those at Troy, had flat roofs and that remains of stairways pointed to access to the roof rather than to a second story. He emphasized that the evidence of heavy burning reinforces the theory that construction methods involved the use of a large amount of wood. The walls were built in the so-called half-timber construction—sun-dried brick in timber framework—and columns and roofbeams were of wood. He points to the Lion Gate sculpture at Mycenae as a likely model of the type of column, with slender proportions and diameter decreasing toward the base.

In addition to broken pottery similar to that found at Mycenae, the ruins of the Tiryns palace yielded numerous fragments of wall plaster on which were paintings in fresco* technique. These and some of the most interesting vase fragments are reproduced in twenty-four excellent color plates in the *Tiryns* publication. Most of the fresco fragments show elaborate nonrepresentational designs of spirals, rosettes and other conventionalized naturalistic and geometric patterns. But some pieces proved that certain walls had been decorated with panels depicting figured scenes. The best preserved composition shows a charging bull and a man performing some kind of acrobatic feat on or over its back (Fig. 33). This scene aroused lively interest because of the references in classical literature to prehistoric bull worship and Theseus' famous encounter with the Minotaur ("Minos Bull") at Knossos in Crete.

Figure 33

ADDITIONAL SITES

Schliemann's boundless energy and driving ambition kept him always on the lookout for new sites to explore. In northern Boeotia a great tholos tomb, like the "treasuries" of Mycenae, had announced its location to the nearby villagers many years before when the dome collapsed with a thunderous roar. The existence of such a monument was realized as a strong indication that the capital of a prehistoric kingdom must have been situated in the vicinity; and the site had been identified as the famous Orchomenos, where Pausanias had admired a "treasury of Minyas." He says of it: "There is no greater marvel either in Greece or elsewhere. It is made of stone: its form is circular, rising to a somewhat blunt top, and they say that the topmost stone is the keystone of the whole building."[21]

"Minyan Orchomenos," as it is called by Homer,[22] had a reputation in mythology for wealth second only to Mycenae. Lord Elgin, who saved (or raped, depending on your point of view) the Parthenon sculptures, had tried to clear the Orchomenos tholos but had been discouraged by the great accumulation of fallen stone. In three short campaigns between 1880 and 1886 Schliemann carried out this task and opened a few graves in the vicinity. The main chamber was badly ruined, but a side chamber like that of the Treasury of Atreus at Mycenae yielded some remarkable sculptured blocks that had lined the walls and ceiling. They were of green schist with exquisitely carved patterns of spirals, rosettes and palmettes. Clearly, this must once have been a royal tomb that rivaled the magnificence of those at Mycenae. But perhaps Schliemann's most lasting contribution at Orchomenos was the recognition of a class of smooth gray wheel-turned pottery, which he called Minyan* after Minyas, the legendary king of Orchomenos. This pottery was to play a crucial role in the reconstruction of an important phase of Greek prehistory; and although Schliemann apparently did not realize it, "Minyan ware" is practically indistinguishable from the pottery that he had found in the sixth ("Lydian") level at Troy.

There were other spots on the mainland—and on islands such as Kythera —where Schliemann made soundings. The two sites that probably interested him most were eventually to loom as large in Greek prehistoric archaeology as Troy, Mycenae and Tiryns. One was in the far southwest, where tradition located Pylos, the capital of Homer's garrulous old hero Nestor. Some very minor probing around the Frankish castle at the north end of the great bay of Navarino (see Map VII) produced nothing spectacular.

The second site was near the north coast of central Crete, which some minor excavation had already connected with the legendary Knossos, capital of King Minos and later the power center ruled by the Homeric hero Idomeneus. Schliemann was sure that the ruins of Minos' palace still lay under a great mound called Kephala (see Map VI) about three miles inland from the town of Candia (Iraklion). In a letter written only two years before his death, he said, "I would like to end my life's labours with

one great work—the prehistoric palace of the kings of Knossos in Crete."
He actually secured an excavation permit from the Turkish authorities
but had trouble in reaching a financial agreement with the owner of the
land. In his posthumously published report on the 1890 campaign at Troy
he confides, "I had thought . . . that I could turn my attention to Crete,
where I hoped to discover the original home of Mycenaean civilisation.
This plan was, however, frustrated by various difficulties, and finally by
the recent disturbances [revolt against Turkish control] in Crete, which
made excavation there impossible."

Fate may have decreed that this ambitious human had already won his
full share of fame and enjoyed his fair quota of excitement. At any rate,
the startling secrets hidden beneath the vineyards at Kephala and under
the olive trees crowning an obscure hill near Pylos were reserved for other
pioneers, in their own way as fascinating personalities as Heinrich Schliemann. Chapters IV and VI will record these later phases of the unfolding
story.

SUMMATION

By 1885 imposing architectural remains and numerous and varied
movable finds from a number of Greek sites were beginning to provide a
basis for a credible reconstruction of a preclassical civilization that seemed
to have at least some valid points of contact with Homeric descriptions.
Schuchhardt recorded:

> There were plenty of discerning people who held that the Homeric
> shields decorated with marvellous art, the splendid cups, the palaces of
> magical beauty, had not all been evolved out of nothing, but must have
> been suggested by things that actually existed. On the other hand, there
> were the faint-hearted, who held all this for idle fantasy and fable, be-
> cause not supported by actual finds. Now we have the great civilisation
> of the Mycenaean period before our eyes, and can no longer doubt that
> this is the civilisation which underlay those Homeric descriptions, where
> every detail is so fondly dwelt upon.

We note that already the term "Mycenaean period" is assuming natural
use, although its wider implications and its chronological limits are not
yet clearly established.

Schuchhardt's summation was no doubt a healthy antidote to skepticism
at the time, but his implication that the question was already settled in
Schliemann's favor is rather misleading. A more perceptive comment on

Schliemann's contribution was written by the great Homeric scholar Walter Leaf. "Dr. Schliemann," says Leaf, "was essentially 'epoch-making' in his branch of study, and it is not for epoch-making men to see the rounding off and completion of their task. That must be the labour of a generation at least. A man who can state to the world a completely new problem may be content to let the final solution of it wait for those that come after him."

III

Before Evans:
The Situation in 1900

WHAT WAS THE SUM of knowledge and theory about Mycenaean civilization when Evans began his first campaign at Knossos in 1900? The personality and achievements of a giant like Schliemann are so overpowering that we are in danger of forgetting that there were others who had also made vital contributions.

One scholar in particular deserves far more credit than he has generally received. Christos Tsountas was one of the very greatest archaeologists of native Greek descent who have excavated in their own country. He was the logical scholar to be designated by his government to continue Schliemann's work at Mycenae. This might have been considered an anticlimactic assignment because of Schliemann's legendary luck and flair for publicity. But Tsountas' efforts revealed important new features of that inexhaustible site; and he achieved notable results in various excavations elsewhere. In addition to his work in classical and Mycenaean contexts, he laid the foundation for the exploration of a brilliant phase of neolithic* civilization that had flourished in northeastern Greece, especially in Thessaly. And on several of the central Aegean islands he found evidence for an important development of "Cycladic*" culture that he recognized as being considerably earlier than the Mycenaean.

Tsountas' most valuable contribution, however, may well have been a brilliant synthesis, called *Mycenae and Mycenaean Civilization,* published in Greek in 1893. His book shows the startling volume of new information that had already accumulated in twenty-three years. But even more valuable than the collection of the data is Tsountas' attempt to systematize and digest the results of that first exciting generation of excavation. The importance of such an overview by an able practicing field archaeologist is obvious enough; but it is a curious fact that for seventy years thereafter, as new information has continued to pour in from many sources, no one of similar background and experience took up the challenge to bring Tsountas' seminal work up to date.

The desirability of making Tsountas' book known to a wider public was immediately realized by an American, Professor J. Irving Manatt of Brown University. Tsountas was willing to authorize a somewhat expanded edition in English; and the names of Tsountas and Manatt appear as coauthors of *The Mycenaean Age: A Study of the Monuments and Culture of Pre-Homeric Greece* (1897). In Manatt's Preface we detect a typical late-nineteenth-century note of confidence—perhaps of overconfidence.

> As I come to date this preface, I am reminded that there could not well be a more auspicious moment for bringing out a work like the present. It signalizes the end of the second decade of Mycenaeology [a term which, fortunately, did not become current]. Just twenty years ago to-day the wires flashed from Mycenae to King George's palace at Athens Schliemann's jubilant message that he had found the Royal Tombs, with their heroic tenants still masked in gold and their heroic equipage about them. That find was the crowning historical revelation of our time, and out of it has sprung a science whose progress is hardly less marvelous than its origin,—a science which has already in great measure restored the landmarks of pre-Homeric Greece, and with them the real background of the Homeric poems.

NEW DEVELOPMENTS AT TROY

Before following Tsountas' account, however, we shall pause to review the new Trojan evidence. But it should be noted that Troy, while it retains a definite relevance to Homeric studies, is increasingly recognized as just one of many sites peripherally in touch with Mycenaean civilization. Dörpfeld was now director of the German Archaeological School in Athens and the leading foreign authority. It is natural that he should have been asked to write the Introduction to *The Mycenaean Age* and also an Appendix called "The Mycenaean Troy."

By this time the campaigns of 1893 (financed by Sophia Schliemann) and 1894 (financed by Kaiser Wilhelm II) were completed. Dörpfeld's "Table of Nine Layers" in his little book *Troja 1893* provides a convenient summary of the new conclusions. Level II is there described as follows: "Prehistoric citadel of Troy; with strong defensive fortifications and large dwelling houses of sundried brick. Three times destroyed and rebuilt. Monochrome pottery. Many objects of bronze, silver and gold. Estimated period 2500 to 2000 before Christ." His characterization of Troy VI, on the other hand, is a far cry from Schliemann's "Lydian" level: "Citadel of Mycenaean times. Mighty fortification walls with a great tower and handsome houses built of well cut stone blocks. The Pergamus of Troy sung about by Homer. Developed monochrome Trojan pottery. With it imported Mycenaean vases. About 1500 to 1000 before Christ."

In so matter-of-fact a tone Dörpfeld announces the new stratigraphical equation foreshadowed in 1890 and proved by 1893. For the first time there was a dependable synchronism provided by Mycenaean pottery in a Trojan level, even though the chronology of Mycenaean civilization itself was still far from precise. The dating bracket now assigned to Troy II was even more uncertain—really little more than an educated guess. It was based on a gross calculation of 500 years for the interval occupied by the intervening of phases III, IV and V. There was still no means of even approximating absolute dates for Trojan material earlier than 1500.

On the northwestern and southwestern slopes of the Hissarlik mound Dörpfeld had now uncovered sizable sections of the fortifications of Troy VI (Fig. 34) with substantial buildings close inside them. Both walls and

Figure 34

houses had been constructed entirely of carefully worked stone. He estimated that the fortified acropolis was about 22,000 square yards, which compares with about the same size for Tiryns, 28,000 for Athens, and 33,000 for Mycenae. On the other hand, the fortified citadel of Troy II was less than 9,000 square yards.

Where their ground plans were preserved, the major buildings of Troy VI showed essentially the same type of freestanding megaron plan already noted in Troy II. Again Dörpfeld is tempted to see in at least one or two of them the Trojan temples mentioned by Homer.[23] In one building a row of wooden columns had stood on stone bases along the main axis, and this same plan had just been shown to have characterized a temple of the early classical period at Neandria, not far from Troy. But he finally inclines to the view that all of the Troy VI buildings are private houses, the "chambers of polished stone" that Homer describes on the Pergamus of Troy.[24] Their closeness in date and plan to the mainland palaces is obvious, though in the small area examined at Troy there were at least sixteen separate examples. In contrast, the main megaron at Tiryns and at Mycenae (which Tsountas had meanwhile discovered) were flanked by a complex of smaller and subsidiary units. Dörpfeld makes a comparison of the size of the main room of the various known megara and finds that at Tiryns it was about 130 square yards, at Mycenae about 166, at Troy between 117 and 194.

In spite of the chronological link, Level VI was in some ways a less attractive candidate for Homeric Troy than Level II. The latter had produced rich treasures, and their abandonment or the attempt to hide them seemed to indicate a sudden enemy attack. This impression was further strengthened by the clear evidence that Troy II met its doom in a furious conflagration. In contrast, there was little trace of fire in the destruction of Troy VI, and it had failed to produce much evidence of wealth, except for its size and the monumental style of its fortifications and buildings. Pottery analysis was still in its infancy, and Dörpfeld merely remarks that on the house floors, along with a fair number of imported Mycenaean sherds, vases of Schliemann's "Lydian" fabric were lying. This smooth gray pottery with metallic profile and appearance still held its secret. Alfred Brueckner, who wrote the chapter on pottery, sees in the gray ware the "old Trojan shapes" and believes there is "no ground for ascribing it to another people."

Dörpfeld was of course an architect and not a philologist, but in *Troja 1893* he dares to enter the age-old controversy. "In my opinion," he writes, "this part of the Trojan Question is solved. I pronounce with increasing confidence . . . that it is the Mycenaean, not a later culture, which lies at the base of the Homeric epics. Now we are concerned with another aspect of the Homeric Question; now it must be established how completely the poet's descriptions correspond with reality. Perhaps we will succeed in this way in gaining a new and sounder basis for research into the origin and development of epic poetry." Dörpfeld here foresees a basic direction that prehistoric archaeology and Homeric studies have taken. Yet the establishment of the correspondence he obviously expected has turned out to be a very complex and often a baffling pursuit.

MYCENAEAN CIVILIZATION: A SYNTHESIS

To return now to the Greek mainland and Tsountas' *Mycenaean Age,* the excavations at Mycenae in the last decade of the century did not seriously upset Schliemann's major conclusions; but they supplemented the earlier work in several important respects. Tsountas cleared the summit of the acropolis and discovered the location of the palace (Fig. 35). Badly ruined foundations of a large building complex were found just southwest of the highest outcropping of rock. A ramp and monumental stairs had led up to it from the Lion Gate. The southern half of the megaron had collapsed into the deep ravine below, but almost all of the preserved features corresponded to those already known from Tiryns. There was the same court in front, the same tripartite ground plan of columned porch, anteroom and main room with column bases near the center. About one-third of the actual curb of a low circular hearth was still in place between the northern column bases, but the floor surface where the throne might have been set had disappeared. So, as Dörpfeld had predicted, a kind of canon of the "megaron type" was emerging from the approximately contemporary sites of Troy VI, Tiryns and Mycenae.

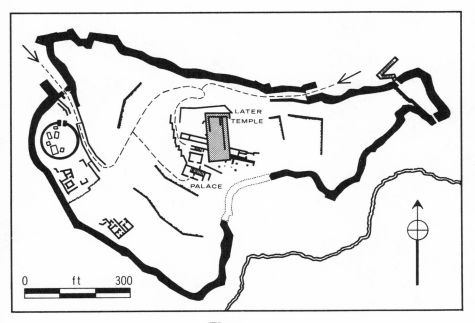

Figure 35

A main corridor and the bases of stairways to the north of the Mycenae megaron indicated that the rest of the palace had lain higher up, on or near the summit; but leveling for a later temple in that area had almost completely destroyed all traces. "If we now . . . reproduce in imagination a Mycenaean palace," writes Tsountas, "our impression of it must be in many respects a brilliant one. There is the Great Hall, with the pillars upholding the roof and inclosing the great round hearth with its rich polychrome designs; the smooth concrete floors, scratched in checkers of red and blue; the walls frescoed in bands, now of animals or linear designs, now of hunting or battle scenes, and crowned with richly carved friezes, while the doorways and the woodwork generally are agleam with noble bronze" (Fig. 36).

The most interesting result of Tsountas' study of the Mycenaean fortifications was that in the eastern part of the acropolis a secret passageway through the north wall led to a series of ninety-nine steps that descended to a deep underground reservoir (Fig. 37). The water was presumably

Figure 36

Figure 37

piped from the famous spring of Perseus about 100 yards outside the wall. This ingenious arrangement would have helped to ensure the all-important water supply in case of a siege.

Deliberate excavation is not by any means the only method by which archaeological evidence is recovered from the earth. An ambitious modern engineering project in the early 1890s drained the big shallow Copaic basin in north central Boeotia and made this rich area available for farming. But the French and English engineers found that they had had predecessors. Tremendous drainage channels or canals had been constructed along the northern and southeastern edges of the lake. Wherever possible, the steep natural slope of rock had been utilized for the outer retaining wall. The artificial banks were mighty earthen structures up to 200 feet in width and reinforced with stone walls. Excess water emptying into the western part of the basin, both from abundant springs and from seasonally swollen rivers, was thus caught and conducted to the northeastern corner of the basin. There the two main channels united and carried the water to one of the natural emissaries or sink-holes from which it found its way underground through the mountain barrier to the sea.

It would appear that the resulting desiccation was most complete in the northwestern part of the basin and archaeologists realized that the chief beneficiary must have been Orchomenos. This ambitious hydraulic system certainly provided a very large and fertile addition to her agricultural resources. And since both tradition and rather meager archaeological evidence pointed to her acme of prosperity in the Late Bronze Age, the Copaic drainage project was termed "the greatest public works of the Mycenaean age." It clearly required as expert supervision and as highly organized a social and political system as did the mighty fortifications of Tiryns and Mycenae or the great tholos tombs.

The southern drainage channel passed close to a rocky eminence, called Gla, which had apparently been an island in the northeastern part of the lake. A mile or so farther to the northeast the two main channels coalesced. Archaeologists for the first time carefully studied Gla's great Cyclopean fortifications and excavated within them. The circuit enclosing Gla is far longer than at Tiryns and Mycenae, measuring almost two miles in circumference, with four gates and protective towers. It appears to have been built at roughly the same time as the fortifications at Tiryns and Mycenae.

A French excavator named A. deRidder worked at Gla for one short season (1893) and showed that a monumental building had been constructed against the north wall and that a large rectangular area to the south of it and in the approximate center of the fortified area had contained other less impressive buildings. This whole area had been enclosed by a second, internal line of fortifications. The so-called palace at the north was quite different in plan from the type established at Tiryns and Mycenae. It was composed of two wings laid out in an L shape. No obvious megaron was identified. There was no evidence of stairways leading to roofs or second stories. Only one room and vestibule showed fragments of frescoed walls. The whole complex at Gla suggested a regional stronghold rather than a royal capital, with much more unoccupied space than in other citadels. The scarcity of small finds indicated that it had not been occupied very long. But, in spite of anomalies, Gla emerged as a third great fortified Mycenaean site, the first discovered north of the Isthmus of Corinth.

Tsountas' most important chapters are those entitled "The Dwellings of the Dead: Shaft Graves" and "The Dwellings of the Dead: Beehive and Chamber Tombs." In the first place we notice that the relative dating of the different grave types is now confidently stated. "The Mycenaean tombs are of two general types. The first is that of the oblong pit [*i.e.,* the shaft grave] sunk vertically in the ground, very much like the modern grave; the second includes the beehive or tholos-structure and the rock-hewn chamber, approached alike by an avenue [dromos] cut horizontally into a hillside. It is the second which offers the great monuments of sepulchral architecture; but the shaft-graves are obviously earlier in origin . . ." Tsountas' relative chronology is not based on the pottery types contained in the different kinds of tomb. This is, of course, the most effective modern proof; but he has to rely, rather tenuously, on the generally richer contents of the Shaft Graves (an odd argument) and on the absence or scarcity in them of such objects as engraved gems, ornaments of ivory, mirrors and razors, all of which were common in the tholos tombs.

Tsountas believes that Schliemann's account of the wonderful state of preservation of at least one body in the Shaft Graves must be taken seriously and that some process of embalming was at least occasionally employed. "From the Homeric poems we know that the bodies of the chiefs lay in state for days, and even weeks, before being consigned to the tomb, and without embalming this would have been impossible." He refers to Thetis' inserting ambrosia and red nectar through the nostrils of Patrokles* "that his flesh might abide the same continually,"[25] and he reminds the reader that Aphrodite anoints the body of Hector* with "rose-sweet oil ambrosial."[26] He points to Homer's use of the verb *"tarchuein"* for "bury,"[27] though its primary meaning is "pickle" or "embalm." So he feels that the Mycenaeans may have taken measures to preserve the bodies of important men for lengthy preburial rituals, although the partial parallel with Egyptian customs should not be used to argue that the Mycenaeans held similar views about the future life.

It was now clear that the Shaft Graves within the grave circle were simply the most important of a whole series of similar burials that had once occupied the slope; but "after the change due to the enlargement of the acropolis, these humbler tombs were neglected and houses were built over them, while the royal tombs were preserved." Tsountas assumes that all six Shaft Graves within the circle of stone slabs belonged to a single dynasty and must form a closely related series. He calls renewed attention to the animal bones found scattered above the graves, which suggest that there was a final funeral feast after the earth was replaced. The sacrificial pit above Grave IV would suggest a continuing cult. Several human burials that were found above the Shaft Graves and were unaccompanied by rich objects are not necessarily from a later period, according to Tsountas, but probably represent "the bodies of slaves or captives immolated on the master's tomb."

After the days of the "shaft-grave dynasty" at Mycenae comes a time when the kings were buried in tholos or beehive tombs (Fig. 38) while the "mass of the people" constructed simpler chamber tombs* for their last

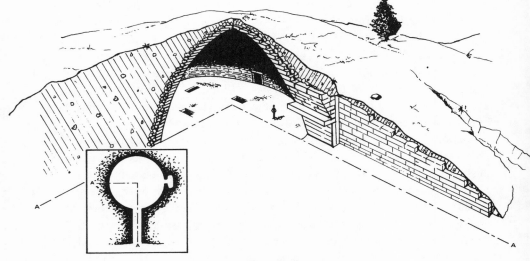

Figure 38

resting place (Fig. 39). Both types have in common the long horizontal entrance corridor, or dromos, cut into a sloping rock face. The chamber tombs are square or oblong rooms excavated in the soft rock at the inner end of the dromos; whereas the tholoi are constructed by sinking a circular shaft from the surface, lining it with a stone wall of gradually decreasing diameter until a single stone closed the dome. The tholos walls were packed with clay mortar and weighted on the outside with earth and stone. Since the dome usually protruded above normal ground level, the earth covering formed a mound, or tumulus*, over the grave. At the time Tsountas wrote, twenty-one tholos tombs were known on the Greek mainland, with by far the greatest concentration (eight) at Mycenae. Three had been discovered near the Argive Heraion (famous sanctuary of the goddess Hera in classical times), which was connected to Mycenae by a carefully built highway leading southward some five miles. Three tholoi had been located at Thorikos in eastern Attica, and single examples were scattered from Dimini in Thessaly to Kampos near the Gulf of Messenia and Vaphio near Sparta. So Homer's picture of a series of kingdoms throughout central and southern Greece was beginning to come into focus.

Tsountas emphasizes the monumental character of the tholos tombs and speculates on the wealth and manpower that must have been at the command of the rulers who ordered their construction. In a detailed description of the so-called Treasury of Atreus at Mycenae, he calls it "the type of the tholos tomb in its highest structural perfection, as well as the most

Figure 39

perfectly preserved monument of Mycenaean architecture." And he adds, "Every visitor must be awed by it, even apart from its august and immemorial story."

Due to their conspicuous mounds, nearly all of the tholoi had been plundered long ago. Tsountas conjectures that the Dorian conquerors were the first robbers, but he seems to feel that the offerings originally placed with the deceased royalty in the tholoi were far less rich than those in the Shaft Graves, which preceded them. This would certainly be the case if he was right that "the tombs of Vaphio, Menidi, Demini, Kampos, and one at the Heraion were found substantially intact." Of these the Vaphio tholos contained the richest grave furniture and, since Tsountas was himself the excavator, we may best follow the discovery in his own words.

"In the doorway . . . we found a pit. . . . This was empty, though a thin layer of ashes covered the bottom. . . . The reasonable supposition is that it was a sacrificial pit for the worship of the dead. Within the rotunda [main circular tomb chamber] . . . there was another pit 7½ feet long, 3½ feet wide, and 3 feet deep—paved, walled and covered with stone slabs. This pit, which we found intact, was a man's grave, and was furnished with a great number of precious offerings . . ."

He then goes on to enumerate the grave goods.

On the floor of the round chamber [*i.e.,* not in the "pit," or cist*] . . . were found thirteen engraved gems, two gold rings, silver and bronze needles, some smaller gold ornaments, and a few leaves of gold. But the most and finest of the offerings lay in the pit . . . and, as they had never been disturbed, it is worth while to describe their arrangement. . . . We found no bones, for they had long ago mouldered away, but everything went to show that the body had lain with the head to the west, just as the Greeks bury their dead at the present day. Doubtless this was only that the dead might face the door of his tomb, which happens to front the east; at least during the *prothesis* or lying in state, it was the custom from Homeric times for the dead to be laid upon the bier facing the vestibule.[28] Near where the head had lain were two bronze vessels (one of them a sort of skillet, possibly for sacrificial uses); a bronze sword, 3 feet long; two spear-heads; seven bronze knives; the bronze scepter-sheath; a large bronze spoon; a mirror disk; ten smaller disks of five different sizes, probably making up five pairs of balances; five leaden disks (possibly used as a sort of currency in trade); two stone basins; two alabaster vases, with a little silver spoon in one of them; two terra-cotta vessels; and three other terra-cottas which look like lamps. All these objects were disposed as if to form a pillow for the head.

As Tsountas continues to list the remainder of the contents of this single cist grave we ought to keep in mind (in connection with his impression that the offerings in tholoi were less rich than in the Shaft Graves) that there were often at least two cists, that burials were usually made on the floor of the circular tomb chamber itself and that Spartan kings were probably not the wealthiest of Mycenaean leaders.

Where the neck and breast must have lain, we found some 80 amethyst beads, with two engraved gems, apparently forming a necklace of two chains. On the left lay a gold-plated dagger, and in the middle of the grave a silver cup with a gold-plated rim. At either hand lay two more cups, one of silver and one of gold: the latter are the now famous Vaphio cups [Fig. 40]. . . . At either hand lay a heap of twelve engraved gems, —the two heaps obviously once forming a pair of bracelets,—with three more silver objects, including an ear-pick, and three rings, one of gold, one of bronze, and one of iron. At the foot lay a bronze knife, two bronze axes . . . and four more lead disks.

It certainly does not appear that this one member of the royal generation using the tholos was any more poverty-stricken than some of the individuals buried in the Shaft Graves.

Turning to the simpler chamber tombs, Tsountas describes the characteristics of more than sixty examples that he had opened in the vicinity of the Mycenae acropolis, as well as others scattered throughout the whole

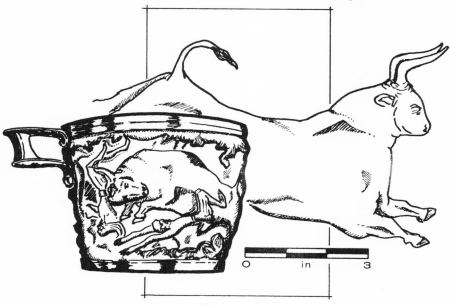

Figure 40

area of east central and southern Greece and some of the Aegean islands. An interesting feature of the Mycenae chamber tombs is that they cluster in clearly differentiated groups, which suggests that the people lived in small villages around the fortified acropolis. The divisions would presumably have been on the basis of clan (*i.e.,* blood relationship), as in later Sparta. The chamber tombs did not have elaborately decorated entrances and doors, as in the finer tholoi, but the doorway was carefully blocked with a wall of stone or sun-dried brick.

In the chamber tombs, as in the tholoi, it is clear that several burials had usually been made. The funeral customs in both types of tomb seem to have been similar. Normally the bodies were simply placed on the floor, usually in a reclining position with the head propped up and the offerings placed around them. They were not covered with earth or placed in a coffin. As additional burials were made, the earlier bones and offerings were likely to be swept aside rather unceremoniously to make room for the newest occupant. Sometimes a pit is cut into the floor, as at Vaphio, and this indicates to Tsountas a special status for the individual so buried. An even more favored position would be in a side chamber with which only a few tholoi and chamber tombs were provided.

Tsountas discusses at great length a puzzling problem implicit in the continuing use of the chamber tombs and tholoi. When a new burial was made and the immediate funeral rituals were completed, did the dromos of the tomb remain open or was it filled with earth? And, if the latter, was it completely cleared on the occasion of the next burial? He firmly argues for the repeated covering and reopening of the dromos in the case of "all the chamber-tombs and most of the tholoi." He concedes that the richly ornamented entrance façades of some tholoi make this hard to believe but finally concludes that even they were "in the strictest sense subterranean, and that their splendors were displayed only on recurring funeral occasions."

He also points to the evidence for subsequent funeral offerings and some sort of continuing cult or at least memorial rituals.

For the funeral sacrifices, we have evidence in the charred bones sometimes found in the vaulted and chamber tombs. These are the bones of burnt-offerings, for we know that the bodies of the dead were not burned. In the doorway of the Vaphio tomb . . . was a deep pit never occupied as a grave. . . . It was doubtless a sacrificial pit: over it the victim's throat was cut, that the blood-offering might stream through it to the dead beneath; and into it were doubtless poured other libations dear to the dead, such as Odysseus offers in that weird underworld scene which throws so strong a light on the whole subject.[29] . . . But the libations of wine, honey, and milk, and the slaughter of victims over the sacrificial pit—all indispensable to the well-being of the dead—did not cease with the solemn funeral. These rites were observed not only on special occasions, but also at fixed times, namely,—if we may carry back so far the known usages of historical Greece,—on the third, ninth, and thirtieth days after death, and annually thenceforward. That these rites were kept up at the Royal Sepulchre [the grave circle] of Mycenae is proven by the circular altar. . . . In Homer the funeral feast—either before or after the burial—is indispensable.[30] . . . That these feasts were customary in the Mycenaean Age is evident. . . . In case of the vaulted and chamber tombs, the bones of animals are found especially in the dromos before the doorway.

On much less dependable evidence Tsountas insists that prisoners, slaves, and even favorite wives may have been forced to accompany the king on his last journey.

Following up the Homeric parallels, we observe that Achilles, when he burns his comrade's body,—not content with holocausts of sheep and oxen, and horses and dogs, to garnish the great pyre a hundred feet square,—adds a yet sterner sacrifice. "And twelve valiant sons of great-hearted Trojans he slew with the sword,—for he devised mischief in his heart,—and he set to the merciless might of the fire to feed on them."[31] This awful immolation . . . [had] apparently now gone out of use and memory, so that the poet, borrowing here from an earlier lay, feels the need of accounting for the act. A like usage prevailed among other peoples related to the Hellenic stock, and must be assumed for the Mycenaeans as well. We have already spoken of the human skeletons found in the *débris* above the acropolis graves, and not infrequently bodies are found buried in the passages of the chamber-tombs. . . . The woman buried in the dromos of the Clytemnestra tomb must have been a slave, and one highly prized. For, while as a rule there are no offerings with the other bodies buried in these passages, this grave yielded two bronze mirrors with richly carved ivory handles . . . as well as several small ornaments of gold. . . . May we not go a step farther and venture the surmise that she was a favorite slain to follow her master to the underworld?

He should, at least, have considered the parallel in the Christian catacombs, where it was considered a coveted honor to be assigned a burial spot (when the natural time came) as close as possible to important personages.

Tsountas next tries to sum up the evidence for "Dress and Personal Adornment," mainly from both scanty and sketchy representations on gems, frescoes and vases. Men are often depicted wearing nothing but a very abbreviated pair of shorts, for which the nineteenth century used such decorous names as "breech-clout" and "loin apron"; but the record is confused by wide variations in the date of the representations and the occasion shown. For instance, the kings buried in the Shaft Graves were dressed very differently from the soldiers shown going off to battle on the Warrior Vase. These later soldiers could perhaps be said to have something in common with Homer's description of Odysseus' father, old Laertes, who was "clothed in a . . . chiton* [a close-fitting shirt], with . . . leggings of ox-hide bound about his knees . . . and on his head he wore a goat-skin cap."[32]

Some kind of sandals with exaggeratedly pointed toes are commonly shown. The hair was worn long and sometimes bound with a ribbon or fillet. Fairly long, carefully trimmed beards are the rule. The upper lip is usually shaved, and we note the bronze razors sometimes found in the graves. On the other hand, some of the gold masks of the Shaft Graves depict luxurious moustaches. Men seem to have been as fond as women of necklaces, bracelets, brooches and other jewelry. Elaborately decorated round metal objects may once have sheathed the handles of the wooden scepters that were the badge of royalty in Homeric descriptions.

The female costume was naturally more complicated. An outer garment fell in full horizontal flounces down to the ankles. The bodice, perhaps of a different material, was diaphanous and followed the lines of breasts and shoulders. Some experts were sure that the artist meant to show the breasts completely nude. Pointed sandals were worn, and the long hair was elaborately curled and braided. Like most of her sex at other times and places, the Mycenaean lady had a whole arsenal of ornaments and toilet accessories, best represented by the fantastic variety from the Shaft Graves.

Of course, it is hardly fair to suggest any generalization from the queens and princesses of the Shaft Graves or even from the priestesses (or goddesses?) depicted on the rings and gems; yet Tsountas' summation is appealing. "We may now picture to ourselves the Mycenaean lady in full dress . . . soft woollen of sea-purple stain, and glistering linen . . . The diadem of gold is on her brow, golden fillets and pins of exquisite technique shining out of her dark hair; golden bands about her throat and golden necklaces falling upon her bosom; gold bracelets upon her arms, gold rings chased with inimitable art upon her fingers, and finally her very robes agleam with gold. Thus she stands forth a golden lady, if we may borrow Homer's epithet for Aphrodite . . ."[33]

Perhaps the best index on the degree of correspondence between actual Mycenaean objects and Homer's word pictures is in the category of weapons and armor. In life, war was the ultimate test of manliness; and apparently a dead warrior needed to be fully armed to continue his prowess in a future existence. While the disintegration of wood and leather has taken its toll, art representations of fighting and hunting piece out the testimony of material objects from the graves. Again, unfortunately, Tsountas' generation was seriously impeded in utilizing the available evidence by their almost total inability to differentiate relative dates within the long Mycenaean time span.

A great man-covering shield, perhaps comparable to that wielded by Homer's Ajax,[34] is shown in two forms on objects such as the inlaid daggers from the Shaft Graves. One type is oblong, the other pinched at the center into a kind of figure eight. These mighty contraptions could not be held in front of one by a handle but were slung over the shoulder with a strap, or telamon. No wonder the warrior so equipped could not move easily and needed a chariot to convey him to and from the battle. The shield shown on the Warrior Vase, on the other hand, is a much smaller, lighter, oval-shaped object, the handle grasped in the left hand, and displaying such blazons as a crescent moon or stars set in a silver field.

A bronze corselet, or cuirass*, covering the upper part of the body is mentioned by Homer,[35] and something of the sort—probably not of metal— is apparently shown on the Warrior Vase; but corselet and greaves* may have been unnecessary with the bigger shields. Homer's favorite epithet for the Greeks is "well-greaved,"[36] and greaves, or shin-protectors, perhaps of leather rather than metal, are depicted on various monuments such as the Warrior Vase. The helmet was usually a conical cap made of the skin of an animal. Several varieties appear, but none seems to be of metal.

The most striking Homeric parallel in this category is between the description[37] of a helmet covered with gleaming tusks of wild boar and archaeological discoveries of boar's tusks and of art objects showing such a helmet (Fig. 41). Schliemann found sixty tusks in a single Shaft Grave. They were ground flat on one side and perforated for attachment. Also, a small ivory head from Mycenae shows a helmet apparently covered with overlapping rows of boar's tusks and with a wide chin strap or cheek piece similarly covered. "This was in all probability an early Mycenaean practice," says Tsountas. The flashing plumes so prominent on the helmets of Homer's heroes are depicted on the Warrior Vase, and some helmets have a kind of button at the apex into which plumes might have been set. On the Warrior Vase, too, some of the helmets are shown surmounted by two "horns," which would further enhance the threatening aspect of the wearer.

Offensive weapons are much better preserved. The basic implement for close-up fighting was the sword or dagger. There are about 150 of these in bronze from the Shaft Graves alone. They are obviously meant for thrusting rather than slashing. Some are more than 3 feet long, but those from later burials tend to be shorter. The most elaborate were magnifi-

Figure 41

cently decorated with inlaid scenes of battle and hunting. Scabbards were no doubt of wood, leather or even linen, and the baldric, or sword belt, of leather. Some of the gold appliqué in the Shaft Graves may have decorated the baldrics. Before engaging at close range, the Homeric hero used his spear. The bronze spearhead had a socket to receive the long wooden shaft, which was riveted to the metal.

Chisel-shaped or double-edged battle-axes are occasionally found. Tsountas is particularly proud of a discovery at Vaphio of a very unusual type of battle-ax (Fig. 42). "It is crescent-shaped, with two large holes (possibly to lighten the blade), while the back is cut out in three teeth. . . . With this unique specimen before us, we can at last understand the feat of Odysseus in sending an arrow through the rings of twelve axes set up in a row."[38] Much later, it was realized that this ax reflects Egyptian influence on a basically Syrian form; but the fact that it was not native to Greece does not necessarily exclude Tsountas' theory.

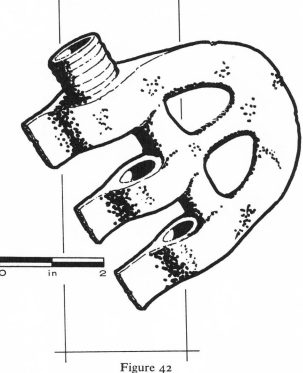

Figure 42

Arrowheads of obsidian and bronze abound in the tombs, and representations such as the siege scene on a badly damaged silver rhyton found in the fourth Shaft Grave show kneeling bowmen and standing slingers. This unique object was, like the inlaid daggers, so encrusted and fragmentary that it was not recognized and cleaned until years after Schliemann's excavations (Fig. 43). The vase had a gold rim and a series of gold figure-eight shields just below the rim. The body was of silver, with the figured scene in relief. "Fortunately, now," says Tsountas, "we have recovered at least one Mycenaean battle-picture. . . . Out of the rocky slope—very much as we see it at Mycenae—springs the fortress wall, and behind rise other squared structures which may stand for towers, or for houses in the citadel; before the wall grow trees which we take for wild olives. Upon the wall are five women . . . in attitudes of frenzy and supplication."

He continues with the description of what is preserved of the battle scene on the Siege Rhyton.

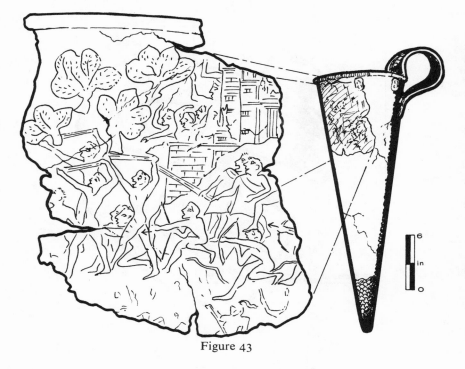

Figure 43

Before the walls we see the archers and slingers in the heat of conflict,
—speeding their shafts and hurling their missiles at the beleaguering
foe, whose figures must have filled the missing foreground . . . and in
the rear, just under the wall, are two figures . . . [who may represent]
aged non-combatants, watching the conflict; and we have a scene the
very counterpart of one wrought by Hephaestus on the shield of Herakles.[39] . . . On other fragments, we make out fallen warriors stretched
upon the rocky ground; others carrying off the dead or wounded. . . .
How vividly it brings before us the savagery and horror of ancient war.
. . . The offending town is beleaguered, and the defense is maintained
with the savage fury of men who feel that all is at stake, cheered on
by women who know too well the doom awaiting them if once the
stronghold be mastered, their husbands and sons put to the sword, and
their homes given to the flames. For war is but a higher order of
hunting, and women the only game worth taking alive. It is this that
nerves the arm of Hector, when Andromache would hold him back
from battle.[40]

Tsountas' account of Mycenaean art and architecture is imprecise, naïve
and occasionally marred by unlikely hypotheses. Yet in 1897 who could
have predicted the startling discoveries so soon to be made on the island

of Crete and their special bearing on this particular phase of Mycenaean civilization? One criticism at least seems to be called for, however, in connection with the early evaluation of Mycenaean art. The nineteenth-century scholars, including Schliemann, showed an extremely casual interest in the evolution of shape and decoration of the omnipresent clay vases. They concentrated almost entirely on objects in precious metals. Yet the latter, because of their very rarity and uniqueness (in terms of survival), offer far less opportunity for any systematic reconstruction of the development of art forms.

One chapter in *The Mycenaean Age* is devoted to a question that was considered more or less settled in the negative for a whole generation following 1900. Were the Mycenaeans literate? The lack of written material seemed to provide yet another parallel with the illiterate civilization depicted in the Homeric poems. At the time Tsountas was writing, only six inscribed vessels of stone or terra-cotta had been discovered. They bore, incised or painted on their shoulders or handles, one to five symbols that were apparently written characters. They seemed to be typical local Mycenaean vessels, and the inscription had preceded the firing. Tsountas himself had published two of them (Fig. 44) and had remarked on the similarity of some characters to those of the "pre-Greek" syllabary* with which some of the inhabitants of Cyprus had written Greek in classical times. Also, at two sites in the Egyptian Fayum the British excavator Flinders Petrie had discovered a good deal of pottery identical with Mycenaean types and "often inscribed with characters similar to, and in some cases identical with, those found in Greece."

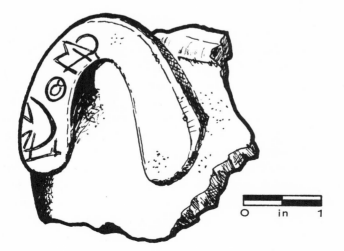

Figure 44

Most significant of all were the recently published results of Arthur Evans' explorations in Crete in the closing years of the century. In a long article in the *Journal of Hellenic Studies* (1894) and then in a book called *Cretan Pictographs and Pre-Phoenician Script* (1895), Evans reviewed the material available at that time. "The evidence which I am now able to bring forward," he wrote, "will, I venture to think, conclusively demonstrate that as a matter of fact an elaborate system of writing did exist within the limits of the Mycenaean world, and moreover that two distinct phases of this art are traceable among its population. The one is pictographic in character like Egyptian hieroglyphics, the other linear and quasi-alphabetic, much resembling the Cypriote and Asiatic syllabaries."

Tsountas accepts Evans' general conclusions; but he shows a prophetic instinct in distinguishing between the mainland and Crete, a distinction which was soon to be highly controversial.

> Mycenaean culture in Greece belongs to the Greeks: this view is daily gaining ground. True, peoples of other stock were drawn within the sphere of its influence; but in Peloponnesus and on the adjoining Mainland, and for the most part in the Islands too, this civilization was Greek, and cultivated by Greeks. For all that, the system of writing to which the "Mycenaean" symbols belong seems not to have been a Greek invention, nor primarily intended for the Greek language. . . . It is of course now well known that the Cypriote alphabet as well was devised by a non-Hellenic stock, and subsequently adapted to the Greek language, whose sounds it could but imperfectly represent.

But when he is forced to take a stand on the meaning of the very minor existing evidence from the mainland, Tsountas decides that these are stray imports. "Three years ago, in publishing two inscribed vase-handles, we stated that facts seemed to show that writing was neither used nor known among the Mycenaean peoples. To-day we must reiterate the same judgment; . . . Perhaps the future may reveal fresh data; but in Greece at least the Mycenaean epoch has been pretty thoroughly explored, and this exploration has yielded us a great mass of monuments,—utensils, ornaments and other products of Mycenaean art; and these afford negative proof against the existence of writing." We smile now to think that anyone could have believed seventy years ago that "the Mycenaean epoch has been pretty well explored"; it would be a debatable statement even today.

So Tsountas took the wrong road, and others followed him for over forty years. It is clear throughout his chapter dealing with writing that Tsountas is unhappy with his reading of the evidence. At the end he says: "This [the absence of writing] is a surprising fact when we consider how splendidly nature had endowed them for other tasks, and how constantly they were in touch with nations that had long known and employed that art." When he tries finally to answer the question "Why did the Mycenaeans not adopt or invent a writing system?" he is scarcely convincing. "It may be that the primitive peoples of Greece felt no need of writing. They had other ways of learning and communicating what they would. Each state, even imperial Mycenae, lay within very narrow bounds; a patriarchal form of government prevailed; social relations were very simple; there were few temples and no sacerdotal class; . . . Finally, there were the winged songs of the troubadours who published the *klea andrōn* [famous deeds of heroes] to a much wider circle than could be reached by inscriptions set up in some one place."

Yet it would be unfair to Tsountas to ignore a remark he made in quite another context, for this pronouncement proved to be truly prophetic. "We may hope, at least," he says, "if this ancient culture ever recovers its voice, to find it not altogether unfamiliar; we need not be startled if we catch the first lisping accent of what has grown full and strong in the Achaean epic." Tsountas' instinct on this point was as near the truth as it was completely missed by the dogma of some of his successors a whole generation later.

In 1897, as to a large extent even now, the religious beliefs and practices of the Mycenaeans had to be deduced from material remains. Tsountas' inventory includes "the actual altars at Mycenae and Tiryns; the funeral offerings and the clear traces of continued ministration to the dead; the adoration scenes occurring in Mycenaean art [especially on rings and gems]; the rude images which are hardly less abundant in Mycenaean remains than the eikon in modern Greece or the crucifix in Catholic countries." He echoes Schliemann's surprise at the relative crudeness of the distinctive little terra-cotta figurines in comparison with the delicacy and perfection of other art forms. The predominantly female representations, with folded or upraised arms, occasionally holding a child, and with garments and ornaments summarily indicated in dark paint show "how religious conservatism had consecrated these divine simulacra as it continued to consecrate the wooden *xoana** in the very presence of the Phidian masterpieces." It is clear, he notes, that "female deities decidedly outnumber the male. With barely the two exceptions . . . [where] we have ventured to recognize Zeus, the monuments give us goddesses exclusively, Aphrodite, Artemis, Hera, Earth. . . . With the exception of Aphrodite, whose cult was brought in by the Phoenicians, all the female deities identified on our monuments are but slightly differing forms of that goddess whose worship is primeval—Mother Earth, the universal life-giver" (Fig. 17).

These deities—at least Aphrodite—apparently had dwelling places built by their worshipers' hands, to judge from such objects as the little golden tripartite buildings with hovering doves that had been found in the Shaft Graves. Yet in excavation no ruined building had yet been found whose plan or furnishing would suggest that it had been a temple or shrine.

As for Tsountas' chapter on "The Problem of the Mycenaean Race," perhaps the less said the better. Not that twentieth-century archaeologists and anthropologists have settled the problem; but they have learned to beware of the broad generalizations and reckless hypotheses so dear to former generations who speculated on this slippery topic. Tsountas is completely under the spell of the "northern mirage." The Mycenaeans must be "Aryans." He tries to connect them with the pile-dwelling peoples who inhabited the marshy areas of northern Italy and Switzerland. Homer's various names for the Greeks and other features of the mythological tradition are pressed into service, with the Danaans representing these earlier "marsh-men" (akin to the Minyans who drained Lake Copais in Boeotia) and the Achaeans* equated with the "lands-men," a later branch of the same race (he speaks also of "two races") who had learned to fortify high citadels. The Shaft Graves could then be conveniently ascribed to the marsh-men (the Perseid* dynasty of mythology) and the tholos tombs to the lands-men (the Pelopid* dynasty). The fusion of these two peoples made up the "Hellenic" race, and they were responsible for a "native growth" of Mycenaean art, "influenced though it was by the earlier civilizations of the Cyclades and the East."

On problems connected with the so-called Dorian invasion, Tsountas' position is the "orthodox" one that has generally prevailed from later antiquity almost to the present. "Can we determine the race or races among the Greeks known to history to whom the achievement of Mycenaean civilization is to be ascribed? In this inquiry we may set aside the Dorians, although many scholars (especially among the Germans) still claim for them the marvelous remains of the Argolid. . . . [This view] cannot stand the test of chronology. For tradition refers that migration to the end of the twelfth century B.C., whereas the Mycenaean people were established in the Argolid before the sixteenth, probably even before the twentieth century."

Against another theory—that the Dorian migration was a myth or belonged to the immemorial past—Tsountas urges that excavation has shown clearly that the Mycenaean civilization perished in a great catastrophe.

> The palaces . . . were destroyed by fire after being so thoroughly pillaged that scarcely a single bit of metal was left in the ruins. Further, they were never rebuilt; . . . How are we to account for this sudden and final overthrow otherwise than by assuming a great historic crisis,

which left these mighty cities with their magnificent palaces only heaps of smoking ruins? And what other crisis can this have been than the irruption of the Dorians? And their descent into the Peloponnese is traditionally dated at the very time which other considerations have led us to fix as the lower limit of the Mycenaean age. Had that migration never been recorded by the ancients nor attested by the state of the Peloponnese in historic times [generally an area of Doric dialect], we should still be led to infer it from the facts now put in evidence by the archaeologist's spade.

By Tsountas' time Greek prehistoric archaeology had already passed somewhat beyond the predicament that he describes as follows: "A dateless era and a nameless race . . . are facts to be accepted only in the last resort. The student of human culture cannot look upon the massive walls, the solemn domes [tholoi], the exquisite creations of what we call Mycenaean art, without asking—When? By whom? In default of direct and positive evidence, he will make the most of the indirect and probable." Schliemann had given prompt and confident, if rather imprecise, answers to these questions. The epoch, he thought, was during and just before the Trojan War, traditionally dated in the early twelfth century. The people were Homer's Greeks, called variously Danaoi, Achaioi, Argeoi. But by Tsountas' day it was realized that the problem was not so simple.

We have followed his rather abortive attempt to pin down the origin of these people. On the question of chronology, however, a firm over-all framework had now been laid. The method employed is still standard for dating as far back as 3000—that is, to establish synchronisms between the culture in question and another culture with an *absolute* chronology that can be calculated from written records. "Here we call in the aid of Egyptology," says Tsountas. "In Greece we find datable Egyptian products in Mycenaean deposits, and conversely in datable Egyptian deposits we find Mycenaean products." He then lists the chief known synchronisms: a late Mycenaean vase in an Egyptian tomb dating within fifty years of 1100; a large group of the "Mycenaean false-necked vase or Bügelkanne*" (we now usually call them stirrup jars* [Fig. 45]), which Flinders Petrie, the first exponent of sequence dating*, had found at various Egyptian sites and arranged in a stylistic series dated between 1400 and 1100; tomb frescoes of Thothmes III (about 1500) at Egyptian Thebes on which were shown "princes of the land of Keftu" (presumed to be Crete) with vases of distinct Mycenaean style in their hands; scarabs found both at Mycenae and Ialysos in Rhodes bearing cartouches of "Amenophis III and of his queen Tiy" (latter half of the fifteenth century).

There had also been some attempt, in addition to Petrie's work, to dis-

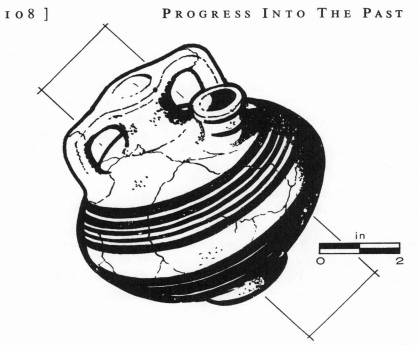

Figure 45

tinguish between an "earlier" and "later" phase. "The earlier period of Mycenaean art is thus shown to be anterior to the reign of Thothmes III; and, as that period cannot conceivably be limited to a few short genera-tions, the sixteenth century is none too early for the upper limit of the Mycenaean age. . . . For the lower limit . . . we have taken the twelfth century, though certain archaeologists and historians are inclined to a much more recent date—some even bringing it three or four centuries farther down." Tsountas refutes the latter theory by pointing out that "if the beehive and chamber-tombs at Mycenae are to be assigned to a period as late as the ninth century, the rare occurrence of iron in them becomes quite inexplicable."

So the destruction of Mycenaean civilization is confidently placed in the twelfth century, and the agents are identified as the Dorians. But Tsountas is at pains to insist that the influence of Mycenaean civilization survived the Dorian destruction. In fact, certain architectural features such as the plan of the megaron and propylon as well as the column and lintel construction became "an enduring possession of Hellenic art, and so of the civilized world."

This theme leads naturally to the subject of his final chapter, "The Mycenaean World and Homer." We hear no more of Schliemann's early and impetuous conviction that the Mycenaean world *is* Homer's world;

but the connection is no less firmly argued. "That Mycenaean art outlasted the social *régime* under which it had attained its splendid bloom is sufficiently attested by the Homeric poems. Doubtless, the Achaean system, when it fell before the aggressive Dorian, must have left many an heirloom above ground. . . . And, again, the poems in their primitive strata undoubtedly reflect the older order . . ." Tsountas sounds an even more modern note in another passage: "Homer avowedly sings of heroes and peoples who had flourished in Greece long before his own day. Now it may be denied that these represent the civilization known to us as Mycenaean; but it is certainly a marvellous coincidence (as Schuchhardt observes) that 'excavations invariably confirm the former power and splendor of every city which is mentioned by Homer as conspicuous for its wealth or sovereignty.' "

In the historical reconstruction that ends *The Mycenaean Age* we detect a characteristic nineteenth-century attitude (possibly to be attributed mainly to Manatt). It was by manifest destiny that the inventive and forward-looking West clashed with and defeated the ancient and conservative East, which sat astride the land and sea routes between Europe and Asia. "The sea power in the Aegean [Mycenae] and the land power on the Hellespont [Troy] could no more avoid an Eastern Question then than can England and Russia to-day."

But the weakened victors of the long struggle celebrated by Homer returned home only to face and succumb to the Dorian threat. "The Dorian migration marks the beginning of long dark ages, the mediaeval epoch of Greece, out of which she emerges only in the Homeric Renaissance. . . . To the isles and shores of Asia Minor, the descendants of the conquerors [of Troy] return as refugees; and of all they carry with them the most precious possessions are the old songs." Tsountas and his contemporaries tended to think of the new colonial milieu in which Homer lived as a "ferment of races and conditions" that gradually produced the complex and more or less unified civilization mirrored in the poems as we have them. "On the establishment of the new order with a new accumulation of wealth, some of the old arts revive, while others have to be created afresh." Political, social and religious institutions described in the Homeric poems are largely the reflection of this post-Dark Ages renaissance rather than of Mycenaean times. Yet it was a far less splendid age than the one that saw the mighty heroic deeds and produced the original heroic songs inspired by them. "As compared with the Mycenaean, the Homeric civilization marks decadence. The arts especially are stationary or even retrograde; and the Phoenicians have resumed their old lead in art as well as in commerce."

Again in the very last sentences, the confident note of late-nineteenth-century optimism is struck. "We set the epic picture against the real background, and the harmony is too close and manifold to have happened [*i.e.,* to be accidental]. To bring out the full measure of that harmony, we have only to go on unearthing the relics of prehistoric Greece and at the same time to delve yet deeper in the inexhaustible mines of Homer." This seems a naïve faith in the light of the archaeological and philological results of the first two generations of the twentieth century. Yet when one reflects on the extraordinary forward leap in solid knowledge documented in Tsountas' book as compared with a generation before, when Schliemann began his excavations, it must be admitted that there *was* considerable reason for such a confident attitude.

I V

Evans, Crete and Minos:

1900-1914

"Evans had come to the site in the hope of finding

a seal impression and a clay tablet, and Time and Chance

had led him to discover a civilization."

W HEN SCHLIEMANN WAS NEGOTIATING for his first excavation at
Troy, a young man of very different background but with many
similar traits of personality was entering Oxford University. Particularly
for his earlier years we shall depend heavily on recollections and documents published by his half sister, Joan, in her book, *Time and Chance*.

Throughout more than half of his life Arthur Evans was simply the
"son of John Evans the great." The older Evans was a Fellow of the Royal
Society, Honorary Secretary of the Geological and Numismatic Societies
of London, a distinguished, wealthy, widely traveled and politically sophisticated businessman and scholar-gentleman. Such books as *The Ancient Stone
Implements, Weapons and Ornaments of Great Britain* (1872) had established his reputation as one of the founders of the new science of prehistory. The son grew up "belonging of right to the world of learning and
the lesser world of archaeology, in having an instinctive judgment of date
and style and use, acquired by living among the collections at Nash Mills
[the Evans manor house]; in possessing a knowledge of prehistory and
numismatics learned so gradually and so easily that it had become unconscious. There were solid advantages . . . in being the son of a man who
provided . . . an allowance of £250 a year without question or condition,
and would always help in a financial emergency . . ."

While profiting all his life from his family's prominence, Arthur was
determined to make his mark on his own terms. In school debates he
criticized the classical curriculum and attacked the Conservative government. He refused to take any interest in the family papermills and after his
college years spent much of his time abroad. Until close to middle age he
lived and traveled mainly in the Balkans. There he combined archaeological
and historical exploration with an ardent interest in the current political
struggle. As correspondent for the *Manchester Guardian* and free-lance
writer, he sent home impassioned dispatches supporting the native aspira-
tions for self-government.

At the age of twenty-seven Evans married Margaret Freeman, whose father was a distinguished medieval historian. They made their home at Ragusa on the Dalmatian coast during the earlier portion of their fifteen years of life together. Actually, the bridegroom continued his constant travels, with or without his bride; and Margaret soon became resigned to frequent separations. Their parents, anxious to lure them back to England, urged Arthur to try to qualify for a new studentship in archaeology at Oxford. An excerpt from his reply tells a good deal about his own attitude and the archaeological climate of the day: "It is quite evident that Athens and no other earthly site is Newton's goal. . . . In that case the studentship ought not to be called a studentship of Archaeology in general. The great characteristic of modern Archaeological progress has been the revelations as to periods and races of men about which history is silent; and for pre-historic Archaeology, no European field is perhaps now more important than the unworked Illyrian one [the area where he was then living] . . . Oxford, however, seems to have set itself to ignore every branch of Archaeology out of its own classical beat."

Evans' resentment of what he felt was a current overemphasis on classical antiquity can again be sensed in his sister's account of a trip to Greece in 1882.

They rode . . . by Orchomenos, where Schliemann had excavated a prehistoric tomb two years before, to Thebes and Athens. . . . They saw the Schliemanns, heard all about the finds at Orchomenos, and laughed a little at the odd little man and his preoccupation with Homer; but Arthur found his gold work from Mycenae beautiful, exciting, and puzzling: it was art of a kind that appealed to him, because it was not classical: but how did its quasi-Assyrian and quasi-Egyptian elements come to be combined with the Aegean octopus? . . . By Aegina and Nauplia they made their way to Tiryns, where Evans was enormously impressed by the Cyclopean walls, and to Mycenae, where he could not get over the extraordinary contrast between its architecture and that of classical Greece.

In 1884 Evans became Keeper of the Ashmolean Museum in Oxford. It is probably fair to infer that the appointment depended more on family connections than on any wide professional reputation that Arthur had earned up to that time. As a matter of fact, the post had for generations been a sinecure, with a motley collection and no funds for its proper maintenance or improvement. But Evans always relished a challenge, and he was soon announcing his intention to collect and display in the Ashmolean a selection of artefacts representing archaeology in the broadest sense. Here was a vision that was far more sweeping than Schliemann's passion to authenticate Homer. It had first stirred a few brilliant and audacious minds in John Evans' generation and was still making slow and painful progress against the weight of orthodox and entrenched dogma.

In his inaugural address, "The Ashmolean Museum as a Home of Archaeology in Oxford," Arthur Evans eloquently sounded the keynote.

> Our theme is History, the history of the rise and succession of human Arts, Institutions, and Beliefs in our historic portion of the globe. . . . The unwritten History of Mankind precedes the written, the lore of monuments precedes the lore of books. . . . Consider for a moment the services rendered within quite recent years by what has been called Prae-historic Archaeology, but which in truth was never more Historic, in widening the horizon of our Past. It has drawn aside the curtain, and revealed the dawn. It has dispelled, like the unsubstantial phantoms of a dream, those preconceived notions as to the origin of human arts and institutions at which Epicurus and Lucretius already laughed, before the days of biblical chronology. . . . We have as yet too little in our Museum to illustrate these early chapters in the history of human arts . . .

The status and prestige of the Ashmolean did improve dramatically under Evans' forceful direction, but the endless negotiating over accessions and funds and building plans bored and exasperated him. Joan Evans writes:

> A new vision was beginning to haunt him: Crete. It is hard to say what chance had first drawn his attention to the unknown island; it seems as if a thousand tiny facts and things had drifted like dust and settled to weigh down the scales of his decision. His father's acquaintance, Henry Schliemann, had revealed a bright new world by his excavations at Troy, Mycenae, Tiryns and Orchomenos: excavations conducted Homer in hand, with no thought of relating them to anything but the epic story. For Evans, as for others, they were not Homeric illustrations but bronze age sites, and for that very reason offered problems more complex than any Schliemann found. There seemed, especially at Mycenae, to be things of many dates, drawn from various sources; and those sources were for the most part still unknown. Schliemann himself had planned to excavate "broad Knossos," but had never done so; and now the same unavowed intention was dawning on the mind of Arthur Evans. On February 3, 1892, he was in Rome, and made friends with Halbherr, an Italian archaeologist who had already explored many of the classical sites in Crete. What he told him of the earlier remains on the island, unexplored and unexplained, fired his imagination and confirmed his interest, though as yet his purpose was hardly formed.

After his wife's premature death in 1893, Evans began to concentrate more and more on Aegean prehistory, particularly on the evidence for a system of writing that he was discovering on engraved gems and seals. "Evans was extremely short-sighted, and a reluctant wearer of glasses. Without them, he could see small things held a few inches from his eyes in extraordinary detail, while everything else was a vague blur. Consequently the details he saw with microscopic exactitude, undistracted by the outside world, had a greater significance for him than for other men." After Schliemann's death, it was possible to work over the finds from his excavations with more freedom, and Evans detected written symbols on two of the objects. Also, in the antique shops in Athens he discovered engraved hieroglyphics on gems that the dealers said had originated in Crete. Similar objects in the Berlin Museum undoubtedly came from Crete, although Adolph Furtwängler, the foremost expert on Mycenaean art, believed that they were to be dated later than Mycenaean times.

Other scholars were also beginning to look toward Crete. The German authority Milchhöfer, in a book entitled *Beginnings of Art* (1883), had inferred that to explain the discoveries at Mycenae and Tiryns one would have to follow the trail back through the Aegean islands (especially Melos) and eventually to Crete. We have already mentioned Schliemann's frustrated plans at Knossos. In 1893 some sherds had been brought to the museum at Candia (now Iraklion, the largest town in Crete) from a cave called Kamares* high up on the southern face of Mount Ida. They were closely similar to pottery that Flinders Petrie had discovered in twelfth-dynasty tombs at Kahun in the Egyptian Fayum and had with marvelous intuition identified as "Aegean imports." So the stage was set to press an investigation in Crete itself as soon as political conditions would permit.

Arthur Evans visited Crete for the first time in 1894, the very year in which his first article on the Cretan inscriptions appeared. His sister draws an interesting contrast in his literary style during the Balkan and Cretan years. The earlier documents were "as much occupied with people and scenery as with objects of antiquity: the records of a desultory quest for interest and adventure"; but after 1894 the letters become "brief and businesslike, devoid of fine writing, and yet imbued with a curious steady purpose." She infers from this sudden change that "before he landed Evans had determined on the archaeological conquest of the island."

A few excerpts from his letters will suggest the exciting atmosphere of those first days on Cretan soil.

The site of Knossos is most extensive and occupies several hills [see Map VI]. The Mykenaean akropolis however seems not to be the highest but that to the south west, nearest to the gorge. . . . Here at a place called *ta pithária* ["the storage jars"] are the remains of Mykenaean walls and passages (where the great pots, Pithoi, were found) noted by W. J. Still-

man [a British diplomat and amateur archaeologist] and others. . . .
I copied the marks on the stones, some of which recall my "hieroglyphics." . . . I was brought a remarkable fragment of a black basalt
vessel. At first I thought it was a bit of some kind of Roman relief
ware, but to my astonishment I found it was Mykenaean, with part of
a relief representing men perhaps ploughing or sowing—an altar?—
and a walled enclosure with a fig tree: a supplement to the Vapheio
vases and contemporary in style!

On March 20 he continues:

Halbherr arrived with the President of the Syllogos [Archaeological
Council] Hadjidakis. . . . [March 22] Long conversation with [Joseph]
Hadjidakis about the excavations of Knossos. Schliemann proposed to
dig here. . . . I took the responsibility of saying he [Hadjidakis]
might buy it [a quarter-share of the site] for me and that I would raise
the money for the entire purchase in England when that was feasible.
The possession of a part can legally compel sale. I said that the "Cretan
Exploration Fund"—at present non-existent—would agree to the same
terms as the Germans at Olympia and that the Cretans should keep
these antiquities only reserving to us the right of publication and such
specimens as were *not needed or could be spared by the Museum of
the Syllogos.* . . . Halbherr would act for the Cretan Exploration Fund
as epigraphic* explorer; he knows of countless places where material
could be gathered and great discoveries made . . .

Having gotten negotiations started in this rather breezy manner, Evans
set out on a long journey of exploration—the first of many—through central and eastern Crete. Everywhere, he recognized the broken potsherds
marking the sites of towns that had existed long before the classical period.
He also bought or took impressions of many engraved seals and gems that
the Cretans called *galopetras* ("milkstones"). Mothers wore them as
charms to guarantee that their milk would prove adequate for their babies.
The antiquities acquired in those first explorations formed the beginning
of the great Cretan collection of the Ashmolean Museum.

One ancient site, at Goulas near Kritsa, particularly impressed Evans.
"What a mighty centre this must have been! There is no one object here
to fix the attention like the Lion Gate; the walls are not so massive as those
of Tiryns, but for vastness of extent, for the preservation of its inner
buildings, for sublimity of site, Goulas throws all competitors into the
shade. . . . There seems to be no trace of anything Hellenic here . . . there
is nothing that is not Mykenaean or prae-Mykenaean." We can already
catch the first glimmer of a theory that was to become Evans' abiding
conviction for the next forty-five years. "What one feels," he writes, "is that

here [in Crete] perhaps was really the great original focus of Mykenaean culture . . ." It is a minor irony that Goulas, the site on which he seems to have first based the hypothesis, was later proved not to be prehistoric at all.

The following year Evans was back in Crete, accompanied by John L. Myres, "a Ulysses of twenty-six, black-bearded and quick spoken, learned in many lores and a fit companion for Homeric adventure." As their explorations continue, Evans sees increasing evidence for close connections with the prehistoric phase already known on the mainland. "The golden age of Crete lies far beyond the limits of the historical period: its culture . . . is practically identical with that of the Peloponnese and a large part of the Aegean world. . . . The great days of Crete were those of which we still find a reflection in the Homeric poems—the period of Mycenaean culture, to which here at least we would fain attach the name 'Minoan.' " Minos was perhaps a generic name for the ruler of Knossos, like Pharaoh in Egypt and Caesar in Rome. The adjective "Minoan" soon came to connote for Evans a culture originating in Crete, particularly at Knossos, and completely dominating its "Mycenaean" counterpart on the mainland. One of our major themes from now on will be the developing evidence for Minoan-Mycenaean interrelations; and for this reason we must be familiar with at least certain aspects of Minoan civilization.

THE SEASON OF 1900

The final Cretan phase of the Greek War of Independence prevented Evans' return until 1899. The next year the acquisition of the Knossos site and the excavation permits were finally in order, and Evans began to dig on March 23, 1900. Like Schliemann thirty years before, Evans was a middle-aged man with practically no experience in excavation when he undertook the uncovering of a crucial site. His half sister frankly admits that he "except at Aylesford [a Late Celtic urnfield in Kent excavated in 1891] had done none but occasional and surreptitious excavation." It is fortunate therefore that he acquired as his assistant a reticent and capable Scot named Duncan Mackenzie.

During the previous four years Mackenzie had been a member of the staff of the first major excavation conducted by the British School of Archaeology at Athens. This was at the deeply stratified and complex site of Phylakopi on the island of Melos. Mackenzie was site supervisor throughout that undertaking and assumed complete charge during the final campaign. We shall later review some of his conclusions and inferences on the Phylakopi discoveries.

At Knossos Mackenzie seems again to have performed the duties that we would now designate as those of the site supervisor. But the exact nature of his responsibilities, the limits of his authority and the personal relationship between him and Evans are something of an enigma. The problem has important scientific implications in view of the controversy that has developed since 1962 about the dependability of some aspects of Evans' publications. The conundrum, in short, concerns the exact roles that the two men played in the gradual evolution of theories from the moment of discovery of crucial evidence until the final arguments and conclusions appeared in definitive publications.

Differences of opinion and personality clashes may occur among the members of any excavation staff, just as in other small groups that are temporarily isolated from normal living and working habits. Whether these tensions were particularly aggravated in the case of Evans and Mackenzie is not clear. According to his half sister, Evans "endured his [Mackenzie's] suspicious temper and his valetudinarian ways with exemplary patience." This would suggest that in the bosom of the family Evans sometimes unburdened certain resentments and frustrations. Yet Evans too was undoubtedly a difficult man with whom to be closely associated. And the situation may well have been aggravated by the almost complete dependence of one scholar on the other for his economic livelihood. One gets the impression, rightly or wrongly, of an annually renewed contract at Knossos, rather than a full-fledged collaboration such as seems to have developed between Schliemann and Dörpfeld.

In any case, we must turn to the chronicle of some of the major discoveries in those fabulous early years. Although one is likely to think of the Knossos excavations as a long series of slow, methodical campaigns extending through the first two or three decades of the century, the fact is that almost all of the major excavation in the palace and much of the exploration of its environs were completed within five years. The season usually lasted from two to four months in the spring and early summer. The nature of the finds soon required the services of a trained architect and a skilled artist. The supervisory staff was always very small and the workmen extremely numerous, by modern standards. And one looks in vain for mention of additional supervisors to direct and control 100 to 200 eager laborers.

Mackenzie, for all his experience and instinct for complete and precise recording, must have been pressed very hard. Evans' own role is less clear; but it would appear that he was more concerned with the preliminary examination of the finds themselves than in methodically checking their exact position and association as they came out of the ground. In short, the early excavation of Knossos was conducted with no more refined technique than Schliemann's later campaigns. No sudden revolution in methodology took place between 1890 and 1900; and it is in fact unrealistic to assume that it should have.

We shall try as far as is practicable to follow the progress of the work by quoting from Evans' letters to his family and especially from his annual reports. The latter were regularly printed in the place of honor at the beginning of each number of the prestigious *Annual of the British School at Athens* for the years 1900 to 1905. First, for a rather more complete description of the geographical setting (see Map VI):

> The site of ancient Knossos . . . about four miles inland from Candia, is shut in by higher hills in three directions. Somewhat South however of the scanty remains of the Roman City, the ground gradually rises into a rounded hill generally known as Kephala. . . . This hill lies at the confluence of a tributary stream with the ancient Kairatos (now *Katsabás*), and descends somewhat steeply towards these channels on the South and East. To the West of the hill . . . runs a road, the antiquity of which is shown by the rock tombs that extend along its further course. This road must in all ages of Cretan history have formed the natural lines of access [to the interior of the island]. . . . Although overlooked by loftier heights beyond the streams and the road, the partial isolation of the hill of Kephala, and the fact that it immediately commanded this natural line of communication, must have made it in early times something of a key position.

Attention was concentrated that first year mainly on the western part of the mound. We cannot hope to provide a detailed and systematic reconstruction of the spectacular finds that came pouring out almost as soon as the surface was scratched. It was not only the quantity and variety that amazed Evans, but above all their quality and novelty. The discoveries on the mainland had hardly prepared anyone for this revelation of a lively, imaginative and exuberant people who had once populated the mythical Knossos. In his formal publications Evans strikes a rather ponderous and detached note, which contrasts strongly with Schliemann's naïve enthusiasm. But the letters show that his reactions were not so very different when he first saw the inscribed tablets, painted pottery, monumental architectural remains and particularly the frescoes.

For instance, in the southwestern section of the hill in what was soon to be called the Corridor of the Cupbearer (Fig. 52), he writes that "two large pieces of Mycenaean fresco" were recovered on which was preserved "far and away the most remarkable human figure of the Mycenaean Age that has yet come to light" (Fig. 46). Later known as the Cupbearer, *she* is described by Evans as follows: "One [fragment] represented the head

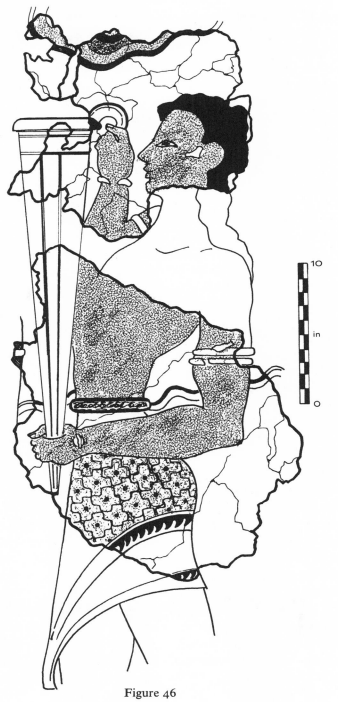

Figure 46

and forehead, the other the waist and part of the skirt of a female figure holding in her hand a long Mycenaean 'rhyton' or high funnel shaped cup. . . . The figure was life size, the flesh colour of a deep reddish hue. . . . The profile of the face was of a noble type: full lips. . . . The eye was dark and slightly almond shaped. In front of the ear is a kind of ornament and a necklace and bracelet are visible. The arms are beautifully modelled. The waist is of the smallest . . ." After cleaning and study prior to the first tentative published report, Evans describes the painting as follows: ". . . on the floor level . . . face uppermost, [lay] two large pieces of fresco. These pieces together formed the greater part of a life-sized figure of a youth clad in the same close-fitting and richly embroidered loin-cloth as those of the 'Corridor of the Procession' . . . The modelling of the face and limbs show an artistic advance which in historic Greece was not reached till the fifth century before our era, some eight or nine centuries later than the date of this Knossian fresco."

A few days later a letter describes the uncovering of a "bath chamber," which was soon recognized as the famous Throne Room.

> On the other side of the North wall was a short bench, like that of the outer chamber, and then separated from it by a small interval a separate seat of honour or throne. It had a high back . . . which was partly imbedded in the stucco of the wall. It was raised on a square base and had a curious moulding below with crockets. (Almost Gothic!) Probably painted originally so as to harmonize with the fresco at its side. This was imperfectly preserved, but showed the upper foliage of a palm tree (No! reeds). . . . On the N. E. wall was another study in foliage, reed like plants in front of a tree (No! hills) and curving lines below apparently indicating flowing water . . ."

Again, in the preliminary publication, a good many changes can already be noticed. The "bath chamber" has become the Throne Room, and the sunken area in front of the throne that suggested the original designation is possibly an aquarium or fish pond (this distinctive feature of Minoan palaces is now usually called a lustral area*). The stone throne itself had been stuccoed and painted, and great wingless griffins with elaborate crests are recognized as the major theme on the frescoed walls. In addition to the throne, "the specially rich character of the relics found in the chamber itself corroborates the conclusion that a royal personage once sat here for council. . . . The stone benches round may have afforded room for twenty counsellors." Furthermore, Evans feels that the room has "an appearance of freshness and homogeneity that makes it improbable that at the time of the great overthrow it had long existed in its present form" (Fig. 47).

Figure 47

The frescoes, whether in place on the lower walls or fallen in tumbled fragments, had to be promptly and carefully cleaned, conserved and copied by an expert. Evans summoned from Athens the Swiss artist Étienne Gilliéron, who had carried out similar work for the French School of Archaeology. For almost a generation the Gilliérons, father and son, were associated with the Knossos excavations. Most of the reconstructions of fresco panels and other art objects are their work. We must, of course, be grateful to the modern artist and the excavator for such striking re-creations of Minoan art. But, as in the case of the restoration of the palace architecture, reconstruction poses serious problems when certainty cannot be attained. How far should one man's imagination and judgment decide for others? Many a visitor to the museum in Iraklion (where most of the movable finds from Knossos are displayed) is startled to discover how little of the original fresco compositions Evans really recovered and how much is restored. And the restored areas are so artfully blended with the original fragments that the innocent student is likely to assume from reproductions in books that the total composition is certain.

As more fresco fragments came out, Evans realized that the Minoan artists had followed the Egyptian convention of using white for the flesh of women and red for men. He also began to suspect that the paintings were not all contemporary. For instance, this is part of his description of the famous "Blue Boy" composition (Fig. 48):

Figure 48

There are eight pieces of this design, which can be put together sufficiently to show the greater part [but missing the head] of a small figure
of a boy in a field of white crocuses, some of which he is placing in
an ornamental vase of "kantharos" shape. This fresco, remarkable in
many ways, apparently belongs to an earlier date than any yet discovered in the Palace. . . . The whole tone of the painting differs from
that of the mature Mycenaean style of the Knossos frescoes, and the
tint of the boy's body, here a pale blue, differs from the regular Mycenaean convention, in which male figures are painted a reddish-brown,
while the women are white.

His instinct about date proved to be right; but a blue *tail* was later detected on one fragment of this composition and the subsequent discovery
of a Knossian scene clearly depicting a blue *monkey* leaves little doubt
that the color convention had not been violated in this case.

Another group of fresco fragments in "miniature style" depicts crowds
of people watching spectacles such as bull baiting or dancing.

At a glance we recognize Court ladies in elaborate toilette. . . . In the
best executed pieces these *décolletées* ladies are seated in groups with
their legs half bent under them, engaged in animated conversation em-

phasised by expressive gesticulation. . . . The men, none of whom are bearded, are naked except for the usual loin-cloth and the foot-gear with banded gaiter-like continuations above the ankle, resembling the buskins worn by the warriors on the fresco-fragments from Mycenae. . . . These unique representations of great crowds of men and women within the walls of towns and palaces supply a new and striking commentary on the familiar passage of Homer describing the ancient populousness of the Cretan cities.[41]

It soon appeared that the Minoans had also used monumental relief sculpture to decorate some wall surfaces. Near the northwest corner of the mound, where Evans suspected that a major entrance to the palace had been located, sizable fragments were discovered of a painted plaster relief of a bull's head (Fig. 49). "It is life-sized, or somewhat over, and modelled in high relief. . . . [It] is the most magnificent monument of Mycenaean

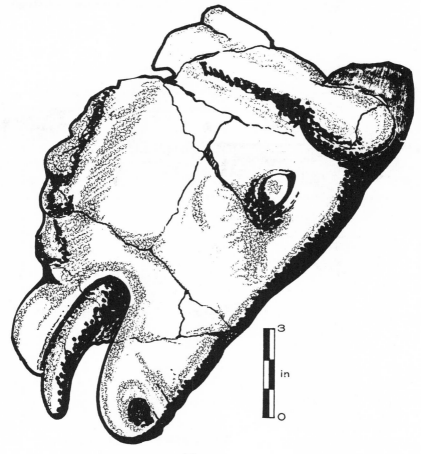

Figure 49

plastic art that has come down to our time . . . full of life and spirit. It combines in a high degree naturalism with grandeur, and it is no exaggeration to say that no figure of a bull at once so powerful and so true was produced by later classical art." Here we can sense again a deep-seated urge to find material not only earlier but "better" than the widely praised original sculpture of the fifth century B.C. that was being recovered in Greece, and particularly at Olympia. And on occasion Evans' imagination is no less fertile than Schliemann's in suggesting historical or mythological associations for his finds. "What a part these creatures [bulls] play here! On the frescoes and reliefs, the chief design of the seals, on a steatite vase, above the gate it may be of the Palace itself. Was not some one or other of these creatures visible on the ruined site in the early Dorian days [after the destruction], which gave the actual tradition of the Bull of Minos?"

In addition to the architectural remains of the palace and the numerous art objects, many inscribed tablets were recovered in the early weeks. When he read the first enthusiastic notice of the Knossos excavations published in *The Times,* John Evans was so pleased that he immediately sent off to his son a draft for £500. In acknowledging the gift, Arthur provided his father with some up-to-the-minute information that shows that written records were still his major concern. "The great discovery is whole deposits, entire or fragmentary, of clay tablets analogous to the Babylonian but with inscriptions in the prehistoric script of Crete. I must have about seven hundred pieces by now. . . . These inscriptions engraved on the wet clay are evidently the work of practised scribes. . . . A certain number of characters are pictographic, showing what the subject of the documents was. Thus in one chamber occurred a series with chariots and horses' heads on them, others show vases [Fig. 50] . . ."

Figure 50

In his first formal report to the scholarly world Evans gives an excellent description of the tablets found in the campaign of 1900.

Of the clay records brought to light the vast majority of pieces, in number over nine hundred, present a linear form of script. The other hieroglyphic class was sparsely represented. . . . Not only were the clay slips extremely friable but the slightest touch of moisture was liable to reduce them to pulp and a few specimens on a tray which had been wetted during a nocturnal storm, owing to a leakage in the roof of the Turkish house which served as our headquarters, became a shapeless mass of clay. The marvel is that any of these clay tablets should have resisted the natural damp of the soil, and in many cases their survival was due to the extra baking they received through the conflagration of the building. In this way fire—so fatal elsewhere to historic libraries!—has acted as a preservative of these earlier records. . . . The linear tablets are for the most part elongated slips of hand-moulded clay with wedge-shaped ends from about two inches to about eight inches in length and about ⅗-inch to about three inches broad. . . . These have the inscription generally in one or two lines along their greatest length. Others, however, are broader, with the inscription in several lines across their lesser diameter. . . . The larger tablets are scored with horizontal lines for the guidance of the scribe. They are generally written only on one side but some show a short endorsement and others present a full inscription on both faces . . .

Evans then proceeds to characterize the inscriptions themselves.

About seventy characters seem to have been in common use. . . . A certain number of quasi-pictorial characters also occur which seem to have an ideographic or determinative meaning. The numerals show a certain parallelism with the Egyptian. The system is decimal [Fig. 51]. The units, consisting of upright lines, are practically the same as the

Figure 51

Egyptian. The tens are generally horizontal lines. . . . The hundreds are circles. . . . The thousands are circles with four spurs. From the frequency of ciphers on these tablets it is evident that a great number of them refer to accounts relating to the royal stores and arsenal. The general purport of the tablet, moreover, is in many cases supplied by the introduction of one or more pictorial figures. Thus on a series of tablets . . . occur designs of a typical Mycenaean chariot, . . . a horse's head and what seems to be a cuirass, sometimes replaced by the outlines of an ingot.

Some of these ideographic symbols appeared to offer the possibility of comparisons with shapes—and therefore dates—of known objects or representations.

Among other subjects thus represented were human figures, perhaps slaves, houses or barns, swine, ears of corn, various kinds of trees, saffron flowers, and vessels of clay of various shapes. . . . On one tablet two ox-heads are seen associated with a vase of the Vapheio type, both of gold, that also occur among the Keft offerings [in Egyptian tombs]. This identity of shape seems to indicate approximate contemporaneity and makes it probable that some at least of the tablets go back to the beginning of the fifteenth century B.C. . . . The words on the tablets are at times divided by upright lines, and from the average number of letters included between these it is probable that the signs have a syllabic value. The inscriptions are invariably written from left to right.

As a matter of fact, after years of intensive work and a major publication, Evans did not really get very far beyond this point in the interpretation of the tablets. Here he goes on to enunciate a policy that, if he had carried it out promptly and fully, might have resulted in a much earlier decipherment. "The full material has first to be collected by the thorough exploration of the as yet unexcavated portion of the Palace. It will then be possible to publish photographic reproductions of the whole, supplemented by careful copies of the inscriptions from the originals, together with complete tables of the letters, numerals and other signs." And as part of a footnote he adds, "No effort will be spared to publish the whole collected material at the earliest possible moment. The Oxford University Press . . . has undertaken the publication, and has already set in hand the preliminary work, including a Mycenaean Fount."

It is reminiscent of Schliemann's experience with loosely supervised workmen that some of the Knossos tablets were smuggled out of the dig and appeared on the market in Athens. Ironically enough, the offending workman's name was Aristides, whose illustrious classical ancestor was nicknamed "The Just." And to intensify the irony, the theft was proved in court by producing other tablets from the same deposit that, though un-decipherable, showed similar formulae.

Although the earlier history of the site does not concern us directly, it may be mentioned that the "Mycenaean" was not the only horizon dis-covered in the first campaign. A deep sounding in the unbuilt area that was later recognized as the great central court of the palace produced "black primitive pottery . . . some incised, and a good many celts [stone hand axes]. . . . Here we have an early site untouched in the middle of a later settlement: from religious reasons (?)." This offhand and tentative theory illustrates a tendency typical of most archaeologists—and particu-larly of Evans—to adduce religious reasons to "explain" any and every enigmatic discovery.

On June 2, 1900, the first phenomenally successful season at Knossos ended. The expedition had dug for nine weeks and had uncovered "about two acres of the Palace site." Evans explains that the very large area laid bare was "largely due to the relatively small depth below the surface at which the actual remains lay." And he continues: "The floor level varied from about 13 inches in the zone immediately above the Southern Terrace to somewhat over 10 feet in the Northern Step-way. . . . It is no exaggera-tion to say, that on no previously excavated site in the Greek lands have so many ancient relics been found within the same space at so slight a depth below the surface of the ground."

Evans is also at pains to point out the careful methods employed.

The earth was removed in layers from the surface, and owing to this method some large pieces of fallen fresco which might otherwise have been ruined by the pick were preserved intact. Wherever the earth showed traces of containing small objects it was thoroughly sifted, . . . Owing to this minute examination many small objects of great value were recovered which would otherwise have been irretrievably lost. Among these may be especially mentioned pieces of inscribed linear tablets, clay "labels" of the hieroglyphic class, and . . . clay impressions of seals, a class of object never before observed in any excavation of a Mycenaean site. That such had existed elsewhere, however, is only too probable, and the example of the native antiquary's [Minos Kalo-kairinos of Candia] dig on the Palace site itself, in which fragments of inscribed clay tablets were thrown out without attracting observation, shows how necessary is a minute examination of all the earth in which finds occur.

While Evans' criticism of the carelessness of earlier excavators is no doubt justified, it is fairly obvious from these remarks that his own attention was concentrated on recovering the objects themselves rather than on minute observation of the circumstances of their discovery *in place.*

Even in the first year Evans could utilize information already available from the Greek mainland and Egypt to place his discovery within at least tentative chronological limits. Above a neolithic level an "early" or "Kamares*" palace should date back at least to 2000; and over its ruins a "late" or "Mycenaean" palace persisted until the fourteenth or thirteenth century. (The chronological chart on p. 167–68 may help here and following.)

> In spite of the complicated arrangement of some parts of the interior of the Palace, a great unity prevails throughout the main lines of its ground-plan. . . . Certain later modifications of the original plan have been noted . . . indicative of various epochs in the history of the building. . . . Many of these more massive constructions really date back to the "Kamáres" period. . . . The Magazines* [long, narrow storage rooms] in their earliest form, and with them their great stone door-jambs, go back to the latest pre-Mycenaean period. A very close parallel to these jambs and magazines has now been found by the Italian explorers in a prehistoric Palace at Phaestos and in that case the great bulk of the associated ceramic remains belongs to the Kamáres period. It is also observable in the great Eastern Court [at Knossos—later recognized as the Central Court] and certain chambers that the pavement level lies immediately over the Neolithic clay stratum and therefore probably represents also the first "Palace level," in other words that already in use at the time when the Kamáres pottery was produced. . . . To this stratum belongs the Egyptian diorite figure [of a certain User, perhaps a merchant or ambassador at the court of Knossos], the date of which has been approximately fixed at 2,000 B.C. . . ."

The period of the "second palace" and particularly the date of its "final" destruction will, of course, concern us most.

> The later changes in the Palace and the arrangement and decoration of the rooms as revealed by the excavations were no doubt the work of the Mycenaean Age. . . . The later pottery was of the mature Mycenaean class, analogous to that found at Mycenae, Ialysos and Tell-el-Amarna, in which latter case the associations take us to the Age of Akhenaten (c. 1383–1365 B.C.). . . . Only a single piece of iron . . . was found. . . . Nothing was more striking . . . than the absence of all remains later than the flourishing Mycenaean period. . . . On the whole it seems difficult to bring down the period of the destruction of the Palace later than the thirteenth century B.C.

The first campaign made Evans realize that complete excavation would require years of work and a great deal of money. Public appeals for funds were not very successful, a result that seems not to have greatly disappointed the director. At any rate, in a revealing and prophetic letter to his father he writes:

> It is just as well that I should be in a more or less independent position. . . . The Palace of Knossos was my idea and my work, and it turns out to be such a find as one could not hope for in a lifetime or in many lifetimes. . . . If you like to give me the money personally that also would be quite acceptable. But we may as well keep some of Knossos in the family! I am quite resolved not to have the thing entirely "pooled" for many reasons, but largely because I must have sole control of what I am personally undertaking. With other people it may be different, but I know it is so with me; my way may not be the best but it is the only way I can work.

THE SEASON OF 1901

Improved political conditions in Crete had opened the way for other excavations too. The Italians Halbherr and Luigi Pernier had begun to uncover another palace at Phaistos in the south. As on the mainland in the case of Mycenae and Tiryns, the Knossos palace had apparently had at least one contemporary rival or colleague. And an intrepid young American female, Harriet Boyd, had begun the explorations that were soon to lead to the discovery of a less pretentious but well-preserved hill-top town at Gournia on the north coast some thirty-five miles east of Knossos.

As one turns to Evans' report on his second campaign, it is startling to glance at Plate 1, "Ground plan of the Palace of Knossos, showing its extent as excavated in 1901." Except for unexplored areas in the northeast and southeast corners, the general impression is that almost the whole ground plan of the palace as we now know it had already been cleared in the first two seasons (Fig. 52).

One urgent problem was that of protecting the architectural remains. The Throne Room was already showing serious deterioration from the weather, and Evans decided that it had to be roofed. In effect, the method used here set the course for the whole program of architectural conservation and restoration at Knossos. "This necessity and the desire to avoid the introduction of any incongruous elements amid such surroundings," says Evans, "determined me to reproduce the form of the original Mycenaean columns. An exact model both for the shape and colouring was happily at hand in the small fresco of the temple façade [in the miniature "Grand Stand" composition] . . ." It was also becoming clear that parts

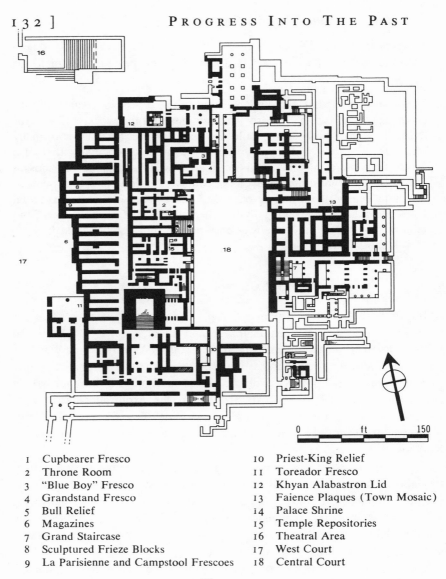

1	Cupbearer Fresco	10	Priest-King Relief
2	Throne Room	11	Toreador Fresco
3	"Blue Boy" Fresco	12	Khyan Alabastron Lid
4	Grandstand Fresco	13	Faience Plaques (Town Mosaic)
5	Bull Relief	14	Palace Shrine
6	Magazines	15	Temple Repositories
7	Grand Staircase	16	Theatral Area
8	Sculptured Frieze Blocks	17	West Court
9	La Parisienne and Campstool Frescoes	18	Central Court

Figure 52

of the palace had had at least two stories above the court level. Evans called in the architect Theodore Fyfe and after him Christian Doll. They set to work to record or calculate the exact position of the vanished wooden columns and beams and to simulate the original crude brick and timber walls with reinforced concrete.

In a later report, when excavation and restoration was further along, Evans eloquently defends his solution.

It being in any case necessary to obtain strong and durable supports
for the upper structures, the *minimum* of incongruity seemed to be
secured by restoring the columns themselves in their original form but
in stone with a plaster facing in place of wood. . . . This work . . .
involved most difficult structural problems and a large use of iron
girders in place of the original architraves and cross-beams. . . . The
actual size of the architraves and beams could be ascertained from some
large charred sections actually preserved. The stones, moreover, of the
upper flight of stairs and of their balustrades had been carefully marked
and numbered so that they could be re-set in their original positions
[Fig. 53]. . . . As a whole, the effect of this legitimate process of recon-
stitution is such that it must appeal to the historic sense of the most
unimaginative. To a height of over twenty feet there rise before us the
grand staircase [in the east or domestic wing] and columnar hall of
approach [in the west or public wing], practically unchanged since they
were traversed, some three and a half millenniums back, by Kings and
Queens of Minos' stock, on their way from the scenes of their public
and sacerdotal functions in the West Wing of the Palace, to the more
private quarters of the Royal household.

Although expert opinion may still be far from unanimous, generations
of visitors to the site would warmly endorse Evans' decision. The excavator
is always duty-bound either to protect the remains of an important building or else to cover it over again with earth. Any type of permanent protection is, of course, very expensive; but funds for this purpose as well as
for adequate publication should be guaranteed before anyone is permitted
to move on to another site. What kind of protection, then? A simple fence
and roof or a genuine attempt at reconstructing the original appearance of
the building? The former solution is cheaper and safer but unlikely to be
as satisfying or evocative for the average visitor. Evans opted for the second and thereby incurred not only very heavy expenses but also inevitable
(and partially justified) charges of going beyond the evidence.

Some of the characteristics of Minoan architecture and its essential differences from the mainland palaces were beginning to impress themselves
on Evans and Mackenzie. To the east of the central court the Hall of the
Double Axes was being uncovered and restored. In spite of certain similarities, Evans is wary about applying the term "megaron" to such halls.

It will be seen that my restored plan does not correspond with that of
the type of Megaron with which we are familiar at Tiryns and Mycenae,
with its quadruple group of columns clustering round the hearth. But
it exactly answers to the "Minoan" halls of Crete as seen in the Palace
of Phaestos. . . . The method of construction answers to a more southern type, in which the hearth no longer forms the fixed centre of the

Figure 53

Megaron, warmth being probably supplied when necessary by some movable brazier like the modern Greek *thermastra*. A central roof-opening, which could also serve as an outlet for smoke, being thus unnecessary, it was found more convenient to have the opening, which was still necessary for light, at the further end of the hall. This broad well for light was probably provided above with a kind of lantern or clear-storey as a partial shelter from rain [Fig. 54].

On the other hand, a close analogy to an architectural feature already known on the mainland was demonstrated by a number of fragments of

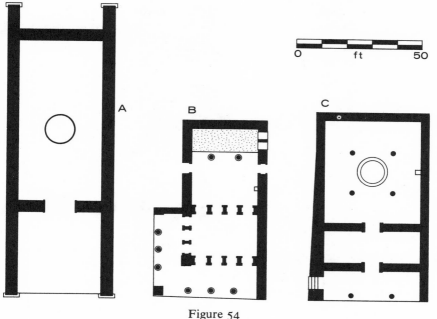

Figure 54

frieze blocks in "porphyry-like limestone" found fallen in the northwest basement area. The pattern in relief consists of elongated half-rosettes separated by vertical members. "It belongs," says Evans, "to the same class as the inlaid alabaster band from the vestibule of the Palace at Tiryns, and the friezes found at Mycenae, as well as that depicted on the small Temple Fresco of Knossos itself. The present arrangement . . . finds its nearest parallel in the small glass paste relief, from the beehive tomb at Menidi [in Attica]." As we have seen, the whole scheme is reminiscent of the triglyph-metope frieze above the columns in the Doric order of classical architecture.

In the same area of the palace Evans and Mackenzie recovered a large number of fresco fragments, originally forming "zones of human figures which when perfect must have been about a fifth the natural height. The figures . . . were more carelessly executed than the Cup-bearer or those of the miniature frescoes." One piece preserved the head and upper body of a figure that was later, under the name "La Parisienne," to attract enthusiastic attention (Fig. 55). But Evans does not seem particularly struck by her at the time of discovery. "The bust of a girl characterised by a very large eye and brilliant vermeil lips as well as by the usual curling black hair displays a high-bodied [bodiced?] dress of quite a novel character. It is looped up at the shoulder into a bunch—blue with red and black

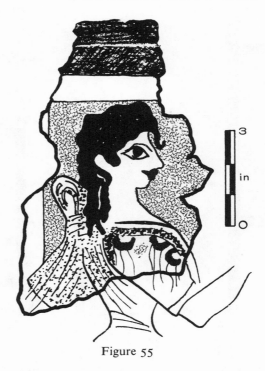

Figure 55

stripes—from which the fringed ends hang down behind . . ." Other associated fragments show still more unusual features, although Evans does not remark on them in any detail. "The men, distinguished by their conventional red tint, seem to have been clad in short-sleeved tunics, blue and yellow with black stripes, which descend to their ankles. . . . Two of the fragments show goblets held in men's hands. Both of these are of the high-stemmed type presenting in outline some resemblance to a champagne glass, but with a handle on either side of the rim" (Fig. 56). This so-called kylix* was one of the most distinctive and popular vase shapes on the mainland in Mycenaean times.

Another fragmentary relief sculpture in painted plaster, as fine in its way as the charging bull, turned up in the southern section; and again Evans points a parallel with the mainland.

The first important piece brought to light showed the back and ear of a male head wearing a crown, the upper part of which consisted of a row of sloping *fleurs-de-lys*. . . . The *fleur-de-lys* ornament recurred in the shape of a collar formed of links of this shape round the neck of a male torso found near the relief of the crown. . . . It is executed

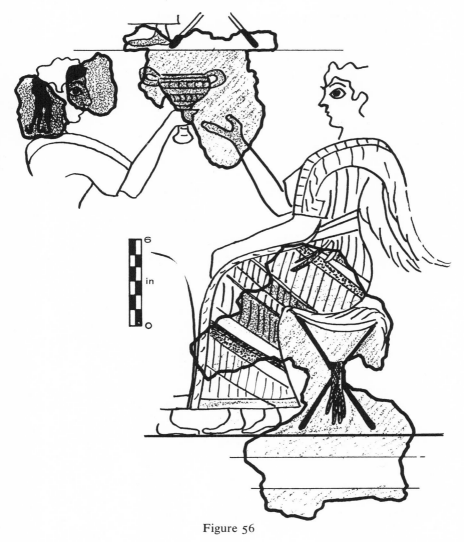

Figure 56

in the same low relief, and . . . shows an extraordinarily advanced style of modelling. . . . The reliefs are all life-size, and the skin was originally coloured a reddish brown. . . . The ornament itself is typically Mycenaean, and its derivation from the pure lily type with the stamens attached may be traced on the gold-plaited inlaid dagger from the Fifth Akropolis Grave [at Mycenae]. Of the natural lily as a Mycenaean hair ornament we have an example in the coiffure of the Goddess and her attendant handmaidens on the great signet from Mycenae. . . . But was the personage who wears it in this case royal or divine? . . . [There is] a real presumption that in this crowned head we see before us a Mycenaean King.

Additional fragments were later discovered, and the reconstructed composition was named the "Priest-King fresco" (Fig. 57).

A stonecutter's workshop held many objects of marble, bone, jasper, steatite and crystal in an unfinished state. Vessels in nearby basement rooms yielded carbonized remains of various seeds such as beans, and heaps of burned grain could be detected. The numerous long narrow rooms in the western basement area were lined with rows of great storage jars for wine and olive oil. It was clear that the palace had been not only a magnificent royal residence but also a more or less self-sufficient center for collecting,

Figure 57

storing and processing agricultural products and for manufacturing luxury goods.

From representations on gems, Evans had for some time been familiar with the favorite Cretan sport of bull baiting. But he is particularly intrigued to discover from fragments of a fine fresco panel that there were female as well as male acrobats (Fig. 58).

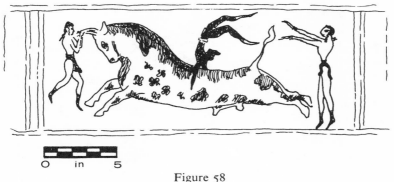

Figure 58

The most interesting feature . . . is the appearance, beside the male performers in this dangerous sport, of female *toreadors,* distinguished by their white skin, . . . the blue and red diadems round their brows, and their somewhat curlier *coiffures,* but otherwise attired in precisely the same way as the "cow-boys," with a loin-cloth and very narrow metallic girdle and striped socks and slippers. . . . We have there nothing of the mere catching of bulls, wild or otherwise, as seen on the Vaphio Cups. . . . They belong to the arena, and afford the clearest evidence that the lords of Mycenaean Knossos glutted their eyes with shows in which maidens as well as youths were trained to grapple with what was then regarded as the king of animals. The sports of the amphitheatre, which have never lost their hold on the Mediterranean world, may thus in Crete at least be traced back to prehistoric times. It may well be that, long before the days when enslaved barbarians were "butchered to make a Roman holiday," captives, perhaps of gentle blood, shared the same fate within sight of the "House of Minos," and that the legends of Athenian prisoners devoured by the Minotaur preserve a real tradition of these cruel sports.

Evans had already distinguished a class of large, handsomely decorated amphoras* (Fig. 59), to which he gave the name "Palace Style*." Since this ceramic style has played an important part in later theories of the relationship between Crete and the Greek mainland, it is interesting to

Figure 59

note his earliest observations. He speaks of it as "the magnificent style of vase-painting prevalent at Knossos in the great days of the Palace." And he goes on to say: "Nothing among the hitherto published Mycenaean ceramic types exactly corresponds with these, but Mr. J. H. Marshall, who kindly undertook the reconstruction of the Knossian fragments, has been able to identify a large vase from a recently discovered tomb of Mycenae, and fragments of another from the Vaphio tomb (left undescribed by its discoverer) as belonging to the same fabric, and with good reason regards these and some other isolated specimens found on the mainland of Greece as of Knossian importation." Who is to say whether this conclusion was originally in Marshall's or Evans' mind? In any case, the conviction was growing on Evans that, given two closely similar artefacts, the one found on the mainland and the other in Crete, the mainland example must be an import and not vice versa.

One of the neatest synchronisms between Crete and Egypt developed in the course of clearing the northwest corner of the palace. Under a floor of "Mycenaean" date, they discovered a

> well-marked archaeological stratum containing a large proportion of charcoal and representing the burnt remains of an earlier structure. In this deposit immediately under the Mycenaean wall-foundations, at a depth of about 16 inches below the later floor-level . . . was the lid of an Egyptian alabastron upon the upper face of which was finely en-graved a cartouche containing the name and divine titles of the Hyksôs King Khyan. . . . The minimum date to which it is possible to refer it, can . . . hardly be lower than 1700 B.C. . . . On the other hand, the early phase of Mycenaean civilisation represented by the chamber built above the earlier stratum in which the lid lay, shows many points of contact with the Egypt of Thothmes III. Yet this later structure, which may thus be taken to go back to the fifteenth or sixteenth century B.C., was separated by over a foot of deposit from the more ancient Palace layer. . . . This result has a very important bearing on the date of the early part of the Palace fabric as a whole . . .

THE SEASON OF 1902

Evans seems to have thought that this would probably be the last cam-paign at Knossos. But the residential or "domestic" area to the east of the central court proved to have extended to a much greater depth than ex-pected, and its excavation posed difficult problems of reconstruction.

Evans was already aware that many of the objects (including inscribed tablets) found in basement rooms were in fact fallen from collapsed upper floors. But an interesting group of plaques made of faience* (colored glass paste poured into molds) proved that even ordinary houses were multi-story. The plaques had apparently been inlaid in zones and panels to decorate a wooden chest, and a large number of the better-preserved speci-mens depict exterior views of houses. They show two, three and even four stories, windows in the upper floors, clerestories and outlines of brick and timber wall construction. Since they were discovered under the pavement of the later phase of the palace, the necessary conclusion was that such pretentious private houses had a long history at Knossos. Other associated plaques, even more fragmentary, showed humans, animals and vegetation. "The warriors and city recall the siege scene of the silver vase [from Myce-nae]. . . . The homes of civic life within the walls, the goats and oxen without, the fruit trees and running water, suggest a more literal com-parison with the Homeric description of the scenes of peace and war as illustrated on Achilles' shield[42] than can be supplied from any other known source."

Inscribed tablets were continuing to appear in large numbers, and new evidence showed that writing had not been confined to formal archives. An inscription painted on a vase as part of the decorative scheme "recalls the inscribed vases of Classical Greece and is the only specimen hitherto known belonging to the 'Mycenaean Period.' " Furthermore, the interior of two plain cups revealed linear writing in ink. "The lines of the letters show occasionally a tendency to divide, which may point to the use of a reed pen. . . . These ink-written inscriptions . . . give us the first direct evidence of the existence of literary materials . . . other than the inscribed clay tablets. . . . Parchment may have been used, and the old Cretan tradition that palm leaves had once been used for writing should not be left out of account."

Almost everywhere, but especially in the western quarter of the palace, Evans saw religious connections. Like many archaeologists, he had a tendency to label as cult furniture almost any object to which an obvious utilitarian function could not be assigned. From such objects and from what he interpreted as cult scenes on rings and gems he was developing a series of ingenious hypotheses about Minoan religion. In the previous year he had published a long account of the evidence for a "Mycenaean Tree and Pillar Cult." Gradually he enlarges the catalogue of religious symbols and representations—the double ax, the bull, the horns of consecration, the Dove Goddess, the Protectress of Animals, the "divine pair." The double ax is the "labrys"; and the palace with a double ax incised on many of its wall blocks is "the place of the double axe," *i.e.,* the mysterious "labyrinth." In this campaign he discovered in the southeastern quarter a "small square chamber [that] proved to be an actual Palace Shrine with the vessels of offering, votive figures, idols, and cult objects still in position" (Fig. 60). He concludes that this installation represents "the latest period during which this part of the Palace was occupied." He points to the "crude" appearance of much of the shrine's furniture (especially the figurines) and suggests that "the contents . . . derive a special interest from the decadent period to which the bulk of them belong, since they afford a convincing proof that essentially the same religious cult . . . survived to the very latest period of occupation."

What absolute date did Evans now have in mind for the "very latest period of occupation" of the palace? He had earlier mentioned the thirteenth century; but it appears that, at least for the inscribed tablets, he is gradually coming to the conclusion that this is too late. At any rate, in describing a group of tablets that show both triangular and leaf-shaped

Figure 60

swords or daggers, he says, "The presence of the leaf-shaped form in the Palace is of great interest, as there can be little doubt that it is of Northern origin. It is not too much to say that the whole chronology of the European Bronze Age is affected by this discovery, which shows that this leaf-shaped type of sword had been developed before the approximate date of 1400 B.C." Thus, as early as 1902 Evans had decided that these particular tablets (and presumably all of the documents soon to be called Linear B) cannot date later than 1400. It is not at all clear how much later he now considered the shrine and other features belonging to the "very latest period of occupation."

It must have been about this time that Duncan Mackenzie submitted an article entitled "The Pottery of Knossos" for publication in the *Journal of Hellenic Studies*. It is a very thorough review of the evidence from the first three seasons at Knossos; and it casts its shadow far into the future. Inevitably, one wonders whether Evans' own developing theories were absorbed into it or whether they were at least in part derived from it. Mackenzie distinguishes "three distinct strata of deposit." The lowest is "prehistoric, neolithic," with a thickness "starting from the virgin soil and extending upwards to the beginnings of the painted series averaging about 20 feet." Above it comes a deposit in which "we have the first appearance of painted Cretan ware . . . and, where undisturbed, underlying the later deposit of the palace. . . . This includes what may be termed the Early and Middle Minoan classes." As for the third major division, "Last of all comes a 'late Minoan' stratum, represented all over the palace region down to the floor-levels. . . . The later phase of this class covers the fabrics elsewhere described as Mycenaean."

We cannot follow the detailed description, but some of Mackenzie's basic points require our attention. He insists on the native character of Minoan ceramics, undisturbed by outside influence, from the beginning to the end of the Bronze Age. There are no "sharp breaks" in its evolution that would signal foreign intrusion. Seemingly abrupt changes are ingeniously explained by what "may be generalised into a law for all undisturbed floor-deposits, to wit, that house-floors being regularly swept do not contain a deposit record of the whole period, during which the floored space was used but only of the close of that period when the floored area for whatever reason came to be abandoned, and that as a rule there is a record of the final period itself only if the abandonment has been an enforced and sudden one. A quiet flitting would never have left behind it the series of beautiful vessels, more or less complete, in fragments found on these Minoan floors."

Mackenzie seems already to be close to the conviction, later to be so firmly held by Evans, that *all* the major pottery types found at Knossos must have been developed there—or at least in Crete. In the case of the distinctive polychrome ware found in the "Kamares" or Middle Minoan levels it turned out that he was correct. "The scantiness and isolation of this ware in all deposits in which it has been found outside Crete are in such complete contrast to the richness of the Knossian deposits that no further proof is needed to bring us to the conclusion that Crete itself is the true source of the similar ware found elsewhere, as in Melos, Thera, Tiryns, Mycenae, Egypt."

But more sweeping assumptions creep into the discussion of the material from the upper levels. He describes the Late Minoan or "Mature Knossian period" as an "era of renewed life . . . which saw the building of the second palace at Knossos." It is characterized by such features as pottery of "a fully developed Palace style native to Knossos [that] occurs in one general context with the magnificent series of stone vases, with the frescoes of the great period, and with the written records of the Palace that now adorn the museum at Candia."

Coming to the latest pottery found in the palace, he can hardly hold that purely quantitative evidence shows that Knossos or Crete as a whole was still the nucleus.

While pottery in the grand Palace style of Knossos is comparatively rare outside of Crete, the style of pottery which is most clearly characterized by its conventional rendering of foliage and flowers is found in a much wider context, embracing the whole of the East Mediterranean basin. This decadent style at Knossos is typical of a period when the palace is only partially inhabited and probably is no longer a royal residence. The Bügelkanne [stirrup vase] which is rare in the great days of the palace is characteristic of this third period. . . . In this latest period thousands of kylix-cups, amphorae and jars exist in this pale yellow clay without any decoration. The perfectly uniform character of style in the Aegean area at this period is at once apparent on the comparison of wares from different centres. . . . If we take the proved instances of importation into particular centres in connection with the perfect uniformity of style prevalent at this period at all the centres that came into account, the hypothesis of production at one centre becomes strengthened. Furtwängler and Loeschcke [who had published in 1886 the authoritative account of Mycenaean pottery as it was known up to their time] with the evidence before them when they wrote, thought this centre must have been Mycenae. With the additional evidence before us now, taken in connection with the fact of ascertained importation into Melos and Egypt, it is more probable that this centre was Crete, to which Melos on the one hand and Egypt on the other are next-door neighbours on either side.

Here we find formulated in 1902 a number of basic ideas on which Evans later staked his reputation—the tripartite chronological scheme; the contemporaneity of the clay tablets with the spectacular Palace Style or "empire" pottery; a partial and later habitation responsible for the "decadent" pottery that was often undecorated and in shapes such as stirrup jars.

THE SEASON OF 1903

During the fourth season the excavation of the Royal Villa, to the northeast of the palace, showed that the complex of monumental buildings extended well beyond the palace proper, and Evans continued to find the ruins of comfortable villas abutting on the palace and presumably belonging to court functionaries. But what he considers "in many respects the culminating point of interest in the whole four years' excavation" was the discovery of the Temple Repositories within the palace itself.

In most of the long narrow basement storage chambers, or magazines (Fig. 61), and in the long corridor onto which they opened, a series of rectangular cists had been cut below floor level and covered with paving blocks. All of the cists showed very careful construction and lining. Most of them had apparently been meant as receptacles to catch the oil or wine that spilled from cracked pithoi or escaped during their filling or emptying. Some may have been for the storage of liquids or grain in years of high productivity when taxes in kind exceeded expectations. But bits of gold

Figure 61

foil in a few cists indicated that they had at some time been used to contain objects of precious metals, of which the palace seemed to have been so thoroughly looted. These considerations "made it desirable to subject the floors of the small chambers about the Pillar Rooms [an area in the central 'religious' section just west of the main court] to the same searching examination. . . . Might there not here too lie concealed beneath the pavements earlier repositories belonging to the Palace Shrine?" Evans was becoming increasingly sure that "there was a sacerdotal as well as a royal side to the Minoan dynasts of Knossos. It would seem that there were here, as in early Anatolia, Priest-Kings; and old tradition, that made Minos son and 'Companion' of Zeus and a Cretan Moses, is once more seen to have a basis in fact."

Sunk into the floor of a room just south of the Throne Room were two small rectangular stone-lined cists, perhaps for the storage of oil, which were apparently contemporary with the latest use of the room. Evans decided to probe around and beneath them. At first the earth was red from the effects of fire; then it became dark and mixed with charred wood and fragments of gold foil. At a depth of about 44 inches was a layer of terra-cotta vases packed closely together. Another 44 inches deeper still the pottery ceased, and the earth grew "fatter and more compact." Finally in a layer about 17 inches thick, at the bottom of what turned out to be a much larger stone-built cist or repository,

> abundant fragments of faience began to come to light. . . . This faience series included figures of a Snake Goddess and votaries, their votive robes and girdles, cups and vases with painted designs, flowers, fruit, foliage, and shells in the round, small reliefs of cows and calves and wild goats with their kids, a variety of plaques for inlaying, and quantities of beads. Among the other relics were an ivory handle and inlays, bone plumes of arrows, doubtless of a votive character, the usual gold foil, a clay tablet and roundels, presenting inscriptions of a linear class different from that of the later period of the Palace, numerous clay seal impressions, many of them of a religious character, and a marble cross of orthodox Greek shape [Fig. 62].

In addition there were painted sea shells, animal horns, burned grain and steatite "Libation Tables," all of which reinforced the impression that the contents of a shrine had been buried here for safekeeping in time of danger or for some other reason.

The presence of a second even more substantially built repository was detected beside the first. The stratification was identical, but the contents were quite different. "Faience objects were here wanting, with one notable exception—a missing part namely of the figure of a Snake Goddess. . . . This circumstance pointed to a considerable disturbance of the contents of the other depository at some period, and was probably due to plunderers at the time of what seems to have been the first great catastrophe of the Later Palace." The contents of the second repository contained a very large amount of gold foil, some of it showing "traces of an elaborate design in relief apparently of circular form and recalling some of the thin gold disks found in the Akropolis tombs at Mycenae." There were gold and crystal leaves and petals, apparently for inlay in chests or other objects of some disintegrated material. Evans suggests that the heavier construction of this repository was "possibly because it contained gold treasure while the value of the objects in the other cist was more preponderantly artistic."

True to his central interest, Evans first discusses the inscribed objects. He recognizes that they represent "a distinctive form of linear writing" as compared to the hundreds of tablets discovered elsewhere in the palace. And he is able to parallel their "typical characters . . . the system of

Figure 62

numeration, the shape of the tablet itself and of the sealed disks" with a newly discovered archive found by the Italians at the "Palace or Royal Villa of Hagia Triada near Phaestos" (Fig. 63). He then proceeds to lay the foundation for a major and important distinction in Cretan writing systems.

This early system of linear script—which may be conveniently termed Class A as opposed to Class B of the latest Palace Period at Knossos—had a wide extension in the island. An inscribed clay tablet found by the British School at Palaikastro belongs to the same class, as also the characters on a clay disk found by Miss Boyd at Gournia in 1903. There can be little doubt, moreover, that the signs on the Dictaean Libation Table [from the Psychro cave in east central Crete] fit on the same system. At Knossos itself certain graffito inscriptions on pottery and those of another isolated tablet prove to belong to the same category.

He naturally proceeds to ask, "What, then, is the relation of Class A to Class B?" After comparing the forms and the distribution and date of

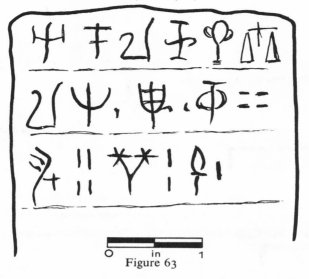

Figure 63

the known examples, he concludes: "We are thus reduced to the conclusion that Class B, though of later appearance in the Palace, is fundamentally a parallel rather than a derivative system. It seems to be an alternative form of linear script, of more or less equal antiquity, which, owing to some political change, came to the fore during the latest Palace period at the expense of the other. At Hagia Triada there is no evidence of any such supersession of Class A."

The remarks that follow echo Mackenzie's earlier pronouncement; and both cast a long shadow into the future. "The change in the official style . . . is a phenomenon which seems best to explain itself on the hypothesis of a dynastic revolution. That there was no change of race appears from various indications. The two systems of script, though divergent, show a large common element. . . . It thus appears that the language was essentially the same. . . . There is no ethnic break, and the culture exhibited by the remains of the latest period of the Palace on the whole represents the natural outgrowth of the penultimate period of its history to which the contents of the Temple Repositories belong." This hypothesis (for that is all it ever was) gradually became dogma during the next half century.

We cannot follow the lengthy description of the unique and lovely faience objects. They now represent Minoan art at its best, and it seems odd to find Evans remarking that "there was nothing to prepare us for [their] extraordinary variety, the beauty and the technical perfection." Yet on reflection we realize that the palace had been thoroughly plundered of movable and precious contents. This discovery was, in a way, as startlingly new as the furnishings of Schliemann's Shaft Graves. Molds found along with the objects made from them left no doubt that they were the product of a native palace industry. They reinforce the evidence for long-term creative use by Cretans of technical processes such as sculpture in faience, which they originally learned from Egypt. The exquisite figurines provided new detail on feminine costume and opened for Evans a new dimension of Cretan religion in the Snake Cult. And he believes that the cross, originally a solar symbol depicting the sun's rays, became an actual object of worship in Minoan cult.

One more revelation of the 1903 campaign calls for mention. In following one of the characteristic narrow paved streets in the deep fill northwest of the palace, a "stepped area" was uncovered consisting of two series of stone steps or seats at right angles to one another and with a rectangular paved area delimited by their lower lines and by walls on the remaining sides (Fig. 64). It became clear that these "steps" did not lead anywhere and therefore must be very low seats accommodating between 400 and 500 spectators. A series of comparable seats in parallel straight lines had been discovered on the north edge of the west court at Phaistos.

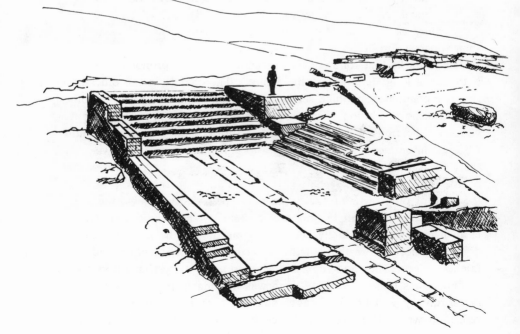

Figure 64

A suggestion, doubtless taken from the great stairs and stepped approaches of the Minoan Palaces, has here developed into a structure which itself is no kind of approach, but the earliest existing example of a veritable theatre. . . . What performances, it may be asked, are likely to have been given in the paved area? The favourite Minoan sport is ruled out, since the enclosure was in no wise adapted for a bull ring. Shows of pugilists . . . may well have taken place here [boxers are depicted in Minoan art]. In spite of its rectangular shape . . . the area would have been also well adapted for dances, possibly of a ceremonial kind like those of the original Theatre in classical Greece.

After reviewing the evidence on gems and frescoes for a high development of the dance in Minoan Crete, Evans suggests that "it is difficult to refuse the conclusion that this first of theatres . . . supplies a material foundation for the Homeric tradition of the famous 'choros' [dancing place] 'like that which once upon a time in wide Knossos Daidalos fashioned for Ariadne of the fair tresses.' "[43] And in a particularly appealing gambit connecting ancient and modern customs, Evans goes on to say that when Dörpfeld and his party came to Knossos on their annual visit to see the newest excavation results, they were entertained in this very theater with a dance by the workmen and their wives, "a dance, may be, as ancient in its origin as the building in which it took place."

THE SEASON OF 1904

The fifth campaign was mainly devoted to examining a large cemetery and to a more detailed study of the palace stratigraphy and chronology. In his report for that year Evans published a "Diagrammatic Section of Strata, below Pavement of West Court," which (though stratigraphic tests continued over the years) was reproduced without change as the major stratigraphic record in Volume I of *The Palace of Minos* seventeen years later (Fig. 65). Whether or not all major phases of the Bronze Age history of the site were as neatly represented as they appear in the chart, the tests established an impressive depth of over 40 feet of habitation debris.

Some 100 tombs were opened in an area called Zapher Papoura about half a mile north of the palace. They belonged mainly to the period immediately after the "final" destruction. Although there were at least three different grave types, Evans strongly resists any suggestion that intruders might have settled around Knossos. "In truth, the high interest of the Zapher Papoura cemetery lies in the fact that throughout its whole duration it attests a striking continuity of local traditions. To whatever cir-

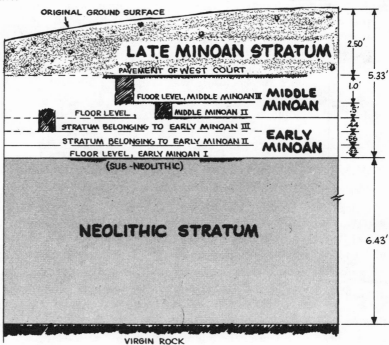

Figure 65

cumstances was due the great overthrow of the later Palace it did not bring with it any real break in the course of the Late-Minoan culture."

About two miles still farther toward the sea a large Royal Tomb was cleared. It was built of well-cut blocks with a dromos, entrance hall with sepulchral niches on either side and a rectangular main chamber. The upper part of the walls was missing, but the roof of both entrance hall and chamber had apparently been in the form of a pointed tunnel vault— probably a Near Eastern trait. Although it had been thoroughly plundered, the chance finds scattered throughout showed clearly enough that the main burial in a cist cut in the floor of the chamber had been a very rich one. Evans dates the original construction to the end of the Middle Minoan age and quotes his architect Fyfe to the effect that "from structural evidence, we are on the whole justified in regarding the Knossos Tomb as of earlier date than any built tomb on the mainland at Mycenae or elsewhere."

Yet Evans was clearly unhappy with the dearth of tombs to rival the palace that he had found. "It can hardly be supposed indeed," he says, "that Minoan Knossos, which to the last seems to have exercised a dominant influence on the arts of mainland Greece, was unable, during the period which is marked by the great domed chambers of Mycenae, to produce at least their architectural equivalent." But he has to admit that in the Treasury of Atreus at Mycenae "the workmanship is finer, the area covered . . . is over three times as great [as in the Knossos Royal Tomb], and the domed vaulting is in accordance both with static and dynamic principles."

Several fine Palace Style amphoras and other objects show that the tomb was still in use contemporary with the later palace, and Evans speculates as to whether Homer's King Idomeneus might have been buried in it. "The site would have been specially appropriate for the tomb of the Cretan prince who led the largest [actually, not as large as those of Agamemnon and Nestor] naval contingent of any of those who took part in Agamemnon's expedition."44 There was also plenty of evidence for its continuing use through the end of the Bronze Age and into the Iron Age. This knowledge seems to cause Evans some pain. "The later history of the Royal Tomb in fact curiously reproduces that of the Palace itself. . . . Just as the once royal and seignorial halls were parcelled out and divided up by poorer denizens, so the spacious vault, originally we may believe constructed as a last resting-place for kings of Minoan stock, became in days of ruin and decline a common burial-pit."

Only one other discovery of the 1904 season need detain us. A test pit had been sunk to try to pick up the course of the narrow paved street that led west from the Theatral Area*. The Minoan level proved to contain inscribed tablets and seal impressions, which led to the clearing of a small section just to the north of the road and to the recovery of a very important group of inscribed records (Fig. 67).

These tablets . . . lay within the opening of what seems to have been a basement Magazine, into which the wooden chests containing them had sunk when the floor above collapsed. Of these about fifty referred to chariots . . . the frames, with or without the poles and yokes, appearing on one set, and the wheels by themselves on another. The large expenditure on the last item entailed by the character of the country may be gathered from the fact that one tablet concerns a total amount of 478 wheels. . . . Still more interesting are a series of tablets showing two curved objects. . . . We have here represented the long curving horns of the Cretan Agrimi or Wild-Goat. . . . To what purpose were these pairs of horns applied? There can be little doubt that we have here the raw material for horn bows, such as that of Menelaos [Pandaros? Paris?] . . .45

But an even more striking coincidence was still in store.

With the above tablets was found the latter part of one referring to a large amount of arrows [Fig. 66]. The subject of this clay document

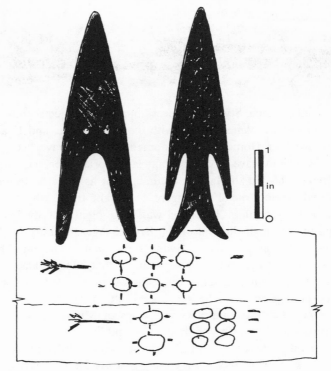

Figure 66

was made clear by the repetition of a pictographic figure of an arrow. The tablets contained a record of two large lots of arrows, one 6010 in number, the other 2630. . . . But what adds an extraordinary interest to the occurrence of this inscription is the discovery in its immediate neighbourhood of the remains of two actual depôts of arrows, at a distance of about 10 feet from one another. The depôts had in each case been contained in wooden boxes with bronze loop handles, and together with the charred fragments of these were found the clay seals with which their string binding had been secured. These sealings were three-sided, the strings passing through their major axis. Both chests had been sealed in an identical manner, and together afforded a more perfect illustration of the Minoan method of controlling and safeguarding deposits of valuables than had as yet been supplied by similar remains from Knossos or elsewhere. . . . Embedded in the *débris* of the chests, once so elaborately sealed and registered, were the carbonized remains of the shafts and, partly attaching to them, the bronze heads of hundreds of arrows. . . . The types of the bronze arrowheads are identical with those of the arrowheads found by Tsountas in a chamber-tomb of the Lower Town

of Mycenae, where they had been laid in two bundles of ten each. . . .
It seems possible that we may be able to locate here the Royal Armoury
and Stables.

THE SEASON OF 1905

The brief report for 1905 is the last to appear as the leading article in
the *Annual of the British School;* and that season was, in fact, Evans' last
major excavation. The very title, "The Palace of Knossos and Its Dependencies," suggests that the operation is spreading out and leveling off (Fig. 67).

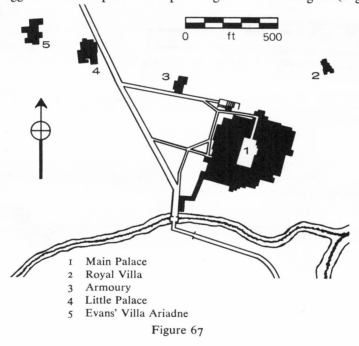

1   Main Palace
2   Royal Villa
3   Armoury
4   Little Palace
5   Evans' Villa Ariadne

Figure 67

Evans had been sure that the roadway running on to the west from the
Theatral Area and past the Armory must have led to a major structure
outside of the immediate palace area. And in fact the ruins of a "large
building on the hill to the West of the Palace," later called the Little Palace,
were discovered. This building "reproduces on a reduced scale the leading
features of the Palace of Knossos as finally remodelled about the beginning of the Late Minoan Period." And Evans' description throws a good
deal of light on his developing theory of the later palace phases.

Here too, as there, were abundant traces of later occupation during the more decadent period of Minoan civilization and of the breaking up of the seignorial halls into the dwellings of humbler denizens. . . . The kings are less, the people more, and the princely building now partially explored, like the great Palace opposite and the "Royal Villa" beyond, is broken up into smaller habitations. . . . But the evidence . . . forbids us to believe that the close of the Palace period at Knossos should be connected with a successful foreign invasion. Rather it points to some internal revolution. . . . In every direction we begin to perceive decadence, but the decadence itself is simply the gradual falling away from the models of the latest Palace style. There is no real break in continuity. . . . But what is still more interesting is the evidence, now for the first time supplied by some fragmentary clay tablets . . . that the fully developed linear script of Minoan Crete continued to be at least partially in use during the later period. It thus appears that the fall of the Palace did not bring with it the absolute extinction of letters, and the true dark ages of Crete were not yet.

He is here definitely leaning again toward a date long after 1400 for some of the Linear B tablets.

We can by now begin to glimpse the reconstruction that was forming in Evans' mind as he finished the first strenuous phase of his Knossos excavations. The Minoan civilization had a strong influence on the Mycenaean mainland from the time of the Mycenae Shaft Graves at least until the destruction of the Knossos palace. But he insists with increasing vehemence that there could be no question of any mainland agency in the destruction itself or in the "decadent" Minoan phase following it.

DEVELOPING THEORIES

A radically different interpretation, however, had occurred to Mackenzie about the same time or perhaps a little earlier. In 1904 the full account of the British excavations at Phylakopi on the island of Melos was published. We will recall that Mackenzie had been a very important staff member there before the Knossos excavations began, and it is natural that he had a share in the publication. He is credited with the chapter entitled "The Successive Settlements at Phylakopi and Their Aegeo-Cretan Relations"; and some of the points he makes are strongly influenced by the finds at Knossos.

In explaining the sudden appearance of a megaron of mainland type at Phylakopi, Mackenzie puts forward the following theory:

The Cretan megaron has a special arrangement for lighting in the form of a light-well at the back, which is absent at Phylakopi as at Tiryns, and it has no hearth in the middle of the megaron such as is present both at Tiryns and at Phylakopi. The presence of the light-well and the absence of the central hearth are universal in Crete, and the light-well at the back of the megaron is as conspicuous a feature in the palaces of Phaestos and of Hagia Triada as it is at Cnossos. . . . The inevitable conclusion then, to which we are driven by all the evidence, is that in the closing era of the Third Settlement at Phylakopi, while the bulk of the population remained the same as at an earlier period, the people who built the palace were of an alien race. Whence these people came it may be possible to conjecture as a consequence of what has been said regarding the affinities of the megaron of Phylakopi. When we have pointed out that this megaron has the closest analogies with mainland types like that of Tiryns, we have virtually said that the latest rulers at Phylakopi were a mainland people, and that these formed part of a general wave of immigration into the Aegean of part of the native population of Greece, consequent on the incursion into their homes of new tribes from the north.

Just who Mackenzie thought were these new tribes from the north is never made clear. But he seems to have had in mind quite a major population movement, since he continues:

That this thrusting into the Aegean region of such sections of the late Mycenaean coast-communities as were unable or unwilling to come to terms with the new comers, or were simply ejected from their homes, was part of a general migratory movement, is proved by the fact that the same phenomenon is observable in Crete. One of the causes which contributed towards the break-up of the Minoan civilization in Crete was undoubtedly invasion from the mainland. And it was the same invasion from the mainland that submerged the earlier native civilization at Phylakopi, and that effectively arrested the course of genuine native evolution on the old lines in Minoan Crete. Thus the last "Mycenaean" people at Cnossos, those who destroyed the palace and then reoccupied parts of its ruins, like those who built the palace at Phylakopi, appear as strangers unacquainted with native institutions and forms of life . . .

Here is a revolutionary change from Evans' and Mackenzie's own repeated assertion that there is "no break" until the very end of the Bronze Age that would permit one to even imagine an occupation of any part of Crete by outsiders.

Between 1905 and 1908 Mackenzie also published four long essays, "Cretan Palaces and the Aegean Civilization." As the title implies, his

starting point was architecture now, not pottery. But he is even more concerned with the broader historical and cultural implications of the whole
complex of recent discoveries on Crete, particularly at Knossos. Again we
sense the operation of a positive and incisive (though sometimes erratic)
intellect that must have played an important part in the interpretation of
the new Cretan discoveries.

The first article was written in reaction to Dörpfeld's theory that, of
the two clearly marked major stages in the palaces of Knossos and Phaistos, the earlier reflects a native Cretan architectural tradition, while the
later shows such strong analogies with the Greek mainland that it must
be the result of an "Achaean" invasion and control of Crete. Following his
position in the Phylakopi publication, Mackenzie attributes "any megara
of mainland type that have ever been identified in the Aegean" to an
invasion and occupation by "Mycenaeans" from the Greek mainland. It
was they who destroyed the later Minoan palaces. "To the same period
and type apparently belongs the late megaron at Hagia Triada which Halbherr himself regards as really Mycenaean."

Then he attempts to draw a fundamental distinction between these
"Mycenaean" invaders of Crete about the time of the destruction of the
Knossos palace and a still later group at the very end of the Late Bronze
Age. The latter, says Mackenzie, must be Dörpfeld's "Achaeans," who
were of Hellenic stock, i.e., Greek speakers.

> The general cumulative tendency of the evidence afforded by excava-
> tion is to prove that the first wave of invading peoples from the main-
> land (who were themselves very apparently of Mycenaean race, of the
> same original stock as the Cretans themselves, and therefore, as we
> shall see in the sequel, not at all of "Achaean" origin), who were re-
> sponsible for the final destruction of the later palaces at Phaestos and
> at Knossos, had themselves appeared too late upon the scene to play any
> reconstructive rôle in the development of the Minoan Civilization; they
> were responsible merely for the work of dissolution which, in com-
> bination with internal causes of decadence, symptomatic of the final
> phase, was one of the potent external influences at work in the final
> break-up of the Aegean Civilization as a whole. When at length the first
> wave of people of Achaean race and of Hellenic stock appeared upon
> the stage of Cretan history, the Palace of Knossos, like that of Phaestos,
> had already long been a venerable ruin. The evidence is fast accumu-
> lating in Crete and in the Aegean in favour of the hypothesis as to the
> continuity of the Mycenaeo-Minoan Civilization down to quite the end
> of the period after the destruction of the Palace at Knossos which we have
> called the Third Late Minoan Period (Late Minoan III.).

The second installment in Mackenzie's series is an extremely speculative adventure in early-twentieth-century ethnography, which might perhaps be better ignored if it had not such a close connection with Evans' later publications involving the North African connections (if not origin) of the Minoans and many of their culture traits. Mackenzie takes the firm position that the "Aegean Race" was essentially unchanged from the time of the newly discovered neolithic at Knossos until the very end of the Bronze Age. "At every later stage in inquiry we have to be on our guard against admitting any such hypothesis of derivation from without, as long as the conception of internal development continues to stand the test in explanation of the phenomena." Crete itself is "so apparently the centre of the Aegean civilization" that if there are no internally inconsistent elements observable in the development there, one can assume practical homogeneity.

But where did the people of the Knossos neolithic come from? There is no neolithic skeletal material, but the evidence for the physical type of the Bronze Age Cretans "turns out to be entirely in harmony . . . with Dr. Evans's views regarding the Egypto-Libyan connections of the Aegean race." In the light of the testimony of modern physical anthropologists to the highly complex and mixed nature of the ancient Aegean skeletal and cranial material, this statement is an oversimplification, to say the least.

Mackenzie then discusses the evidence of origin supposedly provided by Minoan costume. In the scanty clothing of the males "we find the true explanation of . . . a loin-cloth apparel there, on the hypothesis alone that this characteristic attire of a warm climate was original to the people of the Aegean in their original home. And it is apparent that this original home and this warmer climate could only have been in Africa . . . What the people of the North [apparently Dörpfeld's "Achaeans"] looked like in costume, and what they wore next their skins when in the fulness of time they at length appear upon the scene, is clearly shown on the Warrior Vase . . . of Mycenae."

The elaborate female costume presents an even tougher problem, but Mackenzie's Scottish Presbyterian Puritan instincts are fully equal to it.

When we come to consider closely the women's dress of the Aegean, we do not find a different story as to origin and genesis, notwithstanding all the apparent disguise of Parisian-like mode revealed to us in the low bodices, puffed sleeves and multiple skirts worn by the fashionable court dames of Knossos. People have been scandalized by the excessively low dress of these court ladies into serious reflections as to the decadent character of the Late Minoan culture in general, without considering that what looks so shamelessly modern, is really the survival of very primitive custom in dress. . . . We are thus justified in surmising that the . . . ancestresses of these women wore no bodices and no multiple skirts. But they still wore their loin-cloth and belt like the men. . . . This could only have been in torrid Africa!

As the pace of excavation slowed, Evans, too, had more time to devote to the study and comprehensive publication of the Knossos finds. It is characteristic that the materials he first turned to were the written documents. *Scripta Minoa,* Volume I, appeared in 1909. Almost all of the documents published there are of the earliest (hieroglyphic) type. He says in the Preface that "the remaining Volumes—II and III—of this work will be devoted to the detailed publication of the documents of the advanced Linear Scripts of Crete, of both Classes (A and B)"; yet at his death over thirty years later most of these vital documents were still unavailable to other scholars. Perhaps the reason can be guessed from another statement in the same Preface. "In the absence of bilingual inscriptions, the material as a whole has not reached the stage when any comprehensive attempt at interpretation or transliteration is likely to be attended with fruitful results." Evans naturally hoped to decipher the scripts himself, and since he had not made much headway it was unbelievable to him that anyone else could.

Part I of the first volume of *Scripta Minoa* does contain, however, a wide-ranging general discussion of the situation in the later Minoan context, sometimes with a rather tenuous connection to written records. Its tone is reflected by the title, "The Pre-Phoenician Scripts of Crete. Their Mediterranean Relations and Place in Minoan Story." In a preliminary summation of the material to be discussed, Evans points out that

the written documents from the Palace of Knossos and its immediate dependencies now amount to nearly two thousand. The overwhelming majority of these clay documents, including the first discovered, presented an advanced type of linear script—referred to in the present work as Class B—which was in vogue throughout the whole of the concluding period of the Palace history. But the course of the excavations brought out the fact that the use of this highly developed form of writing had been in turn preceded in the "House of Minos" by two earlier types—one also presenting linear characters, described below as Class A, the other, still earlier, of conventionalized pictorial aspect, recalling Egyptian hieroglyphics. . . . We shall not err on the side of exaggeration in estimating the period covered by the successive types of developed script on the Palace site at Knossos at over a thousand years. It must at the same time be observed that the latest of the Minoan documents discovered on this site, those namely dating from the period of decline, when the Palace as a Palace had ceased to exist, are older by several centuries than the earliest known records of Phoenician writing [*i.e.,* in the Greek alphabet]. The twelfth century before our era may be regarded as their latest limit.

Evans seems at this point in his thinking to have been willing to assign to the Linear B tablets a rather wide chronological range, since only a few pages later he says that "the great bulk of the deposits of clay tablets found in the rooms and magazines of the building [*i.e.,* the later palace] . . . represent the form of script in use at the time of its final catastrophe, about the close of the fifteenth or the early part of the fourteenth century B.C." More than that, he apparently had the curious idea that there may be considerable differences in date even for associated groups of tablets. "As to the higher limit of the use of this form of writing at Knossos we have no direct evidence, but some of the larger deposits of clay archives must have been naturally of gradual accumulation. It is possible, therefore, that it [the Linear B script] was already in existence in the earlier half of the fifteenth century before our era."

Evans is quite emphatic that "at Knossos the inscribed documents belonging to the Linear Class A only occur in this particular stratum representing the lowest limit of the Middle Minoan culture," *i.e.,* somewhat before 1600; but he adds that "finds made elsewhere in Crete [particularly at Haghia Triada but also scattered examples at Phaistos, Zakro, Palaikastro and Gournia], however, seem to point to a longer local survival of this type of script." The use of Linear A appears to have spread over all central and eastern Crete and to date from "the transitional age that covers the close of the Middle Minoan and the early part of the Late Minoan Period." On the other hand, "documents of Class B . . . have as yet only been found on the site of Knossos."

His presumption that the two scripts, with many signs in common, were used to write the same language finds a revealing expression at one point. Two different and approximately contemporary documents show the same word group made up of two signs, one of which has a slight peculiarity attributable to Linear A. This, says Evans, "clearly indicates that the language in both cases was the same." No one nowadays would contend that the same *word* occurring in two inscriptions indicates that the *language* of both is the same. In answer to the natural question of why a new script should be evolved to write the same language, he repeats his earlier suggestion that the change is connected with a "dynastic revolution," perhaps also indicated by the "widespread catastrophe that brought to a close the Middle Minoan Period of the Palace."

He has obviously studied the documents very closely and believes that "bureaucratic methods of control here visible are themselves the outcome of a long inheritance of dynastic organization." He speaks of a "Palace School of Calligraphy," and his description of the symbols and method of recordkeeping is characteristically acute yet biased.

> The characters themselves have a European aspect. They are of upright habit and of a simple and definite outline, which throws into sharp relief the cumbrous and obscure cuneiform system of Babylonia. . . . It would seem that the characters stood for syllables or even letters, though they could in most cases be also used as words. Many are obviously compounds, and certain allied groups of signs show a regular systematic variation which betrays the hand of an official grammarian. . . . The spaces and lines between the words, the espacement into distinct paragraphs, and the variation in the size of the characters on the same tablet, according to the relative importance of the text, show a striving after clearness and method such as can by no means be said to be a characteristic of classical Greek inscriptions.

Evans realizes the obvious utilitarian and economic content of the tablets; yet he does not want to deny his Minoans the creation of a real literature.

> Was there more than this? Were there still fuller records, such as chronicles and sacred writings; liturgies, and books of magic, or hymns, possibly . . . ? May we suppose that manuscript copies existed of the Laws of Minos; that Epic tradition was already partly fixed by writing in prehistoric Crete, or that early prose romance had taken literary form as in contemporary Egypt? None of these possibilities can any longer be excluded, but the perishable nature of the materials that must be presupposed for the existence of any extensive literature makes it very improbable that it should have survived the catastrophe of the Cretan Palaces.

One also gains the impression that the "great catastrophe" that took place "not later than the first half of the fourteenth century" (on Egyptian synchronisms) was not complete and final. A few sentences sound as if Evans was half convinced by Mackenzie's recent theory: "That the catastrophe at Knossos itself, and the new condition of things that characterizes the Period of Reoccupation, were partly due to the successful incursions of men representing a closely allied form of culture from the mainland of Greece is in itself quite possible. . . . The new settlers . . . represented a somewhat later stage and a humbler aspect of the same civilization." Yet, in his view, they apparently did not take over political control. "Only in the Domestic Quarter of the Palace—a part of which, perhaps, was almost continuously occupied—are there signs of attempts at restoration on a large scale which make it probable that dynasts of the old stock still maintained a diminished state on the Palace site." Furthermore, Evans is here quite explicit that some tablets belong to this later period. In the "reoccupation phase" of the building called the House of the Fetishes, west of the palace, seal impressions were found "on the later floors" and "in juxtaposition with these, remains of tablets showing inscriptions belonging to Class B, but executed in a somewhat inferior manner."

Evans is now inclined to believe that the Cretan writing system was widely exported along with other Minoan culture traits. "In spite of the negative results obtained by Schliemann at Mycenae and Tiryns, all probability seems in favour of some form of early writing having existed on the mainland side." He is also ready to concede that "during the Third Late Minoan Age [after about 1400] . . . the centre of gravity of the Minoan world tends to shift to the mainland side." Scattered mainland evidence, almost entirely on pottery, would indicate that "during the latest Minoan and Mycenaean period" there must have been in use "a system of script which fits on to a Cretan signary of distinctly earlier date."

Like Mackenzie, Evans believes in a late invasion of the mainland by "Achaean tribes, whose oldest records point to Northern Greece." He apparently thought at this point, too, that they were the people who pushed large numbers of "Mycenaeans" into the Aegean islands, including Crete. As his own contribution to the difficult question of how to distinguish archaeologically between Achaean and Mycenaean, Evans poses a simple but rather drastic theory. "How large a part of the 'Mycenaean' civilization they themselves [the Achaeans] took over from the earlier inhabitants is sufficiently proved by the living record preserved to us in the Homeric poems." The "Achaean period" was at the very end of the Bronze Age (the so-called sub-Minoan), when iron implements and weapons were beginning to appear. "This is precisely the period when the Homeric poems —the apotheosis of Achaean enterprise—take their characteristic shape, and the Idomeneus of the *Iliad* may be taken to reflect Achaean domination of Knossos itself. At the same time the Homeric poems themselves afford a convincing proof that the traditions of the earlier Minoan and Mycenaean culture lived on in that of the Viking race of Greece."

In 1912 Evans was elected to the highest office of the Hellenic Society, and his presidential address, "The Minoan and Mycenaean Element in Hellenic Life," was published in the Society's journal. Here we see clearly how far he is now prepared to go in claiming not only that the Mycenaean inhabitants of the mainland in the Late Bronze Age were completely lacking in originality, but that much of the inspiration in classical Greek civilization, particularly in the areas of art and religion, really goes back to non-Greek, Minoan sources. The anticlassical trend of his earlier years has now matured, and he is confident that his new Cretan evidence has provided the ammunition he previously lacked. Nor does he hesitate to use it bluntly and forcefully.

The flavor of the whole paper can be sensed from a few of the opening sentences.

> In his concluding Address to this Society our late President [Professor Percy Gardner] remarked that he cared more for the products of the full maturity of the Greek spirit than for its immature struggles, and this preference for fruits over roots is likely to be shared by most classical scholars. . . . Yet I imagine that my presence in this Chair is due to a feeling . . . that what may be called the embryological department has its place among our studies. Therefore I intend to take advantage of my position here to-day to say something in favour of roots, and even of germs. These are the days of origins, and what is true of the higher forms of animal life and functional activities is equally true of many of the vital principles that inspired the mature civilization of Greece—they cannot be adequately studied without constant reference to their anterior stages of evolution. . . . I venture to believe that the scientific study of Greek civilization is becoming less and less possible without taking into constant account that of the Minoan and Mycenaean world that went before it."

Evans then announces his theme with obvious relish. "Let it be assumed that the Greeks themselves were an intrusive people and that they finally imposed their language on an old Mediterranean race. But if, as I believe, that view is to be maintained it must yet be acknowledged that from the ethnic point of view the older elements largely absorbed the later. . . . Can it be doubted that the artistic genius of the later Hellenes was largely the continuous outcome of that inherent in the earlier race in which they had been merged?" He alludes sarcastically to those who suggest that Minoans and Mycenaeans belonged to the "Hellenic stock" and who have seen in the "stray specimens of the script [Linear B from Knossos] which have as yet seen the light" evidence that their language was Greek.

Evans' major obsession for the last thirty years of his life is already crystallizing. Mycenaean culture was "only a provincial variant," a "mainland plantation" of the Minoan. Their physical type, their religion and their language were the same. "We must clearly recognize that down to at least the twelfth century before our era the dominant factor both in Mainland Greece and in the Aegean world was still non-Hellenic, and must still unquestionably be identified with one or other branch of the old Minoan race." The major cultural differences between Minoans and Mycenaeans, emphasized by Dörpfeld and even by Mackenzie, have become "slight local divergencies." The theory of Minoan political control of the mainland is much more firmly proposed and is now rather oddly stretched to allow for "a subject race of Hellenic stock during the whole, or a large part of the period of Mycenaean domination." It was against this internal threat that the Mycenaean citadels were so heavily fortified. He does not explain how he proposes to relate these earlier representatives of the Hellenic stock to the "Achaean invasion" at the very end of the Bronze Age.

After pointing to persuasive examples in art and religion where there is apparent continuity between the Minoan-Mycenaean and the classical period, Evans turns to the daring theory that caps his whole argument. It had been vaguely anticipated in *Scripta Minoa* three years before, but one can still imagine the electrifying effect it must have had on his orthodox classicist colleagues. Considerable portions of the Homeric poems, he suggests, were really translations or adaptations of the exploits of an earlier, more gifted people (the Minoans), and they were originally sung (and perhaps even written) in an alien tongue.

> How is it then that Homer, though professedly commemorating the deeds of Achaean heroes, is able to picture them among surroundings, which, in view of the absolute continuity of Minoan and Mycenaean history, we may now definitely set down as non-Hellenic? . . . I venture to believe that there is only one solution of these grave difficulties, and that this is to be found in the bilingual conditions which in the Peloponnese at least may have existed for a very considerable period. . . . Many of the difficulties with which we have to deal, are removed if we accept the view that a considerable element in the Homeric poems represents the materials of an earlier Minoan epic taken over into Greek.

Evans is as sure as Schliemann had been in the case of his Mycenaean discoveries that we can actually see in Minoan art the ultimate visual inspiration of descriptions in Homer's poetry. If there were Greek speakers on the mainland well before the end of the Bronze Age, Evans believes that they had no share in the "inner palace circle of Tiryns and Mycenae, where such works were handled and admired." It is impossible to suppose that "any Achaean bard at the time when the Homeric poems crystallized into their permanent shape [*i.e.,* in the Early Iron Age] had such lifelike compositions [art objects] before his eye or could have appreciated them in the spirit of their creation." Evans reviews a whole series of representations to prove his point. One example is a clay seal impression from

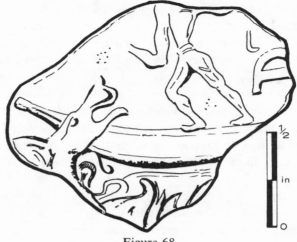

Figure 68

about 1600 found at Knossos (Fig. 68). It depicts a fearful creature with a doglike head, attacking a ship. "This sea-monster," says Evans, "is a prototype of Skylla, and though her dogs' heads were multiplied by Homer's time, we have here, in the epitomized manner of gem engraving, the essentials of Ulysses' adventure depicted half a millennium at least before the age of the Greek Epic."[46]

So Evans holds that Schliemann, although his "views on Homeric subjects were not perturbed by chronological or ethnographic discrepancies," was essentially right in seeing a direct and vivid connection between Mycenaean art objects and the Homeric poems. And Schliemann's most fulsome prose could scarcely outdo Evans' peroration, as he reiterates the glory of that bygone Creto-centric epoch. "By what means could this undimmed reflection [in Homer] of a pure great age have been perpetuated and preserved? Only in one way. . . . They were handed down intact because they were preserved in the embalming medium of an earlier Epos—the product of that older non-Hellenic race to whom alike belong the glories of Mycenae and of Minoan Crete. Thus only could the iridescent wings of that earlier phantasy have maintained their pristine form and hues through days of darkness and decline to grace the later, Achaean, world."

After World War I Evans did not return to Crete until 1922. By that time the first volume of *The Palace of Minos* had appeared. It is wholly concerned with Minoan history before 1600; but sections of the Preface mention Minoan-Mycenaean relations in the Late Bronze Age and can fairly be attributed to Evans' thinking in the prewar period. In fact, he states that "difficulties and preoccupations . . . caused by the Great War delayed the publication of this work, the materials for which were already in an advanced state in 1914." Joan Evans has an amusing paragraph describing the grief that Evans was continually causing his editors. "He had neither secretary nor typewriter, and still used a quill pen. His handwriting was growing more and more stylized, and was of a kind that produced a fertile crop of printer's errors. . . . One reference . . . turned . . . 'exotic' into 'erotic,' with astonishing results. An erratum slip that said 'for *skytotes* read *rhytons*' drew the commentary from *Punch* that they were sorry that the author thought it necessary to part with *'skytotes':* 'it is just the short word we have been wanting for aeroplanes.' "

Volume I of *The Palace of Minos* shows even in the Preface that the thesis of complete Cretan domination over Mycenaean civilization has further solidified. "I have also felt that the view here presented of the Minoan Age . . . could not be adequately drawn out without some attempt to set forth its relation to the Mycenaean culture of Mainland Greece. . . . The results will surprise many. Few probably have yet realized how absolute is the dependence which these comparisons substantiate." One also notes a characteristic forthrightness and at the same time a certain defensiveness about some of his own previous views and the contributions of colleagues. By 1914, of course, a good deal of excavation had been carried out in other parts of Crete by British, American, Italian and Greek colleagues; and syntheses of Minoan civilization were beginning to appear. "The writer has, therefore, some right to be allowed to set down his own conclusions, gradually formed, in the course of years, from a first-hand knowledge of the materials, without seeking to inquire at every turn whether similar opinions may have been already expressed in print in other quarters."

Attention is drawn to Mackenzie's twenty-one years of faithful assistance, and particularly in the preparation of this publication. "My thanks are exceptionally due to him for the continued help that he has rendered to me at every turn in the course of the present work, and for his careful revision of the proofs. His special archaeological knowledge, particularly in the ceramics field, is so widely recognized that it is with great satisfaction that I am able to record that in all main points in my scheme of classification he is in complete agreement with me."

The scheme as it had taken shape by 1921 may be formalized as follows (all dates B.C. and approximate):

Neolithic	8000–3400
Early Minoan	3400–2100
Middle Minoan	2100–1580

*(Early Palaces destroyed
at end of MM II, about 1700)*

Late Minoan I   1580–1475

Late Minoan II   1475–1400

(Later Palace at Knossos destroyed
at end of LM II)

Late Minoan III   1400–1200

In the preliminary pages of this introduction to the distillation of Evans'
lifework, he sketches the history of Bronze Age Crete, particularly as he
has reconstructed it from his own excavations. It is an appealing formulation; and he feels confident that the three major divisions of the Bronze
Age (Early, Middle, Late Minoan), each in turn with three major subdivisions (I, II, III), represent an approach that "is in its very essence
logical and scientific." He insists that "in every characteristic phase of
culture we note in fact the period of rise, maturity, and decay." The interest in origins in general is here combined with a special sentimental concern for the history of the West. "This comparatively small island, left on
one side to-day by all the main lanes of Mediterranean intercourse, was
at once the starting-point and the earliest stage in the highway of European
civilization."

World War I was by no means the end of Arthur Evans' scholarly
career. He had, in fact, still twenty years of a green old age ahead. They
were divided between the comfortable Villa Ariadne, which he had built
for himself on the hillside to the west of the palace ruins, and his English
estate, with its gardens and excellent private library. From these peaceful
retreats came forth volume after volume of the monumental *Palace of
Minos* right up to 1936. At Knossos there were occasional minor tests and
small excavations; and the work of conservation went on. He entertained
friends, students, admirers. He defended with vigor the views he had come
to believe were irrefutable; and he attacked with fervor and sarcasm those
few who were incautious enough to differ with him.

Evans' later years, especially one major controversy, will have a place
in another chapter; but no argument or discovery after the war can be
said to have shaken his confidence in the essential truth of his own reconstruction of historical events in the Late Aegean Bronze Age. Its broad
outlines are laid down in the Introduction to the first volume of *The Palace
of Minos:*

> Thus the time limits with which we have to deal for the Late Minoan
> Age lie approximately between 1580 and 1200 B.C. The early part of
> this epoch . . . is the Golden Age of Crete, followed, after a level inter-
> val, by a gradual decline. The settlement already begun in M. M. III

1700 on the new chronology

[*i.e.,* before 1600] of large tracts of mainland Greece is now continued, and the new Mycenaean culture is thus firmly planted on those shores. . . . The overthrow of the great Palace [at Knossos] took place at the close of the succeeding L. M. II Period [*i.e.,* about 1400], the result, according to the interpretation suggested below, of an internal uprising, apparently of "submerged" elements. It looks as if the Mainland enterprise had been too exhausting. The centre of gravity of Minoan culture shifted now to the Mycenaean side. Finally, some hostile intrusion from the North, which is naturally to be connected with the first Greek invasions, drove away the indigenous settlers who had partially reoccupied or rebuilt the ruined sites at Knossos and elsewhere, and put an end to the last recuperative efforts of Minoan Crete.

From this point on we hear no more from Evans about the possibility that mainlanders (even "kindred" Mycenaeans) might have been responsible for the destruction of the Knossos palace around 1400.

Looking ahead a little, we may here record that Evans' last trip to Crete in 1937 was the occasion for the dedication of a bronze bust set up in his honor at the entrance to the Knossos site. With the plaudits of Cretan friends ringing in his ears and crowned with a laurel wreath, the old man made his acceptance speech in Greek. "We know now," he said, "that the old traditions were true. We have before our eyes a wondrous spectacle— the resurgence, namely, of a civilization twice as old as that of Hellas. It is true that on the old Palace site what we see are only the ruins of ruins, but the whole is still inspired with Minos' spirit of order and organization and the free and natural art of the great architect Daedalos."

We said previously that Heinrich Schliemann was an authentic genius and a man of paradox. It is curious that Joan Evans, with all allowance for sisterly pride and love, describes her half brother in words that are almost wholly applicable to Schliemann too.

Arthur [was] a man of paradox. He was flamboyant, and oddly modest; dignified, and loveably ridiculous; imperious, and surprisingly gentle; extravagant, yet by no means self-indulgent and in some things austere. He could be subtle as an Oriental, and simple as a child. He could be fantastically kind, and fundamentally uninterested in other people; he could be fantastically generous, and extremely self-centred. . . . He was always loyal to his friends, and never gave up doing something he had set his heart on for the sake of someone he loved. He was always true to his principles, and always true, at the same time, to his own unconscious sense of the preeminent importance of the workings of his own mind.

V

Before Blegen: The Situation
in the Early Twenties

A S Tsountas' *Mycenaean Age* provided us with a synthesis of the evidence that had accumulated up to the end of the nineteenth century, so we shall depend mainly on the work of two of his successors in the next generation. Both of them attempted to sum up the impact of new discoveries and new lines of research between 1900 and World War I and to suggest revisions in older theories required by the new data.

One book was part of the ambitious French series called *L'évolution de l'humanité: synthèse collectif*. The preparation of the Greek prehistoric material had been undertaken by a promising young scholar, Adolphe Reinach. After his death in battle at the very beginning of World War I, Gustav Glotz took over the assignment. Glotz's *La civilisation égéenne* appeared in 1923 and was translated into English under the same title, *The Aegean Civilization* (1925). Our second guide will be *Die Kretisch-Mykenische Kultur* (The Creto-Mycenaean Civilization) by Diedrich Fimmen. The author was killed in action in 1916, but he had left the manuscript in the final stages of preparation. It was edited and seen through the press by Professor George Karo (1921).

Unlike Tsountas, neither Glotz nor Fimmen was an experienced field archaeologist. Perhaps this is an advantage in attempting a synthesis, although Tsountas' own excavations do not seem to have lessened his objectivity. To a striking degree, we can see in these two books characteristics that are often alleged to be typical of German and French scholarship. Fimmen's account is terse, concise, factual and methodical, although its notelike quality may in part be explained by the author's premature death. Glotz's book, in contrast, is diffuse, exuberant and imaginative. They therefore form a useful foil to one another. Both, of course, discuss major aspects of the civilization such as palaces, private homes, grave types, pottery, art and economic activities. But Fimmen is more concerned with chronology, foreign contacts and precise systematization of data; whereas

Glotz (like Tsountas) takes a wider approach, with essays on the physical type, costume, weapons and armor, religion, writing systems and political institutions. The purely topical treatment is clearly becoming a drawback since it almost precludes a successful demonstration of the *development* of a civilization within its total chronological range.

The very titles of the two books indicate the wider sweep made necessary by the recent discoveries in Crete. The emphasis has shifted away from Troy and to some extent even from mainland Greece. How overpowering a role Evans himself played in this phenomenon is made clear by a sentence in the Foreword to Glotz's book: "The present volume is devoted entirely to the civilization revealed by Evans in excavations in Crete dating from 1900 and by earlier excavations dating from 1876 on the mainland of Greece and in Asia Minor." Glotz seems almost to be unaware that Italian, American, Greek and other British archaeologists had begun work in Crete at the same time as Evans and had also achieved notable results. It is true, however, that the full text does put the situation in somewhat fairer perspective; and Fimmen's Register gives a complete summary of all the relevant exploration and excavation in Crete, the other islands and the mainland.

Two other general points strike the reader almost immediately. Crete had stolen the stage not only because the revelation of Minoan civilization was novel and exciting, but also because very little new evidence of a spectacular sort had emerged from excavations on the Greek mainland during the first decades of the twentieth century. Steady and important work on various aspects of the Mycenaean material, such as the pottery analysis so prominent in Fimmen's book, had of course been proceeding. But this rather undramatic topic does not receive much detailed attention in Glotz's account. Secondly, it is quite clear that many features of Evans' theories on Minoan civilization and on interrelationships between Crete and the mainland are already approaching the status of unchallenged dogma.

At the same time, both of our authorities have reservations about details of some of Evans' propositions. For instance, we have seen how Evans moved almost full circle in his use of the term "Mycenaean." At first it was applied to everything prehistoric in Crete; but by 1920 it was only grudgingly used to characterize decadent mainland manifestations of "Minoan" inspiration. In this connection Glotz cautiously says, "Since the authority of Evans has invested the word [Minoan] with such respectability, we shall not deny ourselves the use of it, on the understanding that we confine it to Crete and that even in Crete we apply it especially to the period of the hegemony of Knossos."

Glotz also has doubts about certain details of Evans' system of chronology in which we cannot usefully follow him. But, by and large, he is under the spell of the neat "scientific" formulation of the tripartite Minoan scheme. "Evans, it is clear, combines the data of the stratification with the universal laws of evolution and the requirements of the human mind when he assumes with such regularity a period of growth leading to a period of apogee, followed by a period of decadence and transition."

Fimmen, like Glotz, adopts Evans' Minoan terminology and tripartite scheme for the Cretan Bronze Age, but he disagrees in important respects with Evans' absolute dates. His own dates represent a careful reexamination of the Egyptian synchronisms. We must record some of his conclusions, particularly as they affect our Mycenaean focus of attention. In addition to plotting the Near Eastern synchronisms, most of them via Crete, Fimmen underlines a point of view that had been gradually forcing itself on the attention of prehistoric archaeologists. He insists that "the most important basis for the distinction of the developmental features of a culture is the pottery."

Schliemann in his later years had begun to appreciate this crucial fact; and the pioneering German studies, *Mycenaean Painted Pottery* (1879) and *Mycenaean Vases* (1886), by Furtwängler and Loeschcke, had already pointed the way. But up to the end of the nineteenth century attention was mainly concentrated on the intrinsically valuable or unusual artefacts. Archaeologists still had something in common with their predecessors, the tomb robbers, who scorned and trampled the lowly pots. They would have laughed at a prediction that, scientifically speaking, the pottery would one day be quite literally the most precious part of the contents of an undisturbed tomb. In far too many cases the pottery was neglected and never properly published.

Evans had, of course, been a pioneer in the study of Minoan pottery, but he lacked the time—and perhaps the inclination—to devote much attention to that of the mainland. A major portion of Fimmen's book consists of a careful stylistic analysis of ceramic types from the whole Aegean area. And in his studies he works on the explicit assumption, which has appealed particularly to German specialists, that "the decorative motifs [point the distinctions] in greater measure than the vase shapes, since the former have gone through the richest development."

Fimmen proposes the terms "Early Mycenaean," "Middle Mycenaean" and "Late Mycenaean" as a basis for a distinct mainland chronology. His Early Mycenaean period begins about 1700 (more than a millennium after Evans' Early Minoan) and extends down to 1550. This is the time when the distinctive gray Minyan (Fig. 69) as well as matt-painted ware* (Fig. 70) was still flourishing. Both had been represented in the Mycenae

Figure 69

Figure 70

Shaft Graves, along with the earliest actual imports of Minoan ceramics. Fimmen places the earlier phases of the mainland palaces and the Mycenae Shaft Graves before the close of his Early Mycenaean epoch. His dates for the extant remains of mainland palaces have turned out to be much too early.

His Middle Mycenaean period (1550–1400) embraces what he thought was the most flourishing period of the palaces as well as of the great tholos tombs. The Late Mycenaean (1400–1250) marks the final form of the palaces and the strengthening and extension of the fortifications at Tiryns. Troy VI (presumably its latest phases), Troy VII, the intrusive megaron of mainland type at Phylakopi and the destruction of the Minoan palaces are dated to the beginning of this period.

Glotz's chronological scheme is somewhat different in detail, and we shall avoid unnecessary confusion by ignoring it. But in both books we notice very marked progress over Tsountas' generation in relative and absolute dating. And of course a dependable system of dating forms the essential framework of any historical study, whether or not the culture involved was a literate one. It is quite impossible to form rational views of historical development and change unless one can arrange the major observable features in a fairly firm *relative** sequence, preferably with a number of *absolute* dates as anchors for the whole structure.

In beginning his ambitious "historical survey of the Aegean peoples" Glotz poses searching and valid questions. "What place did the Mycenaean civilization have in the whole Aegean world? What was its origin? Was it the end of a world or the beginning, dawn or dusk?" Anyone who attempts a similar synthesis in our own day must make clear how far present information and theory have progressed in finding answers to such basic problems. And, ironically enough, it would probably be true to say that each of the three generations of Greek prehistorians has found clear-cut solutions progressively more elusive.

Glotz frames his answers with a good deal of assurance, as is perhaps necessary if a semipopular account is to inspire confidence in a wide circle of readers. And yet one misses the optimistic view that we have repeatedly noted in the scholars of the nineteenth century, who tend to leave the impression that all of the necessary evidence is in hand—or will be very soon. For example, he points out that "in Asia Minor we are faced with only blackness" and that "excavations that should elucidate this problem [connections between the Aegean area and the Near East] are sadly lacking." Fimmen's Register shows Miletos as the only prehistoric site on the Asia Minor coast below Troy where evidence of Minoan-Mycenaean settlement or trade had been authenticated. And, in fact, though neither of our guides mentions it, most of the Greek mainland and much of Crete were still very inadequately explored.

Glotz accepts without reservation Evans' "Minoan thalassocracy* [rule of the sea]" lasting until late in the Bronze Age, the Minoan colonization and/or political domination of the Greek mainland as well as of much of the east Mediterranean area, and the overwhelming effect of Minoan culture on less developed native traditions. On the other hand, he does not hesitate to question certain aspects of Evans' historical conclusions, though the semipopular format he has adopted prevents any detailed discussion of the evidence.

For example, his view is somewhat different on the date when "Achaeans," *i.e.*, Greek speakers, occupied the mainland, and it diverges still more widely on their continuing role in Mycenaean culture:

> It was above all in the North, in the countries occupied since 2000 by the Achaians, in Hellas which was opened more and more to external influences, that from 1700 onwards Cretan civilization poured in a mighty flood. . . . Everything becomes Cretanized. The ladies dress in fashions of Knossos. In sanctuaries of Cretan type the Cretan goddess is installed, with her usual animals, attributes, and ritual objects; all the ceremonies and all the games celebrated in her honour on the island accompany her to the continent. The princes' dwellings are adorned with frescoes and filled with precious vases and jewels in which there is scarce a trace of Helladic* [mainland] inexperience.

Assuming for the sake of argument that Minoan cultural dominance was as total as this account implies, the obvious question is how such a situation developed. "Is it the effect of an armed invasion," asks Glotz, "of an immigration *en masse?*" He continues:

> No. The mass of the population has not changed. The Achaians still testify to their northern origin by their beard, by their drawers and sleeved *chiton,* by their isolated *megaron* and fixed hearth. Their chiefs . . . impress all the hands needed to carry the gigantic blocks of stone. They delight in war and raids, fine weapons and chariots. By land and sea they go, carrying off cattle and women; but above all they need gold. . . . The sudden metamorphosis of Argolis [the Mycenae-Tiryns region] appears then to be the result of sporadic and peaceful colonization. Elsewhere . . . Cretans could instal themselves as masters . . . but in Argolis they doubtless confined themselves to making the natives accept the blessings of a superior civilization. . . . This Creto-Mycenaean civilization . . . gradually reached every land in Hellas. . . . All the shores of the Peloponnese were visited by the strangers, and at many points they established factories or branches.

Perhaps it is unfair to criticize this general formulation on as tricky a point as Minoan-Mycenaean political relations. But it is difficult to see just what Glotz thinks was the situation. Were the mainland rulers Minoans or Achaeans? Apparently he is saying that only in the Mycenae area did the native kings remain in power. Yet the evidence would seem to indicate that at Mycenae in particular there might have been a Minoan dynasty.

That, at least, is what Evans believed. It is also debatable how Minoan political control could have become established everywhere else in Greece without an armed invasion.

At any rate, Evans would presumably not have been too unhappy with Glotz's account of earlier Mycenaean history. The continuation of the story, however, must have given him acute pain.

In this continual expansion the part played by Cretan traders and colonists was for a long time predominant. But it tended to diminish as the pupils learned to do without their masters, and the power of the mainland chiefs increased. There remained to the Cretans the immense superiority which they enjoyed through their empire of the sea. But even here the Achaians were doing their apprenticeship. . . . A day came when the peoples grew tired of paying tribute to the Cretan thalassocracy. . . . One day of weakness, and the island was conquered. It was. About 1400 the glorious palace of Knossos was overthrown. It was swift and dreadful, a thunderbolt. . . . The catastrophe was universal; Gournia, Pseira, Zakro disappeared; Palaikastro went up in flame. It was no internal revolution this time. Evans would attribute all this destruction to a revolt of the plebs against the monarchy. But everything testifies to the arrival of a new population in Crete. . . . The island which had been mistress of the Mediterranean had become a distant dependency of the mainland. The jewel of the Aegean was to lose all its lustre. . . . When, at the end of a half-century, a few groups of men took possession of Knossos, they could only set up mean hovels in the ruins of the palace.

It is, if anything, more difficult for us now to picture Glotz's (presumably) foreign rulers of Knossos living in the "mean hovels" than Evans' own "miserable [Cretan] survivors." Glotz clearly experiences a letdown of inspiration as he turns to the task of following the fortunes of the rebellious mainlanders. "While the Achaians of Argolis assumed the mastery of the Aegean world the civilization which they had assimilated and transformed to their own use extended further than it had ever gone. . . . New settlements multiply. . . . The Hellas thus formed is the Hellas of the *Iliad,* and the *Catalogue of Ships,*[47] which enumerates its peoples, is a veritable chapter of political geography." Fimmen, too, notes the "thorough-going correspondence of Mycenaean settlements with the places in Homer's catalogue of the Achaeans." In this connection, a puzzling antithesis to Evans' and Glotz's bleak picture of the miserable hovels and pitiful squatters in Crete after 1400 is supplied by the description of Crete not only in this same *Catalogue* but in the general Homeric tradition of the island as "fair, fat, well-watered; and in it are many men, beyond numbering, and ninety cities."[48]

Faced with the apparent shift of material prosperity from Crete to the mainland, Glotz cannot resist a nostalgic and perhaps justifiable eulogy of the Minoan cultural achievement. "Glorious though the spectacle may be which is presented by the Mycenaean civilization if we consider only its extent, it gives the impression of a backward movement if we compare its quality with that of its predecessor. . . . There is the superiority of wealth . . . [but] art grew vulgar and degenerate. It was a characteristic sign of the intellectual decline that writing was very rarely used, and tablets were wanted nowhere outside of Crete."

One of Glotz's surest instincts about Minoan culture concerns the novelty and effect of the great architectural complexes.

> To estimate the level reached by Cretan architecture and to enjoy its charm one must first forget those intellectual qualities of order, symmetry, and balance which give Greek buildings their incomparable beauty. The Cretan architect made no effort to offer to the gods temples worthy of them. He wanted to build comfortable houses and mansions and magnificent palaces, in which the master could conveniently accommodate his whole family, an army of servants, and the offices of a complicated administrative system, and display his wealth by brilliant entertainments. The great artistic skill with which all crafts combined their resources at the call of the Cretan architect is clearly shown not so much in the majesty of the general effect or even in the splendour of the external decoration as in the perfect adaptation to climatic conditions, happy distribution of light and shade, and intelligent ventilation and drainage, in the ease of communication between the countless rooms, the arrangements made to satisfy quite modern notions of comfort [i.e., "flush toilets"] and the harmonious opulence of details, and finally in a sure sense of the spectacular and picturesque which indulges in monumental entrances, the elegant ordering of terrace upon terrace and vistas of noble landscapes on every side. These are the solid and native qualities which appear in the palaces . . . when one tries to imagine them as they were when they had taken on their final form.

When he turns to mainland architecture, Glotz is again not so lyrical.

> Then is the Cretan house of the same origin as the northern house, of which the Mycenaeans bequeathed the type to the Greece of the future? This is the opinion which archaeologists maintained at first, either deriving the Cretan type from the mainland type or vice-versa. But to-day it is generally admitted that between the two systems there are radical differences, due to the climates in which they had their birth. There is nothing at all Cretan about the purely "Nordic" arrangements which appear in the second half of the third millennium at Troy II and in Thessaly, reappear about 1600 at Mycenae and Tiryns [dated far

too early], and extend during the XIVth century to Melos and even to Crete. . . . The essential feature of the mainland palace is the *megaron,* independent and isolated. The addition of one new room after another to the original building [in Crete] is hardly possible except with a flat roofing. . . . The long straight line of the *megaron* [in the mainland] makes it possible to drain off the water by a roof with two slopes. . . . The mainland house is deep, with a single entry in the small side, so as to keep the heat in the cold season. . . . To protect their *megaron* from the weather the Mycenaeans resign themselves to having no light in it but what comes through the doors, the central louver, in which the openings are so narrow that they do not prevent the smoke from blackening the ceiling.[49] . . . Between the principles of architecture applied in Crete and the mainland . . . the difference is profound and absolute, and lies in their very origins.

We notice that Dörpfeld's notion of a flat roof for the Tiryns megaron is here ignored. Although the "northern" pitched roof has had many adherents since Glotz's day, the evidence is now very strongly against it.

Fimmen also insists, as had his earlier German colleagues like Dörpfeld, on a "completely separate line of development in house types," and he points to the change from Cretan to mainland architectural usages both between Phylakopi II and III and even in the latest prehistoric phase at Gournia and Haghia Triada in Crete itself.

Glotz prefaces his chapter "The Social System and Government" with a useful statement of the elusive kind of evidence sometimes available to the prehistorian.

On the organization of the social group the remains of prehistoric times leave a free field to the imagination and do not, it seems, supply any information. It is not impossible, however, to form a rough idea of the lines on which the Aegean societies must have developed. . . . The poet of the *Iliad* tells us that Priam lodged in his palace all his children, his fifty sons[50] and his daughters with their husbands[51]; the poet of the *Odyssey* again shows us in the palace of Nestor six sons, six daughters-in-law, and several married daughters.[52] Here we discover the close relationship which may subsist between social organization and architecture. . . . In the earliest times collective burial was practised; the members of the family were gathered together in the life beyond the grave as they had been gathered together in this world.

There is one notable feature in which Minoan-Mycenaean society seems to show a marked contrast to the contemporary situation in the Near East. Glotz emphasizes "the large part played by women in religious ceremonies and public festivals. . . . They are not recluses. There is nothing corresponding to the harem in Cretan dwellings. . . . The Cretan artists are fond of representing high-born maidens standing up in chariots and holding the reins like Nausikaa.[53] Like Atalante they go hunting." The relatively prestigious status of women is indeed suggested by Late Bronze Age representational art, particularly that in the Minoan tradition. The Homeric poems mirror it to a lesser extent. And one has only to recall the major roles played by women in the myths embedded in Greek classical literature that had their origin in the Bronze Age social situation and that point such a striking contrast with the actual mores of classical Greek society.

Although Glotz's frame of reference in discussing political conditions is largely Minoan, it may be inferred that he saw on the mainland, at least in the region of Mycenae, later developments along similar lines. Political power passed gradually from a large number of heads of local clans to monarchs of a relatively few strategically placed power centers. Shortly after 2000 these independent kings began to build proper palaces. In the end the majority of local chieftains recognized the overlordship of Knossos.

> Only then . . . historical probability permits us to call the king of Knossos by the name of Minos. This name does not seem to have been applied to one personage only. It is less a proper name than a dynastic title. There were Minoses in Crete, as there were Pharaohs and Ptolemies in Egypt and Caesars in Rome. . . . Minos was above all the priest-king. . . . He is the representative of the Bull God, the incarnation of the Minotaur. . . . The king, like the god, had as insignia the sceptre and the double axe, the *labrys*. Two thousand years before it became the symbol of authority in Rome, the axe already held that position in the palace of the Labyrinth.

Evans' view of the Minoan priest-king has now crystallized and become a widely accepted article of faith.

Glotz also summarizes the existing evidence indicating that the later Minoan kingdoms had a very highly developed and complex bureaucratic palace administration. "One thing that gives a good idea of Minoan administration is the multitude of tablets. . . . If we could decipher the tablets we should be thoroughly acquainted with the financial administration . . ." Failing that information, it is still clear that a large number of royal services were installed in the palace.

> Along the ground floor lie the Magazines—what the Homeric epics were to call the "treasure."[54] There, lined up in rows, stand the great *pithoi* containing grain, wine, and more especially oil, and the subterranean cists . . . holding the objects of greatest value. . . . The king's "treasury" was, in the modern sense, the treasury of the State. It was fed by the State revenues and doubtless also by gifts, voluntary or other-

wise. . . . The king . . . owned workshops which had to supply him with objects of art and luxury which . . . bore brilliant witness to his glory, all the world over.

As we have noticed, Glotz follows Evans in believing that Minoan political power extended to the mainland; but he is pardonably unsure about the precise line of command.

According to Thucydides,[55] Minos sent his own sons as lieutenants to his foreign possessions. . . . In any case, on the mainland the command was in the hands of military chieftains, some of whom must have recognized the over-lordship of Minos. . . . The more favoured among them, however, were posted at the ports, such as Pylos, or watched the great roads frequented by merchants at Orchomenos, Thebes, Tiryns, Mycenae, and Vapheio; these became great and mighty dynasts. Each had his retreat on an acropolis surrounded by imposing ramparts. . . . There they lived with all their family in joy and luxury. . . . Such pomp was only possible where the many toiled and moiled for the few. Round the strongholds lived the multitude from whom forced labour could be exacted at will.

Glotz's enumeration of the food resources available to these densely settled communities recalls the Homeric picture of a highly specialized and perfected farming and herding economy. "Wheat and barley were grown throughout Crete as in the Cyclades*, in Asia Minor, and in Greece proper. . . . The olive-tree was of the greatest service to them. In the Homeric poems its oil is only used for the toilet and hygiene.[56] Thus it was believed until quite recently that oil was for a long time a rare commodity in Greece. . . . To-day doubt [about its wide use and economic importance] is no longer possible. . . . The vine was likewise cultivated . . ."

He goes on to mention archaeological proof for the cultivation of figs, dates, flax, poppy, sesame, crocus and saffron. There were flocks and herds of sheep, pigs, goats, and especially of cattle. "All the occupations proper to pastoral life were reserved for the men, and there was doubtless something noble about this privilege then as later, in the time of Homer." Beekeeping is attested by Homer and in archaeological discoveries. Hunting was a favorite pastime and must have lent variety to the food supply. "The ubiquitous sea offered endless resources in the way of fish. . . . Whereas the Homeric heroes scorn fish and leave it for the poor, in Crete it appeared on kings' tables and among the dishes of the gods."

Important evidence for widespread international trade was also accumulating; and it was generally assumed that Minoan ships carried the bulk of it, at least up to 1400. The most reliable index of the various markets is

Fimmen's careful documentation of the discovery of Minoan and Mycenaean pottery found outside of Greece and Crete. Fimmen is quite certain that by no means all the exported Mycenaean and Minoan vases contained wine or oil or some other commodity. "One must certainly not assume that all the vases were traded only for their contents. The expensive painted pottery of Crete and Mycenae with its sense of style formed in itself an important article of commerce. One can certainly dare to assume from the most beautiful vases found in Egypt and from the numerous kraters* with figured scenes in Cyprus that they were purchased for their form and decoration." He goes on to list the major imports, such as amber from the Baltic area, ivory from Africa, and various metals. He admits that it is an "open question" as to how far the Aegean area was self-sufficient in the latter. The main source of copper seems to have been in Cyprus, of tin in Spain and England, of silver in Sardinia and Spain, and of gold in Egypt and Nubia.

In discussing foreign trade, Glotz as usual strikes a more popular note.

Schliemann found at Hissarlik axes of jade and a fragment of white nephrite. Here, then, we have stones which, from stage to stage, have come from the Kuen-Lun Mountains [in central Asia] and perhaps still further to the shores of the Troad. Who can tell by what mysterious roads the amber found its way among the pre-Hellenic peoples, and to such an extent that Pylos before Nestor's day [see chapter VI for the Kakovatos site] contained quantities of it? Through what hands did the tin pass before it reached the bronze-workers of Knossos? . . . Melos, the most south-westerly island [of the Cyclades] . . . from the earliest times . . . exported . . . obsidian, of which it had the monopoly. It became the great half-way house between Crete and Argolis.

Among the most obvious Mycenaean exports were the vases already known from Egyptian tombs in Schliemann's day. "How did these Mycenaean goods make their way into Egypt?" asks Glotz. "It is probable that the Cretans made themselves the middle-men between the whole Aegean and Egypt during the XVIth century and the greater part of the XVth. . . . Before 1420, the Achaians were in direct relations with Egypt. . . . This competition was certainly not unrelated to the catastrophe which ruined Knossos to the profit of Mycenae about 1400. . . . So the trade of Mycenae, once liberated from the hegemony of Crete, poured into Egypt for two hundred years." For example, at the end of the Trojan War, "we find in the *Odyssey*[57] Menelaos and Odysseus, with the men of Crete, Laconia, and Ithaca, setting forth from Pharos [an island off Alexandria], sailing up the Aigyptos [Nile] on ventures which were half commercial and half military, and returning with coffers filled with gold." It should perhaps be injected that Glotz's account of Egyptian trade has turned out to be a particularly distorted reconstruction.

Minoan-Mycenaean traffic with Asia Minor was also coming vaguely into focus. "The Cretans from the XVIth century, and then the Mycenaeans, were constant visitors to the Syrian coast. . . . A complete colony was founded at Miletos, which bears the name of a Cretan city. . . . At the extreme point of Asia Minor, at the entrance to the straits, there was an important market, that of Troy. . . . The opulent city of Priam was for two centuries in continuous relations with the regions dominated by the city of Agamemnon."

Glotz belittles the traditional account of the rape of Helen as the cause of the Trojan War; it was a simple case of cutthroat commercial rivalry. "We already have the competition described later by Hesiod, 'between potter and potter,' but it is international; it is already, on the economic field, the Trojan War. And indeed, when the Achaians, masters of the trade and the coasts from the mouths of the Nile to the Hellespont, grow tired of seeing access to the straits barred to them, Agamemnon need only send out the call to arms and all . . . will come rushing upon the city of Priam."

Glotz also believes, with Evans, that the Minoan thalassocracy had turned its attention to the west. "They [the Minoans] could collect on the [western] coasts still more precious goods, brought from very far by cara-vans—amber, and above all, tin. Italy, Sicily, and Iberia [Spain] thus became the Far West of the Aegeans. . . . In Sicily, then, far more than in Italy, the archaeologist finds all sorts of indications which suggest the establishment of colonies rather than the extension of trade." He even follows Evans' lead in suggesting that there is archaeological evidence to support a rather tenuous later tradition that connects Minos and Daidalos with Sicily.[58] "We have no right to disdain the traditions which mention successive migrations of Cretans to Sicily. Daidalos, it is said, came the first, and then Minos, in pursuit of Daidalos. What Daidalos, who personified the industry and art of Crete, brought with him we see in the painted vases, the weapons, and the jewels laid in the [Sicilian] tombs; what Minos did, who personifies its political power, we know from the concordance of Cretan and Sicilian evidence. . . . Even Minoan writing, according to Evans, was taken up by the Iberians. If there was no colonization here, there was at least commercial contact." Glotz's confident statement of the case for Minoan colonial expansion is by no means echoed by Fimmen, who is not even sure how "colony" can be distinguished from "trading post."

In Glotz's account of Minoan-Mycenaean religion, it is again Evans' hypotheses and to a large extent Evans' discoveries that dominate his thinking. Fimmen, on the other hand, makes a careful independent study of all the grave types through the Aegean area and their dates and localities. By and large, he thinks, hints about religious practices that can be gained from art representations and the like usually prove elusive and baffling, whereas the abundant evidence of funeral ritual in the form and contents of tombs provides at least some dependable material on which to base a reconstruction of a people's religious beliefs. Fimmen comes to the conclusion that, of the three main types—the rock-cut chamber tomb, the cist grave and the tholos tomb—the first occurs in Crete, the islands and mainland Greece (except Thessaly), with the oldest examples on the islands of Melos and Euboea. The second type is especially common in the islands and in northern Greece and is very seldom found in Crete; again, the oldest examples occur on the islands. The tholos type is common on the mainland, unusual in the islands, and (except for a doubtful precedent in Early Minoan times) occurs only in late examples on Crete.

Fimmen also points out other differences between Crete and the mainland. For instance, there are no mainland examples of the common Cretan sanctuary on or near a mountaintop; only in Crete have actual examples been found of the house shrines and chapels shown in art representations; material evidence of continuing hero cults from the Late Bronze Age to classical times seems to be confined to the mainland. While Fimmen does not explicitly say so, the rather obvious conclusion from his review is that extreme caution is indicated before adopting Evans' belief that the Minoan religious tradition eventually preempted the loyalty of all Aegean peoples.

On the question of cremation versus inhumation of the dead, it now seemed safe to say that there is hardly a known case where one can speak with assurance of cremation being practiced in mainland Greece or Crete during the Late Bronze Age. The charcoal, ashes and animal bones in many mainland graves are best understood as evidence for cult offerings to the dead.

Glotz again echoes Evans' judgments in discussing Minoan-Mycenaean art. The Minoans are the creators; the mainlanders, rude and bungling imitators. Crete did, it is true, borrow much from the Near East, but everything was transformed by Minoan artistic genius. "Freedom in respect of all teachings and all traditions—that is the most characteristic feature of Cretan art. It had its conventions; none of them ever hampered personal experiment. . . . The Cretan artist has the confidence of youth and an ingenuous audacity. . . . All these artistic qualities were displayed by the Cretans, as a rule, on objects of small dimensions. They have an eye for truth and for beauty, but not for size. One might say that they reduce everything to their own stature, being small men."

In reviewing the contents of the Mycenae Shaft Graves, Glotz is, of course, puzzled by the lack of homogeneity. But in general the rule holds: Anything "good" is Cretan (or at least foreign), anything "crude" or "simple" is native. But, even granting this dangerous distinction, some peculiar subjective judgments are made.

> Nowhere, not even in Troy, have such masses of jewels been found. . . . Some of them are like nothing in Crete, either in form or in decoration. Others clearly bear the stamp of Cretan influence. . . . The famous gold masks which preserve the features of buried kings speak to the imagination, but they are only clumsy impressions stamped by natives. . . . Simple-minded image-makers cut the grey-brown limestone of the country into clumsy funeral steles. . . . To fill the field the artist could think of nothing better than heavy spirals. The Cretans changed all this. . . . We come thus to certain works which do not merely indicate the influence of foreign models or masters but were actually executed by those masters and were almost all imported.

The siege scene on the silver rhyton shows

> a tale of war which was told in Argos. After the *Iliad* we have the *Odyssey;* on a third fragment of the rhyton there are shipwrecked men swimming for their lives. Thus all the legend which was to be immortalized in the Achaian epic was already immortalized in Cretan art. For the authors of these works, which were buried in the Fourth Shaft Grave, were not the fellow-countrymen of the heavy-handed image-maker who carved the stele of the same tomb. They had come to Mycenae at the call of a dynast who had gold and wanted glory. . . . The art of the cups from Vapheio is more refined and more sure of itself; we pass from the Shaft Graves to the bee-hive tombs . . . One really cannot see where, except in Crete, such complete artistry could have appeared at such a time.

For Glotz, too, the gulf separating Minoan and Mycenaean ceramic products was absolute and unbridgeable for centuries, though native potters finally succeeded in uninspired imitations.

> While the Cyclades and the mainland everlastingly reproduced the same types or altered them only at long intervals, without rising above an industrial technique and an uninspired geometric decoration, Crete soon learned to give superior qualities to ordinary pottery, and above all to transform a utilitarian industry into a luxurious art. . . . The education of the Cycladic and mainland potters was completed during the two centuries [1600–1400] . . . The import of Cretan vases became more and more active all over the Aegean world. Moreover, in many places vases were manufactured which we should call Cretan if certain details did not prove their local origin. These can only have been made

and painted by Cretan immigrants. The native potters kept up their own types, but they became daily more imbued with a technique and a style which they considered superior.

Glotz's remarks on the distinctive Palace Style ceramics might have been written by Evans himself.

> During this time [a generation or two before 1400] the Palace style became known. There is no doubt of the Cretan origin of some of these precious vases, which have been found all over Argolis, at Kakovatos, in Aigina, at Chalkis in Euboia, at Thebes, and at Orchomenos. But others, more numerous, are imitations. . . . From where do these imitations come? . . . The native potters cannot have decorated them; the most advanced of them were still incapable of it. We must, therefore, suppose that master-potters from Crete worked on the mainland in certain centres from which their work was sent far afield.

We may, perhaps, innocently inquire why Cretan "master-potters" could produce originals for export from Crete but were reduced to making obvious imitations when they emigrated to the mainland. The day of distinguishing the provenience* of clays was, of course, still far in the future.

After 1400 the fortunes of Minoan ceramic art mirrored the larger political events. "Just when the pottery of Crete was at its apogee, Mycenaean pottery borrowed its models, carried off its artists, appropriated its processes, and immensely enlarged its domain. The next thing it did was to take its place." The strikingly homogeneous later pottery, one of the leading features of the Mycenaean koinê* (common or shared culture), was exported very widely throughout the eastern Mediterranean area. Glotz has only faint commendation for its best efforts and characterizes the final manifestations as "the last phase of a once glorious art, the death agony of a civilization."

Since Evans and his followers considered the native mainland pottery almost beneath their notice, it will be worthwhile to summarize Fimmen's workmanlike description of the two most important early varieties of what he calls "the pottery of central Greece." One type is characterized by simple geometric or curvilinear decoration applied in "matt" (dull) black or brown paint on a light greenish or yellow-brown ground. This "matt-painted*" ware occurs in its most developed form in the Mycenae Shaft Graves. Another very important contemporary type has already come to our attention several times. It is a monochrome gray or yellow ware, with sharp profiles and sometimes with incised or ribbed decoration. Fimmen notes that Schliemann called this ware "Lydian" when he encountered it in Level VI at Troy and later coined a new name, "Minyan*," for essentially the same pottery at Orchomenos. Fimmen himself prefers the term

"Orchomenos ware." It was approximately contemporary with the matt-painted pottery. It will be remembered that these two very distinctive types of pottery are characteristic of Fimmen's Early Mycenaean period (1700–1550). The developed Mycenaean pottery is essentially a fusion of decorative motifs from both the Minoan and native matt-painted traditions applied in lustrous paint to the yellow Minyan fabric.

The massive impact of the highly sophisticated Minoan art forms had its strongest effect on the mainland in Fimmen's Middle Mycenaean period (1550–1400), and in this environment the so-called Mycenaean koinê began to emerge. "Crete finally developed," says Fimmen, "a completely separate rich and unique culture which soon far outstripped all the other provinces. The fusion which took place in the following period is created through the complete preponderance of Cretan culture. . . . The Cretan naturalistic style of the first Late Minoan Period comprised in a free manner a very large number of motifs which in the ornamentation of the koinê, in time completely stylized, recur again and again." Fimmen is quite prepared to explain this development by the presence of "Cretan colonists," but he does not follow Evans in believing that cultural dominance implies political control. In fact, he believes that the emergence of the koinê style is more likely to imply that the political center of gravity in the Aegean area may have been beginning to shift to the mainland.

Glotz's chapter "Writing and Language" is perhaps the best indicator of the distance we have come between 1925 and 1965 on the question of literacy in the Late Bronze Age. He begins by briefly reviewing the evidence and theories current at the end of the nineteenth century about writing in the Aegean. Evans' excavations "have brilliantly confirmed what was only an inspired divination. . . . Unfortunately these documents are still a dead letter for us and will perhaps remain undecipherable so long as no bilingual inscription is discovered to give the key. All that the penetrating sagacity of Evans has so far been able to do is to distinguish different classes of writing among the *scripta Minoa*."

The long discussion of the connections between Egyptian, Cretan and Phoenician systems of writing is an instructive example of the reckless theorizing that written documents in an unknown language and script are so likely to invite. Glotz's conclusion is that "the simplest thing is to admit, not only that the Phoenicians drew from the Cretan source as well as from the Egyptian, but that the Cretans and Egyptians both drew equally from the primitive source of the Neolithic writings." One wonders how anyone could regard such a suggestion as "simple"! But he takes a more sensible stand in connection with alleged influence from the cuneiform systems in the Near East. "As for Asiatic influence, it appears nowhere in Cretan writing. There is an outward likeness, it is true, between the clay tablets used in Crete and those of Babylonia. One might at first admit, if necessary, that the material form was borrowed, and that only, as in any case the Cretan signs have no resemblance whatever to the cuneiform characters."

Glotz is much more positive than Evans that the clay tablets represent a quite minor class of written documents in a highly literate society. "We must therefore suppose that the documents which have come down to us were not of the kinds most extensively used. The religious and literary writings have disappeared, and of the commercial and legal papers, the stamped documents, nothing remains but the seal-impressions which were attached to them." We find also a somewhat more cautious reflection of Evans' theories of the origin of Greek epic. "When Homer describes the dances which were performed in the theatre of Knossos he authorizes us to think that the bards who sang in the palace of Alkinoos[59] had their forerunners in the palace of Minos, and that the Greek epic, with its artificial language, was inspired by poems far more ancient."

The inferences about the three writing systems of Crete have in general a familiar ring. The earliest hieroglyphic style is succeeded by Linear A "as soon as new dynasties established themselves in the Second Palaces [after about 1700] . . . The new system, perhaps enforced by the royal authority, was alone taught henceforward. . . . This system remained in general use all over Crete. But at Knossos [about 1450] . . . the chancery brought about the predominance of a script which was doubtless reserved for the royal documents, the linear script of Class B. . . . At Hagia Triada, as at Pompeii, we see *graffiti** [in Linear A] scrawled on the walls by idle passers-by. The humblest folk could read and write."

He faithfully reflects, too, the current belief about the language or languages of the tablets. "Judging by the regularity with which writing develops from the end of the Chalcolithic Period [transitional from stone to metal] to the Greek invasions [end of the Bronze Age], we have the impression that the same language is transmitted to successive generations, with inevitable changes. This speech was neither Indo-European nor Semitic. From certain groups of signs it seems to have had alterations of suffix in which we may see word-endings and inflexions; this characteristic makes it similar to the Aryan languages, but proves nothing."

In discussing the diffusion of Minoan scripts, Glotz tries to take account both of the archaeological evidence and of later traditions about the earliest Greek writing systems.

> Since the Cretans took their system of writing with them it is not surprising that they caused it to be adopted all over the Aegean. . . . Everything seems to show that in the islands it is the Cretan language which is expressed in the Cretan script. But on the mainland we do not find

things presented in such a simple fashion. While certain vase inscriptions conform to the linear Class A, others appear to mark a transitional stage between hieroglyphs and linear characters. . . . In Boeotia particularly the archaic system prevailed. The famous "Kadmeian" letters of which the Greeks spoke were indeed used on the Kadmeia [acropolis of Thebes], as at Orchomenos, and it is these no doubt which were engraved on the bronze tablets which Agesilaos found at Haliartos in the "Tomb of Alkmene," and took for Egyptian hieroglyphs.[60]

We shall be reviewing the Theban inscribed jars later; but Glotz's inferences about them are quite wrong.

There is also something prophetic (although curiously inverted) in Glotz's reconstruction of the process by which Greek speakers of the classical period in Cyprus used a syllabary derived from Bronze Age Crete for their own writing system. "This local form of the Cretan writing followed its proper destiny. When it was reduced to a syllabary Achaians from the Peloponnese [who settled in Cyprus toward the end of the Bronze Age] adapted it in a rough and ready way to their own idiom; but it always showed, by its inability to denote certain gradations, despite its 54 characters, that it had not been created to express the Greek language." He agrees with Evans that certain symbols in the later Lycian and Carian alphabets of southwest Anatolia "come direct from linear scripts A and B." And in this connection he points out that "By a curious coincidence, which has an allegorical value, the only passage in which Homer clearly mentions writing is that in which Bellerophon, leaving Argos for the shores of Asia, hands to the king of the Lycians tablets covered with signs."[61]

Glotz's final chapter, survivals of Aegean civilization, ought to be the most important for our theme of Homeric connections; but unfortunately it is far from his best effort. He characterizes the Dorian invasion that destroyed the Mycenaean strongholds as the "*Drang nach Osten* of a continental civilization, that of Hallstatt*." The conventional Dorian culture characteristics are rehearsed—use of iron, cremation burial, geometric ornament on pottery and the use of fibulae* to fasten garments. The invaders also brought with them a "very different religion," in which "a great god prevailed over the great goddess of the Cretans." Protected international trade gave place to piracy on the high seas.

Yet there were elements of the Bronze Age culture that survived the Dorian hordes. "One of the features which give the Aegeans such an original aspect is just one of those which distinguish the Greeks from the other peoples of Indo-European race, that is the liking for the gymnastic and musical contests which accompany the great festivals." He goes on to cite prehistoric associations of the later religious cults connected with important athletic contests—Corinth (the Isthmus), Olympia, Delphi, Delos. "There is as direct a connection between the boxing-matches carved on the *rhyton* from Hagia Triada and those at which Achilleus[62] and Alkinoos[63] preside as between the games described by Homer and the Olympic games."

In Glotz's summation of the relationship between Mycenaean times and the Homeric poems, one senses a firm enough commitment to the proposition that there *was* a strong thread of continuity; but one misses the late-nineteenth-century conviction that the connection was close and vital. "When the days of trial came the last of the great victories won by the Achaians, the taking of Troy, assumed legendary dimensions in the imagination of the peoples who inhabited the neighbouring region, and gradually the Aiolian* bards attached all the warlike epics to that which most flattered and best consoled the new generations. Then, when the migrations in their turn receded into the past and took on a marvelous colour, all the tales of sea-journeys were fitted into the 'Returns' from Troy, and especially into the adventures of Odysseus."

In spite of the author's learning, his notable ability to synthesize and generalize, and his stylistic flair (which comes through even in translation), Glotz's book was not a completely reliable and balanced historical reconstruction even in terms of the evidence available in the twenties. Yet it deservedly appealed to the student and general reader and was a wiser choice than most of the attempted overviews of its day. On the other hand, it is a rather alarming indication of how slowly many in the profession adjust to current developments that Glotz is still prescribed for innocent students and recommended to unsuspecting general readers. The 1952 edition (in French only) is not revised—and scarcely could have been. Professors C. Picard and P. Demargne provided *notes additionnelles;* but such an expedient cannot represent a satisfactory adjustment to the insights of a new generation.

In closing this chapter, we may refer briefly and (we hope) instructively to a publication with the interesting title *A Century of Archaeological Discoveries* by Professor A. Michaelis. The English translation of the original German text appeared in 1908, half a generation after Schliemann had died and when Evans' major excavations were already well known. Indeed, the sponsors of the English version were among those scholars whose approach to classical studies irked Evans so deeply. A few excerpts will make his reasons clear enough.

The tone is set even in the Preface written by Professor Percy Gardner, who delivers himself as follows: "Light won from most of these [Aegean] sites has been thrown on the prehistoric age in Greek lands, rather [than] on what is really Hellenic. It is a Darwinian age, when the search for origins seems to fascinate men more than the search for what is good in itself; and the fact is that our eyes are somewhat dazzled by the brilliant discoveries of Schliemann, Dörpfeld and Evans."

Michaelis, in the author's Preface, defines archaeology in rather peculiar terms, even in reference to classical art. "By the term archaeology is meant the archaeology of art; the products of civilization in so far as they express no artistic character will only be mentioned incidentally." One would be interested to know just how Professor Michaelis would have defined artefacts that have "no artistic character." In any case, he states in his single chapter on prehistory and primitive Greece that the archaeology of art "is not concerned with the questions whether the people were dolicho-cephalous or brachycephalous, whether there was inhumation or crema-tion, or whether cist graves existed, nor does it inquire into their mode of living, their dress, or their furniture . . ." Prehistory is concerned with "anthropology, ethnology, and the history of civilization"; and these sub-jects, says Michaelis, are "as foreign to our studies as the questions of currency, trade, and history would be to numismatics*." One can only hope that the present-day historian of classical art will have the same startled reaction to this revealing admission as would the numismatist.

Michaelis has some high praise for Schliemann's discoveries, but the reservations are ominous. "But there is a reverse to the medal. Schlie-mann's education and talents were quite foreign to all scientific thinking and method. He cared neither for history nor art, as his indifference to the Hermes of Praxiteles proved; primitive cultures, curiosities, and vague imaginings exhausted his interests." Michaelis admires the samples of Minoan art discovered by Evans. "Every new find deepens our sense of a great civilization and of an art which, by virtue of its frank naturalism, united to a well-trained artistic eye and a technical skill by no means contemptible, succeeded in representing men in as individual and charac-teristic a manner as Hellenic art only attained nearly one thousand years later . . ." He is much less enthusiastic, however, about the contents of the Mycenae Shaft Graves. While admitting "the impression of an art fresh in perception and in reproduction," he feels that "one must deny it any capacity for development. Evidently certain conservative influences have to be taken into consideration . . ." Nowadays at least, the reader is more likely to sense rather more obvious "conservative influences" elsewhere.

The ideological chasm between "prehistoric" and "Hellenic," which infuriated Evans and which we shall see A. J. B. Wace deploring as late as 1956, was already wide and deep in Michaelis' thinking. "This culture [Minoan-Mycenaean] was richer and more ancient than that called forth by the so-called Dorian Invasion, which required several centuries before it produced the beginnings of the true Hellenic art, . . . This newly discovered art in its technical perfection, its definite and at times excellent designs, anticipated actual Hellenic art. This art then had to be placed before the beginning of Greek history . . ." Evans, Wace, Michaelis and Gardner would have found the greatest difficulty in arriving at a mutually acceptable definition of "true Hellenic art" or assigning an approximate date for "the beginning of Greek history."

VI

Blegen, Priam and Nestor:
1915-1939

"A man who rivals in wisdom and experience,

though not in loquacity, the ancient hero

whose home he discovered."

CARL WILLIAM BLEGEN WAS BORN IN 1887, the second of a family of six children. His father was Professor of Greek and German at Augsburg College in Minneapolis, Minnesota, so the son came naturally by his interest in higher education and especially in classical studies. The Blegen family is well and favorably known in Minnesota, particularly among scholars, educators and the numerous residents of Norse descent; and the present generation has added to its prestige. It is probably no accident that Carl Blegen is particularly remembered by his brothers and sisters for his absorption in devising and solving puzzles as well as his ability in organizing and supervising childhood games and activities.

Blegen's introduction to classical archaeology followed the usual training in Greek and Latin languages and literature. He studied at Augsburg, at the University of Minnesota and at Yale University. After completing the course work for the Yale Ph.D. in 1910, he was awarded a traveling fellowship that allowed him to enroll at the American School of Classical Studies in Athens. His ability and promise so impressed the director of the school, Dr. Bert Hodge Hill, that he was invited to stay on as secretary. He held that post from 1913 to 1920. In those years Hill and Blegen became close personal friends as well as colleagues in administration and excavation. The friendship persisted with unfailing devotion on both sides up to Hill's death in 1958.

Blegen served his apprenticeship in excavation during the early part of World War I when neither Greece nor the United States was directly involved in hostilities. At the same time another of Blegen's close and lifelong friendships was forming with A. J. B. Wace, director of the British School of Archaeology in Athens. Already a seasoned excavator and explorer for prehistoric habitation sites—particularly those of the neolithic period in the plains and river valleys of east central Greece—Wace had learned excavation techniques from older British colleagues and

in 1912 had coauthored a pioneering study called *Prehistoric Thessaly*.
Blegen's first major excavation was in 1915 and 1916 at Korakou, a
prehistoric mound on the gulf coast about 2 miles west of New Corinth.
Wace was present for a large part of the time during both campaigns, and
Blegen warmly acknowledges his assistance both in the field and in the
systematic study of the pottery before publication.

Indeed, one of Blegen's most striking characteristics is a capacity for
loyal friendships. In this sense he may present a fairly fundamental contrast with his predecessors, particularly in their younger days. In spite of
fame and countless acquaintants, Schliemann and Evans seem to have
been essentially "loners." In Schliemann's autobiography this impression
is strongly conveyed in his long separation from his family and childhood
sweetheart and in his lonely passion to prove his own worth to them and
to the world. And in the reminiscences of Evans' sister, as well as in the
anecdotes about his relationships with colleagues, there are hints of personal
charm and warmth offset by a certain Olympian aloofness. Blegen, on the
other hand, in spite of a reserved, almost shy manner, has a notable capacity for making devoted friends and for preserving close family ties.
Yet members of his staff, like his brothers and sisters in childhood days,
are always aware that he is in charge. Discipline and single-minded concentration on the job at hand are quietly but effectively enforced.

Another strongly marked contrast involves Blegen's caution and Schliemann's audacity. In this respect Evans' instinct was something of a mean
between the extremes. Perhaps the difference is mainly a sign of the times
in which they lived. Because of its essentially wide-open nature and lack of
adequate controls, a young science encourages bold theories and radical
interpretations of meager evidence. But as its outlines become firmer and
a dependable basis of fact gradually emerges, the ideas of even the most
imaginative participants are to some extent restrained and channeled. It
is probably true that Evans made fewer gross mistakes than Schliemann,
both in excavation and interpretation; and, in general, the controversies
in which he was involved in his lifetime were less strident. One does not
need to browse very far in the early scholarly literature to realize that
sharp and even acrimonious personal exchanges in print were far more
common than nowadays. The trend toward restraint is no doubt a healthy
symptom of maturity. In the heat of an open and bitter argument one is
much more likely to be forced into an extreme position that must later
be precariously defended or ingloriously abandoned. Yet human nature
being what it is, strong differences of opinion always exist; and scholarly
tempers sometimes boil over even yet in unfortunate public quarrels.

Blegen's record, at any rate, is a model of caution. His is always the method of understatement. Conclusions or theories, even when radical in their implications, are expressed in a quiet and disarming style. In this respect he presents an interesting contrast to his friend Wace, who was always the impetuous crusader against complacency, easy generalities and outworn viewpoints. Perhaps Blegen's bluntest challenge to established authority was very early in his career; and it involved Walter Leaf, the great Homeric critic. Leaf had stated that the Corinth area was relatively depopulated in the Late Bronze Age. Blegen pointed out that, while there was indeed no evidence for Mycenaean habitation on the exact site of classical Corinth, the surface of several mounds in the vicinity was strewn with abundant Mycenaean pottery. In fact, the mound at Korakou may well have been Homer's "wealthy Ephyra,"[64] apparently the most important settlement in the Corinth area during the Late Bronze Age. "Wherever it [Ephyra] was," wrote Blegen, "it was no doubt the capital of the Corinthia in Achaean times and as such probably exercised sovereignty over a district which was certainly well populated and prosperous, and which from the evidence we have might appropriately be called wealthy."

This exchange between Blegen and Leaf again underlines a serious problem (which we have already mentioned) involving topographical and geographical research in classical lands. The traditional philologist often prefers to remain in his study, depending on ancient literary authorities, out-of-date secondary sources and inadequate maps. The newer breed of field explorer, on the other hand, insists on going over the ground in person and relies increasingly on the evidence of his own senses. He checks the surface pottery and is increasingly likely to ask the advice of scientists in allied fields like geography, geology, civil engineering, aerial photography, agricultural economics and biology. When philologist and field archaeologist learn to cooperate effectively and complement each other's methods, a long forward step will have been taken.

EARLY EXCAVATIONS: 1915–1927

Blegen's success in tactfully challenging established dogmas can be partly explained by the fact that his earlier excavations were carried out at relatively unknown sites. Gonia, Korakou, Hagiorgitika, Zygouries—what do these names convey in comparison with Troy, Mycenae, Knossos, or even somewhat less famous centers like Tiryns, Pylos and Orchomenos? In fact, most of the towns and villages whose ruins Blegen investigated between 1915 and 1927 were obscure in two senses. In the first place, their ancient names are unknown; and so the toponym used by the present-day inhabitants has to serve. Sometimes excavation and research may reestablish the correct ancient name, as when Hissarlik was finally proved to the satisfaction of most scholars to be the site of ancient Troy, or Ilion. But, historically speaking, many large and important ancient sites, particularly those that flourished only in prehistoric times, are still nameless. For example, the great Minoan palace in Crete that has been in process of excavation by French archaeologists since the early 1920's and is fully comparable in importance to those of Knossos and Phaistos is still designated by the local modern name, Mallia (though *possibly* ancient Milatos).

Most of Blegen's early excavation sites are obscure in this accidental sense; but they are probably also obscure in terms of their original, relative historical importance. This, of course, has to be judged from what is often very inadequate evidence surviving in epic poetry, mythology and later tradition. If, for example, we could somehow learn the original names of the mounds now called Gonia or Zygouries, it is quite possible that they would have no historical associations for us. Yet Blegen's patient and methodical excavation of these "nameless" habitation sites has proved to be tremendously important for the reconstruction of the prehistory of the Greek mainland, and particularly for northeastern Peloponnese. Precisely because they were not major political centers in prehistoric or later times, the earlier strata of occupation are less disturbed by extensive leveling to accommodate ever more ambitious complexes of buildings.

To make a gross and obviously inexact generalization, Schliemann was most interested in identifying famous ancient places and in finding treasures of precious metals; Evans, in recovering monumental architecture and the finest ceramic, sculptural and epigraphic remains; Blegen, in observing stratification and analyzing ordinary potsherds. Perhaps this transition shows most clearly the direction in which Greek prehistory has been gradually moving. From the hundreds of thousands of broken bits extracted from carefully noted levels in these unpretentious mounds, Blegen and Wace reconstructed a sequence of ceramic fabrics, shapes and decorative motifs that recurred in roughly the same relative order at different sites. Before the end of World War I they had jointly authored an epoch-making article entitled "The Pre-Mycenaean Pottery of the Mainland."

It is difficult in such a review as ours to present these forward steps in pottery analysis in sufficient detail so that the general reader will grasp both the method and the results. Admittedly, such material lacks the glamour and popular appeal of Schliemann's treasures or Evans' mysterious writing systems. But one simply cannot understand the accomplishments of the third generation without a reasonable background in the essentials of ceramic dating.

Blegen and Wace, in fact, proposed what is still the basic stylistic and chronological framework of major pottery types in central and southern Greece during the whole Bronze Age. As the title of their paper would suggest, they paid minimum attention to the better-known and latest "period of widest diffusion of Mycenaean pottery," which they characterized as the "silver age of Mycenae and Tiryns." The system owes much to Wace's work in Thessaly and to the still earlier British work at Phylakopi and in Crete. It is their primary aim to set up a mainland analogue to Evans' Minoan framework. They examine critically the widely accepted theory that mainland culture during the Late Bronze Age was simply a pale provincial imitation of the Minoan. And they emphasize the need to study mainland developments *before* the period of strong Minoan influence. "The glory of Tiryns and Mycenae was the climax of prehistoric art on the mainland of Greece and, as shewn conclusively by Sir Arthur Evans . . . is derived from Crete. Yet though Minoan in origin, the Mycenaean civilisation is not merely transplanted from Crete, but is the fruit of the cultivated Cretan graft set on the wild stock of the mainland. . . . The underlying mainland element influenced the dominant Minoan art so as to make it Mycenaean as opposed to Cretan." So, even before the first volume of *The Palace of Minos* had appeared, these two young students of mainland prehistory were challenging Evans' basic assumption about Minoan-Mycenaean interrelations from 1600 onward.

Blegen and Wace propose for their area the substitution of the term "Helladic" (*i.e.,* applicable to mainland Greece or Hellas) for Evans' "Minoan." His three major divisions of the Bronze Age (Early, Middle and Late) are retained, though in their scheme the latest pottery classed as Early Helladic is contemporary with Middle Minoan I. Evans' further subdivisions (I, II and III) for each major unit of time are not attempted, nor are his absolute dates mentioned. Furthermore, Blegen and Wace do not claim validity for their sequence of pottery types over the whole mainland. They admit that their conclusions are based "mainly [on] the result of careful observation of the stratification of the Corinthian excavations [*i.e.,* in the vicinity of Corinth] which we have followed together"; but they do take into account published material from other rather widely scattered mainland sites. Thus, they feel, the system ought to be useful "to illustrate the development of civilisation in the Peloponnesus and East-Central Greece during this long period."

Though the implications of their new classification are more epoch-making for earlier phases of the Bronze Age, we are of course directly concerned only with the later developments. Toward the end of their Middle Helladic period, corresponding to Middle Minoan II, the earliest burials were being made in the Mycenae Shaft Graves. About the same time, gray Minyan pottery was being imitated in a closely similar ware called "yellow Minyan" (Fig. 71). Fairly early in their Late Helladic period, corresponding to Late Minoan I, the last burials were made in the Shaft Graves, and the characteristic matt-painted mainland pottery ceased. The Late Helladic period saw a rapid development from the simpler Middle Helladic civilization into the "Golden Age of Mycenae and Tiryns," with the tholos tombs at Mycenae, Vaphio and Kakovatos, and under continuing powerful Minoan cultural influence.

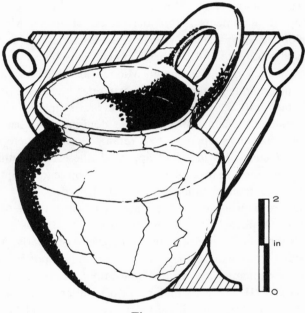

Figure 71

In the mature phase of Late Helladic, corresponding to Late Minoan II, the production of undecorated gray and yellow Minyan pottery ceased and Minoan imports decreased. In this period the mainland was producing an especially fine class of two-handled goblets on a high foot with sparing decoration of graceful floral or marine patterns. The motifs were apparently borrowed from Crete and were painted on a polished yellow Minyan fabric (Fig. 72). "This new kind of Mycenaean pottery was first distinguished at Korakou (which may be the Homeric Ephyra) and has for the sake of convenience been arbitrarily christened 'Ephyraean ware*.'" To generalize rather drastically, the combination of increasingly stylized

Figure 72

Minoan decorative motifs applied to Helladic shapes and fabric became the basis for the later Mycenaean koinê so widespread throughout the eastern Mediterranean in the succeeding phase of Late Helladic corresponding to Late Minoan III.

Evans had always insisted that the sequence of Minoan pottery styles was so gradual as to rule out major intrusions of new settlers or conquerors in Crete. There were no "breaks." Blegen and Wace, on the other hand,

see evidence—at two points especially—for real discontinuity in the mainland pottery. "The appearance of [gray] Minyan Ware in the Middle
Minoan [their Middle Helladic] period marks, as regards the mainland at
least, a break away from the earlier phase characterised by Early Helladic
Ware. The period of Minyan Ware indicates the introduction of a new
cultural strain, the origin of which is not yet clear . . ." We shall soon be
hearing a good deal more about these intrusive makers of gray Minyan
pottery. Blegen and Wace go on to describe the second major dislocation.
"Not so long after the culture marked by Minyan Ware had taken root on
the mainland, Cretan (Minoan) influence made itself felt and profoundly
modified its [the mainland's] character by the introduction of a far higher
standard of civilisation."

Although their estimate of the originality of mainland prehistoric culture differs from Evans', Blegen and Wace definitely support him in his
insistence on the cultural carry-over from prehistoric to classical times.
"All recent research tends to show that archaic and, consequently, classical
Greek art was a renaissance—after it had lain dormant during a dark
period [approximately 1100–800 B.C.] of invasion and disturbance—of the
same artistic spirit that inspired Knossos and Phaestos, Tiryns and Mycenae."

Blegen's first book, *Korakou: A Prehistoric Settlement near Corinth,*
was a development of his Ph.D. dissertation. It was published in 1921, the
same year as the first volume of Evans' *Palace of Minos.* By this time
Blegen had been promoted from secretary to assistant director of the
American School. Even in the Introduction we sense the scientific value
of the thorough examination of this relatively unknown mound. The various classes of pottery, revealed in deep pits sunk right down to bedrock
and in more extensive clearance of limited areas of the upper levels, were
in general not new. The novelty consists in the stress laid on recording the
precise layer or stratum in which they occurred, *i.e.,* on scientific stratigraphy. Blegen is quite specific. "Their exact relation to one another, however, has not hitherto been accurately ascertained. The importance of the
site at Korakou lies in the fact that, supplying the evidence which was lacking at Tiryns and Mycenae, it now definitely establishes the sequence of
these prehistoric wares."

Throughout *Korakou* Blegen uses the new terms "Early, Middle, and
Late Helladic" (EH, MH, LH) and remarks that each of these periods
may be in turn subdivided as the stratification on the particular site dic-
tates. And he does, in fact, recognize subphases of each major division at
Korakou. Although the publication is particularly important for the earlier
Bronze Age, we must confine our attention to the Late Helladic, which is
more or less chronologically parallel to Evans' Late Minoan I, II, III. Not

only are the *relative* dates of the various types of pottery established, but a "roughly correct" chart of *absolute* chronology is worked out by means of direct or indirect synchronisms with the Cyclades, Crete and the Near East. He suggests that Late Helladic I covered the sixteenth century, 1600–1500; Late Helladic II, the fifteenth, 1500–1400; and Late Helladic III, a much longer span, from 1400 to 1100 (see chart on p. 301).

Speaking of the finest mainland pottery at the transition from Middle to Late Bronze, Blegen firmly insists on its local production. "Save, possibly, for one or two sherds from Tiryns, none of this ware can be claimed as genuine Cretan, but the ultimate Minoan source of the patterns on many of these vases cannot be questioned. Since it seems equally free from doubt that most of this ware was fabricated on the mainland, Minoan originals must have been imported for use by the mainland potters. Whether any of these actual originals, which were obviously not numerous, is ever brought to light by further excavation or not, the fact of connections with Crete is nevertheless established."

Another statement is even more explicit about the nature of the cultural interplay. "Late Helladic or 'Mycenaean' pottery . . . evolved through a gradual and regular development of Yellow Minyan ware under constantly growing Minoan influence. The early shapes are thus for the most part those taken over from the Minyan stock, chiefly the goblet on a stem, and a deep bowl with high, splaying rim; but, once the new technique has passed the experimental stage and established itself, it rapidly prevails over the older methods and, as it progresses, it undoubtedly imports from abroad along with its designs many new shapes as well" (Fig. 73).

As he surveys the ceramic evidence for the whole sweep of the Late Bronze Age, Blegen perceives a gradual waxing and waning of Minoan influence.

> Although the evidence of such [Cretan] trade relations becomes exceedingly strong in the First Late Helladic Period, it is not until the Second Late Helladic Period that the height of Cretan influence seems to be reached at Korakou. . . . In fact, in the Second Late Helladic Period the ceramic artists of Korakou apparently strive to attain as nearly as possible the standards set by their Minoan colleagues in Crete. And, finally, in the Third Late Helladic Period, when Mycenaean pottery reaches its widest distribution, the fusion of mainland and Minoan art is complete; but a return swing of the pendulum has intervened, and it is now the mainland element which is seen to be dominant over the Minoan.

One can imagine Evans' reaction to the claim that as early as 1400 the mainland exerted any kind of cultural dominance over Crete.

When he extends the survey to the results of excavation on Late Bronze

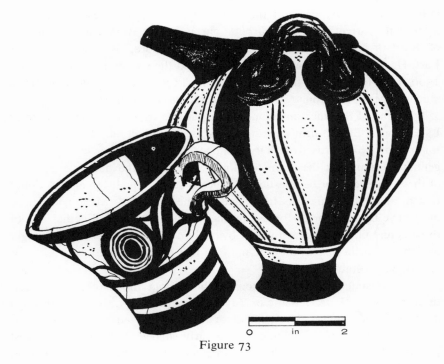

Figure 73

habitation sites in other parts of central and southern Greece, Blegen finds no important discrepancy with his classification or with his appraisal of Minoan-Mycenaean relations. Cretan influence may have been strongest in western Peloponnese. At Kakovatos, which was to have a special relevance to one of his own most important discoveries twenty years later, he feels that the material from LHII and the end of LHI indicates that "Minoan ascendancy appears to be practically complete, and few, if any, of the northern elements so characteristic at Corinth can be distinguished." Yet the Kakovatos pottery as well as that from another tholos tomb farther south at Messenian Pylos is still "almost certainly of mainland manufacture."

In the Aegean pottery assigned to the last centuries of the Bronze Age, there is a mainland-oriented "essential uniformity" of style that Evans himself had partially admitted. Blegen makes no attempt to give a de-tailed list of the very numerous places where such ware occurs; but he underlines the extent of Mycenaean trade and influence by mentioning "numerous places throughout the Greek mainland, on the islands of the Aegean, at several points on the coast of Asia Minor, in Cyprus, Syria, and Egypt, in Southern Italy, Sicily, as well as Sardinia . . ." And he adds that "a related type, at least, appears in the extreme west, in Spain." It is hardly

accidental that a footnote refers obliquely to Evans' insistence on the great
extent of Aegean-centered trade. But Blegen does not openly challenge
Evans' view that the Minoans were the pioneers of this widespread commerce and that Minoan ships were still the main carriers during the heyday
of Mycenae and Tiryns.

On the vital question of what happened on the mainland during the
earlier phases of Late Helladic, however, Blegen leaves no doubt of his
position.

> In explanation of the evolution of the simple, sturdy culture of the
> Middle Helladic Period, as we first see it at Korakou, into the regal
> magnificence of Mycenae, there is no necessity, nor is there evidence, for
> assuming an armed Minoan invasion followed by actual Minoan domi-
> nation. On the contrary, the development, as we have examined it,
> seems rather due to peaceful penetration, chiefly of Minoan commerce
> and Minoan standards, and perhaps of colonies of Minoan artisans,
> among a people ready and eager to seize upon new ideas and new
> inventions, and willing to modify its own. The stimulus came from the
> south, but it acted on a mainland race which had a vigorous spirit of
> progress. The importance of the evidence from Corinth lies in the new
> light it reflects on the evolution of Mycenaean civilization. Korakou
> explains Tiryns and Mycenae.

As he concludes his book, Blegen feels compelled to emphasize the importance of studying the past in the broadest possible perspective. In this
sense, too, he is something of an innovator and foreshadows the day when
sites and whole cultures without glamorous historical connections will be
explored for their own inherent interest and importance. One infers that
he is fairly sure that Korakou is the "Corinth" of the Late Bronze Age and
probably the "Ephyra" of Homer. Yet, even if it remains a "nameless" site
from the point of view of myth and legend, we have much to learn from
its ruins.

> Agamemnon and his noble peers have long enjoyed the prominence
> that was their due; now light is shed also on the conditions of life of
> the humble commoner—the nameless *tis* ["somebody"] of the Homeric
> poems, who with his fellows formed the bulk of the population and
> rendered Agamemnon's glory possible. We have recovered his modest
> house, though its clay walls have long since fallen away. We can picture
> him conducting his household worship about the pillar in his megaron.
> We have seen his simple bed, raised but slightly above the earthen
> floor. We have found the storage jars in which he kept his oil and grain;
> the quern on which he ground his flour; the hearth where he prepared
> his food; the vessels in which he cooked, and the dishes from which he

ate his meal, and the cup from which he drank his wine. And in the disorder of his abandoned house we may recognize the haste with which he fled before that mysterious peril which, under the name of the Dorian Invasion, we believe engulfed his waning civilization.

As assistant director of the American School until 1926 and as acting director in the following year, Blegen had an opportunity to carry out a whole series of further explorations and excavations in northeast Peloponnese. At Zygouries, Phlius, Nemea, Hagiorgitika and Prosymna he uncovered settlements and cemeteries of many periods. Yet, with the exception of Nemea (the site of one of the famous Panhellenic festivals in the classical period), nearly all of them produced mainly prehistoric evidence. And there can be no doubt that, as he shifted operations from place to place, Blegen was increasingly confirmed in his interest in the history of Greece before the Iron Age.

In 1924 Blegen married Elizabeth Denny Pierce, a faculty member of Vassar College and a career archaeologist in her own right. She has continued ever since to share in his almost annual field expeditions and to contribute her part to the study and publication of the finds. In his marriage as in his relationship with his own family and close friends like Hill and Wace, Blegen unfailingly shows a quiet and steady affection. He has a remarkable capacity to inspire loyalty. His sister Anne has helped him with several books, and close academic colleagues like John L. Caskey and Marion Rawson are his constant collaborators.

The text for *Zygouries: A Prehistoric Settlement in the Valley of Cleonae* was completed before Blegen left Greece in 1927 to accept a professorship at the University of Cincinnati. This position proved to be as nearly an ideal situation as any archaeologist can hope for, even if he is independently wealthy (as Blegen is not). Schliemann and Evans had the advantages of wealth and leisure and the prestige that striking success carries with it. But in at least one important respect the impact of their work was lessened—they had no means of regular formal contact with students. It is true that the experience of actually sharing the day-to-day problems of an excavation or working in a museum with a seasoned specialist is an indispensable part of the training of the aspiring archaeologist. But so are the academic contacts in the library, classroom and seminar. For a whole generation of students of archaeology at the University of Cincinnati, Blegen alternated the indispensable role of teacher with his program of excavation. The chairman of the Department of Classics at Cincinnati for many years was Professor W. T. Semple. In negotiating the appointment, both Professor Semple and his wife had been interested in arranging that Blegen's field work should continue; and they had the private means to make this possible. Even after the death of the Semples, the Taft Memorial Fund, which they set up in the Department of Classics, continued to underwrite Blegen's excavations and publications.

The mound called Zygouries lies along the highway in a defile not far north of Mycenae. The rather odd name comes from a particular kind of wild shrub that flourishes there. The two campaigns in the early twenties showed that the town was particularly prosperous in the Early Bronze Age. In Late Helladic III, however, a modest village had existed on and around the mound. It overlooked a limited amount of good agricultural land and, as we have mentioned, lay near a main land route from Corinth to Mycenae. Little towns at that period seem to have had limited scope for either political autonomy or cultural originality. "The rise of great strongholds and the concentration of royal power on the mainland," according to Blegen, "had no doubt completely subjected all the outlying small towns and reduced them to a common Mycenaeanized cultural level. . . . The dependency of Zygouries upon Mycenae, at any rate, is complete . . ."

Blegen excavated several basement rooms of a fairly large building that may have belonged to the local "mayor." At any rate, its size and the fragments of colored fresco would suggest that it was an important building. The basement rooms contained over 1,300 painted and plain vases of about twenty different shapes. Blegen refers to it as the Potter's Shop because the pots had never been used and seem to have been meant for sale. They had almost certainly been manufactured locally, perhaps in or near the building where they were found. They thus form a very valuable "closed deposit" (*i.e.,* all were exactly contemporary) illustrating almost the full repertory of shapes, size and decorative motifs of pottery that householders in this little community found attractive and useful. By this time, Blegen could date them fairly closely within the Helladic sequence worked out at Korakou and elsewhere; but he also refers to the important new dating criteria (which we will review later) being evolved by Wace at Mycenae in those same years.

By the time *Zygouries* was published, some critical reaction to the proposed Helladic system of chronology had begun to appear. Blegen is particularly unhappy about the insistence by some critics that the mainland scheme should correspond in every detail with the Cretan formulation. In a long footnote he writes:

The system is naturally modelled on Sir Arthur Evans' Minoan classification, which laid the foundations for all subsequent study in the field of Aegean chronology, but when applied to the mainland or to any other area outside of Crete, the subdivisions should and must correspond, not with a system worked out on the basis of internal evidence for Crete itself, nor with any fixed mathematical formula, but with the actual facts as revealed by excavations in the region in question. If they are to have any meaning in themselves they should and must correspond with the stratification.

So, in a sense, Blegen is already reflecting uneasiness about the rigidity of Evans' system, although he does not question its general applicability to the whole of Crete.

Two of the three campaigns at the Argive Heraion just south of Mycenae were carried out when Blegen was still on the staff of the American School; the last followed very soon after his move to Cincinnati. One can observe his commitment to prehistory, so clear in the proposal of an over-all formulation for Helladic chronology, gradually intensifying as time goes on. In the preliminary publication of the 1925 season at the Argive Heraion, for example, he refers politely to the "first major enterprise of the kind undertaken by the American School" at that same site from 1892 to 1895. Actually, in spite of Schliemann's startling prehistoric discoveries at nearby Mycenae and Tiryns, the whole interest and emphasis of that first American expedition had been on the later, classical ruins of the great sanctuary of Hera. Very little attention seems to have been paid to the evidence that the site had already been an important one in prehistoric times. Blegen simply points the contrast with characteristic charity and adds: "In the years which have passed since 1895 the wonderful discoveries of Sir Arthur Evans at Cnossus and of his Greek, Italian, English, and American colleagues in Crete, of the British School at Phylakopi in Melos, of the Germans at Tiryns, the researches of Tsountas, Wace and Thompson in Thessaly, of Professor Soteriades in Phocis [the Delphi area], and recently of the British School at Mycenae, to mention only a few, have added a vast amount of material and truly opened a new vista in prehistoric archaeology."

Before the end of his first season Blegen was convinced that "the pre-Hellenic settlement on the site, covering the whole extensive hill, was a very large and flourishing one, worthy to maintain its place in the Argolid beside the strongholds of Mycenae and Tiryns and possessed of a citadel of no mean strength." He believes that the dearth of imposing ruins is "due in large measure to the fact that the site continued for centuries to be occupied by the famous shrine of Argive Hera . . ." And he feels that the two epochs must somehow have a common denominator. "It hardly seems too bold a conjecture to hold that the cult of Hera is itself an heritage from this prehistoric settlement." Such continuity between prehistoric and later phases at several famous religious centers is now (1966) so obvious that coincidence is practically excluded.

A series of Middle Helladic graves and Late Helladic chamber tombs to the north and west of the habitation site had survived much better than the inhabited area. And it is largely the contents of the tombs that Blegen published so meticulously in *Prosymna: The Helladic Settlement Preceding the Argive Heraeum*. The first word of the title is the name that still clung to the site in Pausanias' day, and it has an authentic prehistoric sound. The expensive and beautiful publication, with a whole separate volume of plates, did not appear until 1937, nine years after the last campaign. Two busy years were occupied in cleaning and photographing and studying the tremendous variety of funeral offerings recovered from fifty chamber tombs. The text and illustrations were virtually complete in 1930, and the views expressed should be interpreted as belonging to Blegen's "pre-Troy phase."

The careful description of thousands of individual objects in *Prosymna* does not stand in the way of a synoptic view, although Blegen in his usual modest way understates his accomplishment. "This detailed account of the facts, which forms the major part of the present volume, is offered to meet the obligation that rests on every excavator to set forth in plain terms the results of his work, with the hope that it will prove useful to scholars who may be more competent than the writer to interpret the evidence in its broader historical, cultural and religious significance."

Blegen notes, for instance, that the Mycenaean cemetery was strung out for the better part of a mile to the northwest of the settlement. "Its position had apparently been determined by the course of an important highway connecting 'Prosymna' with Mycenae, and the tombs were evidently constructed on either side of the route, in the fashion that was still customary in the classical Greek period a thousand years later." And indeed, it is always worthwhile to search for the main cemetery of a Mycenaean site just to the west of the inhabited area—a location perhaps conceived as the first stage of the long western journey that the spirit of the dead must take when time had separated flesh and bones.

Clear-cut groups of chamber tombs at Prosymna may represent, as Tsountas thought at Mycenae, the presence of several different clans within the community. There were a few cases of cists dug in the dromoi, and they had clearly been used to accommodate material from earlier burials for which there was no longer room on the floor of the chamber tomb. In one case only, a burial of approximately the same date as those in the tomb was made in the fill of the dromos right above the doorway. "Was this perhaps," asks Blegen, "a slave or servitor, the victim of sacrifice or of self-destruction, who was laid to rest as the faithful guardian before the door of his master's sepulchre?" We recall that Tsountas had the same idea about burials found in a similar position at Mycenae. Solid evidence to confirm or refute such theories is very hard to obtain; and in fact we still do not know but are likely to be very skeptical nowadays.

Blegen is sure that the dromoi were completely filled in after each burial. He points out that the more numerous the burials inside the tomb, the more miscellaneous sherds occurred in the earth fill of the dromos. Some of these fragments definitely represent parts of vessels originally placed as offerings in the tomb, because sherds from the dromos and from the tomb chamber sometimes join. But Blegen also believes that the fill of the dromoi testifies to a custom of drinking a last toast or pouring a libation to the dead, and then smashing the cup against the door of the tomb. The door was always blocked up with a stone wall; and in the very few cases where one or more side chambers opened off the main one, their doors were similarly blocked. A few chambers contained niches (of uncertain use), and benches along one wall sometimes provided a kind of raised bed for a burial. The careful blocking of the entrance may have been meant to prevent the ghosts of the dead from disturbing the living (Fig. 74).

In about half of the tomb chambers a shallow cist had been cut in the floor. Occasionally there were several cists. In two cases they contained primary* (original) burials; in all others the burials were secondary*, *i.e.,* the bones had been moved after the flesh had rotted away. Often multiple remains, usually rather carelessly swept together, were found in a single cist. Broken pottery also occurred in the cists, with some pieces fitting on to others remaining on the floor of the chamber. Blegen notes that the remains from previous burials were often swept back around the walls to provide space in the center for a fresh burial. "It was clear," he writes, "that the actual physical remains of the dead were held in little respect, when the time came for a subsequent burial, at any rate." And he theorizes that the more precious offerings from previous burials were sometimes removed at the same time.

Even in the case of the final burial, the disposal of the body was often impossible to determine because of the collapse of the roof. But enough evidence was preserved to show that the orientation and posture varied. Some corpses had been extended on their backs, others laid on one side or the other; the legs were sometimes extended and sometimes flexed. Only one example occurred where the upper body had been propped up, as Tsountas believed was common at Mycenae. In one case, a wooden bier had apparently been left under the body, but the deceased was regularly laid directly on the floor. The Prosymna tombs contained only one example of the clay coffin, or larnax*, which was so popular in Crete. Blegen remarks that it is "the only larnax yet discovered in actual use in a Mycenaean chamber-tomb on the mainland of Greece. It was clearly not a

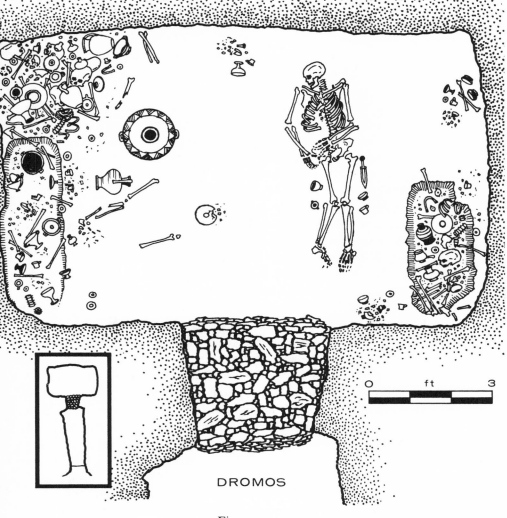

DROMOS

Figure 74

Mycenaean custom to bury in coffins of any kind." This sort of evidence should already have disturbed those who believed with Evans in a thoroughgoing "Minoization" of the mainland.

Only ten of the fifty Prosymna tombs showed evidence of fire, and two reflected rather heavy burning. In not a single case, however, could there be any question of cremation of a body on a pyre. Bones that had been exposed to the fire were burned only on the upper side. Blegen disagrees with those who interpret the burning as a regular part of funeral or commemorative ritual. If that were the explanation, he points out, all tombs ought to preserve traces of fire. His own explanation is that these fires were built for fumigation. "It must have happened occasionally that two or more members of the same family died within a comparatively short time of one another and that sepulchres sometimes had to be re-opened fairly soon after a preceding burial. Under such circumstances it is easy to imagine that need may have arisen for a drastic fumigation of the atmosphere in the chamber, and no better means toward this end could have been devised than to bring in a heap of brush or other fuel and to light a good fire in the tomb, perhaps thereby even combining a ritualistic with a practical purpose." In other tombs a layer of earth was strewn at intervals over the contents of the tomb, thus forming a series of stratified "floors." This practice, too, may have had the same effect as a fumigation by smoke.

The total number of individuals whose remains could be recognized in the fifty chamber tombs approached 500. Besides jewelry, weapons, tools, implements and terra-cotta figurines, almost 1,100 vases were reconstructed. They range in date all the way from the end of Middle Helladic to Late Helladic III. Blegen again underlines the strong element of mainland originality in Late Helladic pottery. "The rapid development of the local Middle Helladic style into the fully evolved Minoan-Mycenaean is particularly clear. This evolution under Cretan influence, although remarkably swift, appears from the evidence of the pottery to have been brought about through the deliberate initiative of the mainlanders themselves."

Presumably all or practically all of the vases had originally contained food or drink or other ingredients to minister to the comfort of the dead person. "It must be admitted," Blegen writes, "that no certain traces of food were observed in any vessel; but many of the large amphoras were found still closed with a tightly fitting lid—usually the inverted foot of a goblet or cylix—and it is not probable that such care would be taken to close an empty pot." In tombs where bones of children were observable, a characteristic spouted vessel interpreted as a "feeding bottle" was particularly common (Fig. 75B), as were terra-cotta figurines.

Even allowing fully for valuable funeral offerings being removed later by relatives, Blegen feels sure that the families who built and used the Prosymna chamber tombs were not wealthy and powerful nobles. "These tombs are those of ordinary citizens in the humbler walks of life: independent farmers, or artisans, rather than serfs or labourers. . . . We have, as it were, a cross-section of the average life of their time. And we see that the bearers of the culture known as Mycenaean were not a small band of feudal lords who had led a successful invasion from abroad and made themselves masters of the country, but the yeomen or burghers themselves, if the terms may be permitted, who must have constituted the sturdy sub-

Figure 75

structure of Mycenaean civilization." This is the typical quiet method of questioning Evans' pan-Minoan theories that Blegen is learning to use so effectively. His more outspoken friend Wace, as we shall see, had meanwhile tried the more direct challenge.

In 1928, the same year as his final campaign at Prosymna, Blegen published with Professor J. B. Haley an essay called "The Coming of the Greeks." It is an interesting attempt to combine the results of linguistic research with archaeological field exploration; and it had a strong influence on the discussion (which still continues) as to when the Greek mainland was first occupied by speakers of the branch of the Indo-European language family later known as Greek. Haley utilized evidence collected throughout the Aegean area for the occurrence of a large number of distinctive place-names that preserve suffixes such as -nthos (Corinth[os]) and -ssos (Parnassos). It had been generally agreed that they represent non-Indo-European, "pre-Greek" survivals; and Haley's data suggested that "the distribution of these names points to a pre-Greek linguistic family occupying in force Crete, the Cyclades, southern and eastern Peloponnesus and central Greece, with offshoots extending beyond to the north, northwest and west into the adjoining provinces."

Blegen's assignment was to test this evidence from the place-names against the known population distribution (as indicated by excavation or the study of surface pottery of habitation sites) of all prehistoric periods from neolithic down to Late Helladic. He found that concentrations of pre-Greek names seem to coincide most closely with the pattern of habitation in Early Helladic times. And he suggested that this congruence might have a significant connection with the archaeological evidence for a cultural "break" when many Early Helladic settlements were burned or abandoned, and the Middle Helladic gray Minyan pottery appeared about 1900. Blegen and Haley concluded that the "Minyan" newcomers most likely spoke an early form of the Greek language that was gradually adopted by most of the survivors among the conquered race. It would be natural, however, that a fair number of pre-Greek place-names and certain other common vocabulary items for plants, trees and the like would have been retained from the older language family.

Linguists like Professors P. Kretschmer and C. D. Buck had already inferred from the distribution of dialects in historical times that the Greek language must have been spoken on the mainland at least as early as 1400, and perhaps 1600. Blegen holds that after the coming of the "gray Minyan people" there is no comparable discontinuity in the development of mainland culture until after 1200, at the very end of the Bronze Age. And so Blegen and Haley strongly support the equation: makers of gray Minyan pottery = first speakers of the earliest dialect (or dialects) of Greek in the peninsula.

Here again we note the challenge to Evans' widely accepted theories. In fact, Blegen outlines the clearest counterreconstruction he has so far attempted.

In Crete the Early and Middle Minoan race and language presumably still continue to exist; but on the mainland we have almost certainly a different race, the descendants of those invaders who brought Minyan ware into Greece. They have now [*i.e.,* by LHI] come under powerful Minoan influence—so strong that many, with Evans, believe in a Minoan conquest of the mainland. . . . In Crete, perhaps as the result of invasion from abroad, perhaps from internal catastrophe, the great palaces were destroyed by fire at the end of Late Minoan II, and the succeeding stage shows only a feeble survival, probably under mainland domination. Some sites were undoubtedly abandoned for a time, at least; at any rate it looks as if henceforth two elements in the population must be taken into account: a subject class and a ruling caste, the latter not necessarily very numerous. It [the ruling class in LMIII Knossos] was presumably an offshoot from the powerful dynasties established at Mycenae and Tiryns in the Argolid; while the bulk of the population was almost surely still constituted by the survivors of the indigenous Minoan stock, who had surely not been exterminated. . . . These [pre-Greek] names [in Crete] surely go back to genuine Cretan traditions and records of an earlier age, and must have existed long before the invasion of the island by the people of the mainland in Late Helladic III.

So the lines are drawn. Evans' reconstruction postulated complete Minoan cultural domination of the mainland, beginning about 1600 with the Shaft Grave period and almost certainly including political control by a Minoan minority. At some point, probably long after 1600, Greek-speaking "Achaeans" did enter the mainland area from the north; but they did not achieve political ascendancy in Greece until after—probably long after—the destruction of the Minoan palaces. Evans reluctantly admitted in most of his publications that at some point in Late Minoan III (after 1400) the tide turned, and cultural dynamism as well as political power was centered on the mainland. But he regarded the possibility of any mainland political control in Crete before the very last phase of the Bronze Age as unproved and unlikely.

Blegen and Wace now openly advocate a clearly antithetical view. According to them, a Greek-speaking minority took over mainland political control soon after 2000. The invaders gradually fused with the Early Helladic survivors and the Greek language became dominant. After 1600 this blended mainland culture was under intensive Minoan cultural influence for a couple of centuries; but a sturdy mainland element can always be detected, and eventually it strongly reasserted itself. Minoans never had any widespread political control of the mainland. At some point fairly early in the third subdivision of Late Bronze and *possibly* as early as the time of the destruction of the great Minoan palaces about 1400, however, the Mycenaeans conquered Crete and became a ruling minority there.

TROY

No depreciation is intended of the sites that Blegen dug in his earlier career when we say that fate seems to have reserved his best years for the sites with the most important historical ties, *i.e.,* Troy and Pylos. When the University of Cincinnati Archaeological Expedition began work at Troy in 1932, Blegen was forty-five years old. Schliemann had turned forty-eight during his first Trojan campaign; and Evans was forty-nine at the beginning of the excavation of Knossos. By normal biological standards, all three were at the height of their physical and mental vigor as they began to probe these complex sites. Yet the contrast in terms of professional experience is vast. As we have seen, both Schliemann and Evans were completely innocent of previous training in excavation technique. Blegen, on the other hand, had more than twenty years behind him, most of it as director of major excavations. He had published definitive accounts of the results; he had the benefit of the accumulation of knowledge and improved methodology from two generations of pioneer investigations; and he had for years been closely associated with men like Hill and Wace with whom to discuss problems and share theories. Furthermore, he had an established position in a large university, the support and encouragement of his colleagues and all the time and financial backing he could desire.

These are tremendous advantages and Blegen made full use of them. Yet they do not fully account for the extraordinary importance of his excavations at Troy and Pylos; and the lack of previous experience and established reputation does not dim the luster of the earliest work at Troy and Mycenae and Knossos. There seems to be a deeper affinity, not fully explicable in terms of luck or experience, between the greatest excavators and the sites where they had their rendezvous with destiny. In a sense, perhaps, a great opportunity conscientiously seized may make the reputation of a man of no more than ordinary ability. But there is something almost mystical about the remarkable success of all three of these extraordinary men.

In the case of Troy, it was usually assumed after the appearance of Dörpfeld's monumental publication *Troja und Ilion* (1902) that, as far as excavation could prove decisive, the last word had been said about its major occupation phases and their historical connections. Before coming to Blegen's work, we must briefly carry on from a previous chapter the record of Dörpfeld's discoveries, particularly of the last campaign in 1894. For it was some nagging uncertainties connected with Dörpfeld's inferences that impelled Blegen to return to that patient mound and to extract from its still-undisturbed depths important new insights, particularly in connection with the Homeric songs. It is a measure of Dörpfeld's stature that he took an unselfish interest in the renewed excavations, thereby demonstrating the sincerity of what he wrote in 1902: "Later generations, which surely will be better equipped in the technique of excavation and in the understanding of the various finds than we, can through new excavations control and eventually improve on our work."

Dörpfeld first gives a useful review of Schliemann's discoveries up until 1890 as a basis for the discussion of his own campaigns in 1893 and 1894. Everywhere his affectionate respect shines out, along with a clear realization of the limitations under which the great pioneer worked. Both of Dörpfeld's own campaigns were concentrated on Troy VI, and the publication is adorned with his meticulous architectural plans. The well-preserved lower sections of the beautifully built fortifications, gates and towers were brought to light throughout more than half of the southern perimeter, and some sixteen contemporary houses were explored in the lower terraces just inside the walls. On the date of Troy VI, Dörpfeld can only repeat in 1902 what he had said ten years before. He is sure that the phase had a "long existence" and that the imported Mycenaean pottery places it roughly in the second half of the second millennium (1500–1000). "Finally," he writes, "one need scarcely mention that this dating is in harmony with the time-setting now held for the Trojan War and the destruction of the citadel by the Greeks." But such chronological calculations are still very obviously vague.

Dörpfeld proceeds to describe the new evidence for Schliemann's Level VII. The latest excavations showed that it comprised "two pre-Greek settlements," which were labeled VII¹ and VII². It is the earlier (lower) phase, VII¹, that Blegen was to find particularly interesting. Dörpfeld points out that its inhabitants probably repaired the fortifications of Troy VI and that its house walls often rest on the destroyed foundations of houses of Troy VI. Many houses of VII¹ were actually built against the old city wall, and he admits that in his preliminary reports they were mistaken for storerooms of the very last years of Troy VI. This mistake is in itself evidence of the lack of any clear layer of burning between.

The new settlement has in general smaller houses with more rooms. Dörpfeld thinks that they had belonged to "ordinary people," whereas the sturdier and roomier houses of Troy VI would have been occupied by "leaders and their dependents." Yet he is impressed by the general similarity, especially in pottery, and comes to the conclusion that the two settlements must have had "a similar population as inhabitants." He also explains his previous view that the small rooms were used for storage by pointing to the extraordinary number of large pithoi sunk up to their rims in the floors of many of them.

As for dating Troy VII¹, Dörpfeld says that the examination of the finds shows that "in the older houses of Level VII practically only such objects were found as also occur in Level VI." And he concludes that "the beginning of Level VII surely goes back, as the vase finds show, to the time of Mycenaean influence. Therefore, it is not impossible that the founding of Settlement VII falls in the last century of the second millennium . . ."

Hubert Schmidt wrote a separate report, entitled "The Pottery of the Various Layers," in Dörpfeld's publication. Schmidt had published in the same year a catalogue, the *Schliemann Collection of Trojan Antiquities* (a gift to the Berlin Museum). In discussing the pottery of "the Sixth, the Mycenaean Level," he maintains that, quite apart from the imported pottery, the native material betrays in its shapes and decoration strong influence from Mycenaean contacts and would by itself show that the culture of the mainland and Troy VI were contemporary. He stresses the association of Mycenaean pottery with the characteristic native monochrome ware that Schliemann had called "Lydian" and that was found on the house floors of Troy VI. And he insists on the "completely similar character" of the pottery of VI and VII[1]. In his judgment, "a distinction between older and younger layers [in terms of ceramics] is completely impossible."

In the same publication, Alfred Götze provides a catalogue and brief analysis in the "Small Finds of Metal, Stone, Bone, etc.," covering all phases of the Trojan excavations. This is, above all, a convenient review of the rich contents of Schliemann's various "treasures" from the second level. But, coming to Levels VI and VII[1], Götze contrasts the rarity of the small finds with the abundance of pottery; and he consequently believes that these levels had been thoroughly pillaged. Finally, he observes that such small finds as there are, especially those from Level VII[1], often betray the influence of Mycenaean models.

It is understandable, therefore, that as Blegen saw the situation almost a generation later, certain questions occurred to him that might be settled by further excavations. Above all, the last word had scarcely been said on the transition from Troy VI to VII[1]. Exactly what was the relationship, now that Mycenaean pottery was so much better known, between the imported pottery in the two levels? Could further evidence be discovered about the way in which each had been destroyed or abandoned? Could such new evidence, if forthcoming, be used to establish a sharper and clearer connection between the archaeological history of the site and the epic story of its destruction by Agamemnon and his Greek allies? Nor was Blegen's interest exclusively confined to the history of Troy in the Late Bronze Age. He was eager to reexamine the basis for the reconstruction of Trojan prehistory at every stage, since its position marked it as a natural link between the Aegean area and the still relatively unexplored hinterland of northwest Anatolia.

So in the spring of 1932 a University of Cincinnati Expedition arrived at Hissarlik, with Professor Semple as general director, Blegen as field director and a large staff of able young archaeologists, most of whom had been trained under Blegen himself. For seven successive seasons they returned to continue excavation in areas not too much disturbed by their predecessors. The full account of the results was published between 1950 and 1958 in a series of four bulky volumes called *Troy: Excavations Conducted by the University of Cincinnati, 1932–38.*

This very detailed report is superior in most ways to those that Schliemann and Dörpfeld had left for the guidance of future scholars. But it is only fair to say that, between the days of Schliemann and Blegen, archaeological publications have—perhaps inevitably—been written more and more for specialists. An interested layman of Schliemann's day might—and no doubt did—read the bulky publications on Troy and Mycenae from cover to cover. But even the most enthusiastic nonspecialist would be very unlikely to get very far with Dörpfeld's or Blegen's multivolume reports. So, it is fortunate—and perhaps a symptom of a renewed awareness between specialists and interested laymen—that Blegen has himself written a short factual account, *Troy and the Trojans* (1963), which is meant to provide a simplified but trustworthy summary of the newest evidence on Trojan prehistory.

In his review of previous work, Blegen too pays a sincere tribute to Schliemann: "The glory of discovering Troy and making it known to the world is his, and his fame was fairly won. . . . From his own mistakes he himself learned—and he was very quick at learning. He was a pioneer, and all those who have come after him have profited from his experience. By the end of his career he had made himself an experienced, trained, observant excavator who could hold his own with anyone . . ." Of Dörpfeld, too, he speaks with warmth; and in *Troy and the Trojans* there is a photograph of the sturdy old man taken during a visit to the Cincinnati excavations.

Using all the newest techniques of stratigraphy, Blegen learned from his painstaking researches how extremely complicated is the full story of the history of human habitation at Hissarlik. He was able to retain the nine major levels distinguished by Schliemann and refined by Dörpfeld. But he showed that each of them included two to eight subphases, representing, in all, forty-nine major and minor catastrophes and reconstructions over at least some areas of the site.

We can dispose very quickly with the new discoveries regarding Levels I through V, since there was no longer any question of their connection with Homeric Troy. But those whose curiosity was aroused by our review of Schliemann's discoveries and theories concerning the earlier levels will be interested in a brief survey of the newer interpretation. Detailed pottery analysis proved that these phases represent over 1,000 years of habitation, corresponding to the Early Bronze Age in the Aegean area, *i.e.,* before about 1900. Schliemann had been right in his inference, based mainly on the pottery, that there had been no detectable cultural disruption (and presumably therefore no major incursion of new people) during all that time. The megaron plan, for instance, has a continuous vogue from Troy I right down to Troy VII; and it now appears likely that this distinctive ground plan reached the Aegean from or via Anatolia. Virtually the same type of "idol," or amulet*, persists from Troy I through V.

A settlement not far away, where the Scamander River empties into the Dardanelles, shows characteristics similar to the earliest copper-using culture of Troy I; but in still lower levels it had a purely neolithic, stone-using population. So it is a fair inference that people from this or similar communities were the first inhabitants of the site that was later to become so famous and important. The hill of Hissarlik, far lower of course at that time, was soon fortified and presumably continued from then on until the end of the Bronze Age to be *the* stronghold in northwest Asia Minor. Though admittedly insufficient, exploration of the interior of Asia Minor so far suggests that Troy's major cultural contacts were always with the west and mainly by sea, rather than with the Asiatic hinterland. Comparable sea-oriented communities have been discovered since Schliemann's and Dörpfeld's day in the northern Aegean, most notably at Thermi on the island of Lesbos and at Poliochni on Lemnos.

The great megaron in the center of the fortified area of Troy II with its flanking dependencies is curiously reminiscent of the much later Mycenaean palace. It must represent the headquarters of a dynasty that had succeeded in acquiring political control over a prosperous agricultural, industrial and trading center. In addition to income from legal trade, these early Trojan chiefs may have added to their "treasures" by piratical expeditions. The tremendous fire that brought the final (seventh) phase of Troy II to an end about 2300 was clearly so sudden that the inhabitants had no time to carry away their valuables and so complete that the survivors, if there were any, were not able to rescue them later. Hence, Schliemann's fabulous discoveries more than 4,000 years later.

The Cincinnati expedition carefully preserved and recorded all the animal bones for analysis by a zoologist, Professor M. N. Gejvall. The remarkable number of sheep bones in the debris of Troy II indicates that sheep raising was a major occupation of the population. Connecting this evidence with the tremendous number of spindle whorls found in this and succeeding levels, Blegen makes the very attractive suggestion that the production of woollen textiles was a major Trojan industry.

A hint at the extent of Trojan trade, direct or indirect, is provided by the fact that the finest of Schliemann's magnificent polished battle-axes of nephrite and other exotic material find their closest parallels in far away Bessarabia. Perhaps, too, the bronze weapons from the "treasures" are royal imports or loot to be distinguished from the run-of-the-mill copper artefacts made and used by the Trojans themselves.

Another interesting result of analysis of the animal bones is that in the time of Troy III the diet was supplemented to a spectacular extent by the consumption of venison. Blegen suggests that this might be explained by the invention of some much more effective hunting technique or by an ecological change such as a shift of climate.

Blegen fully agrees with the verdict of his predecessors that Level VI marks the advent of a new people who had little in common with the culture of earlier phases. It was, he says, "a town which in its buildings seems to have followed a wholly independent plan that took no account of walls of houses and streets that had gone before. . . . A survey of the ruins . . . and of the miscellaneous objects and pottery recovered from them reveals at once striking differences and innovations. . . . The changes seem to me so unheralded, so widespread, and so far-reaching that they can only be explained as indicating a break with the past, and the arrival and establishment on the site of a new people endowed with a heritage of its own."

He admits that in Troy V "the ruins showed no recognisable signs of a devastating fire, nothing to suggest an attack and capture by enemies with the use of force and violence." But there is always the possibility of a relatively peaceable take-over by powerful newcomers or of a new occupation after a period of abandonment. In any case, Blegen points to such novel cultural features in Troy VI as technical changes and improvements in fortifications, solid freestanding houses that are widely spaced on gradually rising concentric terraces and the general use of bronze in contrast to copper. A particularly interesting innovation is the advent of the domesticated horse, shown by the scientific study of the animal bones. This trait has important implications for the origin of the newcomers and suggests the appropriateness of Homer's epithet, "horse-taming," for the later Trojans.

The most important novelty, however, was the sudden appearance in Troy VI of a very distinctive smooth gray wheel-made pottery with new, more angular shapes. This fabric had of course been recognized since Schliemann's "Lydian" designation. Blegen shows that in the earlier phases of Troy VI it is identical with the well-known gray Minyan mainland pottery, the hallmark of the newcomers to Greece at the beginning of the Middle Helladic period. So it appears that the people who had invaded Greece and those responsible for the new culture of Troy VI were either identical or closely related. We realize at once that such a situation has intriguing implications for the identity and language of friend and foe at the time of the Trojan War.

Blegen also notes the gradual increase in Troy VI of the importation of the second distinctive type of Middle Helladic pottery, the so-called

matt-painted ware. And, as time went on, the Trojan potters copied
Mycenaean vase shapes in their gray Minyan fabric. He recovered a whole
series of locally made and imported pottery that was fairly closely datable
from mainland analogies. So he was able to set the time limits for the occupation of Troy VI much more accurately, from the early part of the Middle
Bronze until well on in the Late Bronze Age. The gray Minyan of the
earliest level seems to be best paralleled by mainland ware of about 1800,
and the actual Mycenaean imports of the latest phase are identical with
mainland pots of the beginning of Late Helladic IIIB, about 1300. So
Troy VI had a long and complex existence through eight major phases for
somewhat over half a millennium.

It is remarkable how little evidence has ever been recovered for the
burial customs of the prehistoric Trojans. The few adult burials found
within the walls were clearly exceptional, and there can be no doubt that
the cemeteries were outside the fortifications. All three of the excavators
have successively searched carefully but without much success. Schliemann
mentions this specifically as a major purpose of one of his campaigns, and
Blegen too had it prominently in mind.

Although earlier cemeteries still eluded him, Blegen did discover a badly
disturbed cemetery belonging to a late phase of Troy VI. It lay about a
third of a mile south of the acropolis and contained a fair number of pottery
jars or urns in which had been placed burned bits of human bones along
with a few gifts and offerings. The proof that cremation was the burial rite
in Troy VI is a significant discovery, and its use might help to explain the
lack of evidence for burials from earlier levels. But the most interesting
implication concerns "Homeric" versus Mycenaean burial customs. The
archaeological evidence, of course, shows that inhumation was practically
universal on the Mycenaean mainland, whereas rites of cremation are
invariably described in the *Iliad*. We shall have more to say on this theme
at a later stage.

Blegen was also able to settle, to his own satisfaction and that of most
specialists, the problem of how Troy VI was finally destroyed. The upper
sections of the monumental fortification and house walls were toppled over
and flung about as if by a giant hand far more powerful than any human
agency. There were no convincing signs of a general conflagration, in spite
of Dörpfeld's contrary though not very firmly expressed opinion. And there
was evidence (which Dörpfeld had freely admitted) that the site was
immediately reoccupied by the same people. To such a set of circumstances,
particularly in the Aegean area, there is a fairly obvious explanation. Troy
VI, the mightiest stronghold ever to crown the mound of Hissarlik, was
completely destroyed about 1300 by a violent earthquake. Therefore, if any

confidence can be felt in myth and tradition, the Troy of the final phase of Level VI could not be the Troy captured by the Greeks. Poseidon, the lord of the rumbling earth tremors, not Agamemnon and his host, ruined Troy VI.

But was there another candidate that could be associated with the Greek siege? After all, ancient tradition placed the capture of Troy a century or more after 1300. What about the fortress that was built so quickly over the ruins of Troy VI? Dörpfeld had been clearly embarrassed by the questions raised and left unanswered by his Level VII[1]. Blegen's new discoveries and observations about that phase, which he relabeled VIIa, suggested a plausible solution.

The last inhabitants of Troy VI were apparently warned in advance and were able to save their lives and their more valuable goods. They returned "within a few days" to the ruined site and hurriedly rebuilt the fortifications with rather heterogeneous materials. They utilized other fallen blocks and scraps to build themselves shelters, not on the plan of the heavy structures of Troy VI but consisting of a maze of small crowded rooms. Into the floors they sank large numbers of storage jars covered with slabs, which further reinforces the impression of crowding and of the expectation that they might soon have to withstand a siege.

The pottery on the house floors indicates that Troy VIIa may have existed for no more than a single generation. The forms and fabrics carry on uninterruptedly the fashions of the final phase of Troy VI. There was continuing contact with mainland centers, though the quantity of imported pottery was perhaps somewhat reduced. Blegen analyzes it as follows: "The associated Mycenaean pottery includes many fragments with painted decoration in the style of Mycenaean III A, although the greater part belongs to the early stages of III B; the Grey Minyan Ware, moreover, differs little if at all from that of Phase VIh [the last phase of Level VI]. The overthrow of Settlement VIIa must surely have been brought about by 1250 B.C., if not a decade or two earlier." Other scholars have since suggested that the latest Mycenaean pottery associated with Troy VIIa is somewhat later, in fact too late to be accommodated with other evidence for the date of the Greek siege; but Blegen holds firmly to his original opinion and has in fact slightly raised his estimate recently (1962) to "the decade around 1270 or 1260."

And how was Troy VIIa destroyed? Blegen's firm answer is that "the destruction was undoubtedly the work of human agency, and it was accompanied by violence and by fire. A great mass of stones and crude brick, along with other burned and blackened debris, was heaped up over the ruined houses as well as in the streets . . ." Amid the wreckage the Cincinnati excavators came upon several human skeletons or parts of them that gave the impression that these people had been the victims of violent death.

Blegen believes that only one conclusion fits the new data.

Here, then, in the extreme northwestern corner of Asia Minor—exactly where Greek tradition, folk memory and the epic poems place the site of Ilios—we have the physical remains of a fortified stronghold, obviously the capital of the region. As shown by persuasive archaeological evidence, it was besieged and captured by enemies and destroyed by fire, no doubt after having been thoroughly pillaged, just as Hellenic poetry and folk-tale describe the destruction of King Priam's Troy. . . . It is Settlement VIIa, then, that must be recognised as the actual Troy, the ill-fated stronghold, the siege and capture of which caught the fancy and imagination of contemporary troubadours and bards who transmitted orally to their successors their songs about the heroes who fought in the war. There were no doubt many additions as well as excisions of incident or detail from time to time in the long course of transmission until in the hands of a poetic genius the various separate lays were fused together into the epics that have come down to us.

And so another episode has been added to the record of how archaeological evidence and the Homeric tradition are linked in the famous tale of Troy. Whether Blegen has written the final chapter is not yet clear. But rumblings in some quarters would suggest that not everyone is satisfied with his reconstruction. Like Schliemann and Dörpfeld, Blegen no doubt hopes and believes that he has finally settled the problem. But all three have always sought the truth above all else, and each would be willing to abandon his position if later evidence proved that the truth was not in it.

At about the time that he was completing his excavation at Troy, Blegen coauthored with Wace an important article that appeared in a German historical journal. Entitled "Pottery as Evidence for Trade and Colonisation in the Aegean Bronze Age," the essay is a plea for greater care and precision by archaeologists and historians in drawing sweeping conclusions about trade relationships from ceramic evidence. They show that there is already a basis to distinguish the likely origin of certain vase shapes and decorative motifs. "The stirrup vase, the low alabastron* [Fig. 76], a particular form of squat jug, and the kylix, though the first at least originated in Crete, are far more popular on the Mainland side and certain patterns, the ogival canopy* for instance, are practically unknown on vases of undoubted Cretan manufacture."

They also point to the pressing need for more study to distinguish provenience (point of origin) in terms of fabric—that is, types of clay,

Figure 76

presence of impurities, techniques of manufacture. They deplore the ambiguity in the writing of some historians and archaeologists who use the terms "Mycenean" and especially "Late Minoan" to refer to the whole Aegean area in the Late Bronze Age. "Late Helladic" and "Late Minoan" should be used, they insist, for the mainland and for Crete respectively, if the origin can be ascertained; otherwise, the more neutral "Late Bronze" would be less misleading.

Blegen and Wace are also concerned about the persisting belief in Minoan control of trade with the Near East far into the Late Bronze Age.

> The great spread of Mycenaean influence down the coasts of Syria and Palestine and to Egypt during and after the Amarna period, that is after the fall of Knossos, came from the mainland and not from Crete and probably via Rhodes and Cyprus and the south coast of Asia Minor. There is even evidence that the mainland was in touch with these regions before 1400 B.C. In Egypt several L.H.I and II vases have been found . . . No certain Cretan pottery of later date [than Middle Minoan] has yet been found on either the Syrian or the Palestinian coast. In Egypt Late Minoan I and II pottery is very rare. . . . Recent research shows that most of the so called L.M.I pottery from Egypt is not Cretan but Helladic. This to some degree parallels the discoveries in Syria and Palestine and shows that the plentiful L.H.III imports into Egypt were anticipated to a certain extent by L.H.I and II imports. . . . More than eight times as many mainland (Helladic) as Cretan (Minoan) vases from Egypt in the period L.B. [Late Bronze] I and II, the sixteenth and fifteenth centuries B.C., are now known.

So Blegen and Wace raise serious doubts about the widely accepted thesis of a "Minoan thalassocracy" in control of the whole eastern Mediterranean at least as late as the destruction of the Cretan palaces. They are equally skeptical about the assumption that the occurrence of pottery of "Mycenaean" type in Sicily and south Italy proves that there was regular Minoan trade with the west. "Mr. [Thomas] Dunbabin who has carefully examined these vases agrees that they are not Cretan. . . . They seem to him . . . to resemble the wares of Argolis and Rhodes and therefore more likely to come from an Aegean centre."

Also, interesting historical implications about early rivalry between mainland and Cretan traders are opened up by the pottery from both areas discovered in the Aegean islands, particularly at Phylakopi on Melos. "Already in the Middle Bronze Age," Blegen and Wace insist, "the people of the Mainland were in touch with the Islands, but the extreme scarcity of their pottery in Crete hints that direct relations between the Mainland and Crete were rare and not cordial. In the first two phases of the Late Bronze Age Mainland and Cretan pottery occur at Phylakopi side by side. In the temple repositories at Knossos, where Melian vases were found, Mainland pottery is conspicuous by its absence."

They continue to question the common assumption—based almost entirely on Evans' interpretation of the archaeological evidence—that Crete had political control of the mainland, at least in the earlier phases of the Late Bronze Age.

The theory of a Cretan conquest or colonisation of the Mainland has been taken too much for granted. There is no greater Cretan influence in the Peloponnese than there is Greek in Etruria and the Greeks never conquered or occupied Etruria. In L.H.I and II the vases of undoubted Cretan manufacture found on the Mainland are extremely few, though it is true that Cretan shapes and patterns were widely imitated on the Mainland just as Greek models were copied and adapted by the Etruscans. Further there are signs of Mainland reaction on Crete. Professor [Aeilko Sebo] Snijder has suggested that the big "Palace Style" amphorae which in Crete seem to have been made only at Knossos, but on the Mainland occur almost everywhere, Mycenae, Kakovatos, Vaphio, Argive Heraeum, Berbati, Thorikos, really have their origin on the Mainland. The Ephyraean goblets of the Mainland are imitated in Crete in L.M.II in a conventionalized manner. The differences seen by Snijder, [Martin] Nilsson, [Gerhart] Rodenwaldt, and Karo in the psychology of art, in burial customs, in architecture and in many other points between Crete and the Mainland all tell heavily against the theory of a Cretan conquest or colonisation which has been based on archaeological evidence that will not stand serious critical examination. This theory should therefore no longer be allowed to cloud the historical implications of the archaeological evidence of the Late Bronze Age in the Aegean.

By the time this article appeared Evans was a very old man, and World War II was imminent. No counterattack issued from the Minoan camp; and indeed the mounting evidence had already made Evans' position difficult to defend.

PYLOS

Blegen's excavations at Troy ended in 1938, *Prosymna* had finally appeared the year before and the preparation of the definitive publication on Troy would require years of preparation. For the first time in almost a decade the spring and summer of 1939 were free to follow up another problem that had for years piqued his curiosity. It had, in fact, intrigued a good many scholars ever since antiquity. Where was Nestor's Pylos? Blegen and Dr. Konstantinos Kourouniotis, director of the National Museum in Athens, had for some time held an unpopular belief. They thought there was a good chance that Nestor's capital had been located somewhere close to the great bay of Navarino (see Map VII) in southwest Messenia. And they believed that careful field exploration in that area might be worthwhile.

It is a striking reminder of the youthful state of Mycenaean archaeology (or of the ravages of time—or of the lack of Homeric historicity) that very few of the capitals of the thirty-odd rulers of independent kingdoms listed in Homer's Catalogue of Ships have yet been discovered. If tradition can be trusted, each king had a citadel and palace. The general location, even the exact acropolis, is fairly safely identified in a number of cases. Yet in 1939 only three such citadels had been extensively explored. Agamemnon's Mycenae was the starting point. The kings who ruled at Tiryns and at Gla in Boeotia were not certainly known. The ruins of the palace once occupied by Oedipus' family were known to lie beneath the modern town of Thebes; but according to tradition borne out by minor excavation it had been in ruins before the Trojan War. A good deal of exploration had failed to locate convincingly even the palaces of notable leaders such as Odysseus, Menelaos and Achilles.

Old Nestor, King of Pylos, is of course a figure of comparable prestige to these protagonists in the Homeric songs; and most of the handbooks of the first half of the present century list his palace as one of the few that

are definitely known. But the results of Blegen's explorations strongly challenged this confident assumption, just as he had shown the error of the
identification of Troy VI with Priam's capital.

The early stages of the Pylos controversy carry us back at least as far as
the classical period. Blegen states the problem in his usual precise manner.

> The Dorian Invasion, whatever its source and however it ran its course,
> has left a broad gash, like a fire-scar in a mountain forest, cutting
> through the archaeological panorama of ancient Greek history. Many
> towns and settlements that flourished in the preceding Heroic Age were
> henceforth abandoned or declined to a state of insignificance. Even
> some of the great and noted strongholds sank into virtual oblivion, and
> the places where they had stood were lost from the view of men. In
> late antiquity the site of Troy itself, in spite of all literary fame, was
> no longer remembered, and academic circles disputed as to its identifi-
> cation. Exactly the same fate overtook Pylos, Sandy Pylos, the seat of
> the Neleid King Nestor, where Telemachos was so hospitably enter-
> tained on his famous journey described in the Odyssey.[65]

In classical times it was almost universally believed that Nestor's capital
had been built on the high rocky citadel of Koryphasion (now called Palaio-
kastro, "Old Castle") at the northwest corner of the bay of Navarino (see
Map VII). Those frowning cliffs are now crowned with a ruined fortification
dating back at least to Frankish, Venetian and Turkish days. In the northern face of the cliff Pausanias saw what is still called the Cave of Nestor,
and somewhere nearby he was shown the House of Nestor.[66] But doubting
voices had already been raised centuries before Pausanias' time. The chief
objector to the Koryphasion site was the geographer Strabo. We have
noticed that he played a similar role in the Hissarlik controversy, and in
each case he seems to have been simply expanding on the views of certain earlier scholars. Strabo apparently enjoyed jolting popular opinion by
supporting an unorthodox view. And he was, above all, a firm believer in
the literal truth of the Homeric poems. Compared to Strabo, Schliemann
was almost a skeptic! Strabo had absolutely no doubts that Homer was
personally acquainted with every detail of geography and topography
referred to in the poems.

Strabo pointed out that there were actually *three* spots on or near the
west coast of the Peloponnese to which the name Pylos belonged.[67] He
immediately eliminated the northern one because its location does not fit
the Homeric account. But he set out with great energy and persuasiveness
to prove that the middle, or "Triphylian," Pylos accords far better with
Homer's allusions than does the generally accepted "Messenian" Pylos on
the great southern bay. The crux of his arguments concerns specific dis-

tances and routes of communication. The southern site, he thinks, is much too far away from Ithaka and the Alpheios River to fit Homer's description of either Telemachos' voyage[68] or the driving of the captured flocks and herds to Pylos after Nestor's victory on the banks of the Alpheios.[69] Also, the southern site is unsuited to Telemachos' journey by chariot from Pylos to Sparta,[70] since the lofty Taygetos mountains bar the way; whereas a much easier route from the Triphylian site skirts the northern end of the higher mountains. And, in addition, Strabo's notion of the location of the other eight "cities" of Nestor's kingdom, listed in the Catalogue of Ships,[71] suggested to him a cluster of major towns in the vicinity of the central, Triphylian Pylos.

It is difficult to say how much impact Strabo's view had on his contemporaries; but if one takes literally some of Homer's geographical descriptions, it can be argued that singers (and audiences?) in the interval between Mycenaean times and Homer's own day may have confused or conflated the two locations. In any case, we can return to the topographical problem more profitably when new facts, utterly unknown to Strabo, have been assimilated.

The general tendency between Strabo's time and the beginning of the present century was to hold with the prevailing ancient view that Nestor had lived at the southern (Messenian) Pylos. Then a new factor swung opinion heavily to Strabo's thesis. Wilhelm Dörpfeld plays the leading role in this episode, and it is one of the many ironies of our story that Blegen was destined to revise Dörpfeld's conclusions about Pylos just as he had in the case of Troy. In 1907 Dörpfeld was informed that peasants in the village of Kakovatos had discovered a tholos tomb and were carrying off the stones from its walls. He hurried to the rescue and began a careful excavation. It turned out that three large tholoi had been constructed in a slope looking down toward the sea across a fertile coastal plain some two miles in width. As usual, the tombs had been robbed in antiquity, and the domes had later collapsed; but a number of small finds and a mass of broken pottery remained. From the fragments Dörpfeld was able to reconstruct several large amphoras of the Palace Style, closely comparable to those that Evans was finding at Knossos and that he dated in Late Minoan II. So it was a fair inference that somewhere near the Kakovatos tholoi at about the same time as the latest palace phase at Knossos, at least three generations of a mainland dynasty had lived and died. Evans and his followers saw in the pottery and other contents of the Kakovatos tholoi further evidence of Cretan domination of the mainland, in both cultural and political terms.

Dörpfeld examined the flat hilltop that faced the tholoi immediately to

the south, and on its badly eroded surface he discovered the ruins of fortifications within which were the foundations of at least one sizable building. Dörpfeld remembered Strabo's theory and realized that Kakovatos is
in the district called Triphylia in ancient as well as modern times. So he
quite understandably believed that he had discovered Nestor's capital. The
mediocre ruins on the acropolis became a "palace," and he persuasively
reargued Strabo's case, adding some ingenious points of his own. Hardly
a dissenting voice was raised. Strabo and Dörpfeld were right; the almost
unanimous ancient and modern opinion had been mistaken. The capital
of the Homeric kingdom of Pylos was at Kakovatos. The ninety ships that
Nestor led against Troy had been launched from the broad sandy beach
near Kakovatos. The local inhabitants enthusiastically renamed the site
Nestora.

But there were soon a few minor discordant notes. In 1919 Kourouniotis
excavated a tholos tomb that had been discovered near Tragana, a village
located on the rim of hills about three miles north of the bay of Navarino
(see Map VII). Excavation showed that it had been built at approximately
the same time as those at Kakovatos and that there had been a succession
of burials—or at least offerings—in it until the early Iron Age. Kourouniotis
also located but did not excavate a second tholos nearby. So the southern
Pylos had a pair of royal tombs to rival Kakovatos.

Six years later a local tomb-hunter, Charalambos Christophilopoulos,
led Kourouniotis to the site of a third tholos in the southern area. It lay in
almost flat ground, just south of the modern village of Koryphasion which is
located slightly closer to the bay than the Tragana tombs. Its dromos
could not have been horizontal, unless the whole domed chamber had
been built above ground. And, in fact, the entrance proved to have sloped
downward quite steeply to provide access to a chamber deeply hollowed
below ground level. Its original exterior appearance would have been
similar to that of the usual tholoi built into a side-hill; that is, the dome
above the level of the lintel would have protruded above ground and been
covered with a protecting mound of earth. There was another novel feature about the Koryphasion tholos, although it was not recognized at the
time. Some of the vases put together from the broken pottery on its floor
date considerably earlier than any pottery in previously discovered tholoi.
In fact, some of them seem to belong to the last years of the Middle Helladic period. This would mean, unless there was a very long cultural lag
in Messenia versus Argolis, that the Koryphasion tholos was approximately
contemporary with the Shaft Graves at Mycenae.

As time went on Kourouniotis and Blegen confirmed the existence of
several additional tholoi in the southern area; but these discoveries near

Messenian Pylos did not cause many scholars to shift their allegiance from Kakovatos. Tholos tombs were turning up fairly frequently in many parts of south and east central Greece. It was vaguely conceded that their presence should indicate that a royal citadel had existed in the vicinity; but the Triphylian connections of Nestor had by then become an article of faith that few had the courage to challenge.

Blegen and Kourouniotis, however, were becoming increasingly skeptical. It seemed to them that the Homeric evidence, taken as a whole, does not rule out the southern site; and indeed this is proved by the fact that antiquity, so slavishly devoted to the literal truth of the poems, generally opted for the Messenian Pylos. They also saw that the southern location had various natural advantages. Here was the biggest, best watered and most fertile plain along the whole west coast south of the Alpheios River. Here was the magnificent sheltered bay, an invaluable base for the naval power that sent the second-largest contingent of ships to Troy. While taking seriously the strong ancient tradition about the general location, they did not agree with it that Nestor's capital would necessarily have been built on the great rock of Koryphasion, so exposed to storms and sudden attack from the sea. They preferred to begin by searching the hills and ridges that lay inland from the plain in the general vicinity of the tholos tombs.

So, in the spring of 1939 Blegen organized a very modest exploratory campaign. Kourouniotis kept in close touch with developments and managed to snatch a few days from his duties in Athens for a visit to Messenia. Blegen and his associates ranged the country by car and on foot, not searching blindly but with certain definite aims. By that time, the Mycenaean pottery that had been used in the days of Nestor and the Trojan War was well known. One characteristic sherd could by its shape or fabric or decoration provide a clue to a habitation site. A concentration of such pieces on the surface of a plowed hilltop or a weathered slope provided sure evidence. The expedition was able to locate several new habitation sites and tholos tombs, in addition to those that had been previously located.

There were other criteria, too. Nestor's palace would probably have been located on a defensible hill commanding a clear view all around, and especially toward the bay. It would have had to be readily accessible from the sea by road. There should still be a good supply of fresh water within easy reach. Perhaps one could even hope to find some fragments of fortification or house walls still protruding above the surface or recently exposed by cultivation or an earth slide.

After a thorough search, Blegen decided that a hilltop about five miles north of the bay best suited these requirements. It is called Ano (or

Epano, *i.e.,* "upper") Englianos, and it lies right beside the main highway
—actually a miserable, bumpy, winding track in those days—which leads
inland along a ridge and approximately at right angles to the coast. The
road had been cut into the south side of the hill, exposing characteristic
Mycenaean pottery of the thirteenth century. And on the hilltop there was
a spot among the olive trees where a big solid knob protruded above the
ground. Although it looked like Roman concrete, it could be limestone
calcined by fire. At a slightly higher level a quarter of a mile farther inland
there was a fairly good spring that was fed by a whole line of copious
sources extending right up to the Aigaleon mountains paralleling the
coast.

On April 4, Blegen laid out the first trench across the hilltop of Ano
Englianos. The sequel is the dramatic stuff of which movies are made
but that seldom happens in the real context of slow, unexciting, uncomfortable and often disappointing archaeological exploration. Within a
couple of hours Blegen knew that toward the end of the Bronze Age a
very large building (or complex of buildings) had stood on the hill and
had been destroyed in a great fire. This discovery seemed likely to be the
evidence he and Kourouniotis had hoped for in the search for Nestor's
palace. But that was not all. By incredible good luck the first trench exposed the ruins of a little room that still contained broken clay tablets
inscribed in a writing system that seemed on first impression to be identical
with Evans' "Minoan" Linear B. So, here in Messenia, far distant from
the Mycenaean "heartland" of northeast Peloponnese, Blegen discovered
the earliest cache of written records then known on the continent of Europe.
Tsountas and others had apparently been wrong. The Mycenaean civilization, at least in the Pylos area, *was* a literate one.

The repercussions of this epoch-making discovery were wide enough,
but it must be remembered that the Linear B script had not been deciphered. Evans had tried for forty years and failed. Furthermore, he had
published only a fraction of the Knossos material, which meant that other
scholars anxious to work on the decipherment were seriously handicapped.
Practically everyone took it for granted, as Evans did, that all of the Cretan
tablets, both those written in Linear A and Linear B, presented the puzzle
not only of unknown scripts but also of an unknown "Minoan" language.
The Linear B tablets at Pylos did not directly challenge that assumption.

Blegen's preliminary publication of the results of the 1939 campaign
naturally reflects extreme caution on this point. "We need not hesitate to
say, with all due reserve, that the script used in our palace is almost certainly a modified or adapted form of the Knossian Linear B. Whether our
documents were written in the Minoan language or in a quite different

tongue cannot yet be stated with safety, though the former alternative seems to be almost certain." We wonder if his friend Wace would have agreed with that final clause.

In fact, the Pylos tablets could be and were taken by some to reinforce Evans' long-held theory of Minoan domination of major mainland centers. Could they not reflect the administration of a Cretan "government" of Pylos? But the date proved troublesome. Few doubted the orthodox view that the destruction of the mighty palace of Minos should be assigned to about 1400, and that only "miserable squatters" inhabited the ruins thereafter. The Linear A writing system may have been continued to a very limited degree in other parts of the island; but Evans had decided, after a good deal of vacillation, that Linear B came to an end with the "final" destruction of the Knossos palace about 1400. Yet the pottery on the floors of the burned palace at Pylos, including the archives room, seemed to date much later. "We think," says Blegen, "this destruction cannot have occurred before 1200 B.C., in round figures, and that it may indeed have come about considerably later. . . . We are thus inevitably led to the conclusion that the tablets must be dated at the earliest to the close of the thirteenth century B.C., that is, to a period when, it is almost universally agreed among archaeologists and historians, an early strain of Hellenic stock has already long been established in control of the Greek mainland."

A Knossian governor and a Minoan-speaking palace bureaucracy at Pylos were rather difficult to accept at so late a date, but Evans had lately theorized (as we shall see) about just such a move from Knossos to Mycenae. Cretan control of mainland centers might have become localized and have held on, at least at Pylos, for two centuries. This is said to have been the immediate reaction of the aged Evans. Yet evidence had been accumulating for a generation that it was the mainlanders who were masters of the eastern Mediterranean after 1400, if not earlier. Martin Nilsson, one of the greatest authorities on Greek prehistoric culture, thought that the Pylos tablets perhaps represented the spoils of a piratical strike against Crete by Pylian ships. But would they not be strange booty? And where on Crete were documents being inscribed in Linear B not long before 1200? Apparently not in Knossos, although we have seen that Evans had once thought some of his Linear B tablets were considerably later than 1400! It was all very disturbing.

Blegen's summation of the immediate impact of the discovery is indeed a masterpiece of understatement. "Whatever its full bearing when the evidence has been more thoroughly studied, the recovery of so great a collection of written records in a Mycenaean context—the first deposit of its kind to come to light on the mainland of Greece—will necessitate some revision of certain current theories regarding the state of culture in the late Mycenaean world."

During the remainder of the 1939 preliminary campaign at Pylos small groups of broken tablets were laboriously cleared with delicate tools, left in place for a few hours to dry in the sun, photographed, sketched, numbered and gingerly removed. Ominous war clouds were looming, and systematic excavation of the building complex did not seem to be an immediate possibility. The trench where the first tablets had been found, only inches below the modern surface, was gradually widened. Everywhere in an area of a few square feet they lay, broken and topsy-turvy. And even the fragments were in a truly "delicate condition," permeated with moisture and riddled with rootlets. Their outline was barely distinguishable from the surrounding soil of which they had been made and to which only by a miracle they had not quite returned. No wonder if previous excavators of major Mycenaean sites, taking it as an article of faith that no palace archives had existed on the mainland, may have allowed their workmen to dig right through similar deposits.

From the moment of their discovery the Pylos tablets were assumed to be administrative records, like their counterparts at Knossos. They were clearly a homogeneous group from the very last year of the palace's existence. Such tablets were quickly and cheaply made of local clay as the need arose. The surface was inscribed while the clay was still damp, left to dry in the sun, and provisionally stored in the archives room. When they had served the immediate purpose, significant totals were presumably transferred to more permanent records on other writing materials. Then the original clay tablets were useless and would be thrown out or reduced to pulp for the next year's records. In any case, their life would normally be short. It was only the irony of fate that had preserved this final group by partially baking them in the tremendous fire that ruined the palace and most of its contents.

As at Knossos, most of the Pylos tablets are long and narrow, the simplest shape to roll out by hand and adequate for a short entry (Fig. 77). Another type is much wider, with a correspondingly large writing surface. From Cretan parallels, it could be assumed that the writing had been in

Figure 77

one or two lines along the length of the smaller tablets, and in as many as twenty neatly ruled spaces across the shorter dimension of the larger ones. Actually, the written surface could not be seen in the excavation stage, since a hard white lime accretion completely covered the surface. The inscribed content and the similarity to the Cretan Linear B writing system had at first to be inferred for all of them from the very first fragment found. It was so near the surface that it had partially dried and therefore held together when a workman noticed its rounded upper edge and picked it up. Before he could be prevented, he had drawn his hand across the surface. That one stroke revealed the written symbols and also came perilously near to obliterating them.

After they had dried out in the sun for a few hours, however, a group of tablets could safely be removed, packed in cotton wool and taken to the excavation house in modern Pylos. Dr. Hill, Blegen's closest associate then, as twenty-five years before, had constructed wire drying racks. In a few days the tablets were rock hard and could be safely handled; but they were still illegible. It was only then that Blegen, cautious as always, allowed a few to be carefully scraped until the writing could be made out. So it could finally be safely inferred that all were inscribed, and telegrams were sent off to Athens and Cincinnati to announce the news.

In the widened trench, meanwhile, a hint of the physical context was beginning to emerge (Fig. 78). Under only one or two layers of less frag-

Figure 78

mentary tablets a narrow stuccoed bench was uncovered. It was in the form of an open rectangle facing southeast, with one arm broken off irregularly and the other ending in a neat, squared fashion. In the area enclosed by the bench broken fragments continued to appear at lower levels. Behind the bench the stone foundation of the walls of a little room was cleared. The upper walls, of sun-dried brick in timber framework, had been destroyed by fire and weather, as had happened throughout the great building. There had once been a door where the bench ended so regularly. The floor was finally reached about 10 inches below the top of the bench, and the inventory of broken tablets reached almost 700. The section of the room beyond the door had clearly suffered even more; but there was no time to investigate further in that direction.

Blegen was now able to make a preliminary reconstruction of what had happened. The tablets had been stored neatly on the bench, possibly contained in wooden boxes or wicker baskets that may have been protected against unauthorized prying by clay sealings such as those found among the tablets. When the fire struck, the roof and walls of the little room collapsed, and the tablets were hurled pell-mell to the floor. Naturally, even if the inhabitants survived to come back and comb the ruins for valuables, they would not have bothered searching for such remnants. And the attackers who were presumably responsible for the fire would not have been interested in salvaging the tablets before they set the torch.

The clearing of the archives room was not the only activity of Blegen's first campaign. A second trench was laid out at right angles to the first, and it became clear that under the surface over the whole northwestern half of the hill lay massive foundations of a complex of rooms making up a very large building indeed. Naturally, very little could be made out of the plan of rooms and corridors that were intersected in the trenches. A few tablets found in other areas showed that the concentration in the archives room did not represent all of the preserved clay records; and one or two beautiful fragments of frescoed wall paintings with figured design hinted at luxury that might rival Knossos and Mycenae. In the 1939 campaign, too, the location of at least two more tholos tombs was discovered, and the one that lay alongside the highway some distance down the ridge toward the sea was cleared by Mrs. Blegen and Mrs. Hill. It proved to contain the usual assortment of small finds and pottery overlooked by robbers; and in its floor were two cists, a large one and another barely big enough to contain the body of a child. A total of five tholoi had now been authenticated in the immediate Pylos area, a number surpassed only by "golden Mycenae."

So Blegen felt justified in ending his preliminary report of that first season's work at Ano Englianos with a confident historical reconstruction.

Through the whole body of Hellenic tradition relating to the Heroic Age a single dynasty of rulers is accredited with the overlordship of southwestern Greece, and the most famous king of the Neleid line, sage Nestor, is a peer and equal among the Achaean leaders at Troy. Though presumably represented by subordinate chieftains in his many towns, so far as the literary records tell, he clearly had no rival of like standing anywhere in the district. His royal residence might then confidently be envisaged as a palace, built on a scale commensurate with that of the abodes of the other Achaean kings, including Menelaos and even Agamemnon himself. It is just such a palace that has now been discovered at Ano Englianos, the chief citadel of Western Messenia in Mycenaean times. . . . We venture therefore without hesitation, even in these early phases of our investigation, to identify the newly found palace at Ano Englianos as the home of King Nestor, the Sandy Pylos of Homer and tradition.

That first season at Pylos was probably the climax of Blegen's long and productive career; but a paper he wrote in 1940 contains his most "philosophical" general insights on the present status and future development of the science to which he has devoted his life. The occasion was a symposium on the arts and architecture in which a number of well-known scholars participated to commemorate the bicentennial of the founding of the University of Pennsylvania. Blegen's contribution, "Preclassical Greece," was first on the program.

He notes that Schliemann had begun his own archaeological career exactly seventy years before. "With Schliemann, one may fairly maintain, a new spirit entered into archaeological research, and modern field archaeology was conceived." Blegen proceeds to pay tribute to other pioneers, especially to Dörpfeld, Tsountas and Evans. He outlines the perspective on Greek prehistoric civilization to which they and many others had contributed so much. "A long and gradual development preceded the flowering of Hellenic [classical] civilization, which cannot be regarded as a spontaneous phenomenon wholly isolated from the past. Greek genius had deep roots going far down into the early layers of culture in the land; and many of the physical and mental characteristics of the Hellenic stock were surely inherited from forgotten antecedents of a remoter antiquity."

Three main ethnic "metals" had "fused together," he suggests, during prehistoric times to form the "peculiar Hellenic alloy." The archaeological record suggests that remote neolithic ancestors could be responsible for "the superstition, coarseness, and occasional unbridled passion and cruelty exhibited in the Hellenic nature." The temperament of the Early Bronze Age people, seen in its most undiluted form throughout Minoan history, suggests the origin of "the delicacy of feeling, freedom of imagination, sobriety of judgment, and love of beauty, which endowed the Greeks with a magic touch in all forms of art." The racial stock of the Greek speakers who probably entered the peninsula in the Middle Bronze period may equally account for "that physical and mental vigor, directness of view, and that epic spirit of adventure in games, in the chase, and in war, which so deeply permeate Hellenic life."

One brief paragraph on Minoan-Mycenaean relations shows that his and Wace's reaction to Evans' preconceptions has finally attained a fully confident statement.

> With the opening of the sixteenth century Mycenae became the main-land capital, and henceforth the upper ranks of Mycenaean society, at any rate, seem deliberately to have adopted and absorbed a great many of the refinements of Minoan civilization, adapting them, when necessary, to their own needs and tastes. The culmination of the process may be seen in the overthrow of Cretan power and the capture of the chief Minoan centers by an expedition from the mainland early in the fourteenth century, perhaps the last and most effective in a series of warlike raids. The kings of Mycenae now preside in the Aegean world as arbiters of a civilization compounded of Minoan and mainland heritages. It is likely that some early form of Greek was the current language.

He seems already to be rethinking his statement of only a year before that the language behind the Pylos tablets is probably "Minoan."

Blegen also concisely reviews current assumptions about the later course of events.

> Mycenaean civilization as evolved at the outset of the fourteenth century maintained its existence some three hundred years, during which a slow progressive decline is manifest both on the material and the artistic sides. Exactly what forces were at work to bring about this internal decay we are not yet in a position to determine. When the end came, however, it was clearly the result of action from outside and not from within; for all the late Mycenaean towns seem more or less nearly synchronously to have been destroyed by fire, surely the victims of hostile attack and capture. From literary sources we know that this was the Dorian Invasion, and it is interesting to note that the archaeological evidence confirms essentially the dating handed down by tradition.

It is true that the destruction of Mycenaean centers in the twelfth century does generally coincide with the date assigned by Greek tradition to the Dorian invasion; but we shall find that the agents of that destruction now appear to be much harder to identify than Blegen thought in 1940.

In concluding his Philadelphia address, Blegen makes two vital points about lines along which prehistoric archaeology should move in the future. After a quarter of a century spent in continuous field work, no one could have been better qualified to diagnose weak points and no one had a right to a more respectful hearing.

> The amplification of any synthesis in the present state of our knowledge has urgent need, apart from further actual digging, of a systematic comprehensive survey of the districts of Greece, province by province, with the recording and mapping of all ancient sites. Most of the large centers have long ago been noted, but scores, not to say hundreds, of smaller settlements still await discovery. Almost infallibly the numerous potsherds that lie strewn superficially over the slopes of such mounds before any digging is done, give evidence of all the periods represented by the accumulated debris below. When the whole country has thus been methodically and thoroughly explored and the results have been properly tabulated and made available, we shall know infinitely more than we now do regarding the extent of occupation and the movements and distribution of population from period to period. In each district where investigations have hitherto been inadequate, two or three promising sites might then be carefully excavated for supplementary detailed information.

This recommendation is thoroughly in the tradition of Wace's and Blegen's own early and careful survey work, which was followed by such productive excavation.

A second admonition has perhaps an even more prophetic ring in terms of what has actually begun to happen in Greece since 1940. Even before that time Blegen had followed Schliemann's precedent by collaborating with scientists, particularly physical anthropologists and palaeozoologists. "In the future I believe we shall come more and more to rely on pure science for help in solving many of the problems that face us. Anthropologists, metallurgists, chemists, and zoölogists have already been called in to collaborate, to the great advantage of many excavations; and there are tasks for physicists, botanists, and geologists as well. . . . By combined effort we shall ultimately ascertain far more than we yet know regarding the formative period in the history of the Greek people."

These two methodological prescriptions were, indeed, long overdue in the Aegean area. Efforts are being made in some quarters since World War II to repair the lag; but it is puzzling to note how often the reaction to proposed cooperation with social and natural scientists ranges from skepticism to outright opposition. Blegen's energetic leadership, however, has ensured that the Pylos area where he is now working is in the forefront.

Professor Spyridon Marinatos, who succeeded Dr. Kourouniotis as Blegen's colleague, has carried on a program of exploration as well as excavation. Dr. Nicholas Yalouris, ephor (supervisor) of the Greek Archaeological Service for western Peloponnese, has also kept a careful check on all new discoveries and has cooperated closely with Blegen and his staff.

Finally, a Messenia expedition, organized at the University of Minnesota but closely coordinated with Blegen's own postwar activities, is conducting an intensive and wide-ranging program of surface exploration, topographic mapping and land-use study. In line with Blegen's prediction, more than 150 habitation sites contemporary with the palace have been located within the area which can be reasonably assumed to have been ruled by Nestor. And more tholos tombs are now (1966) known in the same area than had been recorded in all of mainland Greece as late as 1940. The population distribution of other periods, before and after the Late Bronze Age, is also beginning to come into focus. In terms of Blegen's second prescription, the Messenia expedition includes on its staff (in addition to archaeologists and historians) specialists in civil engineering, geology, paleobotany, ceramic technology, anthropology, geography, geophysics, geochemistry and agricultural economics. Each of them, as Blegen predicted, is making a contribution to the elucidation of the archaeological picture.

Blegen himself, a generation after his greatest discovery, continues to excavate annually at Ano Englianos; and the first volume of his monumental publication of the palace of Nestor is about to appear. We shall follow the postwar results in due order; but the conclusion of this chapter seems the most appropriate place to chronicle a significant event that took place on December 29, 1965. The Archaeological Institute of America has established a prestigious annual award "for distinguished archaeological achievement." The Institute's first gold medal was presented by its president with the following citation:

> Carl W. Blegen, excavator, author and teacher, throughout his long and distinguished career has fulfilled magnificently all the manifold responsibilities of an archaeologist's profession. Excavations of major importance, beginning with Korakou and ranging from Zygouries and Prosymna through Troy to the Palace of Nestor, have steadily revealed more and more of the identity and relationships of the cultures of prehistoric Greece. . . . The stately volumes which record his excavations, clear, precise, thorough, ever illuminating their wider historical and cultural implications, stand as enduring models of scholarly publication. And beyond these achievements extends the pervasive influence of the teacher and the man . . .

We have come to know Blegen's character well enough to feel the appropriateness of his response to this greatest honor that the leading American archaeological organization can confer on one of its members.

My feelings are deeply touched and I have difficulty in finding suitable words to express them. From my heart I thank you for this recognition of my somewhat plodding and prosaic endeavors. I wish I had accomplished much more to merit this award. Field archaeology—that is, excavating—is an uncertain and fickle mistress. In addition to work, application and perseverance, many other factors too are essential for success: among the most important may be counted good luck and good comrades. Most of my failures resulted from the lack of one or both of those two elements; and most of my enterprises that somehow turned out reasonably well owed it to my able colleagues . . .

Those who know him best will testify that the modesty is as genuine as the success, and that the success is as deserved as the first AIA gold medal.

VII

Developments Between the Wars: 1919-1939

FOR OUR REVIEW of the new knowledge that had accumulated between the two great wars we shall again, as in Chapter V, depend on syntheses by two recognized scholars—in this case J. D. S. Pendlebury and Martin P. Nilsson. But to understand them adequately and to continue our chronicle of the emerging evidence from the key sites of Mycenae and Knossos, we must first follow up a resounding controversy. A. J. B. Wace's work at Mycenae in the earlier 1920s (as well as later) is in the great tradition of Schliemann and Tsountas, his predecessors there. Also during the period under review Evans not only continued some limited excavation at Knossos but published his multivolume *Palace of Minos*. It would hardly be fair to deny to either Wace or Evans the opportunity to state his own views. The bulk of this chapter, therefore, will be concerned with that "Great Debate."

WACE AT MYCENAE

Schliemann had discovered the Shaft Graves; and his own insight along with that of various later experts, particularly the German scholar George Karo, had contributed much to the understanding of their marvelous contents. Tsountas' main contribution had been the clearing of the ruined palace on the acropolis and the opening of a very large number of chamber tombs in scattered concentrations among the hills to the west of the citadel. Both Schliemann and Tsountas had shown considerable interest in the tholos tombs in the same vicinity; but despite the architectural grandeur of the tholoi, the meager contents left behind by ancient robbers had made these great monuments less attractive to full-scale study and publication. Wace's work effectively filled this gap.

There were other outstanding problems, too—particularly those concerning the chronology of various important features at Mycenae, which further excavation might help to elucidate. So Wace, as director of the British School of Archaeology, applied for permission to continue the work, and two very important campaigns between 1920 and 1923 initiated a long series of British excavations. The staff included a number of talented young scholars such as Helen Lorimer, Winifred Lamb, Ida Thallon (later Mrs. B. H. Hill), Axel Boethius, R. W. Hutchinson, W. A. Heurtley, L. B. Holland, J. P. Droop and A. W. Gomme, all of whom later became well known in their own right. Piet de Jong, a gifted British artist and draftsman, divided his time between Mycenae and Knossos. Tsountas and Blegen were generous with assistance and advice.

Such a large and able staff—American as well as British—was a relatively new phenomenon in Greek prehistoric digs. The possibility thus offered for student training and careful supervision of the work force and the division of labor for intensive field study of various classes of finds were favorable omens for the future. The labor force never exceeded fifty-five, a salutary contrast to the great gangs working under one or two supervisors in earlier days. The results of the first two seasons were fully published by Wace and his assistants in the *Annual of the British School* and in the journal *Archaeologia*.

Supplementary excavation under the Cyclopean walls at two points between the Lion Gate and the Postern Gate as well as under the threshold of the former provided useful and somewhat surprising evidence. "In every case," says Wace, "L.H.III. sherds were found. It thus seems that the circuit wall of Mycenae should be dated to this same period; in other words, it cannot be older than the beginning of the fourteenth century B.C., since the finds at Tell-el-Amarna give us a fixed point for the date of L.H.III. pottery." He points to the results of the latest German excavations under Kurt Müller and G. Rodenwaldt, who were continuing and refining Dörpfeld's work at Tiryns. Their investigations indicated a similar date for the main walls of that fortress. "The walls of both citadels have always been recognized as alike in style," says Wace, "though those of Tiryns have generally been thought the older."

Wace's allusion to the sculpture in the relieving triangle* over the Lion Gate is also worth quoting. "Sir Arthur Evans has shewn the significance of the type of this relief, the Sacred Pillar with the guardian lions, and has given illustrations of parallel types. The column is the sacred pillar of strength and protection, and is an aniconic form of a deity. . . . In this case . . . the sacred pillar possibly stands for the Great Mother Goddess. . . . The placing of such a relief over the citadel of Mycenae probably meant that it was placed under the protection of the Great Mother, and that she was the establisher of Mycenae." We might anticipate here by mentioning an attractive recent conjecture that the missing heads would have identified the beasts over the Mycenae gate as griffins rather than lions. The heraldic griffins behind the Pylos throne and the wingless griffins in the Throne Room at Knossos do suggest a very intimate connection with Mycenaean royalty.

Everywhere throughout the publication one is impressed by Wace's detailed enumeration of the pottery and its careful assignment to the newly established categories and subcategories. He and Blegen and others of their generation are pioneering in a less spectacular way, perhaps, than their predecessors; but they are establishing the basis on which the chronology— and therefore the intelligible history—of Mycenaean civilization is to be founded. For instance, Wace proves that the building just to the right inside the Lion Gate was destroyed when the citadel was finally sacked and burned. From the remnants of grain in storage jars in its basement corridors, reminiscent of the storerooms of Crete, Wace concludes that it was an official supply depot and so christens it the Granary.

In describing the pottery found in the Granary, Wace was laying the groundwork for dating levels at the very end of the Mycenaean Age, later called LHIIIC. "In the same two Corridors . . . was found the deposit that had collected on their floors during the last period when the building was in use. This consequently is particularly interesting as it shews us the kind of Late Mycenaean (L.H.III.) pottery in use at Mycenae at the time of its ruin. The pottery from these two Corridors shews the same characteristics as that from the East Basement [of the palace] and we therefore have one homogeneous class of L.H.III. ware, of such a strongly marked style that we have called it the Granary Class . . ." (Fig. 79).

The British probings in the area of the ramp leading up to the palace from the Lion Gate showed that the citadel had had a long history of occupation. The excavators discovered pottery that could be safely assigned, as a result of the stratification established by Blegen at Korakou, to an early phase of the Early Bronze Age "about the beginning of the Third Millennium B.C." And above this was found the familiar matt-painted and gray Minyan ware of the Middle Bronze Age. Because of later intensive building activity, no intelligible remains of buildings could be associated with these early classes of pottery.

Important results for the history of the site and especially for the true understanding of the Shaft Graves come from the examination of the LHIII houses, presumably belonging to courtiers and important palace officials, which occupied the lower part of the fortified area. Below the level of these houses, several shallow single cist graves could be safely assigned to Middle Helladic times. They correspond to others discovered

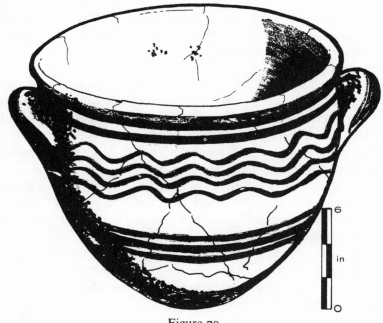

Figure 79

earlier within or near the Grave Circle; and Wace proved that this whole slope had contained an extensive MH cemetery long before its upper part had been enclosed within the fortified area.

More than that, Wace sees a direct development from these simple antecedents to the famous Shaft Graves. The earlier graves "are in form primitive shaft graves, and apart from the rough stone wall which lines the latter, it is of the same general type as the Second Shaft Grave [Schliemann's #5]. The Shaft Graves in themselves are after all only elaborate versions of the ordinary M.H. cist grave hollowed out in the rock." So, in spite of the profusion of rich burial furniture, the very form of the royal Shaft Graves would indicate a long occupation of Mycenae by the ancestors of those wealthy and ostentatious monarchs. If (as had sometimes been inferred) they had come from abroad, bringing their riches with them, they would most likely have been accustomed to a different type of tomb and would have insisted on using it.

As he begins his account of the British researches in connection with the Grave Circle itself, Wace sums up the work of the past generation as follows: "Although much has been written on this subject since the excavations and researches of Schliemann, Stamatakes and Tsountas, the greatest advance towards a fuller understanding of its history was made by Karo, whose able paper has unfortunately not yet been published. Thanks to his unselfish courtesy we had the opportunity of conducting our researches in the Grave Circle with the assistance of the proofs of his article."

In the first place, it is pointed out that the higher and lower levels at which Schliemann found stelae should mark two separate periods in the history of the cemetery. The stelae at the lower level represent the ground level of the original rock surface, when the graves were first dug and used, but the stelae found higher up show that a major artificial change had later been made in the contour of the slope. Wace reconstructs the earlier situation as follows: "Thus assuming that in early times there was a settlement on the summit of the citadel, where the Palace was afterwards built (and we have plenty of evidence for such an early settlement in the Early and Middle Helladic pottery found below the walls and floors of the Palace) the area of the soft rock of the Grave Circle and its neighbourhood was the nearest spot to the summit of the acropolis where it was possible to cut graves. The hard limestone rock of the upper part of the citadel was naturally most unsuitable."

The development of this cemetery of simple Middle Helladic cist graves is then carried a step further.

At the end of this period, not long before the beginning of the sixteenth century B.C., part of this cemetery became reserved for royal interments. Perhaps just about this time a new dynasty occupied the throne of Mycenae. At all events from this time onwards Mycenae, which had certainly been flourishing before, now began to be extremely prosperous. From the fact of their having been laid in these graves we may call this, the first Mycenaean dynasty that we can envisage, the Shaft Grave Dynasty. During the course of the sixteenth century B.C., six royal graves were dug here close to one another, and in them nineteen persons were buried. Further to the north of the Grave Circle under the Granary, yet another was dug, and to the south of the Grave Circle . . . there was probably once another Shaft Grave. . . . Of these graves the Sixth is now recognised, by the pottery found in it by Stamatakes, as undoubtedly the earliest, and the first interment in it should be placed at the end of the M.H. period. . . . The two latest would be the Third and First [the latter is Schliemann's #2] Graves, but even these do not come down so late as the end of the sixteenth century B.C. That is to say this series of the six royal Shaft Graves stops before the end of L.H.I. . . . It is possible that this cemetery may have no longer been used for royal interments because a new dynasty now sat on the throne of Mycenae.

In order to follow the reconstructed sequence of events, we must at this point anticipate Wace's new chronological evidence from the tholos tombs.

"From about the end of L.H.I. begins the series of Tholos Tombs which from their impressive size and noble architecture we can only regard as the tombs of kings. The Tholos Tombs, beginning towards the end of L.H.I., continue right through the next (L.H.II.) and well into the last phase (L.H.III.). The different method of burial inclines us to the belief that a change of dynasty took place at Mycenae, and we may call this, the second dynasty, the Tholos Tomb Dynasty."

Yet the altar that Schliemann found within the Grave Circle and other evidence as well suggested that the royalty buried in the Shaft Graves continued to be remembered and placated with offerings. "It seems clear," says Wace, "from the investigations of Sir Arthur Evans and others that Minoan kings were regarded as semi-divine personages. The Mycenaeans seem as far as we can tell to have adopted the Minoan religion. Thus naturally the graves of the kings buried in the Shaft Grave cemetery would have been regarded as sacred. The kings were the temporary human manifestations of divinities, and to them as such all due rites and offerings were paid." It is clear that Wace was at this point deeply under the spell of at least some of Evans' preconceptions. Within a decade Martin Nilsson and others were stressing notable differences between mainland and Minoan religion.

About the beginning of the fourteenth century, according to Wace, a particularly rapid development can be noted in the whole mainland area. By then the palace of Knossos had been destroyed and the center of political power had shifted to the mainland. In Wace's view, Mycenae itself apparently benefited most dramatically. "It would then have been under the rule of a rich and powerful prince of the Tholos Tomb Dynasty. He rebuilt the palace on the summit of the acropolis, and replanned the whole citadel and enlarged its area. We assume one king to have been responsible for all this building activity, for so far as the archaeological evidence goes, all these buildings must have been constructed within a comparatively short time."

The natural line of the new fortifications would have cut right through the revered royal Shaft Graves, and so the wall was bellied out at considerable expense to include the whole area. But even greater pains were taken to show respect.

It was resolved to enclose and preserve as a kind of temenos* the sacred area where the kings still lay in state. This was done by enclosing the sacred spot with the elaborate double ring of vertical slabs with their massive covering stones and monumental entrance leading from the Lion Gate . . . but since this was a sloping hillside special constructions had to be undertaken to level the ground. . . . When the ring wall was completed . . . the sculptured grave stelai which had stood over the graves at the original level on the sloping hillside were reerected over the graves at the new level on even ground.

This imposing fourteenth-century monument seems to have remained—honored, protected and undesecrated—through the later Bronze Age. Wace theorizes that its memory, if not the actual structure, explains the story of the graves of Agamemnon and his companions that was told to Pausanias when he visited Mycenae. Wace's reconstruction ends in a characteristically modest way.

> The intuition of Schliemann enabled him to divine the existence of royal graves within the Lion Gate, and rediscovered to the world the brilliance of the civilisation which Homer had celebrated. Schliemann, however, could not, with the scanty knowledge then at command, see his wonderful finds in their true perspective. The work of Tsountas and Evans, to mention the two most prominent investigators only, has given us an outline of the history of those times. Our knowledge is still extremely imperfect; but the little we have done towards unravelling the history of the Grave Circle, in itself an epitome of the history of Mycenae, will, we hope, make the way a little clearer for our successors.

Perhaps this rather painful awareness of the disparity between what we know and what we would like to know best characterizes not only Wace himself but also most archaeologists of the twentieth, as compared to the nineteenth century.

W. A. Heurtley made a careful study of the sculptured stelae. To explain the curious discrepancy between the perfection of the geometric decoration and the clumsiness of the naturalistic figured element he suggests that the stelae must have been sculpted by mainland artists who had as yet imperfectly assimilated the new Cretan influence. And he points a comparison with the mainland vase painters.

> The feature which distinguishes the decoration of later Middle Helladic Matt-painted pottery from that of the Cyclades on the one hand, and from the contemporary wares of Crete on the other, is the persistence of the geometric tradition. Long after the naturalistic impulse from Crete had profoundly affected the art of the Cyclades, the vase painters of the mainland were dividing the surface of their vases into vertical and horizontal compartments in the earlier manner. . . . The decorative scheme of the stelai . . . is in close relationship with this tradition. . . . It is indeed clear that during the first half of the first L.H. period, three distinct artistic currents existed side by side at Mycenae, the Helladic proper which includes the makers of Matt-painted pottery and Minyan goblets, the Creto-Mycenaean represented by the potters and metalworkers, working under Cretan teachers, and the Minoan, which is

represented by the numerous objects either made by Cretans at Mycenae or imported from Crete.

Heurtley thus places the mainland and Cretan artistic productions in the perspective of two very different traditions and rejects Evans' broad generalization that everything "good" on the mainland must be Minoan or under Minoan influence, while the locally inspired productions were beneath notice. Heurtley says:

> The stelai confirm the impression which many of the gold objects from the graves and the polychrome Matt-painted vases produce, viz. the independent character of Mycenaean art. . . . Even when Cretan art was becoming paramount at Mycenae, and almost before the last Shaft Graves were finally closed, the earlier tholos tombs were rising, and though the stelai, as such, have no successors, the architectonic genius which they foreshadow was to find, at a later period, its full expression in the Lion Gate and the great tholos tombs of the third group, and in the application of sculpture to their façades.

In his final sentence Heurtley makes a prophetic inference. "Perhaps a reflection of the same [mainland] spirit may be seen in the Palace Style [pottery] of Crete."

The British excavations in the Mycenae palace were mainly a reexamination of Tsountas' conclusions, with the advantage of more precise ceramic analysis. This rocky acropolis, however, with very little depth of earth remaining and that in a disturbed state, was a very difficult place to apply the new methods. Wace sees some evidence of a new over-all rebuilding of a much larger second palace, contemporary with the new fortification walls and the finest tholos tombs. But his proposed chronology is doubted by his colleague L. B. Holland, who thinks it more likely that the changes were gradual and piecemeal. Yet Wace's suggestions are at least appealing to the imagination.

> In L.H.I. under the Shaft Grave Dynasty a First Palace stood on the summit of the acropolis. This, with alterations, would have served in L.H.II. for the earlier kings of the Tholos Tomb Dynasty. Later, at the beginning of L.H.III., under the most powerful and wealthiest kings of the Tholos Tomb Dynasty, a Second Palace was built here and we have before us to-day the ruins of one of its sections. This Second Palace seems to have lasted till the fall of Mycenae, and it would thus have been the home of the Atreidai [descendants of Atreus, including Agamemnon], if, as we now believe, they were historical. Schliemann's imagination, which dreamt of the home of Agamemnon and Clytemnestra, was not far wrong. If there was an Agamemnon, if Homer did

not write pure fiction, it was in this Palace that the King of Men lived and hither he brought home his bride Clytemnestra from the banks of the Eurotas [a river flowing through Sparta].

We can agree with Wace on the LHIII palace; but his "First Palace" contemporary with the Shaft Graves rests on very little solid architectural evidence.

We have already reviewed Tsountas' description of the preserved ground plan. The British researches did not seriously modify the earlier work, but one new discovery must be mentioned. On an upper terrace in the northeast part of the palace, which had apparently been the royal living quarters, one room contained "a curious stepped construction covered over with red stucco" and a stone-built drain. The similarity to the tank baths or lustral area in Cretan palaces led them to christen it the Red Bath. We can imagine what Schliemann would have made of this discovery, in the light of the tradition about Agamemnon's murder in the bath on his return from Troy!

Coming to the megaron, Wace suggests that the columned porch had a flat roof, which served as a balustraded loggia or upper veranda reached from the higher level of the south corridor. He imagines that from this loggia "the royal household could watch games in the Court below, as seen in the well-known fresco found by Schliemann below the Ramp House" (Fig. 80). The porch had a doorway in the center of its east wall, as well as double doors communicating with the anteroom and, through it, with the megaron proper. The side door that connected with the Domestic Quarter was apparently covered only with a curtain (Fig. 81).

The great hall was about 43 by 40 feet and had brightly painted stucco floor and walls. In the center was the ceremonial hearth flanked by four columns, as at Tiryns. Although it had been partially destroyed when the supporting wall of the southeastern section had fallen into the gorge below, the diameter of the hearth could be calculated as about 12 feet. Where it had been broken, ten separate layers of painted stucco could be distinguished. In spite of constant redecoration, conservative taste or religious associations reproduced each time the identical "wave and star" or "notched plume" motif. This depiction of rays or flames was also used to decorate movable hearths and tables of offering at Knossos. There was, as we saw, no evidence of provision for a throne in the preserved section of the floor. Possibly, it was movable, like the rest of the furniture.

Wace speculates on the peripheral position of the Mycenae megaron as compared to that at Tiryns. He assumes (and again the fascination of pan-Minoan theories is clear) that the higher central terraces, where one would expect it to have been located, were already occupied with buildings in a

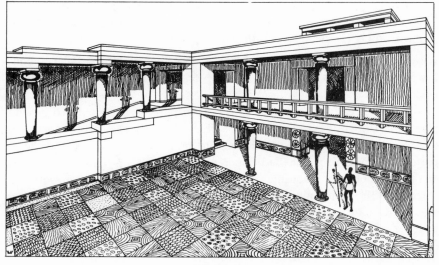

Figure 80

different tradition. "If the First Palace at Mycenae—as seems reasonable, though we know practically nothing about it—depended largely on Cretan models, and if the Megaron, as held by Dr. Duncan Mackenzie and others, is a Mycenaean and not a Minoan feature, then we can understand the late introduction of the Megaron at Mycenae and Tiryns." He also discounts the suggestion that this was the "men's megaron" and that there had been a corresponding, somewhat smaller "women's megaron" (as at Tiryns) on a higher terrace. He insists that "the old theory . . . that the men and women had separate quarters in megara in Mycenaean Palaces" must now be discarded completely. We shall see later that the newest palace plan at Pylos forces a reexamination of this problem.

The lighting and ventilating of the great hall also raise problems. Wace believes that there may have been windows in the south and east sides that "would, of course, have given a magnificent view down the precipitous Chaos ravine and over the Argive plain beyond." But the escape of smoke from the hearth is more difficult, since he rather firmly holds out for a second story over both vestibule and hall. Dörpfeld's theory of a higher section of the roof (clerestory) supported by the four columns around the hearth does not appeal to Wace.

On the other hand, L. B. Holland, in his architectural commentary, doubts that the outer megaron walls and the four interior columns would have been strong enough to support either a second story or a clerestory. He feels that a fair amount of smoke from the hearth was taken for granted,

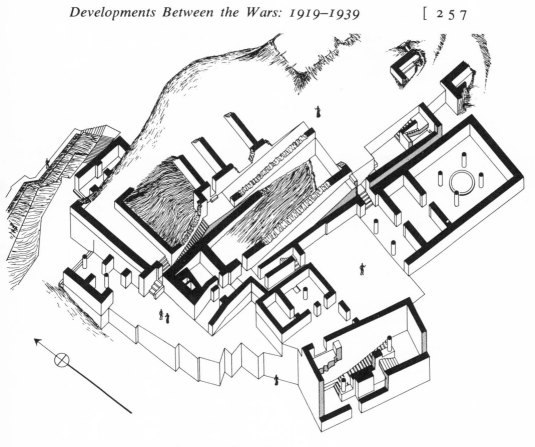

Figure 81

as is suggested by Odysseus' advice to his son. If the suitors ask why Telemachos is removing the weapons from the megaron, he is to explain that they were getting injured by the smoke.[72] Holland proposes instead that the spacing of the four interior columns both at Tiryns and Mycenae suggests the presence of a large rectangular opening in the center of the megaron. "The arrangement is similar to that of a Roman *atrium*, which was a living room in a colder climate. There what amounts to a small court is surrounded on all four sides by porticoes of nearly uniform depth."

An amusing feature in Holland's report is that Wace keeps inserting disclaimers in footnotes. For instance, at this point he rather sensibly inter-jects: "Assuming the Megaron to be a living-room, a hole in its roof about 15 x 13 feet in area would be extremely inconvenient in the rainy season, when a fire on the hearth would be most needed." Yet, here again, one senses a free and healthy interplay of theories and ideas. It would be difficult to imagine a publication by Schliemann or particularly by Evans in which a subordinate openly challenged the director's point of view.

The British excavators were also able to discover new evidence for the fresco decorations on the walls of the megaron. Tsountas' material from 1886 had already been supplemented by Rodenwaldt, who in 1914 had discovered new fragments near the north wall. The British recovered still more; and it was clearly established that the megaron had been decorated with a continuous frieze or separate panels representing battle scenes. Miss Lamb published the following reconstruction: "The fresco represents a building of several stories, marked into narrow vertical divisions by walls of which the ends are seen in section, and with women standing either at the windows or outside. . . . It has some of the characteristics of the high, many-towered type of building . . . The framework is of wood, probably filled with rubble and decorated with stucco imitating stonework. Below, to the right, is part of the rock on which the castle stands . . . and faint traces of a tree. The resemblance to the silver rhyton from Mycenae . . . is particularly striking."

In a footnote she emphasizes the Homeric parallel: "Fighting before the walls of a besieged castle is in accordance with Homeric practice as described in the *Iliad*. There, the Trojan army is camped before the walls of Ilion, which we know from the excavations of Schliemann and Dörpfeld to have more nearly resembled a castle than a fortified city. . . . Here we have a frieze with the besieged castle at one end of the wall, the armies fighting before it, and the camp of the besieging army beyond. It may well be considered as illustrating a siege like the siege of Troy." Can we imagine Schliemann exercising such restraint with this tempting opportunity?

The most important feature of the earliest British excavations at Mycenae, however, was surely Wace's new classification of the nine great tholos tombs in a typological* sequence. By his day it was generally agreed that they were all later than the Shaft Graves; but there was no consensus as to the outside dates of the series or where individual tombs fitted within such a span. It will be remembered that Schliemann had briefly examined the only uncollapsed tomb, the so-called Treasury of Atreus (its later label, the Tomb of Agamemnon, is still a pure guess). Stamatakes completely cleared it in the following year. Close to the Lion Gate, Sophia Schliemann had also partially excavated the dromos and chamber of another tomb (later assigned with no more evidence to Cly- temnestra). Beginning in 1886 Tsountas cleared all the previously known tholoi as far as he could safely do so; and he raised the total to nine by the discovery of three more. No addition has since been made at Mycenae, and it is usually assumed that there were no others.

Wace and his colleagues carefully reexamined all nine (Fig. 16). Evans' keen interest in mainland developments is shown by a financial contribution to this project. The Greek authorities forbade complete excavation of the so-called Aegisthus Tomb because it was feared that further digging would dangerously weaken the surviving structure. Another tomb, called by the local toponym Epano Phournos, could not be safely cleared. ("Epano Phournos" means "Upper Lime Kiln," and the resemblance of ruined tholoi to these common structures is close enough that the local peasants can hardly be blamed for confusing them.)

Wace describes his own work as an attempt to reconstruct the "history of the tholos tombs at Mycenae from the point of view of construction and material." He admits that his favorite method of dating by pottery analysis has only limited application here because sherds of far earlier and later periods got washed down or thrown into the tombs. Later cult seemed to have involved ritual offerings; and tomb robbers, modern shepherds, earlier investigators and collapsing domes had completely disturbed any stratification there might once have been.

The analysis includes one other tholos, which was located at the Argive Heraion (Prosymna) only five miles or so to the south. Wace sensibly points out that his criteria may very well be inapplicable to edifices at a greater distance. "Methods of construction are bound to vary from district to district with the variations in the local material ready to hand. It is therefore inadvisable to argue from constructional peculiarities of tholoi elsewhere in the Peloponnese, in Attica or in Thessaly, unless there is other evidence available, in support of theories as to the Mycenaean tholoi. Still more so should the architectural parallels of Crete be used with great caution, since the whole environment of the Minoan civilisation in that island was different from that prevailing at Mycenae and on the mainland."

To explain the method of building these great circular tomb chambers, we can hardly do better than quote Wace's summary of the observations made in the early nineteenth century by the architects of the French *Expédition Scientifique de Morée*. Their description, it should be added, applies particularly to those of regular ashlar* construction.

The sides of the facing blocks of the dome are not cut to fit one another so as to make a kind of horizontal arch. They merely touch at their inner angles, and the resulting interspace is packed tight with small stones driven in to make all solid. At the back the big blocks of the tholos wall are counterweighted so far as can be seen with a heavy mass of rough stones packed in behind them. The blocks in the lower courses are larger than those in the upper, and the eye or final course is capped by a large slab which has a hollow on its under surface to continue the line of the dome to a rounded point. The top of the dome projects above the surface of the hillside and is covered with a mound of earth which naturally serves to hold the masonry in place. Built on this system with well-dressed rectangular blocks of hard stone, the dome ought not to collapse if reasonable care is taken. Each successive ring of masonry should support itself if the joints are true, and it is well packed and counterweighted so as to make it fit tight within the circular excavation.

Wace's scheme divides the nine Mycenae tombs into three convenient groups of three each, with the Heraion example falling in the second category. The first group includes the so-called Cyclopean Tomb, that at Epano Phournos and the Aegisthus Tomb. In the second are those called the Kato (Lower) Phournos, the Panagia and the Lion Tomb; while the third group comprises the Treasury of Atreus, the Tomb of Clytemnestra and the Tomb of the Genii (sometimes called the perfect tholos). All of the names are entirely fortuitous. There is, of course, not the slightest evidence to assign any of the tholoi to specific individuals whom tradition associates with the royal families of Mycenae.

Wace's major typological criteria are clear and crisp (Fig. 82). The three tombs of Group I are built of limestone (or "poros") rubble, with somewhat larger blocks around the doorway. Only the tomb of Aegisthus has a stone-lined dromos; and that feature, plus a later façade of ashlar masonry in regular horizontal courses, suggests that it is transitional to Group II. Those in the second group have a stone-lined dromos, a door frame of large dressed blocks of the much harder local conglomerate and long lintel blocks that indicate the presence (proved in one case) of a relieving triangle above the doorway. Group III displays dromoi completely lined (in two cases) with conglomerate blocks laid in ashlar technique. The doorways are built of massive and regular conglomerate blocks cut with the saw. The sparing use of sawed blocks in the Treasury of Atreus ought to make it the closest to a transition from Group II. The stone lining of the circular tomb chambers is of very carefully cut conglomerate laid in regular courses. The tombs of Group III have precisely set thresholds and frames for separate doors, whereas in all the others except the transitional Lion Tomb the entrance had simply been sealed with a stone wall.

Wace himself reviews the distinctions as follows: "The second group is characterized by the discovery of the relieving triangle and by ashlar work in poros. The third group is distinguished by the discovery of the possibility of sawing hard stone like conglomerate and by great advances in engineering skill, which facilitated the handling of gigantic blocks." The

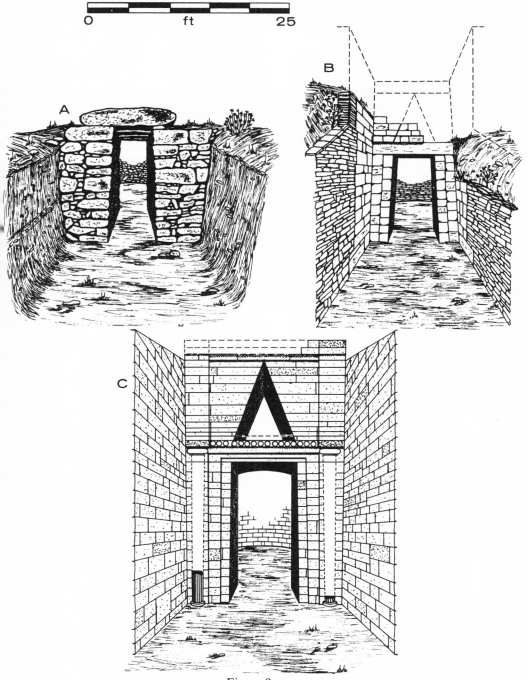

Figure 82

line of development, or *relative* chronology, seemed the natural one, *i.e.,* from the simpler to the more complex. But it was soon to be vigorously challenged.

On the question of *absolute* chronology, however, Wace finds much more difficulty. He begins with Group III and points out a parallel with the use of sawed conglomerate in conspicuous places in the latest phases of the palaces and fortifications (both at Tiryns and Mycenae) that are securely dated in LHIII. Since the Treasury of Atreus shows only sparing use of the saw, it ought to date at the beginning of that period, *i.e.,* about 1400. At this point he adduces some ceramic evidence gained from a small test under a section of its massive threshold, where one might expect to find no sherds later than the original construction. In the shallow bedding trench, packed with small stones and the characteristic tough yellow clay that served the Mycenaeans for mortar, a number of potsherds were found. "All are of L.H.III. date and compare well with those from the first or earliest strata by the Lion Gate, and so date from the beginning of L.H.III., or the early fourteenth century B.C." It should be noted that Wace later lowered the date to about 1330. Professor George Mylonas has recently offered evidence that would lower the date of the latest monumental phase of the fortifications (including the Lion Gate) to about mid-*thirteenth* century. And he further believes (without much more definite evidence than Wace had for his equation) that the Treasury of Atreus should be about contemporary.

Wace then goes on to assign dates to his first two groups by almost Euclidean reasoning.

> Having thus acquired a fixed point for the third group, it is easy to give approximate dates for the other two. . . . The tholos tombs are almost certainly the tombs of kings. If they are the tombs of kings, they cannot well be contemporary with the Shaft Graves, as it would be absurd to imagine two dynasties ruling simultaneously at Mycenae. The princes buried in the tholos tombs . . . must therefore have been either earlier or later than the Shaft Grave Dynasty. The tholos tombs are not Middle Helladic and so cannot be earlier, but must be later. The Shaft Graves are Late Helladic I., and the third group of tholos tombs is Late Helladic III. Thus the first and second groups should fall between the Shaft Graves [the end of the sixteenth century] and the beginning of the fourteenth century B.C. . . .

Holland adds a very brief architectural commentary in which he fully supports Wace's criteria for tracing the development of the tholos. And his concluding paragraph, although not concerned with his specialty, is particularly interesting.

There are, in all probability, few, if any, more tholos tombs to be found in the vicinity of Mycenae, though there are probably a good many more chamber tombs still undiscovered there. This is due to the fact that the latter were built entirely below ground, while in the tholos tombs, as has been shown, the lintel was regularly set at the level of the natural grade of the hillside, bringing nearly half of the structure above ground. Even with a collapsed dome the presence of such a tomb could hardly have escaped notice in all the very thorough investigations of the region. We can say safely, then, that there were at Mycenae a series of nine or at most, say, a dozen tholos tombs, built over a period of something above two hundred years; and of the nine known ones no two are contemporary. This means that on the average they were built twenty to thirty years apart, or one, and only one, to each generation. The inference is obvious: they are the tombs of a dynasty of kings who ruled, from the downfall of the Shaft Grave Dynasty, until themselves overthrown when the Palace was destroyed. For nobles, and perhaps for a short-lived king—unless laid in his predecessor's tholos—chamber tombs had to suffice; the commoners probably were content with still more humble resting-places, while tholoi were reserved for royalty alone.

We notice a difference of opinion here between Holland and Blegen. The latter had insisted that the occupants of the chamber tombs at Prosymna were not nobles but ordinary citizens. And we wonder, too, if chronological considerations on Wace's reconstruction would not require that the last kings before the final destruction were buried elsewhere or in reused ancestral tholoi.

Some additional secondary questions are raised or implied by Wace's study. One concerns access to the tholoi. The clearly artificial conical mounds were noticeable in modern times above the Heraion, Lion and Clytemnestra tombs, as is still true of the uncollapsed Treasury of Atreus. Such mounds are a reliable indication to the trained eye of a surface explorer in every corner of central and southern Greece. They must have been a sufficient clue, also, to the tomb robbers of antiquity. But how did the thieves—or even the legitimate users—enter the tomb? Was the dromos filled in after each burial and reexcavated before the next? Or was it left open so that the passerby could see its façade, adorned in the latest examples with architectural and sculptural decorations? Were the tholoi, in fact, accessible through the dromos until classical or even later times, and did the entrances only gradually fill up with wash from the hillsides?

The evidence is not easy to interpret, and Wace does not face the question directly; but he does provide important clues. In several cases, potsherds found on the floor of the dromos, some of them trodden into it, belonged to vases of which the remaining pieces lay on the floor of the tholos chamber. This could only happen when the dromos was clear, but it hardly proves whether the dromos was left open or simply reopened temporarily for another burial. Again, what is the purpose of a wall built across the outer end of the dromos in the later Mycenae tholoi? Wace says it was "probably . . . so made that it could be easily taken down when the tomb was re-opened and could be replaced later." But what would be its function if the dromos was filled between burials? On the whole, it seems likely that the dromoi *were* completely filled in after each burial; and the analogous procedure in the case of the Shaft Graves may be relevant here.

In this connection we should note the relatively rich burial that Tsountas discovered at the inner end of the dromos of the Tomb of Clytemnestra. He saw in the grave goods, particularly the bronze mirrors with carved ivory handles, clear evidence that the single occupant had been a woman; and he speculated that she was a favorite slave who was forced to accompany her royal master to the next world. At any rate, the grave goods belong to relatively late Mycenaean times, and the burial was undisturbed. At that time, the inner part at least of the dromos must have been filled and never reopened. Wace believes this was a "secondary interment*," that is, presumably, that this skeleton with its possessions was removed from the tholos chamber (or some other place) and reburied in the dromos. But if she really was a slave, would she have been buried in the tholos in the first place?

Wace also notes rather enigmatic evidence concerning late finds in the tholos chambers, though again he does not face the problem directly. Mycenaean tombs often contain pottery from geometric, classical and even Hellenistic times. Usually it was deposited before the collapse of the dome. Does it indicate reuse for later burials or a hero cult of the dead king, or both? Wace seems somewhat in favor of the cult hypothesis, which of course would not necessarily prove that the dromoi remained open. The offerings might well have been inserted through a hole just below the lintel of the doorway or through a small opening in the top of the dome. "The quantity of Geometric [Early Iron Age] ware is also very striking, and might indicate that in this tomb [that of the Lion] . . . the cult of the dead princes buried here continued long after their earthly kingdom had passed away." The parallel of the altar above the Shaft Graves and the circular wall is mentioned in a footnote. The question of a continuing hero cult, at least in the sense of an uninterrupted tradition, is still unresolved.

A further source of some uncertainty involves the cists, or pit graves, dug in the floor of the main tomb chamber in the case of at least three of the later tholoi (those of the Lion, Heraion and Genii). In each case there are three cists, varying from a size large enough for several adult burials to what could barely have accommodated a child's body. In addition, there may have been a cist just inside the door of the Aegisthus Tomb, and there was another in the side chamber in the Treasury of Atreus. They are common, too, in tholoi outside of Mycenae. In at least two of the Mycenae tombs, heavy stone slabs either covered the cists or lay nearby. What do these cist graves reveal of the royal burial ceremonies?

As Blegen was later to conclude in the case of the Prosymna chamber tombs, Wace is quite sure that they were used for reburial when a new occupant was installed on the floor of the tombs. "The number and size of these grave-pits [in the Lion Tomb] suggest that the tomb was in use for some little time, and that secondary interment was practised in these tholoi as in the private chamber tombs." But could this explanation be squared with Tsountas' description of the careful arrangement of the rich remains in the cist of the Vaphio tomb?

Wace also points out that secondary burial is very rare in Minoan tombs and suggests that "this difference in burial customs may indicate a racial distinction between the Cretans and the Mycenaeans, in spite of the fact that the latter had almost entirely adopted the religion and civilisation of the former." The last clause again emphasizes how deeply Evans' dogma had penetrated, even into independent minds like Wace's, by the early 1920s.

The theory of secondary burial is believed by Wace to be strengthened by the use of a side chamber in the Atreus tomb as well as in the Orchomenos example.

This side chamber [in the Atreus tomb] if one can judge by the grave-pit found in the floor and by the analogy of the chamber-tombs, was probably intended to be used as a charnel chamber to receive the remains of earlier interments when the main chamber (the tholos) was being prepared for a fresh burial. It thus served as a kind of elaborate substitute for the grave-pits [cists]. . . . The procedure seems to have been that the bodies were first laid in the main chamber, and remained there till it was necessary to reopen the tomb for another interment. Then the skeleton of the first tenant with the funeral offerings which had been laid around him were removed to a pit in the side chamber, or merely piled up in a heap in one corner. Apparently it was during the process of removal that the relatives of the deceased took away any of the funeral offerings that pleased them.

A few of Wace's comments on the remaining contents of the tholoi also merit our attention. In describing an amphora in the so-called Palace Style, Wace insists firmly that these vases were local products and not imported from Crete. In his opinion one such vase "cannot be dated earlier than the end of L.H.I. and, like the Kakovatos, Vaphio and Thorikos vases, it is clearly of mainland fabric." In a footnote he adds, "The design is common on the mainland . . . but of course originated in Crete . . ." He also points to the relatively long period of popularity of this ceramic class and its value for chronology. "They are . . . characteristic of the Second Late Helladic period . . . and thus would have been in use for at least a century."

In describing the pottery from the Aegisthus Tomb, Wace (like Blegen) emphasizes the survival and vitality of the mainland ceramic tradition and its probable resurgent influence on the imported Cretan style. "These considerations seem to hint that even by the end of L.H.I. the native tradition of the mainland as exemplified in the shapes and patterns derived from the earlier Minyan and Matt-painted wares had already begun to influence the imported Minoan style, and was tending to create a distinctive Mycenaean type." In the same vein but in a larger context, he remarks that the Mycenaeans blended their own ideas with the imported Minoan culture and by the Third Late Helladic Period had evolved a specifically Mycenaean culture differing significantly from the Minoan civilization from which it had sprung.

One feature of the offerings found in the Tomb of Clytemnestra was especially involved in Evans' coming attack on Wace's chronology of the tholoi. A group of fifteen fragments of large vessels of the pithos type carved in green steatite* had been recovered, partly in Mrs. Schliemann's dig and partly during repairs carried out in 1913. They proved to belong to two very similar vases that Wace describes as "imitations in stone of one of the large medallion pithoi of Knossos, which belong to the transitional period at the end of the M.M.III. and the beginning of L.M.I." (Fig. 83).

Wace has some trouble, however, explaining this find in a mainland context that he believes is LHIII.

> No previous examples of this type of pithos in any material have been found on the mainland, so one is at a loss to date them. They would certainly be later than the Cretan originals in clay. . . . Ambitious stonework of this type corresponds well with the character of the Treasury of Atreus and the Tomb of Clytemnestra with their façades of elaborately carved stone of many colours. . . . We may therefore attribute these vases to the beginning of L.H.III. . . . In any case the vase cannot be earlier than L.H.II., as stone vases are excessively rare in the Shaft Graves; the supposition that an L.H.II. vase was placed in an L.H.III. royal tomb as a kind of heirloom would cause no difficulty.

On the origin and development of the tholos, Wace is sure of two points. He believes most emphatically that its monumental phases are to be attributed to mainland architects. And, although it was probably borrowed in

Figure 83

an undeveloped form from outside the mainland, the direct source was not Crete.

Both before and since the 1920s, scholars have suggested a connection with the so-called tholoi of the Early Minoan period in south central Crete. None of these stands to any great height; all that is usually left is a low ring of rubble masonry. There is thus no absolute proof that these tombs were roofed, or if so, how the roof was constructed. Dr. Stephanos Xanthoudides, who had excavated many of them, believed, from the enormous quantities of fallen stone found within the walls, that they were once vaulted like the tholoi of the mainland. The Cretan round tombs, however, do not appear to come down later in date than Middle Minoan I, *i.e.,* they were no longer built by the beginning of the second millennium. Yet only at the very end of LMIII, according to Wace, do true tholos tombs appear in Crete, and they seem more likely to be due to the influence of the mainland than to the reemergence of an earlier indigenous type after long disuse. "So far then as the Cretan evidence goes," Wace concludes, "it does not seem possible that the tholos tomb was brought to Mycenae from Crete, more especially since the earliest Minoan objects from Mycenae are those of the Shaft Graves."

Although he could scarcely foresee the all-out nature of Evans' reaction, Wace does try to forestall pro-Minoan arguments. "In Crete the great period of ashlar masonry . . . is the First Late Minoan Period. It might therefore be supposed by those unfamiliar with the sites of the mainland that the ashlar work of Mycenae should be assigned to a corresponding date." But he insists that imitation, especially in such monumental modes as architecture, takes considerable time to establish itself in a totally different environment; and he points to the continuing use of ashlar construction in much later Minoan building.

Wace mentions the possibility of some connection with the small Early Bronze domed tombs of the Cyclades. He also refers to the discovery of a LHIII tholos by an American expedition at Kolophon on the Asia Minor coast; and he suggests that "when the exploration of the early remains of Western Asia Minor can be undertaken, some clue to the origin of the tholos tomb may be found there. On the other hand, the late tholoi of Asia Minor, like those of Crete, may be only an importation from Mycenae."

More than forty years after Wace's pioneering study, the origin of the tholos tomb is still unresolved. A strong case has recently been reargued for a more or less continuous development from the Early Bronze "tholoi" of southern Crete to the earliest examples on the mainland; but opinion is divided on its validity. Perhaps the best statement is still Wace's final paragraph, although we would not be so sure that the earliest mainland stage appeared first at Mycenae itself.

> For the present we have no information to guide us to the home of the tholos tomb: but whatever its origin, it was certainly still in a primitive form when it was first introduced at Mycenae. It was the genius of the Mycenaean engineers and architects that, without the aid of any metal harder than bronze, transformed the mean vaults of the first group into marvellous subterranean cupolas like the Treasury of Atreus, which astonish the traveller to-day as much as they did Pausanias of old. The treasures of Atreus and his sons, which he [Pausanias] dreamt of, have long since been scattered to the four winds, but the Mycenaeans in these triumphs of structural ingenuity have bequeathed imperishable treasures to the world.

Wace makes only one or two oblique references in print to the sudden halt of the British excavations at Mycenae in 1923 and to the equally abrupt termination of his tenure as director of the British School at Athens. Few details were made public at the time, and it would serve no useful purpose to review them. Wace may have been less than tactful in private reactions against Evans' dominating personality; but it was Wace's message, not his manners, that was the real irritant. We have seen him (along with Blegen and others) groping for a synthesis that would both admit the pervasiveness of Minoan cultural influence on the mainland in LHI and II and at the same time identify a concurrent mainland individuality that strongly emerged toward the end of the Bronze Age in the full-blown Mycenaean period.

Evans' reaction, as we shall see, was to challenge in print the validity of any basis for this belief and also to make it impossible for its proponent to continue his leading part in the British School and its program of excavation. We can understand and even applaud the one action; but it is impossible to condone the second. Fortunately, saner counsel finally prevailed in British archaeological circles. Wace became a professor at Cambridge University and eventually returned to Greece as an excavator of proved and exceptional ability.

EVANS' POSTWAR POSITION

In 1927, four years after Wace's study of the royal tombs at Mycenae, Evans published a handsome, slender monograph called *The Shaft Graves and Bee-hive Tombs of Mycenae and Their Interrelation*. His thesis had already been outlined at the general meeting of the Hellenic Society in the very year following Wace's publication. After a brief review of Wace's historical reconstruction, Evans sums up his own reading of the evidence as follows:

> In one case, then, we find magnificent mausolea without contents, in the other case mere stone-lined pits huddled together, but containing the richest group of burial deposits that has ever been brought to light. . . . But may there not be a simple explanation at hand which avoids the necessity of calling in a second dynasty at all? It had occurred to me independently long since, and the idea, indeed, had been tentatively put out in an early Ashmolean Lecture, that the two sets of monuments in fact represented the remains of one and the same dynasty, the contents of the bee-hive [tholos] tombs [including the stelae] having been transferred to the grave pits [Shaft Graves] as a measure of security in view of some external danger. The same explanation had already occurred to Professor Percy Gardner . . .

It is hardly necessary to review in detail the majority of Evans' arguments to support this reactionary view that ignores mainland evidence established as early as Tsountas' day. To Evans' credit, "the very careful enumeration and description [of the Mycenae tholoi] by Mr. A. J. B. Wace" is characterized in a footnote as "a great advance on any preceding accounts"; and some sound observations and acute comparisons are made. But a sarcastic and overbearing tone and a persistence in regarding mainland cultural features in Minoan terms clouds the whole unfortunate essay. Furthermore, although the disturbed condition of the tholos tombs made ceramic dating less dependable than usual, Evans reverted to the far more imprecise (and generally outmoded) method of trying to establish synchronisms by analysis of style in major art forms.

Evans' over-all analysis of the date and characteristics of the contents of the Shaft Graves does not claim much more for Cretan influence than had Wace's own. "In the earlier stage represented in the Shaft Graves a considerable native ingredient, as we learn from the pottery, was still perceptible. By the later phase, corresponding with L.M.Ib, however, the predominant Cretan element triumphs all along the line . . ." A couple of sentences later, however, Wace's and Blegen's whole concept of an independent mainland scheme of chronology is challenged. "Parenthetically, it may be observed," wrote Evans, "that to call this civilization 'Helladic' is both untrue to fact and misleading to students." And he continues in the same vein: "The higher aspects of the culture revealed to us at Mycenae must in any case be recognized as belonging to the Minoan world. That world doubtless included provincial areas. . . . But Minoan Crete is still its centre, and . . . the influence of Knossos itself, the 'Great City,' was still predominant."

The real bombshell, however, is still to come. Wace's criteria for his three groups of tholoi may be acceptable, but his relative dates are backwards. "Greatly as the archaeological world is indebted to Mr. Wace for his painstaking study, and logical as the above results may be regarded *per se,* the gravest objection must be taken to his chronological conclusions." Then Evans points to a very real consideration—that, after a typological series has been set up, one must still be very careful to establish the *direction* of the development. So, for instance, rubble masonry is clearly a less sophisticated technique than ashlar; but rubble may just as well represent a degeneration from, as a forerunner of ashlar. "The truth is," says Evans, "that much of the evidence can be read both ways. The 'Atreus' and 'Clytemnestra' Tombs at Mycenae, structurally the most advanced, are probably the earliest on the site in point of time . . ."

Evans insists that the round tombs in the Cretan Messara are true tholoi and that the time interval between the latest of them and the mainland tholoi is not so great as is generally assumed. Yet he cannot point to Cretan examples that, by the wildest stretch of the imagination, could be the direct ancestors of the Treasury of Atreus. So he falls back on the "argument from silence," to which there can be no empirical refutation. "It seems probable that a part of the Anatolian coast [*i.e.,* Caria in the southwest] came within the area of true Minoan culture at an early date, and this might explain how it is that the finest and earliest of the Mycenae vaults make their appearance in an already Minoized form."

Evans' first precise argument concerns the technique of stone cutting. "On the technical side the most conspicuous instance of reading the evidence backwards is Mr. Wace's contention that the use of the saw was carried to the greatest proficiency in the latest structures. . . . The use of the saw in cutting conglomerate and other materials, so far from being a late characteristic, is a typically M.M.III technique [apparently on the mainland], parallel with similar work at Knossos." He also insists that fine carving in hard stone, such as that preserved on fragments from the façade of the Treasury of Atreus, is best paralleled in MMIII work at Knossos. He continues:

> In view of the existing evidence, it is perhaps hardly necessary to dwell on Mr. Wace's attempt to bring down the date of the "Treasury of Atreus" over three centuries later than that indicated by the decorative parallels above given, mainly on the ground of a painted sherd discovered by him beneath its threshold. This sherd . . . belongs . . . to the latest Mycenaean class, equivalent in date with L.M.IIIb in Crete. To use it as a base for dating this magnificent structure . . . is peculiarly unfortunate, since the ceramic group to which it belongs shows a complete divergence from the current style of Late Minoan Crete.

Evans then discusses the fragments of steatite jars that, as mentioned above, had clearly bothered Wace himself. "The correspondence in details and contour, visible in the steatite example with those of the finest class of M.M.III jars of this type, combined with the plaitwork decoration answering to that of M.M.III stone vessels of another form, supply sufficient warrant for concluding that we have here a contemporary counterpart in stone, belonging to the earlier M.M.III phase." In a footnote that refers to Wace's attempt to explain the fragments as LHIII, he inquires rhetorically, "How then, it may well be asked, did this master lapidary of the Mycenaean decadence obtain his models? By excavation in the Palace Magazines of Knossos?" And he treats with equal disdain Wace's suggestion that the vessel may have been an heirloom.

The case against Wace is reviewed in a final summation.

The "medallion" pithoi from the "Clytemnestra" Tomb . . . like the inlaid pot and bull's head "rhyton" from the "Atreus" *dromos,* as well as the comparisons suggested by the decorative sculptures of its façade, take us back to the earlier phase, *a,* of M.M.III, to which the most ancient Minoan elements found in the Shaft Graves also belong—in other words, well back into the seventeenth century B.C. Thus the two groups, so far from representing successive chronological stages, were contemporary with one another, and the theory of a "Tholos Tomb" dynasty succeeding one represented by the Shaft Graves falls to the ground.

Thus ends the essay that, more than any other publication, shows how warped Evans' once sound judgment had become in his later years, at least in relation to questions involving the mainland versus Crete.

We have already reviewed some of Evans' developing theories about Minoan-Mycenaean interrelations as formulated in the Introduction to the first volume of his *Palace of Minos.* This work had appeared in 1921 and belongs explicitly to his pre-World War I years. Probably the same could be said for most of the contents of the three bulky volumes (in five parts) that appeared between 1928 and 1935. In this sense, it would have been neater to consider them in the context of the previous chapter. Yet it is inevitable that the later volumes reflect increasingly his reactions to postwar discoveries and theories. They also present the results of some new small-scale excavations and tests at Knossos.

By long and careful study of the Minoan pottery and of foreign synchronisms, especially with Egypt, Evans has refined his chronological scheme and assigned extremely close absolute dates to the later phases. He now feels confident that it was a severe earthquake that destroyed the early palace toward the close of MMIII. Thus, it does not represent the dividing point between Middle and Late Minoan, but is followed by a short "epoch of Restoration" before the appearance of the first features to be associated with the Late Minoan period.

After experiencing personally one of the recurrent earthquakes in 1926, Evans feels he has gained new sympathy for the religious awe with which Cretans at all periods seem to have regarded the powers of the underworld. And he suggests that earthquakes rather than the fury of human foes may explain at least some of the catastrophes in antiquity. "To archaeological science it will be certainly a new suggestion that the successive destructions at Knossos, of which we have the stratified evidence, and which can indeed be approximately dated, correspond with successive seismic overthrows."

Severe earthquakes have occurred about twice a century in historical times and are likely to have been at least as frequent in antiquity. They could, he feels, have a direct bearing on the popularity of the ubiquitous "sanctuaries" with their massive pillars in the palace basements. They might also explain the Minoan veneration of bulls, which are often connected with the worship of Poseidon the Earth-Shaker. "Nor can the possibility be ignored that these great natural convulsions had political consequences, and that they may have been productive of the uprising of depressed elements in the population, or of a change of dynasty."

Excavation in the environs had made clear that at its zenith in LMI the palace was surrounded by villas of a "prosperous burgher class," and soundings farther out suggested that beyond these were smaller homes of "poorer inhabitants," crowded into close-packed blocks. Such a centripetal scheme had already been suggested by the excavation of towns like Gournia and Palaikastro. On the basis of the known Knossos examples of each class, Evans assigns to the villas an average size of 244 square yards and to the ordinary houses, 99 square yards. The Inner Residential Quarter seems to have occupied a total area of about 145,000 square yards and the "poorer outlying Zone" perhaps three times as much. Another very rough estimate is that the villas might have had an average of eight inhabitants and the ordinary houses somewhat more. "Without endeavouring to attain any too precise results, we may yet, on the basis supplied by the existing remains and the comparative materials, conclude that the Minoan town of Knossos at its most flourishing period, including its haven [harbor town], had held a population not much, if at all, under a hundred thousand souls." Most experts would now be inclined to believe that this estimate is a serious exaggeration.

Evans draws an attractive picture of the comparative safety of the Minoan city and its freedom to expand because of the absence of cramping fortifications. "The Homeric description—eureia Knōsos[73]—'Broad Knossos,' is specially distinctive as compared with the fenced-in cities of Mainland Greece. Of the populousness of Knossos again, 'the Great City,' we have a true record in the famous passage of the *Odyssey*,[74] where the 'Ninety Cities' of Ancient Crete are mentioned."

Proceeding to archaeological comparisons, Evans sees no contemporary equal, at least in the Aegean area. "Minoan Knossos in its great days was a centre of human habitation to which no rival, certainly, could have been found on the European side. Mycenae as a great and civilized city was only just in the making at the hands of Minoan conquerors and colonists. The position of Knossos must have been in many respects unrivalled even on the East side of the Mediterranean basin. No fenced city, surely, on the Syrian coast, shut in by walls and with its fields the constant prey of the passing invader, had either its expanse or its population." This concept of a fenced city is surely a misleading one, at least for mainland Greece. Without suggesting that the population of Mycenae approached that of Knossos, no one believes that the bulk of its population lived within the fortified acropolis.

Evans is not willing to commit himself too far in regard to the internal political situation in Crete, but there are frequent hints that in the "true Golden Age of the Island" Knossos probably had more than local control. "In Crete itself some superior sway may well have been wielded by a Minoan dynasty, and the general agreement that we find in all the externals of life throughout a wide area of the Island . . . speaks in favour of some central administration and organization. . . . There is much in all this that recalls to mind the general well-being fostered by the *Pax Romana* in the best days of the Empire."

The last volume of *The Palace of Minos,* published in 1935, contains Evans' final pronouncements on mainland-Minoan relationships. As he wrote the Preface in the previous year, he looked back nostalgically over the past. "Just forty years from the beginning of my first exploration of the site of Knossos it has been given me to complete this final Volume . . ." He points to the tremendous amount of comparative material drawn together from "far beyond the Aegean and even the Libyan Sea" and notes that without the help of many colleagues the task he was now completing would "transcend the limits of individual capacity." It is indeed natural that its author should claim for this great work "some title to be regarded as an Encyclopaedia of Minoan cultural features, of its Art, and of its Religion."

The same Preface also contains a touching tribute to several associates whom death has removed from the scene. The volume is dedicated to Federico Halbherr who had been so helpful when "the urge towards exploring what lay behind the traditions of Minos and Daedalos, and of the fabled Labyrinth, together with the quest of a still earlier form of writing, had led me to Knossos." A still more poignant passage refers to Mackenzie, who had been archaeological curator at Knossos as late as 1928. If there had been friction between the two long-time associates, it was now completely erased. No warmer tribute could be written, and excerpts can scarcely give the full flavor.

It has been my grave misfortune to have been deprived through a now lengthening space of years—owing to a mental affection that had left no avenue for hope—of the invaluable services of my friend and colleague Duncan Mackenzie. . . . Nothing could replace the friendly personal contact and availability for consultation on difficult points with one of such great special knowledge. His Highland loyalty never failed, and the simple surroundings of his earlier years gave him an inner understanding of the native workmen and a fellow-feeling with them that was a real asset in the course of our spadework. . . . No wedding ceremony, no baptism, no wake was complete among the villagers without the sanction of his presence . . . [And then, a short separate paragraph]

Even as these words return from the printers' hands there reaches me from Italy the brief announcement that, a few days earlier, on August the 25th that vexed Spirit had found release at last.

But there is no softening here toward at least one living colleague. Evans repeats at great length arguments advanced six years before in connection with Wace's excavations at Mycenae. If anything, increased exasperation is betrayed with a theory that "actually refers the finest example [of the tholoi] . . . to the last age of decadence!" Such lack of taste and perception "is of a piece with the terminology—still in vogue among those who approach the Minoan world backwards, from the Mainland side— which describes the products of that unified culture, when found North of the Aegean, as 'Late Helladic.' . . . The Roman Wall itself becomes 'Late British' with equal reason!"

It is clear that Evans' final position in 1935 had hardened far beyond the prewar years. Now he not only denies any notable cultural independence on the mainland before 1400, but contradicts the position that he and Mackenzie had earlier taken about the shift of cultural as well as political leadership to the mainland in the last two centuries of the Bronze Age.

He also firmly rejects a theory that was gaining very strong support— that the "final" destruction at the end of his LMII phase at Knossos might imply the presence of newcomers from abroad.

The popular idea of the fall of the Knossian Palace [at the end of LMII] seems to be that it was due to some hostile irruption from the Mainland side, and the explanation of the new fusing process that now seems to have set in [in early LMIII] would naturally be based on this view. But the ceramic data before us . . . lend no countenance to such a conclusion. . . . Whatever local break was caused by the overthrow of the Great Palace, there was no real interruption in the local culture, and indeed the Residence of its Priest-kings may simply have been shifted to another site. It will be seen that many current ideas regarding the beginnings of the succeeding L.M.IIIa phase—to use the Cretan terminology—must be radically revised.

The only detailed information Evans ever published on the Linear B
tablets from Knossos occurs in the second part of the final volume of *The
Palace of Minos*. He recalls that their discovery, a generation earlier,
"excited more general interest than any other." But he himself is obviously
discouraged, and his prognosis for their decipherment is not bright.

> The widespread hopes of its early interpretation were not verified. No
> one, indeed, who understood the real conditions could expect such a
> speedy solution of the problem. According to every indication . . . the
> root affinities of the original language lay on the Anatolian side. The
> phonetic value of the signs themselves was itself unknown. . . . The con-
> ditions, indeed, are by no means so favourable as in the Etruscan
> inscriptions, where we have to deal with a known alphabet, yet in that
> case—after over three generations of research—how vain on the whole
> has been the effort at decipherment! Of the Minoan script, not only the
> language but the greater part of the phonetic values of its characters are
> both lost. . . . All that I have been able here to attempt—after copying
> over 1,600 documents of which the whole or some material part had
> survived, and as the outcome of prolonged researches into their details
> and as to the various applications of the signs themselves—is at most
> of a preliminary nature.

Actually, he provides line drawings and a few photographs for slightly
over 100 examples; and he includes a series of tables of the complete
syllabary, as well as a comparison with that of Linear A. There is also a
careful analysis of the symbols and ideograms, their possible connection
with other writing systems (especially that of Egypt), the system of numeration, the tablet shapes, the business methods and the economic and agricultural practices that they illustrate. Very little is said here about the ideas
formerly expressed that some of the Linear B tablets might be considerably
earlier than the destruction about 1400, and not a single word is mentioned
about the possibility that others could be considerably later.

He then turns to the sparse examples of writing that had been discovered
on mainland pottery, mainly stirrup jars.

> The inscriptions of the Mainland offshoot of Class B . . . in some cases
> give evidence of such close agreement with their Knossian palatial pro-
> totypes as equally to entail the conclusion that they were separated from
> the other by only a short interval of time [*i.e.*, the mainland examples
> must date close to 1400]. . . . It is clear that both at Knossos and the
> Mainland sites we have to do with the same language. This absolute
> correspondence, indeed, of a series of name-groups—out of the very
> limited number recorded—on the "stirrup vases" of the Boeotian Thebes

and Tiryns, belonging to the period immediately succeeding those on the latest clay documents of the Knossian Palace, might even suggest that in certain cases we have to do with the same individuals.

Evans' historical theories based on this new mainland evidence might almost be anticipated.

That Script B of Knossos—the system of writing that reflected the highly elaborate bureaucratic methods of its later Priest-kings—should reappear in the principal Mainland centres—at Tiryns and Mycenae, as well as Thebes and Orchomenos—in the period that succeeds the fall of the Great Palace is itself an arresting phenomenon. Its reappearance on so many urban sites would naturally imply that the language and script was current at this time not only at the Courts but among the ordinary citizens, both in the Peloponnese and throughout a large tract of Northern Greece beyond the Gulf. It follows that, to at least the middle of the Fourteenth Century B.C., there is no place either at Mycenae or at Thebes for Greek-speaking dynasts. Apart from certain innovations due to the climate and environment, including the reaction of the older indigenous element [Greek speakers?], the culture, like the language, was still Minoan to the core.

He proceeds to cast doubt on the hypothesis that Linear B continued in use on the mainland until the end of the Bronze Age and that it may have been via the mainland that Cyprus borrowed the script that continued to be used to write Greek as late as classical times. He admits that a carelessly inscribed jar rim from Asinê (firmly dated about 1200) bears three undoubted Linear B symbols, but "it seems probable that the Asinê potter—though himself illiterate—had before him some existing document of the old script, the signs of which he may have used as decorative models . . ." Evans concludes that the Knossian script is a more probable source of the Cypriote, and he suggests that "the only real hope of even approximately learning the values of the Minoan signs" rests with a careful comparison of the known phonetic equivalents of the Minoan-derived symbols in Cyprus.

In addition to the distinctive pottery types and writing system in the "last palatial phase" (LMII) at Knossos, Evans was aware of a phenomenon to which he refers as "a military and indeed militaristic aspect." Many of the tablets clearly refer to a corps of charioteers and to the issuing of weapons and armor to a garrison. Equally unmistakable is the emphasis on soldierly equipment in contemporary Knossian tombs, such as the Warrior Graves. He provides a thorough review of the available evidence for the form and development of the bow and arrow, sword, dagger, helmet, cuirass, chariot and horse's harness. It is equally characteristic that, though allowing the earlier Helladic inhabitants the use of perforated boar's tusks for necklaces, he insists that "their claim to have initiated this use for Minoan helmets must be altogether disallowed." Indeed, it is somewhat of a shock to find him conceding that "the use of the horse . . . was earlier diffused on the Mainland side, where the Argolid Plain offered more special facilities than in Crete itself."

Clearly some explanation was needed for the military emphasis during the final phases of the palace, which is in such stark contrast to the apparent peacefulness of earlier Minoan times and even to contemporary Crete, except for Knossos. Evans believes that the answer lies in the sudden accession of a new and aggressive dynasty of native priest-kings. They had not only forcibly subdued their own island but probably much of the mainland too. An ominous clue is the LMII fresco fragment that shows a red-skinned "Minoan officer" at the double with at least one black-skinned follower (Fig. 84).

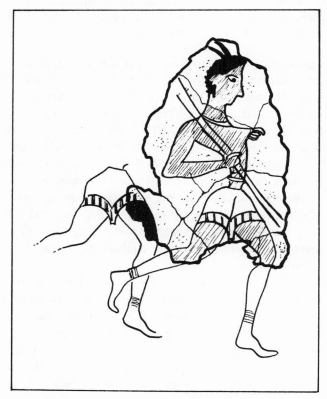

Figure 84

It seems highly probable that these docile and easily drilled negro bands were actually employed in Minoan military enterprises on the Mainland side in much the same way as the swarthy troops of Ibrahim Pasha [a Turkish general during the Greek War of Independence]. Had black mercenaries, under Knossian leadership, overrun the Morea [Peloponnese] some thirty-three centuries earlier? . . . May we not here, indeed, recognize the "Second Minos" of later story—the tyrant of Athens who, according to the grim traditions, fed the Minotaur with its tribute children, but who also rose to fame as the first organizer of the "Empire of the Sea"? Had Athens, too, like contemporary Canaanite cities under Pharaoh's sway, held a negro garrison?

The militarism, the new pottery types and the intensified bureaucracy aided by the new script were not the only signs that something different was going on at Knossos in the two or three generations before 1400. Clear evidence had been found for major changes in palace architecture. The Throne Room complex now stood out as a "revolutionary intrusion, effacing all previous remains" and a "wholesale invasion of new elements." In its stylized and formal griffin mosaic, the shading of the lower contours of the body represents "the first recorded instance of a regularized attempt to render Chiaroscuro." The wonderful gypsum throne flanked by two wingless griffins faced a sunken lustral area, and a door to the right flanked by another pair of griffins gave access to the goddess' own inner shrine, though "the images of the Goddess and her votaries, the Sacral Horns, and Double Axes, such as had once been placed here, had disappeared."

Evans attains considerable suspense as he described "the Closing Scene" in the Throne Room (Fig. 47).

It would seem that preparations were on foot for some anointing ceremony in the "Lustral Basin" in which the Papa Rè [Priest-King] himself may well have been called on to play a leading part. For this it had evidently been found necessary to refill most of the alabaster oil vessels, usually placed, as the marks of their bases on the pavement show, along the wall to the left of the entrance to the Inner Shrine, where there was a convenient nook for this purpose. Five out of six of these had been removed . . . from their place of storage and set down irregularly in the area in the entrance opening of the "Room of the Throne." One of the large oil *pithoi* from the Magazines, the contents of which were conveniently low, had been carried in here and laid down on its side so that the oil could be easily ladled into the *alabastra*. But this initial task was never destined to reach its fulfilment. . . . What happened here seems exactly to have resembled what . . . took place in the "Sculptor's Workshop" . . . where the alabaster and limestone "amphoras" were left unfinished on the floor. The sudden breaking off of tasks begun—so conspicuous in the first case—surely points to an instantaneous cause.

Evans believes quite firmly now that a sudden and major earthquake explains the disaster better than an enemy attack. There was evidence of severe burning, with clear indications that a strong wind was blowing from the southwest; thus, the month was probably March. But he points out that a lamp or brazier upset by the quake could easily account for the fire after the inhabitants had fled to the open fields. And the scarcity of precious objects on the floors could be as well explained by the survivors' combing the ruins as by hostile pillagers. Furthermore, if foreign attackers had stayed, there should be evidence of cultural novelties in the following period, but "the evidence of neighbouring cemeteries . . . [shows that] the general course of civilization was not sensibly interrupted."

Why, then, was the palace not rebuilt, as it had been after several equally severe earthquakes? Evans' answer to this is startling at first, but actually not out of line with the train of reasoning that he had been gradually developing over thirty-five years.

On this occasion the catastrophe was final. Squatters, indeed, after a short interval of years, occupied the probably considerable shelter still offered by the remains of the fabric. But the Minoan augurs may have at last satisfied themselves that the Powers of the Underworld were not to be exorcized. The long experiment was given up, and there are some reasons for supposing that the residence of the Priest-kings of Knossos was, perhaps not for the first time, transferred to a Mainland site, quite probably, indeed, to Mycenae, at this time re-decorated according to the latest Knossian fashion.

It was surely the decree of some merciful Providence that this aged pioneer who had contributed so long and brilliantly to the rediscovery of Aegean civilization did not have to face the final clinching evidence that utterly destroyed his increasingly fantastic theories.

P E N D L E B U R Y ' S   S Y N T H E S I S

Probably no human being, certainly no archaeologist, has known Crete as well as J. D. S. Pendlebury. He had worked for several seasons at Knossos and seemed to be Evans' heir apparent just as surely as Dörpfeld had succeeded Schliemann at Troy. Pendlebury's early experience in Egyptian archaeology gave him an important advantage in problems involving connection between the Aegean and the Near East. He had published, with Evans' approval and support, the useful *Handbook to the Palace of Minos* (1935). Like Schliemann, Evans and Blegen in their younger days, Pendlebury was an avid field explorer. He was a familiar and respected figure in every corner of Crete and had conducted important excavations in his own right. No one could have written with greater first-hand knowledge and recognized authority on Minoan prehistory. When *The Archaeology of Crete* appeared in 1939, it was immediately recognized as not only an up-to-date summary of Evans' bulky publication, but a more balanced synthesis of the equally important evidence that had accumulated since 1900 from many other quarters of the island. The reprinting of *The Archaeology of Crete* in 1964 shows the enduring quality of his scholarly attainments.

In addition to academic competence, Pendlebury had special qualities of personal magnetism, perseverance and courage. His heroic stature was climaxed, in the eyes of friends everywhere and particularly of all Cretans, by his death during the abortive resistance to the German parachute invasion of Crete in 1941. Cretans will never forget his valor.

In his Introduction Pendlebury makes it plain why he has decided to follow the chronological method of presentation. He fears that the topical method, as used by Glotz for instance, may obscure the understanding of over-all historical development and change. Yet within each of Evans' nine time periods Pendlebury does discuss separate topics such as architecture, sculpture, ceramics, burial customs and foreign relations. He also includes very useful site lists and maps of population distribution for each chronological subdivision. And his latest chapters follow the chronicle of ancient Cretan civilization down to Roman times.

In general Pendlebury supports the conclusions and theories drawn by Evans from the archaeological material. Nevertheless, he asked Wace to read his text in manuscript and acknowledges "many valuable criticisms and suggestions." There may be a connection here with a remark on terminology. "I have unrepentantly used the term Late Helladic I, II and III for Mycenaean I, II and III. L.H. is more convenient than Myc, it does not attempt to ram the name of a city down the throat of a country, and, as we shall see, we must have some distinction between Crete and the Mainland, so L.M. will not do." This point of view required a good deal of courage in Evans' associate, although by 1939 no other position could be defended.

On the other hand, Evans' basic chronological framework for Minoan Crete is vigorously upheld against current criticism. "In the present state of our knowledge," says Pendlebury, "it would be absurd to confuse matters by altering the arrangement. . . . Until we have got something better to put in its place the terminology which has acted so well for so long must be kept." Pendlebury states clearly, too, the basis for both absolute and relative chronology, which is so vital a framework for Aegean prehistory. "The positive dating of the Bronze Age Periods in the Aegean depends entirely on foreign contacts—mainly with Egypt. Sometimes this is simple, as for example when objects bearing the name of Amenhotep III and Ty [his queen] are found in L.H.III deposits at Mycenae and L.H.III vases are found in the city of their successor, Akhenaten, in Egypt, or when a M.M.II vase is found in a XIIth Dynasty grave and a XIIth Dynasty statue in a M.M.II deposit."

Pendlebury is somewhat less rigid than Evans in regarding the evidence from Knossos as the touchstone and measure for developments throughout Crete.

> For comparative dating in Crete itself pottery is of course our chief criterion, and the duration of the periods . . . is determined by changes of style. Naturally everything is based on Knossos, for not only was that the first and most important site to be excavated but also at Knossos alone is the series complete. But . . . we must always be prepared to accept divergencies from the Knossian series, particularly on the smaller sites. . . . Evidence from stratification and from style must go hand in hand. It is fortunate that Knossos was excavated by two men who realized this. So, also, it must be recognized that the styles and periods often slide almost imperceptibly one into the next. It was slow progress, not the town crier, that ordained the change from E.M.III to M.M.I. We must not expect watertight compartments . . .

Pendlebury is equally forthright on the vital matter of basing theories, however tentative, on the archaeological evidence at hand. "In the absence of documents which we can read and believe we are bound to progress by means of theories. Any theory is justifiable which agrees with the greatest number of facts known at the time and contradicts neither a vital fact nor human nature and reason. The most reasonable theory, which gives a connected history, should hold the field until a better one is produced or until it is flatly contradicted by some newly discovered fact." He might have added, however, that tentative theories sometimes have an unfortunate tendency to become dogma, first with the originator and then in the minds of contemporaries and successors if the originator has attained great prestige.

We are particularly interested, of course, in Pendlebury's assessment of the relationship between Crete and the mainland during the Late Bronze Age. Here he shows considerable flexibility and a willingness to accept evidence that forces him to differ from the views of Evans and Mackenzie.

He admits many of the facts already brought out in our review of Wace's and Blegen's article on trade, which appeared in the same year as *The Archaeology of Crete*. Yet he will not go nearly as far as their modest conclusions as to the implications of this evidence about mainland independence and originality long before 1400. He supports Wace in the controversy with Evans over the development of the tholos tombs, stating flatly, "Architecturally the greatest contribution of the mainland was the Tholos tomb. Nothing like this was constructed in Crete until L.M.III."

Yet, in fact, Pendlebury adopts almost completely the Evans thesis about the political situation.

> So Minoanized does the rest of the Aegean become that it is impossible for the present writer at least to avoid the conclusion that it was dominated politically by Crete. Athenian tradition, always the most vocal, remembered the tyranny of Minos over the Saronic gulf. We cannot separate the legend of the youth and maidens, sent to be devoured by the Minotaur, from the bull-sports of Late Minoan Crete. . . . The peace of the seas is essential to an empire whose wealth is based on trade, and the thalassocracy of Minos is no myth. But that the empire was not obtained by a deliberate policy of fire and sword seems clear from the lack of a general catastrophe on the Mainland at the beginning of the Late Bronze Age.

The admitted dissimilarity in mainland palace architecture is explained as remodeling on essentially Minoan lines. As for the striking differences in the frescoes, a parallel is drawn with India under British colonial rule. "But equally, as in India, the native princes must have been allowed to continue ruling as vassals. Otherwise the intensely mainland character of the known frescoes could hardly have existed. Just as in the palace of an Indian Prince European artists will be employed on the condition that their subject-matter is of interest to the Indian, so with the Mainland dominions of Crete the style is Minoan, but the subjects are Mainland." Thus Pendlebury, too, reflects the lingering vestiges of modern colonial preconceptions that clouded the vision of so many nineteenth-century historians of earlier epochs.

A particular interest attaches to Pendlebury's description of the short period of a couple of generations just before 1400 that Evans called LMII. Its culture, characterized by Palace Style pottery and Linear B script, had proved to be quite exotic to the rest of Crete; and Evans had seen in it the final stage of Knossian control over the whole island with a kind of special regal exclusiveness at the capital itself. Pendlebury reveals the same Knosso-centric obsession when he remarks that "the L.M.II style appealed to the Mainland, whereas it was practically confined to Knossos

in Crete . . ." How near he was at this point, however, to considering the
fairly obvious reverse possibilities is shown by a footnote. "Snijder . . . indeed goes so far as to consider L.M.II an offshoot of the Mainland style,
and having regard to the fact that this short-lived, locally restricted style
can only have overlapped the latter part of L.H.II, it is hard to argue against
him."

We are equally concerned about Pendlebury's views on the destruction
of the center or centers of this Minoan "empire." Here again he differs considerably from Evans.

> The catastrophe which overtook the Cretan cities at the end of L.M.Ib
> (or L.M.II at Knossos) was practically universal. Knossos, Phaistos,
> Agia Triadha, Gournia, Mokhlos, Mallia, and Zakros all show traces of
> violent destruction accompanied by burning. At Palaikastro, Pseira,
> Nirou Khani, Tylissos and Platé there is a distinct break in the habita-
> tion, though no trace of burning was found. This overwhelming disaster
> must have taken place at one and the same time and it has been attrib-
> uted to a severe earthquake. Earthquakes, however, in ancient times
> are not liable to cause fires . . . Everything, indeed, points to a deliber-
> ate sacking on the part of enemies of the most powerful cities in Crete.
> We have seen the prosperity of the period and it is obvious that no
> mere Viking raid could have accomplished such destruction. It must
> have been a highly organized expedition with an avowed purpose. That
> this purpose was not to invade and colonize the island is clear from the
> way in which the Minoan culture continues, though in a very minor
> key, without any Mainland influence until the very end of L.M.III.
> The object of this thorough, relentless destruction must have been purely
> political.

Pendlebury then proceeds to outline two current theories that might
account for the above facts. He admits that "both have much to be said
for them and, curiously enough, they are diametrically opposed." Pendlebury thinks that one theory, proposed by Wace, has not previously appeared in print. According to it, Crete never had political control over the
mainland, but in LMII the mainland was strong enough to conquer Crete,
presumably without serious resistance. The widespread destruction about
1400 might then represent a Cretan nationalist revolt that threw off the
foreign yoke. Pendlebury does not agree with Wace's theory, but neither
does he attempt to refute it.

The alternate explanation, which Pendlebury accepts, could be called
the orthodox one in 1939 and for some years afterward. It held that Crete,
under Knossian leadership, had attained essential political control of the
whole Aegean area before 1400 and that the destruction of Minoan sites

about that time reflects a successful mainland revolt carried to the island itself. Pendlebury believes, in spite of the evidence for extensive mainland participation in foreign trade before 1400, that the main motivation for the invasion was mainland resentment against taxation and exclusion from foreign markets.

He carries on the historical reconstruction of the last days of Knossos in an even more dramatic fashion than Evans.

> Now there is a name which is always associated, if not with the sack of Knossos, at least with the liberation of its subjects—Theseus. . . . It has already been suggested that the seven youths and seven maidens may have been the Mainland quota for the bull-ring at Knossos. That is just the type of detail that would be remembered, the more so in that it may well have been the sentimental reason without which no purely commercial war can ever take place. No doubt the rape of Helen was a very good rallying cry when the Mycenaean Empire wished to break through to the Black Sea trade which Troy was keeping for itself. And in the last decade of the fifteenth century on a spring day, when a strong South wind was blowing which carried the flames of the burning beams almost horizontally northwards, Knossos fell. The final scene takes place in the most dramatic room ever excavated—the Throne Room. It was found in a state of complete confusion. A great oil jar lay over-turned in one corner, ritual vessels were in the act of being used when the disaster came. It looks as if the king had been hurried here to undergo too late some last ceremony in the hopes of saving the people. Theseus and Minotaur! Dare we believe that he wore the mask of a bull?

NILSSON'S VIEW

Martin P. Nilsson is not a field archaeologist, but he follows the results of excavation closely and is an expert critic and synthesist. Now retired from his professorship at the University of Lund in Sweden, he still continues his active scholarly career. His *Homer and Mycenae* (1933)—an expansion of the Sather lectures at the University of California—presents better than any other single volume a judicious appraisal of the whole sweep of Homeric and Mycenaean studies between the wars and even before. Above all, we shall be interested in his chapter "The History of the Mycenaean Age," but throughout the book there is material that concerns our theme. Nilsson is primarily an authority on mythology and religion, but he is fully in control of the current arguments from linguistic and archaeological evidence. These three sources—mythology, linguistics and archaeology—are judiciously utilized to reconstruct Mycenaean history.

He recognizes that they offer very incomplete and often ambiguous evidence; but they are the only means available and "in dealing with the origin and development of epic poetry, which ultimately goes back to Mycenaean times, we must try to form some idea of the outlines of the history of that age." He wisely avoids the circular arguments sometimes used in which the content of the poems themselves is used to reconstruct a particular historical period. "Our best method will be to try and see what can be reasonably stated and inferred in this respect independently of Homer and to apply the results to the understanding of the genesis of the epic poetry."

To Nilsson, the main questions are: Who were the Mycenaeans? What can be inferred about the political and social contributions of the Mycenaean Age, especially about the migration of Greek speakers?

He approaches the first question with the salutary warning that there is no more perilous undertaking than the attempt to equate an archaeologically defined prehistoric group showing common traits in its material culture with a particular race and/or language. Alien languages are often adopted from or by conquerors or conquered. Race is a slippery concept even with living subjects and is especially difficult if all one has to depend on is a few skulls or stylized representations in art. Pottery, the prehistorian's most valuable evidence, is too fragile to have been used as containers by people constantly on the move. "It may be considered as pretty certain that the invading Greeks had no pottery of their own . . ."

Nilsson agrees with Blegen and others that the people of the Aegean area before 2000 definitely were not Greek speakers. "To this pre-Greek population the Minoan people belonged. . . . The Minoan language was certainly non-Greek, for if it had been Greek the efforts of the most competent and sagacious scholars to decipher the Minoan script would certainly not have failed." This last remark is surely a naïve one in view of Evans' continued delay in publishing the Knossos tablets.

At what points after 2000, asks Nilsson, does archaeology show "breaks" in civilization and the introduction of foreign elements of culture, indicating the presence of a foreign people? Like Blegen and others, he sees three such "breaks" in the record—the advent about 1900 of the "gray Minyan people," who apparently caused widespread destruction of earlier sites; the sudden appearance about 1600 of Minoan culture on the mainland; the destruction of Mycenaean strongholds between 1200 and 1100, traditionally connected with the Dorian invasion. He rules out the last because of the unanimous tradition that other Greek dialects had been spoken in the peninsula before Doric. Turning to the second, he points out that there are two explanations for the Minoization of mainland culture. We have already reviewed the theory of Minoan political supremacy championed by Evans and the explanation in terms of mainland political autonomy but cultural dependence held by Wace and Blegen. Nilsson strongly supports the latter.

In fact he goes further than Wace and Blegen in underlining mainland initiative in the early Mycenaean period. "Greek tribes, barbarous but open-minded, and very subject to the lure of a superior civilization, as Aryan peoples always have shown themselves, warlike and fond of booty, may have occupied Greece and come into contact with the Minoans. Roving and pillaging they may have raided Crete and taken booty, and they may also have carried on some trade with the Minoans. They may have acquired a taste for the rich and splendid Minoan culture, and they may have brought not only valuables but men also and among them craftsmen to their strongholds in the mainland."

He then proceeds to outline his famous "eleven points," which in sum strongly suggest that Mycenaean civilization—although heavily Minoized —had decidedly un-Minoan aspects, some of which point to a northern origin. Mackenzie and Evans had tried to refute some of these arguments, such as those about the megaron type of architecture and costume, but Nilsson is unconvinced. The use of amber, especially for beads, is another point of difference. Amber is very common in early Mycenaean graves but is practically never found in Crete. Similarly, the mainlanders were very fond of sewing rows of boar's tusks on their leather helmets, but no tusks or art representations of tusk helmets occur in Cretan contexts until Late Minoan III.

Writing, on the other hand, is very scarce on the mainland and widespread in Crete. "If the Mycenaeans had been Cretan colonists we could not imagine them allowing the art of writing to fall into disuse, but if they were barbarians who invaded Greece it is quite natural." Nilsson also feels an important "difference in spirit" between what seems to have been a Minoan emphasis on peaceful pursuits and an obvious Mycenaean liking for war, hunting and raiding. He notes an elaboration about the Mycenaean burial customs and the cult of heroes that cannot be paralleled in Crete. Again, the names of almost all those who figure in the myths going back to the Mycenaean age are Greek, not pre-Greek in etymology. And Minoan art is "essentially small art," while there is a definite tendency toward monumentality in such Mycenaean remains as the tholos tombs and the Lion Gate.

Generally speaking, Nilsson's distinctions are clear, reasonably precise and essentially sound. In sum, they lead him to a firm contradiction of Evans' view that Mycenaean civilization is essentially a watered-down colonial version of the Minoan. "So many differences exist between the Mycenaean and the Minoan civilization which cannot be explained by an organic development of the Minoan culture under different conditions, and which very definitely point northwards, that we may state confidently that they were brought in by a people with northern connections who over took [he means "took over"] the Minoan culture but mixed it up with elements of their own."

Assuming that there really was an un-Minoan and presumably Greek element in Mycenaean civilization, the question still arises as to when and how the first Greek speakers reached the peninsula. In fact, Nilsson avoids taking a stand. "The opinion embraced by many scholars, especially those of a later generation, that the first immigration of the Greeks coincides with the break between Early and Middle Helladic [about 2000] cannot be definitely disproved nor can it be proved." But, by a process of elimination, one must assume that he considered this the most likely juncture for the arrival of Greek speakers.

After discussing the successive destructions of the palace at Knossos and their apparent connection with the vicissitudes of other Minoan sites, Nilsson suggests certain connections with the mainland situation. Cretan disasters contemporary with the earlier Mycenaean period, when Minoan culture is becoming paramount on the mainland, may be explained as the raids of earlier Greek-speaking "Mycenaeans" whose dialect was Ionic. It is perhaps to this time that the Theseus myth belongs, with its implications of a strong Crete that posed a threat to the mainland, and especially to Ionic Athens. The total collapse of Minoan civilization after the destruction of Knossos about 1400 coincides with a new vigor on the mainland. "No doubt seems to be possible as to the correlation of the fall of Cnossos with the bloom of the Mycenaean centres of the mainland. It points to a vigorous and successful attack of the mainland tribes on Cnossos. This is justly the general opinion. The people to whom this war is to be ascribed are, of course, the Achaeans who certainly were the dominating population of the mainland in the late period of the Mycenaean Age."

Nilsson also tries to interpret the opinion of Near Eastern scholars as to how much, if at all, the Mycenaeans are mentioned in contemporary Hittite and Egyptian documents. He concludes that the least debatable equation from Hittite sources is that "Ahhijawā" refers to Achaea. King Mursil, who ascended the throne after 1336, wrote to his "brother, the king of Ahhijawā." This king was apparently on much the same footing with the Hittite empire as the kings of Egypt, Babylonia and Assyria. "There is, of course, no place for this great empire in Asia Minor. . . . It must be the Achaean Empire of Mycenaean Greece, members of which had taken possession of part of the southern coast of Asia Minor."

Toward the end of the Bronze Age, as the Mycenaeans intensify their trade and perhaps even colonial activities along the main route to the Near East through Rhodes and Cyprus, there are also apparent references in Egyptian documents. The Tell-el-Amarna letters of the early fourteenth century mention that the tribe of "Danuna" had settled on the coast of Palestine. Nilsson seems favorable to the suggestion that the Danuna may be equated with the "Danaoi," one of Homer's commonest names for the Greeks who attacked Troy. Toward the close of the thirteenth and in the early twelfth century a motley collection of "peoples from the sea" was attacking Egypt. The names of those who were beaten off in a great land and sea attack on the delta in 1221 include the Luka (Lycians), Turusha (Tyrsenoi = Etruscans?), Shardana (Sardinians) and "Aqaiwasha." Nilsson tends to agree with the suggestion that the last-named may again be the Achaeans.

Nilsson feels that the late Mycenaean period "was really the Heroic Age of the Greeks," and in such a context the attack on Troy is a natural event. He strongly supports the historicity of the Trojan War but is very skeptical about the economic reasons alleged by modern scholars. It is true that Schliemann's Hissarlik is in a strategic position to control trade by land and sea between Europe and Asia. But we should not read modern, highly developed economic motives into the ancient record without more justification. The Mycenaeans were ambitious, quarrelsome, avaricious plunderers without long-range economic or military strategy. We have to do with "an age of wars and of strife, of extensive wanderings and oversea expeditions, the Heroic Age of the Greeks. This is the background of the Greek myths and of the Homeric poems."

After the unsuccessful attacks on Egypt the raids of the Sea People subsided. In Greece itself Nilsson thinks that the exhaustion caused by these exertions is visible in the poverty of the sub-Mycenaean period. And Nilsson implies that the last Mycenaeans were in no condition to withstand the hardy northerners whom tradition associated with the Dorian invasion.

What is Nilsson's assessment of the main points of contact between the Mycenaean age and the Homeric poems? He notes that all Homeric scholars now believe that the poems were composed in more or less their present form at the beginning of the historical period, though exact chronological estimates range all the way from the tenth to the sixth century.

Shortly after the discovery of the Mycenaean civilization it was realized that certain descriptions in Homer correspond closely to and are explained by objects and elements appearing in the Mycenaean civilization but not in the [later] Archaic Age. . . .

But he also insists that

> On the other hand, other and not less conspicuous elements in Homer refer certainly to the Archaic Age. . . . It is very unwise to treat Homer as chiefly a product of the Mycenaean Age, and to consider the elements from this age as survivals which may be put on one side is as unwise as to consider the passages referring to the Archaic Age as irrelevant additions. . . .

Serious problems are raised by the discovery that

> The Homeric poems contain elements from widely differing ages. . . . [but] we have to accept it without circumlocution and to try to comprehend this state of things and to explain how it is possible and how it came about.

His examples are categorized as "definitely late" (*i.e.,* post-Mycenaean), "definitely early" (*i.e.,* Mycenaean) and "controversial points." In the late category he puts, for example, elaborate brooches like that worn by Odysseus[75] and references to the Phoenicians, especially in the *Odyssey*. Among the "elements deriving from the Mycenaean Age" he lists the cup of Nestor; the boar's-tusk helmet of Meriones; the kyanos (blue glass paste) frieze in the palace of Alkinoos; the big body-shield ("tower" and "figure-eight" types). In addition to material objects, he states quite positively that "there are references to political and geographical conditions which cannot possibly belong to the Archaic Age of Greece or the intermediate period but only fit in with the Mycenaean Age."

On the other hand, Nilsson regards as unprovable Evans' contention that Minoan art is reflected in the Homeric poems. "Descriptions of works of art are often said to refer to the Minoan art. It would not be astonishing if they did. . . . But the question being so controversial they cannot be adduced as reliable evidence."

Burial customs pose a particularly difficult problem for those who hold the general belief that Homer faithfully reflects Mycenaean practices. The bodies of Homeric heroes are always cremated in a great pyre, and of course cremation was common in the Iron Age. On the other hand, archaeology seems to show that the universal Mycenaean rite was inhumation. Nilsson suggests a compromise and illustrates it by referring to the recent Swedish discovery of an almost unplundered tholos tomb at Midea, near Mycenae.

> Professor [Axel] Persson's interpretation seems to be fully justified, viz. that the bones in the smaller pit are those of men and animals slaughtered at the funeral, and that a pyre had been erected over the

larger pit in which various precious objects were burned. To the same custom of burning offerings to the dead in the tomb, are certainly related the traces of fire, which have often been observed in Mycenaean chamber tombs and have caused so much discussion. I have no hesitation in referring the description of Patroclos' funeral to this Mycenaean custom. It is only natural that in an age in which cremation was the rule for stately funerals, the poet misunderstood the old custom and mixed it up with those prevailing at his own time, letting the corpse of Patroclos also be burned on the pyre.

In spite of such prestigious support, however, Persson's observations have not been generally accepted as typical of Mycenaean burials.

Nilsson concludes that, although certain early and late cultural elements can be isolated, the various strata have been in general inextricably blended in the poems that have reached us. "How is it credible," he asks, "that the former Mycenaean elements were preserved through the centuries and incorporated in poems whose composition may be about half a millennium later?" We cannot follow his review of epic technique among other peoples at varying times in the past; but he insists that "from the examples quoted it is easy to understand that the epics which originated in this [Mycenaean] age were preserved throughout the subsequent dark and impoverished centuries." And he believes that "with the aid of the epic technique they preserved not only their memory but certain archaizing features, in spite of an inevitable accommodation to a new environment . . ."

The migration across the Aegean Sea to Ionia at the beginning of the Iron Age "prepared the ground for a renascence of epics," and finally "a great poet appeared who infused new life and vigour into epic poetry." Neither this poet nor his audience could have had any direct knowledge of Mycenaean civilization. But echoes of it, sometimes authentic and sometimes confused, had come down in the unbroken oral tradition. Agamemnon and Nestor would no doubt have trouble in recognizing in Homer's version the songs that bards may have sung in their courts at Mycenae and Pylos. But it seems absolutely sure to Nilsson that the kernel of the action and much of the circumstantial detail did not originate in poetic imagination.

VIII

The Fourth Generation of Aegean Archaeology:

1940-1965

Another book, rather than the remainder of this one, would be required to do justice to the task attempted in these three final chapters. As with so many areas in modern life, so with archaeology. The pace of new discoveries and new theories seems to increase in some mysterious geometric progression. Perhaps the increased tempo is not so mysterious if we acknowledge the changing position of archaeology: no longer ancillary to other disciplines, archaeology has become a rigorous discipline in its own right. Alliance with specialists in various fields has both broadened the scope of archaeological inquiry and involved more individuals in its tasks. Thus it is no longer accurate to describe advances as the work of those few key figures who have dominated the story up to now. Schliemann has been dead for nearly a century; Evans died at the ripe old age of ninety during the early days of World War II. After retirement from his university post, Blegen continued the excavations at Pylos and completed the three volumes of the final publication before his death in 1971.

A true exception to this trend is the work of Michael Ventris. Unquestionably, the major development in the fourth generation of Aegean archaeology was his decipherment of Linear B in 1952, and subsequent revelations about the content of the documents, especially those from Pylos and Knossos. Several archaeological discoveries rank close behind the decipherment in their significance for an understanding of the Bronze Age. This quarter century witnessed the gradual uncovering of the extensive ruins of the palace at Pylos as well as the detection and early exploration of a well-preserved Mycenaean palace at Iolkos, modern Volos. Equally important was the excavation of a second grave circle just outside the fortified citadel of Mycenae. Burials with contents similar to some of those found in the Mycenae Shaft Graves were uncovered at Peristeria, near the west coast of the Peloponnese. A large building, apparently constructed for religious purposes and containing almost life-size statues, was discovered on the island of Keos. In terms of continuing excavations, the French pursued their productive efforts at Argos; the Germans and Greeks renewed their investigations at Tiryns; further work at Mycenae and at Thebes produced Linear B tablets, and from

Thebes also came seals bearing the first cuneiform inscriptions to be found in Greece since the nineteenth-century discovery on Kythera of a cuneiform inscription bearing the name of Naram-sin, ruler of Akkad in the late third millennium. Important new evidence came to light in the closely related Minoan sphere, at Zakro and Arkhanes. It was a period of drastic, and sometimes acrimonious, review of Evans' chronological, typological and historical conclusions.

Intensive surface exploration, renewed in the late 1940s, carried on the tradition of Wace, Blegen and Pendlebury. The aim of surface exploration is, of course, to record evidence of habitation at every period in the past, but exploratory missions were of particular interest for their indication of a real "population explosion" in and around Mycenaean centers in the Late Bronze Age. The need was recognized to examine regions other than Attica, Argolis, Laconia and Messenia to test the prevalence of similar population concentrations. In fact, the mechanization of Greek agriculture began to force the pace on survey work before deep-ploughing destroyed surviving surface indications. Extensive drainage, irrigation, road building and other construction projects also speeded the pace of exploration.

Gradually, too, the second objective to which Blegen pointed in 1940 gained adherents. Specialists in a wide variety of the natural and social sciences increasingly came to join survey teams and excavation staffs; archaeologists were trained to observe, record and preserve specimens so that they could ask specialists the right questions and provide necessary data for scientific analysis in the laboratory. The most valuable of the scientific aids developed in this period was the Carbon 14 technique, by which, if conditions are right, fairly close absolute dates can be assigned to samples of organic material.

While increasingly scientific in its methods, the study of Aegean prehistory also rather suddenly became, as in its first thirty years, a subject of wide popular interest. The discovery and decipherment of the Linear B tablets must be credited with much of the new appeal. Also, several books became available in which specialists and popular writers provided the general reader in English with more or less reliable and readable syntheses of the present state of the evidence, replacing Tsountas' *Mycenaean Age* of 1897. Bronze Age archaeology had indeed changed both in the quantity and the types of available evidence since the last decade of the nineteenth century. However, there was continuity as well so that theories, inferences and conclusions developing in the seventy years before 1940 served as a foundation for further excavation and discussion during this fourth generation of Aegean prehistorical study. Perhaps it will be worthwhile at this point to gather together the main threads of this pursuit from its inception before examining the new evidence of these twenty-five years.

Schliemann's work at Troy, Mycenae, Tiryns and elsewhere established beyond doubt that a highly developed civilization had existed in the Aegean area many centuries before the Classical era. In this sense, at least, his efforts authenticated Homer, and there was considerable evidence that the earlier culture had points of contact with Homeric epic as well as later Greek developments. But Schliemann failed to convince most scholars that Homer had firsthand knowledge of Mycenaean Greece or Troy II; before he died, Schliemann himself had practically abandoned this belief. Dörpfeld showed that it was Troy VI that was approximately contemporary with the most prosperous phases of the citadels like Mycenae and Tiryns on the opposite side of the Aegean; but his case for a close correspondence between the material remains of that later Trojan level and the Homeric account was not much more convincing. After Dörpfeld's Trojan excavations, however, there seemed to be somewhat more reason to believe the kernel of the Homeric account, *i.e.*, that an army from Mycenae and Tiryns and other major Mycenaean centers might have attacked and conquered Troy. At the very least, Mycenaean pottery found on the house floors of the destroyed site testified to fairly close contact between the mainland and the later inhabitants of Troy VI.

Tsountas discovered evidence for habitation in Thessaly and the Cyclades long before the Mycenaean efflorescence, and he contributed materially to a more rounded picture of cultural conditions in the "Mycenaean" period, which was by then roughly defined as the last half of the second millennium. Tsountas' book showed dramatically how much had been learned in a single generation. It was reasonably clear by his time that this civilization had extended far beyond the Argolid and that the exploits of these wealthy, restless and warlike people had provided the basis for much in the tradition of Greek myth and heroic song. But he scarcely came to grips with the prickly problem of the time lag between the Mycenaean Age and the Homeric epics.

Then the Cretan chapter opened out, with the revelation of an even earlier and in many ways more creative and opulent society, which in its later phases had much in common with the Mycenaean. Evans saw in the Cretan palaces of the Middle Bronze Age the first highly developed European civilization, and he associated the Minoan acme around the middle of the second millennium with a persistent tradition of a "control of the sea" established by King Minos of Knossos over the whole eastern Mediterranean and even beyond. An intimate connection was obvious between art objects from the Shaft Graves and tholos tombs of the Mycenaean mainland and those of proven Minoan origin and development in Crete. No one contested the conclusion that Cretan fashions, particularly in art, had very deeply affected the mainland beginning about 1600. But Evans believed that this wave of Minoan cultural influence was sufficient proof of total domination in every significant aspect of mainland civilization, including political control of at least the major population centers. And he won the assent of most scholars to his theory.

As to the last 200 years or so of the Aegean Bronze Age—which comprise the more critical period for Homeric connections—Evans' views became increasingly Creto-centric. According to his calculations, the great age of the Minoan palaces had come to an end about 1400, and this catastrophe was interpreted by most scholars as proof of some sort of major shift in the balance of power toward the mainland. But Evans insisted that at no time until the very end of the Bronze Age was there any archaeological evidence for a cultural "break" that would be needed to mark invasion and political control of Crete by "Achaean" (*i.e.,* Greek-speaking) mainlanders. He adopted the theory that the frequent destruction, burning and rebuilding of Cretan palaces—perhaps even the "final" destruction at Knossos—was best explained as the result of recurring serious earthquakes.

Evans admitted that for two or three generations before the "final" destruction, an aggressive and militaristic dynasty had been in control of Knossos and perhaps most of Crete, but he held that these were native rulers. In his last publication he even advanced the view that after 1400 the incumbent "priest-king" transferred the capital to the mainland, probably to Mycenae. The last two or three centuries of the Bronze Age, both in Crete and on the mainland, were in Evans' view a continuation and gradual degeneration of an essentially Minoan civilization. If Greek-speaking people were already present, they were a subject race. The heroes of Greek tradition were presumably Minoan leaders or puppets, and the first epic poems about their exploits may have been written down in the Minoan language. A long literate tradition had existed in Crete, and the Linear B script had been developed at Knossos and used on the mainland at least as early as 1400.

Practically no one else was willing to accept all of the implications of these hypotheses. In spite of Evans' awesome reputation and prestige, his own assistant, Pendlebury, believed the "final" destruction of Knossos could be explained by a successful mainland revolt against Cretan colonialism. Many who had long studied the mainland evidence were skeptical of Evans' repeated insistence on its total dependence on Minoan models. Nilsson published his "eleven points" of important dissimilarities in the very year that Evans' last and most extreme pronouncement appeared (1933). But the case for a sturdy native "Helladic" cultural tradition, never totally submerged even at the height of Minoizing fashion and strongly reemerging after 1400, was put most persistently and cogently by Blegen and Wace. Their system of mainland chronology, though closely coordinated with the Minoan, was a symbol of mainland integrity.

A second crux was Wace's dating of the finest tholos tombs at Mycenae after 1400 and the insistence that the later stages in this monumental form of architecture developed in a non-Minoan environment. Even in the pottery, where they freely admitted widespread importation and imitation of Minoan ceramics over a long period, Blegen and Wace felt that mainland motifs and shapes could be traced in every period. The massive Minoan influence apparent in the fifteenth and sixteenth centuries was, they insisted, rather out of proportion because the surviving evidence tends to underline a single cultural aspect, that of minor arts, especially ceramics. They believed in an almost total loss of Minoan international power after 1400 and speculated that strong mainland competition in foreign trade had been developing considerably earlier.

In an unbiased view, no really convincing case could be made for Minoan political control of mainland power centers at any time. The dominant language of the Mycenaeans, in the opinion of most scholars, was probably an early form of Greek that had most likely been introduced to the peninsula at the beginning of the second millennium when cultural traces preserved in the material record suggest the arrival of new people. Although not primarily concerned with Homeric connections, mainland archaeologists like Blegen and Wace believed that an authentic mainland Greek traditon of heroic songs originated in the Mycenaean context with clear echoes—however they were to be explained—in Homeric epics.

This was more or less the status of the problem when the Linear B tablets were unearthed at Pylos in 1939. The news did not have any immediate and serious effect on existing theories except to contradict the common view that the mainlanders were essentially nonliterate. Evans himself had declared that a few inscribed vases found earlier on the mainland (especially at Thebes) showed that at least as early as 1400 the Minoan bureaucratic palace system and the Linear B script had been transferred to the mainland; and he had implied that the failure to find tablets might be attributed to the fixed idea among mainland excavators since Tsountas' time that there were no tablets to find. To be sure, the date assigned to the Pylos records, around 1200, seemed unexpectedly late; but after all, this was close to the time of most intensive Mycenaean economic activity at home and abroad, and it was then that they would have felt the greatest need for a viable system of record keeping. There was no absolute proof to rule out the possibility that, if Minoan-speaking minorities had seized control of mainland centers around 1400 or before, they might still be in power two centuries later. In fact, Evans must have been cheered during his last months by the Pylos discovery, which seemed to lend confirmation to his views.

The preoccupations of World War II interrupted and slowed normal scholarly progress and cooperation in archaeology, as they did in many other scholarly areas. Field work in Greece was particularly affected because of the long agony of the civil war that followed its heroic defense and foreign occupation. Some activity continued in spite of the war and even as part of the military effort; Nicholas Hammond and others continued to walk through the Greek and Balkan terrain even though it was now behind enemy lines; particularly in Macedonia, one-time members of British and French archaeological schools continued their reconnaissance work as British and French military officers. Yet the work was secondary to more pressing needs and, thus, minimal. Even after organized fighting ended, renewed archaeological activity was long hampered by devastation, poor communications and outlaw bands. Many museums were damaged or destroyed, and their contents in some cases were not accessible for decades.

FURUMARK'S CERAMIC ANALYSIS

The most important publication during the war years came out of Sweden, a country not directly involved in the conflict, and even in this case the research had been done in peacetime. Arne Furumark's monumental feat of analyzing and classifying the evolution of ceramic shapes (typology) and decorative motifs (stylistics*) is a landmark. Almost inevitably his system is complex, and modifications have since been advocated, but *The Mycenaean Pottery,* which he published in two volumes in 1941, provided an organized context for comprehensive discussion into which new material could be incorporated and by means of which misunderstood positions might be discarded.

As far as technical terminology is concerned, Furumark rejected both the all-inclusive Evans-Mackenzie "Late Minoan" and the distinctive Wace-Blegen "Late Helladic" to designate the Late Bronze Age on the mainland. He preferred the more general term "Mycenaean," which has been used with varying degrees of precision as to time and area ever since Schliemann's day. Furumark's major objection to "Helladic" was that it implies an exclusively mainland character that does not take into account influences from various quarters, especially from Crete and other south Aegean islands. Here Furumark gained few followers, although the general designation "Mycenaean Age" came to be used interchangeably with "Late Helladic period." Late Helladic has clearly emerged as the usual technical ceramic designation, especially when complicated subperiods (I, II, III; A, B, C.; 1, 2, 3) are involved.

Furumark's scheme of classification naturally owed a good deal to previous formulations, but the more refined (some think too refined) subperiods were mainly the result of his own meticulous studies. The equivalent absolute dates were based on the best evidence available through synchronisms with Crete and directly or indirectly with Egypt and the Near East. Without following it in full detail, we reproduce the main features, which will be an indispensable basis of much of the discussion in the remainder of the book.

LHI	about 1550–1500
LHIIA	about 1500–1450
LHIIB	about 1450–1425
LHIIIA	about 1425–1300
LHIIIB	about 1300–1230
LHIIIC	about 1230–1100

Furumark's book appeared in the year of Evans' death, and it completely demolished Evans' thesis that mainland pottery throughout the Late Bronze Age was simply a "colonial" version of Minoan. A necessary part of Furumark's task had been to analyze both mainland and Minoan pottery of the preceding Middle Bronze period, as well as the Minoan developments throughout the Late Bronze Age. He was therefore able to state quite authoritatively that even during LHI, when Minoan influence was rapidly gaining ground in the mainland, some vases were being made in the unadulterated mainland tradition of shape and decoration and technology, while still others showed a mixture of the two traditions. Apparently the lustrous applied paint of LHI is a Cretan novelty. The mainland potter's repertory of shapes was derived nearly equally from Cretan and native sources. As one might expect, the imported shapes are generally those of "luxury" vessels, while local shapes are retained for common "utility" pots. Yet some finer mainland-derived shapes like the stemmed cup (kylix) and deep bowl (krater) not only survived but eventually became popular in Crete. There are also a few shapes, like the pilgrim flask* (Fig. 85), that were borrowed from Near Eastern sources. Furumark believed that mainland potters were much less likely than their Cretan colleagues to imitate new shapes from other media, such as metal vessels.

LHIIA represents the nearest to complete period of Minoan domination in Furumark's eyes; contemporary Cretan fashions almost preoccupy the attention of mainland pottery. On the other hand, the style of LHIIB is essentially a mainland creation that Furumark saw as the first genuine Mycenaean ceramics in which the native mainland and the Minoan traditions are successfully fused into a new style.

An increasing tendency toward typically mainland stylization and simplification is observable in LHIIIA, even though fairly strong influence from Crete resumes. The technical processes of selecting, preparing and firing the clay are being continually improved. In general, mainland and Cretan products are becoming easier to distinguish. The extremely wide-spread LHIIIB pottery shows a logical development of previous tendencies. It is, in general, notably homogeneous, although a recognizable eastern (Levanto-Mycenaean) style can be differentiated. Cretan influence practically ceases and mainland artistic propensities are in full control. Shape and decoration are more standardized. Design is becoming abstract and stereotyped, so that the naturalistic origin of many motifs is scarcely recognizable. These are the tendencies that earlier generations of archaeologists were inclined to characterize as "decadent."

LHIIIC is more varied and complex, reflecting the breakdown of the Mycenaean koinê and the fragmentation caused by turbulent political and cultural conditions throughout the east Mediterranean area. Two almost antithetic tendencies implicit in LHIIIB are separately developed. The one involves simplification, the other elaboration in decoration. They were in fact represented in the

Figure 85

same time sequence at Mycenae and called by Wace, respectively, the Granary Class and the Close Style* (Fig. 86). LHIIIC pottery exhibits far more distinct regional features, too, and a new wave of Cretan influence is apparent. A strong element of representative art also appears in some of these vases and is apparently derived from the tradition of mainland fresco painting. The best-known single example is the Warrior Vase from Mycenae. But the style is most at home on chariot kraters (now proved to have been made and painted in the Peloponnese), which seem to have been especially popular in Rhodes and Cyprus (Fig. 87).

The final phase of LHIIIC, often called sub-Mycenaean, reflects the last attempts at elaboration and pictorial representations, which occasionally show a surprising vigor. At the same time, the prevailing trend toward a radical use of simple geometric designs develops. Here within late Mycenaean art can be found the basic elements of the so-called protogeometric* style of the earliest Iron Age.

It is difficult to breathe life and popular interest into these drastic simplifications of Furumark's conclusions. And yet it is often from such unspectacular evidence that sweeping historical generalizations can be affirmed, modified or refuted. For instance, it can no longer be seriously held that "Dorians" or any

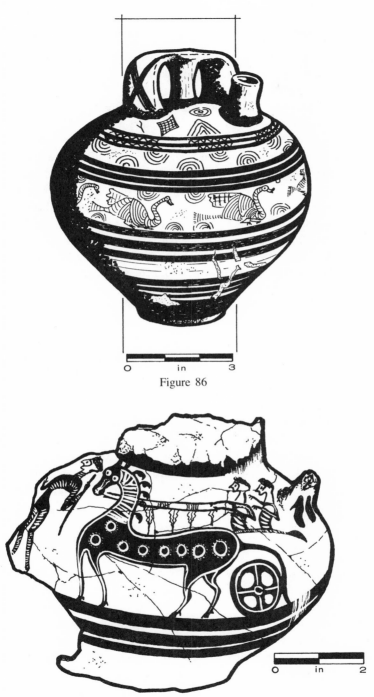

Figure 86

Figure 87

other group of newcomers introduced an intrusive style of "geometric" pottery at the end of the Bronze Age. This issue of continuity of the Mycenaean tradition into the first millennium continues to grow in complexity as material evidence accumulates. In the next chapter, we will take stock of opinion as the last decade of the twentieth century begins.

Furumark also showed that, although there was extremely strong Cretan influence on mainland ceramics in the sixteenth century and particularly in the earlier fifteenth century, it was never a completely overpowering phenomenon. The native tradition survived and reasserted itself. There is nothing here that could not be explained by close and fairly rapidly developed economic and cultural relations between politically independent peoples, the one possessing a more sophisticated artistic tradition. In any case, a more closely reasoned and controlled reconstruction of the relationship between Crete and the mainland began to emerge in the 1940s and 1950s: a period of intensive contact from about 1550 to 1450 was followed by a shorter period of stabilization and fusion from 1450 to 1425 after which the next two centuries witnessed increasing mainland self-confidence and material prosperity. From about 1200, a more complex, diffuse and decentralized situation prevailed until the end of the Bronze Age. The ceramic evidence provides an indispensable basis into which additional cultural material may be fitted and with which broader historical theories must be reconciled.

In the immediate post–World War II years there were several important developments similar to Furumark's ceramic analysis that bore little or no relation to the resumption of excavation. They were, on the contrary, the result of seasoned reflection on the published results of earlier field work. This vital kind of archaeological activity may or may not be carried on by practicing excavators. It is usually the quiet sort of contribution that is seldom in the headlines. Yet without the synthesis that it does so much to provide, the rapidly expanding bulk of evidence from excavations would soon become chaotic and unmanageable. Indeed, there is much to be said for some kind of schedule to impose a moratorium on new excavation at stated intervals and allow excavators and their colleagues a respite for reappraisal.

KANTOR'S ANALYSIS OF CONTACT
WITH THE NEAR EAST

A significant shift in opinion on the question of Minoan-Mycenaean leadership in economic activities followed the publication in 1947 of an important monograph by Helene Kantor. Being in the enviable and rather unusual position of knowing at first hand the artistic traditions in both the Aegean and the Near East, she could authoritatively review the interrelations in *The Aegean and the Orient in the Second Millennium B.C.* (1947). As a historian of Near Eastern art, her interest centered on the evidence for direct importation and imitation of Aegean decorative motifs. Her analysis showed that, contrary to Evans' belief, the critical shift in Minoan versus Mycenaean contact with Egypt and other countries of the eastern Mediterranean seems to have occurred between 1700 and 1600. In the MMII period there is a fair amount of evidence for direct or indirect trade in Cretan pottery and metalwork, probably in patterned textiles and no doubt in other raw materials and processed goods that can no longer be traced. On the other hand, the moderate amount of Aegean imports into the Near East in the earlier part of the Late Bronze Age, *i.e.,* 1600 to 1400, would seem already to derive almost exclusively from the Greek mainland. There is even some transitory impact discernible from mainland art on the conservative Egyptian tradition.

Kantor considered the evidence sufficient to prove that direct trade connections between the Mycenaeans and people of the Near East were solidly established during LHI and II, although she viewed with some skepticism Persson's attempt to show strong reverse influence from Egypt on Greece (Persson, 1942). She further maintained that the pottery and even the celebrated Egyptian tomb paintings of the Eighteenth Dynasty, which show offerings of Aegean type being presented by "Keftiu," indicate that Crete by this time had a very limited share in trade with the Near East.

Blegen and Wace had stressed the Mycenaean origin of most Aegean pottery found in the Near East. Pendlebury had acknowledged the direction in which this evidence was pointing, but he had sidestepped the complementary political implications. Kantor bluntly stated that it is impossible to reconcile these facts with any theory of Mycenaean payment of tribute to Cretan overlords. In fact, the whole concept of a Minoan thalassocracy in LMI and II became dubious. Kantor referred obliquely to Wace's bold suggestion that LMII at Knossos might even represent a period of mainland political control and, without directly supporting it, said that the (by this time) orthodox explanation of the destruction of Knossos by mainlanders about 1400 cannot be correct, since it postulates a mainland revolt against an economic monopoly that clearly did not exist in the late fifteenth century.

The greatly expanded trade contacts between the Greek mainland and the Near East in the last centuries of the Bronze Age now appeared in the perspective of a gradual buildup over the preceding century or two, rather than as a sudden burst of pent-up energy released by the conquest of Crete about 1400. During LHIII, Asiatic artisans were affected by Mycenaean imports; in ivory carving, Aegean motifs exercised a particularly notable influence. Kantor's summation was in its way as sweeping as any of Evans' frequent generalizations—and it directly contradicted one of his major premises. "After the close of the MMII period, and throughout the later part of the Second Millennium," she insisted, "only the sailors, merchants, and craftsmen of Mycenaean Greece can justifiedly lay claim to the honor of forming the links connecting the Aegean with the Orient" (1947: 103).

ADDITIONAL EVIDENCE ON TRADE

Perhaps in response to the preceding years of intense and worldwide interaction, the years after World War II saw an increased interest in such large-scale Bronze Age economic interrelationships. One frequent question was the nature of goods traded. A related query was the location of trade routes.

In the eastern Mediterranean, there was mounting evidence of extensive foreign trade in the sixteenth and fifteenth centuries. Mycenaean products, reflected mainly in the indestructible potsherd, were penetrating to more and more distant points, and exotic objects appear increasingly in Mycenaean contexts. In a thorough study of the Aegean pottery found in the East, Frank Stubbings essentially confirmed the thesis of Wace, Blegen, Kantor and others that Minoan trade, at least insofar as pottery is an index, seems to have yielded to Mycenaean competitors almost from the beginning of the Late Bronze Age (1951). Stubbings explained the phenomenon through intermediaries: Mycenaean trade was carried on by independent colonies on islands like Rhodes and Kos (1951: 102). This position required modification after the spectrographic analysis of H. W. Catling and two of his associates in the Research Laboratory for Archaeology and the History of Art at Oxford University (1963: 94–115). The analyses indicate that the later Mycenaean pottery in the East originated largely in the mainland, not in the islands of the southeast Aegean, and it would be extremely unlikely that this situation was reversed in the earlier centuries.

The evidence for trade in the West has accumulated more slowly. However, William Taylour's *Mycenaean Pottery in Italy and Adjacent Areas* demonstrated well the earlier indications that Mycenaean traders turned in that direction at least as early as they did to the more civilized East (1958). It may have been easier to find markets and sources of raw materials in the relatively unexploited West than to break in on the long-established trading patterns of older economies. For instance, Middle Helladic vases of the matt-painted style were already reaching southeastern Sicily and one or two of the Aeolian Islands off the north coast of Sicily in the seventeenth century; and an exact duplicate of a scepter from Grave Circle B at Mycenae was found in the grave of a British chieftain in Wessex. Contact with central Europe and southern England is proved by the influence of

Mycenaean vessels and armor on the flourishing native metal-working tradition as early as the sixteenth century.

On a deeply stratified acropolis on the island of Lipari in the Aeolian group, so much Mycenaean pottery of the sixteenth and fifteenth century (along with a modest amount of contemporary Minoan ware) has been found that an important trading station must have been located there. The nearby island of Filicudi has also produced a moderate amount. The Aeolian Islands lie at the center of the Mediterranean basin and appear to have been a strategic focus for early long-distance sea traffic. Small islands do, of course, provide an ideal situation for trading entrepôts.

Spyridon Marinatos envisaged Lipari as the intersection of a great inverted T (1962). To the east across two almost equal stretches of water lie Kephallenia/ Pylos and Rhodes/Cyprus. To the west at approximately equal distances are Sardinia and the Balearic Islands off Spain. Looking north, the islands of Ischia and Vivara off the Bay of Naples are somewhat closer to Lipari, and there are indications of Mycenaean contacts there at least as early as the fifteenth century. Marinatos might well have added still another hypothetical stage toward the north, from Ischia to the Etruscan coast, with its abundant copper.

Pottery is our main evidence for trade with coastal points, and the vases themselves must have been attractive as well as useful to native peoples. Stubbings suggested that the demand for Mycenaean pottery may have been due partly to the fact that it was fired at higher temperatures than most contemporary pottery. Marinatos contended that the ceramic types found on Lipari indicate that the Pylos district was the chief source. He assumed that pottery and other trade goods were carried in Mycenaean ships, and he suggested that long familiarity with such voyages would explain Homer's emphasis on Nestor's daring in sailing straight across the open Aegean on the return from Troy.[76]

Yet we need not conclude that the ceramic containers or even their contents such as oil and wine constituted the only, or even the major, Mycenaean export. Since pottery is confined almost entirely to coastal sites, it used to be taken for granted that Mycenaean trade goods did not penetrate far inland. Marinatos pointed out quite logically, however, that overland caravans, unlike ships, cannot afford to transport cheap articles. Since pottery would (he argued) by and large fall into this category and is also extremely fragile, its scarcity does not necessarily prove that valuable and durable goods—particularly metal weapons, implements and jewelry—did not move inland. One might also observe that a fair proportion of the goods received in exchange at a foreign port must have come from the interior, and caravans would not willingly return empty-handed.

An easily recognizable class of segmented blue faience beads (Fig. 88), manufactured in the Aegean or the Near East, has been found sparsely in southern France in the neighborhood of Narbonne and very frequently in the British Isles,

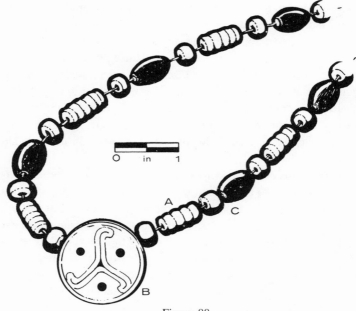

Figure 88

with a concentration in southern England. They represent a type of trade goods that is much more easily transportable over land than pottery and may be proof of a trade route from the Mediterranean to Britain, probably across southwestern France by the Narbonne-Carcassonne-Loire route to the Atlantic and on to southern England. British gold and copper as well as precious tin could have been moved to the east Mediterranean along this route.

A second concentration of trade goods emerged far inland in eastern and central Europe, generally north of the Danube and stretching from Hungary to Czechoslovakia. In addition to the distinctive faience beads, decorated bonework bearing characteristic incised Mycenaean patterns has been identified. Similar scattered finds, as well as a few Mycenaean metal objects, have come to light at or near the north end of both the Adriatic and the Aegean, suggesting that as much as possible, these trade routes lay over water. Here again abundant copper, tin and gold seem to have been the major attraction for Mycenaean merchants, who were tapping this great area by the fifteenth century.

Another object of regular trade was amber. Marinatos argued (1962) that the importance of the early trading station on Lipari was owed mainly to the amber trade. This substance, which held such fascination for many ancient peoples, occurs in various parts of northern, central and southern Europe. Various trade routes from as far as the southern shores of the Baltic Sea are believed to have converged at the head of the Adriatic Sea, where ships based in the western Peloponnese or the Ionian Islands seem to have been especially active in the amber trade. The early tholoi in that part of the Greek world, robbed as they are, still yield disproportionately large quantities of amber beads.

A most striking indication of long-distance commerce in amber concerns a distinctive type of small flat plate or spacer bead with complicated perforations (Fig. 88). Examples in Mycenaean contexts were found in both circles of the Mycenae Shaft Graves and in the tholos tombs of Kakovatos. Similar objects also occur in south Germany and in southern England. In 1957, R. Hachmann claimed that the Greek and British plates belonged to necklaces and collars, whereas the German examples came from a longer kind of pectoral. He argued, therefore, that the Greek and British plates must have been manufactured at the same center (1957: 1–36).

LORIMER'S REVIEW OF HOMERIC CONNECTIONS

A major synthesis appeared in 1950 when H. L. Lorimer published the work of a lifetime in *Homer and the Monuments* (Lorimer, 1950). Her purpose was to bring up to date a subject much in the thoughts of earlier excavators and Homeric scholars. The available evidence had been summed up sixty-three years before in a German work, *The Homeric Epos Illustrated from the Monuments,* by Wolfgang Helbig (1887). Unfortunately, Schliemann's work was then just getting under way, and Helbig's masterly synthesis was deprived of the results of the first organized excavations. Part of the subject was carefully handled a few years later in Wolfgang Reichel's book *Homeric Weapons,* also in German (1894). Lorimer became their distinguished successor in attempting to sort through the vast problem of the relationship between material remains of varying periods as revealed by archaeology and the complex culture depicted by Homer. Since this issue has become even more central to Aegean prehistory in the years since 1965, it will be useful to examine Lorimer's major conclusions as they set the tone for continuing debate.

Schliemann's impetuous enthusiasm had identified Troy II with the city of Priam, and the occupants of the Shaft Graves at Mycenae with Agamemnon and his contemporaries. In the Homeric poems he saw (at least in the earlier years) such direct descriptions of these places and objects as could only be the result of personal experience. But few, even at that time, fully shared his conviction, and two generations of further research completely ruled out this conclusion. Closer dating showed that Troy II had been destroyed many hundreds of years before the Shaft Graves were constructed. The Shaft Graves in turn had held their hallowed dead for centuries before the days of intensive Mycenaean contact with Troy VI and VIIa in the thirteenth century. If, as was increasingly believed after Schliemann's day, the Trojan War was a real historical event, it had probably taken place between 1300 and 1200. Were there, then, in the poems authentic echoes of the culture of that period or of the immediately preceding centuries as it was revealed by archaeology? If so, it would be fair to assume a continuous tradition in oral songs originally circulating in Mycenaean courts and persisting until Homer's time when nobody had firsthand knowledge of Mycenaean civilization.

It was to these problems that Lorimer directed much of her research, although she was equally interested in identifying the latest cultural elements of the poems, as indicated by archaeological parallels in the Early Iron Age (after 1100). The latter line of inquiry was clearly a very important means of assigning an approximate date to the poet or poets responsible for giving the *Iliad* and the *Odyssey* their more or less final form. From this evidence Lorimer inferred that Homer lived in the second half of the eighth century. Some cultural features of the *Odyssey* seemed to her to be a little later than any in the *Iliad*, but the time lag need not exceed the span of one lifetime. This general position on one aspect of the Homeric Question had many adherents even before Lorimer's book was published, and the support of her meticulous handling of the archaeological evidence buttressed it considerably. As we shall see, continuing study up to the present has lent it additional weight.

Lorimer's major conclusion on the problems that directly concern us would have been somewhat disappointing even to Schliemann's more cautious successors like Dörpfeld and Tsountas. She found, in short, that the poems do indeed preserve certain features of Late Bronze Age culture, but that the correspondence is not nearly as consistent as was once supposed. Perhaps the most striking examples of archaeologically verified objects described in the poems occur in earlier Mycenaean contexts, especially in the Shaft Grave period. Such artefacts as the great body shield, the "cup of Nestor" and the boar's tusk helmet certainly did not physically survive the Bronze Age. The helmet, which she considered the most decisive Homeric echo, was covered with four or five rows of tusks arranged with the curve in alternating directions in each row. Thirty to forty pairs of tusks were used in making a single helmet. Lorimer wrote: "For four centuries at least [before the eighth century] no one could possibly have seen a boar's tusk helmet; only in the amber of traditional poetry handed down with an astonishing verbal fidelity could its image have been preserved" (1950: 453).

She also concluded that the exotic niello technique of metal inlay, which is believed to have originated in Syria and is best illustrated in early Mycenaean daggers and described in connection with Achilles' shield, died out before the end of the Bronze Age. More general considerations, like the repeated references to bronze weapons centuries after that metal had been largely replaced by iron, also have validity.

The discrepancy between Mycenaean inhumation burial and Homer's rites of cremation has been a stumbling block for many who sought to establish a continuous tradition. It caused no particular problem in Lorimer's perspective of a long time span involving mixed culture traits that are reflected, sometimes in rather undigested form, in the final product. She pointed to Blegen's discovery of a cemetery of cremation burials contemporary with Troy VI and to the probability that the Greeks attacking Troy VIIa saw and perhaps practiced the same rite on foreign soil. During the chaotic decades toward the end of the Bronze Age, cultural novelties were disturbing many long-cherished customs, and cremation seems to have been one of them. It is probably no accident that cremation became popular in and near Athens, apparently the rallying place of many Mycenaean refugees and the springboard for the Ionic migration to Asia Minor.

Lorimer's chapter "The Age of Illiteracy in Greece" dramatically reflected the lack of preparation of most scholars for the shock that was to come only two years later. She inclined to Evans' theory of foreign oligarchies in mainland centers, "where Minoan would be the court language," and regarded the Pylos archives as confirmatory evidence. Preliminary work on the tablets, she judged as "wholly unfavourable to any hope entertained that the language of the inscriptions might be Greek" (1950: 123).

Although a rather cumbersome system of writing was in use in at least some of the later Bronze Age Aegean power centers, a period of nonliteracy seems to have followed the end of the Bronze Age, except in Cyprus where there was a continuing use of a modified version of linear script. When writing was reintroduced in Greece, the script was a quite unrelated alphabet borrowed, directly or indirectly, from the Phoenicians. Lorimer accepted the theory that dated the historical Greek alphabet no earlier than about the middle of the eighth century. It was therefore probable that the Homeric poems were composed in a milieu where renewed literacy was in its infancy, but Lorimer does not speculate on the possibility that the new system may have been used to record the poems in or soon after Homer's lifetime. The society that Homer describes is clearly nonliterate, and this would point to a continuation of oral heroic poetry during the so-called Dark Age between the end of the Bronze Age and the eighth century. Echoes of the past, consequently, could be explained by a continuous oral epic tradition.

VENTRIS AND LINEAR B

In the year 1952 an epoch-making discovery was announced that has every right to be ranked with Schliemann's at Troy in 1870 and at Mycenae in 1876, Evans' at Knossos in 1900 and Blegen's at Pylos in 1939. Michael Ventris was not an excavator or a "desk archaeologist" or a philologist, but an architect by profession. Already an avid linguist and amateur cryptographer, Ventris as a boy of fourteen had heard Evans lecture in 1936 on the mysterious Cretan scripts and had then made up his mind that he would someday solve the puzzle.

Unfortunately, there was not much material to work on before the war. As we have seen, Evans had published little more than 100 of the 3,000 or so Linear B tablets he had found at Knossos. And he was extremely indignant when a Finnish scholar, Johannes Sundwall, copied and published a few more without explicit permission (1932a; 1932b; 1936). Photographs of a half-dozen Pylos tablets had appeared in Blegen's preliminary report in 1939, but most of the tablets from both sites were unavailable, although plans were being made for their publication as rapidly as possible (1939: 557–576).

Several premature, even weird, attempts at decipherment had been made, but few experts were much impressed. The underlying language had been identified as anything from Basque to a rather odd kind of primitive Greek. Several scholars were inclined to see in Linear B (and even in Linear A and Minoan hieroglyphics) some kind of Indo-European pattern at least related to Greek; but the overwhelming tendency was to follow Evans in visualizing a pre-Greek, non-Indo-European, non-Semitic "Aegean" or "Minoan" language with vague origins and perhaps survivals in southwest Asia Minor. Some saw the most attractive possibility in the Etruscan language, itself a puzzle, although the alphabet at least was familiar. In 1940, Ventris, at age eighteen, published an article in the prestigious *American Journal of Archaeology* in which he supported the Etruscan equation.

Then came the war years, when only a few scholars were able to devote their attention to the decipherment. Fortunately, there had been time for the Pylos tablets to be cleaned and photographed before they were taken off to the vaults of the Bank of Greece along with treasures from the National Museum in Athens. In 1939 excavation photographs and notebooks as well as a full set of professional photographs of the cleaned and mended tablets had been brought back to Cincinnati. Blegen had entrusted this material to one of his graduate students, Emmett Bennett, Jr. A formidable amount of work needed to be done before the tablets could be made available to scholars, and both Blegen's and Bennett's efforts were interrupted by military service. Gradually, however, line drawings were made from painstaking tracings of each fragment, joins of one fragment to another explored, a table constructed of normative forms of each symbol of the syllabary* and a word index compiled. It is a tribute to Blegen's determination to make the full evidence quickly available to scholars and to Bennett's industry and revision that the first edition of *The Pylos Tablets: A Preliminary Transcription* appeared as early as 1951.

Immediately, the amount of available material was multiplied by five, since it had been reasonably clear from the first that, though there are minor differences, the Pylos texts and the documents in Linear B from Knossos could confidently be studied together. The impact of the new Pylos material is reflected in the rapidity of Ventris' progress toward their decipherment in the next few months. An admirably clear account of that fascinating process was provided by Ventris' closest colleague, John Chadwick, in *The Decipherment of Linear B* (1958, 1967).

There seems, in retrospect, to be no completely rational explanation for the fact that between 1939 and 1951 almost all scholars continued to exclude the possibility that the Linear B script was used to write Greek. Even as Ventris was building the grid* of phonetic equivalents for the syllabary, he took it for granted that the underlying language would turn out to be an unfamiliar one. On the other hand, Tsountas had long before insisted that the Mycenaeans spoke Greek, and linguists such as C. D. Buck had reinforced the idea (Tsountas and Manatt, 1897; Buck, 1926: 1–26). Blegen and many colleagues believed that Greek speakers had first entered the peninsula as early as 1900. Wace's theory that several anomalous culture traits of the LMII phase at Knossos might be explained by the presence of mainlanders (presumably Greek-speaking) had been recorded by Pendlebury in 1939 and accepted, although it was not published until after the decipherment was announced, by Sterling Dow (Pendlebury, 1939: 229; Dow, 1954: 77–129, esp. 115ff.).

Evans himself had once observed that the two-syllable word that accompanied an ideogram* of a young horse on some of the Knossos Linear B tablets, if assigned phonetic equivalents that these symbols had in the later Cypriote syllabary, would be PO-LO, which is startlingly close to the Greek *polos* (a cognate of English "foal"). In 1927 A. E. Cowley had inferred from the content of certain Knossos tablets that two frequent word groups of two syllables and having the first syllable in common must represent "boy" and "girl"; and he compared the phenomenon to Greek *kouros* ("boy") and *koure* ("girl"). Furthermore, a serious question about the usual theory that Linear A and B were used to write the same language was raised by Bennett in 1950. He had shown that the system used to indicate fractions was entirely different in Linear A and Linear B (1950: 204–222).

Yet when Ventris circulated a questionnaire to a dozen or so of the leading world authorities in 1949, few who replied seemed to have looked seriously on the possibility that the language of the Linear B tablets could be Greek. However, at least one—Tom Bard Jones—detected Indo-European characteristics. It would be difficult, indeed, to point to a more glaring example of how one able and dynamic scholar's interpretation of inconclusive evidence so thoroughly dominated the thinking of nearly all colleagues for half a century.

Nor were the philologists alone in this error. It is equally embarrassing to quote a judgment such as that published in 1950 by Furumark: "The most conspicuous manifestation of this Cretan period [*i.e.,* LMII], its art, has indeed been considered so peculiar that it has been suggested that it was due to an inspiration from abroad; this assumption has, in its turn, led to the theory that at this time Knossos (and Crete) was under foreign rule. But a systematic study of the material shows such views to be untenable" (1950: 256). The real stumbling block, by hindsight, was the acceptance of the political consequences that would have to accompany the idea that Greek might have been spoken or mainland artefacts used at the court of Knossos before 1400.

In any case, by mid-1952 Ventris was forced to believe that more than chance was involved when in so many cases the substitution of the values in his experimental grid was producing attractive Greek equivalents. Place-names like Knossos (phonetic equivalent KO-NO-SO) and its port Amnisos (A-MI-NI-SO) were assumed to be present in the Knossos documents and were used to provide the values for the grid. The critical point, however, was reached when Ventris' phonetic equivalents for the common two-syllable word known to mean "total" came out as TO-SO (masculine) and TO-SA (feminine), which are inflected forms of the common Greek adjective meaning "so much." Other equations, though they may appear somewhat strained at first glance, produced standard Greek nouns like PO-ME, *poimen* ("shepherd"), KA-KE-U, *khalkeus* ("bronzesmith"), KU-RU-SO-WO-KO, *khrusoworgos* ("goldsmith").

It was this evidence that caused Ventris to suggest on the BBC's Third Programme in early June, 1952, that he had found the key to the decipherment of Linear B. "During the last few weeks," he said, "I have come to the conclusion that the Knossos and Pylos tablets must, after all, be written in Greek—a difficult and archaic Greek, seeing that it is 500 years older than Homer and written in a rather abbreviated form, but Greek nevertheless" (Chadwick, 1958: 68).

Somewhat ironically, the occasion of that broadcast was an invitation to review the long-awaited Volume II of *Scripta Minoa,* the preparation of which was a labor of love performed by Evans' old friend Sir John L. Myres. Unfortunately, the bulk of the Knossos tablets, finally published after Evans' death, appeared too late to play a major part in Ventris' decipherment.

Ventris' modest announcement had a particularly galvanizing effect on one of his hearers, Dr. John Chadwick of Cambridge University; and within a few weeks Ventris and Chadwick had become collaborators. Chadwick had been working on Linear B for some years, and his expert linguistic knowledge of the facts already established or inferred about early Greek was exactly the right foil for Ventris' brilliance and inventiveness. Before the end of the year they submitted to the *Journal of Hellenic Studies* a historic article with the cautious title "Evidence for Greek Dialect in the Mycenaean Archives." The use of the adjective "Mycenaean" had a stronger authority because of recent news that Wace's newest excavation in a row of houses or palace annexes just outside the Mycenae citadel had produced tablets inscribed in the same Linear B script.

After stating the linguistic, historical and archaeological reasons why their thesis had a claim to a fair hearing, Ventris and Chadwick printed the grid in which phonetic equivalents were supplied for sixty-five of the more than eighty different symbols in the syllabary. They then explained their "assumed rules of Mycenaean orthography" (*i.e.,* spelling rules), which to users of an alphabet seem complicated and clumsy and inexact. For instance: (1) the same symbol serves for the syllables, *pu, bu* and *phu;* (2) L and R are not distinguished; (3) consonants at the end of a word are not written; (4) S is not written at the beginning of a word if the next sound is a consonant; (5) certain combinations of consonants have the following vowel anticipated by a "dead" vowel, KO-NO-SO illustrates rules 3 and 5 and may be presumed to represent Knossos. PU-RO illustrates rules 1, 2 and 3 and must from context designate Pylos (*Pulos* in Greek), although the same two symbols would also be used to write Bylon, Phylor, Spyros (rule 4) and so on.

It is immediately apparent that the theoretical possibilities for various combinations and permutations are numerous; and when this difficulty is compounded by many unfamiliar features of bookkeeping shorthand, archaic grammar and obsolete vocabulary, one can begin to see why jokes have developed, radically different serious translations are current, and the meanings of many words, phrases, clauses or even whole tablets remain mysterious.

Ventris and Chadwick gave numerous samples of words that fit the rules and context neatly, like PA-TE and MA-TE for *pater* ("father") and *mater* ("mother"), where lists of parents and children seemed indicated. They also hazarded translations and interpretations of a few longer passages. And finally they pointed to numerous significant instances where this Mycenaean dialect is closely related to the so-called Arkado-Cypriot dialect of Classical times. Arkado-Cypriot had long been assumed to represent enclaves of refugees who survived the dark days at the end of the Bronze Age in two very widely separated areas of the Mycenaean world, Arkadia in central Peloponnese and the island of Cyprus off the Syrian coast.

The first exposition of the decipherment convinced some scholars immediately; most experts (including Bennett) still withheld judgment, and a few were very skeptical. Almost all of those in the second category, however, were persuaded by a new and dramatic confirmation of Ventris' system. In 1952, Blegen had finally been able to begin the full-scale excavation of the palace at Ano Englianos. One of the first areas cleared was the vicinity of the little archives room uncovered in 1939. Immediately to the south and east, an area that had been disturbed by a great trench dug by later seekers for building stone yielded more than 300 additional tablets. When they were cleaned and mended the following spring (1953), Blegen experimented with the proposed system of decipherment and was so impressed with the results in one particular case that he wrote immediately to Ventris. It should be emphasized that Ventris had no knowledge of the document in question until after he had completed his original grid and announced the tentative decipherment.

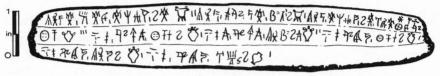

Figure 89

This tablet (Fig. 89) is identified as Ta 641 in Bennett's rather complicated classification system. The alphabetic letters identify it as one of a series of records inventorying containers and furniture. As is fairly often the case, this scribe added pictures of the objects being inventoried, described them carefully and recorded the number in each distinct group. The first word, followed (after three descriptive terms) by the picture of a vessel shown with three supports and the numeral "2," turned out on Ventris' system to be TI-RI-PO-DE. In the second entry (midway in the top line), only one vessel of exactly the same type is inventoried, and the corresponding word here is TI-RI-PO. Only an extremely stubborn opponent of Ventris' decipherment could refuse to agree that we have here the Greek word for a three-legged vessel, or "tripod." Its singular form is *tripos*, and the dual number (common in Homer and still occasionally found in later Greek when pairs are involved) is *tripode*. Furthermore, in the second and third lines another pair of inflections of a single word—DI-PA and DI-PA-E—occurs, along with pictures of a vessel of different shape, which narrows sharply toward the base. The word reminds us of Homer's *depas*, a bowl or goblet for libations; and the dual form DI-PA-E occurs in the only entry (midway in the second line) where two of them are inventoried.

Nor does the persuasiveness of Ta 641 end here. The DI-PA shape is pictured with four handles, three handles and no handles at all. In the entries opposite the four- and three-handled varieties respectively are the words QE-TO-RO-WE and TI-RI-O-WE; while A-NO-WE occurs with the plain vessel. These words are surely compound adjectives describing the vessels. The O-WE element is easily identified with the Greek word for "ear" that continued to be used in later Greek to denote "handle"; and QE-TO-RO, TI-RI and A(N) must be Greek *tetra* ("four"), *tri* ("three") and *a(n)* (a negative prefix).

Could any neater and more opportune confirmation of Ventris' system be imagined? It is so overwhelmingly convincing, in fact, that one persistent critic hinted at collusion; but such an allegation is unworthy of a member of the scholarly community. The established sequences of events as well as the reputations of Ventris, Chadwick and Blegen made the insinuation impossible and unthinkable. There are still unresolved problems but the Greek-ness of the underlying language is beyond doubt.

The 1953 article by Ventris and Chadwick did not fully explain how the grid had been built up, and some clarification and amplification was desirable. Further, the new tablets from Pylos and Mycenae had to be taken into account. The excavators allowed Ventris and Chadwick free access to the newly discovered tablets, so that in the same year they were hard at work on a much more ambitious project. Their bulky book, *Documents in Mycenaean Greek,* dedicated to Heinrich Schliemann, appeared in the autumn of 1956, a few weeks after Ventris' tragic death in an automobile accident.

Ventris and Chadwick first provide extensive chapters dealing with the development of the decipherment, the writing system, the language, the very large proportion of personal names and place-names and the new data on Mycenaean civilization. But the nucleus, as the title suggests, is a translation (with commentary) of 300 selected texts from Knossos, Pylos and Mycenae. The choice of this particular group out of a total of over 4,000 was based mainly on their judgment of the most interesting documents that were then available and at least partially intelligible.

Documents in Mycenaean Greek marked the zenith of the initial interest and enthusiasm produced by the decipherment. The first rush led to some excessive hopes and sometimes to rash and untenable proposals, but steady progress has rectified as well as increased knowledge painfully extracted from the syllabary. In fact, a second edition of *Documents* was needed less than twenty years after initial publication.

Apart from the continuing problems of interpretation, the decipherment brusquely decided the "Great Debate." It must have been a kindly fate that decided that Evans should die before 1952 and that Wace should survive to write the Foreword to *Documents.* He may be pardoned for showing in it a certain belated exasperation with the widely accepted "pan-Minoan theories." And he had even stronger criticism for certain classical archaeologists and philologists who continued to insist on an almost absolute gulf between the cultures of Bronze Age and Iron Age Greece. On this quite separate issue he and Evans had long been allies. Wace wrote:

The importance of Mr. Ventris' decipherment can hardly be overestimated, for it inaugurates a new phase in our study of the beginnings of classical Hellas.

> We must recognize the Mycenaean culture as Greek, and as one of the first
> stages in the advance of the Hellenes toward the brilliance of their later amaz-
> ing achievements. We must guard against the facile assumptions of the past
> and look at everything afresh from the new point of view. In culture, in history
> and in language we must regard prehistoric and historic Greece as one in-
> divisible whole. The way has been prepared for us by the pioneer archaeologi-
> cal work of Schliemann, Tsountas and Evans, and we must follow boldly in
> their footsteps under the guiding light now provided for us by Mr. Ventris and
> Mr. Chadwick. (1956: xxxi)

Wace particularly emphasized the growth of the conviction that Greek speakers
had entered the peninsula as early as about 1900, the evidence that Mycenaean
culture always preserved native mainland traits and the error of regarding LMII
Knossos as the wide-ruling Minoan capital of the Aegean world.

Wace invited another controversy, one that has become a major issue in the
present generation of pre-classical studies, by assuming that the mainland Greeks
never completely lost their literacy in the period between the end of the Bronze
Age and the assimilation of the new alphabet some three or four centuries later.
Citing the parallel of the survival of a modified form of the Minoan syllabary in
Classical Cyprus, he insisted, "it is incredible that a people as intelligent as the
Greeks should have forgotten how to read and write once they had learned how to
do so" (xxviii). Another of his assertions has likewise provoked debate: was
writing done on materials other than clay in late Mycenaean times? The flowing
curves of the Linear B syllabary seem to have been developed on a more tractable
material and are only possible on clay by the use of a very thin sharp stylus in a
practiced hand. The idiosyncracies of scribal hands were noted by Bennett
shortly after the decipherment and more recent analysis has revealed additional
marks of individuality. Such idiosyncracies may support the thesis of a somewhat
more widespread calligraphy on perishable materials like papyrus or skin (parchment). The clay tablets were apparently not used for permanent records, even of
a local economic nature. They contain no year date and seldom even identify the
month. There are references to "this year," "last year," "next year," but that is
all. It may be that other materials were used for more permanent economic
records, and it is at least possible that there was written diplomatic exchange at
the inter-kingdom level within (and perhaps beyond) the Mycenaean orbit. Certainly other contemporary cultures communicated with one another through written records.

The position of John Chadwick in *Documents* and others like Sterling Dow is
that the Mycenaean world knew only restricted literacy, a situation that would
explain the absence of writing implements from the archaeological records, the
lack of monumental inscriptions, the paucity of inscribed vases, the disappearance of writing following destruction of the palaces at the end of the Bronze

Age, and the apparent specialization of writing among a small scribal group. As we will see, the issue is still far from being resolved.

Wace's belief in the continuity of literacy and his hypothesis of a variety of materials led him to an extreme position. After outlining the orthodox idea that Homer stands at the end of a long tradition of epic song that probably extended back in an unbroken line to Mycenaean times, he added, "we need not therefore be surprised if excavation or some casual find in Greece gives us an early document—a letter, or a literary text, a history or a poem—from some long-forgotten forerunner of Homer" (xxix). Wace's position gave rise to even more intensive study of the technique of epic poetry. This study suggests very strongly that the long epic tradition culminating in Homer was from the first—and almost if not quite to the last—an entirely oral one. The hope of finding a written bit of pre-Homeric poetry shows misunderstanding of the potentials of oral tradition.

The theories of an American philologist provided an explanation for the character of Homeric poetry that began to find supporters in the 1930s. Venturing onto the battlefield known as the "Homeric Question," Milman Parry defined the seemingly peculiar characteristics of the Greek epics as usual features of oral composition. The severe critics of the nineteenth and early twentieth century—known as analysts—had seen repetitions, discrepancies of plot, and inappropriate language as tokens of the poor quality of Homeric verse. For Parry, on the other hand, the conditions of oral composition were the clue to the formulaic nature and metrical patterning of the *Iliad* and *Odyssey*. With the assistance of Albert Bates Lord, Parry undertook a comparative study of Yugoslavian Serbian ballads and the Homeric epics, believing "when one hears the Southern Slavs sing their tales he has the overwhelming sense that, in some way, he is hearing Homer" (Parry, 1933: 179–97; rpt. in Parry, A., 1971: 378). "In a society where there is no reading and writing," he concluded, "the poet, as we know from the study of such peoples of our own time, always makes his verse out of formulas. He can do it in no other way" (Parry, 1932: 1–50; rpt. in Parry, A., 1971: 329). The oral bard is conservative; he works with an inherited store of material, shaping it by traditional devices of meter and language patterning. Although each telling of a tale brings change both conscious and unconscious on the part of the bard, oral poetry does not strive for innovation. Instead, it gradually, slowly reworks the inherited tradition, making it intelligible and pleasurable to the present hearers. A tale of the Trojan War sung by a bard of the eighth century could well have its roots in the Mycenaean age, though much of the foliage would date from later centuries.

Nor were all prehistoric archaeologists of the third generation in accord with Wace's severe criticism of many of their colleagues working in the later, classical horizons. "From the beginning of Schliemann's discoveries at Mycenae," Wace charged, "the conservatism of classical archaeologists has obstructed progress in the study of Greek civilization as a whole. . . . It is this spirit which has impeded progress in our studies of pre-Classical Greece. . . . Greek art is one and indivisible, and has a continuous history from the first arrival of the Greeks." What Wace called the "orthodox" classical attitude is the position (which we saw exemplified in Michaelis' book) that Mycenaean and classical culture are so completely different that any close organic connection is impossible. These scholars see in the culture of the Early Iron Age the real origin of the "new life of pure Hellenism" (1956: xxvii, xxviii).

Wace believed that the wide cultural "chasm" that some supposed to exist at the end of the Bronze Age and that had been explained traditionally by a Dorian Invasion is a mirage comparable to Evans' pan-Minoan obsession. According to Wace, every step of the development of the form and decoration of the crisp, economical geometric artistic style so admired by Hellenists can be traced on Greek soil growing from the late Mycenaean repertory.

In retrospect, the nature of Wace's assertions demonstrates a common—perhaps even healthy—pattern in Aegean studies. The pattern is, simply, the dialectic. New evidence produces an extreme position which, in turn, gives rise to an opposed, similarly extreme position. Eventually a middle stance prevails. As we will see, the question of continuity from the Bronze Age to the Classical period is another illustration of this tendency in a list that begins with Schliemann's interpretation of the Trojan War and Evans' assertion of Minoan supremacy.

THE DATE OF THE LINEAR B
TABLETS FROM KNOSSOS

Those who had previously faced the problem usually spoke of scribal conservatism in a closely guarded art passed on from one generation to the next in restricted palace "schools." Parallels for an almost static writing system could perhaps be found in cuneiform texts on clay. However, Blegen argued, Linear B is a very different kind of script that seems to have been developed and used mainly for writing on more tractable materials than clay. Thus development of form would be more likely to occur in the Greek system than in Near Eastern scripts. And later Greek alphabetic records, even on stone, show quite rapid changes in writing styles. Blegen therefore suggested that the advances in stratigraphic excavation during the half century since the Knossos tablets were discovered and the profound increase in our knowledge of Minoan-Mycenaean relations in the Late Bronze Age may provide good reason for a careful review of the evidence for dating the Knossos tablets.

There is, of course, nothing incompatible now about the association of documents written in Greek with LMII levels at Knossos, since strong mainland cultural influence at Knossos is already very clear before the "final" destruction. But Blegen was inclined to believe that the closest parallels, not only for the tablets but for other features like the architectural planning and fresco decoration of the Throne Room at Knossos, are found in the securely dated context of the LHIIIB mainland palaces (*i.e.,* after 1300). Furthermore, various artefacts that were apparently found in the same context as the Knossos tablets appear to have their best parallels in mainland objects to be dated somewhat later than 1400.

Finally, Blegen emphasized the serious dilemma involved in Evans' theory that fragile tablets, partially burned in a destruction around 1400, could have survived during Evans' lengthy "period of reoccupation" at Knossos. "I have long wondered," wrote Blegen, "if there is not a strong probability that all the Knossian texts in Linear B really came from the debris heaped up in the burning of a palace which had been reconstructed and occupied by a Mycenaean conqueror from the mainland in Late Minoan III, or—shall we say?—Late Helladic III. . . . A thorough reexamination of all evidence available for the circumstances of discovery in each specific place where tablets were found at Knossos is certainly needed to test this suggestion" (1958: 64, 66).

The issue was soon taken up by several scholars, but one of them would take a commanding position in the escalating debate. This was L. R. Palmer, then Professor of Comparative Philology at Oxford University, who had immediately accepted Ventris' decipherment and contributed a great deal to the task of interpreting the content of the tablets as well as to the elucidation of the early stage of the language there documented. Indeed, philology would seem to have a proper role in helping to solve the chronological problem, and philologists generally agree that in linguistic features as well as script the two sets of tablets show very few significant differences. Again, therefore, a gap of two centuries appears strange.

However, the crucial problem of the stratigraphical context at Knossos is clearly an archaeological one. There are, roughly, two possible methods for solving the issue. One is to make new stratigraphical tests in unexcavated areas at Knossos in the hope of discovering new and securely datable tablets; the other is to try to review and reconstruct the circumstances of the original discoveries in Evans' and Mackenzie's early excavations. Palmer spent a great deal of ingenuity on the second approach, showing that there are serious discrepancies between the original field records, the excavators' immediate inferences and Evans' final summation of the evidence and conclusions. A rather heated exchange of views, first in the British press and later in pamphlet and book form, between Palmer and some of Evans' successors and supporters did little to clarify the problem. Palmer's book *Mycenaeans and Minoans* (1961, revised 1965) set out to show that the tablets not only belong to the last "reoccupation" phase of the palace, but that the general archaeological context and some internal evidence in the texts point to a destruction date actually later than 1200.

On the other hand, a reexamination of the record by archaeologist John

Boardman, Reader in Classical Archaeology at Oxford, upheld Evans' general conclusions (1963); and new stratigraphical tests by Sinclair Hood were cited as further confirmation (1962). Preliminary information on the excavation at Thebes beginning in 1963 placed the few tablets discovered there in a context around 1300. The Greek supervisor, Dr. Nikolaos Platon, believed that the date and content of the Theban documents would strengthen Evans' dating of the Knossos tablets (Platon and Touloupa, 1964: 859–861). Clearly, the issue was an open question at the end of the fourth generation of Aegean studies. In fact, as we shall see, the fifth generation of scholarship has not reached uncontested conclusions on the matter.

MAJOR EXCAVATIONS

At the end of World War II, archaeological activity resumed at sites where investigation had begun before the war and began at new sites. Indeed, "resumed" is far too mild a description since activity accelerated at a rapid pace. Several new schools and institutes for archaeology were chartered in the postwar period, and their energies would yield results in the field as well as in the world of publication. For the period under review in this chapter, some of the most striking results came from Mycenae, the southwest Peloponnese, Keos, Dendra, Athens, Thebes, Iolkos (modern Volos) and off the coast of southwestern Turkey.

THE SECOND GRAVE CIRCLE AT MYCENAE

As late as 1951 the six Shaft Graves inside the Grave Circle and the fabulous burial offerings that Schliemann had found at Mycenae remained virtually unique. It is true that fairly close parallels to the grave type had been discovered at Eleusis and Lerna; and roughly comparable circular structures enclosing cemeteries had been explored on the island of Leukas. But Schliemann's discovery continued to represent the preeminent insight on the crucial point of time, the transition from Middle to Late Helladic, when the heretofore independent and distinct mainland and Minoan traditions first met.

Although most scholars adopted Wace's view that the Shaft Grave type was simply a more monumental form of the older and simpler individual Middle Helladic cists that had been scattered over the same hillside, there were other notable innovations not easily explained as natural developments. One could point to the sculptured stelae erected over the graves, to the special reverence that seems to be indicated in the later construction of the circular parapet and also to the striking richness of the original burials. It is no wonder that Mycenae has remained the site for the study of early "Mycenaean" civilization. Its power and wealth seem to have surpassed those of any other area of the mainland in the same period. The new evidence did not alter the impression of Mycenae's commanding position, but it showed dramatically that the occupants of Schliemann's Shaft Graves did have earlier roots at Mycenae and that their "dynasty" did not represent quite as sudden an efflorescence of wealth and power as had been assumed.

The repair and restoration of the great tholos tomb of Clytemnestra, which Mrs. Schliemann had first excavated long before, led to the discovery. The tholos lies on ground sloping down to the west almost immediately outside of the citadel wall. Here a new Shaft Grave was discovered. This was not an entirely unexpected development, but it directed attention to the area immediately to the south, where several stone blocks formed what could be a segment of a circle. Was it possible that there had originally been another Grave Circle lower down on the slope? The implications were so important that the Greek Archaeological Society named a special committee, which in turn entrusted the supervision of excavation to two of its most trusted members: Dr. John Papadimitriou, then director of the Archaeological Service; and Dr. George Mylonas, a faculty member both of Washington University in St. Louis, Missouri, and of the University of Athens. Their three campaigns between 1952 and 1954 not only brought to light the second Grave Circle, but have provided vital comparative evidence on Schliemann's Grave Circle. The final publication by Dr. Mylonas appeared in 1973. Their work provides us with an understanding which is next best to being able to reexcavate Schliemann's Shaft Graves using painstaking modern techniques (Mylonas, 1973).

Papadimitriou and Mylonas called the new circle B and used A to designate the one so long known. The twenty-eight graves in Circle B were further distinguished by letters of the Greek alphabet to avoid confusion with Graves I to VI in Circle A. Circle B was surrounded by a rather roughly built wall of almost identical diameter with that of Circle A. Fourteen graves in B can be classed as true Shaft Graves. Mylonas was reasonably sure that the construction of the wall of Circle B (as well as an original, lower wall forming Circle A) preceded the digging of the graves within them. The entrance to Circle B was probably at the west, and sculptured stelae seem to have faced in that direction.

The burials in Circle B date somewhat earlier than those of Circle A, beginning in the seventeenth century and overlapping to a considerable extent with the earlier sixteenth century graves of Circle A. The overlap is difficult to explain if (as had been usually assumed) the Shaft Graves contain the bodies of royalty only and if there was a single ruling dynasty at Mycenae. Both circles show clearly a common tradition of burial rites, and the wealth so conspicuous in A is already accumulating in the earliest graves of Circle B.

Modern excavation of the new Grave Circle provided welcome authentication for current interpretations of Schliemann's rather scanty and confused evidence. All the major features of the later burials are present in Circle B: the methods of construction and roofing, the laying of the corpse (usually at full length) on the pebble-lined floor with food and weapons and ornaments around it, the lack of any sign of cremation or embalming, the immediate filling in of the shafts, the funeral feast with fragments of food and dishes thrown over the grave, the heaping up of more earth into a low mound with a plain or rather awkwardly carved tombstone on its apex and the building of a low stone wall around its edge, the frequent reopening of the grave for later burials and, when necessary, pushing earlier burials and gifts aside to make room for the new occupant.

Apparently, however, the final resting place of these earlier "kings" was not so reverently remembered as in the case of Circle A. The wall surrounding the graves in A was monumentally rebuilt at a higher level inside the later fortification walls and may have been visible as late as Pausanias' time. On the other hand, Circle B seems to have been neglected and forgotten at least as early as the time that the Clytemnestra tholos was built, because the new construction encroached on its area. The great mound of the Clytemnestra tholos deeply buried most of the earlier graves, protecting them in the same way as the later fill inside the wall had done for those in Circle A.

Some of the graves within Circle B are simple, individual Middle Helladic cists with very sparse grave furniture. So Wace's theory of a local origin of the so-called Shaft Grave dynasty seemed to be reinforced by the new evidence. At the other end of the time spectrum represented, one of the largest Shaft Graves was reopened and enlarged, apparently in the fifteenth century; and a long, narrow tomb chamber and entrance passage with vaulted saddle-roof of cut stone blocks was constructed. This type of tomb was unique in Greece; the closest parallels were with slightly later structures at Ras Shamra on the Syrian coast. The close trade contacts that had already developed between mainland Greece and the Near East may explain both the form of the grave and the wealth of the graves generally.

As in the case of Grave Circle A, the contents of these deeply dug and rather inconspicuous tombs were practically intact. Most of the gold is again thin foil, which originally covered objects of lesser worth. Weapons are a predominant item of contents, as in Circle A. The pottery, however, seems to be almost entirely in the mainland tradition, especially the later Middle Helladic matt-painted and gray and yellow Minyan fabrics. One of the most interesting among the many important grave gifts is an amethyst bead with a tiny, beautifully carved portrait of a handsome bearded man. The single electrum death mask discovered in Circle B is another indication of direct continuity with the contents of Circle A.

Dr. Lawrence Angel, a physical anthropologist who examined the bones of these early Mycenaeans, concluded that they were generally big, tall men, quite different from the smaller, lithe, beardless Minoans. Perhaps their stature set them apart even from their own subjects. One skull showed a trepanation, presumably done to relieve pressure caused by a brain concussion. Two gallstones lay neatly in position with one skeleton, and several individuals had suffered from arthritis.

It was natural that, when Grave Circle B was discovered outside the fortified acropolis, its position should bring to mind Pausanias' statement that he was shown the graves of Clytemnestra and Aegisthus "outside the walls." Indeed, Wace and others inferred that part of the surrounding wall of Circle B or some of the stelae were still visible in Pausanias' time in the second century A.D. when Pausanias reported on ancient remains he had seen (Wace, 1949). Mylonas made a persuasive case for believing that this could not have been so (1964); however, it is at least possible that the mounds over some of the tholos tombs were pointed out to Pausanias as the burial spots of Clytemnestra and Aegisthus.

NEW FINDS IN THE SOUTHWEST

An even more recent discovery provides strong support for the theory that the contents of the Mycenae Shaft Graves represent a phenomenon that was by no means confined to the Argolid. Dr. Spyridon Marinatos, then Professor of Prehistoric Archaeology at the University of Athens, discovered in 1965 at Peristeria, some twenty-five miles north of Pylos, an unlooted trench that is presumably to be connected with the badly destroyed tholos tomb above it. Finds included a gold plaque with a procession of young men in relief, gold dress ornaments decorated with rosettes, birds, a gold diadem and three gold cups. The best of the cups is decorated with linked spirals in relief and Marinatos believed that it may have been made in the same workshop as a comparable cup from the Mycenae Shaft Graves. The associated pottery indicated a date for graves and contents at the end of MH and in LHI, *i.e.*, contemporary with the Mycenae Circle A.

Schliemann's excavations had first dramatized the importance of the northeastern Peloponnese, and Evans and others continued to regard it as almost the only mainland area worth considering in the Late Bronze Age. Yet finds like Tsountas' at Vaphio and Kampos and Dörpfeld's at Kakovatos had shown quite early that rich and powerful Mycenaean centers had been located as far away as southeast and west Peloponnese. Blegen's discovery of a ruined palace at remote Messenian Pylos underlined the fact that major Mycenaean power centers were by no means confined to the Argolid. In fact, sporadic finds and organized exploration in many areas have revealed an increasingly wide scattering of tholos tombs and Mycenaean pottery, which in turn strongly support the testimony of the Catalogue of Ships in *Iliad* II that the whole of central and southern Greece had been thickly populated in later Mycenaean times. Continuous and energetic exploration of southwestern Peloponnese in the postwar years revealed that from Early Helladic times until the end of the Mycenaean period fertile areas were intensively occupied. The Pylos region began to emerge as a prosperous and highly developed area equal to the Argolid, not a peripheral rural cousin. Beyond its own inherent value, the investigation of Pylos gave rise to expectations that similar intensive regional exploration might reveal a comparable situation for other Mycenaean kingdoms recorded in Homeric epic.

Dr. Kourouniotis, who had been Blegen's associate in 1939, died during the war. His successor, Professor Marinatos, carried out a series of excavations in the Pylos area coordinated with Blegen's concentration on the palace site itself. Marinatos' attention was mainly devoted to numerous tholos tombs that cluster, usually in groups of two or three, about various peripheral regional centers. A picture began to take shape of independent capitals of small political units that gradually succumbed to the sovereignty of the palace center at Pylos.

It is in this context that Dörpfeld's site at Kakovatos was understood. Whether or not this general area was confused with Nestor's Pylos in post–Bronze Age times, there is no archaeological evidence that the capital of the kingdom was transferred there after the destruction of the palace at Messenian Pylos. The political system in the twelfth century and for some time thereafter would seem to exclude any large unified Pylian kingdom. On the other hand, the floruit of the site at Kakovatos is probably too early to allow the possibility that the Neleid dynasty settled there before locating at Messenian Pylos.

The general impression from the postwar excavations in the Pylos region was that it was in close touch with Crete almost as early as was the Argolid and that Minoan influence and trade relations continued to be very strong. The initial impression has been confirmed by subsequent exploration, as we shall see.

The pottery discovered in a tholos tomb near modern Koryphasion, which was cleared by Kourouniotis in 1925, suggests that it is as early as any yet known on the mainland, contemporary with the later Shaft Graves at Mycenae. A some-

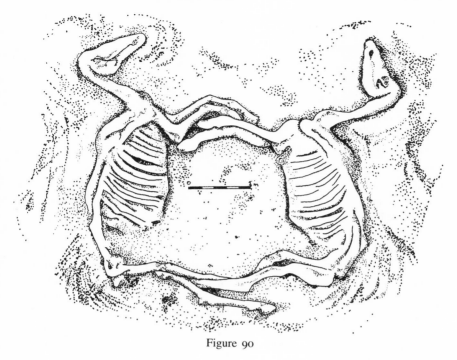

Figure 90

what later tholos at Peristeria, originally almost as monumental as those at Mycenae, has a facade composed of carefully cut limestone blocks, two of which bear incised Linear A signs like those on Cretan buildings. Still another at Routsi, which had somehow escaped the tomb robbers, revealed the last burial still laid out in orderly fashion on the floor in the center of the chamber. Bones and offerings from several previous sepultures had been deposited in shallow cists. Among the contents, perhaps the finest were two inlaid daggers in the same marvelous "metal painting" technique as the earlier examples from the Mycenae Shaft Graves.

One of Marinatos' interesting observations is that in at least some tholoi, wheel ruts were cut in the dromos near the doorway of the tomb chamber, apparently indicating that the body and its accoutrements were conveyed to the last resting place in a chariot or wagon. This theory was later supported by the discovery in 1969–70 of the antithetically placed skeletons of two horses lying beneath the floor of the dromos of a tholos tomb near Marathon in Attica (Fig. 90). They may have been sacrificed after drawing their dead master to the tomb, and perhaps it was believed that these badges of luxury thus continued at his command. The practice of burying chariot and horses in later Cypriot tombs may also be a survival of Mycenaean practice.

THE PALACE AT PYLOS

In the excitement of the retrieval of the Linear B tablets at Pylos in 1939, attention was temporarily distracted from the importance of the fairly well-preserved floors and lower walls that showed up in the trenches, but Blegen's painstaking clearing of the hilltop between 1952 and 1964 fully redressed the balance. The palace associated with Nestor has emerged as the most coherent and impressive building complex of Mycenaean times. Roofed over and protected, it gives the modern visitor who traverses its rooms and corridors a vivid sense of physical contact with the past. The clarity and completeness of the ground plan and the excellent preservation of the lower walls and various permanent installations is owed to the fact that no later habitation, as at so many important sites, destroyed or obscured the ruins of the latest monumental Mycenaean phase. At Pylos one gets far the best picture of how a Mycenaean king's household was arranged, but one must still go to Mycenae and Tiryns to see the massive fortifications by which such installations were usually protected. Perhaps Tiryns might have provided both aspects if modern techniques of excavation and preservation had been available when it was first cleared. But its palace ruins could scarcely have compared to those at Pylos, even when Schliemann and Dörpfeld first uncovered them (Fig. 91).

On the other hand, the visitor to the palace should not expect too much. The whole complex was burned to the ground in a raging conflagration fed by the great structural timbers and such especially flammable contents as big jars filled with olive oil. No doubt, either the inhabitants (if they had time) or the captors (if any were responsible for the burning) carried off almost every movable object of value—vessels of precious metals, inlaid furniture, jewelry, weapons—before the fire was set. Any surviving organic materials like wood and leather and textiles have long ago disintegrated. What remains are the more or less indestructible ruins of an architectural nature and certain equipment that could not be removed or was not considered worth saving. In the latter class are the thousands of pottery vases that were smashed to pieces as the building collapsed. The majority had fallen from the wooden shelves of the "pantries" where they had been stored for local use or (just possibly) for export. Inscribed clay tablets, though concentrated in the archives areas, were also in use in other parts of the building. Together with the clay sealings and particular types of pots, they sometimes help identify the original use of certain areas in the palace.

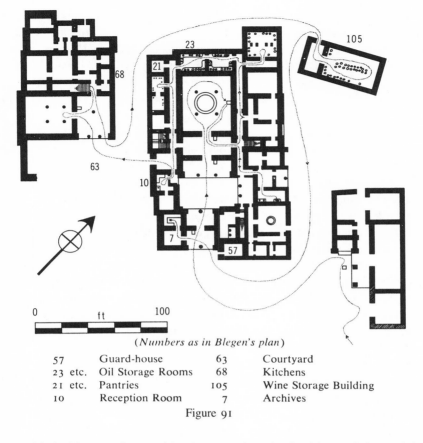

(*Numbers as in Blegen's plan*)

57	Guard-house	63	Courtyard
23 etc.	Oil Storage Rooms	68	Kitchens
21 etc.	Pantries	105	Wine Storage Building
10	Reception Room	7	Archives

Figure 91

In a kind of intermediate position between these lowly objects of clay and the preserved architectural features are the innumerable fragments of fresco paintings. Blegen found masses of the decorated plaster facing fallen from the walls and not completely obliterated by the fire. But he was doubly fortunate to locate a large deposit of less damaged fragments discarded from an earlier decorative scheme and tossed over the edge of the acropolis. Many of the more important palace rooms on both the first and second stories must have presented a gay, not to say garish, appearance. Most walls and even some floors (as well, no doubt, as ceilings) were painted. Many of the wall panels, sadly fragmentary though they are, provide a good deal of information about the people themselves—their physiognomy, costumes, implements, occupations. Presumably the paintings were based mainly on contemporary local models, but we seem to detect a conservative tradition going back to Minoan originals. Other compositions show glimpses of buildings, animals (real and imagined), stylized plants or purely geometric motifs.

Finally, a visitor sees the blackened stumps of the walls, the stuccoed floors, the drains and water pipes under the floors, the built-in clay hearths and stairs and benches and counters, and the gaps in the floors and walls that once accommodated wooden beams, columns, door frames, sentry boxes and even the king's throne.

Out of such spare material the archaeologist (and the visitor) must try to reconstruct the original appearance of the buildings and the life of the people who lived in them. Blegen had the advantage of a lifetime of familiarity with the remains of Mycenaean civilization, from both his own and others' excavations. Throughout the years at the Pylos palace he worked with meticulous care and associated with him a variety of able assistants in the task. Others have been able to continue efforts of reconstruction in the present generation.

Piet de Jong did many of the Knossos illustrations during Evans' later years and assisted in the study and illustration of the results of a whole generation of British and American excavations. He was responsible for many of the architectural drawings of the Pylos palace, for the architectural reconstructions, for the illustrations of restored fresco panels, fresco fragments and some of the finer pottery. Mrs. Blegen and Miss Marion Rawson did not miss a season of excavation as section supervisors and specialists on the pottery and such material as jewelry from the nearby tombs. Miss Rawson cooperated with Blegen in editing volume 1 of *The Palace of Nestor at Pylos: The Buildings and Their Contents,* which appeared in 1966. Professor Mabel Lang of Bryn Mawr College became an expert in cleaning and reassembling fresco fragments and was entrusted with the 1969 publication of the fresco material in volume 2 of the same work. Volume 3, edited by Blegen and others, treats the lower town, tholoi and chamber tomb cemetery and was published in 1973.

The history of the site came more clearly into focus, meshing remarkably well with tradition. The acropolis and its western slopes were occupied continuously from MH times. It is probable that in the LHI phase heavy fortifications guarded the hill itself. A thorough-going destruction of LHIIIA buildings about 1300 can be plausibly connected with the tradition of Neleus' arrival and suggests that his new Pylian kingdom was not won without violence. It is perhaps significant that all of the tholoi in the immediate vicinity of the acropolis antedate this event, while the chamber-tomb cemetery bridges the two periods without obvious interruption. After a drastic leveling process, the new palace would be represented by the older part of the surviving ruins at the western end of the hills, and it is probable that from then on no private homes were allowed to intrude on the acropolis. Well before the middle of the thirteenth century, "Nestor" (to use a name from tradition for an anonymous figure) would have added the unified rectangular structure directly to the east. Perhaps some of the minor buildings are even later.

The whole complex on the acropolis as well as the lower town was put to the torch about 1200, just as the last LHIIIB pottery styles were merging into LHIIIC. We will have a good deal to say later about the possible agents of that final destruction.

But let us go back in time before the end of the palace, using as our guidebook the Homeric account of Telemachos' visit to Pylos.[77] Some ten years after the end of the Trojan War, Telemachos has come from Ithaka in the hope of learning from Nestor some news about his father, Odysseus, who is still missing from home. The ship runs up on the beach where we find the venerable king and hundreds of his people engaged in sacrifices to their patron god, Poseidon, who was reputed to be Nestor's grandfather. Nestor greets us hospitably at the water's edge, asks us to share in the ritual meal and then insists that we go up to the palace to spend the night.

Our destination is five miles or so away—too far for distinguished guests to walk. A line of gorgeous chariots with bodies of brightly painted wood inlaid with ivory and drawn by matched pairs of gaily harnessed horses awaits us. We whirl off the beach and join the coast road, which soon turns inland along a high ridge. As the grade steepens and the road twists its way upward, the horses slow down and we can look back through the clouds of dust from other chariots and catch glimpses of the flat coastal plain and the Pylian navy drawn up snugly on the sheltered beach. Soon we see artificial tholos mounds and chamber tombs beside the highway and we know we are approaching an important town.

Suddenly we round a slope and see ahead of us a fairly steep hill crowned with a large building (Fig. 92). Its west side faces us, presenting a flat-roofed façade of two stories with rows of windows. The heavy dun-colored walls of mud brick and timber seem almost to be a higher continuation of the hill slope. As we come closer to the acropolis we see that there is a good-sized town spreading around and below it. The chariots roll through the street below the south slope of the acropolis and turn up the easier grade at its east end. Looking inland across a little saddle we see a smaller hill crowned with another of the familiar tholos mounds. Behind it, catching the evening light, a noble range of mountains apparently about five or six miles farther inland is parallel to the coast.

We clatter up onto the acropolis and notice that the nearer eastern half is free of buildings. We realize that this is where the people in the lower town would congregate in time of danger. Ahead of us looms a massive building complex with a couple of smaller separate structures intervening (Fig. 93). Grooms run out from the nearest building and catch our horses' bridles. From inside this building we hear the hum of voices and the busy sound of hammer and anvil. The grooms unhitch the horses and push the chariot through the doorway. As we leave this building, we see a small room recessed in the wall and open in front, with an altar

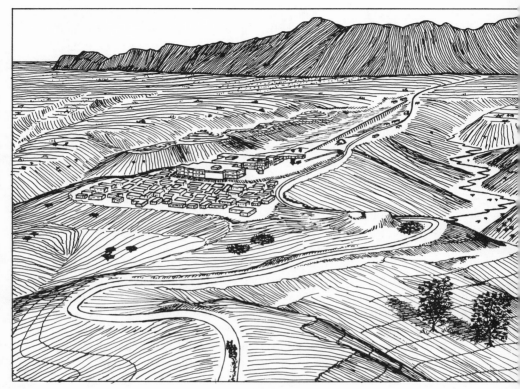

Figure 92

just outside. Here we catch up with Telemachos and Nestor, who are carrying out
the initial rites by which a guest is introduced to the protection of the palace deities (compare Fig. 91).

Our little group then passes around to the south side of the main building and
we realize that the main entrance faces in this direction—and no wonder, for it
presents a magnificent sweep of undulating countryside covered with olive trees,
vineyards and grain fields. Several distinctive mountain peaks etch the horizon.
The sea is in view off to the right. We congratulate Nestor on the beauty and
fertility of his country. He is obviously pleased and proud as he leads us toward
the main block of the palace. One question which we cannot restrain seems to
leave him a bit troubled. Why, we ask, is this rich administrative center not fortified like most of its rivals? He hesitates for a moment, and then says that the
main problem is water supply. There is a long tradition that the citadel itself cannot withstand a close siege since there is no spring on the hill or its immediate
slopes. The only feasible defense, he assures us, is to take advantage of the con-

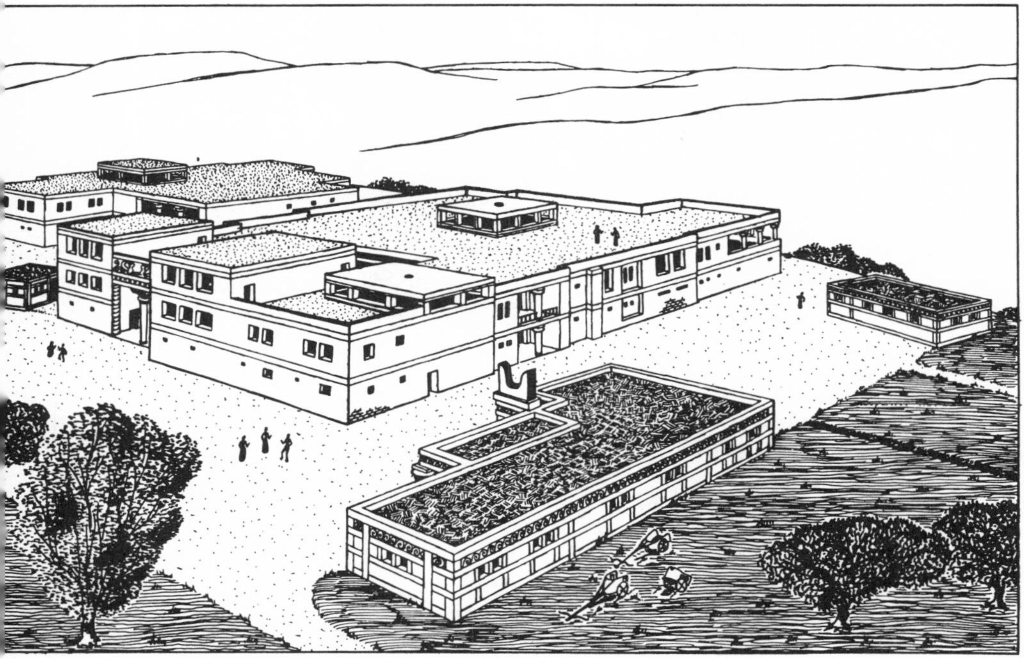

Figure 93

tours of the narrow ridge, with its steep slopes to north and south. The spring up the road to the east must be defended at all costs and contact maintained if possible with the harbor to the west. Nestor admits to some camouflaged fortifying. Pointing toward the southwest, he tells us that the large building had been quite separate from the main building of the palace until recently when several buildings were joined by the addition of new rooms and walls. And originally, he continues, there were several additional entrances to the palace. They have been closed so that the outer wall of the buildings is very like a protective shell, although it does not resemble the massive walls at Tiryns or Mycenae.

Passing a strongly built guardhouse on our right and continuing through the columned main entrance, we find ourselves in a handsome courtyard. Facing us is the columned porch of the megaron, which is a familiar nucleus of every royal palace; and there is also a shady columned porch to our right. We pass between the two columns of the megaron porch, are saluted by a sentry on guard and enter an anteroom with doors in the center of each of its four walls. Nestor leads the way through the door facing us. We pass another guard and find ourselves in as handsome a throne room as any Mycenaean king possesses (Fig. 94).

Since we have seen other palaces, almost every feature is familiar—the great

Figure 94

circular ceremonial hearth in the center with the four columns supporting a raised section of the roof, the throne against the wall on our right, the stuccoed floor divided into squares that are decorated with various painted designs, the colorful frescoed walls and painted ceiling. We particularly notice the protecting griffins and lions behind the throne and the graceful octopus in the floor panel directly in front of it. Additional wall panels depict other animals and humans. One distinctive scene portrays a harpist sitting on a rock while a bird hovers near, charmed by his song (Fig. 95).

Nestor takes his seat on the wooden throne decorated with costly inlay, and a servant brings him a cup of wine. He pledges us a welcome and passes the cup to us. When it is handed back to him, he pours the remainder of the libation into a depression in the floor at his right from which it trickles along a channel to a second depression. His wife and family, servants and courtiers gather in the throne room or look down from a sort of gallery or mezzanine with its railing framed by the tall slender columns. We are formally introduced and offered light refreshments, after which we enjoy the use of the palace's second-floor bathing rooms, and are given linen clothes of native manufacture.

Nestor courteously breaks off the business he has been attending to and dismisses the clerks. He asks us if we are too tired for a tour of the palace before dinner. Curiosity prompts our ready request for a tour, and we follow Nestor as he leads the way into the same corridor. He turns left along the side wall of the throne room. We pass a number of storerooms, and at the end of the corridor he shows us three big rooms (23) lined with great jars containing olive oil. He tells us that this is one of the major agricultural products of his kingdom and that the finest oil is boiled up with aromatic herbs and sent all over the world in stirrup jars made by the potters in the palace. From the oil stores we pass into a long corridor on the opposite side of the megaron and come to a series of small rooms (21) in which tremendous numbers of vases, most of them unpainted, are arranged by size and shape on wooden shelves. Nestor laughingly confirms our guess that in one little pantry alone there are almost 3,000 kylixes or wine cups of various sizes. Clearly, grapes are also widely grown in Pylian territory.

Beyond the pottery stores and opposite a door leading into the megaron porch is a room (10) equipped with a comfortable bench and a big jar of wine. The room is empty now, but Nestor says that tomorrow it will be crowded with people waiting for an audience with the king or his most trusted administrators.

We move on into a larger courtyard (63) near the southwest edge of the hill, a

Figure 95

complex recently joined more closely to the palace. Nestor seems to be particularly proud of it and tells us that early in his reign he himself supervised its construction. He says that the older section we are about to enter is the main part of the palace, which his father, Neleus, built a generation earlier when he first established control of the district. We had first sighted its outside wall as we drove up the road. The plan here seems to be less unified than that of the new section. There are two big rooms in front with interior columns. Nestor still uses these halls for state dinners and other occasions, particularly when the weather is hot. The small rooms (68) behind continue in use as the main palace kitchens. As we go up the stairway we hear the clatter of the preparation and smell the delicious odor of a meal being prepared. Some of the rooms on the second floor are reserved for guests, and through the windows of those assigned to us we feel the evening breeze and get a lovely view of the bay and the sea far beyond in the southwest.

We descend again and stroll down an open shaded area between the old and new palaces. A turn to the right behind the oil storage rooms brings us to a long, freestanding building (105) close to the precipitous north edge of the acropolis. Here Nestor's wine is stored in rows of big terra-cotta jars, each with a label indicating origin and age. We continue our tour along the northeast side of the new palace and notice its particularly fine outer wall of square-cut, carefully dressed limestone blocks.

Nestor leads us toward the main entrance again as on first arrival, saying we have time to take a look at an important part of the palace. We turn left opposite the guardhouse and enter a room (7) where scribes are taking dictation from inspectors who all day have been receiving and storing goods brought to the palace by people from various parts of the kingdom. Clay sealings indicate the people throughout the kingdom who are held responsible for the several activities. A huge, ribbed pithos in one corner has received a quota of fine olive oil, which will be ladled into smaller containers for transfer to the palace storerooms. An inner room (8) is the archives proper (Fig. 96). On a low clay bench are neatly stacked newly inscribed clay tablets. Still others are stored in baskets, labeled and in order.

Finally, just as darkness is falling and torches and lamps are lit, we are summoned to dinner in the great hall. Tables have been set up and are loaded with food. As eating gives way to serious sampling of the products of the Pylian vineyards, Nestor calls for a song. A distinguished figure rises from his place at table and picks up his lyre. Leaning on a column and with the torchlight fitfully illuminating his fine old face, he begins the epic tale of the Neleid conquest of the Pylos region. We all sit enchanted as the story unfolds. Some minutes after the singer has stopped his tale, Telemachos finally leans over to Nestor and reminds him of the purpose of our visit. The old man obviously considers this as busi-

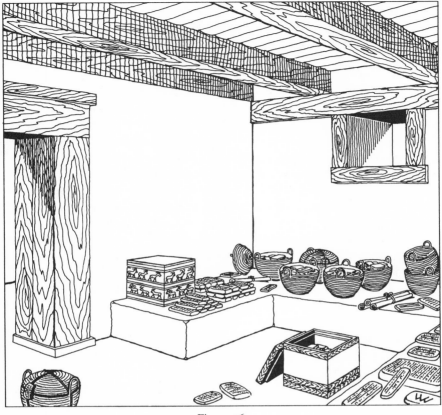

Figure 96

ness for tomorrow. But he does ask the singer to give us some of the stories of Odysseus' exploits in the Trojan War. So we sit, far into the night, sipping our wine, entranced by the spell of the singer.

A Temple at Keos

The uncovering of the palace of Nestor, the new Grave Circle at Mycenae and the decipherment of the Linear B script provided much of the major excitement of the postwar years, but important work carried on elsewhere resulted in unexpected and significant discoveries. One of the most interesting find spots is on the island of Keos, just off the southeast tip of Attica. The excavation began in 1960 under the direction of John L. Caskey, director of the American School of Classical Studies in Athens, a former student of Blegen's, his colleague at Troy, then his successor as chairman of the Department of Classics at the University of Cincinnati. Caskey devoted much of his energy of the last two decades of his life to Keos excavation. After his death, preparation of the final publication continued under the supervision of his former students and colleagues.

The discovery was of major importance in several respects: in addition to revealing the earliest Bronze Age Aegean example of a temple, the town demonstrates the nature of Aegean cultural interaction during the second millennium. In the sixteenth century (and perhaps even earlier), maritime towns like that on Keos seem to have been under strong Cretan cultural influence. Minoan pottery found on Keos—and even more recently on the island of Kythera—suggests that Cretan cultural and commerical (if not political) influence was still strong in the fifteenth century. The apparent use of the Linear A script confirms this impression. Contact with the mainland even before the end of the MH period is also attested. On the other hand, the results of Caskey's excavations did not indicate that the culture of the islands was simply local adoption or adaptation of features already identified in Greece or Crete.

The building identified as a temple also indicates the individuality of the island cultures. Among the buildings in the main town of Keos, one large structure appears to have been a temple from the time of its foundation. It was in continuous use from the beginning of the sixteenth century until the end of the Bronze Age, through the Iron Age and into the Hellenistic period. Furthermore, in the earlier strata lay the broken remains of at least nineteen terra-cotta female statues, some of which are almost life-size. So at one blow two long-held generalizations about the Aegean Late Bronze Age were shown to be untenable.

An "argument from silence" is always uneasy, and yet, until Keos, it was impossible to ignore the fact that three generations of extensive excavation had not produced a single certain example either of a monumental freestanding building devoted solely to religious purposes or of a truly monumental statue in the round. In spite of some equivocal cases (particularly at the very end of the Bronze Age), it was natural to infer that these features were unknown in Mycenaean times. Indeed, this statement was regularly made by leading authorities. Numerous indications of cult installations and religious paraphernalia in addition to the statues—particularly in one room at the inner end of the Keos building that Caskey identified as the most holy shrine or *adyton**—and the clear evidence of continuing religious use extending down past the Classical period left little doubt about its major purpose from the time it was built. Several of the statues were repaired from the fragments: the stance, the full skirt, and the open-fronted jacket exposing ample breasts are quite clearly in the authentic plastic tradition of the Aegean. The oval face and jutting chin may hark back to Cycladic marble sculpture of the Early Bronze Age, and other features such as the archaic smile may

Figure 97

anticipate Greek sculpture of the Iron Age (Fig. 97). The presence of numerous female representations in a single shrine has Bronze Age parallels, especially in Crete. In such cases we might perhaps recognize all of them as representations of "the goddess" or her priestesses or devotees.

The Keos excavations proved that small shrines in private homes or palaces were not the only places of worship. The work at Keos also showed that miniature representations of deity were not the absolute rule. Subsequent to the Keos find, structures identified as temples (at least by some scholars) have been excavated at Phylakopi on Melos; Arkhanes, Mallia and Myrtos on Crete; and possibly Mycenae, Eleusis, Pylos, and Tiryns on the mainland. There were, in fact, scattered (and generally late) indications from earlier excavation that a few freestanding structures might have been wholly dedicated to religious use, and the occasional monumental relief sculptures and rare fragments of large-scale sculpture in the round prepared scholars to some extent for the new evidence.

B R O N Z E   A R M O R   A T   D E N D R A

Similar revision in another area of our understanding of the Bronze Age was produced by a rich and almost unrobbed chamber tomb at Dendra just east of Mycenae, where Swedish excavators uncovered in 1960 the burial of a Mycenaean warrior with his full battle dress placed beside him in the tomb. Buried about 1400, he had worn a helmet, onto which were neatly sewn rows of boar's tusks. The upper part of his body had been protected by a bronze cuirass (Fig. 98) consisting of a separate front and back section laced together at the sides. His neck had been shielded by a separate bronze collar, his groin by overlapping flexible bands of bronze and his legs by bronze greaves. Another pair of bronze greaves was found in a late Mycenaean tomb in the northwest Peloponnese shortly after the Dendra discovery, and among discoveries at Thebes in 1962 were recognizable parts of another bronze cuirass. The general design of this body armor ties in neatly with an ideogram in a series of Linear B tablets from Knossos, which record the issue to individuals of horses, chariots and what has long been recognized as some kind of corselet with loops over the shoulders (compare Fig. 50).

Before these discoveries, it was often said that Mycenaean defensive body armor must have been made of some perishable material like leather; and no doubt most of it was. Again, however, one can see in retrospect that it was dangerous to rule out metal armor completely. Nearly all of the richer Mycenaean tombs, where such precious objects might have been deposited, have been robbed. And, in fact, metal was so costly and the skill to fashion such formidable and difficult equipment so rare that it would have required extraordinary restraint and respect for the dead if relatives had abandoned such precious objects in a grave or failed to retrieve them when the grave was reopened.

The armor suggested revision of another opinion: Homeric descriptions correspond in a convincing manner with the complicated fabrication of Mycenaean body armor. In specific cases such as the boar's tusk helmet, the poems embody

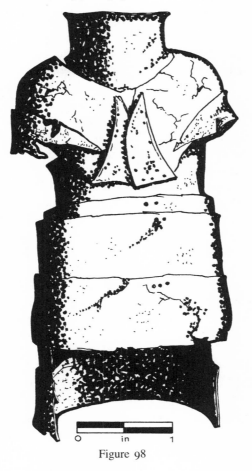

Figure 98

an authentic Mycenaean tradition. The fact that details were so little distorted by generations of bards who must have been increasingly out of touch with the actual objects is a powerful confirmation of the conservatism and veracity in oral transmission of the epic.

MYCENAEAN ATHENS

Among the many interesting post–World War II discoveries was new evidence found at three other important centers—Athens, Thebes and Iolkos. Farily intensive surface exploration has shown that Attica was heavily populated in Mycenaean times. Numerous widely scattered tholos tombs may indicate the truth of the tradition that it was only toward the end of the Bronze Age that Athens became the political capital of the whole region, with the unification traditionally attributed to Theseus. Due to constant and intensive later occupation, very little early evidence except broken pottery has survived on and around the Athenian acropolis. But there can be no doubt that a Mycenaean palace occupied the north central section of the "well-built fortress of great-hearted Erechtheus," [78] not far from where the classical temple called the Erechtheion still stands.

We are also sure that a great Cyclopean fortification more or less on the lines of the later classical walls protected the acropolis in the late Mycenaean era, and indeed sections of it were incorporated in the later construction. Professor Oscar Broneer discovered traces of an ingenious "water stair," very reminiscent of the well-preserved arrangement of Mycenae and rather similarly placed alongside the north wall. Like its counterpart it seems to have been built to ensure access to a water supply in time of siege. Private houses clustered below the fortress, and ruined chamber tombs in the Areopagos hill to the west and in the Agora just north of it give us a glimpse of where and how the wealthy inhabitants were buried. The large number of Mycenaean graves discovered provide at least a suggestion of Athens' important status during the later Bronze Age.

THE PALACE OF KADMOS AT THEBES

The existence and vicissitudes of Gla, which we reviewed earlier, are almost surely tied in to some extent with the history of Thebes as well as with Orchomenos. The Theban acropolis rises in the heart of the flat and fertile south Boeotian plain, and it has had a much longer record of occupation than Gla, both before and after Mycenaean times. Until recently, however, most of what we knew of Theban prehistory depended on legend and myth. Excavation has been difficult because a modern town covers the ruins left from continuous earlier habitation.

Very limited and tentative excavation in the first three decades of the present century showed that an extensive Mycenaean palace had once stood on the acropolis; it seemed plausible to see in it the home of the mythical Kadmos, who is said to have come to Greece from Phoenicia in search of his sister Europa. According to one legend, Kadmos settled in Thebes in obedience to an oracle from Apollo of Delphi and introduced "Phoenician letters" to his adopted countrymen. The so-called Theban cycle of Greek mythology recounts the tragic fate of Kadmos' descendants, especially the ill-starred Oedipus. The destruction of

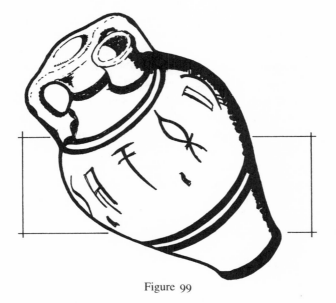

Figure 99

Thebes in a fratricidal struggle between Oedipus' sons two or three generations before the Trojan War seems to account plausibly for the striking absence of Thebes and Thebans in the *Iliad*.

The earliest excavator, Keramopoullos, thought, on rather limited evidence, that the destruction date was early in the fourteenth century, a date that did not contradict the legendary tradition that Thebes had been destroyed considerably earlier than Mycenae and Tiryns. The few basement rooms and corridors that could be explored suggested that this had been a storage and industrial area of the palace. In one room, fragments of an early Mycenaean fresco panel (perhaps fallen from an upper story) showed a procession of women in costume striking poses reminiscent of Evans' discoveries at Knossos.

Perhaps the most significant find, however, was a series of about eighty large stirrup jars, of which some thirty had short inscriptions painted on their shoulders (Fig. 99). The script was recognized as comparable to Evans' Linear B, and Sir Arthur made full use of this discovery to support his thesis of Knossian political control of important mainland power centers. Another, more recent conclusion about the origin of these vases will be reported at the end of this chapter.

Just before World War II, a second minor excavation confirmed previous indications that the ruins of a great Mycenaean building underlay additional areas of the center of modern Thebes. But it was not until a deep foundation for a new modern building was being sunk in 1963 that archaeologists had a better opportunity to probe a limited new area. The results of this work reported by Dr. Platon and Mrs. Eva Stassinopoulou-Touloupa of the Greek Archaeological Service were immediately tantalizing.

It was not surprising that a few Linear B tablets were discovered. The Pylos archives, Wace's discovery in palace annexes just outside the acropolis at Mycenae and the subsequent British discovery of a few fragments inside the Mycenae citadel conditioned scholars to expect tablets and inscribed objects in any new excavation of an important administrative center. The Thebes examples were found in what seems to have been a separate annex, perhaps an arsenal, some distance to the east of the earlier excavations and apparently separated from the palace by a wide roadway. Their date is very important. Platon assigned the destruction of the "arsenal" to about 1300 and, if this dating is correct, the tablets from Thebes would be the earliest yet found on the mainland and would fall midway between Evans' date for the Knossos tablets and Blegen and Wace's for those from Pylos and Mycenae. The Theban tablets show no significant difference from the Pylos archives in script and in what they reflect of the particular stage of the language, so that, if the date is right, the Linear B system will indeed have been shown to be a very conservative one. In that case, as far as internal evidence is concerned, an even longer gap between the Knossos and Pylos tablets is not ruled out.

In addition to the tablets, the excavations at Thebes produced gold jewelry, carved ivory plaques, onyx beads, numerous bronze implements, vessels and weapons and the defensive armor mentioned earlier. Fragments of horse harness represented another "first." In the main area of the 1960s excavation, a mass of closely datable pottery lying on floors in two distinguishable layers of ash indicate that the main Mycenaean building was destroyed by fire at least twice. Reports on the destruction dates remain somewhat contradictory, but Platon assigned the first to the later fourteenth century and the second almost at its end. The complex in which the inscribed stirrup vases were found in earlier excavations had a similar orientation to the older structure. Platon referred to the latter as the "Kadmeian" palace, though Kadmos is supposed to have arrived in Greece as early as the sixteenth century. Tradition tells us that its destruction was caused by lightning. The rebuilt palace destroyed later had a different orientation. In legend, it would represent the one over which Oedipus' sons fought and died.

Platon's major discovery, which guarantees that the fabled Theban palace ranked with those of Priam, Agamemnon, Minos and Nestor, was a "hoard" fallen from a higher floor into a basement room connected with the later building. The cache includes typical Mycenaean and "Aegean" seals, as well as jewelry of gold and faience and ivory; but the really startling presence is a group of almost thirty Near Eastern cylinder seals of lapis lazuli and agate. They bear characteristic carved representations of gods, demons, humans and animals; fourteen have cuneiform inscriptions. A preliminary classification by E. Porada indicated that all can be dated before 1300 and that they are a mixed lot—mostly Babylonian, Kassite and Mitannian. One inscription published early on identifies a certain Kidin-Marduk, an official of King Burraburrias II, twentieth king of the Kassite dynasty, who reigned 1367 to 1346.

As with previous "bombshells" like Schliemann's Shaft Graves and the Pylos archives, it required time for the archaeological community to assimilate the new evidence. As we will see in the next chapter, two decades of interpretation have defined the significance of the material in several respects. Still, the discovery of Near Eastern seals in a Mycenaean context did not cause undue surprise. It has long been known that there were close trade relations between Mycenaean centers and markets at the east end of the Mediterranean, and the Naram-sin cuneiform inscription from Kythera was found in the mid nineteenth century. Objects manufactured in one milieu occasionally occur in the other, and art forms and techniques were mutually borrowed. It would not be at all difficult for a wealthy Theban king to have his agents collect and send to him this fine selection of inscribed Near Eastern oriental seals.

THE PALACE OF JASON AND PELIAS

More tentative and much less sensational results were obtained still farther north between 1956 and 1960 at the town of Volos, a busy modern seaport at the head of a deep protected gulf on the east central coast. The great acropolis, formed almost entirely from the debris of millennia of continuous human occupation, has usually been identified since Tsountas' day with the famous Mycenaean capital of Iolkos, from which Jason and the Argonauts set out to recover the Golden Fleece. Iolkos was also the original home of Nestor's father, Neleus, brother of Pelias. The overlying modern buildings have presented the same problem to excavators as in the case of Thebes. The Greek archaeologist Demetrios Theocharis decided to try to cut into the northwest edge of the acropolis below the overhanging medieval fortifications.

Theocharis was able to substantiate that a thick layer of debris from the Late Bronze Age contains well-preserved foundations of a monumental building with typical Mycenaean remains, including fragments of fresco painting. Again, two major phases were indicated by layers of ash and destruction. The later building apparently survived longer than most of the power centers farther south. A heavy stone foundation over 90 feet long was uncovered, and partitions dividing the building into three large rooms extend under the fill. No more than the edge of the structure can be explored without the removal of the modern buildings above.

Even then a monumental operation of examining and removing later walls and deep overlying deposits of debris—not yet undertaken—will be necessary before reaching the prehistoric levels.

Yet other northern sites produced Mycenaean pottery, sometimes in association with chamber tombs or tholoi or walls, in the 1950s. Gritsa, south of Volos; Ktouri, Chasambli and Petra to the north; and Gremnos in Thessaly all were indicators of the wider spread of Mycenaean culture than archaeologists had previously envisioned.

A   B R O N Z E   A G E   S H I P W R E C K

A fascinating new area of archaeological discovery made major advances in this generation of investigation in the development of scientific underwater exploration and salvage. The most valuable evidence bearing on our period was produced by a University of Pennsylvania expedition under the direction of Dr. George Bass and with the assistance of Peter Throckmorton. Local sponge divers led them to the wreck of a small ship which (it turned out) had sunk about the end of the thirteenth century off the rocky coast of Cape Gelidonya in southwest Turkey.

The general nature of the contents and, particularly, the standard employed for the hematite weights suggest that its home was some east Mediterranean port and that it was proceeding westward, stopping off at coastal points to bargain and barter. It was apparently a kind of floating blacksmith's shop, carrying its own supplies of copper (probably loaded in Cyprus) in the familiar form of stamped ingots occasionally found in Aegean sites and portrayed on the Linear B tablets. Tin oxide was used to temper the copper, and bronze scrap in such form as broken implements seems to have been acquired along the way. (When they returned to the site in 1987, the excavators found a lump of metalic tin, even more convincing proof of the ship's cargo and activity.) New tools such as hoes, plowshares, axes, adzes, chisels, spades and meat grills were available on board for the customer's inspection. If a desired object was not obtainable ready-made, it could have been forged to order on board. Bigger craft no doubt transported most of the raw copper direct to mainland markets, where they picked up a return cargo of perfumed oil and other mainland specialties.

S C I E N C E   A N D   A R C H A E O L O G Y

No more appropriate conclusion could be chosen for this chapter than a glimpse at the tentative results of just one of the many areas where new scientific techniques are being applied to archaeological materials. As early as 1939 Blegen and Wace, among others, had foreseen the possibility and importance of scientific research applied to ceramics. Dr. H. W. Catling and two of his associates in the Research Laboratory for Archaeology and the History of Art at Oxford University reported in 1961 and 1963 on the spectrographic analysis of a group of over 500 Mycenaean and Minoan potsherds dated after 1400 and collected from some thirty known sites. The purpose was to determine whether there are detectable differences in chemical content of the clays that might identify place (or at least area) of manufacture.

The preliminary results were most encouraging and continuing analysis has enriched the findings. Researchers distinguished thirteen distinct kinds of composition, which were labeled Type A through Type M. Two major points were established: 108 out of 110 samples from sites in the Peloponnese fell within their Type A; and nearly all the samples from Knossos and central Crete could be assigned to Type B.

Pottery of Type A (Peloponnesian) was identified in relative abundance in Rhodes, Melos and in the sites in Egypt and Syria. Conversely, pottery of Type B (central Cretan) did not occur at all in the east Aegean and Near Eastern sites. This neatly confirms other evidence we have reviewed for the supersession of Minoan by Mycenaean traders in the east Mediterranean, particularly during the fourteenth and thirteenth centuries. A somewhat unexpected corollary seems also to be indicated, that is, that Mycenaean "colonies" in the Aegean were importing large numbers of pots (or their contents) from the mainland and that the fine Mycenaean pottery reaching the east end of the Mediterranean was largely manufactured on the Greek mainland rather than in the much closer island settlements. For example, the distinctive kraters with chariot scenes, found much more frequently in Cypriot graves than on mainland sites, were apparently manufactured in the Peloponnese.

The preliminary analysis also seems to confirm a widespread belief in minimum contact between Crete and the mainland after 1400. Pottery of Type A was extremely rare in Crete; and that of Type B was very uncommon on the mainland, except at Thebes. Catling was inclined to explain the latter anomaly as an accidental similarity of the local clays rather than as evidence for some exclusive trade connection between Knossos and Thebes (Catling et al., 1963).

The results of the tests in the Oxford laboratory suggested a good many other interesting possibilities about the minor centers of trade and manufacture. An immediate problem was to find means of distinguishing pottery manufactured in different parts of the Peloponnese. It will be vital to know, for example, how much of the Type A pottery found in the Near East came from particular mainland centers.

A similar problem of distinguishing between sherds from Thebes in Boeotia and central Crete was solved in 1965 (Catling and Millett, 1965: 3–95). Catling (with A. Millett) described the reanalysis of the Theban sherds and the addition of a further group of twenty from more recent excavations at Thebes. Nineteen of the latter proved to belong to Type B. The breakthrough came in isolating a previously uncounted component in the spectrum: germanium. This element was found to be consistently present in a very small quantity in all of the Type B sherds from central Crete. Furthermore, the scattered Type B sherds from elsewhere on the mainland are of the Theban variety now distinguished as Type "B.*"

An equally absorbing result of the research reported in the mid 1960s concerns the inscribed stirrup jars found at Thebes in 1921. The date originally assigned (early fourteenth century) has been both supported and attacked on the basis of both shapes (typology) and inscriptions (epigraphy). But neither criterion is yet precise enough for close dating, and the original context of their discovery (like those of some possible parallels at other sites) is poorly documented. Estimates all the way from 1400 to 1200 are current. Spectrographic analysis cannot pin down the date; but, as we have seen, it is most useful to indicate origin (or provenience), and there can be no doubt that the inscriptions were painted on the jars at the time and place of their manufacture.

Evans, of course, believed firmly that the Linear B inscriptions were in the "Minoan" language and that these jars found at Thebes (as well as scattered examples at Mycenae, Tiryns, Eleusis and Orchomenos) proved that the mainland sites were under Minoan political control. The fact that no inscribed jars were known from any Cretan site and that Linear B tablets had been found only at Knossos convinced him that the Minoan rulers came from Knossos.

After the decipherment, Evans' view had to be abandoned, but the supposed connection with Crete persisted. Typically the inscriptions consist of three words—a personal name (perhaps that of an official?), a place-name (origin of jar and contents?) and an adjective indicating "belonging to the wanax (king)." Palmer had already pointed out that several of the personal and place-names recur in the Knossos Linear B tablets, and that the presumption should be that the jars and their contents were shipped to Thebes and other mainland sites from Crete.

The Oxford scientists were allowed to take drillings from twenty-five of the Theban jars. Spectrographic analyses revealed three distinct groups of twelve, six and five examples, with the remaining two jars perhaps forming another group. There are additional significant variations within each group; but, overall, Group I is closest to Type F of the 1963 analyses and Group II to Type O. Both of these types, therefore, indicate a provenience in the extreme eastern part of Crete, Type O in the neighborhood of Palaikastro and Type F in or near Zakro. In Group III, three jars appear to have been manufactured in Thebes itself and two are closely comparable to Type A (Peloponnese). Not a single jar seems to have come from Knossos or central Crete.

The repercussions of this analysis go far beyond the obvious commercial implications. More intensive excavation in western Crete, increasing from the 1960s, shows, for instance, that the Linear B writing system was used in western Crete as well as at Knossos. If the date of the jars were eventually narrowed to around 1400, this would have very interesting implications about the political situation contemporary with Evans' dating of the "final" destruction of the Knossos palace. A date a century or more later, on the other hand, would suggest revising the traditional view of Cretan literacy as well as overseas trade in the closing part of the Late Bronze Age.

Whatever the specific questions and answers, the new alliance between archaeology and the exact sciences would fundamentally affect the investigation of Bronze Age Greece in the next generation of study.

IX

Recent Developments:
1965-1988

P*rogress into the Past* was first published in 1967. In theory, then, that year marks the division between the previous and the present generation of Aegean prehistoric scholarship. Of course, the realities are somewhat different. Publication delays and problems in the interpretation of finds impose a time lag of several years or even decades between artefact discovery and dissemination of descriptive and analytical material. Still, using the year as a theoretical division between generations, 1967 points to several paths of scholarship that developed during the last two decades.

One major direction has been the continuation of work at known sites particularly aimed at clarifying finer points of chronology and determining contact with other sites. For example, in 1967 excavations were resumed at the important sites of Tiryns and Knossos. Some splendid new discoveries have been made in the bargain. The cult area in the vicinity of Tsountas' House at Mycenae is but one instance.

The same year also saw the start of new excavations. Preeminent on this list is Akrotiri on the island of Thera; buried under volcanic ash and pumice up to 150 feet deep, the site is a dramatic find in its own right. Additionally, it appears to hold clues to the relationship between the mainland civilization and that of Minoan Crete. Continuing work on Crete has located new sites that may also hold the key to relationships between the Minoan and Mycenaean cultures.

A third path is illustrated by the excavations at Nichoria in Messenia. Not only is it interdisciplinary—a trend visible in earlier archaeology but a particular mark of the practice of the present generation—the project is diachronic on a grand scale. Nichoria's history extends from the Bronze Age into the Dark Age and, after an interval, into the Byzantine period. Work at Nichoria demonstrates exceptionally well the expanded vista of scholars: as developments of the Bronze Age have become clearer, investigators are increasingly interested in establishing the relationship of those developments to earlier and later sequences. As a result, there is considerable progress into the more remote past of Neolithic,

Mesolithic and Paleolithic stages. Investigations at the Franchthi Cave in the Argolid, where trial trenches were sunk in 1967, and at Klithi in Epirus similarly demonstrate the depth of the cultural roots of Greece. At the other end of the time scale, attention to the Early Iron Age is making the Dark Age of Greek history less dark. Excavation at Lefkandi on Euboea, for example, has done much to alter the previous notion of an absolute break between the late Bronze Age and subsequent centuries.

By comparison with earlier generations of Aegean archaeology, however, the present generation's results have not been marked by a great many dramatic finds. Instead, its contributions are the understanding and consolidation of existing data enhanced by development of ancillary skills. Applications of scientific techniques may have been slow to win general acceptance in Greece, but they have gained ground nonetheless. Dating techniques, the geophysical study of sea-level changes, and archaeometry especially, have given new precision to the evidence. Dating the eruption of Thera is a dramatic illustration of the productive alliance between scientific techniques and archaeological evidence. Since 1984, excavation of the oldest known shipwreck off the southern coast of Turkey at Ulu Burun demands the precision of scientific techniques adapted to underwater archaeology. While archaeological work has grown to encompass a greater geographical area and a broader range of types of sites, it has also expanded both technically and as a discipline.

In fact, the whole of classical archaeology (not just its "Mycenaean" subdivision) is being challenged to reexamine its fundamental aims and methods. The development of the "new archaeology" has stimulated heated debate upon the merits and identities of traditional versus new archaeology. In 1980 Colin Renfrew, a major proponent of the new archaeology, addressed the centennial celebrations of the Archaeological Institute of America on "The Great Divide" between advocates of both approaches.

"Ladies and Gentlemen," Renfrew concluded,

> if it is true to say that the Great Tradition has been insufficiently aware of the intellectual challenge offered by recent developments in anthropological archaeology, it is also the case that the New Archaeology has been largely blind to, and remains in considerable ignorance of, the immense potential offered by the archaeology of the Ancient World. It is time we all got our act together! (1980: 297f.)

Since the issues which have been raised play a significant role in Bronze Age Aegean archaeology, it will be well to review the basic ground of this debate and its ramifications for current and future developments in the field.

THE "NEW ARCHAEOLOGY"

"To concentrate on higher culture to the exclusion of the more humdrum aspects of life distorts the archaeologist's role, which is surely to reveal the past in as many facets as possible, rather than to treat it as a 19th century museum. Palaces, temples and artistic objects still dominate the Classical archaeologist's thinking to an unhealthy degree." These were the conclusions of S. Mitchell and A. W. McNicoll as recently as 1978–79, when they reported on archaeology in Asia Minor for *Archaeological Reports* (61). Primarily because of the impact of the "new archaeology" and the increased application of a primary tool of its practitioners, namely, archaeological survey, this assessment is less correct a decade later.

Given its name in the 1960s to distinguish recent developments in the discipline from older practices, the new archaeology was described by one of its first proponents, the English archaeologist David Clarke, as "a new level of disciplinary consciousness, critical self-consciousness" (1973: 7). New methodologies, observations and philosophies have extended the discipline in a host of directions, enlisting the skills of other disciplines and drawing on recent technology for the collection and analysis of data. With the recently employed tools have come new questions. In other words, the dimensions of the field have expanded: new archaeology seeks a larger contextual analysis than description of individual objects or sites while acknowledging the need for specific object or site information as part of the necessary data base.

Not single objects or individual events but processes and entire systems are the favored objects of attention among new archaeologists. A society can be viewed as a system, a "network of intercommunicating attributes forming a complex whole" (Clarke, 1968: 43). The attributes of the culture are its main aspects—its subsystems—influencing one another in ever-changing relationships. Since subsystems are simply aspects of the same system, they can be variously defined and counted. Often five or six main aspects are isolated. A given culture is defined by the sum of these subsystems and by its relationship to the external setting of the environment which is itself a system composed of subsystems. There are three levels of equilibrium in a functioning system or culture: within each subsystem, between subsystems, between the system and the environment. Practitioners of new archaeology are interested in understanding the individual parts together with their relationship to the whole. Thus the tools of several disciplines must be employed; assumptions and hypotheses must be framed and tested; investigation must account for changes through time; various parts in a complex combination must be viewed as interacting with one another.

In the Sather Classical Lectures of 1984–85, Anthony Snodgrass described "the present state and future scope of the discipline of classical archaeology." This became the subtitle of the lectures published in *An Archaeology of Greece* in 1987. Snodgrass concluded with several pleas: for greater cooperation and respect between traditional and non-traditional archaeologists; for more attention to the archaeology of the Greek landscape; and for increased integration of art historical, archaeological, and other types of evidence. An increasingly popular way of attaining all of these ends is through survey archaeology.

Survey archaeology is not itself a new field; in fact, it was one of the earliest practices of the discipline. Not excavators, but travelers like Jacob Spon and George Wheler began the rediscovery of ancient Greece. Schliemann was an inveterate traveler, even after his excavations were well underway; he recognized the advantage of a better understanding of the whole region in which he was excavating or considering excavation. Even as excavation became the primary focus of archaeological exploration, survey expeditions continued. Now, during the past two decades, survey has become a formal division of the discipline.

One main development is associated with the size and complexity of surveys. Until recently, topographical surveys were usually projects of one or two people. Such individual enterprises are increasingly giving way to larger projects that involve several people who collectively possess a wide range of expertise. In 1983, it was estimated that while small projects involving one to three people accounted for almost 50 percent of the surveys in the Mediterranean area, medium-sized ventures bringing together between four and fifteen members were a full 50 percent of the total. Even larger projects of sixteen or more people represented a few percentage points of all surveys (Keller and Rupp, 1983: 5).

The size of the teams has grown in response to the aim of present-day surveys: "The growing emphasis is on interdisciplinary research projects which address the broader issues of patterns of settlement and resource exploitation, demography, economics and political organization, trade systems and the relationship of man to his environment on a regional scale" (Keller and Rupp, 1983: 5). The area of exploration, questions about the evidence, and the period of time covered are all larger than the similar concerns of excavation archaeology. The area of survey is regularly extended over more than one site; search ("intensive survey") extends over a smaller or larger block of landscape that is laid out in transects and inspected closely by workers who walk as closely as 15 meters to one another. Within that region, questions are asked about settlement patterns, spheres of cultural influence, extent of trade. Survey archaeology is inherently diachronic: surface remains provide the evidence catalogued or collected by the surveyors, and such remains cut across broad periods of time. In addition to material remains, survey archaeologists are especially concerned with the interaction between human and environmental conditions.

For all these reasons, an archaeological survey team must be interdisciplinary. One of the first large efforts of this sort was the Minnesota Messenia Expedition. The subtitle of the published findings defines the research goal of the expedition as "Reconstructing a Bronze Age Regional Environment." While special attention was addressed to the Late Bronze Age, the team studied the habitation pattern in a region of 1,400 square miles for all periods from the Neolithic to the Roman era. Personnel included both archaeologists and para-archaeological personnel represented by specialists in ethnology, epigraphy, metallurgy, civil engineering, geology, history, geography, ceramic technology, soils, agricultural economics, and palynology.*

Methods of survey teams vary from project to project, of course. What most surveys have in common is "use of pedestrian search tactics to recover information about the extant surface archaeological remains in a region" (Cherry, in Keller and Rupp, 1983: 381). In other words, members of the project walk in predetermined patterns over a specific amount of territory, recording information about archaeological, geographical and geomorphic finds. Information gathered by individual members is consolidated on maps prepared for the project. For the Minnesota Expedition, maps using four different scales were employed: regional with a scale ranging between 1:500,000 to 1:100,000 sq. km; micro-regional, 1:100,000 to 1:25,000; site, 1:25,000 to 1:200; and micro-site, 1:200 to 1:1.

Survey archaeology has become increasingly popular for a number of reasons. Its logistics are easier than those of excavation, it is far less costly than research excavation, and it has been less difficult to secure permission to carry out survey investigation than to acquire a permit to excavate.

There is an obvious need for collection of information that surveys can provide as the ancient landscape is altered rapidly by road construction, major building projects, and massive irrigation schemes, as well as by normal land use by modern inhabitants. Equally important, survey provides a different perspective than excavation: as John Cherry summed up the difference between the two endeavors, "Excavation reveals a lot about a little of one site; survey can tell us a little about lots of sites . . ." (Cherry, 1983: 387). Since many of the sites selected for excavation have been major centers, results emphasize the activities and culture of densely populated (if not truly urban) settlements. With its regional focus, survey concentrates on rural, non-elite sites. Its results point to environmental, social and economic developments of all strata in the region defined for investigation.

It is most unlikely that survey will replace excavation archaeology. In fact, some archaeologists believe that it has value only as a preliminary tool and is thus ancillary to excavation or in rescue operations where time does not allow full-scale excavation. Richard Hope Simpson is perhaps most emphatic on this point of view. In the introduction to his own 1981 survey of Mycenaean Greece he argued, "while the new techniques and the new zeal are to be welcomed, it must be pointed out that there are obvious limitations inherent in all survey work, especially when not accompanied by excavations" (1981: 1). Some areas cannot be surveyed and surface patterns have been distorted, so that the evidence itself is distorted.

Even committed advocates of the value of survey archaeology admit to problems. A more or less standard technique is only now evolving. Members of survey teams have the same problem communicating with one another as do excavation archaeologists, both because of the lack of a uniform approach and because publication of often unglamorous finds is difficult. Would-be surveyors must be funded, even though costs are not as high as those of a major excavation. To be effective, specialists from a number of fields must be involved. Site accessibility is equally problematic for survey investigators and for excavators.

The results of survey cannot provide answers to all of the questions posed. Chronology is even less exact than that of an excavated site. Definition of a site is no easy matter; surveyors are not in agreement about the quantity of materials needed for definition of an area as a site. Just as sites arose and disappeared in the past, so they come and go in the present. Surface remains visible one season may be gone by a second; alternately, routine plowing by a farmer may reveal "new" evidence not previously detectable. Even when a site is recognized, information about its internal organization and function is difficult to obtain. Very much at issue is the relationship between intensive and extensive examination.

Even with such limitations, regional surveys have become an important part of Greek archaeology, particularly in the Peloponnese, east central Greece, Attica, Crete, the Cyclades, the Dodecanese, Cyprus, and southwestern Asia Minor. Important results have been produced by surveys in Euboea (1974, 1981–82), central Boeotia (from 1978), Laconia (1983–85), Nemea, Thesprotia and Epirus, the southern Argolid, Phokis-Doris, Methana, Megalopolis, Andros, Naxos town, Keos, Thasos, and, on Crete, the western Messara Plain, the Agiopharango Gorge (1971), Lasithi Plain, and around Roussolakkos in the eastern part of the island.

The Minnesota Messenia Expedition was the first large-scale project. Field work continued from 1959 to 1969, with findings published in 1972. The approach of its directors, William McDonald and George Rapp, Jr., is illustrated in Figure 100 (McDonald and Rapp, 1972). Another major expedition has been carried out on the island of Melos under the direction of John Cherry. Analysis linking ancient habitation patterns with medieval and modern practices was published by C. Renfrew and J. M. Wagstaff, eds., *An Island Polity: The Archaeology of Exploitation on Melos* (1981). The Cycladic island of Keos is the site for a survey project of several years' duration. Preliminary findings have been pub-

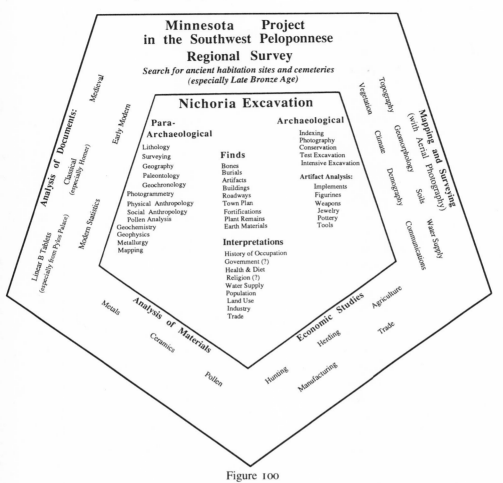

Figure 100

lished by J. Davis. The Kommos area of south Crete was surveyed between 1970 and 1980 by the Kommos Excavation Team coordinated by J. W. Shaw and R. Hope Simpson. Published results of survey work in the southern Argolid are now beginning to be available. Explorations in the area were undertaken in the 1950s by Michael Jameson, then Professor of Classics at the University of Pennsylvania. When Jameson moved to Stanford, the work continued as the Argolid Exploration Project from 1979 (van Andel and Runnels, 1987). Richard Hope Simpson was mentioned earlier in connection with his own extensive survey work on the mainland. His compendia of site information illustrate one of the most useful directions taken by the present generation of prehistoric Greek archaeology.

The perspective of the Minnesota Messenia Expedition will serve as a useful case in point. The Expedition investigated the region that fans out from Pylos, which occupied our attention in chapter eight. Just as the discovery of additional centers of Mycenaean civilization was a characteristic of the previous generation of early Aegean archaeology, so the present generation has started to study the more extensive territories in which those centers flourished.

Blegen's excavation at Ano Englianos made it possible to describe, in some detail, the nature of the palace center as well as earlier building phases. Association of the archaeological site with legendary evidence resulted in a recreation of the visit of Odysseus' son Telemachos to the home of his father's Trojan War comrade, Nestor. The fruits of regional surveys add a further dimension to the picture. We can now visualize the nature of life that supported the palace and its occupants; that is, the pattern of land settlement and use throughout the entire kingdom of Nestor. As one member of the team put it, the soil itself is a source of information. And the picture is not limited to one reign: it cuts through chronological phases, allowing students to watch the process of development from the Neolithic period as well as to sense changes after the twelfth century destruction.

In the spirit of our visit to Nestor's palace (see chapter eight), we can now accompany Nestor on a tour through his kingdom. Its size is great enough that it will require several days, with nights spent in the homes of local officials (*basileis*) throughout the region. The seacoast obviously sets limits to the west and south; the Taygetos Mountain Range marks the eastern boundary; and, to the north, regular communication with the Alpheios Valley extends the kingdom at least as far as the Nedha River. Throughout this 1,400 square mile realm, Nestor can travel with some ease on the network of "roads" that links the more important towns with one another and with Pylos. While many of these roads are little more than well-worn paths, others were constructed to carry wheeled vehicles. His subjects and the products of their agriculture also circulate regularly. All encourage communication, including the periodic tours of inspection that help to maintain the flow of raw and finished goods.

We will not visit every village, since their number is almost 200, with a total population of at least 41,000 subjects. Nestor can boast a sharp increase in both figures during his own lifetime; a few generations earlier the total population of Messenia was about 16,000 people living in 120 villages. And, he can reminisce, the increase in both the number of settlements and their size has been continuous from the Early Bronze Age into the thirteenth century. Much of the explanation lies in the security of the kingdom; villagers have felt safe enough to move their settlements from isolated inland hilltops to more accessible sites. "And there are twice as many towns on the coasts of the kingdom as there were 350 years ago," Nestor boasts. "Our fleet protects the shores and takes our products far afield."

Figure 101

Traveling along the road from Pylos eastward, we pass through village after village (Fig. 101). The Pylos district is exceptionally densely populated, as are the Kyparissia River Valley to the north and the area west of the Pamisos Valley. "Most of my people live with family and neighbors in small villages of about 200 souls," we are told. "Of course, you have seen Pylos and I can assure you that we have several other towns of size and character," the king adds. "We will spend the night in one of them so that you can compare it with MY town." "We have had to clear land to provide sites for more villages," Nestor relates. "Unfortunately, it was necessary to chop down large numbers of trees in order to bring land near Pylos under cultivation. We have even started to settle the remote Mani peninsula: the land is not as good as river valley land but it is well suited to flocks of goats and sheep."

Sheep and goats especially, but also larger animals such as horses and oxen and smaller animals like pigs are visible throughout the land. They are clearly very important to the maintenance of life in Mycenaean Pylos. We learn that most farming families keep a number of animals for their own use. On occasion, however, we see huge flocks whose care is a full time responsibility for their tenders who in turn are responsible to palace officials for these royal herds.

Still, most of the subjects of Nestor seem to be farmers. Many of the villages have about 1,500 hectares of land (one hectare = 2.47 acres); we note that approximately a quarter of the land around a village seems to be intensively cultivated. On the best farm land, we see a great deal of grain, especially barley and some wheat, while less fertile terrain is given over to tree crops and vines. The gray-green of the olive is especially noticeable. We now have a better understanding of the need for so many storage areas at Pylos, since Nestor's subjects pay taxes in kind (agricultural products and animals), not in cash.

As we drive through the lowland plain we are puzzled by an unusual crop with beautiful blue blossoms. Nestor explains that many of his flax fields are located in the well-watered land close to the capital of his kingdom. In addition to the natural advantages of the land, the location allows close supervision from the palace. "This happy combination of circumstances has produced a linen industry that yields the most abundant and the best products in Greece," Nestor quietly assures us.

Other specialized crafts are in evidence. Many of the villages have furnaces for baking clay and for melting ingots of copper and tin. "Our clays are plentiful and of high quality," Nestor tells us. "Unfortunately, we are without metal resources so must import them from other areas. In spite of our land clearing projects, we continue to have a good supply of timber for fueling the furnaces." Large holding pens indicate collection points where sheep are sheared and, in one town, we stop to inspect a building where several women are spinning and weaving the wool into cloth. We see, too, pens of goats and learn that they are especially valuable for their long curving horns as well as their hair, hides and, when slaughtered, their meat.

The three days with Nestor have been enlightening, if not altogether comfortable. Nestor hopes to do something about the paths in the hillier areas so that a chariot can pass more smoothly! Still we have seen the extent of the system and can appreciate the need for careful regulation from the center at Pylos.

B R O N Z E   A G E   A N T E C E D E N T S

Beyond its changed methodological emphases, the "new archaeology" has enhanced our understanding of the depth of Greek prehistory. Features of these remote millennia are part of the cultural heritage of later centuries and, consequently, their discovery and definition add much to our picture of the final Bronze and Iron Age civilizations. Evidence from the remote Stone Ages is particularly significant for our understanding of the Mycenaean era in tracing the sources of language affinities with other regions of Europe and for correcting the earlier view of the respective roles of Crete and the mainland. Two decades ago, it was claimed that Greece had few traces of human life during the upper, middle and late Paleolithic phases. Until the Neolithic era, it was then believed, the few wanderers to enter Greece were splinter groups from more heavily populated areas of Europe, although no part of Europe had a dense population during the Old Stone Age. On the basis of this evidence arose theories concerning the arrival of the Greeks and their indebtedness to the Minoans. As we shall see, the earlier views must now be modified.

One implication of the new evidence concerns the basis of the population and the language of Bronze Age Greece. A new theory, which we will examine in chapter ten, ascribes the spread of Indo-European languages to the time and people of the Neolithic agricultural revolution. Since Indo-European languages and farming techniques spread simultaneously through Europe, the cultural affinities of the inhabitants of Greece can be seen in clearer focus. If the new thesis is proven correct, we will be able to do without some of the later invasions to explain the development of the Mycenaean Age (Renfrew, 1987; Bernal, 1987).

The modified picture of earlier developments in the Aegean also has historiographic importance for our story. Through the first half of the twentieth century, the generally accepted picture of events in the Aegean gave a leading position to Crete. From the time of its settlement in the Neolithic Age by people already practiced in agriculture and animal husbandry, inhabitants of Crete served as a bridge of cultural diffusion to less advanced cultures in the north and west. Greece, it was thought, had few inhabitants in the Paleolithic period; agriculture came rather late to the northeastern region and gradually spread to the rockier southern areas of the mainland. Progress was more rapid when the mainlanders met the culturally advanced Cretans. If, on the other hand, the past of Greek developments is as deep as or deeper than that of Crete, Minoan ascendancy is not so easy to argue. Let us briefly review recent finds to demonstrate the outlines of present evidence.

Many more paleolithic finds have been made in the past twenty-five or thirty years; important excavations have recently been completed at several cave sites. In the early 1960s, inveterate walker and archaeologist E. Higgs located several sites in Epirus with evidence of Paleolithic industry. In 1964, the Greek Archaeological Service carried out trial excavations at one of them, a rock shelter known as Asprochaliko. Excavation continued the next season when evidence from the base of superimposed hearths produced a Carbon 14 date of 40,000 B.C. Traces of man-made structures dated between 15,000 and 9000 B.C. Another Epirote site at Kastritsa yielded a date of 22,000 B.C. as well as Bronze Age burials.

Since 1983, a team headed by G. Bailey of the British School has been investigating the rock shelter in northwestern Greece known as Klithi to clarify problems brought to light by Higgs' earlier excavations in the region. The Paleolithic site is the focus of investigation ranging from study of the site itself to analysis of its role in the larger local, regional and even continental setting. Indications of human occupation were found in the first season of investigation and, since then, the quantity of data has soared. In the 1985–86 season alone, 75,000 flint artefacts and 120,000 animal bones were recovered. Radiocarbon dates indicate that much of the material dates from the upper Paleolithic between 12,000 to 10,000 B.C.

Occupation of the Franchthi Cave on the coast of the Argive peninsula dates to

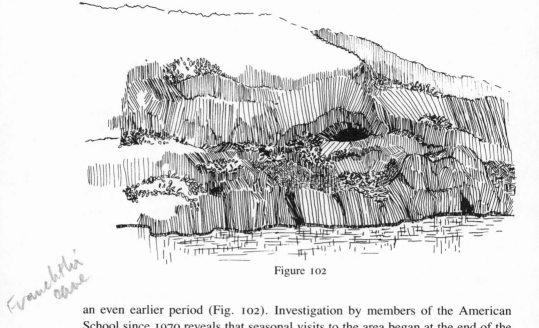

Figure 102

Franchthi cave

an even earlier period (Fig. 102). Investigation by members of the American School since 1970 reveals that seasonal visits to the area began at the end of the European ice ages, about 20,000 B.C. Perennial springs were probably an important attraction for animal and human visitors; successive occupants arrived over a period of 17,000 years, down to approximately 3000 B.C. when the site appears to have been abandoned because of earthquake. The Franchthi site reveals changes from the hunting-gathering life of small bands of seasonal visitors through more complex cultures that gathered a wider variety of plants and animals, fished and engaged in trade, to early domesticators who had tamed goats and sheep as well as wheat and barley.

Elsewhere, a 1963–64 survey in Elis by the French School produced evidence of Paleolithic industries at nineteen sites; a number of sites have been identified on the Mani peninsula; and Lower, Middle and Upper Paleolithic finds are increasingly plentiful on Euboea as well as in caves in Boeotia. Specifically, the Kephalari Cave south of Argos has Upper Paleolithic remains; Nauplia evidences material from the Middle Paleolithic period; from Ayios Athanasios in Thessaly have come the first cave drawings in Greece; Kozani in western Macedonia was the find spot of two elephant skeletons and accompanying stone tools; and, perhaps most controversial, the Petralona Cave of the Chalkidice contained two human skeletons claimed to date to 800,000 years ago. Whatever the final verdict on those skeletons, it is certain that, in recent years, our progress has been even deeper into the past.

Neolithic evidence was fuller than Paleolithic in earlier decades of the present century, but equally important new data have accumulated for the first farming communities of the Aegean. New Neolithic sites have been located, and Neolithic remains have been found at deep levels of known sites. The Kastri settlement on Thasos started life in the Late Neolithic period. Ayios Petros in the northern Sporades has an important Late Neolithic level with three occupation levels that correspond to the pre-Dimini mainland culture. The islands of Samothrace in the northern Aegean, Rhodes in the southern Aegean and Cyprus in the eastern Mediterranean have produced evidence of Neolithic settlement. In the last case, the earlier material goes back to Meso- and Paleolithic times and comes from a growing number of sites. Of the Ionian Islands, Kephallenia and Lefkas attest Neolithic occupation.

On the Greek mainland there are many sites with Neolithic finds on Euboea, in east-central Greece, especially near Lake Copais, and in Thessaly. Tiryns has significant Neolithic pottery; there are Neolithic houses known from Aegina and Athens; Mycenae, Corinth, Argos, Nauplia, Thebes, the Saronic Islet of Varkiza, all show signs of habitation prior to the Bronze Age. A number of caves were occupied or used for cult purposes during the Neolithic period: use of the Dreros Caves excavated by the Greek Archaeological Service since 1970 dates back to 4000 B.C.; A. Sampson has identified more than twenty caves on Euboea occupied in Paleolithic and Neolithic times. Additional identifications include two caves at Nauplia with Neolithic burials; a cave on the slopes of Mount Pelion; Maries in the northern Sporades; Maroneia in Thrace; the cave of Kitsos near Laurion; the "cave of Nestor" in Messenia; the Corycian Cave in Phocis; the cave in Mt. Mathias on Kerkyra; and the cave at Koumeda on Rhodes.

The Bronze Age debt to the earlier culture of Greece is clearer when we are able to list specific sites occupied in both the Stone Age and the Mycenaean era. Were there more continuity of particular names, the weight of the legacy would increase correspondingly.

NICHORIA AND LEFKANDI

Work of the present generation has been directed as much to the post-Mycenaean era as to its antecedents. A major issue of Bronze Age studies concerns the end of the Mycenaean and Minoan civilizations. That issue is intricately connected with subsequent developments in the Aegean area in the Early Iron Age. Hence, the need to study the history of sites across several centuries is particularly important in attempting to reach an answer about continuity between

Mycenaean and later Greek culture. One of the most important issues of the question of continuity concerns the Homeric epics. The poems describe the Age of Heroes, that is, the time of the Trojan War, but they date in their final form to the late Dark Age. The entire Homeric Question is bound up with the continuity between the Bronze and Iron ages. Evidence from actual settlements of the later period will help answer that question, to which we will turn in chapter ten.

The first Dark Age settlement on the mainland to be intensively excavated is Nichoria in the southwest Peloponnese. Work at that site demonstrates clearly the value to be derived from merging the techniques of excavation with those of survey archaeology. Investigation here constituted the second phase of the Minnesota Messenia Expedition; in fact, in volume I of the final excavation report (published in 1978), much of the emphasis is on the local physical environment and the adaptation by the inhabitants of Nichoria to this terrain. Volumes II and III deal with the more traditional evidence found at the site itself: volume II, treating the history of the site to the end of the Bronze Age, was published in 1989; volume III, dealing with the Dark Age and Byzantine settlements, appeared in 1983 (Rapp and Aschenbrenner, 1978; McDonald, Coulson and Rosser, 1983).

The objective of the seven seasons of excavation was to gain a clear idea of the extent and plan of individual settlements on the hilltop site located above the modern village of Rizomilo. Equally important was the picture of change over time; it is evident that the site played various roles during different phases of its history. During the Bronze Age, for instance, it probably became part of the larger socioeconomic unit we have called the Kingdom of Pylos. Cynthia Shelmerdine has made a convincing case for the identification of Nichoria as TI-MI-TO-A-KE-E in the Pylos Linear B tablets (1981: 319–325). In the Dark Age, by contrast, the villagers determined their own destiny. Evidence from each phase of the settlement's history has enlarged our understanding of the broader context of developments throughout Greece during that particular period. Since our previous knowledge of the Dark Age was so limited, the evidence from Dark Age Nichoria has been especially valuable. The Dark Age is not nearly as dark as it once appeared.

Temporary abandonment or extreme reduction in population at Nichoria accords with the established picture of a disintegration of the Mycenaean kingdoms in the late thirteenth and twelfth centuries. However, evidence from the site does not point to a cause for Mycenaean collapse. The excavators concluded, "our evidence does not rule out any one (or a combination) of the human and ecological factors variously alleged to have been responsible for the general Mycenaean collapse . . ." (McDonald and Coulson, 1983: 322).

Even if it may have been uninhabited for a century or so, the site was not forgotten. It lay at the intersection of two major land routes and possessed several natural advantages: proximity to two rivers fed by perennial springs as well as to a protected harbor and the security of elevation. It is not surprising, then, that a small village persisted throughout the Dark Age right up to the mid-eighth century.

The first Dark Age village, in existence no later than the eleventh century, evidences continuity from the Mycenaean Age: the Mycenaean townsite and cemetery were reused, ceramic and bronze working techniques persisted, a small tholos was built for a series of burials. However, life was greatly simplified and the population considerably reduced. During the first phase of its Dark Age existence, excavators estimate a population of about thirteen to fourteen families, or eighty-five to ninety people, rising to some forty families, or two hundred people, in the second phase and falling again to about twenty families, or one hundred people, in the final phase. A variety of crops was grown, although some of the Bronze Age products may well have disappeared. There is evidence of cereal grains, grapes, olives, pea legumes, acorns, figs and perhaps wild cherries. Of greater importance during the Dark Age than during the Mycenaean era were the herding activities in the environs of Nichoria. Bones of cattle and red (later roe) deer increase markedly, indicating a shift in the main economic base of the community from mixed farming to cattle ranching. There is a corresponding decrease in the proportion of sheep and goat bones. In chapter ten, we will examine the far-reaching consequences of this evidence.

Some specialization seems to have been practiced—making of ceramics and textiles, building, metallurgy, production of stone tools and leather working— although much of the craft production must have been carried on within the home. The products show some, but not much, contact with other parts of Greece; Laconian influence in the second phase of Dark Age Nichoria is clear. There may also have been some political specialization; a much larger than average structure may have been both the home of a village chieftain and his family and a religious center for the little community. In general, the Dark Age dwellings were simple, one-room huts with stone foundations, wattle and daub or mudbrick walls and pitched, thatched roofs (Fig. 103).

The excavators have reconstructed the daily order of life at Dark Age Nichoria, and it is instructive to compare this picture with our two earlier reconstructions, the visit to Nestor's Pylos and the tour of his kingdom. While Nichoria has few features in common with Pylos, it may be very like the smaller Mycenaean villages controlled *from* Pylos.

The women would spend most of their time on the ridgetop, except when carrying out the age-old female task of bringing water up from the river or perhaps from a couple of closer springs. . . . Preparation of food and the various home crafts would be carried out in or near their huts. Since the latter

Figure 103

occupied only a small part of the ridgetop, a good deal of land was available on the ridge for tree crops, pasture for sheep and goats, and for gathering plants and fuel. Summer kitchen gardens, if such were cultivated, would have had to be situated nearer water. Most of the men no doubt worked farther from home, tending cattle in the bottomlands and crops on the slopes that were safe from seasonal floods. Hunting was probably a part-time occupation in seasons when the major tasks were lighter. (McDonald and Coulson, 1983: 328)

Nichoria is no longer the only Dark Age site to have been intensively exca-vated. Evidence from sites on the island of Euboea has been similarly instructive for our knowledge of the Dark Age. Eretria, examined jointly by members of the Swiss School and the Greek Archaeological Service since 1964, shows occupa-tion back to the last phase of the Early Bronze Age, when affinities with the east-ern Aegean are pronounced (1968–85). The next phase sees the first gray Minyan ware. There were three building phases toward the end of the Mycenaean era; the site passed out of use without destruction at the end of the third phase. During the following Dark Age, the site was occupied again. That area has been excavated since 1974. One discovery is a U-shaped building set on a stone founda-tion bearing resemblance to the apsidal structure at Nichoria. The Eretrian struc-ture has been identified as the first in a series of temples on the site (Fig. 104).

Finds at Lefkandi (modern Xeropolis) on Euboea are also helping to lessen the darkness of the Early Iron Age (Popham, Sackett and Themelis, 1980). Like Nichoria, occupation of the Euboean site extends from the Late Neolithic Age to the end of the Dark Age. From the Middle Bronze Age, it was a town of consid-erable size and importance. However, it is the Dark Age site that has been espe-cially revealing. Indeed, it has been described as "perhaps the most important excavation of an Early Iron Age site in Greece since World War II" (Snodgrass, 1987: 65).

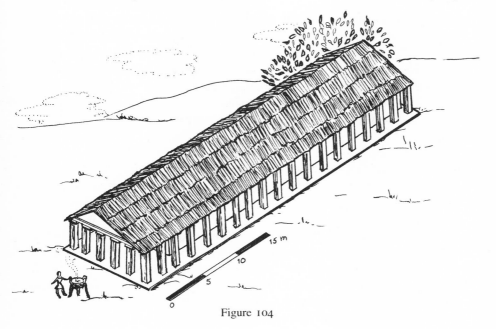

Figure 104

The site has been known for some time, but excavations did not begin until the 1960s. Even now, only a small portion of the site has been uncovered. Before the settlement was discovered, it was known that there were several cemeteries, close together, in the vicinity. The total of 150 tombs pointed to the presence of a settlement nearby. The settlement was discovered and investigated from 1964 to 1970.

Occupants of the area chose a promontory on the eastern edge of the Lelantine Plain. A narrow plateau 500 m x 120 m is about 17 meters above sea level but has a bay suitable for mooring ships at each end. Such inducement to sea travel seems to have been a major factor in the importance of the site; imported goods figure in both the Bronze Age and Iron Age settlements. What is more, the pottery of Lefkandi was exported as far away as Al Mina in the Levant.

The significance of the site can be seen in several features; one of the most surprising was discovered accidentally in 1980 when traces of a very significant structure were found. An apsidal building measuring 10 meters wide by 45 meters long rested on a stone socle and contained Near Eastern objects as well as fine jewelry. Not only its size but a date of approximately 1000 B.C. struck a blow at then-current notions of Dark Age architecture. Graves beneath the floor of the building have prompted identification of the structure as a "heroon" or center of a hero-cult. If the identification is correct, the phenomenon of hero-worship is pushed earlier than previously thought by about two centuries.

In its prosperity, too, Lefkandi has altered our view of the Dark Age. Rather than being isolated and impoverished, the town enjoyed considerable foreign contact and, as a result, a degree of wealth and prosperity not generally found in Greek sites of the Early Iron Age. Products from a bronze and iron foundry at the site dated to ca. 900 B.C. show clear indications of contact with Cyprus and the Levant; gold and faience have been found in several graves; pottery indicates contact with other mainland sites, particularly Athens but also Thessaly and even Macedonia.

The finds from the settlement and cemeteries have been sufficient to reveal the broad lines of development of the site. Its importance continued from the Middle Helladic into and through the Late Helladic Age. When other settlements were witnessing destruction in the Late Mycenaean period, Lefkandi saw rebuilding and an increase in population. In the twelfth century the site was burned, but a new settlement followed without a break. Only at the end of the twelfth century was the settlement abandoned for approximately a century. However, use of the cemeteries continued during this break in occupation. Rebuilding of the town is dated to approximately 1000, after which it was inhabited continuously until 700 B.C., when it was sacked and abandoned. During its last stage, from 825 to 700, the situation of town and cemeteries was reversed: that is, no burials have been discovered that date after 825.

Thus, along with new evidence Lefkandi raises its full share of puzzles. Who were the Lefkandiotes of the Iron Age? Were they survivors of the Bronze Age population of the region or were they newcomers? Did the site decline in importance as a result of the struggle over the Lelantine Plain by Chalcis and Eretria? Why did the later inhabitants of Lefkandi no longer use their accustomed burial grounds? Where did the survivors of Lefkandi resettle in 700 B.C.? Following the verdict of the excavators, it is necessary to suspend judgment until more evidence is available. What is of crucial significance, at the present state of our knowledge, is that the received interpretation of the poverty and isolation of Greece during the Dark Age may need to be reexamined.

THERA (MODERN SANTORINI)

The most exciting new excavation has been at Akrotiri on the island of Thera. It is not, to be sure, a Mycenaean site and so, in the strict sense, an account of its discovery does not belong solely to the story of the recovery of the Mycenaean civilization. However, the evidence indicates Mycenaean cultural connections as well as Minoan associations so that the site may help our understanding of the interaction of island, mainland, and Cretan civilizations in the later Bronze Age. Just as important is the dating of the eruption on which many points of interpretation depend.

Ever since the middle of the nineteenth century, prehistoric remains have been known to exist at this site. Digging for pumice for use in the construction of the Suez canal brought a number of traces to light. The same volcanic activity that created the pumice also buried Akrotiri, and other parts of the island, in an ash layer more than 150 feet deep. An explosion, which is now claimed to be quite precisely dated to 1628 B.C., collapsed two-thirds of the island, producing a caldera of 83 square kilometers and spewing lava of a temperature estimated to have been more than 1470 degrees Fahrenheit. The force of a tidal wave that resulted from the shock of the explosion would also have been crushing. Indeed, the volcano's force has been described as the equivalent of detonating 150 megatons of TNT. Volcanic material has been found on other islands as far away as Crete, Rhodes, and Cyprus, and pumice (identified as Theran) was also found at Nichoria and at Sardis. While the pumice may have drifted to the beaches decades or centuries after the explosion, the uniformity of contexts in which it was found indicates that it was spread by the eruption that rendered Thera itself temporarily uninhabitable. What appears to have been the Bronze Age center of the island was virtually encased in a block of cement (Fig. 105).

This seemingly impenetrable site was taken on by Spyridon Marinatos in 1967, who began to dig by tunneling into the pumice from a gully bed that straddles the site. He had argued, as early as 1939, that the volcanic eruption of Thera had destroyed the Minoan civilization centered on Crete. Marinatos was searching for evidence to support his theory in his examination of Thera. In the very first season, Marinatos found highly promising remains: buildings of two or three stories, ceramics and metal goods. Continuing excavations under the sponsorship of the Greek Archaeological Society have revealed a Bronze Age equivalent to Pompeii; it is one of the most completely preserved towns of antiquity. Marinatos directed the excavations until 1974, when Akrotiri claimed his life as the result of a fall in the excavated area. Since his untimely death, Christos Doumas has supervised the investigations, which he believes will require at least several decades to complete.

After more than twenty years of work, the general nature of the site can be reconstructed with some certainty (Doumas, 1983). The site was occupied from about the middle of the third millennium; its location encouraged development so that by the time of destruction, it merits description as a city. Doumas has estimated its area as 200,000 square meters where a population of several thousand lived. In appearance, Thera was probably quite like modern Cycladic villages with narrow, winding streets, irregularly shaped buildings and variable levels. Basic building materials were clay, timber, and unworked and dressed stones. Windows at the ground level as well as in upper stories provided ventilation and light. Some of them may also have served as "counters" for shops, inasmuch as ground-floor rooms were used as workshops and storage areas for goods. Living quarters were in the upper stories, and water closets have been identified in sev-

Figure 105

eral buildings. Drainage channels led to a sewer beneath the city street, and there are indications that both tubs as well as toilets were linked to the drainage system.

Such high standards of comfort have been reinforced by finds, in many of the houses, of magnificent frescoes described by Doumas as "the ultimate artistic creations of Late Bronze Age society in the Aegean" (1983: 56). The technique is the same as that practiced on Crete. Some of the figures are comparable to those in Cretan frescoes—the Blue Monkeys and the Young Priestess, for instance. Yet there are important differences. The naturalism of the young boxers and the fisherman is striking. Equally vivid is the narrative quality of several of the paintings. In the flotilla, a fleet of ships is sailing into or from a harbor where townspeople watch from the roofs of buildings or from the land. A miniature fresco shows the same active quality: warriors are marching while women and unarmed men watch; herdsmen drive animals; contorted bodies of naked men appear to be flailing in the sea.

The artistic and social value of the Thera paintings is great. We learn, for example, that the frescoes come from private houses and usually were located in the upper residential stories. Beyond these important lessons, there may be historical evidence to be gained from the scenes. Debate has been particularly lively over the flotilla and sea battle frescoes: are the figures to be identified as Mycenaeans or Minoans by physiognomy and dress? Is the artist recalling capture of a town, perhaps even his town, by foreigners? Marinatos interpreted the battle fresco as showing Mycenaean warriors invading a Libyan village, since the scene also depicts North African sheep, a shield of ostrich feathers and the Libyan fashion of circumcision (Marinatos, 1974: 44–57). Quite another interpretation identifies the painting as a scene from a sea festival; the flailing bodies are swimmers displaying their skill, and the warriors are an honor guard (Sakellariou, in Doumas, ed., 1980: 147–154).

Disagreements like this are unavoidable, given the nature of the evidence and its state of preservation. The scenes may be vignettes of daily life portraying actual people in specific situations, but we lack both the range of physical evidence and any literary evidence to make conclusive identifications. The frescoes do reinforce a conclusion of the last generation of archaeological interpretation, one that we discussed in connection with Caskey's work on Keos. The island cultures had strong individual personalities, even though contact with Minoan Crete and, later, mainland Greece was regular and frequent. When excavation has been completed, it may be possible to plot the stages of contact between the three cultures. At present, development appears to have been from largely independent cultural status to increasing influence from Crete to growing Mycenaean presence. However, actual mainland control of Akrotiri is less likely if the seventeenth-century dating of the Theran eruption proves to be correct. While such a date is coeval with the Shaft Grave era, mainland activity abroad seems to increase after the seventeenth century. Even the sixteenth century seemed to Doumas too early for mainland penetration of the southern Aegean. Surely it is less likely during the seventeenth century. The case of Akrotiri, while perhaps providing a location for Atlantis, has produced new questions for the sixth generation of Aegean prehistorians.

One of those questions concerns absolute dating. The magnitude of the explosion makes it a useful peg for other developments of the second millennium. Until the present decade, the eruption could be firmly placed in the second millennium B.C., but exact dating was impossible. Many scholars argued for a date near 1500 B.C. on the grounds of objects found in the destruction level at Akrotiri that seemed similar to Minoan items assigned to that time frame. For others, 1450 seemed a more likely date: the force of the volcanic explosion would thus account for the widespread destruction in Crete about the middle of the fifteenth century. Perhaps, some maintained, there were two or even three eruptions separated by intervals of as much as fifty years. Or, as Angelis Galanopoulos proposed, separate eruptions occurred about 1450 and 1200 B.C.; thus the effects of the Thera explosion help to account for the decline of Aegean civilization at the end of the Bronze Age (1981). Leon Pomerance has pressed the case for a single eruption ca. 1200 B.C. (1970).

This variation in opinion was due, in no small part, to what seem still to be imprecise dating techniques. Carbon 14 dating of charred wood of a pine tree buried in the volcanic tephra on Thera yielded a date of 3370 years $+-$ 100, or a date between 1500 and 1400 B.C. Even less exact was the evidence of cores taken from the sea floor. They were found to contain layers of volcanic ash, and one layer was dated to "later than 3000 B.C." By contrast, developments of the 1980s have proposed a much earlier and very precise date and, along with it, have posed new problems. Stuart Manning has discussed the evidence thoroughly and as clearly as such technical data permits (1988).

The earliest development occurred in C¹⁴ dating. Although this method has been used since 1946, important refinements have since been made. In 1946, W. F. Libby suggested that measurement of the isotope of carbon remaining in no-longer-living organic matter will allow a close calculation of the amount of time elapsed since the death of the object. All living things take in carbon from the atmosphere; part of that carbon is a radioactive form known as carbon 14. When organic matter dies, it no longer absorbs carbon and thus its C¹⁴ diminishes at what was believed to be a regular and predictable rate. Measuring the amount of C¹⁴ present will indicate the approximate date at which the matter died. The date is only approximate; $+-$ 30 years, for example, yields a sixty-year range within which the specific date should be fixed.

Beyond this fairly wide margin of probable date, there was a flaw in the original method of calculation. Until recently, it was not known that the ratio of radioactive to ordinary carbon is not constant but varies over the years according to fluctuations in the environment. Thus an organism alive when conditions led to higher production of radioactive carbon will contain more after it has been dead 500 years than will an organism alive during a period of different conditions. When the known environmental fluctuations are taken into account, the C¹⁴ dates can be adjusted accordingly (Renfrew, 1976).

A series of C¹⁴ dates from Akrotiri is especially long and a subset of dates is particularly interesting for dating the volcanic eruption. Sixteen dates of short-lived objects like twigs and seeds have been calculated. The mean age, adjusted to account for environmental fluctuations, was announced as 1615 B.C. Since this result was more than a century earlier than the artefact-based dating of the eruption, many archaeologists were not convinced of the accuracy of the results.

Work in two other dating techniques produced a stronger case for the results of C¹⁴ analysis. Dendrochronology and ice dating have yielded results that accord almost exactly with the carbon dates. Since 1929, the observation of annual growth rings in trees has been used to date archaeological material. By overlapping the evidence of living trees with old wood—timbers in buildings for example—with trees preserved in bogs, two remarkably long series of rings have been compiled. A series based largely on the California bristlecone pines extends over 8,500 years, and in 1984 a 7,272 year chronology was completed in Belfast using oaks preserved in Irish bogs.

In addition to ordinary annual growth, dendrochronology reveals environmental abnormalities. Narrow rings correspond to poor growth conditions. There is a

wide range of possible causes for growth variation, from purely local conditions
to global environmental changes. One such cause is volcanic eruptions. Vol-
canoes create dust veils that have the effect of lowering temperatures, thus affect-
ing growing patterns. Frost rings can be detected in the size of tree rings as well
as in the form of the vessels of the wood. In 1984, scientists examining evidence
from the California series claimed that a significant frost ring dated to 1626 B.C.
might relate to the eruption of Thera (La Marche and Hirschboeck, 1984: 121–
126). The actual explosion would have occurred a year or more earlier. Detection
of narrow bands through much of the decade of the 1620s B.C. has led Irish
dendrochronologists to a similar conclusion (Baillie and Munro, 1988: 344–346).

Finally, dating by means of annual ice deposits gives the same result. Working
with samples from southern Greenland, a Danish team has studied seasonal variations in layers of ice deposits from 1300 back to 1900 B.C. One feature of volcanic eruptions is the ejection of large amounts of sulfur dioxide into the atmosphere. When mixed with water, the sulfur dioxide becomes sulphuric acid that
will be embedded in a layer of ice as it is forming. When the sulfate content of
ice is high, it is abnormally conductive of electricity.

The eruption column of Thera is estimated to have extended twenty nine kilometers; thus it penetrated well into the stratosphere and would have carried thousands of miles. In the Greenland cores, three conductive layers were found:
1428, 1644 and 1688. The first and third were high in nitric, not sulphuric, acid;
the second—which had the highest level of acidity—alone was associated with
sulphuric acid. Thus, if the sulphuric layer resulted from the volcanic eruption on
Thera, that explosion can be dated to 1645 +− a seven-year standard deviation
and +− a twenty-year estimated error limit. In other words, ice dating identifies
the same decade in which tree rings show abnormal growth very probably caused
by a major volcanic eruption (Hammer, Clausen and Dansgaard, 1980: 230–235).

The much higher date is not altogether welcome to Aegean specialists. It is a
century earlier than chronology reached through pottery dating, and, as we have
seen, the edifice built on analysis of ceramic evidence has been painfully erected.
In a candid admission, at least one Minoan pottery specialist has confronted the
new evidence. Philip Betancourt concluded in 1987:

> . . . if we were to ignore earlier prejudices completely and erect a new
> Aegean chronology today, it would be somewhat different from the received
> tradition. This author withdraws many of the opinions he expressed a decade
> ago . . . ; the Aegean Late Bronze Age probably began during the Hyksos
> period, and radiocarbon was correct all along. (Betancourt, 1987: 48)

The primary thrust of the new chronology would be to place the start of the
Late Bronze Age a century earlier for all the Aegean cultures. Then, all later
periods at least to the end of the Bronze Age must be either expanded to absorb

the hundred years or similarly dated to earlier absolute dates. Betancourt proposes a tentative chronology for Crete and Greece based on the seventeenth-century dating of Thera:

Crete	Greece	Dates
LMIA	LHIA	ca. 1700–1610 B.C.
LMIB	LHIIA	ca. 1610–1550 B.C.
LMII	LHIIB	ca. 1550–1490 B.C.
LMIIIA:1	LHIIIA:1	ca. 1490–1430/10 B.C.
LMIIIA:2	LHIIIA:2	ca. 1430/10–1365 B.C.
LMIIIB	LHIIIB	ca. 1365–1200 B.C.

[handwritten annotations in the margin: "Thera destroyed", "Cretan sites", "only @ Knossos", "is n rooms destryd"]

There are some firm absolute dates for the later phases of the Late Bronze Age, particularly Aegean finds in datable Egyptian contexts or datable Egyptian materials discovered in Crete or on the Greek mainland. For the earlier phases, there are no Aegean goods in well-dated eastern Mediterranean contexts. Consequently, the earlier centuries can better accommodate stretching than can the later centuries of the period. What is more, the new dating solves other chronological problems that have existed in the relationship between Aegean and northern European cultures. In the revised dating scheme, the Aegean-related metalwork of northern Europe is closer in time to similar finds from the Aegean. And, as Betancourt has argued, the earlier dating explains why there is no report of the explosion in Egyptian records. There are no records from the Hyksos/ Second Intermediate period, which lasted through the seventeenth century B.C. (1987: 48).

Reaction to this information has been mixed. Since the new scheme entails a number of highly specialized techniques, a final verdict is likely to be delayed some years. As we have had occasion to observe, established interpretations are not quickly overturned. After all, the views of Heinrich Schliemann and Arthur Evans have their adherents even today.

SANCTUARIES AND RELIGIOUS SITES

In the past two decades, important new finds have come from previously explored sites, and many of these "surprises" concern religion. Evidence from Crete, the Greek mainland and the islands has both altered earlier assessments of religious practice and given insights into the mentality of the practitioners. Many scholars have concluded that the Mycenaeans were influenced by Minoan religious forms, if not actual religious beliefs. The throne rooms of the palaces were earlier instances of such borrowing; the new evidence suggests that there may have been similar influence leading to freestanding temples.

In chapter eight we discussed the importance of excavation at Ayia Irini on the island of Keos. Until the discovery, there was no certain example of a freestanding building devoted to religious purposes. Cult activity was thought to occur in parts of the palaces, in caves or at peak sanctuaries. Consequently, the identification had its challengers. Recent work has produced several new examples of probable temples from both Crete and the mainland. Although the identifications are not unanimously accepted, there can be little doubt of the function of a three-room building near the modern village of Arkhanes on the island of Crete.

There have been clues to the importance of the site since the time of Arthur Evans' investigations nearby at Knossos. As recently as 1967, McDonald wrote, "it is too soon to speculate as to whether a new discovery at Arkhanes might have any bearing on the political situation. A sixteenth-century building, possibly a palace, is reported to have been 'larger and finer' than the contemporary palace at Knossos" (385). In other words, perhaps it was the center from which newly arrived Mycenaeans assumed control over parts of Crete. Unfortunately, it is still too early to determine its precise role in the puzzle of Minoan-Mycenaean interaction.

Located just seven kilometers south of Knossos, the village stands at the foot of Mount Iuktas. Beyond its natural beauty, the peak had major religious associations, since it was remembered as the tomb of Cretan Zeus. Evans discovered a peak sanctuary on Iuktas early in the century; its architectural design has become clearer through reinvestigation from 1973 on. Peak sanctuaries are not unusual in Crete. In fact, the present generation has witnessed discovery of a number of newly identified sanctuaries. Rather, the exceptional nature of this particular sanctuary suggested the importance of the surrounding area, and excavators were not disappointed in their expectations. At the foot of Iuktas, Yannis and Efi Sakellarakis started to uncover an important site in 1965. Dominating the settlement was a building defined as either a small palace or a large mansion. The former possibility gained strength the next year when excavation of a large Minoan cemetery began northwest of the modern village on the hill of Phourni. Multi-roomed buildings, some with second stories, contained burials extending from the third through much of the second millennium. The necropolis produced numerous and rich finds: one sealed larnax alone contained 140 pieces of gold jewelry. The importance of the burials was demonstrated in another way during the first season of excavation: the skeleton of a horse and the head of a bull testify to interment of people of high status. Since the discovery of the horse burial at Marathon, it may be assumed that those people had something to do with the mainland.

A more recent find was even more astonishing, causing Mycenaean specialists to hope that there was no link to the mainland. In an area west of the village known as Anemospilia, or "Caves of the Winds," workers from the Phourni excavation found traces of an old wall in 1979. Immediate excavation revealed a temenos wall surrounding a small building of 10 x 10 meters, probably with two floors. Three narrow rooms did not interconnect but did open on to a corridor where pottery vessels, some still holding charred seeds, contained food stuffs. Other vases were found in the central room where the excavators discovered a pair of life-size clay feet. Here, finally, was proof that cult images played a part in Bronze Age religion: a wooden image—implied by the pieces of burnt wood—would have rested on the feet. Near the feet was an unhewn rock that may have had ritual significance that has a counterpart at Mycenae.

Traces of a stepped altar found in the east room strengthened the identification of the building as a temple, but it was the west room that provided conclusive evidence. It too held an altar. Additionally, the excavators discovered three skeletons within the room (and a fourth in the corridor). It was obvious that the first two discovered had been victims of an earthquake; fallen debris had broken the legs of one. The third skeleton in the room—the remains of an eighteen-year-old youth—lay on its side on a low masonry platform, and what was first identified as a bronze knife lay in the skeleton. (Subsequently, the weapon has been described as a spearhead.) Supported by the finds of anthropologist Alexandros Kontopoulos and criminologist Antonios Koutselinis, the excavators have made a compelling case for ritual human sacrifice. The youth was slain, the arteries of his neck severed by the weapon. Before they could leave the building, the others were overcome in the catastrophic earthquake that destroyed the temple ca. 1700 B.C.

More than astounding, the report was painful to many modern students of antiquity. Present-day Greeks were appalled by the spectre of their ancestors participating in human sacrifice. In fact, the excavators engaged in an unprecedented public debate in Athens in April of 1980. That debate centered on what was suggested to be an exceptional event: in the face of grave impending disaster, a supreme sacrifice was made. The announcement of a find from Knossos during the 1979 season raised new spectres. Discovery of a quantity of children's bones brought the verdict: "cannibalism seems clearly indicated" (Warren, 1980: 49).

Beginning in 1978, members of the British School undertook excavations of a building complex on the west side of the stratigraphical museum. The site promised to be instructive in the matter of dating throughout much of the second millennium B.C. At the Late Minoan level, they uncovered a small rectangular basement cell 1.76 x 1.08 m. The floor of the cell contained 299 human bones, subsequently determined to belong to two children approximately eight and eleven years old at time of death. The context of the bones indicates that the bodies were on the floor at the moment of the destruction of the building; nothing suggests a cemetery or funerary situation. The presence of twenty-seven fine knife-cut marks on certain of the bones indicates removal of some, though not all, of the flesh. The marks were not caused by the blow of a weapon; there is nothing about the state of the bones to indicate survival cannibalism. In fact, an adjacent room contained a pithos in which children's bones were mixed with snail remains and burnt earth, which suggests cooking.

Neither find can be explained away, although some have attempted to do so. Even if such finds appear to be "The Unacceptable Face of Minoan Crete"—in the words of a 1982 article by Keith Branigan—the evidence advances our understanding of Bronze Age religion generally. Moreover, the discoveries may have a bearing on our specific pursuit of the nature of Mycenaean civilization; especially in the case of Knossos, the palace may have been in the control of mainlanders at the time of the destruction.

There are examples of probable temples from mainland sites as well. In fact, new excavations in 1968 and 1969 brought to light independent cult buildings at Mycenae. The area around Tsountas' House is now seen to have been the religious center of the late Mycenaean settlement.

Uncovering the area between Tsountas' House and the South House on the southwestern part of the acropolis, Lord William Taylour revealed a temenos on three levels of the hillside. A path, described by George Mylonas as a processional corridor, led from the courtyard of Tsountas' House to an area in front of another building, called the House of Idols after its most startling contents, a trove of unique clay figures of varying sizes, some as large as 0.6 m (Fig. 106). With one possible exception, the figures are female; those with painted designs show strong similarities of decoration with vases belonging to LHIIIA and B periods, that is 1425–1230. A cartouche of Amenophis III (1412–1376 B.C.) accords with these limits. The clay statuettes are akin to figures found by Marinatos in Crete and by Caskey in Keos. In addition to the figures, the Mycenae building contained two coiled, ceramic snakes and fragments of four others; pottery, including a bowl holding such treasures as an ivory figurine, amber beads, lapis lazuli, rock crystal, and glass beads. An alcove was found to contain even more figurines, including two male statuettes and additional fragments of snakes. A natural rock embedded in the floor was surrounded by a quantity of broken and unbroken clay figures (Fig. 107). It is interesting that an unhewn rock similar to that at Mycenae was discovered at Anemospilia. A cult role is not unlikely. The small room containing the figures was separate from the main chamber of the building (Mylonas, 1972; Taylour, 1970: 270–280).

The House of Idols, in turn, is separated from another building on the same level, an irregularly shaped structure measuring 11 x 4 m. The largest room measures 5.30 x 3.50 m. A hearth of elliptical shape occupies the center and postholes at either end mark locations of columns. A bench of earth with a border of large undressed stones running along the south side contained vases dated to LHIIIB2

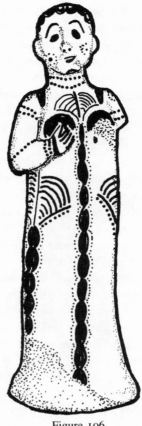

Figure 106

and two fine ivories. Extending almost two meters, a fresco of a standing female figure with two smaller figures decorated the east wall. The three figures have been identified as goddesses. Their style of dress is Minoan, and two of them hold objects: one holds what appears to be a spear, the other holds in both hands bright red objects, which have been described by Taylour as almost certainly some kind of cereal (Fig. 108). At right angles to the wall was a low step up to a higher platform. An adjacent L-shaped room was named the Room of the Ivories since it contained a number of partly worked ivories as well as vases on its east-west arm. The north-south arm seems to have been a shrine. A painted figure was found in place on a dais in the southwest corner.

Southwest of the House of Idols were remains of two altars: a horseshoe-shaped altar of clay 1.40 x 1.35 m was later replaced by a rectangular altar which, as late as 1972, was the only certain case of an altar identified as belong-

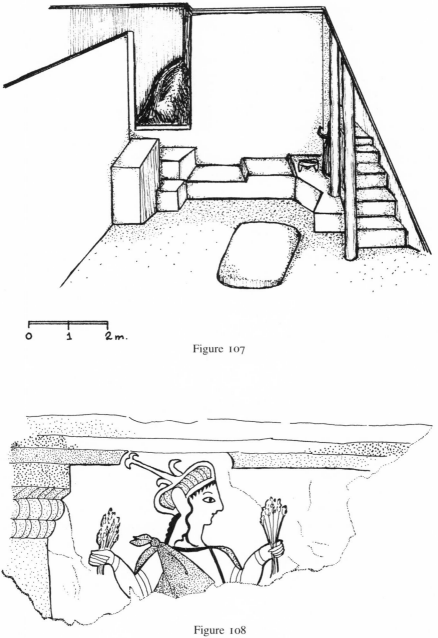

Figure 107

Figure 108

ing to the Mycenaean period. Further south, another building called the South-East House, was identified by Mylonas as having cult purposes, perhaps serving the needs of a priest.

A similar sacred area has been identified in the lower citadel at Tiryns. During the rebuilding that followed destruction at the end of LHIIIB, traditionally ca. 1230 B.C., several small buildings were constructed next to the fortification wall. First a small chamber was built; it was replaced by a structure almost 3 m square, identified as a temple by the excavators. The stuccoed interior may have been painted red; it contained figurines, miniature vessels and an animal-shaped rhyton. North of the building was an altar measuring 2.08 x 1.0 m; the ash surrounding the altar contained bits of an idol and rhyton. Later in LHIIIC, a larger building was erected. It measured 5.10 x 2.20 m and contained goods similar to those found in the smaller structure. In other words, its use for cult seems certain.

Pylos, too, appears to have had a shrine near the main entrance to the palace. A stuccoed and painted altar stood in front of a small recess that is identified as having served religious purposes. At Epidauros, the Mycenaean shrine was long-lived and important. It has two phases; an altar was used frequently and it produced some fine items, including several very large wheelmade animal figures. N. Valmin identified a Late Helladic sanctuary at Malthi, where he excavated. At Berbati near Mycenae, two chambers have been identified as a chapel and a repository. As early as 1932, Mylonas and Kourouniotis supported the identification of Megaron B at Eleusis as the first temple at that important religious site. Other scholars, including Nilsson, disagreed with the proposition, arguing that the building was a residence. In light of recent discoveries of separate cult buildings at other mainland sites, the earlier identification has gained adherents (Rutkowski, 1986).

Another sanctuary was identified in the British School reexcavation at Phylakopi on Melos between 1974 and 1977. The building, originally about 11 x 6.5 m, was constructed during the LMIIIA period. Eventually it had two main rooms, the earlier west shrine roughly 6 m square and the east shrine, added later, containing half as much floor area. An open court formed part of the complex. The building was destroyed in LHIIIC after several architectural changes in the two centuries of its use. The rooms contained altars, benches, figurines—male, female and animal—seals and pottery. The complex is quite modest. However, as Colin Renfrew, the director of the excavation, pointed out, its size and furnishings are quite in accord with the nature and size of the settlement, whose total population is estimated to be between 1,400 and 2,100 people (Renfrew, 1985).

Much more impressive are the temples at Kition on Cyprus; three Mycenaean temples were uncovered in 1969–70 and two more were found in 1974–75. All of them appear to date to the period in which Mycenaean merchants or colonists or refugees were living at several locations on the island. The largest was built at the end of the thirteenth century and abandoned near the end of the eleventh century. A very grand 35 x 22 m, it was reused by Phoenicians as a temple of Astarte from the ninth century. The second structure was earlier, dating to the beginning of the thirteenth century, though it too was abandoned near the end of the eleventh century. It is smaller—15.50 x 9 m. A third building measures 6.76 x 4.15 m; it lasted most of the thirteenth century.

These finds have done a good deal to increase our information on Bronze Age religion. While the data cannot reveal the beliefs of Bronze Age worshippers, they do show how those worshippers practiced rituals related to the beliefs. Separate buildings not very different from dwellings were a part of the practice, and much of the ritual was carried on in the open air, at altars situated near the cult buildings. Clay figurines and, at least in one location, a large wooden image celebrated deities either by depicting them or by representing their worshippers. Figurines of animals also played a significant role as did special vessels such as rhyta.

In a word, there is much in the archaeological record to remind us of Classical Greek religion. In fact, evidence of cult continuity is one of the major results of the present generation of Bronze Age investigation. The evidence from Eleusis and Epidauros has already been mentioned. At least twenty other sites in all parts of the Aegean tell the same story. On the mainland, apart from Epidauros and Eleusis, there are indications of continuity of cult at Rhamnous in eastern Attica. A location of the cult of Nemesis in the Classical period, the site has revealed pottery as early as the Early Helladic period continuing into Late Helladic, Geometric and Archaic. West of Attica, the island of Aegina has produced Mycenaean pottery on Kolonna Hill, the site of the later Temple of Apollo. The temple of Athena at Philia in Thessaly has Mycenaean levels that continue into Early Christian times. Members of the German School have found a late Bronze Age sanctuary under the Classical temple at Kalapodhi in central Greece. Mycenaean and Protogeometric pottery has been found in the northwest quarter of the Demeter Sanctuary at Corinth. The eighth-century Menelaion near Sparta may well have been built amid Late Helladic ruins. Excavations have brought to light imported Mycenaean sherds as well as local imitations dating from the Late Bronze Age at the site of Zeus' temple at Dodona in northwestern Greece. At Dodona, a large elliptical structure 9.5 meters long dates to the Early Iron Age.

There are also indications of cult continuity away from the mainland. While this evidence does not have such a direct bearing on the Mycenaean civilization, it is important for the debt of later Greek culture to the Bronze Age, a subject to which we will return in chapter ten. There are Early Bronze Age sherds at the Asclepeium of Pergamon, and the first monumental sanctuary of Aphrodite at Palaipaphos on Cyprus is now dated to the end of the thirteenth century. And at Kato Syme Viannou on Crete, A. Lembesis has been excavating the rural shrine of Hermes and Aphrodite, well known from the Classical period. She has discovered levels dating back to Middle Minoan III/Late Minoan I and proposes that worship of a Minoan goddess and male consort was replaced by the cult in honor of Aphrodite and Hermes whose practice continued into the third century A.D. A many-roomed cult building (fifteen rooms have been identified as of 1984–85) containing thirty-one offering tables was the seat of ancillary cult activities. Even when the building was destroyed in the Bronze Age, the site continued to be used for open-air observances. A strong Minoan flavor attached to the practices even in the later Classical period.

As a result of such mounting evidence, the line dividing religious practice of the Bronze Age from that of the Classical period is no longer so fixed. The decipherment of Linear B revealed proper names of familiar deities; present excavation demonstrates the continuity of cult practice honoring those deities.

CONTINUING EXCAVATIONS

Excavations have continued at most of the major sites originally investigated before 1967. Questions requiring resolution regularly include dating, limits of the settlement site, continuity between periods and innovations suggesting cultural change. New sites, too, have been identified and excavated, as we have seen in the case of Akrotiri.

On the Greek mainland, continuing investigation at major sites has helped to clarify our understanding both of developments at particular sites and of connections between sites. A great deal of attention has been paid to dating, both absolute and relative. Moreover, since the Mycenaeans were increasingly active in other areas of the Aegean and Mediterranean, recent excavations have detected their presence at various sites of Crete and the Cyclades.

We have discussed the important discoveries in the vicinity of Tsountas' House at Mycenae in examining developments in our knowledge of Bronze Age religious areas and buildings. Tiryns, too, has been the scene of continuing activity by members of the German School. The upper citadel, or Oberburg, has been studied anew for a better understanding of dating and phases of use. The Unterburg, or lower citadel, has been thoroughly examined during the last two decades. Traces of many open-air activities came to light as did a freestanding shrine with associated large terracotta figures. The site is now understood to have been thoroughly reorganized during the last phase of the Mycenaean Age due to extension of the settlement to the north and the south. Continuity of pottery styles from late Mycenaean into sub-Mycenaean received substantiation when traces of sub-Mycenaean occupation were found in 1979.

Excavation was resumed in 1971 at Asine after a forty-year interval. Recent finds by members of the Swedish School go back to the Middle Helladic period; and at Argos, recent work by the French has shown its importance as early as the Middle Bronze Age continuing into and beyond the Late Bronze Age. There is Neolithic and Early Bronze Age material as well. The site exhibits features common to other sites: a tomb recalls the previously unique tomb Rho at Mycenae; an enclosure wall surrounding a burial area may be like Grave Circle B at Mycenae. However, Argos has produced unique finds as well: from the Middle Helladic phase comes a cremation trench burial. In 1971, more than eighteen human skeletons were found mingled with animal bones in a constructed well. Animals and humans may have been victims of a natural disaster.

Perhaps the four humans found in situ in a Mycenaean house at Plakes, 150 meters north of the Mycenae postern gate, were victims of the same disaster. The excavators suggest earthquake as a cause near the end of LHIIIB. It is now clear that the disaster was not sufficient to end or even greatly reduce occupation. The LHIIIC phase is thought to have lasted three generations, until about 1120 B.C. During this period the northwest slope of the acropolis was still closely packed with houses, and there was continuous occupation of higher sections of the citadel.

As with Argos, Attica's prominence in the Bronze Age has expanded. Not only Athens, but other settlements appear to have been important centers. Thorikos, in the southeast corner of the peninsula, was certainly one such center, as recent work on the part of the Belgian Mission has revealed. Its position overlooking two harbors surely was a factor. Perhaps more important were metal resources of the vicinity. Lead and silver seem to have been extracted at Thorikos as early as the third millennium. Traces of hammering along the veins of ore are still visible. Although the importance of the site was indicated by a tholos discovered in 1893, the past two decades have brought to light three additional Mycenaean tombs (Fig. 109). A tumulus 25 meters in diameter and an oblong tholos are dated to the Middle Helladic period; the most recently discovered tomb, although looted, still contained a few gold ornaments similar to those found in Circle A at Mycenae. Like the Mycenae tomb, the Thorikos structure is dated to Late Helladic I. Thorikos is significant for our understanding of the Iron Age also: more than 150 Geometric tombs have been discovered, and it was the location of an heroic or funerary cult established by the Archaic period.

North of Thorikos, Marathon has been shown to have been an important site during the Bronze Age. The years 1969 and 1970 witnessed dramatic discoveries here: in 1969 Marinatos excavated four grave circles of Middle Helladic and Mycenaean dates, in one of which the skeletons of two horses were found, suggesting heroic burial. In the same vicinity, there is a Middle Bronze Age settlement at Plasi and an Early Bronze Age cist tomb cemetery at Tsepis. Several tholoi and

Figure 109

chamber tombs have been identified in various parts of Attica including Athens itself, where an early tholos dates to LHI. Even earlier, Middle Helladic remains from the agora have been announced. On Salamis, a Mycenaean cemetery has come to light showing some connection with Crete in the form of a Minoan lentoid seal.

Pioneers in Aegean archaeology failed to discover a palace center for Odysseus and Menelaos; efforts have continued in this generation. At the Aetos site on Ithaka, S. Symeonoglou has been looking for the town of Odysseus. The seekers of Menelaos' home have met with more immediate success. While it may not be a palace center (only one possible Linear B painted inscription has been found),

Figure 110

an important site was excavated during the 1970s by the British School at the Menelaion, the location of a hero cult from the late eighth century. The unwalled main settlement, 100 meters above the Eurotas River, was occupied from the Middle Helladic period. It was intensively settled in the Late Helladic phase when the site was dominated by a large mansion first constructed in the second half of the fifteenth century. The complex was rebuilt after a calamity in the late fifteenth century, when new walls were buried beneath one meter of fill. Then it was abandoned for approximately a century; it was refurbished and reoccupied until its destruction near the end of the thirteenth century. In spite of destruction there is significant LHIIIC1 pottery, some of which is handmade ware (Fig. 110). We will consider the implications of this handmade ware in some detail in chapter ten. Development of the entire region of southern Laconia seems associated with Cretan influence in Kythera. At Ayios Stephanos remains associated with a MHIII/LHI house, excavated in 1973–74 under Lord William Taylour's direction, show strong Minoan influence. There is a great deal of MMIIIB and LMIA pottery similar to that found on Kythera. The Minoan site on Kythera itself seems to have had no occupation after the middle of the fifteenth century.

Finds from Messenia continue to be particularly rich both in terms of numbers and quality. Professor George Korres has been active in the excavation of tombs, especially at Peristeria, continuing Marinatos' earlier work. The so-called tholos tomb of Thrasymedes at Voïdhokilia is now known to have been set into pre-

Mycenaean remains on this promontory; the later tholos was inserted into the existing structure.

In the north Peloponnese, discoveries have also mounted. Neolithic and Early Helladic material from Corinth and Nemea demonstrates that the fertility of the region was recognized from an early period. The high number and the size of known Mycenaean settlements in the Corinthia can be interpreted as testimony to the productivity of the area. A number of Bronze Age finds have been made recently in neighboring Achaea, a region that had a major influx of population in the Late Mycenaean period. While some of the new discoveries reinforce the picture of movement of people at the end of the Bronze Age, others suggest that the region was important throughout the Bronze Age. An Early Helladic settlement has been discovered at Chalandritsa, and Agoulinitsa has produced a mass of Middle and Late Helladic pottery sherds. Arkadia, too, has long been thought to be a place of refuge during the difficulties at the end of the Bronze Age. Recently Pheneos in Arkadia has produced Middle Helladic as well as Late Helladic remains. A population movement into Elis has been strengthened by recent evidence: in addition to continuing occupation in the LHIIIC period, new sites were built during the same time.

In central Greece, the present thrusts are both regional and localized. As for the northern Peloponnese, survey work has revealed a greater density of population for much of the area than was earlier realized. Increased productivity as a result of drainage around Lake Copais may have been either the cause or the effect of growth; no matter which sequence is correct, appreciation of the accomplishment has led to reexamination of the drainage works. Identification of a well-paved road of the Mycenaean period provides additional evidence for communication between sites.

The pattern of centralization that occurred elsewhere took place in Boeotia, and the two major sites of the Mycenaean era have been intensively studied. In central Greece, Orchomenos has been reexcavated since 1974 by the Greek Archaeological Service. Its importance throughout the Late Helladic period is now clear: a cemetery comparable to the grave circles at Mycenae has been discovered, while a palace and little palace with frescoes date to the Late Helladic IIIA and B phases. The second major center was Thebes, where work has been continuous, if difficult. Fortifications up to 5 meters wide date to the end of the fourteenth century and are being studied by Vassilis Aravantinos. Even the Early Helladic complex seems to have had a fortification wall surrounding structures as fine as a massive apsidal building. The mysterious site of Gla has been reexamined beginning in 1978, by Sp. Iakovides, who dates construction and use of the site to the first half or three-quarters of the thirteenth century. Not a normal palace center but a fortress is the usual description of "this barren and rocky 'island' with Cyclopean walling over a circumference of about two kilometres (enclosing an area over ten times that of Tiryns)" (Hope Simpson, 1981: 64).

When they constructed Gla, Mycenaeans were active in regions far distant from the mainland. Consequently, to tell the full story of the Mycenaean Age it is necessary to look at results of investigations carried on elsewhere, particularly on Crete and on the Cyclades. The question of Mycenaean presence at Knossos has continued to occupy the attention of excavators, while discoveries in western Crete provide valuable data for other Mycenaean presence on the island. The harbor site of Kommos in southern Crete holds clues of another sort.

Knossos, however, is at the center of controversy, as it has been so many times in the past. New evidence has come from excavations carried out by members of the British School between 1967 and 1972, when they examined what was known as the Unexplored Mansion behind the little palace. (It retains that name even now that it has been explored.) The building's facade was found by Evans, but it was not excavated immediately, due to an extremely deep accumulation of post-Minoan occupation. When excavated, it proved to be a Late Minoan building measuring 24.5 x 14.5 meters. A major destruction occurred during Late Minoan II, and there was a further disaster in LMIIIA. However, final abandonment did not occur until approximately 1200. The excavators tell of the "sad story of slow decline" when the pillar hall was reused as a workshop for smelting and the upper story was the collection point of scrap metal for resmelting. A stirrup jar from this period had a painted inscription on its shoulder testifying to continuity of literacy even within these conditions. In the words of one of the excavators, M. R. Popham, the assemblage of the evidence led to the conclusion, "that it was the presence of Mycenaeans at Knossos which led to these changes" (Popham, 1973: 58). We will return to this evidence in chapter ten in reviewing the present theories of Mycenaean presence at Knossos.

Evidence from western Crete has a bearing on the same question. In fact, this region of the island has been the source of several surprises in the past twenty years. While sites were known earlier, it was generally thought that the western part of the island was out of the mainstream during the Bronze Age. The choice of Chania as the location of the second International Cretological Congress in 1966 may have been fortuitous; but it is interesting to note that finds in the western region have been rapid since then. Of particular importance for the question of island/mainland interaction is the site of Chania, excavated since 1970 by a joint team of Greek and Swedish archaeologists. Building remains go back to the late Neolithic period and continue across most of the Bronze Age. Important discoveries at the site include a Linear A archive in 1971 and, in subsequent seasons, sealings with Linear A signs and Linear B tablets. The Minoan complex at Kastelli seems to have been an important administrative center. The presence of

objects from Knossos as well as imports from the Cyclades and the Greek mainland also attest the site's role in cultural interaction. Additionally, the use of Linear B implies mainland presence at the site at approximately the time when the
Mycenaean evidence at Knossos increased (Tzedakis and Godart, forthcoming).

Chania was not the only settlement in western Greece, as the evidence demonstrated by Jennifer Moody's survey work in the Chania region clearly shows.
Minoan settlements have been identified at several locations, and there are tombs
and burials at others. Since the sites bear testimony to use in the Early or Middle
Bronze Age, we must revise the earlier opinion vividly stated by Pendlebury. He
summarized the view of many scholars that the disaster marked by the destruction of Knossos

> had broken the spirit of the Minoans. . . . At all events the map clearly shows
> the tendency for the population to scatter. Particularly noteworthy is the exten-
> sion of habitation in the West. Thrown back on to their own resources, their
> great fount of wealth, Egypt, apparently cut off from them and their trade in
> the hands of others, the Minoans were forced to exploit and tame the wild
> country West of Ida, where before there has been only isolated outposts.
> (Pendlebury, 1939, rpt. 1965: 237ff.)

Rather than being the result of an act of despair, the settlement of the west part of
the island now seems to have been within the overarching system of Minoan
Crete from an early period. Thus, a reason for Mycenaean activity in western
Crete is not hard to find.

Excavation at Kommos began in 1976 and has resulted in expanded knowledge
of the nature of the connection between Minoans and others, inasmuch as Kommos seems to have been the chief port of entry on the Libyan Sea for Minoan
Phaistos. Its importance in maritime trade is attested by such unusual features as
a huge structure of at least five galleries opening onto a court. The excavators
suggest the galleries were used for storing ships in the winter months (Fig. 111).
Clear traces of paved road also came to light indicating trade links with other
parts of the island. Another stoa-like building 55.4 m long has at its east end a
number of bins and slab enclosures. It coincides with the period showing the majority of imported ceramic items, namely LHIIIA. While many of these items
were Cypriot, the time is one in which Mycenaean presence is attested elsewhere.

In the continuing investigation on Crete, some earlier opinions have been modified. Several of these have a bearing on our understanding of the Mycenaean civilization vis-à-vis that of Crete. For example, fortifications no longer seem so
unusual for Minoan Crete. Protective walls are now surmised for Vasiliki; Roussolakkos, an islet of Kouphonisi; Kastro Kephala near Almyros; and Pyrgos, a
long-lived village in southern Crete uncovered between 1970 and 1977. We must

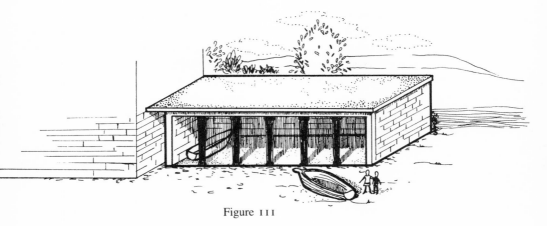

Figure 111

conclude either that these sites are atypical or that the earlier picture of Minoan society is incorrect. The picture that pervades accounts until the present generation of scholarship is summarized by R. Higgins:

> The peaceful character of this civilization is noticeable even before the Palace period. It was to remain a Cretan peculiarity and contributed to no small extent to the rapid development of her culture. (Higgins, 1967: 18)

To account for anomalous finds, it was necessary to resort to arguments that accorded with the received picture. Thus:

> A wealth of decorated weapons could scarcely be expected in a community as peaceful as Crete between 2800 and 1500 B.C., yet the palaces must have had their ceremonial guards and the rulers their insignia of office, and the ruins of the first palaces at Mallia have in fact yielded three ceremonial swords of about the eighteenth century B.C. (Higgins, 1967: 42)

By contrast, the culture of mainland Greece has regularly been described as warlike and militaristic. Groups of people relied on their swords to establish control over limited territories; they built walls around natural fortresses; their martial spirit carried them to other parts of the Aegean and the larger Mediterranean world. This dichotomy between the two Bronze Age Aegean cultures has been employed to explain the history of their development and interaction. Thus, a Minoan trading empire collapsed when the Mycenaeans intruded with their greater force of arms; Knossos itself fell to redoubtable Mycenaean warriors; the attackers shown on the Akrotiri frescoes *must* be Mycenaeans, not peace-loving Minoans.

The new evidence will occasion review of the once-standard contrasts. And it strikes another blow at one of the strangest theories presented during the present generation of Aegean studies: in 1971, H. G. Wunderlich proposed that the Minoan centers were not palaces for the living but sites where preservation of the dead was carried out (Wunderlich, 1974). Lack of defenses may be strange for settlements of the living, the argument maintains, but is not surprising for communities of the dead. Wunderlich's thesis has not been accepted, essentially because there is no trace of all those dead supposedly preserved at the "palace centers"; nor are there indicators of the real lives of those engaged in the massive tasks of preservation. Moreover, the recent evidence undercutting Minoan pacifism further weakens this theory. As Chester Starr has cautioned:

> In sum, we may properly continue to believe that the Minoans cherished the flora and fauna of nature. Both positive archaeological evidence and the comparative testimony of other civilizations, however, should not lead us to the dangerous further step of idealizing their relations with foreigners or captives, slaves, and other unfortunate victims. (Starr in Hägg and Marinatos, 1984: 12)

Minoan and Mycenaean activity in other parts of the Aegean should serve as a similar corrective to overstated descriptions of pacifism. Some encounters were peaceful; others clearly were not. The recent generation has done extensive work on the Aegean islands. We have mentioned the new excavations on Thera. Other major work includes reexcavation at sites such as Phylakopi on Melos, and significant surveys on Melos, Keos and elsewhere. Several of these sites are helping to clarify our picture of the pattern of interaction between the three main cultures of the Aegean region.

We have seen hints of a pattern in the earlier investigation by John Caskey on Keos, where Minoan influence was gradually replaced by Mycenaean influence. Members of the British School reexcavated Phylakopi on Melos between 1974 and 1977. They studied the Mycenaean megaron or palace of the Late Helladic IIIA period as well as the earlier building levels, which show greater affinity to Minoan and other Cycladic cultures. The identification of the first tholos found in the Cyclades at Ayia Thekla on Tenos is yet another clue to the presumed pattern. The tholos is Late Helladic in date. Lisvori on Lesbos apparently had a similar history: the settlement was occupied throughout the Bronze Age and toward the end shows Mycenaean pottery. On Siphnos, the Ayios Andreas acropolis had a small settlement in the Middle Bronze Age when its cultural connections point to Minoan Crete, whereas a later fortified settlement, continuing from the Mycenaean into the Geometric period, shows what appears to be a pattern of expanding mainland influence. A Mycenaean settlement and necropolis at Naxos flourished from the early thirteenth century.

Koukounaries on Paros points to a like situation. The settlement was important throughout the Late Bronze Age and was apparently the island's center of power in the thirteenth century. Excavation of the site, which began in 1976 under the direction of D. Schilardi of the German School, has demonstrated its importance to our understanding of the period of destruction and transition between Mycenaean and Dark Age culture as well (Schilardi in MacGillivray and Barber, 1984).

The site, occupied in the Early Bronze Age and again during the Late Helladic period, shows evidence of Cycladic culture in its first phase, and Mycenaean in its second. It was fortified with Cyclopean walls toward the end of the thirteenth century. The main building has been identified as a palace and shows a clear resemblance to mainland buildings. The area was overcome by destruction described by the excavator as having occurred slightly later than mainland destructions. Human and animal bones found together within the remains of the palace suggest that it served as a last hope of refuge for inhabitants at the time of difficulty. A second, short phase of the site is identified as post-destruction; walls belong to structures that were built either by survivors or agents of the earlier destruction. At some point the site was deserted until the early tenth century. The third phase belongs to the protogeometric period; architectural remains are apparently walls of houses and perhaps a temple. A degree of prosperity is attested by the materials imported from Attica. It was during the late Geometric period that the settlement assumed its final plan. Though still small, the site appears to have prospered primarily through farming and herding and related crafts. A larger than usual building may have been the house of a local leader superintending the community until it was peacefully abandoned in the course of the seventh century. The question of abandonment remains unanswered, although there are parallels with other contemporary communities. As we will see in the concluding chapter, our picture of on-going change from Bronze Age into Dark Age is growing clearer as a result of investigation of "less significant" sites like Koukounaries.

UNDERWATER ARCHAEOLOGY

Another recent development in Bronze Age archaeology, underwater excavation, is an area of great interest. George Bass, who directed the expedition off Cape Gelidonya (compare chapter eight), has more recently guided the investigation of a fourteenth-century B.C. ship wrecked off the southern Turkish coast near the promontory of Ulu Burun. A sponge diver discovered the ship at a depth of some 150 feet in 1982, close to the limit of practical detail work using scuba diving at this time. Beginning in 1984, the wreck was excavated jointly by members of the Institute of Nautical Archaeology, Texas A & M University and Turkish associates of the Museum of Underwater Archaeology.

The variety of objects found indicates an international trading enterprise (Fig. 112). There are pottery pieces from Cyprus and Syria-Palestine; metal objects with Egyptian, Cypriot, Canaanite and Mycenaean designs; tin ingots and 200 copper ingots; Canaanite glass; a quartz cylinder seal similar to known Kassite seals; a scarab with Egyptian hieroglyphs containing the name Nefertiti; beads of Baltic amber; two hippopotamus teeth and a length of elephant tusk; fragments of tortoiseshell; and a small folding tablet of wood thought to have once contained a text pressed in wax.

Some of the individual finds are unique: the tin ingots are the oldest yet discovered, the gold scarab is the first known with the complete name of Nefertiti "the Exquisite Beauty of the Aten." Studied as a whole, the finds tell us a great deal about the nature of contacts between cultures in the Late Bronze Age. Ships like the one wrecked at Ulu Burun may well have sailed from port to port around the eastern Mediterranean into the Aegean and perhaps as far as the Tyrrhenian Sea, gathering goods—and perhaps crew—in each harbor. Bass has described the shipwreck, still only partly excavated, as an archaeologist's dream come true. It contains information for scholars of individual Bronze Age cultures, for students of ship construction, economic history, ancient metallurgy, and social history, and for geographers and art historians.

Less spectacular, the underwater study of the island of Saliagos began in 1964. This islet between the Cycladic islands of Paros and Antiparos was found to be the site of the first Neolithic settlement excavated in the Cyclades, and it continued to be occupied during the Bronze Age. Since it was waterless, the excavators were puzzled as to why it would have been selected for habitation. Since it was a coastal site, divers were called in to investigate the off-shore area. They found that in antiquity, the site had been situated on an isthmus linking Paros and Antiparos; a three-meter rise in relative sea level since Roman times has fundamentally altered the terrain. Rather than an isolated site without water, Saliagos can be understood as a settlement with two harbors, comparable to Corinth with its commanding position on the isthmus.

The importance of underwater archaeology has been recognized in the establishment of a new division of the Greek Archaeological Service, the Ephorate for Underwater Archaeology. The first major project of the ephorate was exploration of an Early Helladic wreck off Dokos (between the mainland and the island of Hydra). In 1982, the establishment of a new Centre for Greek Underwater Archaeology was announced, to be housed at Pylos in the former Turkish fortress of Neokastro. The Centre includes a museum to display finds.

Several Bronze Age sites, now underwater, have been discovered but not thor-

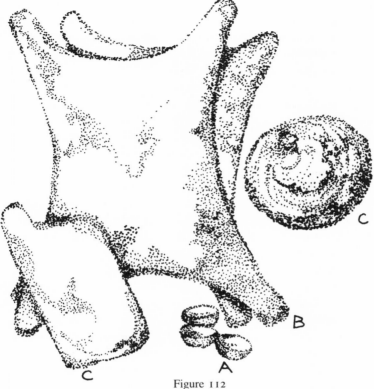

Figure 112

oughly explored: at Elaphonesos in southern Laconia, Mycenaean walls have been detected along with Roman and Byzantine remains, and an Early Helladic settlement has been found off Astakos in western Greece. Sites on Crete include a Bronze Age settlement extending some 400 x 60 meters in Platygiali Bay; a site at Paralia tou Mylou; and others at Stalos (Kydonias) and Stavromenos (Rethymnou). In the islands, there is an underwater site north of Grotta on Naxos and two others at Paroikia Bay and Naoussa Bay on Paros.

WRITING

Nothing comparable to the decipherment of Linear B in 1952 marks the present generation of Aegean studies in the area of written materials. Instead, the past two generations have seen refinement of detail and quite remarkable cooperation among scholars.

The corpus of data has not grown very much. Some Knossos Linear B fragments were rediscovered in 1984: they had been wrapped in newspaper and
stored away since Evans' original discovery of them. Crete has produced additional Linear A inscriptions from several sites; Chania, Zakro, Mallia, stone tablets of offerings from Mt. Iuktas, Mt. Vrysina in western Crete, Kato Syme
Viannou and the Phourni cemetery. Fragments of Linear B inscriptions have
come to light from Chania, and hieroglyphic inscriptions have come from Mallia
and Knossos. Beyond Crete, more Linear A is reported from Kythera and Kea.
Objects with Cypro-Minoan signs have been excavated at several sites on Cyprus,
and there is possibly one piece from Kea with Cypro-Minoan signs. Apart from
the Linear B from western Crete, the largest new find is fifty-five sealings inscribed in Linear B excavated at Thebes. In a protogeometric context, the cemetery at Tekke on Crete was the source of a bronze bowl with an incised inscription of thirteen letters of the Phoenician alphabet. An alphabetic cuneiform
inscription was found at the late Cycladic site Hala Sultan Tekke in Cyprus.

Nothing comparable to the sizable Linear B archives discovered earlier has
been found during the present generation of Aegean studies. The quantity of Linear A is still insufficient to enable much progress toward decipherment. A sensible procedure has been to compare signs with similar forms in Linear A and B.
For instance, when decoded according to the values of Linear B, some Linear A
groupings produce names almost identical with place-names found on the Knossos
Linear B tablets. Since names of places tend to persist even when people living in
those places change, such similarity between tablets is not surprising: both Linear A and Linear B tablets seem to deal with commodities and people that are
regularly identified by location. Comparison between Linear A and Linear B has
been enough to confirm the belief that the language of the former is not Greek.
An important clue to the nature of the language of the Linear B script is the word
for "total," TO-SO or TO-SA, used before a reckoning. The word used before a
reckoning in Linear A tablets is KU-RO when transcribed according to Linear B
values. KU-RO has no meaning anything like "total" in classical Greek.

Even though there is more Linear A material than there is of the forms on the
single Phaistos Disk, the decipherment of Linear A requires a great deal more
data. John Chadwick's 1987 assessment for the Disk is appropriate for Linear A
as well:

Only a large increase in the number of inscriptions will permit real progress
towards a decipherment. Meanwhile, we must curb our impatience, and admit
that if King Minos himself were to reveal to someone in a dream the true interpretation it would be quite impossible for him to convince anyone else that his
was the one and only possible solution. (1987: 61)

With more numerous but still limited materials, Linear B scholars have turned to other approaches to gain as much information as possible. Publication of the texts so far known has been impressive. The Pylos tablets were published in two parts in 1973 and 1976; a new edition of the Knossos tablets appeared in 1987. The Mycenae, Tiryns and Thebes tablets have also been published as has the corpus of vases with Linear B inscriptions. Consequently, information on specific subjects has been advanced by the availability of the evidence. Joins among fragments of tablets, thereby creating larger grammatical contexts, have clarified points of detail although, as Lydia Baumbach has put the current status, "in the interpretation of vocabulary words we seemed to have reached the point where the 'law of disminishing returns' becomes established." She predicts that "the many publications that have appeared recently using sets of tablets as evidence for various aspects of Bronze Age life is in my opinion an indication of the way future research in Mycenology will continue to proceed" (Killen, Melena and Olivier, 1987: 75).

Several scholars, particularly J.-P. Olivier, Y. Duhoux and T. Palaima, have examined differences between the Minoan and Mycenaean archives. While Linear A is found at all types of sites throughout Crete and beyond, Linear B is concentrated at major mainland sites. Linear A inscriptions occur on votive offerings, ceramic and stone vases, metal objects, seals and sealings, plaster fragments as well as on tablets. By contrast, Linear B occurs on tablets, sealings, labels and pottery. Such differences suggest distinctions in the administrative structures where the various writing systems were employed. They also indicate that literacy had penetrated deeper into Minoan culture than it had on the mainland. John Chadwick is of the opinion that "the finds show that writing was not in widespread use in Mycenaean Greece. . . . Writing seems to have been exclusively a bureaucratic tool, a necessary method of keeping administrative accounts and documents, but never used for historical or even frivolous purposes" (1987: 11). Linear A, on the other hand, apparently had religious and decorative as well as administrative uses.

Comparison with written records from other Bronze Age cultures has become a useful means of examining the Aegean materials. By comparison with the Near East, the records of Crete and Greece are limited: there is nothing personal, commemorative, legal, literary or propagandistic in the Aegean collections as there is in the Near Eastern accounts. Nevertheless, the tablets are a strong clue to the nature of the Mycenaean economy: centralization characterized Mycenaean Greek economic, social and political organization just as it did contemporary Near Eastern economies. Recent scholarship has done much to elucidate the types of goods that were controlled from the palace centers. The work of John Killen and José Melena with the sheep and textiles tablets is an important example; Cynthia Shelmerdine has demonstrated the major role for perfumed oil production at Pylos; and Margareta Lindgren has undertaken prosopographical study of individual names (Killen, forthcoming; Melena, 1975; Shelmerdine, 1985; Lindgren, 1973).

Cooperation between textual scholars and archaeologists has also brought greater insight in the use of written materials. Fundamental to their cooperation is the view that the architecture and contents of places in which tablets were found will shed light on the tablets while, reciprocally, the tablets will shed light on the find-spots. For example, a complex of seven rooms excavated at Pylos in 1957 was first described as a garrison or palace guard quarters. An examination of the contents of the complex together with tablets listing groups of men, herds of animals, skins, one tablet dealing with bronze and another referring to wheels, leads to the conclusion that it was a workshop.

Relationships between parts of the larger palace complex can be demonstrated by means of another clue provided by the tablets. Identification of scribal hands has made it possible to follow the activity of specific individuals ("hands"). The same hand can be detected in tablets describing different commodities; or the same hand can be recognized on tablets located in certain parts of the palace. Thomas Palaima has found "an apparent versatility in the range of subjects treated by the better-attested record-keepers" and argues, "this wide range of 'assignments' must be kept in mind when considering the role of scribes, whether well-attested or not, in specialized industries" (Palaima and Shelmerdine, 1984: 34).

Establishing a context for the tablets has a methodological importance. The result of archaeological excavation is a static picture: archaeology provides evidence of once-dynamic processes; for us, however, that activity has vanished. Examining the context of the tablets, or any single category of evidence for that matter, restores some of the original dynamism. There has been much effort given to another contextual question concerning the tablets. Morphology, etymology and phonology along with associated issues are primary focuses of Mycenaean philological studies today. One of those issues is the relationship of Mycenaean Greek to the Classical dialects. Antonin Bartonek, who has done a great deal of work in this area, has stressed the significance of the decipherment in the study of the Greek language:

. . . the discovery in 1952 of the only recorded Greek dialect from the second millennium B.C., Mycenaean Greek, opened up unexpected perspectives for the diachronic study of the relations between the dialects, whose possibilities were considered virtually exhausted twenty-five years ago. (1979: 113)

Several scholars now believe that some differentiation occurred during the second millennium: specifically, the language of southern Greeks diverged from that of northern Greeks. However, linguistic developments were more rapid at the end of the Bronze Age. Ernst Risch joins Bartonek in looking to the "darkening" century following the collapse of Mycenaean rule as "the great period of linguistic ferment" (Risch, 1979).

There is general agreement that, of the later dialects, Arkadian and Cypriot are closest to Mycenaean. There is less agreement about the association between Mycenaean and the other dialects of the first millennium B.C. We will have more to say in the last chapter about a thesis advanced by John Chadwick that attempts to trace the relationship of Mycenaean to the Doric dialect.

Another contextual question is the time and place of the origin of the scripts. The first evidence came from Crete, and Evans explained the development as a succession of forms of writing within the Minoan civilization: pictographic writing gave way to Linear A which led to Linear B. The discovery of large quantities of Linear B on the Greek mainland suggested that some revision was necessary, but even the Cretan evidence argued against a view of simple succession. It is likely that earlier scripts continued in use even when later forms had evolved.

But what situation led to a script to write Greek? Those who believe that mainlanders established themselves on Crete during the second millennium have a ready explanation: Minoan scribes altered their own script, Linear A, tailoring it to the needs of a different language. The result was Linear B, which shows similarity to Linear A in almost half of the signs. Use of Linear B was carried from Crete to the mainland centers.

Others are persuaded that Linear B was developed on the mainland of Greece. Minoan scribes as well as Minoan artisans practiced their skills—either voluntarily or through compulsion—in the emerging centers on the mainland. It was at Pylos or Mycenae that scribes adapted their knowledge of writing to accommodate Greek. James Hooker argues that expanding trade led to the introduction of a Minoan script to the mainland as early as the sixteenth century (Hooker, 1979). As the script continued in use it was gradually modified. Most significantly, it was shaped to accommodate the language of the mainland Greeks, as well as other peoples, who were increasingly part of a cultural koinê. More Greek words, even notations of weights and measures, were introduced. Linear A, in other words, became proto Linear B, then fully Linear B. Thus, for Hooker, the use of Linear B at Knossos does not betoken control of that site by mainlanders. Rather it demonstrates the mixture of culture and languages that typifies the second half of the second millennium.

There are other contenders for place of origin, particularly locations where Minoans and Mycenaeans came regularly into contact with one another: Kythera, perhaps, or Thera. On the basis of present evidence, Crete or the mainland seems a more likely source. As in so many areas, a final verdict must await major additions to the body of evidence.

X

Some Current Theories
and Problems

W HEN HE WROTE THE CONCLUDING CHAPTER of the first edition of this book, William McDonald cautioned that it was not intended as a summary and synthesis of the information then available on Mycenaean civilization. Nor will this discussion attempt to summarize the state of our knowledge more than twenty years later. Instead, our purpose is to review the major historical problems that have emerged during five generations of Aegean archaeology and to examine them in the context of the most recent evidence. Some of the issues that were problematical in 1966 remain unresolved; others have been solved to the satisfaction of most specialists; certain questions are now posed as well as answered in quite different ways than they were two decades ago; and, of course, new areas of controversy have arisen.

In examining the theories advanced by authorities in the field of Aegean studies, the two secondary aims that were announced in the first edition of *Progress into the Past* remain the same. The first is to warn readers that several vital issues remain unresolved. The second is to indicate from time to time specific directions that future research might usefully take in efforts to attack some of the more troublesome outstanding questions. In addition, we want to mention certain new directions in Mycenaean studies. Adhering to the original purpose of this chapter, the account is addressed to both nonspecialist and specialist readers, which brings the same double vulnerability that McDonald recognized in 1966. It is one of the mixed blessings of the field that it attracts the attention of such a variety of students. As we have repeatedly seen, however, communication between varied specialists is absolutely essential to the health of our discipline. These paragraphs are intended to further that kind of cooperation.

This later chapter embodies another form of cooperation inasmuch as it is an amalgam of the discussion of current theories and problems examined in the 1967 edition, modification of certain areas in light of developments since that date, and a review of literature and theories since 1967.

The situation on Greek prehistoric archaeology is never static; as in any lively science, it changes and shifts in a kaleidoscopic series of developments with every passing year. We now have much solid knowledge unavailable to Schliemann, Evans, Blegen, and even to members of the fourth generation of Aegean archaeologists and prehistorians. This advantage allows us to recognize and correct certain inferences and conclusions reached by them and their contemporaries. But it would still be grossly misleading to give the impression (as J. Irving Manatt and C. Tsountas did as early as 1897: 347) that we are now or very soon will be in possession of "the facts" about Mycenaean civilization. Certainly, we have made great strides as we have acquired new tools. The evidence of the Linear B tablets, the insights of survey archaeology, and the solutions offered by specialized scientific techniques provide whole new dimensions to our understanding of the Greek Bronze Age.

Yet, the nature and limited quantity of evidence suggest that some questions are likely to remain forever unanswerable. Illicit excavations and looting, especially of tholos and chamber tombs, continue. The pollution of the modern atmosphere and the pressure of tourism adversely affect archaeological remains. Repair and conservation are essential but costly activities. The demands of salvage operations make rescue archaeology increasingly important; it has been called by some "nightmare archaeology." In 1967 alone, more than forty such operations were carried on in Thebes, while eighty were undertaken in Athens. And these pressures have been increasing because of the modernization of Greece. The massive irrigation project in the northwestern Peloponnese is only one illustration of modern improvement causing destruction of ancient evidence. The site of Agrapidochori was quickly investigated before submersion: it was found to be the location of a Mycenaean chamber tomb. In Crete, a large, important cemetery near Knossos dating to the Dark Age was brought to light in 1975 when a large trench was dug to bring water to Herakleion. Then, to make way for a new hospital, emergency excavations in 1978 investigated nearly six acres of burials extending across the controversial Late Minoan/Sub-Minoan phase. They showed continuing links outside Crete that argue against the notion of isolation after the palace period, a major point of debate in the past. Near the Knossos palace, deep ploughing in preparing the ground for a new olive grove did much damage.

Beginning in 1974, ancient remains as well as the modern structures on Cyprus suffered the ravages of war. The political power of the colonels in the late 1960s and early 1970s affected archaeological research in another way: the director-general of the archaeological service was removed along with five of his senior colleagues and seventy scientific assistants. Few new projects could be initiated nor could work in progress be adequately continued. Nevertheless, there is a wealth of new material that must be published, stored and kept in good repair. All of these are costly operations. Publication is often delayed by several years, causing problems for scholars who require access to it. One notable delay in publication retarded interpretation for two generations; material found in a tomb in 1896 was finally published in 1974!

The quantity of recent finds has resulted in the construction of a number of new museums and additions to existing museums. The Stratigraphical Museum at Knossos was dedicated in March 1966 by Joan Evans, sister of Sir Arthur Evans. Two decades later, a museum to house the Goulandris collection, with primary emphasis on Cycladic art, opened in Athens. There are new museums also at Vathi on Ithaka (1965), at Famagusta and Kryenia on Cyprus (both 1967), on Kerkyra (1968), at Brauron (1969), at Larnaca on Cyprus (1969), at Kalamata (1971, but so badly shaken by the earthquake of 1986 that its contents had to be transferred to museums in other areas), at Polyiros in Chalkidice (1971), at Kilkis (1971), at Olympia (1972), in Messene (1976), at Komotini in Thrace (1976), on Poros (1979), and on Kythera (1981). Galleries have been added to the National Museum in Athens to display finds such as the Thera frescoes as well as a huge influx of less spectacular additions.

In the face of the mounting evidence, probably Schliemann and Tsountas would be somewhat surprised, yet on the whole pleased with what has been built on their foundations. In fact, it is Homer who would be most astonished, as Professor Palmer has remarked, for it is quite misleading to suggest, as Joseph Alsop did, that "Homer has now been justified by the archaeologists, and every bit as fully as old Schliemann could have wished" (1964: 81). We will consider this issue at greater length later in the chapter. Dörpfeld might be disappointed to find that his identifications of Priam's Troy and Nestor's Pylos have been upset; but he would be recompensed with the assurance that the integrity of his work at those and several other sites has not been seriously questioned. In fact, in his Sather Classical Lectures, Anthony Snodgrass took Dörpfeld as a prime example of classical archaeology's distinctive strengths: "It is hard to imagine a better spring-board than Dörpfeld's (at least for its period) for further work on prehistoric settlement and land use in the area in question" (1987: 33f.).

Evans and Mackenzie, on the other hand, would be almost incredulous to learn that many scholars now believe that mainlanders had gradually encroached on Minoan trade and finally occupied the Knossos palace. But they might be mollified to realize that no one takes lightly the fundamental influence that the brilliant Minoan culture had on so many aspects of mainland life. Wace lived to see most of his major theories vindicated, and the present situation would hold no real surprises for him. Blegen's work, too, established foundations that have been built upon in several directions. His excavations at major centers like Troy and Pylos as well as at smaller sites like Korakou and Zygouries are widely admired by archaeologists of the present generation. Blegen would also be pleased by the results of a surface survey of the whole region of Messenia which McDonald organized and led. That survey by the Minnesota Messenia Expedition has been described as a "watershed" project by a major archaeologist of the present generation, John Cherry, and MME excavation at Nichoria is of fundamental significance to our understanding of the Iron Age history of Greece (1987).

In the preceding chapters we have reviewed, selectively but as fairly as we could, the major discoveries over the past 120 years. Now, looking at the Mycenaean Age more specifically as a historical phenomenon, what are the firm facts and where are the major areas of uncertainty and controversy?

ORIGINS

The population of central and southern Greece and the neighboring islands during the Late Bronze Age was already a very mixed one, as the evidence of language and skeletal remains both demonstrate. Probably there was still a considerable admixture of blood from ancestors who inhabited the area as far back as Neolithic times (about 6500–3000). Almost certainly descendants of the gifted and progressive people of the Early Bronze Age (about 3000–2000) formed an important element. According to the "orthodox" view, it was these early inhabitants who would have spoken an "Aegean" language (or family of languages), which was also widely used in Crete, in the islands and in western Anatolia. Many words by which this "Aegean" language designated islands, mountains, towns, trees, plants, animals and mythological persons persisted as a distinctive substratum in later Greek. The classical Greeks vaguely referred to these languages and their speakers as "Pelasgian" and considered them autochthonous (*i.e.,* the original inhabitants of the area).

In the 1960s several scholars (Palmer, 1961; Huxley, 1961, and others) proposed to connect at least some of these words and suffixes with the newly discovered Indo-European Luwian language of western Anatolia. Palmer associated its introduction into Greece with Middle Helladic invaders, since the existence of Luwian cannot be traced in Asia Minor before about 2000. In his reconstruction, another movement of Indo-Europeans from Anatolia brought the earliest Greek-speakers to the Aegean close to 1500 B.C.

Other scholars identified the disturbances dating to approximately 2000 B.C. as marks of the arrival of the earliest Greek-speakers. Several sites were destroyed, new sites were established, and there are certain innovative features in the pottery and architecture associated with this Middle Helladic period. What is more, there was a distinct drop in the cultural level in many parts of the mainland. The interpretation that won increasing favor saw these Middle Helladic newcomers mixing with their predecessors over some 500 years, and, with Minoan influence, eventually creating the foundations of the powerful civilization of the Late Bronze Age. Initially, the century 2000–1900 was the usual date assigned to the arrival of these "proto-Greeks," but John Caskey (1964) made a strong case for putting their occupation of several sites some two centuries earlier. The first signs of the new culture traits associated with the "proto-Greeks" were located in east central Greece whence they gradually spread through the peninsula. Indications of similar changes have not been found on the Aegean islands or on Crete.

These Middle Helladic folk were associated mainly with a very distinctive wheel-made, gray "Minyan" pottery. We recall that this is the ware that Schliemann first identified and named at Orchomenos. He had found even earlier a very closely related ware in the sixth level of Troy, and there he called it "Lydian." Dörpfeld and Blegen later confirmed the sudden appearance of gray Minyan pottery in the earliest levels of Troy VI; and it continued in use throughout that long phase, dated by Blegen from about 1900 until 1300 (1963). The shapes of gray Minyan pots, with their characteristic sharp angular profiles and ribbed surface, seem in many cases to have been copied from metal prototypes, and it is possible that the distinctive color and fabric were meant to simulate silver. A special surface sheen was produced by firing the clay under reduction conditions by which smoke penetrates the fabric. The makers apparently brought with them to Greece both the potter's wheel and the knowledge of this special technique of firing their pottery. Earlier and rather desperate theories that the pottery itself or the "molds" or even the clay was imported should be completely discarded.

The occurrence in the Troad and in Greece of pottery made by the same technique and in the same distinctive shapes had larger significance. Examination of similarities led Blegen to the conclusion that "two invading groups, one on the east, one on the west of the Aegean, make their appearance at the same time. . . . Must we not, therefore, conclude that these two groups were kinsmen, branches of one and the same stock?" (1963, 145–146). Since no earlier stages of Minyan ware are detected in Greece and prototypes were available for the Troad, the direction of folk movement was thought to be from east to west (Forsdyke, 1914; Guthrie, 1964).

After closer examination of the ceramic evidence, however, the case has lost some of its force. Caskey has shown that several mainland sites (Lefkandi, Berbati, and Lerna) evidence a local development of gray Minyan ware from earlier, cruder pottery. And studies by J. Mellaart and D. French have demonstrated that the gray Minyan ware of Troy VI is not intrusive but is a development of gray pottery already present in Troy V. What is more, the shapes of gray ware from the Troad and the mainland of Greece are not identical, as previously thought. Consequently, we must now admit that these pottery styles probably developed independently on both sides of the Aegean. However, it is entirely possible that contact through modest trade played a role in the later development of the gray Minyan ware as well as in other cultural areas (French, 1973: 51).

Other features of Middle Helladic culture which have regularly been associated with newcomers are houses with a megaron plan and an apsidal rear wall, intramural burials around or even under the houses, and domestication of the horse. The cumulative significance of these features is impressive but, at present, it appears that they may have been acquired at different times. In some cases, similar features have been detected in the Early Helladic period, as we have seen to be the case with Minyan ware. And as excavation continues, some aspects of the evidence change. For example, when Professor McDonald wrote his conclusion in 1966, there was very little (if any) dependable evidence for the presence of horses in mainland towns of the Middle Helladic period. Horse bones are now attested for some Middle Helladic sites, for example Lerna and Marathon. In other words, the picture is not uniform throughout the mainland. The artefacts used to demonstrate immigration may have been introduced at widely different times and be completely without interconnection, or they may have evolved locally.

As we have seen, it has been widely believed that the introducers of the new practices and products were the first "Greek speakers" in the peninsula. For example, Sterling Dow insisted in 1960 that "Greeks came to Greece by the start of MHI: that may be regarded now as certain" (4). This proposition, however, rests on inference and not on direct evidence, archaeological or otherwise. The relevant points usually cited are: (1) that about 1400 (if Evans' date for the Linear B tablets from Knossos is accepted) an early form of what is unmistakably Greek was in use; and (2) that before 1400 no major cultural "break" has been detected in the archaeological picture until one backs up to the advent of the "gray Minyan people." Actually, the second point has been challenged by those who infer considerable cultural disturbance at the time of the appearance of the Shaft Grave dynasty of Mycenae in the late seventeenth century; but this view has not been widely accepted.

In any case, those who believe that the equation "makers of gray Minyan pottery = speakers of an Indo-European language" is certain, or nearly so, must support it with an assumption that a change of language is likely (or even certain?) to be indicated by radical changes in the material culture. Or, to put it another way, they assume that in a prehistoric setting, when no actual written documents can be expected, one may use archaeological evidence for the intrusion of distinctive new traits in material culture as a basis for an otherwise inferred change in language. This was the argument Evans and Mackenzie used for denying Achaean (Greek) control of Crete, insisting that in the Minoan cultural record there is no archaeological "break," which they believed would have to accompany such a change. But, it has been pointed out very forcefully by scholars like Fritz Schachermeyr (1935), James Hooker (1976) and Colin Renfrew (1987), that this assumption remains in general a most insecure basis for asserting or denying changes of either population or language.

Joseph Alsop directly challenged the validity of such an inference on the basis of comparative analysis. He insisted that, given a conquering minority at a cultural level inferior to the subjugated inhabitants, recorded history shows hardly a single example where the language of the newcomers has prevailed. In fact, he argues, "in all cases the conquerors ended by learning the language and carrying on the administration in the writing of the conquered higher civilization" (1964: 218).

Another view of language development emphasizes the nature of present evidence. The striking metaphor used by Colin Renfrew is that our present picture is a palimpsest, the end product of millennia of development during which some languages disappeared without leaving any trace whatsoever for us to find today. The persistence of language might depend upon density of people speaking it; it might equally be due to a very few tenacious, isolated speakers. In other words, languages develop and disappear for social and demographic reasons as well as out of the linguistic processes studied by most experts (Renfrew, 1987: 268).

Such cautions are salutary warnings against a second assumption that is implicit in some curent formulations of the development of the Greek language. There is no compelling reason to believe that a new language (whether introduced by military, political, economic or religious means) quickly spreads to all areas and social levels. An Indo-European dialect could not have been imposed by fiat on the older population in Greece, nor have we any reason to assume it was so "naturally superior" or carried such prestige that it quickly crowded out competitors. Indeed, it is possible that, even in the later second millennium when the language of the Linear B tablets was Achaean Greek, speakers of one or more non-Greek languages still formed a considerable proportion of the total population.

John Chadwick's view of the situation recognizes these possibilities. He maintained that the period of cultural change around 2000 marks the arrival of "an Indo-European idiom which, after influence by the surviving indigenous peoples, emerged as Greek" (1963: 15). And in 1976, he wrote of the "proto-Greeks" who entered the peninsula no later than the nineteenth century where "they mixed with the previous inhabitants, whom they succeeded in subjugating, and borrowed from them many words for unfamiliar objects; and the mispronunciation of Greek by these aboriginals led to permanent changes in the phonetics of the language" (1976: 3).

Renfrew has recently formulated a bold new thesis that would place the origins of the Greek-speakers much earlier. In fact, his investigation deals with the origin of early speakers of all Indo-European languages. Joining the evidence of artefacts and of linguistics, Renfrew links the spread of Indo-European languages to the spread of the major economic and social changes associated with the "Neolithic Revolution." From an original location probably in Anatolia, the practice of agriculture seems to have been carried across almost the whole of Europe beginning about 7000 B.C. Renfrew argues:

> People have to have a reason for moving, and often they go somewhere where the resources they need are more easily available than at home. When

we are talking of agricultural populations, that generally means land and, other things being equal, people move from an area of higher population density to one of lower. (1987: 124f.)

While admitting that other things are not always equal, Renfrew demonstrates that newcomers must have some type of superiority if they are to make an impact, particularly when they are outnumbered by the existing population. In this case, the "powerful factor which outweighs almost all others when we are discussing the large-scale dispersion of a new population" is the increased numbers that can be supported by farming techniques over hunter-gathering practices. It is calculated that the subsistence techniques of early farming can support an increase in the population density of up to 5000 percent. Of course, population did not immediately or uniformly take such upward surges. Instead,

> the new economy of farming allowed the population in each area to rise, over just a few centuries from perhaps 0.1 persons per square kilometre to something like 5 or 10 per square kilometre. As the model predicts, with only small, local movements of twenty or thirty kilometres, this would gradually result in the peopling of the whole of Europe by a farming population, the descendants of the first European farmers. (1987: 150)

In the process of movement, the language of those earliest farmers would have also spread across Europe, changing over the centuries into dialects and eventually into distinct though cognate languages (Fig. 113). In some cases, the languages of the earlier, Mesolithic people who may have spoken "relict" tongues like Etruscan, Basque and Iberian may have prevailed.

Renfrew's argument is far more sophisticated than this bare summary suggests. He postulates various models to explain language displacement and argues for differences in the actual process of transformation, particularly between the development of western and eastern Indo-European languages. The recentness of its statement means that it is still under judgment. In 1988, *Current Anthropology,* for example, devoted thirty-one pages to its précis and review (volume 29, no. 3). Because of its magnitude, the thesis will also generate a variety of opinions. As Renfrew concluded his book, if theory is proven correct, it "impinges upon all those areas of study where the early histories of peoples and of nations are considered to be of significance" (1987: 272).

What does this daring hypothesis suggest in terms of reconstructing developments in early Greece? In the first place, it relocates the origin of the Greek-speakers to a far earlier time. The latest archaeological evidence indicates that farming techniques were being practiced in Greece well before 6000. There are strong indications of contact between Anatolia and the earliest Neolithic cultures of Greece, including Crete. Evidence from the Franchthi Cave, for instance, sup-

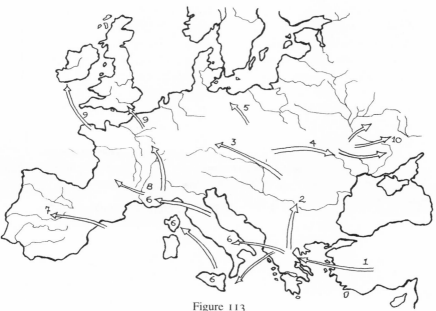

Figure 113

ports the hypothesis that the village-farming way of life spread westward across the Aegean. However, Renfrew's new theory also dates to the seventh millennium the linguistic transformation that ultimately led to the Greek language in its earliest known form. If accepted, this idea will radically change our interpretation of subsequent culture "breaks" that have been identified as indicating the arrival of the first Greek-speakers.

We have seen that there are several periods in which such breaks have been identified, particularly the end of the fourth millennium, the end of the third millennium, and at some point in the last two centuries of the second millennium. In fact, the belief that newcomers arrived at all three points in time was conducive to a "wave theory" of invasion, with each wave bringing a different form, or dialect, of Greek. A major objection to such a view is that there are either too few waves or too many. Must we, for example, insert another arrival at the start of the Late Bronze Age in Greece, as Palmer argued? Are all important cultural changes to be associated with population movements? There are very good grounds for answering "no," as we shall see in reviewing events at the end of the Mycenaean Age. Renfrew holds that, apart from an assemblage of pottery found at several maritime Greek sites dating to ca. 2200, "it is difficult to find any major assemblage of finds from prehistoric Greece which shows an outside origin, such as would indicate a displacement of people." Instead, "the story in

Greece . . . seems to be one of substantial continuity, with some occasional dis-
placements" (1987: 176).

The formation of the Greek language seems to accord with this view of cultural development. Geographical place-names identified as "pre-Greek" are
firmly embedded in the language; the Greek dialects were in process of formation
at least as early as the second millennium, and traces of differentiation can be
found in the Linear B tablets. In other words, Greek has been in process of transformation for a very long time before and after its Classical form. As Sir John
Myres sensed many years ago, all criteria demonstrating Greek unity fail (1930:
531). "The Greeks of classical times were of mixed descent, spoke different dialects of a hybrid language, combined Olympian with chthonic cults and rituals,
contrasted Doric and Ionic manners and ideas . . . and their traditions intermixed
indigenous stocks, which were not Greeks, with immigrant culture-heroes. . . ."

Not only the Greek language but the Greeks themselves were ever in the process of becoming. On present evidence, we can now theorize that prehistoric incursions into Greece may well have taken place at the end of the Early Helladic
or the beginning of the Middle Helladic period; but massive cultural and racial
change probably did not occur after Neolithic times.

THE EARLY MYCENAEANS
(ABOUT 1600 – 1400)

There appears to have been a quite sudden burst of energy, prosperity and foreign contacts in at least some Middle Helladic communities a generation or two
before and after 1600. This phenomenon is still most startlingly exemplified in
the fabulous contents of Schliemann's Shaft Graves, although its presence is by
no means confined to the evidence of that single site. It is no wonder that the
fortunate finder concluded that these kings must belong to the era of "golden
Mycenae" and "wide-ruling Agamemnon." Nor should we be surprised that
Schliemann's friends as well as critics reached such incompatible conclusions in
trying to analyze and explain the contents of the Shaft Graves, since at first they
seemed to have developed without precedent.

The slightly earlier Grave Circle B does not solve, even for Mycenae, the
enigma of the rapid transformation from Middle Helladic stagnation to Early
Mycenaean dynamism. In fact, the new discovery adds a further problem as to
why there were two circles partially overlapping in date. But the newer evidence
does make less likely the theories of scholars like Nilsson, V. Gordon Childe,
Schachermeyr, Palmer and Stubbings (1965), who have seen in the kings buried
in Schliemann's Shaft Graves an intrusive dynasty whose founder had seized con-

trol and brought his own burial customs and wealth with him from abroad. The situation at Mycenae seems rather to have been one of sharply rising prosperity, as measured by kingly ostentation, over several generations. And the thesis championed long ago by Wace in regard to the local evolution of the royal Shaft Graves from the ordinary Middle Helladic cists has gained added weight with the discovery of the slightly older Grave Circle.

A phenomenon related in time and significance is the appearance of the tholos tombs. The origin of the essential features of the tholos may be even more controversial than that of the Shaft Grave. The earliest examples now known on the mainland surely had a long tradition behind them and may have evolved outside of Greece. The two areas often cited as sources are southeastern Europe and Crete. In the first view, tumuli found from the Middle Helladic period in Greece may have covered the prototypes of tholos tombs. Nicholas Hammond has attempted to trace the practice of tumulus-burial southward from Albania and Epirus (1967 and 1973) (Fig. 114). More and more authorities are leaning toward Hood's belief that the round tombs associated with the Early Bronze and the earlier Middle Bronze Age in southern Crete and in some of the Aegean islands may represent previous stages in the tholos tradition. As we have seen, in the Cretan/mainland debate Evans led the argument for Minoan influence, but he was not referring to Early Minoan origins. Major structural differences between the Cretan circular tombs and the mainland tholoi caused that source of derivation to lose ground in the 1950s and 1960s. Refinements in dating have shown that some of the Cretan tombs were built as late as MMII and that they continued in use into the Late Minoan period. It may be that it was the skills of sophisticated construction, not the exact form, that the Minoan engineers provided. As Oliver Dickinson has argued, "the architectural skills required to build a tholos were certainly not to be found on the mainland at this period, where there are no possible prototypes, whereas they are amply demonstrated in the Cretan tombs. The tholos, then, could well have been evolved on the mainland as a special form of tomb by Cretan architects" (1977: 61). According to the investigations of Marinatos, being continued by Korres, the earliest mainland examples of tholoi seem to come from Messenia. Similar tombs were soon being constructed in the Argolid and other parts of the Peloponnese, Thessaly, Boeotia and Attica. Beyond their rich grave goods, the amount of material and labor required in their construction bespeaks new wealth, greater organization and increasing stratification in mainland society. This is surprising especially in light of "culture's low standards of technology, limited range of artefacts, and lack of a strong artistic tradition" in the Middle Helladic period (1977: 66). There have been various explanations of the rather sudden and unprecedented wealth in the hands of a presumably native ruling class.

Evans was right in pointing to the strong Minoan influence, if not actual

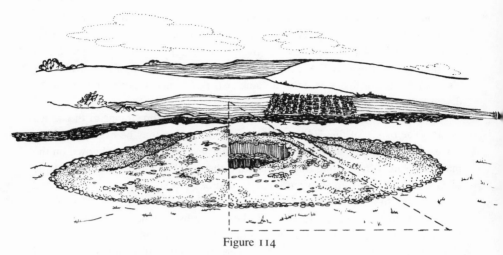

Figure 114

Cretan origin of many objects in Grave Circle A at Mycenae. The same conclusion can be drawn from a number of goods from Messenian tombs such as Peristeria and from the Dendra tombs. Items from the earlier Mycenae Grave Circle B show less Minoan influence, although the rock crystal duck bowl found in Grave Omikron is one example. We have noticed that Minoan skills must have directly influenced the mainland artisans at first. It is highly improbable that the later mainland artisans could have learned the new techniques so fast and so well without Minoan coaching, and there is little if any evidence on the mainland suggesting a believable native transition.

On the other hand, much of the pottery, especially in the Circle B graves, seems to have authentic, direct Middle Helladic parallels and antecedents. In this connection, we might profitably remind ourselves of Blegen's warning against fixing our attention on royalty alone. He suggested by implication that in the Prosymna chamber tombs there is a more reliable record of unbroken cultural development from MH to mature LH times. He did not detect in this record any abrupt change or "break" in culture patterns at the beginning of the Shaft Grave phase; and he regarded this as a strong indication of essential continuity in the ruling power at nearby Mycenae. Evidence from Nichoria, forthcoming in *Nichoria* II, apparently gives an unbroken sequence from Middle Helladic to and through Late Helladic pottery.

Yet another characteristic is apparent: much about the more elaborate Shaft Graves is new in terms of both normal Middle Helladic and Minoan culture traits—the deeper, bigger graves with multiple burials, the method of roofing, the profusion of weapons, the face masks, and the sculptured stelae. Clearly, new ideas were astir and new external contacts were developing. How are they to be explained?

Perhaps the emphasis on weapons among the grave goods of the period is a clue that the new wealth was not so much gained in legitimate trade as extorted directly or indirectly by threat, piracy, raids or outright war from weaker neighbors in Greece and apparently far beyond its borders. As we have mentioned, some scholars believe that the change is too sudden and sweeping to be explained on any basis but the seizure of power by foreign usurpers. Some used to believe that they were the first Greek-speakers in the peninsula. On the other hand, Stubbings proposed that the legendary Danaos* may represent a kind of collective folk memory of a limited number of Hyksos adventurers who seized control of backward Middle Helladic centers like Mycenae when they were forced to leave Egypt. He also suggested that the story of Kadmos' coming to Boeotian Thebes from Phoenicia (Syria) represents a similar and perhaps closely contemporaneous historical event. More recently, Martin Bernal has advanced an even stronger case for eastern Mediterranean, particularly Egyptian, influence on Greek civilization (1987). He sees much evidence for the Classical Greek view of their own past that links developments with Egypt and the Levant, and he suggests that this tradition was undermined by the modern historiographic tradition of western Europe that spurned a Semitic origin for their distinctive culture. For the second millennium, Bernal sees a variation in the intensity of Greek cultural borrowing from Egypt and the Levant. High points occurred in the twenty-first century, at the start of the eighteenth century when he believes Hyksos presence in the Aegean began soon after the Hyksos arrival in Egypt, in the mid-fifteenth century, at the start of the fourteenth century and in the twelfth century.

The emphasis on the importance of contact between the Aegean and the Levant is certainly correct, as we saw in several specific instances in the last chapter. However, it is difficult to identify a point of origin for the Shaft Grave developments on the basis of material remains. As Piggott has shown (1965), the external contacts betrayed by their contents are amazingly diverse. The gold and silver ornaments can be linked stylistically with the Caucasus and Iran, the amber with the far north, the horse-drawn chariot, some of the swords and various small luxury articles with the Near East, the form of the graves themselves and the burial posture with western Anatolia and south Russia. Closer to home, increasing contact with island centers is proved not only by the contents of the Shaft Graves, but by the mainland (Middle Helladic) pottery found at Phylakopi and Keos.

Perhaps it was not new but long-established leaders who were the final owners of the often luxurious objects. One theory explains the wealth as pay for mercenary service. Marinatos suggested that mainlanders were hired to assist in the expulsion of the Hyksos usurpers from Egypt (1960: 181f.). Pay for their services might have come in the form of luxury goods and raw materials drawn from many sources but collected in Egypt. Evans argued that the sudden change may be explained by the relationship between Crete and the mainland: Minoans now "colonized" mainland sites, he thought. Consequently, a sudden increase in Minoan products would naturally be seen in the archaeological record. The goods might have been produced either on Crete or on the mainland by craftsmen who were themselves trained in the Minoan tradition.

The relationship in reverse would have mainlanders obtaining the goods from Minoan centers, either peacefully through trade or by force. One could even suggest that all of the exotic contents of the Shaft Grave era derived from Crete, where they had been amassed from various sources by legitimate Minoan trade. And the objection that no parallels for many articles in the Shaft Graves have been found in Crete might be met by pointing out that the survival and discovery of the Mycenae treasures is an almost unique accident and that comparable hoards of portable wealth were probably stored in the strong rooms and deposited in the graves of more than one Minoan Minos. A theory of Minoan craftsmanship is also compatible with this view of mainland initiative. Minoan artisans may have been brought to the mainland, either willingly or as captives, to work for mainland employers. Their presence in considerable numbers would explain better than would continued raids or even intensive (one-way?) trade the extent of the Minoan influence by the later sixteenth century. It would account for the perfection of certain objects made in the current Minoan tradition as well as the more tentative experimentation with new materials and techniques and motifs that mainland taste and resources seem to have dictated. Undoubtedly, such émigré artisans might be expected to train mainland pupils, and it would have been the grandsons and great-grandsons of these masters and pupils who gradually attained a blending of the Minoan and mainland traditions to produce the finest examples of indigenous Mycenaean art. This result was, of course, achieved in the context of continuing intimate contact with the developing art of Crete itself.

The question of sudden wealth at the mainland centers is bound up with Crete's role in the Aegean and Mediterranean during the second millennium. As we have seen, that role has been debated during every generation in the study of Aegean prehistory. For the sake of simplicity, it can be defined as the issue of "Minoan thalassocracy," a view that was derived from the ancient tradition of a strong Minoan fleet that protected the island's "empire" and imposed Minoan naval supremacy around the eastern Mediterranean. The question of Crete's military power in the Aegean area as well as in the eastern Mediterranean during the first half of the second millennium is still unresolved. So is the extent of Minoan presence in the western Mediterranean.

Evans, of course, believed that the Minoans controlled the seas at this time. However, there was mounting evidence that, at least in the west, the sixteenth- and fifteenth-century Aegean vases and other artefacts were Mycenaean, not Minoan. It was impossible, however, to prove that Minoan ships did not have a monopoly or a share in transporting these goods. The evidence for the amber trade casts considerable doubt on the theory that Cretan ships were active in western trade. Amber appears suddenly in the transition from Middle Helladic to Late Helladic in Shaft Grave burials, and soon afterward in rich tholos burials in Messenia. The total number of pieces in LHI contexts is approximately 1,560. By contrast, the few amber finds from Crete tend to cluster in the Knossos district (Todd, 1985: 258, 265). The most logical conclusion is that it was Mycenaean ships that were transporting goods, including amber from northern Europe, from ports in the western Mediterranean. If there is a historical basis to the legendary Cretan expedition to southeast Sicily to bring back Daidalos, the context may be a period when a Mycenaean Minos occupied the throne of Knossos.

This was admitted by Huxley, but he remained a vigorous proponent of the position that at an earlier stage Crete was the dominant Aegean power while Greece was a tributary ally. He pointed not only to a strong tradition in later Greek history about a Minoan thalassocracy but also to a number of specific tales about successful Minoan expeditions against islands like Keos and mainland strongholds like Athens, and to various places "colonized" by the Minoans (some apparently preserving the memory by their name, Minoa). "In the Aegean," he says, "trade was followed by colonisation in Middle Minoan III. In that era, about 1600 B.C., the palaces of Crete achieved their greatest prosperity, and to it we may assign the creation of the Cretan thalassocracy by the kings of Knossos. . . . The Minoan navy rid the seas of pirates and made them safe for commerce" (1961: 3).

Without intending to preclude the judicious use of tradition, one must still insist that it be supported by some other kind of evidence before being accepted as essentially historical. First, there is the problem of whether this tradition is based on the exploits of a Minos who is a Mycenaean Greek or a Minoan. As we just saw, Huxley himself ascribed to the former the tradition of the "Minoan" expedition to Sicily. Also, one could construct from equally believable traditions a fairly strong case for a Mycenaean Greek thalassocracy from the exploits of the older heroes like Bellerophon, Jason and Herakles. They, too, travel widely from the Black Sea to Troy to Lycia and to the Pillars of Herakles (Strait of Gibraltar) in the far west. And, if the legends of their "colonies" are fewer than those of Minos, the archaeological evidence for the spread of Mycenaean culture in the Aegean area more than evens the balance.

Before we turn to the archaeological record, however, it may be worthwhile to think for a moment about the whole concept of "rule of the sea." Is the notion really applicable to a prehistoric situation? May we not be reading much later ideas of navies and fleets and armadas and maritime policemen into Thucydides' remarks, which themselves were made in the very different context of the Athenian empire a thousand years after the time with which we are concerned? Chester Starr asked this question in 1955 in "The Myth of the Minoan Thalassocracy." He argued that "neither logically, archeologically, nor historically can the existence of a Cretan mastery of the seas be proved. . . . The presuppositions which underlie the concept—dynamic expansion, trade preserves, a strategy designed to ward off the enemy at sea, developed warcraft—have virtually no justification when placed in the actual structure of economic and political life in the second millennium B.C." (282, 291).

One of the answers to Starr's challenge was a compromise between the two extremes. R. J. Buck asked, "Is it too far-fetched to see Kythera, the Cyclades, and a few outposts along the coasts as a Cretan defensive zone—a combination of buffer, forward bases, client-kingdoms, and trading posts?" (1962: 135). A fair portion of the trade could have been a carrying trade; there would have been no need of special warships or extensive military power if the activity was, by and large, peaceful trade. What is more, this interpretation gives scope for others to engage in similar activity without fear of reprisal from Minoan warlords on ships of war.

This position has found growing confirmation. The archaeological record demonstrates the occurrence of Middle Minoan pottery at many sites around the Aegean, including Lerna, Nichoria, Keos, the Cyclades, Miletos, Rhodes, Samos, Kythera, Melos, Cyprus, Thera, Byblos and Egypt, as well as possible contact at Delos, Megara and Krisa. Minoan influence is found in everyday items as well as in luxury goods and there are features echoing Minoan architecture, tombs, religious ritual and even the use of Linear A at a number of sites. The cultural influences were not uniform, suggesting that the relationships were not the same in every case. As John Cherry has demonstrated (1986), the first palatial period in Crete witnessed major changes in the scale and nature of palace organization. These changes seem to be associated with rapid population growth—whether as cause or effect cannot be determined. There is no doubt that the palaces served as redistribution centers, and it appears that the processes involved in redistribution spurred further advances in economic activity and organization. Those advances extended beyond the immediate territory of the palaces, even beyond the island of Crete. Overseas activity and influence appear to have flourished through the first Late Minoan phase, when there is a decline in imported Minoan products at many sites. At just this time, the list of Mycenaean pottery found east of the Greek mainland begins to grow. Over the past century, mainland products have been recovered from several Aegean sites; and, as we shall see, that number has grown rapidly in recent years. There is also the evidence, which we have reviewed, of Mycenaean activity in the west-central Mediterranean.

Although a case can thus be made for the presence of early Mycenaean traders outside the Greek mainland, we still must consider how they paid for the imports and how they acquired such "purchasing power." The same consideration seems to make it very unlikely that the precious objects in the Mycenae Shaft Graves represent a collection of gifts to the kings of Mycenae from their counterparts around the known world. Even though it is possible that the system of gift exchange so prominent in the Homeric epic was already well established among Greek monarchs and the once fabulous contents of the tholos tombs may have consisted very largely of gifts, it is doubtful that the kings of the sixteenth century could have commanded the respect of distant monarchs or carried on diplomatic negotiations with foreign powers or possessed the necessary countergifts to account for the contents of the Shaft Graves.

Another set of theories associates the appearance of wealth with successful exploitation of minerals. Wace's suggestion that Mycenae controlled copper mines in the Nemea district has been disproved by members of the Minnesota Messenia Expedition, who concluded more generally that "the type and extent of the deposit [at areas of copper deposits in the Peloponnese] makes it certain that there was little or no recovery effected in the Bronze Age" (McDonald and Rapp, 1972: 232). A related explanation was that of O. Davies, who was familiar with metallurgy; he claimed to have discovered near Delphi evidence for tin mining and smelting in context with Mycenaean pottery (1932–33). He noted that in the Homeric catalogue the area immediately south of the Gulf of Corinth belonged to Mycenae, and he suggested that Mycenae might have controlled the production of this vital commodity on the opposite side of the gulf. Although sources of tin in the Aegean are an enigma even today, James Muhly, a leading authority on Mediterranean metallurgy, believes that northwestern Europe, especially southwest England and Brittany, remains the most plausible source of tin for the Bronze Age Aegean, probably with other sources in the western Anatolia and Sardinia (1985). Yet another theory—that the salt-pan method of evaporating precious salt from seawater was a Minoan-Mycenaean patent (and if so of course an important source of wealth)—still needs expert study. It certainly was practiced in later periods of Greek history and is likely for the Bronze Age. But even if it is demonstrated to have been an important industry, it seems unlikely that salt production alone could explain the wealth and social organization of the Shaft Grave era. Commercial tolls exacted by those strategically placed power centers is another possible, although unprovable, explanation. It has been specifically advanced for both Mycenae and Troy.

A balanced view might be that in the sixteenth and fifteenth centuries Crete lost its former predominance in Aegean and east Mediterranean commerce. Whether Minoans resisted this trend in a military sense, we have no sure way of knowing as yet. It would appear to have been a gradual process rather than a sudden shift, but that does not prove that the transition was peaceful. In this connection, the events revealed by excavation at Trianda on Rhodes may be instructive. A Minoan settlement seems to have been followed by a nearby one founded by Mycenaeans perhaps a century later. For several generations the two groups apparently lived side by side quite peacefully, until the Minoan settlement was hurriedly abandoned. One inference is that the agents responsible for their departure were their Mycenaean neighbors.

Minoans and Mycenaeans interacted in several spheres, and so we must review current theories about the relationship between Crete and the mainland. If we ever unravel this story to general scholarly satisfaction, we are likely to have an explanation for the wealth of the Shaft Graves and much else. The background of events on the island is closely tied in with the two palace periods, separated by destruction at many important sites. A second period of destruction affected most of the palaces, with the curious exception of Knossos, which continued as an administrative center. The mainland situation centers on the sudden display of energy at the end of the Middle Helladic and the beginning of the Late Helladic period.

Devastating earthquakes recurring on Crete itself suggest possibilities for new local political alignments, as well as a tempting target for outsiders to take advantage of a temporary vacuum caused by shock and paralysis. Even before excavating on the island of Thera (modern Santorini), Marinatos was a leading follower of Evans in seeking to explain destruction levels on Crete by such natural phenomena (1939). He linked this theory with the tremendous volcanic disturbances on Thera, suggesting that the greatest eruption, which he dated to about the mid-fifteenth century, caused heavy destruction and loss of life on Crete and temporarily ruined the Minoan economy. If so, this would have made Crete an easy target for large-scale raids from the mainland, and it might have been the time when the Greeks asserted control of Knossos and eventually other parts of Crete. The proposed new dating of the great Thera eruption to the last quarter of the seventeenth century might then push mainland presence on Crete closer to the Shaft Graves. And it seems likely that there were earlier visits by mainlanders to the island, perhaps mainland raids, bringing goods and artisans to the emerging centers of strength in Greece. Successful mainland raids may have been followed by a shorter or longer period in which the Minoan way of life continued to develop wholly or largely independently of mainland political control. The first contacts may have created such a demand in Mycenaean centers that Minoan artisans and/or their products continued to be attracted to the mainland. The tenor of this hypothesis owes much to a general observation that the Minoans seem to have been essentially unwarlike, and the Mycenaeans a warlike people. There are some who challenge this characterization of the Minoans, but one can suggest two theories that might provide a historical basis that modern consensus still seeks in the attribution of these characterizations. Either a vigorous Minoan power was really centered at Knossos (as Evans thought he had proved) or some non-Minoan dynasty that occupied Knossos succeeded in attributing its ambitious acts to a legitimate Minoan power.

Some scholars still believe that the former is more likely. For example, Stubbings believed that the Theseus legend proves that Athens was at one time under genuine Minoan political domination. Those who support this position tend to conclude that the Minoan thalassocracy flourished early in the millennium, that is, before signs of mainland influence on Crete grew strong. This argument may be strengthened by the earlier dating scheme proposed on the basis of the revised date of the great Thera explosion.

An alternative explanation is that a group of Achaean-speaking mainlanders, perhaps with a veneer of Minoan culture already acquired through sporadic contact, took over political control at Knossos some time in the sixteenth or earlier fifteenth century. The "intrusive" mainland culture traits that Wace first pointed out at Knossos in Evans' LMII period (beginning perhaps before the mid-fifteenth century) still represent in the "orthodox" view the earliest time for such a takeover. But it is possible that they are simply signs of a later intensification of mainland control. Again, if absolute dates are raised by approximately a century, LMII begins ca. 1550. In this case, the first assertion of mainland control may have occurred in the wake of the eruption of Thera at the end of the seventeenth century.

Whenever the mainlanders first seized power, the process outlined by Alsop whereby a conquering minority on a lower cultural plane adjusts to controlling a more sophisticated people would have gone into effect. The previous Minoan dynasty at Knossos may already have been extracting taxes from much of that fertile and prosperous island, and the new Achaean Minos may have taken over the whole area intact or regained it with a minimum of violence. So far, he and his fellow adventurers would have been acting as we have reason to believe similar bands of Achaeans were (or soon would be) in other areas, particularly among the southeast Aegean islands.

No immediate jealousy or friction with other Achaean powers need have developed. But this particular group succeeded to no ordinary situation. They inherited a well-developed, highly organized administrative system, and it would have been very much in their own interest to preserve and even extend it. The Linear B tablets make it perfectly clear that they eventually regulated production and distribution of goods, although it is at present impossible to be sure how far back this situation goes. It may well be that the many features of Cretan palace building and administration made their way to the mainland centers after the Achaeans took control of Knossos.

Alsop contends that the first Achaean-speaking rulers would be likely to adopt the current language ("Minoan") and script (Linear A) as well as most other features of the sophisticated Minoan culture. In any case, we have to reckon with the fact that Achaean Greek is the basic language of the Knossos Linear B tablets and that Greek was therefore the official language in which the administrative machinery was conducted by the time of the "final" destruction of the palace. In chapter nine we discussed the several theories for the development of Linear B and we will shortly consider the questions associated with the dating of the Knossos Linear B tablets.

Not all scholars agree that the mainland features found on Crete indicate mainland control. In an examination of the material evidence, Hooker concluded, "the alien elements, though undoubtedly present, are not so numerous or so striking as even remotely to suggest that there had ever been an invasion and a period of control by a Greek-speaking people from the mainland. They indicate nothing more than a continuation of that symbiosis of the Helladic and the Minoan which, beginning in the Shaft Grave era, became still closer in the ensuing period" (1976: 77). Hooker further maintains that Linear B is a product of this same symbiosis: as objects, people and processes from the mainland sphere gained wider circulation, they were incorporated into the records of centers where they were known. Linear B is thus a *lingua franca* or commercial jargon resulting from the interaction between mainland and island cultures. Hooker makes the salutary observation that the kind of reasoning that led to a dismissal of Evans' theory of Cretan dominance on the mainland ought to be practiced in the issue of mainland control on Crete. While it is important to bear this observation in mind, many scholars continue to believe that mainland presence on Crete seems certain.

The larger question cannot be finally decided on present evidence. The scale may be inclined in the direction of occupation of parts of Crete by Greek-speakers from a consideration of subsequent developments. Crete was essentially a Greek-speaking island by the Classical period. If we are unable to use "Dorian Invasion" to bring Greeks to Crete, we may profitably envision a process occurring over several centuries. Some of the Achaeans arriving on Crete in the second millennium are likely to have stayed permanently. Over time their language tended to prevail, probably as their numbers increased. A thousand years later, though enclaves of "EteoCretans" were still identifiable, the island was predominantly Greek in culture and language.

Whatever the nature of their interaction, the cultures generally retained their own identities in the Bronze Age. Burial practices strongly suggest that mainland religion remained essentially distinct from Minoan. Although mainlanders borrowed much from Minoan artisans and architects, their products and buildings show noteworthy differences. And, even though it may be unwise to press too far the dichotomy of peaceful/martial, the militaristic character of mainland culture is everywhere apparent. As Vermeule has concluded, "from the end of the Middle Bronze Age, militarism was so congenial to the mainland temperament that both its aesthetics and its technology focused on the trained soldier with his equipment . . ." (1964: 258). Nor should this trait be regarded as an isolated phenomenon. From western Asia to eastern and central Europe through the second millennium a martial and aristocratic stratified society was developing. Like their counterparts in the Near East, the kings of early Mycenaean times were very proud of their horses and chariots. Everywhere, the kings or chieftains and their families were buried with utmost ostentation and luxury. Like their successors of the "empire" period, these kings were violently acquisitive of precious possessions and interested in them as objects of beauty and fine craftsmanship as well as for their intrinsic and prestige value. They mustered large labor forces and skilled architects to build monumental tombs that would one day house their families and their possessions.

In fact, the Age of Heroes in Greece can properly be said to extend back as far as the end of the Middle Helladic period. It seems initially to have had more in common with Piggott's "High Barbarian Europe" than with the sophisticated societies of Crete and the Near East to which Greece turned increasingly in the succeeding "empire" period. Yet, because of their proximity to the sophisticated cultures of Crete and the Near East, the Mycenaean kingdoms had a head start in technology, trade and opportunities for plunder. In time they adopted such civilized culture traits as literacy and bureaucratic palace administrations. In the Middle Helladic period, the borrowings had barely started.

Recent scholarship tends to regard culture change as a process extending over centuries and encompassing all aspects of life. The several hundred years of the Middle Helladic period were not static but witnessed the growth of consolidation of several basic skills: control over agricultural production, more sophisticated knowledge of metallurgy, recognition of trade possibilities and, probably, the practice of increasingly effective military techniques. The Shaft Graves and tholoi mark the results of the long years of consolidation. The earlier Mycenaeans, who diverted so much of the resources of their kingdoms to constructing and equipping an impressive receptacle for their mortal remains, were apparently willing to live in relatively modest homes and to guard the treasure they were amassing with much less monumental fortifications than in later Mycenaean times. We can be reasonably confident that most houses, from the humblest to the most ostentatious, carried on the Middle Helladic traditions. They were usually set on a stone base and had walls of puddled clay or sun-dried brick, occasionally set in a timber framework. Such structures seem to have been considered safest in countries like Greece, where earthquakes are frequent. The distinctive roof tiles so popular in classical times and later are never found. Roofs seem to have been flat or nearly so with wooden rafters covered by reeds, clay and perhaps thatch. The typical Middle Helladic megaron house with forecourt seems later to have been most usual for the dwellings of royalty. The general effect of a Mycenaean house was very different from the Minoan cellular constellation of rooms clustered around a central court.

The remains of the early tholoi prove that Mycenae was by no means the only mainland center that experienced a rather sudden rise in its standard of living, at least the royal level. It may be that rulers of no other kingdom in the early Mycenaean age could have provided as rich a complement of possessions to molder with their bodies as Schliemann found in the Shaft Graves; but kings in many another center were incomparably better off in material possessions and in the means to amass them than the most powerful ruler of Middle Helladic times seems to have been.

The distribution of the early tholoi also suggests that the territory that most of these kings controlled was much larger than that of the average Middle Helladic village. In Messenia, for instance, the results of the Minnesota Messenia Expedition indicate continued growth in territory as well as in population that was controlled from one of the new power centers.

Although the early Mycenaean kingdoms did not reach the extent of those carved out after 1400, the aggrandizement of a strong king's territory at the expense of weaker neighbors must have begun long before. It is fairly clear that most of the offensive weapons buried with the occupants in the Mycenae Shaft Graves had not been used in their owner's lifetime solely for ostentation. The scanty contents that remained in most of the early tholoi tell the same story. It is altogether likely that such weapons were turned against mainland neighbors at least as often as they were used overseas. Lord William Taylour's observation has not been contradicted by any new evidence: "It would almost seem as if they loved strife for its own sake. This element in their nature is conspicuous from the very first . . ." (1964: 135). Archaeological evidence as well as legendary accounts suggest that there was a recurring pattern in the rise and fall of various kingdoms, with no evidence of outside interference. An obsession with building bigger and bigger political units by force of arms was already typical and may perhaps be echoed in tales of the exploits of the "older" generations of heroes like Perseus and Herakles, who lived long before the Trojan War.

To organize and maintain the military power necessary to control far larger territories, the kings of the early Mycenaean period were probably able to exploit natural resources more effectively than their Middle Helladic predecessors. This age is likely to have witnessed notable improvements in methods of agriculture and stock breeding that were necessary to support the expanding population. For Messenia, the number and size of known Bronze Age habitation sites indicate an Early Helladic population of approximately 4,000, increasing to about 10,000 in the Middle Bronze Age and reaching at least 50,000 before the end of the Late Bronze Age.

This could well have been the period, too, when the Copaic basin was first drained (see chapter three), although excavation at Gla by J. Threpsiadis and Sp. Iakovides confirmed the previous impression that it was not extensively occupied or fortified until LHIIIB. Traces of roads leading to the gates of Gla, found in the plain created by drainage, might suggest a date later in the Mycenaean Age for the massive fortification project. In any case, a Mycenaean origin of the main system of dykes and canals is now generally accepted.

Even though our information on land use and on the technical competence of engineers is still meager, it seems plausible to argue that the spectacular improvement in monumental tomb architecture and in the ability to produce or procure articles of ostentation and luxury in the early Mycenaean period suggests that the bigger political units were made possible by corresponding improvements in the economic basis of the society. Whether or not piratical raids are the most likely explanation of the wealth in the Shaft Graves, piracy could never have formed the stable basis of Mycenaean prosperity. And trading, especially in the days of barter, requires that one have a surplus of desirable commodities to exchange. There is general agreement that the Mycenaean economy, even in its most advanced stage, continued to depend mainly on agriculture and stock raising. Goods manufactured from these products probably paid for most of the standard imports— raw materials like copper, tin, ivory and amber, as well as luxury goods manufactured abroad. We may at least theorize that the carefully supervised agriculture and huge flocks reflected in the Linear B tablets and the descriptions of lovingly tended gardens and orchards and vineyards in the Homeric poems already had their modest counterparts in the small but ambitious early Mycenaean kingdoms. The on-going search for solid evidence along these lines, utilizing all the analytical and comparative resources of modern science, is one of the most important directions now beginning to receive greater attention in survey techniques; future archaeological research should amplify present evidence considerably.

Improved farming and stock breeding would have formed the basis for manufacturing and processing enterprises based on surpluses of such products as oil, wine, wool, flax and hides. No doubt there was a certain amount of exchange of agricultural and manufactured products between independent Mycenaean kingdoms, but the increasing homogeneity of the material remains shows that foreign trade was a necessity. Basic raw materials that were unobtainable in Greece as well as many luxury goods had to be imported from abroad; and most of them had to be paid for in goods or services, even if piracy and war booty continued to account for some of the royal treasures. There is, in fact, mounting evidence of extensive foreign trade in the sixteenth and fifteenth centuries. Mycenaean products, reflected mainly in the indestructible potsherd, were penetrating to more and more distant points in every direction, and exotic objects appear increasingly in Mycenaean contexts. Appreciation of the significance of this whole process is as important to our understanding of the Bronze Age as recognition of the brilliance of the Shaft Graves.

THE LATER MYCENAEANS (ABOUT 1400–1200)

In the uncertainty about Late Bronze Age chronology in the Aegean, a date around 1400 still serves as a marker between the early and mature Mycenaean phases. In spite of Evans' vehement denials of growing Mycenaean strength vis-à-vis Crete, many scholars in the 1940s and 1950s reached the opposite conclusion. Some argued that the "final" destruction at Knossos represented a successful mainland revolt from Cretan political control. And these later scholars rather naturally inferred that a sudden upsurge in mainland fortunes, comparable to that of the Shaft Grave period, would have occurred almost immediately after 1400. In the next two decades, however, quite a different interpretation emerged: rather than being controlled by Minoans, Achaean-speaking mainlanders may have established themselves at Knossos well before 1400. Increased Mycenaean activity in the eastern Mediterranean may have stemmed from their recent challenge to the Minoan trade network.

Changes on the mainland should, of course, reflect this new activity. Developments on the mainland, however, do not appear to have been revolutionary. The early pottery styles merge gradually into the so-called Late Helladic III, with increasing mainland independence from Cretan models. During this phase records in Linear B began to be kept at the mainland palaces, indicating that the political, economic and social system was moving toward the level of centralization long known in the Near East and in Crete. Foreign trade was becoming more intensive, the population was growing rapidly, and the smaller kingdoms of early Mycenaean days were being absorbed into larger units.

It was once fashionable to account for these developments by noting the "short pedigrees" given to most Homeric heroes whose genealogies are usually traced back through only three human generations before the family claims divine ancestry. While students of the oral tradition like Jan Vansina (1985) have demonstrated that accurate remembrance generally encompasses about a century, the span has been used to explain major changes in Greece. Sir John Myres, for one, accounted for the abbreviated ancestry by suggesting that the families were newcomers to Greece who had seized political control only a century or so before the Trojan War (1930). Or a new ruling aristocracy might have been composed of native families who seized control from older local dynasties, although it would be rather odd if the same phenomenon was repeated in so many centers. Nilsson thought that a single group of determined and ambitious warriors originating abroad took over control of Mycenaean kingdoms. A variation is that those foreign warriors originally controlled just one mainland center such as Mycenae and later extended their sovereignty.

The role of Mycenae in mainland affairs is a particularly important issue for the later Bronze Age. Vincent Desborough was perhaps the most outspoken advocate for placing Mycenae in a special position. He maintained that only in terms of an overall unified political structure can one explain the remarkable phenomenon of the Mycenaean cultural koinê; and he believed that Mycenae was the center from which numerous culture traits, including pottery styles, were diffused to the rest of the Mycenaean world. He concluded, "I am firmly convinced that there was one ruler over the whole Mycenaean territory, with his capital at Mycenae" (1964: 218). Features of a unified Mycenaean kingdom have been identified in the Homeric poems where the King of Mycenae has a certain primacy in relation to other Achaean kings. For example, Agamemnon offers Achilles seven "cities" located on the Gulf of Messenia, which is far removed from the area assigned to the kingdom of Mycenae.[79] Certainly, the archaeological record, ever since Schliemann's day, has continued to suggest that no other center in the Greek orbit equalled Mycenae.

The position of Mycenae has been reappraised in the present generation of Aegean scholarship (Thomas, 1970); and, while the issue has not been decided, it appears mistaken to speak of Mycenaean political hegemony in the sense that Desborough described it. While there was regional consolidation around several important centers, that process does not appear to extend beyond each region. Present information indicates that road systems existed within but not between kingdoms. Of course, sea routes connected most capitals, which were usually on or near the coast. But, especially when navigation was closed by winter storms, supplementary land routes would have been necessary to maintain effective control from one center.

The remarkable cultural uniformity of the Later Bronze Age does not imply political centralization from one center. Moreover, as Desborough admitted, there is no indication that any one district took the lead in fostering this uniformity. It is possible to account for the cultural unity through trade and even migrating craftsmen. Consideration of one specific example will make the matter more concrete. Halford Haskell has recently studied (1984) the 119 stirrup jars from Epano Englianos published by Blegen and Rawson. It is clear that the purpose of this type of vase was storage and/or transport of oil in bulk; thus from their numbers it is reasonable to conclude that Pylos participated in large-scale oil trade. So did other centers using vases of the same shape. The Pylos stirrup jars do not differ significantly from examples found at other Mycenaean centers.

However, "all but two of the stirrup jars seem to be of local manufacture, match-ing in fabric the masses of plain pottery found in the palace" (103). There are some imported vessels, although not in significant numbers. In other words, ele-ments of a common culture and similar activity do not seem to involve permanent ties or a political relationship with another mainland center. As we have seen also in the case of the Ulu Burun shipwreck, the international character of trade need have no political implications.

What is more, there are indications that the Mycenaean world was not unified. The archaeological evidence reveals a discernible pattern in the rise and fall of individual Mycenaean kingdoms, especially during these two hundred years of the Late Bronze Age. The destructions that occurred at Knossos, Thebes, Pylos and other sites are not accompanied by evidence of foreign culprits. In other words, the agents may have come from within the mainland world. Added to the simple fact of destruction is the phenomenon that the sites destroyed appear to have been experiencing exceptionally good fortune just prior to destruction. If not the center of all of Crete, Knossos certainly was a leading organizer of eco-nomic and commercial activity on the island as well as beyond it. After the diffi-culties at Knossos, Thebes became an important merchant city until its destruc-tion, dated to the early thirteenth century. In the first half of the thirteenth century, much of the activity seems to have been concentrated on Argolid cen-ters, at least in oil production and trade. Pylos enjoyed greater activity in the second half of the thirteenth century. Coupled with the material data is the evi-dence of legend: Minos, a cruel tyrant, was undone by Theseus of Athens; the "Seven against Thebes" included heroes from Argos and Kalydon as well as exiles from Thebes itself; the ruling house of Mycenae seemed bent on destroy-ing itself; Neleus fought with his brother in central Greece, then moved to Mes-senia where he defeated the ruling king and established his own dynasty. If these traditions represent an authentic memory, they suggest a world not unlike that of Classical Greece, where fortunes of individual states shifted and rivalries be-tween states fluctuated with great rapidity.

A consideration of Agamemnon's exceptional position in the epic tradition does not necessitate belief in an actual Bronze Age political hegemony from My-cenae. In the *Iliad*, Agamemnon holds a position of military leadership for the purpose of waging a particular war. Agamemnon organized a force by traveling to the lands of other kings, asking them to join forces with himself and Mene-laos. When a considerable army had gathered, of which Agamemnon supplied the largest contingent of men and ships, the local kings made a vow to Agamem-non "to go home only after you have sacked strong-walled Ilion." [80] To these reasons was added the practical observation of Odysseus that "the kingship of many is no good thing; let there be one leader, one king." [81] That Agamemnon's position continued only for the duration of the expedition is made clear in several passages in the *Odyssey*. Once Troy had been sacked, Agamemnon's control appears to have vanished, and when he and his followers were killed by Aegisthus and Clytemnestra, the responsibility for vengeance rested solely with family members. No contest for Agamemnon's throne occurred.

Finally there are the Hittite references to Ahhijawa which have been used to argue Mycenaean unity. The kings of Hatti and Ahhijawa exchange gifts; the king of Ahhijawa is listed (but later erased) in the same context as the kings of Egypt, Babylon and Assyria; the god of Ahhijawa is summoned to cure a Hittite king; a Hittite exile is sent to Ahhijawa; the two royal families were intimate enough that Ahhijawans were sent to Hatti to learn chariot driving. In particular, the two kingdoms carry on negotiations, which gradually become less friendly, concerning a town (or country) called Millawanda (or Milawatas). Millawanda seems to be more or less under the political control of Ahhijawa and to have been located on the Anatolian coast. Most authorities now believe that the name represents Miletos, which in this period was a fortified settlement in which the pottery indicates that a good many Mycenaeans were living and that it might have been a Mycenaean "colony."

Yet, several difficulties surround the Hittite references; still vexing is the accuracy of the equation Ahhijawa = Achaia. The Hittite specialist Hans Güterbock confessed, in 1986, that "the Ahhiyawa problem is still a matter of faith: there is no strict proof possible either pro or contra" (33). Güterbock, however, belongs to the believers. Even if the equation is sound, the exact referent cannot be firmly established. Was it Mycenae or another mainland center? Some believe that hints in the documents fit better with an island (or islands) nearer Anatolia in the southeast Aegean. Rhodes is a leading candidate. Cyprus seems to be excluded because it was called Alasiya by the Hittites. The Hittite scholar O. R. Gurney suggested a Greek Minos installed at Knossos in Crete as another possibility (1961). The dating of the references further complicates the identification. In a recent re-evaluation, several of the references have been dated to the fifteenth, rather than the thirteenth century; and the situation prevailing in the earlier period may have been quite different. For instance, the Hittites might have known several different kings of Ahhijawa and may have sent messages to several locations, as Ahhijawans carried their products and themselves to new locations on and near the Anatolian coast.

Whatever can be concluded about Mycenaean hegemony, it is clear that mainland products were carried far afield during the Late Bronze Age. The fourteenth and thirteenth centuries mark the high point of Mycenaean prosperity. Increasing population as well as commercial ventures abroad apparently encouraged a good deal of emigration. Our picture of the spread of Mycenaean influence has been enlarged with finds of the past twenty years. While the Aegean may not have been a Greek lake, there are Mycenaean finds from the northern Sporades to the

Dodecanese, and there is increasing evidence of Mycenaean activity in Asia Minor. Similarly, the picture of lively trade with the central Mediterranean has been reinforced by new evidence. It is now clear that even on the Greek mainland the sphere of Mycenaean influence had expanded.

Mainland contact with Rhodes has been known for a number of years. Other islands of the southeastern Aegean now show similar contact as well as settlement. In a survey of Karpathos, Saros and Kasos, forty-four sites with Minoan/ Mycenaean material were identified. Even the tiny island of Psara had a Late Minoan/Mycenaean cemetery of cist tombs, implying settlement. There are Mycenaean walls as well as ceramics from Kos, and two Mycenaean chamber tombs were found in 1975 on Astypalaea.

As for the Anatolian mainland, settlement is now well attested at Miletos, where there was excavation of Mycenaean and Archaic levels in 1968. A megaron of more than 200 square meters, other living quarters and agricultural buildings date to the fourteenth century. In the next century, a massive fortification wall enclosed a sizable area of the site. Settlement is also attested for Samos, where three settlements have been identified. The excavator of the site of Iasos, where Mycenaean buildings are associated with LHIIIA pottery, believes that evidence there demonstrates the Anatolian derivation of Cycladic and Cretan civilization. A site near Erythrai has been identified as a Mycenaean settlement. Some fifty Mycenaean chamber tombs were discovered in 1962 near Muskebi, west of Bodrum, and were excavated in 1963–64. The pottery ranges between ca. 1500 and 1200, with a concentration of LHIIIA2-B. More of the same kind of tombs with Mycenaean pottery were found by Yusuf Boysal in excavations from 1963 to 1966. No contemporary settlement has yet been identified.

New pottery and tomb finds have been made at a number of additional sites from the Troad to Knidos and into the interior—at Besigetepe, the Bronze Age port of Troy, as well as at Pitane, Çandarli near Elaea, Klazomenae, Kolophon, Ephesos, Kuşasdası, Pergamon, Mylasa, Halikarnassos, Sardis and Tarsus. Further away, the Pontic site of Masat has produced Mycenaean flasks and stirrup jars along with Hittite cuneiform. At Burdur in the southern interior, Mycenaean-type ware has been found in cemetery remains. Of course, Mycenaean pottery does not prove Mycenaean habitation or even trade. However, it does reveal eventual cultural interaction, if only by such indirect means as down-the-line trade.

On the mainland of Greece, Mycenaean influence has been noted further north and east than previously known. In 1986, a large Mycenaean cemetery was discovered at Ayios Dimitrios in the Petra Pass, on the northeastern face of Mount Olympos. It is the first Mycenaean cemetery found in Macedonia and contains more than twenty-four cist tombs with several burials in each cist. Sealstones are among the grave goods. While not basically Mycenaean, a cemetery at Stathmos Angistis in eastern Macedonia contained imported Mycenaean LHIIIB and C pottery as well as local imitations. In central Macedonia, Assiros was excavated between 1975 and 1981 by the British School. Its twenty building phases span more than a millennium (2000–900); imported and locally made Mycenaean ware was found in phases 6 and 7. Kargani, near Thasos, has possible Mycenaean imports. In the area of Thessaloniki, there is imported Mycenaean ware.

Important Mycenaean evidence has been found in Thessaly too. A small Mycenaean tholos indicates the penetration of the remote area of Mount Ossa; there are chamber tombs at Mega Monastirion, where a toy chariot was recovered; Krannon and Elasson show only Neolithic and Early Bronze Age remains so far, but there was a Mycenaean settlement near Magoula Bunar Baschi. The site of Demetrias, excavated from 1967 by a German Archaeological team, shows a great deal of imported material; there is impressive Mycenaean material now from Pherai; Volos has remains of a palace under the modern town, as well as a Mycenaean tomb; Pretromagoula has Mycenaean material.

A similar wealth of finds is forthcoming from Boeotia: Lithares was a major settlement even in the Early Bronze Age; there is Mycenaean pottery from Kirrha; a cemetery at Lamia, previously thought to be no earlier than the fifth century, has Middle and Late Helladic material; a site at Drosia was occupied throughout the Bronze Age; Ypatai has an Early Helladic settlement and cemetery. In the northwest too, the horizons of Mycenaean contact have been extended to Prodan in Albania, where two bronze knives of late Mycenaean types have been found. Excavations directed by Th. Papadopoulos at Ephyra in Epirus since 1974 have produced Mycenaean materials associated with tumuli and cist burials. Mazaraki, also in Epirus, is the location of a rich LHIIIB cist grave with much Mycenaean ware; and in Acarnania at Mila a Mycenaean tholos has been discovered. Further west, additional evidence from the Ionian islands testifies to Mycenaean influence. Zakynthos has Early Bonze Age sites and a Mycenaean cemetery near Kambi.

The mounting evidence of contact between eastern and central Mediterranean has been sufficient to produce the assessment that "a new chapter of Mediterranean archaeology is in process of being written" (*Archaeological Reports for 1981–82: 83*). Islands seem to have been particularly important points of contact. From Lipari, 327 Aegean sherds published in 1980 suggest that island's importance in the first stages of the Mycenaean Age, after which Vivara's role increased. There are now more than 150 fragments of LHI-IIIB vases from Vivara. Sardinia, especially Sarrok, had strong links with the Aegean and Cyprus, as demonstrated by substantial Minoan and Helladic ware. In Sicily, more Mycenaean influence has been detected at Thapsos, and Late Helladic pottery was found near Syracuse. A Late Minoan seal was recovered as far afield as Tocra in Cyrenaica.

As excavators have turned to earlier levels of Italian sites, the Mycenaean materials have increased. The acropolis of Broglio di Trebisacce overlooking the plain of Sybaris has Late Helladic IIIA/B sherds. Several sites in Apulia show Mycenaean influence in pottery remains: Leuca, Otranto, Terminito, Torre Mordillo, Luni, San Giovenale, Monte Rovello, Narce. There are bronzes as well as Mycenaean pottery from Punta della Terrare in south Italy.

Mycenaeans appear to have been in regular contact with highly sophisticated cultures of the eastern Mediterranean as well. Egyptian references to Keftiu, often identified as Cretans, are replaced in the fourteenth century with references to inhabitants of "the islands in the middle of the Great Green Sea" and to Tanaja. The increased quantity of Mycenaean goods from the fourteenth century lends credence to the equation of Mycenaeans with some of these dwellers in the Great Green Sea. Mycenaean contact with Cyprus grew steadily in this period; and at trade depots such as Tell Atchana (Alalakh) and Ras Shamra (Ugarit), in Byblos in Syria and at Gezer and Lachish in Palestine, Mycenaean merchants seem to have formed part of a varied foreign population. As we have seen, the fourteenth century ship wrecked off the coast of Turkey provides even more concrete evidence of the interaction of the major cultural traditions of the whole eastern Mediterranean.

The major products moving in trade over this relatively large area included the important Mycenaean exports of perfumed olive oil, textiles, weapons, metal work, ceramics, and wines. The slow-pouring stirrup jar was a favorite container for transporting liquids, and its fragments are prime evidence for the extent of Mycenaean trade. Return products probably consisted chiefly of raw metal— copper, tin, gold, silver—dyes, spices, ebony, ivory, lapis lazuli and exotic manufactured products like textiles, fine wines, faience objects, ceramics, cylinder seals, bronze statuettes and carved ivory. Even the Greek words for some of these commodities were borrowed from the Near East. Direct trade contact with the Near East as well as indirect influence via Crete is also indicated by a good many of the favorite motifs in Mycenaean art. Hybrid animals similar to Syrian creatures were particularly popular.

Emily Vermeule and others have suggested that food staples, particularly grain, may have formed a major import, just as sections of mainland Greece and the islands in later times depended heavily on the Black Sea region, Egypt and Cyrenaica. The nature of the evidence virtually precludes a certain answer. As we saw in chapter nine, more land was brought under cultivation in Pylos, so perhaps a sufficient quantity of foodstuffs was provided locally or needs were reduced through emigration. Even if foodstuffs were not a major part of trading activity, the Mycenaeans were an integral part of the international culture of the Late Bronze Age. This fact will be important in our understanding of events at the end of the Mycenaean period. During the fourteenth and thirteenth centuries, however, Mycenaeans participated economically, culturally and militarily in this larger world.

Vermeule described the later Mycenaeans as merchants, soldiers and kings. We have just seen the appropriateness of the first description. The second has also been continually reinforced in the present generation of archaeological study. The massive fortifications belong to the later Mycenaeans. In fact, Sterling Dow theorized that the rise of the great fortified citadels may be interpreted as proof of increasing inter-kingdom competition and the desire to safeguard royal possessions. The evidence for growth in the size of kingdoms points in the same direction. The quantity and sophistication of weapons and armor, the use of battle scenes as decorative elements, and the thrust of the legendary evidence all reinforce the accuracy of the portrait. And, as we have seen in the Hittite records, it was during this period that Ahhijawans were particularly troublesome in Asia Minor. What of the third description; how did the Mycenaeans organize their kingdoms?

In 1959, Denys Page wrote that the organization was through "monarchies unlike anything that we associate with the Greeks or anything that ever again existed in Hellas" (179). Contact with older civilizations, combined with features fostered by their own earlier history, resulted in a series of kingdoms centered on a citadel strongholds in mainland Greece and perhaps in much of the Aegean islands. It remains an open question whether unification was successfully enforced by any one center over the others during late Mycenaean times.

The evidence of archaeology, especially the Linear B tablets, has shown that the citadels were redistribution centers, the focal points of life within the kingdoms. Raw materials from outlying districts and from abroad were stored, goods were produced and military authority emanated from these strongholds. Certainly, political authority also derived from the palaces. In the last decade of the nineteenth century, Tsountas asserted "that monarchy was the Mycenaean form of government is sufficiently attested by the strong castles, each taken up in large part by a single princely mansion" (1897: 336). With the decipherment of the Linear B tablets, that assertion has been proven correct. What is more, specific aspects of the nature of that monarchy have been revealed.

There are repeated references in both the Knossos and the Pylos records to the *wanax,* who seems to have been the supreme ruler in his own kingdom. In Classical Greek the initial digamma was dropped and the term *anax* was employed for gods, Homeric heroes, kings and in metaphors like "lords of the oar" (Aeschylus, *Persians,* 378). There has been a fair amount of discussion concerning the status of the Mycenaean *wanax,* particularly his connection with religion. The conclusion McDonald reached in 1967 remains sensible: "The Mycenaean *wanax* seems to have had at least some divine prerogatives or associations, as is still dimly remembered in Homer" (327). The elevation of the term in the Dark Age and Classical period so that it is most appropriate to gods favors this conclusion. Archaeological evidence indicates that the Mycenaean kings may have received what was considered divine protection and that they played an important role in ritual and ceremony. From the Linear B tablets it is clear that deities associated with the palace were of signal importance. The lords of mainland Greece—which certainly included *wanaktes*—were buried with elaborate ceremony and accompanied by rich funeral gifts. It is likely that these Bronze Age rulers had priestly functions as well as military and administrative responsibilities; but none of the evidence requires us to adopt a theory of sacral kingship akin to the status of rulers in some Near Eastern kingdoms.

The tablets contain a number of other terms, apparently for various officials. It would seem that in a Mycenaean kingdom there were two basic types: the more important state officials and lesser functionaries who exercised only a local authority. One Pylos tablet records the distribution of special "cuts" of land or *temene;* an official known as the *lawagetas* is ranked next to the *wanax* in holdings of temenos land, and it is generally believed that the *lawagetas* was second in command in the Pylian kingdom. A similar term appears in the Knossos tablets. The specific function of the *lawagetas* is not spelled out, but etymology of the word ("leader of the people") suggests that he had something to do with warfare.

In the same Pylos tablet that lists *temene,* officials called TE-RE-TA or *telestai* are listed in the third rank of holdings. Since they individually receive the same amount of land or seed as does the *lawagetas,* they are officials of some importance. There are a number of them listed in the tablets, and they have been variously identified as fief-holders and as religious officials. Another official called E-QE-TA or *hequetas* is associated with what are called the "Rower and Watcher" tablets that concern the deployments of watchers to guard the coast, as well as rowers. In this case, the E-QE-TA seems to have been a military position.

In addition to officials connected with the central administration of the palace, there were a number of subsidiary officials who exercised authority in outlying areas. The kingdom of Pylos was divided into two major "provinces," designated as "hither" (*i.e.,* closer to the capital and so probably the western part of the kingdom) and "further" (apparently to the east, around the Gulf of Messenia and inland from it). The hither province was made up of nine districts (designated by what is perhaps the name of the principal town), and the further province of seven districts. The official called KO-RE-TE has been described as akin to provincial governor; the PO-RO-KO-RE-TE as his deputy.

One other term is especially significant, since it appears to have had an important history subsequent to the Mycenaean Age. The office of the PA2-SI-RE-U or *basileus* was then a minor, local position. There are a number of such officials listed on the tablets; sometimes they are concerned with allocation of bronze or are listed as holding a certain type of land. In some tablets they are associated with a QA-SI-RE-WI-JA, variously identified as a retinue, an establishment, or a household. It is not difficult to believe that, as Finley argued, both the role and title of the *basileus* became more important with the collapse of the centralized control of the *wanax*.

Mycenaean society appears to have taken the shape of a pyramid, with a concentration of wealth and power in a few hands at or near the apex. Substantial houses within and outside the citadels, numerous chamber tombs and the complicated officialdom revealed by the tablets demonstrate the existence of an aristocratic element within the kingdoms. In Messenia, for instance, tholoi are too numerous to be associated only with the major political families. Here, and probably elsewhere, wealth seems to have spread to families of lesser status. It remains uncertain whether this stratum included "new merchant and professional classes," as Vermeule believed (1964: 156), or was composed primarily of near peers to the king linked by feudal ties of obligation, as T. B. L. Webster argued (1958), and Chadwick has increasingly come to accept (1980).

What is certain is the careful oversight of the palace economy. The tablets reveal that central control governed the use of the land, natural resources, labor and finished products. Archaeological evidence confirms the importance of supervision: both workrooms and storage areas are integral parts of the normal Mycenaean palace complex, and it may be presumed the ultimate responsibility for the supervision of these areas rested with the *wanax*. Slaves seem to have been numerous and appear to have been assigned to a wide variety of specialized tasks. The tablets show that over 500 slave women plus their children were attached to the palace at Pylos. Their daily rations of grain and figs are precisely recorded on the tablets.

The major crafts in which both free and slave workers were engaged appear to have been connected with various stages in the manufacture of textiles, especially woolens and linens. Other activities included the production and trade of oil; the making of weapons and other objects of metal; carpentry; shipbuilding; and the manufacture of jewelry, pottery, inlaid furniture and perfumes. The scale of industry is captured in details such as the 19,000 sheep (most of them apparently castrated males) listed on a single tablet from Knossos (Fig. 115). And the high quality of the manufactured products is demonstrated not only by many that survive but by descriptions on tablets, such as one that describes "one ebony (?) footstool inlaid with figures of men and lion in ivory." We have already noted the quantities of specialized shapes of pottery containers for oil.

In general, the economic, political and social conditions indicated by both the archaeological evidence and the Linear B tablets are remarkably similar to the highly centralized kingdoms of the Near East. In his 1984 analysis of the economic organization of Mycenaean Greece, John Killen concluded that the tablets give evidence that "the palaces controlled at least the bulk of the 'industrial' production of the kingdoms, and very likely all 'industrial' production that involved a substantial degree of craft specialization" (252). And he continued, "there is little question that . . . the palaces themselves played a major entrepreneurial role in the economy, and had a deep involvement both in the movement of goods and in the employment of labour in the kingdoms" (252). "There is clear evi-

Figure 115

Sheep tablet, Knossos 463
This incised clay tablet refers to over 19,000 sheep.

dence that the central authorities in the kingdoms maintained a direct control
over the taxation process" (260). Moreover, while it is quite possible that there
was some private bartering at the local, village level in the kingdoms, it is surely
difficult to believe that such activity was prevalent. Although there are some indications that the palaces generally may have exercised less direct control over
land in more remote areas, there are also indications of a continually tightening
centralized control of labor and resources. Especially toward the end of the thirteenth century there are signs of further consolidation of palace control over production and storage.

Blegen and others believed that the chamber tombs belonged to members in
lower strata and society, even the peasants. And it is true that the "people" (apparently referred to as DA-MO, *damos* or *demos*) are listed as land holders on
the Linear B tablets, on one occasion challenging the claim of a priestess to certain land. Peasants living in small villages must have comprised the largest portion of the population, and their economic situation may well have improved with
increased production and trade in the late Mycenaean Age. But a leveling of economic distinctions does not seem to accord with the evidence. We do not know

the status of people buried in the chamber tombs, which constituted the major argument for leveling. The number of tombs is not excessive for the use of a relatively small class of nobles with considerable wealth. Certainly, there are not enough known, even with recent finds, to accommodate a fraction of the free peasant population.

It is not easy to assess the social status of soldiers like those buried in the later Knossos cemeteries or depicted on the Warrior Vase. They scarcely give the impression of army privates. But most armies have elite corps and all armies need commanders. Chadwick believes that the *hequetai* or "followers" filled this need in the Mycenaean kingdoms. Their status would have been high, and the tablets show that a follower could own slaves. The tablets do not allow us to determine whether ordinary soldiers were drafted when required or whether there was a standing, professional force.

The question of "professionalism" has a bearing on the whole administrative structure of the Mycenaean kingdoms. How long-lasting and well organized were the systems we can dimly perceive in the Linear B tablets? The evidence makes it extremely difficult to determine how long record keeping was practiced at the Mycenaean centers. The tablets were not deliberately baked but were preserved only when accidentally baked in fires that destroyed the buildings where they were kept. Thus the preserved records date to the last year of life of the palaces. Some scholars believe that there are several tablets from Pylos that do not fit with the rest of the tablets; it has been suggested that they are much earlier. On the other hand, it has also been argued that record keeping was not particularly advanced on the mainland even in the later thirteenth century. Writing was not in widespread use; there was no private use of writing—not even graffiti—and the administrative accounts that have been recovered are essentially lists. Aspects of life where writing was employed in other contemporary cultures are without record in Greece. Oversight of communal justice, for example, was apparently not aided by literacy as it was in the Near East.

The absence of clear indications of extensive literacy has led some scholars to another interpretation. In their view, specific events occurring in individual centers led to the compilation of special records. Since all centers did not experience the same situations, records were not compiled uniformly or everywhere. The sense of emergency which pervades the Pylos tablets may be the occasion prompting the creation of that archive. Such a view does not dismiss record keeping from the Mycenaean kingdoms; rather, it proposes that literacy was a recent and sporadically used acquisition on the mainland. Written records surely would have been employed more widely had the difficulties of the late thirteenth and early twelfth centuries not interrupted, and in some cases terminated, the growth of the

Mycenaean states. But circumstances prevented this expansion and, in fact, seem to have completely eliminated the use of the Linear B writing system in any capacity. The Mycenaeans were absorbing lessons from other cultures around the Mediterranean where they were themselves so active. There was simply a time lag in putting the new information to work.

THE DATE OF THE KNOSSOS TABLETS

The question of cultural interaction is closely tied to the relationship during the later Bronze Age between Crete and the mainland. It is important to review the range of opinions concerning this situation.

We have discussed earlier the uncertainties that cloud the issue of Mycenaean political control at Knossos. Controversy is as heated on another problem concerning Knossos; in fact, the issues are closely related: What is the destruction date for the phase of the palace to which the surviving Linear B tablets belong? We have seen how Blegen questioned the basis for Evans' date of about 1400 and have noted the furor that followed. Tempers became even more heated in the 1960s, and nearly thirty years later, though the tone of the debate is quieter, the issue is not resolved.

In the early 1960s, there were three proposed dating brackets for the Knossos tablets. Evans' own final position was perhaps the most widely supported. He was sure that the tablets belong to the "last palace," which was burned about 1400, although at least part of the site was later reoccupied by "miserable squatters" who were presumably illiterate. At the other extreme, Professor Palmer insisted that the tablets belong to the reoccupation era, that the site was then occupied by the palace of a Mycenaean king (Idomeneus) and his descendants and that this palace was destroyed at least as late as its counterparts on the mainland, probably around 1150 (1963). A compromise position was closer to Evans but its supporters seemed divided on the reality of a reoccupation period. Sinclair Hood, for example, argued (1965) that the reoccupation period is a "mirage" and that the date of the destruction of the "last palace" and of the tablets must be reconciled with that of the latest pottery which is now usually assigned to a reoccupaion period. He suggested that the pithoi and Palace Style vases were already heirlooms at the time of the destruction and that the painted stirrup vases and undecorated household pottery should date in the Amarna period, around the middle of the fourteenth century or a little later.

In the most recent generation, the debate has assumed somewhat different parameters. Most scholars agree that a reoccupation period is not a mirage: after the destruction between 1400 and 1370, parts of the palace were reoccupied and used down to 1200 or even later. Disagreement centers on the state of this "palace" and its occupiers. Was Minos' grand residence reused as a palace, or had it become the miserable remains of collapsed walls and scattered rubble in which people still lived?

Few scholars press the case for squalid poverty. Peter Warren, while maintaining that the fourteenth and thirteenth centuries were post-palatial, believes that there was a thriving community at Knossos, as at many other locations on the island. Eric Hallager and W. Niemeier interpret the evidence to show reuse of the palace as an administrative center. A compromise position was offered by M. Popham at the Fourth International Symposium at the Swedish Institute in Athens held in 1984. He suggested the analogy of "the Ministry of Supply, evacuated from London during the last war and accommodated in one of the stately country houses of Britain, with clerks sitting in the ballroom . . . and in alcoves along the corridors filing cabinets and all, amid the ancestral possessions of the owners; the cellars firmly locked against intruders . . . and the family chapel available at hand for religious attendance" (1987: 298).

Support for this last interpretation came from British School excavations, between 1967 and 1972, of the Unexplored Mansion at Knossos, which we reviewed in chapter nine. Its "sad story of slow decline" points to continuity of use accompanied by reduced circumstances. Even with this new evidence, however, the case is not closed. What is needed is an accurate dating of the Knossos tablets. If the tablets were written during the reoccupation period, an administrative center seems to be the best definition of Knossos in the Late Bronze Age. However, if the tablets are remains from the fifteenth century or early decades of the fourteenth, which were then mixed indiscriminately with later debris, the administrative functions of Knossos are likely to have ceased before the reoccupation.

A decision on the issue of the date of the Knossos archive bears significantly on the role of Mycenaeans at Knossos. The presence of Linear B tablets indicates the presence of speakers of the language the script embodies. If the Knossos records date to the fifteenth century, the thesis of Mycenaean rulers at Knossos in the mid second millennium is probable. If the records date to the fourteenth or thirteenth century, the Mycenaean presence at Knossos may have to be connected with this later period.

The archaeological evidence is not conclusive. Similarity of pottery can result from trade as well as domination or co-settlement; increased numbers of weapons could be the product of internal developments; the chamber tomb may be a Minoan development rather than an import from the mainland. To be sure, the argument runs, individual mainlanders may have lived on Crete, employed as mercenaries, perhaps, or in other capacities.

Quite another interpretation of the physical remains emerges when the tablets are dated to the fifteenth century. Then a new militaristic spirit, shown in the Knossos arsenal, points to the mainland as does the appearance of the Palace Style of pottery. Certain innovations in fresco painting and architectural features parallel examples from Mycenaean sites. Further indications of Mycenaean influence in the fourteenth century may be seen as the fruits of initial settlement.

Most scholars believe in a period when a sizable number of Mycenaeans resided at Knossos. More than residents, the Mycenaeans are usually, but not always, pictured as rulers of at least some portion of the island. Such a picture raises the further question of the destructions at Knossos in the fifteenth and fourteenth centuries. Were Mycenaeans responsible on one or both occasions?

Professor Dow theorized (1960) that Minoan resistance to Achaean control in those days proved as desperate as the modern Cretan reaction to Turkish and (most recently) to German occupation. He suggested that in utter exasperation the Achaean forces themselves put the torch to Knossos and other Minoan centers and left the rebellious islanders to their own devices. But this is surely as desperate an explanation as the supposed plight of the occupation forces. Would those in control, no matter how harassed, voluntarily give up the ample income that the tablets prove was being collected in the very year of the destruction? And, as mentioned above, the picture we have rightly or wrongly formed of the Bronze Age Cretans suggests that last-ditch resistance was hardly their forte. If it was, Professor A. Severyns' theory (1960) of a massive native rebellion and capture of the capital held by the hated interlopers would be a more likely explanation. But in either case, there is no hint of impending difficulties in the tablets.

It seems somewhat more likely that the fate of Knossos is to be attributed to the same general cause as is reflected in the legends about Troy and Thebes and Kalydon. If there is anything we know of the Mycenaeans from myth and archaeology, it is that they were restless, aggressive, thin-skinned, acquisitive. If Mycenaeans gained control of Knossos, we know from the tablets how rich a prize they seized. It is altogether believable that another group of mainlanders should have decided to pillage this rich center, even though it was controlled by their own kinsmen. There is archaeological as well as traditional evidence to suggest that the Greek world was no more unified in the Bronze Age than it was during the Classical period. As at Troy and apparently at Thebes, the attackers may have planned simply to destroy and not to supplant. Whether they had a deeper economic motive than pillage is not clear. Possibly the Knossian Achaeans posed a threat or impediment to the conquerors' trade routes or to a planned manufacturing monopoly or source of raw materials, but it is at least as likely that the motive was endemic piracy, perhaps coupled with some personal or dynastic feud. To Dow's question "Why did Mykenai kill a goose that was laying golden eggs?" we can perhaps answer that one group of Mycenaeans killed the goose that was laying golden eggs for another group of Mycenaeans.

The known facts might even be manipulated to conform to the Minoan thalassocracy and the Theseus legend. Might the Achaean dynasts at Knossos have seized control of one or more vulnerable areas outside of Crete? Unfortunately for our theory, very few, if any, non-Cretan place-names have been authenticated in the Knossos tablets. But after all, there is the tradition of the expedition against Sicily that Professor Huxley believed was led by an Achaean Minos. Could an Achaean Minos have for a short time exacted tribute from Athens? If so, might Athens have taken the lead in organizing an expedition from the mainland to rid the Aegean once and for all of the oppressors who were identified in later legend as Minos and his bull?

Even if the destroyers of Knossos were Achaeans, did mainlanders remain in any significant numbers? The island's history toward the end of the Late Bronze Age is still not well known. In 1964, Desborough reflected the standard opinion when he described the Cretan situation in the last two centuries of the Bronze Age as a "period of stagnation" (229). More recently, archaeologists write of peaceful, even prosperous conditions in the fourteenth and thirteenth centuries. Even though palatial life had largely, if not entirely, disappeared, settlement continued at older sites and new settlements were founded, many of them inland rather than coastal. Continuity from the Minoan past is clear, yet there are also signs of Mycenaean influence such as the megaron at Ayia Triada, another megaron house at Gournia, the house with central hearth at Chania, the fixed hearths at Kommos, the Shaft Grave construction at Arkhanes. All these features date to LMIIIA2.

A relatively prosperous Cretan economy explains several curiosities not understandable within the context of the earlier view of stagnant conditions. We recall Furumark's insistence on a renewal of Cretan influence on mainland ceramics toward the end of the Bronze Age. Again, Catling's analyses prove that some of the stirrup jars found in the palace at Thebes were made and identified with Linear B writing in eastern Crete; and there seems to be at least an even chance that their date is later than mid-fourteenth century. Also, if the muster roll in *Iliad* II can be trusted (and informed opinion increasingly supports its authenticity), Crete was one of the most prosperous areas of the Mycenaean orbit at or not too far from the time of the Trojan War. It is portrayed as having some kind of unified political organization under King Idomeneus of Knossos. Numerous passages in the Homeric poems offer additional testimony of Cretan wealth and importance. These passages would seem on their face to have as good a chance of representing authentic Mycenaean echoes as the references to the mainland kingdoms. Even without a proper palace, an Idomeneus may have commanded a sizable domain that was able to furnish sufficient aid to Agamemnon at Troy.

Interaction of the Minoan and Mycenaean cultural traditions is certain; it is the nature of the interaction and the chronology of its tempo that remain unclear. Popham has written:

> We still require some selfless and conscientious scholar, experienced in excavation, who will continue the work of Boardman, Palmer and others, and who will compile for us an excavation report of the Palace based on the excavation notebooks, Evans's photographic archive and the surviving finds, some of which, like the sealings, have yet to be fully published. Until this is done, it may be that not much progress can be made towards answering the problem which puzzles me or towards testing the validity of some of the theories about the Palace. . . . (1987: 298f.)

In many ways, Minos' palace remains an enigma wrapped in mystery.

THE TROJAN WAR

Very few authorities nowadays doubt that Schliemann correctly identified the site of Hissarlik as Troy. There are, however, skeptics who see no compelling reason to believe that the Greeks ever attacked and destroyed the fortress at Hissarlik. Moses Finley, for example, argued (1964) that Hissarlik may have been destroyed in the Late Bronze Age but that the agents were either marauding Sea People or other inhabitants of Asia Minor. "Achaeans" may have been among the marauders. Memory of their participation in this raid, Finley continued, was later distorted into the heroic tradition of the Homeric epics. Finley has been challenged by both archaeologists and students of the epic tradition who maintain that there is more evidence for a traditional view than there is for the marauder thesis.

Others are dissatisfied either with the date assigned by Blegen to Level VIIa or with its identification in preference to Level VI as the object of the siege. Gray, for instance, stressed the "curious accuracy" of the description of Troy in the *Iliad* and suggested that it is based on Mycenaean memory of the power and wealth of Troy VI somehow conflated with its poorer successor (1954). Recent reevaluation of the evidence suggests that defenders of both positions may be correct: that there really was an organized war during the thirteenth century when

Troy flourished, but that its final destruction occurred in the random raiding activities that characterized the twelfth century.

As we have seen, there is increasing evidence of frequent contact between mainland Greece and the Asia Minor coast from the fifteenth century. But these activities seem to have been curtailed in the later centuries of the Bronze Age. For some scholars like Emily Vermeule, this picture, together with pre-Mycenaean elements in the poetic tradition, suggests that the tradition of the Trojan War grew out of conflicts of the early Mycenaean era. "Suppose what we always thought is wrong, that the *Iliad* is pre-palatial after all, and really belongs in the generations when the Greeks and Cretans were joining and clashing, at Knossos or Trianda or Miletos, and rioting in Anatolia like Atarrissyas and his one hundred chariots?" (1986: 90). Certain Hittite tablets, with references to Wilusiya and Taruisa (Ilion and Troia?) in a list of places that combined forces against the Hittite king, recently have been redated from the thirteenth century to ca. 1400 B.C. If the new date is correct and if the Hittite references have anything to do with the Trojan War, the tablets may offer support of an earlier dating for the historical event that gave rise to the memory of war. On the reading of Alaksandus as a Greek name written in Hittite form in the cuneiform (Güterbock), it is possible to settle a Greek ruler on the Wilusan throne!

Hittite difficulties with Wilusa seem to have occurred several times, one of which may be reflected in the material evidence from Hissarlik during the last main phase of Troy VI. There are indications of partial destruction before the final disaster to Troy VI. Thus, even if earthquake were responsible for the end of Troy VI, as Blegen believed, there may have been a major attack on Troy earlier in the thirteenth century. Hittite specialists have dated the accession of Alaksandus as king of Wilusa to the period just before Qadesh, placed in 1275 on the newest reconstruction of Egyptian New Kingdom chronology. During the time of Alaksandus at least one of the attacks seems to have occurred: the text of the treaty concluded between Alaksandus and the Hittite King Muwatallis implies that Muwatallis assisted Alaksandus against some aggressors before the treaty was made.

If these aggressors were Achaeans and if Wilusa was Troy, Troy VI may have been the source of the epic remembrance. This solution accounts for the strange mixture of pottery found in both Troy VI and Troy VIIa: the last stratum of Troy VI produced more than 300 sherds of pottery from the transitional ceramic period Late Helladic IIIB-C along with predominantly IIIA and IIIB material, and Troy VIIa included imported LHIIIB pottery as well as LHIIIC ware. According to the traditional scheme, IIIB ware dates to approximately 1300–1230 or 1200 while IIIC pottery begins in the late thirteenth century, continuing through the twelfth. To account for the overlapping of pottery traditions, many scholars propose lowering the date for the fall of Troy.

However, if the first calamity to befall Troy was an attack but not total destruction, it is entirely reasonable to find IIIC pottery remains from the site. Inhabitants would have carried on as best they could until the final destruction occurred
several decades later.

Discussion also continues over a cause of hostility between Achaeans and the
inhabitants of Troy. Such a venture is completely in character with what is known
of Mycenaean psychology and exploits around and beyond the Aegean. If Troy
was vulnerable at a particular juncture, the Achaeans many have been encouraged to attack. As in early phases of the Bronze Age, Troy seems to have had
reasonably close and constant trade connections with the Achaeans during the
final centuries of the Bronze Age. There has long been an implicit assumption
that much of Trojan prosperity was due to its strategic position, controlling the
water route between the Aegean and the Black Sea as well as the easiest land
route between Asia and Europe. It was further believed that the Greeks finally
acted to remove this impediment to their expanding trade. Professor Rhys Carpenter has argued, however, that the most direct north-south land route crossed
the strait farther east and that heavily loaded merchant ships of the type used in
the Late Bronze Age could not negotiate under sail the swift currents in the narrows of the Hellespont (Dardanelles) and particularly of the Bosporos. Light, fast
craft with a strong crew of rowers might have managed it, he suggested, and
perhaps the story of Jason and the Golden Fleece is an authentic echo of such a
daring and dangerous enterprise.

Actually, if east-bound seaborne goods had to be transshipped near Troy, the
old theory of exacting tolls on commerce would make more sense. However,
Carpenter's argument has been categorically denied, and the scanty evidence that
Mycenaean goods penetrated to the Black Sea area throws increasing doubt on
long-range economic motives for the war. Not commerce but fishing (especially
for the tunny) has been proposed as the attraction that led the Mycenaeans to
Troy (Bloedow, 1987). Remains of fish are abundant in later Trojan levels, suggesting that the resource existed during the Bronze Age. Michael Wood has proposed that "the archaeology of Hissarlik could support the idea [of] a sort of
Bronze-Age cod war" (1985: 166). A careful examination of the excavated evidence, however, has shown that the tunny is all but absent in Troy VI and VII. In
fact, representations of any kind of fish are rare on the mainland throughout most
of the Bronze Age (Mee, 1978, and Bloedow, 1987). The inclination now is to
attribute Trojan prosperity mainly to shrewd management of resources such as
raising horses and sheep within its own immediate territory and to see this kind
of success as arousing Greek mainland cupidity. In other words, events at Troy
may have been similar to earlier events at Knossos.

T. B. L. Webster maintained that the amount of Mycenaean pottery at Troy
indicates that there might have been a Greek trading station at Troy, as there ap-

parently was at Ugarit. He even considered it possible that "Troy VII A was a Greek-speaking kingdom and a member of the circle of Mycenaean kingdoms like Knossos and Pylos" (1958: 116). We have seen that several scholars argued for affinity of population at Troy and on the mainland at the start of the Middle Bronze Age. It is indeed an intriguing fact that, among the names so far identified in the Linear B tablets, about one-quarter are names that Homer assigns to Trojans. In Webster's opinion, too, it is quite possible that the well-documented "story of the siege of a town by the sea was elaborated for centuries in the Mycenaean circle, and then given a new setting in the East when Troy VII A was attacked" (116).

Denys Page (1959) produced an ambitious synthesis of the evidence on the Trojan War from contemporary Near Eastern documents, the Homeric poems and the archaeological data. Several of his main points have been accepted by many scholars of the present generation. An increasing number of them believe, for instance, that the Catalogue of Ships in Book II of the *Iliad* is an authentic muster roll of Mycenaean forces mobilized against some overseas target. Page emphasized the survival of many authentic Mycenaean echoes elsewhere in the poems. Only recently has there been a concerted revision of Blegen's conclusions about Troy VI and VIIa, all of which Page accepted. He studied the Hittite documents in which a power called Ahhijawa is mentioned, and concluded that it was to be equated with Rhodes. To be sure, there are other strong candidates.

Wherever it was located, Ahhijawa had dealings in Asia Minor. Page found evidence in the Hittite records that there was a strong rivalry (or at least antipathy) between Ahhijawa and a power coalition called Arzawa, which seized control of western Asia Minor as Hittite power crumbled. He suggested that, willingly or unwillingly, Troy finally joined this hostile coalition and thus became one of the targets of Achaean attack. This is at least a credible historical reconstruction and has come a long way from a war to avenge Paris' ravishing of the fair Helen. Page concluded that "our two sources—the Hittite records written at the time, and the Iliad four hundred years later—fit easily enough together. The Iliad is concentrated on one incident, the siege of Troy . . ." (1959: 111).

While the reality of a Trojan War may have become more agreeable to scholars, a few in the present generation have struck a sharp blow at the first excavator of the site. Schliemann is once again the target of the same virulent hostility that he contended with in his own lifetime. Since the attack on the man has a direct bearing on his excavation, we must briefly consider the new charges.

We have seen that Schliemann was regarded in a variety of lights even before his death. He was never fully accepted by the academic establishment of his own day; the Berlin Archaeological Society was particularly hostile. He was a frequent subject of satire published in the popular press, like the verse in the *Kladderadatsch,* "Pithoi mit Sauerkraut" (Döhl, 1981: 61):

Hier sieht man schon die Lithoi,
Die Priamus einst gebaut,
Und dort stehn auch die Pithoi,
Gefüllt mit Erbsen und Sauerkraut.

Probably Schliemann himself would not have been surprised to learn that debate about his work at Troy continues more than a century after his initial explorations. He admitted his own serious difficulties in identifying "Homer's Troy," deciding first on one level, later on another. He *would* be surprised, however, to know of the contention surrounding his own life and character. Not only is there a Homeric Question, and a Troy Question; there is now a Schliemann Question. In fact, Aegean archaeologists of the second and third generation may have made better progress in completing the task that Schliemann and his contemporaries began than they have in reaching a unanimous assessment of Heinrich Schliemann's contribution to the investigation.

The problem in reaching a verdict is twofold: the field of investigation has matured, as we have seen, discarding many of the techniques employed in its earlier days. It has become a rigorous discipline demanding specialized methodology that was unknown in Schliemann's day. On the other hand, Schliemann's efforts were truly those of a pioneer, supplying the base on which subsequent prehistoric Aegean archaeology still rests. Thus Schliemann cannot be ignored.

Personally, too, Schliemann was the sort of "colorful" figure who attracts and enjoys attention: a perseverer against huge obstacles, he was irascible, temperamental, unsure at times, yet full of conceit at others. So pronounced were these traits that they have attracted continuing attention. In his own lifetime, the hostility of the Berlin classical scholars was balanced by support from German anthropologists like Virchow and from archaeologists such as Dörpfeld. Later, even as German psychoanalyst W. G. Niederland was studying Schliemann's childhood conflicts as the source of his later obsession for digging, Carl Blegen was conceding Schliemann full credit for identification of Hissarlik as Troy. Recently, allegations of Schliemann's inability to tell right from wrong, coupled with charges of deliberate distortion of the archaeological record, have produced defenders from the ranks of both archaeologists and ancient historians.

Does the differing assessment truly matter? Terence, the Roman writer of comedy, matter-of-factly wrote, "Quot homines tot sententiae: suos quoique mos" (*Phormio*, 454)—As many opinions as there are men: to each his own custom. It would be easy to accept Terence's verdict but, unfortunately, that attitude would seriously affect all evidence that has any association with Schliemann. The current argument was first broadcast in 1972 by William Calder III, who has since been joined by others, perhaps most prominently by David A. Traill. They have concluded that Schliemann created a myth of himself; there was, for instance, no trace of a consuming desire to find Troy until he had actually found something. In creating his story, Schliemann lied about a number of things: witnessing the great San Francisco fire, for instance, and being entertained by President and Mrs. Fillmore. Such mendacity, the argument continues, is one trait of a character tinged with psychopathy. Other tendencies include superficial charm and good intelligence; unreliability, untruthfulness and insincerity; inadequately motivated social behavior; poor judgment and failure to learn by experience; pathological egocentricity and incapacity for love; general poverty in major affective reactions; failure to follow any life plan. The deductions drawn from this recreation of Schliemann's character are of most concern to us: "It would be remarkable indeed if an individual so inclined to fraud and deceit proved consistently truthful in his archaeological reporting" (1986: 27 and 130).

In light of such serious recent accusations, there is need for a careful re-examination of Schliemann's career. One such investigation was Hartmut Döhl's study *Heinrich Schliemann, Mythos und Ärgernis*. An archaeologist himself, Döhl concentrated his attention on Schliemann's archaeological activity during the years 1869–1890. He found much that is admirable in the record, including a willingness to admit errors both in excavation and in publication. While relying on Homer, Schliemann's dependence on the poet was neither blind nor total, since he recognized that Homer *was* a poet, not a historian. Schliemann valued the independent testimony of topography and traveled widely to gain firsthand knowledge of geography. Although some of his methods of excavation arouse panic in the breasts of modern archaeologists, Schliemann knew the importance of monetarily worthless finds such as potsherds. While traveling in Nubia, for instance, he learned how handmade pottery was produced in a faithful tradition thousands of years old. He acquired some of these modern examples of an ancient skill and offered them to the Berlin Museum for their comparative value. The speed of publication of his finds is especially impressive, even today.

Döhl's assessment is more convincing than the case of those who insist that Schliemann was a liar and a cheat. And, more recently, Edmund Bloedow has analyzed the case against Schliemann in a thorough fashion, deciding in favor of the defendant (1986 and 1988). Quite simply, in most cases the evidence does not exist to prove beyond doubt the truth or falsity of the individual charges. Moreover, the case as a whole is ahistorical. Accomplishments and individuals must be seen in their own historical perspective and they must be judged accordingly. Thus, to produce a sensible study of Schliemann's career, it must be set against nineteenth-century scholarship and opinion. Schliemann's character should also be evaluated within its historical context: the type of person attracted to archaeology in the nineteenth century is an important part of nineteenth-century intellectual history. Schliemann's rages, bragging, divorce, friendships, and wealth were not uncommon traits of a man who was successful in defining a new field. Is it necessary to judge the man before we examine the fruits of his labors? If so, we must pass personal judgment on the character of all of our sources. According to this standard, all anonymous accounts are at least suspect, if not worthless.

Analysis of this sort belongs to the field of psychobiography, a technique that shares the failings of psychohistory in deriving its facts from psychoanalysis, not from history. While practitioners of a discipline like archaeology or history have a subject other than themselves, analysis does not. Schliemann's subject was the material evidence of several sites that turned out to be important in the Greek Bronze Age. Thus, his legacy has an identity that can be evaluated apart from the man; it has been tested, corrected and augmented by the work of others, for nearly a century. The tests have been rigorous, yet the foundations still stand. Testing will continue and, in the process, Schliemann's conclusions will be proved wrong on some counts and right on others. Indeed, Schliemann's work must be assessed as part of the present and in light of the present, for it has been incorporated into the data of current archaeology. Psychohistorical analysis of the man will also undoubtedly continue, but Schliemann's character must be set in the context of his own time, without being allowed to distort our assessment of the archaeological legacy. Schliemann died in 1890, but his legacy is still alive.

THE COLLAPSE OF MYCENAEAN POWER

The fall of a great civilization is a particularly fascinating subject for both professional historians and reflective laypersons. Elements of mystery solving are combined with vague hopes that previous mistakes can be recognized and avoided. The fate of the Mycenaean power centers certainly holds its share of mystery, which we shall review but not succeed in solving. If there is any lesson to be learned from the following account, it is left to the individual reader's perception.

The events associated with the collapse took place during the century from roughly 1250 to 1150. Contemporary Near Eastern documentary sources seem to be relevant to the story, as Greek legend and early epic poetry may also be. But, as usual, this kind of evidence is extraordinarily difficult to interpret with assurance.

The archaeological material, too, is fragmentary and inconclusive. Nevertheless, it is clear in its main statement: most of the Mycenaean centers collapsed or were destroyed in a relatively short period, and there ensued several centuries that justify the description of a Greek "Dark Age." Since it defines the outcome, the archaeological data should hold a clue to its cause and we may begin with a review of the present evidence for the Greek mainland.

In the late thirteenth century energetic repairs and reinforcement and extension of fortifications are proved for such key centers as Mycenae, Tiryns and Athens. Even at Pylos, which remained without a fortification wall, buildings were restructured, making the palace complex a more tightly-knit, inward-looking unit. At several sites, large depots were constructed apparently for the storage of provisions, and elaborate arrangements were made to ensure that a safe water supply was accessible from inside the walls. What seems to have been a line of fortifications was at least partially carried across the Isthmus of Corinth at approximately the same time. Although some scholars believed that these were remains of a retaining terrace for a road, they are now generally accepted as forming part of a Cyclopean-style wall. These seem to be reasonably clear indications that a number of Mycenaean power centers anticipated some kind of serious attack. The fundamental problem is to identify the threatening foe.

Also, as we have seen, the Linear B tablets from Pylos may provide some information on the issue. In the first place, they were preserved by a fire that completely destroyed the palace. There are several hints that all was not well just before the fire: rowers are stationed; watchers are dispatched; resources and manpower of the kingdom are being tabulated. One tablet lists what Chadwick described as "an unprecedented group of offerings, thirteen gold vessels and ten human beings to three groups of deities." And the document is clearly "a hastily compiled record." (Chadwick, 1976: 96).

Later Greek literature, certified by Thucydides' authority, has long been regularly joined to the physical evidence to provide an answer to the question of the destroyers' identity. Every reader of Herodotus and Thucydides knows of the Dorian invasion and the return of the descendants of Herakles. Sixty years after the Trojan War, Thucydides recounts,[82] a group of Greek-speakers, on being expelled from Thessaly, entered Boeotia, and twenty years later the Dorians entered the Peloponnese. The entrance, according to Herodotus, was one hundred years after a first attempt to enter had failed, when Hyllus, a son of Herakles, was defeated in hand-to-hand combat by the Mycenaean Arkadian hero Echemus. Adhering to an agreement by which they would enter only if their hero were victorious, the Dorians withdrew. The most common traditional date for the latter event was Eratosthenes' calculation, which can be equated with 1184. Thus the "Dorian invasion" was placed about the end of the twelfth century. Until recently it had always been taken for granted that, although the ancient calculation is rather too late, the invaders were indeed the Dorians of legend who arrived by land from the general direction of northwest and central Greece. They were said to have bypassed or failed to capture Athens and then proceeded to conquer practically all of the Peloponnese before going on to occupy Crete, most of the southern Aegean islands and the coast of Asia Minor opposite them. Especially in the Peloponnese, we are told, they immediately carved out new kingdoms. Since these are the areas that gradually evolved into the Dorian states of historical times, it was quite naturally assumed that these invaders spoke a primitive Doric dialect of Greek.

Although scholars from classical times until World War II believed implicitly that this "Dorian invasion" was responsible for the ruin of Mycenaean power, the Homeric poems ignore it. There is no mention in them of a Dorian conquest of the mainland; only the Herakleidai * (descendants of Herakles) figure as attackers of certain power centers. As we have seen, Nestor remembered that his eleven brothers had been killed by a rampaging Herakles.[83] Their advent is described as a *kathodos,* which has usually been interpreted as a "return" but which can also mean a "coming down" (presumably from the north). Could the Herakleidai have been the same Greek-speaking invaders as the Dorians, or could the two have joined forces to attack the Peloponnese? If either is the case, did attack come from the north so that the wall across the Isthmus of Corinth was constructed in anticipation? But if so, why were the Pylian rowers and watchers stationed along the coast?

Problems such as this have emerged only recently. Until the recent generation, archaeologists and historians accepted Dorians and Herakleids as the agents of destruction, although they might differ about route and timing. Neat and impressive archaeological evidence for the Dorian arrival in the late thirteenth or twelfth century was confidently enumerated, in much the same manner as that for the invasion of the "gray Minyan people" almost a millennium earlier. In fact, for a considerable time, invaders were the usual solution to major cultural change of any and every type.

In the earlier view, new cultural traits were introduced between the Bronze and Iron ages. The most striking, it was argued, were the smelting, forging and casting of iron tools and weapons, cremation burial, and geometric pottery. These features seemed to mark as persuasive a cultural "break" as one could wish for, since they were associated with material, aesthetic and intellectual characteristics. Reassessment during the last two decades, however, has shown that these supposed hallmarks of the Early Iron Age came into gradual use in the transitional years of the later Bronze Age. Iron technology was practiced in Anatolia in the mid-second millennium and spread gradually from there to other areas of the eastern Mediterranean. The new metallurgy radiated southward long before it was known in Greece. Iron objects are found at Egyptian sites and are mentioned in written documents as early as the fourteenth century, and forged iron artefacts are found in Greece at the very end of the Mycenaean period. Cremation is known from the Bronze Age; in some Mycenaean cemeteries cremation burials begin to occur side by side with the usual inhumations. There is no hint that the families that chose the new rite were notably differentiated in origin or traditions. It may be that contacts with alien cultures, through war and trade, had long familiarized some of the Mycenaeans with cremation. A situation where warriors died in foreign lands or where refugees were living apart from their ancestral homes may have linked up with new religious beliefs to encourage its use. Moreover, cremation of the dead was not uniformly adopted even in regions where later the Doric dialect was used.

Moreover, in the pottery from the latest Mycenaean cemeteries and settlements, a gradual transition in most vase shapes as well as the beginning of the new "tectonic" decorative tradition characteristic of geometric times can already be detected (Fig. 116). Thus, not a "break" but a continuous evolution best describes the development of pottery so that the roots of Geometric pottery can be found in Late Mycenaean times. The final products of the eighth century look quite different from the thirteenth century work, but study of examples from the centuries between clearly shows the evolutionary stages.

There is more debate over a type of handmade, unburnished pottery occasionally found in late Mycenaean levels especially in the Argolid and the Corinthia. The view of some archaeologists is that it is intrusive, while others interpret it as part of the local, handmade tradition that persisted alongside the finer wheel-made pottery. (A sample of the debate is the exchange between J. Rutter and G. Walberg in *AJA* 79 [1975] and 80 [1976].) Increasingly, samples are being found in fully Mycenaean levels. For example at Tiryns, a nearly complete handmade hydria copying a Mycenaean wheel-made shape was found in 1981; at the Menelaion site there is significant Late Helladic IIIC1 pottery, some of which is handmade; at Aegion "barbarian ware" was found in apparently peaceable circumstances of LHIIIC.

As once certain indicators of newcomers have been called into question, practically the only archaeological evidence that may now be connected with the traditional Dorian invasion is the destruction and burning of Mycenaean centers. An important advocate of the Dorian invasion theory, Vincent Desborough, was increasingly troubled even by this evidence and in 1968 asked,

> if [invaders] remained and settled, why have they left no trace? Can one only really suppose that they were so primitive as to leave no evidence, whether in some new custom or at the very least in some new artefact? . . . If they moved on, where did they go to? If they went back, why did they do so, leaving the good land which they could have occupied?" (1076f.)

Desborough's questions placed the situation of Greece into a larger context, a perspective that is essential to properly understand the Late Bronze Age. Just as the Mycenaeans were associated with other contemporary cultures through trade and warfare, so too did contemporary cultures experience major decline at the end of the Bronze Age. It is more than likely that the situation in Greece had some relationship to conditions elsewhere. Concluding her study of the problems

Figure 116

at the end of the Bronze Age, Nancy Sandars reflected, "There are no clear-cut solutions to the problems discussed in these chapters, no rolling up of the map by a Genghis Khan or Attila, only a number of very complicated actions and interactions" (1978 and 1987: 197).

The records of Egypt describe attackers in some detail. Libyans and northerners from all lands attacked the delta region in 1231, and again in the early years of the twelfth century, Libyans joined forces with others attempting to invade Egypt. At least one group of would-be invaders is known to subsequent history:

the "Peleset" eventually settled in Palestine and appear as the biblical Philis-
tines. The weakened Hittite kingdom was destroyed near the end of the thirteenth
century. Major towns in Syria were also beset, and many were destroyed at
roughly the same time that larger kingdoms were threatened.

Collectively the attackers have been called "the Land and Sea Peoples" (Fig.
117). The names of some of the allies who made up the motley hordes of Sea
People are preserved in Egyptian documents; and a few equations such as Lycians, Sardinians, Tyrrhenians and Sicilians have been proposed, although most
Near Eastern specialists are very uncertain of their validity. Even if the equations
are correct, the names may refer to places where certain groups eventually settled,
not their places of origin. Some scholars have suggested that the Achaeans are represented by a group called Akawasha, but it remains problematical whether
Achaeans joined the Sea People in their attacks on the Near East and/or were
themselves among the objects of these attacks.

Even if not attacked by bands of these "Land and Sea Peoples," the wealthy
Mycenaean citadels, most of which were near the sea, must have been tempting
targets in a lawless era of large-scale piracy. Some scholars have suggested that
pressure from farther north may have forced the fierce barbarians of Illyria into a
destructive invasion. There may also be some truth in the assumptions so often
made that enterprises like the Trojan War had lessened Mycenaean resilience
against attack. However, as in the case of the Dorians, there is no archaeological
confirmation of outsiders in the destruction levels.

While the agent is still in doubt, it is possible to describe the results of destruction with some accuracy. These results may be helpful in answering the fundamental question of what produced them.

There was heavy destruction within the citadel of Mycenae, but some of the
inhabitants either held out or reoccupied the citadel almost immediately. Work in
the present generation indicated that the LHIIIC phase lasted three generations,
until about 1120 B.C. The northwest slope at Mycenae was still closely packed
with houses in this latest Bronze Age phase. The Pylos palace was burned about
the end of the thirteenth century. The era of Tiryns' prosperity seems to come to
an end about the same time: there are now indications of two phases of destruction in the LHIIIB period (about 1300 and 1230), although the lower citadel was
thoroughly reorganized in LHIIIC (after 1230) when the settlement was extended
north and south. The settlement on Aetos Hill near the Menelaion shows a pattern similar to Tiryns and Mycenae: violent destruction at the end of LHIIIB was
followed by renewed occupation of some considerable numbers. Strong points in
central Greece like Gla and Thebes suffered destruction in the thirteenth century;
Gla may have been abandoned, but chamber tombs attest continued occupation in
the vicinity of Thebes. The excavator believes that the final destruction of the
citadel of Iolkos took place at about the same time. Even smaller settlements

Figure 117

such as Zygouries, Prosymna, Berbati and Nichoria were burned or deserted, although there are known exceptions like Korakou.

In the Argolid and Attica the old way of life continued, although at a lesser level of prosperity. According to legend, Athens served as a point of refuge during the difficulties at the end of the Bronze Age. The Neleids of Pylos escaped to Athens, where Nestor's descendants Melanthos and Kodros became *basileis*. Melanthos is said to have won his rank after victory in single combat over a leader of the Boeotians. Kodros died defending Athens against an invasion by the Peloponnesians. Traditions also link the Argolid with Athens through the story of Theseus, who returned to his real father's home from Troezen during the confusion surrounding succession to Aegeus. It is interesting to find an intensification of contact with the Argolid in Athenian pottery at the end of the thirteenth century; additionally, there are a number of parallels between the Athenian fortress and those of the Argolid. In fact, it has been argued that Mycenaean Athens rose to prominence only toward the end of the Bronze Age, achieving leadership in a wider territory partly by default.

We cannot even estimate the proportion of Mycenaean inhabitants who survived the tribulations of the twelfth century. Wherever intensive exploration has been carried out in the areas of the Mycenaean kingdoms, there is impressive evidence of drastic depopulation in the decades following 1200, when the LHIIIB pottery phase was evolving into LHIIIC. In 1972, Desborough wrote that much of Greece had but "a shadow of the departed greatness" (25). More recently,

Anthony Snodgrass has described "a picture of depopulation on an almost un-imaginable scale" (1980: 20). Lefkandi on Euboea, which we have seen to have been a prosperous community by Dark Age standards, had a population of about fifteen people in the eleventh century. Mycenaeans who had apparently fled to, or already lived in, marginal and inaccessible areas such as the central and north-west parts of the Peloponnese (Arkadia and Achaea) seem to have fared better. Teichos Dymaion was a vigorous, fortified settlement that persisted until the late twelfth century. Numbers in these regions appear to have been increased by refu-gees from other areas. In these enclaves a simplified version of the Mycenaean way of life continued for several generations. We have mentioned the strong tra-dition recording that many refugees, especially from Pylos, reached Athens. The Athenian acropolis does appear to have survived intact, and there were some fairly populous late Mycenaean settlements like Perati along the east coast of Attica.

Both tradition and archaeological evidence inform us that many refugees from major centers escaped by ship. The Ionian islands sheltered a fair number, and there are indications in the following generations that some trade developed be-tween Kephallenia and central and eastern Europe. Although the Aegean Islands did not escape the difficulties, as the recently excavated settlement at Koukouna-ries on Paros shows so graphically, there was strong Mycenaean continuity east-ward across the central Aegean.

There is increasing archaeological confirmation for two waves of new My-cenaean settlers on Cyprus in the late thirteenth century, and an interesting lin-guistic phenomenon fits neatly with this situation. Scholars have long distin-guished a so-called Arkado-Cypriot branch of classical Greek that preserved very old features of the language. The survival of two closely related enclaves of ar-chaic Greek in areas as widely separated as mountainous Arkadia in central Pelo-ponnese and Cyprus very near the eastern end of the Mediterranean now finds a plausible explanation in the fact that these were major havens for Mycenaean sur-vivors. And although the current tendency is to derive the Cypriot syllabary from the Minoan Linear A, the language of the Linear B tablets shows elements of close connection with the later Arkado-Cypriot dialect. We should also note that as late as the third century B.C. a syllabary derived from the linear scripts of the Bronze Age was still employed on Cyprus to write Greek.

A major puzzle involves what happened to the rich agricultural areas formerly occupied by the great Mycenaean powers. Few of the burned or abandoned My-cenaean sites seem to have been immediately reoccupied, and new settlements dating from the twelfth and eleventh centuries are scarce. Were the majority of these once fruitful lands lying untended? As we have seen, the cultural features once linked with the supposed Dorian invaders have proved undependable. Those who still believe in an immediate Dorian occupation argue that the conquerors were just another group of Greeks with an essentially similar though much less sophisticated culture. Also, the Early Iron Age villages are supposed to have been small and scattered, with buildings constructed flimsily of perishable materials and whose inhabitants had little in the way of portable wealth or durable artefacts. Another thesis is that pastoralism, particularly cattle raising, increased significantly in many areas, not replacing but supplementing settled agriculture. In a 1987 review of the evidence, Snodgrass concluded that the apparent desertion of hundreds of Mycenaean sites, together with later reoccupation and memory of their names, could be explained as the result of intermittent visits by pastoralists. One Mycenaean site that was reoccupied in the Early Iron Age, Nichoria in Messenia, has produced evidence of a major increase in the proportion of cattle to other animals.

At several other sites, including Eretria and Lefkandi, there are remains of small, simple structures beneath the more permanent structures of the later Dark Age. These could be explained as seasonal structures of short-term visitors. Even the problematic handmade pottery has been seen as a product of migratory peoples who did not regularly use a potter's wheel. Dedications at sanctuaries may point in the same direction: Klaus Kilian argued that types of small bronzes found in Thessaly at the sanctuary of Artemis could be best understood as dedications by seasonal visitors traveling between Thessaly and more northern regions. Another site in Thessaly provides evidence of a different sort: at Iolkos, early seeds are almost entirely pulse seeds, most plausibly viewed as animal fodder; later the remains are primarily carbonized grain seeds. And in an examination of animal figurines dedicated at Olympia, Snodgrass found that the proportion of oxen and sheep steadily declines throughout the Dark Age, while horse figurines increase. Herding itself seems to have become less important in the latter part of the Dark Age (Fig. 118).

Is there anything that could be described as the sign of newcomers? Are the Dark Age pastoralists the descendants of rude Dorians who pushed southward into Greece toward the end of the Bronze Age, destroying the Mycenaean centers and replacing the sophisticated culture of the second millennium with the impoverished life of the first millennium? But we have seen that there are no clearly "intrusive" elements, that continuity at a reduced level is a more apt description than innovation for the twelfth and eleventh centuries. Moreover, Chadwick (1976b) has adduced linguistic evidence to demonstrate features of Doric Greek in the Linear B tablets and has argued that this evidence reveals the presence of Dorians during the second millennium. The Doric elements suggest that the dialect was that of the common people and, thus, their presence is little attested in the world of tablets. Dorians enter our historical and archaeological horizon only when the administrative superstructure of the palaces disappeared. We will return to the issue of continuity in our concluding section; but for now, it is enough

Figure 118

to say that search for links between Bronze Age and later Greek culture is one of the significant features of this present generation of Aegean scholarship.

Agents of destruction need not have come from outside Greece. Civil war is not ruled out as an explanation nor is an attack by a coalition of Mycenaean powers. The notion of strife within the Mycenaean world is no longer far fetched, as there appears to be a discernible pattern to the rise and subsequent collapse of individual power centers. Events at Knossos, Thebes and Pylos support this view of internal destruction occurring periodically and randomly throughout the height of the Mycenaean era. Perhaps we can look within the Mycenaean world to locate the agents of the difficulties at the end of the thirteenth century. The tales of the difficulties Agamemnon and Odysseus faced on their returns from Troy may be remembrances of civil strife. Perhaps a great revolt had been led by the middle-class merchants (if there was such a "class") or by the free peasants (perhaps of different racial stock and even language) or by the masses of slaves. Possibly they all made common cause against the autocratic Achaean kings and nobles. Or could the destroyers have been Achaean kinsmen, perhaps a combination of the numerous and prosperous Mycenaean "colonies" in the southern Aegean? It has been objected that tales of strife are not widespread and thus do not accord with the general destruction; for example, Nestor apparently had no trouble in reasserting his control at Pylos. Nor is there a single likely source—no earlier-day Sparta or Athens—if the agent was one Mycenaean center. What would explain the burning of smaller settlements if those who attacked the fortresses were subjected population? How could slaves or peasants overturn the military fortresses that the major centers had become?

Still other proposed explanations partially or wholly eliminate human agents. Could the deforestation that may have followed the construction boom and spreading agriculture of LHIIIB have caused such serious erosion of the soil that famine, perhaps coupled with a cessation of foreign trade, produced revolution?

Might there have been a tremendous plague or series of epidemics that hastened the fall of Mycenaean power and could perhaps be tied in with the increased practice of cremation burial? Rhys Carpenter advanced the thesis (1966) that the Mediterranean experienced a major drought in the twelfth and eleventh centuries: melting of the polar ice altered the trade winds and brought a warming trend and desiccation. Others have held that there was a change to a cooler and wetter climate beginning about 1100. While the evidence does not support any theory of major climatic change, shorter term anomalies in precipitation may have seriously impeded agricultural productivity. For a time it seemed as if the volcanic eruption of Thera might provide an answer. However, by the 1960s most scholars dated the eruption to the fifteenth century and, as we have seen, some scholars now date it to the late seventeenth century. Still, Angelis Galanopoulos has argued (1981) for a later eruption of Thera, contemporary with an explosion of Vesuvius, about 1200; both eruptions, he believes, would have contaminated Greek soil. Earthquake is another possible culprit, and there are several recent indications of earthquakes in the thirteenth century: at Mycenae, Tiryns and Argos, convincing evidence of destructive earthquake about this time has recently been found. Yet if nature were the only culprit, how do we explain the feverish construction of fortifications, the provision of access to water supply from within the walls, the dispatch of watchers along the Pylian coasts, the apparently urgent distribution of metals to Pylian smiths for the manufacture of weapons?

The thrust of the "new archaeology" has been described as a factor of first-rate significance in the field of Aegean history, and it may help to solve the question of Mycenaean collapse. Several scholars see Bronze Age Greece as an excellent instance of "systems collapse." Colin Renfrew has made a strong case that general features of collapse and aftermath are apparent in the case of the Mycenaean kingdoms (1979). According to this interpretation, the central administrative organs are adversely stressed until they collapse; the elite class disappears; a centralized economic structure ceases to function; and population decline and settlement shifts of notable proportions follow. The aftermath is marked by a transition to a lower level of sociopolitical organization along with the emergence of a romantic myth that attempts to link and legitimize present conditions with a glorious past. Several other features predicted for systems collapse appear in the Mycenaean case: the collapse often requires about a century for completion; dislocations, often expressed in human conflicts, are evident in the early part of the process; boundaries may weaken and thus invite invaders; societal organization is likely to become more complex initially only to fall off suddenly; there is no clear, single "cause" for the collapse.

Continuing the reasoning advanced earlier by Vermeule, Philip Betancourt (1976) made a strong case that the Mycenaean collapse is best understood in this manner. After reviewing the evidence for growing complexity and specialization in the Mycenaean economy, he suggested that the kingdoms may have become too specialized to adjust to economic difficulties. The Mycenaeans may have relied too fully on a few items in their agrarian production, a particularly ominous situation in view of the dramatic increase in population that we have seen for Messenia and that was paralleled in other kingdoms. "Thus a destruction or a series of crop failures from any cause would not only have eliminated much of the food supply for an entire year, it would also have seriously upset the industrial picture and the trade that depended on it" (44).

An attractive feature of this explanation is that it allows for differing local conditions and reactions. It also correctly links events in Greece with those of the larger Mediterranean. The "Land and Sea People" may have been moving because they had experienced similar economic disasters; similarly, their movements may have precipitated fundamental upsets in the productive systems of the advanced cultures of the eastern Mediterranean. Certainly, the activities of marauders would have disrupted trade. We have seen how international trade activity had become by the fourteenth and thirteenth centuries and how fully the Mycenaean participated in Mediterranean commerce. The economy would have been hard hit by harassment and interruption of foreign trade.

Interruption of trade and crop failure do not explain the actual destruction of the palaces, but the collapse of the entire system does suggest an answer. The mechanisms of the redistributive economies were controlled by centralized administrative systems. If the palace officials were unable to correct malfunctions, the local units comprising the kingdom could have become severed from the administrative machinery and thrown on their own resources. Imre Tegyey has argued that the latest system in the Pylos kingdom was too strictly organized, not allowing any self-reliance to the local towns of the kingdom. Thus, ineffectual action by the central rulers would have decapitated the kingdoms, and the disruption of the intricate administrative system would have furthered economic and social breakdown. Some sufferers may have fled, some may have attacked neighbors, some carried on as well as they could at much lower economic, political and social levels of activity and organization. The points at which food reserves and other resources were concentrated would have been especially vulnerable to attack by starving people deprived of even meager rations.

We have noticed possible signs in the Pylos tablets that all was not well within that kingdom: some (perhaps unusual) arrears in taxes owed to the *wanax;* bronzesmiths short of raw materials; lavish gifts to divinities. Also tantalizing are the cryptic entries about assignment of rowers and watchers to certain coastal locations. At the same time, the palace appears to have been intensifying its control over production. In other words, there are a number of hints that the system is not functioning as it should. There appear to be attempts to use the system in new ways, perhaps even to mobilize as many available resources as possible. The ultimate failure of the Neleids is shown, not in the Linear B records, but in the archaeology: the Pylos palace was completely destroyed, not to be found again until the present century.

Most of the Mycenaean kingdoms were affected in much the same way. There are no tablets to provide details about mobilization of watchers or collection of bronze, but the archaeological evidence clearly reveals collapse of both major and minor settlements accompanied by a great deal of movement and much reduced levels of cultural activity. If we are persuaded by the explanation of systems collapse, lack of cooperation among kingdoms is no longer puzzling. While it may have been contrary to Mycenaean psychology to unite, even against a common enemy, in this situation there would have been no single, recognizable common enemy. The enemy was both external and internal, human and natural. There was plenty of warning of difficulties. In fact, the situation may well have worsened in some regions because of the flight and attack of people from other collapsing kingdoms. Some kingdoms may have even cooperated. Tradition tells us that the Athenians accepted survivors from Pylos. The wall across the Isthmus may have been a cooperative defensive measure. But since the enemy had many forms, regionalism marks the period of Mycenaean collapse just as it characterized earlier developments. By its very nature, destruction occurred at varying rates. So too did cultural continuity into the sub-Mycenaean period vary between areas.

THE FINAL PHASES

In appraising the major directions in the present generation of Aegean Bronze Age archaeology, we suggested that the expanded vista of scholars is an outstanding feature. Investigators have become increasingly interested in establishing the relationship of the Bronze Age to both earlier and later developments. One of the consequences is that the transition from the Bronze to the Iron Age has been more fully documented, and our understanding has improved considerably about the generations immediately following the great disruptions of the thirteenth and twelfth centuries. Among the important published collections of the evidence are those of Vincent Desborough (1972), Anthony Snodgrass (1971) and Nicholas Coldstream (1977).

There is less inclination to find intruders today than there was as little as two decades ago. As we have seen in examining the question of "Dorian invasion," even advocates of the invasion thesis, like Desborough, came to the conclusion that the intruders, after they had burned, pillaged, killed and enslaved to the limit, withdrew and left the most productive areas of central and southern Greece to the few native survivors. This view calls into question the reliability of the tradition cherished in later Dorian communities that their ancestors had conquered and immediately occupied large parts of the ancient Mycenaean kingdoms, especially in the Peloponnese. Accepting the general trustworthiness of this traditional evidence, scholars of the stature of Hammond and Schachermeyr continue to defend the position that Mycenaean Greece suffered its final destruction at the hands of northern enemies; and, as we have seen, those archaeologists who believe the handmade pottery of the late Mycenaean phases to be intrusive also argue for the presence of northern invaders.

As evidence has become fuller, however, more scholars are puzzled by the absence of new cultural elements as well as of indicators of people bringing those innovations. As Snodgrass said, it is a "baffling situation of an invasion without invaders" (Snodgrass, 1971: 312). Those items once thought to betoken newcomers have been shown to have evolved within the context of the Bronze Age civilizations. Certain novelties such as shield-bosses, flame-shaped spearheads, long bronze dress-pins and arched fibulae can be interpreted as imports coming in by different routes or as cultural borrowings or as traces of a short-lived period of particularly strong nothern influence on objects already used in Greece.

The use of the fibula (Fig. 119) and the straight pin to fasten heavy garments was long thought to point to newcomers from a colder climate. Both violin-bow and arched fibulae are common in Italy and the Balkans, suggesting that their use began earlier, and in the north. However, as in the case of other apparent innovations, the violin-bow shape was already used in Greece in the Mycenaean IIIB period and straight bronze pins found in IIIC graves seem to have local antecedents in the long bronze pins with crystal globes found as early as the Shaft Grave context of Circle B at Mycenae. Tombs of the Mycenaean era commonly contained small pins of bronze and other materials such as bone and ivory. Thus, many are inclined to agree with J. Deshayes (1966) that there are serious obstacles to the accepted account of the source of the twelfth-century pins. If there was major climatic change, their increased use in Greece may have been due to the beginning of a period of cooler and wetter weather alleged by some to have lasted from about 1100 to 800. Disruption of the highly developed Mycenaean textile industry might provide another explanation.

Certain types of weapons and armor are seen by some to provide evidence for contacts with the north. The distinctive slashing sword (Fig. 120) had an unbroken development in earlier sword types of Central Europe. Until recently, the appearance of this type of sword in the Aegean was thought to coincide with the period of destruction. Piggott wrote that the presence of the slashing sword in Greece demonstrates that "here we must have central and west European adventurers and mercenaries forming part of the raiding bands along with the Luka and

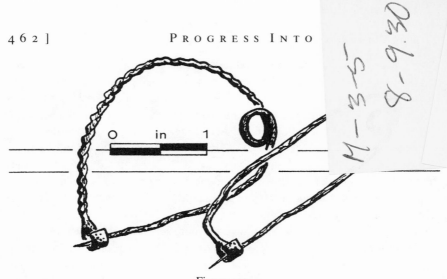

Figure 119

the rest [*i.e.*, the Sea People]" (1965: 159). As evidence has accumulated, however, Aegean specimens of the slashing sword have been found in certain IIIB
contexts. Snodgrass now concludes, "the only possible interpretation of this evidence is that the swords were known to, and used by, the Mycenaeans distinctly
earlier than the great wave of destructions of the palaces" (1971: 307).

In other words, new culture traits are as difficult to find as invaders in the late
thirteenth and twelfth centuries. Rather, there appears to have been general continuity of Mycenaeans and Mycenaean culture, together with the destruction of
most of the palaces and the kind of control they represented. In a recent study of
Mycenaean pictorial pottery, Emily Vermeule convincingly described the new
confidence of painters, their skill and even humor. As she argued elsewhere
(1968), the destruction of the palace organization may have been liberating and,
in fact, energizing. We have seen that Athens may have been most vigorous during just this period of difficulties, and mounting evidence from sites in the Argolid shows continued habitation of sizable numbers of people. And there were
new settlements, like that of Lefkandi where frequent, if not regular, contact
with outside areas is well attested.

However, it cannot be denied that there were serious difficulties, that population declined dramatically either through death or flight, and that many settlements were abandoned or decayed in the course of the twelfth century. Between
1150 and 1125 there were fresh disturbances at a number of sites; for example,
Mycenae experienced more destruction. Settlements like Lefkandi and Koukounaries appear to have been deserted for some generations. There was further dimi-
nution of foreign contacts. With these Dark Age developments, persistent features of the old Mycenaean culture, such as multiple burials in family chamber

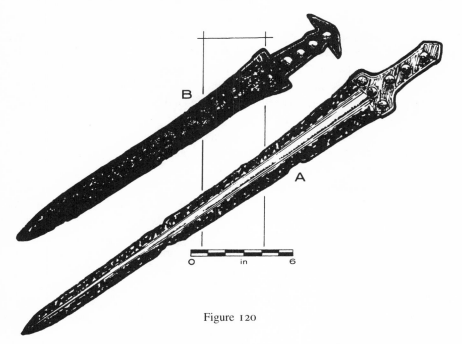

Figure 120

tombs, seem finally to have disappeared at many places. The common mode of burial became individual or double cist graves and occasionally in pithoi.

Desborough concluded that the sum of these features strongly suggests the arrival of newcomers from outside the Mycenaean sphere. There may, he argued, have been several groups of intruders, and they apparently originated in the northwest and arrived by land. Some confirmation was seen in the verdict of two physical anthropologists that skeletal remains from Athens and Argos include characteristics of a new strain of northern origin in the population. Certainly, as Desborough suggested, newcomers would have met little opposition from weak Mycenaean survivors, who may have gradually fused with them to produce the so-called protogeometric culture. This fusion would explain the pottery of the eleventh century which was fundamentally and almost entirely Mycenaean: it would owe a debt to the newcomers as well as to the latest (so-called sub-Mycenaean*) style of the original inhabitants. Desborough implied that one or more groups of these newcomers may have spoken a primitive Doric dialect of Greek; other scholars have seen in this later folk movement the real Dorian invasion.

In the past two decades, interpretation of this evidence has dampened enthusiasm for invasion at the end of the twelfth century, as it earlier questioned a thirteenth-century influx. The skeletal remains provide no proof: the evidence is very slim, and physical anthropologists differ over its classification. For Athens, one expert found evidence of one possibly "Nordic" skull type in the sub-Mycenaean remains. Another expert, who described "Alpine" skull types as intrusive, found an increase of "Nordic" specimens. A third expert maintains that "Alpine" types are an established category during the Greek Bronze Age. In the case of Athens, one reading of the evidence gave an actual decline in skull types thought to be "northern."

Nor does the cultural assemblage of the late twelfth century appear to represent a new population element. Borrowings there certainly were, such as the embossed and impressed decoration on metal objects. Yet, the growing use of cist graves occurs in places with clear Mycenaean continuity such as Athens, Perati and Lefkandi. Rather than intrusive, as Desborough believed, the cist grave is now believed to have been a revival of a Middle Bronze Age practice. Cist cemeteries are located in fresh places, sometimes actually lying above old habitation sites. While these changes indicate altered burial practices, they do not seem to imply the arrival of newcomers.

One explanation is provided in the thesis argued by Snodgrass and others that Greeks increasingly turned to animal husbandry during the early Dark Age. The average life of sites—both settlement and cemetery—of this period is short by comparison with earlier and later periods, approximately 150 years. An apparent movement of people regularly began or ended use of the sites for either habitation or burial. New use of "old" habitation sites either by the former occupants or by people from neighboring regions, is quite predictable. Several locations where new tombs were cut into earlier settlements are former palace sites: Mycenae, Tiryns, Thebes, Iolkos and the Athenian acropolis. And since it was the continuity of *palaces* that was already seriously undermined in the thirteenth century, memory of previous use of certain areas may have weakened.

In 1967 McDonald wrote, "one of the most pressing problems in Greek archaeology is the discovery of the location and careful excavation of several habitation sites where these newcomers settled—if possible at spots where Mycenaean survivors had still held on" (420 f.). He pointed to Lefkandi as holding much promise in this connection. Twenty years later, a fair amount of Lefkandi has been explored, and excavation of Nichoria has begun under McDonald's own direction. In both places, Mycenaean tradition is tenacious. Of Lefkandi in IIIC, Snodgrass says, "If the new builders were immigrants, they were Mycenaean immigrants." Of the settlement there that was rebuilt at the end of the twelfth century, he continues, "once again it is clear, above all from their pottery, that the newcomers were still Mycenaeans" (1971: 361). At Nichoria too there is an unbroken cultural thread, with outside influence suggested for certain ceramic features, the individual apsidal cist graves, the apsidal dwellings and the heavy emphasis on herding. As we have seen, it is animal bones from Nichoria and other places that may eventually substantiate the theory of increased pastoralism in the early Dark Age. The other apparent innovations can be explained variously. While there appears to have been considerable movement during the late Mycenaean period continuing into the next centuries, much of it was apparently internal movement by people already resident in Greece. It is too early to reach a final verdict, but an explanation that sees internal decline rather than destructive invasion by outsiders also accounts for the tradition in later times of an "age of heroes." That tradition seems to represent a folk memory of what we call the Mycenaean Age, and it was enshrined, at least in part, in Homeric epics.

HOMERIC AND LATER CONNECTIONS

The earliest stages of the Greek Dark Ages that followed the collapse of Mycenaean civilization lead us naturally to a discussion of another difficult question, namely the relationship between the culture of the later second millennium, which we have been reviewing, and the Homeric epics. Closely linked to this question is the whole issue of the degree of continuity between the Mycenaean Bronze Age and the Archaic and Classical ages of Greece.

The *Iliad* and the *Odyssey* tell of the Trojan War and the return of the surviving Greek heroes, especially Odysseus, following the destruction of Troy. Before the archaeological excavations that began in the last third of the nineteenth century, classical scholars tended to regard the poems as reflections of "the fabulous age of Greece," which "must have no place in history." The excavations of Schliemann demonstrated that there had really been a rich, long-lived culture in Greece during the Bronze Age. And, as we have seen, Homer was an important guide to Schliemann's discoveries at Hissarlik and Mycenae. Finds were described as the "palace of king Priam," "Priam's treasure," "Agamemnon's Mycenae," a goblet that "vividly reminds us of Nestor's cup." In fact, we have seen that Schliemann believed that Homer "must have been born and educated amidst a civilisation which was able to produce such works as these."

The opinion of some contemporaries swung immediately in favor of the close parallels between certain Late Bronze Age artefacts and Homeric descriptions. However, many classical scholars strongly resisted and resented Schliemann's efforts to prove that the context of Homeric epics was derived directly from that period of Greek history. The confused and anachronistic nature of many elements of Homer's account gradually led to a view that blurring of what once were clear memories had occurred during the centuries-long oral transmission of the poetry. However, the poems betray not only confusion; some very distinctive traits of Mycenaean times like tholos tombs, fresco painting and literate palace bureaucracies seem to be completely unknown to Homer. Rhys Carpenter represented the extreme critical position when he wrote that, from the Mycenaean age, "we are left with a single helmet constructed of boars' teeth; and if that is really all that Homer knows about the material actualities of the great Late Helladic culture, it is tantamount to nothing at all" (1962: 31).

The findings of Milman Parry were particularly important in unravelling the thread of continuity. Arguing that Homeric poetry was composed orally without the assistance of writing, Parry described the use of formulaic language to aid the memory of singers. These formulas helped to conserve the fundamental elements of the stories that were retold generation after generation. Thus, the oral technique was conservative of older elements but also constantly changing, since the nature of oral composition entails that each retelling will vary, if only slightly. If the poems were transmitted orally from the late Mycenaean Age to the eighth century when, as many believe, they were finally written down, countless alterations would have occurred.

Parry's thesis was not uniformly welcomed. As recently as 1968, Sterling Dow wrote, "the human brain works slowly, if at all, and there are signs that although the Parry doctrines are getting to be fairly well absorbed in England, farther away, as in Vienna, the light has not yet dawned" (124). However, most scholars were persuaded, and more recent studies in the Greek oral tradition, particularly those of Eric Havelock (1982), have shown how and to what extent oral song is "modernized" in order that it be immediately comprehensible to its auditors. Not only individual words but an institutional framework and code of behavior will be reshaped in order to be immediately recognizable in a world where a second, more reflective "reading" is not possible.

Another important element in the question of continuity resulted from the realization that the language of the Linear B tablets is basically Greek. The evidence of language shows that Greek was the language of the Mycenaean Age as well as of the Classical period, demonstrating another strong link between the Bronze Age and later times. This link of "Greekness" has a bearing on a most debated question, that is whether specific words can be shown to be common to the tablets and to the epics.

All of the evidence—archaeological, linguistic, traditional—points to the correctness of the general conclusion that there was a continuous tradition, perhaps poetic from the start, linking the Mycenaean with the early Iron Age and down to Archaic and Classical times. And if not unanimity, there is at least strong consensus that the poems contain episodes, descriptions of artefacts, names, and at least a few linguistic and stylistic traits that can be explained only by the theory that they were handed down from the Late Bronze Age to Homer's time in a continuous oral tradition.

There is a difficult related problem: were the Mycenaean memories preserved because they were embodied in a poetic tradition that was created in the Mycenaean period? T. B. L. Webster argued strongly (1958) for the existence of Mycenaean poetry and even suggested that Linear B was adequate for recording poetry and may have been used for this purpose, although the texts have perished. A further clue to the existence of poetry in the Mycenaean era is the Mycenaean nature, in the Homeric epics, of certain elements that had disappeared from actual use. In other words, if practices or objects went out of use before the end of the Mycenaean age, we can assert that they could have survived only in "a poetic tradition" (Webster, 1958: 91) or perhaps in "a loose prose tradition *later* incorporated in poetry" (Kirk, 1964: 18). Sometimes the "dead" trait appears to have been embalmed quite successfully, as in the case of the "sword silver-studded," [84] which may preserve an actual phrase from Mycenaean Greek describing a metal-working technique that probably went out of use about the end of the fifteenth century. On the other hand, the description in the poems of chariots as a kind of "equine taxi service" cannot conform to strict reality of any period. The poetic tradition (except in a few passages) has lost touch with the way Mycenaean chariots were actually used in battle. Other misconceptions together with linguistic arguments have led some authorities like Kirk to doubt the existence of a Mycenaean poetic tradition. He presented the thesis that heroic tales might have been passed on to the earliest Iron Age in story telling of a more fluid nature.

To reach any conclusion, it is necessary to consider the larger question of actual continuity between the Mycenaean Age and later periods. Aside from the Homeric epics, what was the legacy of Mycenaean Greece to the Archaic and Classical periods? If there was any inheritance at all, how many and how strong and how direct were the connections?

Until recently, the dominant position was that there was little direct connection between the Bronze Age and Classical cultures of Greece. As Chester Starr presented the position, "Mycenaean civilization is not a system from which historic Greek culture emerged on a straight line" (1962: 56). The break at the end of the Mycenaean Age was decisive. It allowed Hellenic features brought in with the earliest Greek-speakers but submerged by foreign influences to grow stronger when released from the grasp of non-Hellenic traits.

We have reviewed Evans' and Nilsson's arguments emphasizing important elements of continuity from Mycenaean and even Minoan times that may have been obscured but were never lost. Evans' claims provoked almost as violent opposition as Schliemann's, but his massive influence, bold hypotheses and brilliant analyses forced most open-minded classicists to admit that the Classical Greeks may indeed have owed a good deal to their own distant past. Nilsson's more cautious and carefully documented claims, particularly in the field of religion, carried still more conviction. Reviews of Minoan-Mycenaean representational art by Webster and Vermeule not only support Nilsson but tend to revert to Evans' hypothesis that at least some of the germs of epic may be Minoan. With respect to the larger question, a position diametrically opposed to that emphasizing break between the periods was argued by Wace in 1956. He asserted that the prehistoric and the later phases of Greek history are one and indivisible.

Resistance, though less prevalent, is still deeply rooted in some quarters. And it has to be admitted that many features of Archaic and Classical Greece show little or no evidence of continuity. In political and social organization, for instance, the structured system of the relatively large Mycenaean kingdoms is comparable to Near Eastern institutions, which are regularly cited as the antithesis of those in the small independent classical city-states. The meagerness of evidence for the early centuries of the Iron Age can be cited as a basis for the lingering belief in the almost total abandonment in Greece of "civilized" living. And this situation reinforces a very long and strongly held assumption that the wonder and perfection of Classical Greek culture had no authentic forebears, that it was a kind of miracle relatively independent of time and space and normal historical processes.

However, the evidence for continuity is increasing and there is a greater willingness to consider developments in Greece in association with processes in contemporary cultures. The plan of the Mycenaean megaron has long been seen as the source of the typical plan of the Classical temple, with the two columns of the porch in line with the ends of the side walls, the main shrine or *naos* replacing the inner room of the megaron, and a central statue base where the great ceremonial palace hearth once stood. The recent discoveries at Nichoria and Lefkandi of independent buildings that seem to have served religious purposes are more concrete clues to the continuous use of architectural elements in the centuries between the Mycenaean and Classical periods. Furthermore, as Guthrie has emphasized, later temples were often built on spots that had been sacred in earlier periods. We have seen, in chapter nine, that more such situations have been identified, at least tentatively, as excavation has progressed. While we usually cannot be absolutely sure whether their location was due to an uninterrupted cult or to a lucky reidentification in the Early Archaic period, when the popularity of the Homeric poems and a general idealization of the heroic past gave a great impetus to hero cults, the choice of certain places like Mycenaean tholos tombs can hardly be accidental.

If one looks to the architectural orders of the Classical period, there is, first of all, the general column and lintel arrangement. And the so-called Doric column and capital bear an unmistakable similarity to earlier examples like the column in the relieving triangle over the Lion Gate at Mycenae, as well as to some of those depicted in fresco fragments from Knossos and Pylos and on Minoan and Mycenaean gems and seals. Even the stone-carved and fresco examples of Minoan-

Mycenaean friezes (Fig. 121) of split rosettes alternating with groups of vertical fasciae are strikingly close to the triglyph and metope pattern of the later Doric order of architecture.

It is certain that pottery styles evolved from the Mycenaean Age through the Dark Age and into the Archaic period. The destructions of the thirteenth century were important in the evolution but did not, apparently, bring new styles into Greece from elsewhere. As Vermeule argued persuasively (1968), it was the formal palace pottery that disappeared, together with the palaces themselves. Palatial forms were replaced by lively products, particularly in those areas where so-called sub-Mycenaean communities preserved their ties with the past. In fact, the "fresh life of spring" that Desborough found in the Protogeometric pottery of the late eleventh century derived from Athens, where continuity from the Mycenaean period is particularly strong. There were changes, of course: some vase shapes passed out of use so that the repertoire was considerably reduced, and new themes were introduced. Scholars are only beginning to study the aesthetic and iconographic relations between late Mycenaean and late Dark Age, but the relationship cannot be denied (Fig. 122).

The physical evidence was examined in detail by Roland Hampe and Erika Simon (1980), who found continuity in a great variety of objects. Grave stelai find descendents from the Archaic to the Hellenistic period. In metal products, the list of shapes includes the cup with high handles, or the *kantharos;* the tripod bowl; the straight and arched pins; and work in gold (attested, for example, by the Eretrian hoard). From the very beginning of prehistoric Aegean archaeology, Furtwängler identified Mycenaean gem carving as Greek in its essential characteristics.

In athletic contests (where there are religious overtones in both prehistoric and later times) and in many details of cult and ritual, the resemblances are equally notable. Webster and others have shown that in Minoan-Mycenaean representational art there are many convincing parallels with singing, dancing and instrumental performances connected with later religious observances. Continuity in religion—particularly in divine names—is strongly reinforced by the Linear B tablets. Worship at the graves of some of the Bronze Age heroes appears to have recurred in the Early Iron Age and to have continued into Classical, Hellenistic and Roman days. The case for continuity may be reinforced by the imitation of earlier customs detected by many scholars in the evidence of the eighth century. The heroic burials in Cyprus and at Eretria echo Mycenaean traditions; art of the late eighth century turns to heroic subjects and themes. In Snodgrass' words, "it begins to look as if this attitude of deference to the heroic past was an important element in the revolution that was sweeping through Greek life [in the eighth century]" (1980: 77).

The evidence of myths and legends also shows us that the Classical Greeks

Figure 121

Figure 122

were quite aware of many non-material facets of their prehistoric heritage. Even the structure of the most fundamental of entities—the polis—may have Mycenaean roots. Terms for rulers, now known from the Linear B tablets, constitute one measure of continuity. Not only *wanax* and *basileus,* but terms such as *telestes* and *lawagetas* survived into the Classical period. Religious functions of the polis also show possible links. According to the tablets, the bronze-smiths (*chalkewes*) had a particular importance. On one tablet they are connected with the goddess Potnia. In Classical Athens, Chalkeia was a regular festival, while the cult of Athena Chalkioikos was practiced in Sparta. The Classical polis was identified with the people (the *demos*), and the Linear B records of Pylos suggest the role of the *damos* (DA-MO) in village affairs. Indeed, even the roots for *polis* and *astu* have been seen in Linear B. It may not be too far fetched to see certain elements of the later polis in the village structure of the Mycenaean kingdoms. Their independence was, of course, curtailed by the centralized structure of the palaces; but when the centralization was removed, the local units could continue unimpeded. Nestor's son, Peisistratos, may have had vital ties in culture and institutions, as well as in blood, with his illustrious Athenian descendant of the sixth century.

In mentioning Nestor and Peisistratos, we have returned to the Homeric epics, an appropriate conclusion to our investigation. Throughout the story of archaeological discovery, another theme has been a review of the evidence accumulating over the past century and a quarter on the nature and dependability of the Homeric evidence. Much caution is needed in making an assessment, but the necessity of dealing with the poems before taking any position is without question. That is clear in the constant references throughout this book to Agamemnon's Mycenae, Nestor's Pylos, Minos' Knossos. At least a partial explanation is provided by the human condition: history as the sum of the deeds of anonymous actors is not very exciting to most of us. The embodiment of history in the shape of people adds life to events and objects. Some of the names in the epics may be true Mycenaean names: a man called Akhilleus seems attested on the tablets from both Pylos and Knossos; the name Hektor occurs in the Pylian records; Alexandros is accepted by many scholars as the name of someone associated with Wilusa, perhaps Ilion or Troy. But, in the final analysis, the exact connection of the people of the epics with the material evidence of the sites cannot be demonstrated. We must continually remind ourselves that in each generation these songs were altered during both the earlier oral and the later written transmission.

Despite all these cautions, the Homeric poems are of incomparable value for insight into the heroic age of Greece. They preserved knowledge of its existence across the Dark Age, instilled values into the culture of Classical Greece and, in modern times, served as a guide to its rediscovery. Through the poems we now possess evidence of another kind that allows us to understand new dimensions of that age. The proud claim of the Roman poet Horace is even more appropriate to Homer:

> I have raised a monument more lasting than bronze
> More lofty than the regal pile of the pyramids,
> Which neither gnawing rain, nor violent Aquilo
> Shall demolish nor even the innumerable
> Succession of years and the flight of the ages.
>
> —*Carmina* 3.30.1–5

Chapter Bibliographies and
Sources of Quotations

MAJOR SOURCES, both books and articles, on which the particular phase of the chronicle is based are first listed in sequence for each chapter. The direct quotations are then keyed in by a triple reference system: (1) page number(s) in our text; (2) identification of the source by its number in the chapter bibliography; (3) page number(s) in the source.

> AJA American Journal of Archaeology
> BSA Annual of the British School in Athens
> JHS Journal of Hellenic Studies

CHAPTER II

1. Heinrich Schliemann, *Troy and its Remains* (London: 1875)
2. ———— *Ilios: The City and Country of the Trojans* . . . (London: 1880)
3. ———— *Troja: Results of the Latest Researches* . . . (London: 1884)
4. ———— *Mycenae: A Narrative of Researches* . . . (London: 1878)
5. ———— *Tiryns: The Prehistoric Palace of the Kings of Tiryns* (London: 1886)
6. Carl Schuchhardt, *Schliemann's Excavations: An Archæological and Historical Study* (London: 1891)

9 .	2 .	xvi	17, 18 .	1 .	194
11 .	1 .	76	18 .	1 .	219
12 .	2 .	213	18 .	1 .	80
13 .	1 .	62	20 .	1 .	304, 305
15 .	3 .	237	21, 22 .	1 .	323, 324
16 .	1 .	68–70	23 .	1 .	335
17 .	1 .	58	23, 24 .	1 .	332, 333
17 .	1 .	41	24 .	1 .	347, 348

CHAPTER III

1. Christos Tsountas and J. Irving Manatt, *The Mycenaean Age: a Study of the Monuments and Culture of pre-Homeric Greece* (Boston: 1897)
2. Wilhelm Dörpfeld, *Troja 1893: Bericht über die im Jahre 1893 veranstalteten Ausgrabungen* (Leipzig: 1894)

84 .	1 .	xviii	104 .	1 .	284
84 .	2 .	86, 87	104, 105 .	1 .	291, 292
86 .	2 .	60	105 .	1 .	316
88 .	1 .	80, 81	105 .	1 .	295
90, 91 .	1 .	83	105 .	1 .	296
91 .	1 .	95	105 .	1 .	302
91 .	1 .	114	106 .	1 .	340
92, 94 .	1 .	117	106, 107 .	1 .	341
94 .	1 .	121	107 .	1 .	316, 317
94 .	1 .	131	107 .	1 .	317
94 .	1 .	130	108 .	1 .	320–322
94 .	1 .	144, 145	109 .	1 .	323, 324
96, 97 .	1 .	148–150	109 .	1 .	338
97 .	1 .	150–152	109 .	1 .	360
98 .	1 .	189, 190	109 .	1 .	365, 364
100 .	1 .	207, 208	109 .	1 .	365
102 .	1 .	212–215	110 .	1 .	366
104 .	1 .	282			

CHAPTER IV

1. Joan Evans, *Time and Chance: the Story of Arthur Evans and his Forebears* (London: 1943)
2. Arthur Evans, "Knossos: the Palace," *BSA* 6 (1899–1900) 3–70
3. ——— "The Palace of Knossos," *BSA* 7 (1900–1901) 1–120
4. ——— "The Palace of Knossos," *BSA* 8 (1901–1902) 1–124
5. Duncan Mackenzie, "The Pottery of Knossos," *JHS* 23 (1903) 157–205
6. Arthur Evans, "The Palace of Knossos," *BSA* 9 (1902–1903) 1–153
7. ——— "The Palace of Knossos," *BSA* 10 (1903–1904) 1–62
8. ——— "The Palace of Knossos and its Dependencies," *BSA* 11 (1904–1905) 1–26
9. ——— "The Prehistoric Tombs of Knossos," *Archaeologia* 59 (1905) 391–562
10. Duncan Mackenzie, *et al.*, *Excavations at Phylakopi in Melos* (London: 1904)
11. Duncan Mackenzie, "Cretan Palaces and the Aegean Civilization," *BSA* 11 (1904–1905) 181–223
12. ——— "Cretan Palaces and the Aegean Civilization," *BSA* 12 (1905–1906) 216–258
13. Arthur Evans, *Scripta Minoa: the Written Documents of Minoan Crete,* Vol. I (Oxford: 1909)
14. ——— "The Minoan and Mycenaean Element in Hellenic Life," *JHS* 32 (1912) 277–297

15. ———— *The Palace of Minos: a Comparative Account of the Successive Stages of Early Cretan Civilization as Illustrated by the Discoveries at Knossos,* Vol. I (London: 1921)

113 .	1 .	338	140 .	3 .	51
113 .	1 .	163	141, 142 .	4 .	22
114 .	1 .	221, 222	142 .	4 .	66
114 .	1 .	263	142 .	4 .	109
115 .	1 .	270, 271	142 .	4 .	95, 105
115 .	1 .	299, 300	143 .	4 .	94, 95
116 .	1 .	308, 309	143 .	5 .	157, 158
116 .	1 .	310	144 .	5 .	170, 171
116, 117 .	1 .	312–314	144 .	5 .	182
117, 118 .	1 .	317	144 .	5 .	191
118 .	1 .	321, 320	144, 145 .	5 .	199
118 .	1 .	329	146 .	6 .	38, 39
119 .	1 .	330	147 .	6 .	40, 41
120 .	2 .	3	147 .	6 .	44, 45
120, 122 .	1 .	331	147, 148 .	6 .	46, 47
122 .	2 .	15, 16	148 .	6 .	52, 53
122 .	1 .	332	149 .	6 .	54
122 .	2 .	42	151 .	6 .	109, 110
124 .	2 .	45	151 .	6 .	111
124, 125 .	2 .	47, 48	151, 152 .	9 .	523
125, 126 .	2 .	51, 52	152, 153 .	9 .	558, 557
126 .	1 .	334	153 .	9 .	561
126 .	1 .	333	153 .	9 .	560
126, 127 .	2 .	55–57	153 .	7 .	57–62
127, 128 .	2 .	57	156 .	8 .	5, 14, 16
128 .	2 .	58, 59	157 .	10 .	270, 271
128 .	2 .	58	158 .	11 .	220–222
129 .	1 .	332, 333	159 .	12 .	225
129 .	2 .	67–69	159 .	12 .	230
129 .	2 .	69, 70	159 .	12 .	235
130 .	2 .	63–66	159, 160 .	12 .	237, 238
130 .	2 .	65, 66	160 .	13 .	x
131 .	1 .	335	160 .	13 .	v
131 .	3 .	2	160, 161 .	13 .	18
133 .	8 .	25, 26	161 .	13 .	38
133, 134 .	3 .	24	161 .	13 .	31
135 .	3 .	54, 55	161 .	13 .	34
135 .	3 .	55, 56	162 .	13 .	38
136–138 .	3 .	15	162 .	13 .	39, 40
139 .	3 .	94–96	162 .	13 .	50

162 . 13 . 52, 53
162, 163 . 13 . 55
163 . 13 . 58
163 . 13 . 60, 61
164 . 14 . 277
164 . 14 . 278, 279
164, 165 . 14 . 283
165 . 14 . 287, 288
166 . 14 . 291
166 . 14 . 293

166, 167 . 15 . xi
167 . 1 . 363
167 . 15 . x
167 . 15 . xi
168 . 15 . 25
168 . 15 . 24
168, 169 . 15 . 27, 28
169 . 1 . 392
169 . 1 . 350, 351

CHAPTER V

1. Gustav Glotz, *The Aegean Civilization* (New York: 1925), tr. by M. R. Dobie and E. M. Riley; 2nd ed. 1926; 3rd ed. 1952, in French only, with additional notes by C. Picard and P. Demargne
2. Diedrich Fimmen, *Die Kretisch-Mykenische Kultur* (Leipzig: 1921)
3. A. Michaelis, *A Century of Archaeological Discoveries* (New York: 1908), tr. by B. Kahnweiler

174 . 1 . v
174 . 1 . 21
175 . 1 . 21
175 . 2 . 125
175 . 2 . 211
177 . 1 . 13
178 . 1 . 44–46
179 . 1 . 47–49
179 . 1 . 50, 51
179 . 2 . 38
180 . 1 . 52
180 . 1 . 119
180, 181 . 1 . 125–130
181 . 1 . 131–134
181, 182 . 1 . 143
182 . 1 . 148, 149
182 . 1 . 150, 152
182, 183 . 1 . 152, 154
183 . 1 . 158
183 . 1 . 162, 163
183 . 1 . 165
183 . 1 . 170
184 . 2 . 118, 119
184 . 1 . 197, 198

184 . 1 . 211, 212
184 . 1 . 226
185 . 1 . 215–218
185 . 1 . 219
185 . 1 . 220, 223
185 . 1 . 223, 224
186 . 1 . 306, 308
187 . 1 . 325, 334
187 . 1 . 336–338
187, 188 . 1 . 347, 348, 364, 365
188 . 1 . 366
188 . 1 . 367, 369
189 . 2 . 75–79
189 . 1 . 371
189 . 1 . 373, 374
190 . 1 . 374
190 . 1 . 388
190 . 1 . 376–380
190 . 1 . 385
190, 191 . 1 . 380
191 . 1 . 383
191 . 1 . 389

CHAPTER VI

1. Carl Blegen, "Corinth in Prehistoric Times," *AJA* 27 (1923) 151–163
2. ——— and Alan Wace, "The Pre-Mycenaean Pottery of the Mainland," *BSA* 22 (1916–17; 1917–18) 175–189
3. Carl Blegen, *Korakou: a Prehistoric Settlement near Corinth* (New York: 1921)
4. ——— *Zygouries: a Prehistoric Settlement in the Valley of Cleonae* (Harvard: 1928)
5. ——— "Excavations at the Argive Heraeum," *AJA* 29 (1925) 413–418
6. ——— *Prosymna: the Helladic Settlement Preceding the Argive Heraeum,* 2 vols. (Harvard: 1937)
7. ——— and J. B. Haley, "The Coming of the Greeks," *AJA* 32 (1928) 141–154
8. Wilhelm Dörpfeld, *Troja und Ilion,* 2 vols. (Athens: 1902)
9. Carl Blegen, *Troy and the Trojans* (London: 1963)
10. ——— and Alan Wace, "Pottery as Evidence for Trade and Colonisation in the Aegean Bronze Age," *Klio: Beiträge zur alten Geschichte* 32 (1939) 131–147
11. Carl Blegen, "Excavations at Pylos, 1939," *AJA* 43 (1939) 557–576
12. ——— "Preclassical Greece," *Studies in the Arts and Architecture* (Philadelphia: 1941) 1–14

CHAPTER VII

1. Alan Wace, *et al.,* "Excavations at Mycenae 1921–23," *BSA* 25 (1921–22; 1922–23) 1–402
2. Arthur Evans, *The Shaft Graves and Bee-hive Tombs of Mycenae and their Interrelation* (London: 1927)
3. ———— *The Palace of Minos . . .,* Vol. II (London: 1928)
4. ———— *The Palace of Minos . . .,* Vol. IV (London: 1935)
5. John Pendlebury, *The Archaeology of Crete* (London: 1939)
6. Martin Nilsson, *Homer and Mycenae* (Berkeley: 1933)

CHAPTER VIII

Bass, G. F. 1967. *Cape Gelidonya: A Bronze Age Shipwreck*. Philadelphia.
Bennett, Emmett, Jr. 1950. "Fractional Quantities in Minoan Bookkeeping."
　AJA 54, 204–222.

————. 1951. *The Pylos Tablets, A Preliminary Transcription.* Princeton University Press for the University of Cincinnati.

Blegen, Carl. 1939. "Excavations at Pylos, 1939." *AJA* 43, 557–576.

————. 1958. "A Chronological Problem." *Minoica: Festschrift zum 80. Geburtstag von J. Sundwall.* Berlin, 61–66.

————, with Marion Rawson. 1966. *The Palace of Nestor.* Vol. 1. Princeton.

————, et al. 1973. *The Palace of Nestor.* Vol. 3. Princeton.

Boardman, John. 1963. "The Date of the Knossos Tablets." In *On the Knossos Tablets,* Oxford.

Buck, C. D. 1926. "The Language Situation in and about Greece in the Second Millennium B.C." *Classical Philology* 21, 1–26.

Caskey, J. L. 1971. "Investigations in Keos, I: Excavations and Explorations, 1966–1970." *Hesperia* 40, 359–396.

Catling, H. W. 1963. "Correlations between Composition and Provenance of Mycenaean and Minoan Pottery." *BSA* 58, 94–115.

————, and A. Millett. 1965. "A Study of the Inscribed Stirrup-Jars from Thebes." *Archaeometry* 8, 3–95.

Chadwick, John. 1958 and 1967. *The Decipherment of Linear B.* Cambridge.

Dow, Sterling. 1954. "Minoan Writing." *AJA* 58, 77–129, esp. 115ff.

Furumark, Arne. 1941. *The Mycenaean Pottery.* 2 vols. Stockholm.

————. 1950. "The Settlement at Ialysos and Aegean Prehistory c. 1550–1400 B.C." *Opuscula Archaeologica* 6, 150–271.

Hachmann, R. 1957. "Bronzezeitliche Bernsteinschieber." *Kommission für Bayrische Landgeschichte, Bayer. Akad. d. Wissenschaft* XXII, 1–36.

Helbig, Wolfgang. 1887. *Das homerische epos aus den denkmälern erläutert.* Leipzig.

Hood, Sinclair. 1962. Report to the British School at Athens, 6 February.

Kantor, Helene. 1947. *The Aegean and the Orient in the Second Millennium B.C.* Monograph #1, Archaeological Institute of America, Bloomington.

Lang, Mabel. 1969. *The Palace of Nestor.* Vol. 2. Princeton.

Marinatos, Spyridon. 1962. "The Minoan and Mycenaean Civilization and Its Influence on the Mediterranean and on Europe." *Atti del Congresso internazionale delle Scienze Prehistoriche e Protostoriche.* Rome.

Mylonas, George. 1964. "Grave Circle B of Mycenae." *Studies in Mediterranean Archaeology* VII. Lund.

————. 1973. *The Grave Circle B of Mycenae* (in Greek). Athens.

Nilsson, M. P. 1933. *Homer and Mycenae.* London.

Palmer, L. R. 1961 and 1965. *Mycenaeans and Minoans.* London.

————. 1963. "The Find-places of the Knossos Tablets." In *On the Knossos Tablets,* Oxford.

Parry, Milman. 1932. "Studies in the Epic Technique of Oral Verse-Making, II: The Homeric Language as the Languages of an Oral Poetry." *HSCP* 43, 1–50. Reprinted in Adam Parry, ed. 1971. *The Making of Homeric Verse: The Collected Papers of Milman Parry.* Oxford.

————. 1933. "Whole Formulaic Verses in Greek and Southslavic Heroic Song."
    TAPA 64, 179–197. Reprinted in Adam Parry, ed. 1971. *The Making of
    Homeric Verse: The Collected Papers of Milman Parry.* Oxford.
Pendlebury, J. D. S. 1939 and rpt. 1965. *The Archaeology of Crete: An Intro-
    duction.* London.
Persson, A. 1942. *The Religion of Greece in Prehistoric Times.* Los Angeles.
Platon, Nicholas, and Eva Touloupa. 1964. "Oriental Seals from the Palace of
    Cadmus: Unique Discoveries in Boeotian Thebes." *Illustrated London
    News,* 28 November, 859–861.
Reichel, Wolfgang. 1894. *Homerische Waffen.* Vienna.
Stubbings, Frank. 1951. *Mycenaean Pottery from the Levant.* Cambridge.
Sundwall, J. 1932a. "Minoischen Rechnungurkunden." *Soc. Scient. Fenn.,
    Comm. Hum. Litt.* 4.
————. 1932b. "Zu dem minoischen Währungssystem." *Mélanges Glotz* II,
    827ff.
————. 1936. "Altkretische Urkundenstudien." *Acta Acad. Abo., Humaniora*
    10, 2, 1–45.
Taylour, Lord William. 1958. *Mycenaean Pottery in Italy and Adjacent Areas.*
    Cambridge.
Tsountas, C., and J. Irving Manatt. 1897. *The Mycenaean Age.* Boston.
Van Andel, T. H., and C. Runnels. 1987. *Beyond the Acropolis: A Rural Greek
    Past.* Stanford.
Ventris, Michael, and John Chadwick. 1956 and 1973. *Documents in Myce-
    naean Greek.* Cambridge.
Wace, Alan. 1949. *Mycenae: An Archaeological History and Guide.* Princeton.
————. 1956. "Introduction" to Michael Ventris and John Chadwick, *Docu-
    ments in Mycenaean Greek.* Cambridge.

CHAPTER IX

Baillie, M. G. L., and M. A. Munro. 1988. "Irish Tree Rings, Santorini and
    Volcanic Dust Veils." *Nature* 332, 344–346.
Bartonek, Antonin. 1979. "Greek Dialects between 1000 and 300 B.C." *SMEA*
    20, 113–130.
Bass, George, Camal Pulak, Dominique Collon, and James Weinstein. 1989.
    "The Bronze Age Shipwreck at Ulu Burun: 1986 Campaign." *AJA* 93,
    1–29.
Baumbach, Lydia. 1987. "Linear B: Retrospect and Prospects." In J. T. Killen,
    J. L. Melena, J.-P. Olivier, *Studies in Mycenaean and Classical Greek
    Presented to John Chadwick,* Salamanca.
Bennett, Emmett Jr., and Jean-Pierre Olivier. 1973, 1976. *Pylos Tablets Tran-
    scribed,* I–II. Rome.

Bernal, Martin. 1987. *Black Athens: The Afroasiatic Roots of Classical Civiliza-tion.* Vol. 1. New Brunswick, N.J.

Betancourt, P. P. 1987. "Dating the Aegean Late Bronze Age with Radiocar-bon." *Archaeometry* 29, 45–49.

Chadwick, John, 1987. *Linear B and Related Scripts.* London and Berkeley.

Chadwick, John, J. T. Killen, J.-P. Olivier, Louis Godart, Anna Sacconi, and J. A. Sakellarakis. 1987. *The Knossos Tablets.* Rome.

Cherry, John. 1983. "Frogs Round the Pond: Perspectives on Current Archaeo-logical Survey Projects in the Mediterranean Region." In Keller and Rupp, *Archaeological Survey in the Mediterranean Area,* Oxford.

Clarke, David. 1968. *Analytical Archaeology.* London.

———. 1973. "Archaeology: The Loss of Innocence." *Antiquity* 47, 6–18.

Doumas, Christos. 1983. *Thera: Pompeii of the Ancient Aegean.* London.

Eretria: Ausgrabungen und Forschungen. Vols. 1–7. 1968–1985. London.

Galanopoulos, Angelis. 1981. *New Light on the Legend of Atlantis and the My-cenaean Decadence.* Athens.

Hammer, C. U., H. B. Clausen, and W. Dansgaard. 1980. "Greenland Ice Sheet Evidence of Post-glacial Volcanism and Its Climatic Impact." *Nature* 288, 230–235.

Higgins, Reynold. 1967. *Minoan and Mycenaean Art.* New York.

Hooker, J. T. 1979. *The Origin of the Linear B Script.* Salamanca.

Hope Simpson, Richard. 1981. *Mycenaean Greece.* Park Ridge, N.J.

Keller, D. R., and David W. Rupp. 1983. *Archaeological Survey in the Mediter-ranean Area.* Oxford.

Killen, John. Forthcoming. *A Mycenaean Industry.*

La Marche, V. C., Jr., and K. K. Hirschboeck. 1984. "Frost Rings in Trees as Records of Major Volcanic Eruptions." *Nature* 307, 121–126.

Lindgren, M. 1973. *The People of Pylos.* 2 vols. Uppsala.

Manning, Stuart. 1988. "The Bronze Age Eruption of Thera: Absolute Dating, Aegean Chronology and Mediterranean Cultural Interrelations." *Journal of Mediterranean Archaeology* 1, 17–82.

Marinatos, Spyridon. 1974. *Excavations at Thera.* VI. Athens. 44–57.

McDonald, William A. 1967. *Progress into the Past.* Bloomington and London.

———, and George R. Rapp, Jr., eds, 1972. *The Minnesota Messenia Expedi-tion: Reconstructing a Bronze Age Regional Environment.* Minneapolis.

———, William D. E. Coulson, and John Rosser, eds. 1983. *Excavations at Nichoria in Southwest Greece.* III. *Dark Age and Byzantine Occupation.* Minneapolis.

Melena, José. 1975. *Studies on Some Mycenaean Inscriptions from Knossos Dealing with Textiles.* Supplement to *Minos* 5. Salamanca.

Mitchell, S., and A. W. McNicoll, 1979. "Archaeology in Western and South-ern Asia Minor, 1971–78." *Archaeological Reports for 1978–79,* 59–90. London.

Mylonas, George. 1972. *The Cult Centre of Mycenae*. Athens.

Palaima, Thomas. 1984. "Scribal Organization and Palatial Activity." In T. G. Palaima and C. W. Shelmerdine, *Pylos Comes Alive*, 31–39. New York.

Pendlebury, J. D. S. 1939 and rpt. 1965. *The Archaeology of Crete: an Introduction*. London.

Pomerance, Leon. 1970. *The Final Collapse of Thera (Santorini), Studies in Mediterranean Archaeology* 26. Göteborg.

Popham, M. R. 1973. In *Archaeological Reports for 1972–73.* London.

———, L. H. Sackett, and P. G. Themelis, eds. 1980. *Lefkandi* 1–4. London.

Rapp, George R., Jr., and S. E. Aschenbrenner, eds. 1978. *Excavations at Nichoria in Southwest Greece*. I. *Site, Environs, and Techniques*. Minneapolis.

Renfrew, Colin. 1976. *Before Civilisation, the Radiocarbon Revolution and Prehistoric Europe*. Harmondsworth.

———. 1980. "The Great Tradition versus the Great Divide: Archaeology as Anthropology?" *AJA* 84, 287–298.

———. 1985. *The Archaeology of Cult. The Sanctuary at Phylakopi*. London.

———. 1987. *Archaeology and Language*. London.

———, and J. M. Wagstaff, eds. 1981. *An Island Polity: The Archaeology of Exploitation on Melos*. Cambridge.

Risch, Ernst. 1979. "Die Griechischen Dialekte im 2. Vorchristlichen Jahrtausend." *SMEA* 20, 91–110.

Rukowski, Bogdan. 1986. *The Cult Places of the Aegean*. New Haven.

Sakellariou, A. 1980. "The West House Miniature Frescoes." In C. Doumas, ed., *Thera and the Aegean World*, II, London, 147–154.

Schilardi, D. U. 1983. "The Decline of the Geometric Settlement of Koukounaries at Paros." In Robin Hägg, *The Greek Renaissance of the Eighth Century B.C.: Tradition and Innovation*. Stockholm.

———. 1984. "The LH IIIC Period at the Koukounaries Acropolis, Paros." In J. A. MacGillivray and R. L. N. Barber, *The Prehistoric Cyclades*, Edinburgh.

Shelmerdine, C. W. 1981. "Nichoria in Context: A Major Town in the Pylos Kingdom." *AJA* 85, 319–325.

Snodgrass, Anthony M. 1987. *An Archaeology of Greece: The Present State and Future Scope of a Discipline*. Berkeley and Los Angeles.

Starr, C. G. 1984. "Minoan Flower Lovers." In *The Minoan Thalassocracy: Myth and Reality*, ed. Robin Hägg and Nanno Marinatos, Stockholm.

Taylour, Lord William, 1970. "New Light on Mycenaean Religion." *Antiquity* 44, 270–280.

Tzedakis, Y., and L. Godart. Forthcoming. *Témoignages archéologiques et épigraphiques en crete occidentale du Minoen Ancien au Minoen Récent, (Incunabula Graeca)*. Rome.

Warren, P. M. 1980. Report on Knossos in *Archaeological Reports, 1979–80*. London.

Wunderlich, Hans Georg. 1974. *The Secret of Crete*. English translation by Richard Winston. New York.

CHAPTER X

Alsop, Joseph. 1964. *From the Silent Earth*. New York.

Bernal, Martin. 1987. *Black Athena: The Afroasiatic Roots of Classical Civilization*. Vol. I. New Brunswick, N.J.

Betancourt, Philip P. 1976. "The End of the Greek Bronze Age." *Antiquity* 50, 40–47.

Blegen, Carl. 1963. *Troy and the Trojans*. London.

Bloedow, Edmund F. 1986. "Schliemann on His Accusers." *Tyche* 1, 30–40.

———. 1987. "Mycenaean Fishing in Troubled Waters." *Echos du Monde Classique* 31, n.s. 6, 179–195.

———. 1988. "Schliemann on His Accusers II." *L'Antiquité Classique* 57, 5–30.

Buck, R. J. 1962. "The Minoan Thalassocracy Re-examined." *Historia* 11, 129–137.

Calder, William M., III, and David A. Traill, eds. 1986. *Myth, Scandal, and History: The Heinrich Schliemann Controversy and a First Edition of the Mycenaean Diary*. Detroit.

Carpenter, Rhys. 1962. *Folk Tale, Fiction and Saga in the Homeric Epics*. Berkeley and Los Angeles.

———. 1966. *Discontinuity in Greek Civilization*. Cambridge.

Caskey, John. 1964. "Greece, Crete and the Aegean Islands in the Early Bronze Age." In *The Cambridge Ancient History*[2]. Vol. 1, chap. xxvi(a). Cambridge.

Chadwick, John. 1963. "The Prehistory of the Greek Language." In *The Cambridge Ancient History*[2]. Vol. 2, chap. xxxix. Cambridge.

———. 1976a. *The Mycenaean World*. Cambridge.

———. 1976b. "Who Were the Dorians?" *Parola del Passato* 31, 103–117.

———. 1980. "The Mycenaean Social System." Paper presented to the annual meeting of the Association of Ancient Historians at the University of Washington.

Cherry, John. 1986. "Polities and Palaces: Some Problems in Minoan State Formation." In C. Renfrew and J. Cherry, eds., *Peer Polity Interaction and Socio-political Change*, Cambridge, 19–45.

———. 1987. "Modern Approaches to Ancient History." Lecture at the NEH Summer Institute, University of Washington.

Coldstream, Nicholas. 1977. *Geometric Greece*. London.

Davies, O. 1932–33. "The Ancient Tin Sources of Western Europe." *Proceedings, Belfast Natural History and Philosophical Society*, 41–51.

Desborough, V. R. d'A. 1964. *The Last Mycenaeans and Their Successors.* Oxford.

———. 1968. "History and Archaeology in the Last Century of the Mycenaean Age." *Atti e Memorie del 1° Congresso Internazionale di Micenologia,* 1073–1093. Rome.

———. 1972. *The Greek Dark Ages.* London.

Deshayes, J. 1966: *Argos, les Fouilles de la Deiras, Études Peloponnesiennes* 4.

Dickinson, O. T. P. K. 1977. *The Origins of Mycenaean Civilization, Studies in Mediterranean Archaeology* 49. Göteborg.

Döhl, Hartmut. 1981. *Heinrich Schliemann, Mythos und Ärgernis.* Munich and Lucerne.

Dow, Sterling. 1960. "The Greeks in the Bronze Age." *XIᵉ Congrès International des Sciences Historiques.* Stockholm.

———. 1968. "Literacy: The Palace Bureaucracies, The Dark Age, Homer." In *A Land Called Crete,* Smith College, 109–147.

Finley, M. I. 1964. "The Trojan War." *JHS* 84, 1–9.

Forsdyke, E. J. 1914. "The Pottery Called Minyan Ware." *JHS* 34, 126–156.

French, D. H. 1973. "Migrations and 'Minyan' Pottery in Western Anatolia and the Aegean." In R. A. Crossland and Ann Birchall, eds., *Bronze Age Migrations in the Aegean,* London.

Galanopoulos, A. 1981. *New Light on the Legend of Atlantis and the Mycenaean Decadence.* Athens.

Gray, D. 1954. "Homer and the Archaeologists." In M. Platnauer, ed., *Fifty Years of Classical Scholarship.* Oxford.

Gurney, O. R. 1961. *The Hittites.* Baltimore.

Guthrie, W. K. C. 1964. "The Religion and Mythology of the Greeks." In *The Cambridge Ancient History*². Vol. II, chap. xl. Cambridge.

Güterbock, Hans G. 1986. "Troy in Hittite Texts? Wilusa, Ahhiyawa, and Hittite History." In Machteld Mellink, ed., *Troy and the Trojan War,* Bryn Mawr, 33–44.

Hammond, N. G. L. 1967. "Tumulus-burial in Albania, the Grave Circles of Mycenae, and the Indo-Europeans." *BSA* 62, 77–105.

———. 1973. *Studies in Greek History,* Oxford, 1–25.

Hampe, Roland, and Erika Simon. 1980. *The Birth of Greek Art.* Oxford.

Haskell, Halford. 1984. "Pylos: Stirrup Jars and Their International Oil Trade." In T. Palaima and C. Shelmerdine, eds., *Pylos Comes Alive,* New York, 97–107.

Havelock, Eric A. 1982. *The Literate Revolution in Greece and Its Cultural Consequences.* Princeton.

Hood, M. S. F. 1965. " 'Last Palace' and 'Reoccupation' at Knossos." *Kadmos* 4, 16–44.

Hooker, J. T. 1976. *Mycenaean Greece.* London.

Huxley, George. 1961. *Crete and the Luwians.* Oxford.

Killen, John. 1985. "The Linear B Tablets and the Mycenaean Economy." In A.

Davies and Y. Duhoux, eds., *Linear B: A 1984 Survey,* Louvain-la-Neuve, 241–305.

Kirk, G. 1964. "The Homeric Poems as History." In *The Cambridge Ancient History*². Vol. II, chap. xxxix(b), Cambridge.

Marinatos, Sp. 1939. "The Volcanic Destruction of Minoan Crete." *Antiquity* 13, 429–39.

————. 1960. *Crete and Mycenae.* London.

McDonald, William A., and George R. Rapp, Jr., eds. 1972. *The Minnesota Messenia Expedition: Reconstructing a Bronze Age Regional Environment.* Minneapolis.

Mee, C. 1978. "Aegean Trade and Settlement in Anatolia in the Second Millennium B.C." *Anatolian Studies* 28, 121–155.

Muhly, James D. 1985. "Sources of Tin and the Beginnings of Bronze Metallurgy." *AJA* 89, 275–291.

Myres, Sir John. 1930. *Who Were the Greeks?* Berkeley.

Page, Denys. 1959 and 1963. *History and the Homeric Iliad.* Berkeley and Cambridge.

Palmer, L. R. 1961 and 1965. *Minoans and Mycenaeans.* London.

————. 1963. "The Find-places of the Knossos Tablets." In J. Boardman and L. Palmer, *On the Knossos Tablets,* Oxford.

Piggott, Stuart. 1965. *Ancient Europe.* Chicago.

Popham, Mervyn. 1987. "The Use of the Palace at Knossos at the Time of Its Destruction, c. 1400 B.C." In Robin Hägg and Nanno Marinatos, eds., *The Function of the Minoan Palaces,* Stockholm, 297–299.

Renfrew, Colin. 1979. "Systems Collapse as Social Transformation." In Renfrew and K. L. Cooke, eds., *Transformations, Mathematical Approaches to Culture Change,* New York, 481–506.

————. 1987. *Archaeology and Language.* London.

Sandars, N. K. 1978 and 1987. *The Sea Peoples: Warriors of the Ancient Mediterranean.* London.

Schachermeyr, Fritz. 1935. *Hethiter und Achäer.* Leipzig.

Severyns, A. 1960. *Grèce et Proche-Orient avant Homère.* Brussels.

Snodgrass, Anthony M. 1971. *The Dark Age of Greece.* Edinburgh.

————. 1980. *Archaic Greece: The Age of Experiment.* London.

————. 1987. *An Archaeology of Greece: The Present State and Future Scope of a Discipline.* Berkeley and Los Angeles.

Starr, Chester. 1955. "The Myth of the Minoan Thalassocracy." *Historia* 4, 282–291.

————. 1962. *The Origins of Greek Civilization.* London.

Stubbings, Frank. 1965. "The Rise of Mycenaean Civilization." In *The Cambridge Ancient History*². Vol. II, chap. xiv, Cambridge.

Taylour, Lord William. 1964 and rev. ed. 1983. *The Mycenaeans.* London.

Thomas, C. G. 1970. "A Mycenaean Hegemony? A Reconsideration." *JHS* 90, 184–192.

Todd, Joan Markley. 1985. Special issue of *Journal of Baltic Studies* 16: *Studies in Baltic Amber.*

Tsountas, C., and J. Irving Manatt. 1897. *The Mycenaean Age.* Boston.

Vansina, Jan. 1985. *Oral Tradition as History.* London and Nairobi.

Vermeule, Emily. 1964. *Greece in the Bronze Age.* Chicago.

———. 1968. "The Decline and End of Minoan and Mycenaean Culture." In *A Land Called Crete,* Smith College, 81–98.

———. 1986. " 'Priam's Castle Blazing': A Thousand Years of Trojan Memories." In Machteld Mellink, ed., *Troy and the Trojan War,* Bryn Mawr, 77–92.

Webster, T. B. L. 1958. *From Homer to Mycenae.* London.

Wood, Michael. 1985. *In Search of the Trojan War.* London.

Homeric References

(including a few later ancient sources)

1. *Il* 22. 147–152
2. *Il* 3. 145–242
3. *Il* 1. 584
4. *Il* 24. 228
5. Herodotus I. 94
6. *Il* 6. 316
7. *Od* 6. 303–309
8. Pausanias I. 16. 5–7
9. *Od* 3. 263
10. *Il* 18. 497–505
11. *Il* 1. 450
12. *Il* 10. 257–259
13. *Od* 4. 524–527; cf.
     Aeschylus' *Agamemnon*
     1–39
14. *Il* 7. 219
15. *Il* 11. 632–635
16. Herodotus VII. 102
17. Pausanias II. 25. 8
18. *Il* 2. 559–564.
19. *Od* 7. 87
20. *Od* 7. 81–106
21. Pausanias IX. 38. 2
22. *Od* 11. 284
23. *Il* 5. 446; 6. 88
24. *Il* 6. 248
25. *Il* 19. 38, 39
26. *Il* 23. 186, 187
27. *Il* 7. 85; 16. 456
28. *Il* 19. 212
29. *Od* 11. 23–36
30. *Il* 23. 28–34
31. *Il* 23. 175–177
32. *Od* 24. 227–231
33. *Od* 8. 337, 342
34. *Il* 7. 219–223
35. *Il* 3. 332
36. *Il* 1. 17
37. *Il* 10. 261–265
38. *Od* 21. 120–123, 420–423
39. Hesiod, *Shield* 139–317;
     cf. *Il* 18. 509–540
40. *Il* 6. 450–465
41. *Od* 19. 172–174
42. *Il* 18. 490–605
43. *Il* 18. 590–592
44. *Il* 2. 645–652
45. *Il* 4. 105–111
46. *Od* 12. 235, 236
47. *Il* 2. 494–759
48. *Od* 19. 172–174
49. *Od* 19. 18
50. *Il* 6. 243–246
51. *Il* 6. 247–250
52. *Od* 3. 387, 412–415
53. *Od* 6. 81, 82
54. *Od* 21. 1–14
55. Thucydides I. 4, 8
56. *Il* 10. 577
57. *Od* 3. 299–301; 4. 355
58. Diodorus IV. 76–79
59. *Od* 8. 256–268
60. Plutarch, *Moralia* 579A
61. *Il* 6. 168, 169
62. *Il* 23. 257–897
63. *Od* 8. 104–194

64. *Od* 2. 328
65. *Od* 3. 1 ff
66. Pausanias IV . 36. 2, 3
67. Strabo VIII. 3. 7
68. *Od* 15. 292–300
69. *Il* 2. 670–762
70. *Od* 3. 475–497
71. *Il* 11. 591–602
72. *Od* 19. 4–9
73. *Il* 18. 591
74. *Od* 19. 173, 174

75. *Od* 19. 226–231
76. *Od* 3. 165–179
77. *Od* 3. 1–486.
78. *Il* 2. 546, 547
79. *Il* 9. 149–153
80. *Il* 2. 286–288
81. *Il* 2. 204–206
82. Thucydides I. 12
83. *Il* 11. 690–693
84. *Il* 14. 405

Suggested Reading

The following list is a combination of the bibliography given in the first edition of *Progress into the Past* and certain publications that have appeared since 1967. The new items are intended to be useful for the interested general reader as well as specialists. The range of items is obviously representative, not exhaustive. In addition to the books mentioned below, the early volumes of *The Cambridge Ancient History* were revised in the late 1960s and 1970s; the third edition includes chapters by major scholars on various aspects of the Aegean Bronze Age. The American publication *Archaeology* is meant for a general readership. The *Illustrated London News* continues to feature accounts of archaeological discoveries. Early Greece is often the subject of articles in the *National Geographic* and *Scientific American*.

Alsop, J. 1964. *From the Silent Earth*. New York.
Barber, R. L. N. 1987. *The Cyclades in the Bronze Age*. London.
Blegen, Carl, with Marion Rawson. 1966. *The Palace of Nestor* 1. Princeton.
———, et al. 1973: *The Palace of Nestor* 3. Princeton.
Bowra, C. M. 1952. *Heroic Poetry*. London.
———. 1955. *Homer and His Forerunners*. Edinburgh.
———. 1972. *Homer*. London.
Chadwick, John. 1958 and 1967. *The Decipherment of Linear B*. Cambridge.
———. 1976. *The Mycenaean World*. Cambridge.
———. 1987. *Linear B and Related Scripts*. London and Berkeley.
Clarke, J. G. D. 1952. *Prehistoric Europe: The Economic Basis*. London.
Daniel, Glyn, and Colin Renfrew. 1988. *The Idea of Prehistory*, 2d ed. Edinburgh.
Desborough, V. R. d'A. 1964. *The Last Mycenaeans and Their Successors*. Oxford.
Evans, Joan. 1943. *Time and Chance: The Story of Arthur Evans and His Forebears*. London.
Fagan, Brian M. 1984. *In the Beginning: An Introduction to Archaeology*, 5th ed. Boston.
Finley, M. I. 1956. *The World of Odysseus*. London.
Glotz, G. 1925. *The Aegean Civilization*. New York.

Graham, J. W. 1962. *The Palaces of Crete*. Princeton.
Gray, D. 1968. "Homer and the Archaeologists." In M. Platnauer, ed., *Fifty Years (and Twelve) of Classical Scholarship*, 2d ed. Oxford.
Gurney, O. R. 1961. *The Hittites*, rev. ed. Baltimore.
Hampe, Roland, and Erika Simon. 1980. *The Birth of Greek Art*. Oxford.
Harding, A. R. 1984. *The Mycenaeans and Europe*. London and Orlando, Fla.
Havelock, Eric A. 1986. *The Muse Learns to Write: Reflections on Orality and Literacy from Antiquity to the Present*. New Haven and London.
Hood, Sinclair. 1978. *The Arts in Prehistoric Greece*. Harmondsworth and New York.
Hooker, J. T. 1976. *Mycenaean Greece*. London.
Hope Simpson, Richard. 1981. *Mycenaean Greece*. Park Ridge, N.J.
Horowitz, Sylvia L. 1981. *The Find of a Lifetime, Sir Arthur Evans and the Discovery of Knossos*. New York and London.
Hutchinson, R. W. 1962. *Prehistoric Crete*. Harmondsworth.
Kirk, G. 1962. *The Songs of Homer*. Cambridge.
Lang, Mabel. 1969. *The Palace of Nestor*, 2. Princeton.
Lord, A. 1960. *The Singer of Tales*. Cambridge, Mass.
Lorimer, H. L. 1950. *Homer and the Monuments*. London.
Luce, J. V. 1975. *Homer and the Heroic Age*. London.
Marinatos, S., and M. Hirmer. 1960. *Crete and Mycenae*. London.
Matz, F. 1962. *The Art of Crete and Early Greece*. London.
McDonald, William A., and George R. Rapp, Jr., eds. 1972. *The Minnesota Messenia Expedition: Reconstructing a Bronze Age Regional Environment*. Minneapolis.
Mellink, Machteld, ed. 1986. *Troy and the Trojan War*. Bryn Mawr.
Mylonas, George. 1966. *Mycenae and the Mycenaean Age*. Princeton.
Nilsson, M. P. 1932. *The Mycenaean Origin of Greek Mythology*. Berkeley.
————. 1933. *Homer and Mycenae*. London.
————. 1950. *The Minoan-Mycenaean Religion*, 2d ed. Lund.
Page, D. 1959 and 1963. *History and the Homeric Iliad*. Berkeley and Cambridge.
Palmer, L. R. 1961 and 1965. *Mycenaeans and Minoans*. London.
————. 1963. *The Interpretation of Mycenaean Texts*. Oxford.
Pendlebury, J. D. S. 1939 and rpt. 1965. *The Archaeology of Crete: An Introduction*. London.
Persson, A. 1942. *The Religion of Greece in Prehistoric Times*. Los Angeles.
Piggott, Stuart. 1959. *Approach to Archaeology*. Cambridge.
————. 1965. *Ancient Europe*. Chicago.
Renfrew, Colin. 1976. *Before Civilisation, the Radiocarbon Revolution and Prehistoric Europe*. Harmondsworth.
————. 1987. *Archaeology and Language*. London.
————, and P. Bahn. Forthcoming. *A Handbook of Archaeological Method*. London.

Samuel, A. E. 1966. *The Mycenaeans in History.* New York.

Schliemann, H. 1875. *Troy and Its Remains.* London.

————. 1878. *Mycenae: A Narrative of Researches.* London.

————. 1880. *Ilios: The City and Country of the Trojans.* London.

————. 1884. *Troja: Results of the Latest Researches.* London.

Schuchhardt, C. 1891. *Schliemann's Excavations: An Archaeological and Historical Study.* London.

Snodgrass, Anthony M. 1971. *The Dark Age of Greece.* Edinburgh.

————. 1987. *An Archaeology of Greece: The Present State and Future Scope of a Discipline.* Berkeley and Los Angeles.

Taylour, Lord William. 1983. *The Mycenaeans,* rev. ed. London.

Thomas, C. G., ed. 1977. *Homer's History: Mycenaean or Dark Age?,* rpt. Huntington, N.Y.

Tsountas, C., and J. Irving Manatt. 1897. *The Mycenaean Age.* Boston.

Ventris, M., and John Chadwick. 1956 and 1973. *Documents in Mycenaean Greek.* Cambridge.

Wace, Alan. 1949. *Mycenae: An Archaeological History and Guide.* Princeton.

————, and F. H. Stubbings. 1962. *A Companion to Homer.* London.

————, and C. Williams. 1962. *Mycenae Guide,* 2d ed. Meriden, Conn.

Webster, T. B. L. 1958. *From Mycenae to Homer.* London.

Wood, Michael. 1985. *In Search of the Trojan War.* London.

Heinrich Schliemann (1822–1890)

Arthur J. Evans (1851 – 1941)
Department of Antiquities, Ashmolean Museum, Oxford

Carl W. Blegen (1887–1971)
Published with permission of the University of Cincinnati

Michael Ventris (1922–1956)

Alan J. B. Wace (1879–1957)

Wilhelm Dörpfeld (1853–1940)

Christos Tsountas (1857–1934)

William A. McDonald

Glossary

absolute chronology   the determination that one object or grave or stratum can be assigned a specific date, at least within a quarter century

Achaean (Achaian)   one of Homer's names for the Greeks at Troy; now often used to denominate speakers of Greek (especially on the mainland) in the Late Bronze Age; also applied to the language of the Linear B tablets

adyton   isolated room in a temple, often used for the safekeeping of treasure and/or for particularly secret rites

Aegisthus   seducer of Clytemnestra in Agamemnon's absence at Troy who planned with her Agamemnon's murder on his return

Aeolic (Aeolian)   a major dialect of Greek (along with Ionic and Doric); spoken in historic times in east central Greece and on the islands and coast of northern Anatolia; had some effect on the language of Homeric epic

Agamemnon   king of Mycenae and leader of the Greek expedition against Troy

Ahhijawā   a political unit (*possibly* Achaea) with which Hittite kings were in diplomatic contact

alabastron   a low, closed vase, usually with three small handles, and probably used as a container for fine oil (Fig. 76)

amphora   a high, closed vase, probably used as a container for wine and water; the name literally means that it has two handles, but three are usually spaced around the shoulder (Fig. 75A)

amulet   an ornament or gem worn as a charm against ill luck

Anatolia   Asia Minor or modern Turkey; literally "the land where the sun rises" (*i.e.,* east to the Greeks)

arch   (see *corbelled arch*)

archaic   in Greek archaeology and history designates specifically the period from about mid-eighth until end sixth century B.C.

ashlar   wall construction in regular parallel horizontal courses; vertical joints are usually at approximate right angles (Fig. 82C)

Athena one of the major deities in Olympian pantheon; protecting goddess of Troy and Athens

bas-relief geometric or figured decoration sculpted in low relief on a flat surface

brachycephalic round-headed, *i.e.,* width of skull relatively great in proportion to length

Bügelkanne (see *stirrup jar*)

cartouche a stamped or incised identification on objects manufactured in Egypt specifying date and other information

Cassandra Trojan priestess and daughter of Priam; seized as Agamemnon's concubine after the capture of Troy and brought back with him to Mycenae where she (with her twin boys) was murdered by Clytemnestra and Aegisthus

celt stone hand ax, one of the earliest general-purpose tools made by Stone Age people

chamber tomb a communal or family tomb cut into the soft rock of a hillside and approached by an open corridor or dromos; *may* have been used by commoners as well as nobles (Figs. 39, 74)

chiton a shirt worn next to the upper body by men; made of wool or linen

chlaina a woolen mantle or cloak

cist grave dug in rock or earth very much as modern graves; sometimes lined with stone and covered; normally rectangular and meant for single burial

classical in Greek archaeology and (technically) in Greek history designates the period from the Persian invasions (490 B.C.) until the death of Alexander the Great (323 B.C.)

clerestory a higher central section of the flat roof of a large building; small windows in its sides would admit light and air and allow smoke to escape (Fig. 90)

close style a fussy but effective over-all decorative scheme, geometric and sometimes figured, on some LHIIIC vases (Fig. 86)

Clytemnestra unfaithful wife of Agamemnon

corbelled arch unlike the true arch (not used by the Mycenaeans), it is constructed by slightly overlapping each course of blocks in two parallel walls until the vault can be completed by wedging it securely with the final course (Fig. 37)

crater (see *krater*)

cross-dating (see *synchronism*)

cuirass   armor covering the neck and upper body (Fig. 95)

Cyclades (Cycladic)   a group of islands in the central Aegean, so named because they were thought to form a circle (cycle) around Delos; Bronze Age civilization in the islands is labeled Early, Middle, Late Cycladic

Cyclopean   fortifications, walls of buildings, etc., in which very large un-worked boulders are used, with smaller stones and clay mortar in the interstices; thought by the ancient Greeks to have been constructed by giants (Cyclopes)

cylix   (see *kylix*)

Danaos   cheated by his brother of his rightful share in Egyptian govern-ment, he migrated to the Argolid with his fifty daughters

depas amphikypellon   Homer's description of a two-handled drinking cup

dolichocephalic   long headed, *i.e.,* length of skull relatively great in pro-portion to width

Dorian invasion   the cause of the destruction of heroic (Mycenaean) civi-lization, according to later Greek tradition; supposedly a single over-whelming thrust from the north overland by speakers of the historic Doric dialect of Greek

Doric   a major dialect of Greek used in historic times in much of the Peloponnese as well as areas colonized from there; also applied to one of the three orders of classical Greek architecture with a somewhat simi-lar distribution

dromos   the "street" or approach to a tholos or chamber tomb; a long corridor, usually cut into a hill slope, open at the top and with its in-creasingly high walls ending at the doorway of the tomb proper (Figs. 39, 82)

Eileithyia   goddess who assists women in childbirth

Electra   daughter of Agamemnon and Clytemnestra

electrum   a natural alloy of gold and silver

Ephyraean ware   a class of pottery first identified by Blegen at Korakou (perhaps Homeric Ephyra = Corinth) (Fig. 72)

epigraphy   the scientific study of written records inscribed on stone, clay, metal, etc.

faience   colored glass paste, poured into molds; used for miniature sculpture, appliqué, beads, etc. (Fig. 62)

fibula (plural: *fibulae*)   ancestor of the safety pin, used in place of buttons to secure clothing (Fig. 99)

fillet   a decorative band to hold the hair in place

fresco   a technique of monumental painting by which the design is applied to wet plaster (*al fresco*)

geometric   decorative design, strictly speaking nonrepresentational, tending to neat repetitive patterns and motifs; used especially to designate the crisp and careful work of the Early Iron Age

glyptic   cutting, carving, sculpting miniature designs, particularly in hard stone, as for seals and gems (Fig. 68)

graffito (plural: *graffiti*)   writing (usually casual) on such surfaces as walls

granary class pottery   vase shapes typical of LHIIIC, with rather sparse, stylized and often careless decoration (Fig. 79)

grave circle   any circular construction in which burials are made; particularly the monumental structure (A) at Mycenae within which Schliemann discovered the Shaft Graves; and also the earlier structure (B) at Mycenae (Fig. 19)

gray Minyan pottery   distinctive, smooth, silvery fabric (with soapy feel) produced by reduction firing in the kiln; angular profiles with sharp transitions (perhaps copying metal shapes) and liking for ribbed stems (Fig. 69)

greaves   armor to protect shins

grid   a series of contiguous rectangles in which one arranges vertically and horizontally syllabic combinations of vowels and diphthongs used in a given language

griffin   hybrid animal combining the body of a lion with the head (and usually wings) of an eagle (Figs. 47, 92)

Halstatt   generic name for a distinctive iron-using culture extending over much of central and western Europe in the seventh and sixth centuries B.C.

Hector   son of Priam and the greatest warrior of Troy

Helladic   chronological term to designate mainland Greece (Hellas) in the Bronze Age

Hellenistic   chronological term to designate Greek culture in its widest penetration from the death of Alexander the Great (323) until the destruction of Corinth by the Romans (146 B.C.)

Herakleidai   the sons (or descendants) of Herakles; they were responsible, according to Greek tradition, for depredations on the Mycenaean kingdoms

Herodotus   a writer of the fifth century B.C. who incorporated in his *History* much legendary material about earlier events and customs (which he did not necessarily believe in full)

Hesiod a poet who lived slightly after Homer's time and who continued to use the epic form for new themes such as genealogies of gods and a handbook on agriculture

hieroglyphics a highly developed and standardized form of picture writing; literally "priestly incising"

Hittites a people speaking a basically Indo-European language who invaded Anatolia at the beginning of the second millennium and controlled most of it until about 1200 B.C.

Homeric Question Who was "Homer"? When and where did he live? Did he compose one or both of the epic poems attributed to him? Were the stories invented by him or are the poems the culmination of a long oral tradition?

Hyksos an intrusive minority who controlled Egypt in the earlier second millennium and were expelled by Ahmose, founder of the eighteenth dynasty

ideogram a stylized picture used in early writing systems (Fig. 88)

Idomeneus king of Knossos in Crete and leader of the Cretan contingent of Greek forces in the Trojan War

Ilion (Ilios) alternate name for Troy

inhumation placing a corpse in a grave or tomb (as opposed to reducing it to ashes, *i.e.,* cremation)

Ionic a major dialect of Greek used in historical times in Attica and neighboring areas as well as in regions colonized by these states; possibly a descendant of the earliest major Indo-European dialect to be spoken in Greece

Jason leader of the Argonauts from Iolkos who sailed to Cholcis in the Black Sea to carry off the Golden Fleece

Kadmos a native of Phoenicia who, according to tradition, occupied Thebes and introduced "Phoenician letters" to Greece

Kamares a cave sanctuary in central Crete from which the first samples of a distinctive type of Minoan pottery were first recovered; by extension sometimes used to designate the period of the early palaces when this pottery was in use

Keftiu a name used by the Egyptians to designate the homeland of people who appear in eighteenth dynasty tomb paintings and bear gifts, some of which are Aegean in appearance; usually assumed to be Crete

koinê the common or shared culture so noticeable throughout the whole Aegean area in the later Mycenaean Age; also applied to a form of Greek language widely used in Hellenistic and Roman times

krater a large open bowl for mixing wine with water (Fig. 75C) *kylix*   a stemmed two-handled goblet resembling a champagne glass (Figs. 56, 72)

larnax   clay coffin or sarcophagos, usually with painted decoration; used in Crete but not in mainland Greece

light-well   rectangular shaft that provided light and circulation of air for interior living units in large Minoan buildings (Fig. 54B)

Linear A   syllabic writing system developed by the Minoans out of the earlier hieroglyphics; used throughout Crete in the early palaces and probably continuing everywhere except at Knossos until at least the fifteenth century (Fig. 63)

Linear B   modified version of Linear A adapted to writing Greek; so far certified in Crete only at Knossos but apparently widespread at mainland capitals (Fig. 88)

Lion Gate   the main gate in the Mycenae fortifications; so named for the heraldic lionesses sculpted on the relieving triangle above the lintel (Fig. 15)

liparite   shiny volcanic stone from the Lipari islands; flakes easily and was used for making sharp blades, etc.

loomweight   artefact of clay or stone, usually conical and pierced vertically, used to exert desired tension on vertical threads suspended from the loom; apparently some previously so categorized are really buttons

lustral area   a small "room" (possibly for bathing) sunk below level of surrounding floors and approached by stairs in Minoan palaces

Luwian   an early Indo-European language used in western Anatolia in the second millennium; believed by some scholars to have been spoken also in Crete

Lydian ware   Schliemann's designation of a very distinctive class of pottery in the sixth level at Troy; later equated with gray Minyan (Fig. 10)

magazines   long, narrow basement storage rooms typical of Minoan palaces (Fig. 61)

matt-painted pottery   basically MH vase shapes in light-colored clay on which rather simple geometric decoration is applied in a dark, dull (*i.e.,* matt) paint (Fig. 70)

megaron (plural: *megara*)   Homeric term for king's palace, or specifically the throne room; in general a relatively long and narrow architectural unit consisting of (columned) porch and main living room with hearth; often a third room lies in front of or (less commonly) behind living room (Fig. 54A, C)

Menelaos   king of Sparta and brother of Agamemnon

Minos   generic (probably) name for the king of Knossos in Crete

Minotaur hybrid monster (literally "Minos-bull") said to have inhabited the labyrinth at Knossos and to have been killed by Theseus

Minoan coined by Evans to designate the culture of Bronze Age Crete and used as the basic terminology for his chronological system

Minyan (see *gray, yellow*) coined by Schliemann to designate a kind of pottery he first recognized at Orchomenos, the home of the legendary king Minyas

Mycenaean (Mykenaian) adjective derived from Mycenae (Mykenai) and originally designating culture traits first recognized there; now regularly denominates the Late Bronze Age culture of south and central Greece as well as its wide extension in the Aegean area

naos Greek term for "temple"; more specifically the main room in which the statue of the deity was located

Near East in general the countries bordering the east end of the Mediterranean from Anatolia on the north through Syria to Egypt; more vaguely may include Mesopotamia

Neleus Nestor's father, who came from Iolkos in Thessaly and founded a kingdom in Messenia with capital at Pylos

neolithic the "new stone age" distinguished by food production and domestication of animals; about 6000–3000 B.C. in Greece

Nestor son of Neleus and his successor as king of Pylos; leader of the Pylian contingent in the Trojan War

niello a complicated technique of "metal painting" whereby geometric and figured designs in various metals are inset on a metal (usually bronze) background (Fig. 30)

obsidian a fine-grained volcanic stone used for small, sharp blades; the most common color is a shiny black; the Aegean supply seems to have come mainly from Phylakopi on the island of Melos

Odysseus king of the island of Ithaka and hero of Homer's *Odyssey*

ogival canopy a distinctive decorative motif, so named by Evans (Fig. 76)

palace style pottery rather "monumental" style both in size of vases and in decorative schemes; found in the "final" palace at Knossos and common in mainland tholoi (Fig. 59)

Palladium the primitive statue of Athena that was particularly sacred to the Trojans

Palynology a branch of science dealing with pollen and spores

Patrokles (Patroclus) Achilles' close friend who was killed by Hector

Pausanias a learned "tourist" of the second century A.D. who wrote a lengthy account of his travels in Greece, noting buildings, monuments and the legends connected with them

Pelopid dynasty   a line of kings at Mycenae beginning with Atreus, father of Agamemnon; Atreus was descended from the legendary Pelops

Peloponnese   literally "island of Pelops"; the whole of southern Greece below the Isthmus of Corinth

peplos   a sewn garment or dress of linen or fine wool worn by women on the mainland

peristyle   columned porches on all four sides of an open court

Perseid dynasty   a line of kings at Mycenae beginning with the legendary Perseus and ending with Eurystheus, who was succeeded by Atreus (see *Pelopid dynasty*)

pilgrim flask   a "drum-shaped" water container fairly common in the eastern Aegean and borrowed from the Near East (Fig. 85)

pithos (plural: *pithoi*)   large terra-cotta storage jars for both liquids and solids (Fig. 7)

Poseidon   brother of Zeus and reputed grandfather of Nestor; patron deity of Pylos; god of the sea and lord of earthquakes

prehistory   all stages in the development of a culture before the availability of written documents that can be deciphered

Priam   aged king of Troy at the time of the Greek attack

primary burial   the original burial of a body in a prepared grave

pronaos   technical name for the porch in front of the main room of a temple (see *naos*)

propylon (plural: *propylaea*)   a columned gateway into a fortified area; the plural is used for a particularly monumental plan with columns both inside and outside the entrance

protogeometric   the earliest culture stage in the Iron Age; roughly the tenth century B.C.

provenience (provenance)   original geographical source from which an object or custom derives

relative chronology   determining that one object or burial or stratum is younger or older than another

relieving triangle   the triangular space above the lintel of monumental entrances; designed to lighten weight on center of lintel; often filled with a slab bearing bas-reliefs (Fig. 15)

repoussé   a technique of relief sculpture in metal whereby the designs or figures are hammered out from the inside; details may be added on the outside by engraving (Fig. 40) *rhyton* a term used for two types of vessel, the one conical (Fig. 43), the other in the shape of an animal head (Fig. 24)

sauceboat a vessel with a handle at one side and a spout (often quite long) at the other; distinctive shape of the Early Helladic period (Fig. 5)

Scaean Gate the major entrance in the walls of Troy, according to Homer

scarab Egyptian sealstone carved in the shape of a beetle

Sea People a motley horde of warriors from the middle Mediterranean and probably beyond to the north and west; they attacked the settled civilizations of the Near East (and possibly Greece) in the thirteenth and twelfth centuries B.C.

seal a small signet (usually of stone) and decorated with a distinctive pattern; when pressed on clay or other soft substance, the impression signified ownership or endorsement

sealing the impression of a seal (Fig. 68)

secondary burial the removal of the bones (and sometimes the funeral offerings) of a previously buried body to another place

sequence dating (seriation) the arrangement of a series of artefacts of the same basic type in the order of their progressive development

shaft grave essentially a large, deep, cist grave in which several burials were made at different times; typically lined with stone walls and roofed over before the earth is filled in; perhaps marked by a low mound, a gravestone and a low circular wall (Fig. 29)

spindle whorl an artefact of terra-cotta or stone, pierced vertically; used to form tight threads from individual fibers; often difficult to distinguish from loomweight or button

steatite a soft stone, usually black but occasionally green, which is shaped easily and often decorated with bas-relief

stela (*stele;* plural: *stelae, stelai*) a stone grave marker or tombstone, usually with fairly flat front and back surfaces and sometimes decorated with bas-relief (Fig. 18)

stemmed goblet (see *kylix*)

stirrup jar a closed terra-cotta container for shipping fine oil; at the top two small handles join a false spout or neck, while the real spout is on the shoulder (Fig. 45)

Strabo a writer on geography who lived about the time of Christ; his book describes most of the Roman Empire

stratigraphy the various techniques by which successive strata (singular: stratum) are identified; in archaeology the reference is to the layers of a habitation site or other deposits of man-made debris

stylistics   (see *sequence dating*)

sub-Mycenaean   the final impoverished phase of Mycenaean culture, covering roughly the eleventh century

syllabary   a series of symbols or stylized ideograms used to write syllabically, *i.e.,* one symbol for each syllable of a word

synchronism   a situation where it is possible to associate an artefact or stratum or closed tomb group (possibly dated absolutely) at one site or in one culture with an artefact or stratum or closed tomb group in another (possibly undated previously)

Telemachos   son of Odysseus; he traveled from Ithaka to mainland Greece, according to Homer, in search of his father

Temple Repository   a cache of objects, many of faience and most, if not all, with religious connection, found by Evans at Knossos; some of the sculpture represents Minoan art at its acme (Fig. 62)

temenos   a plot (literally "cut") of land set aside for the use of a king, god, etc

Terramara (plural: *Terramare*)   Early Bronze culture of eastern Po valley; named for habitations resembling "lake dwellings on land"; perhaps introducers of bronze-working to Italy from central Europe

thalassocracy   "rule of the sea"; according to a Greek tradition as recorded by Thucydides and others, King Minos of Knossos had once controlled the whole eastern Mediterranean with his fleet

Theatral Area   a series of seats (L-shaped at Knossos) closely connected with Minoan palaces (Fig. 64)

Theseus   son of Erechtheus; prince and later king of Athens; according to tradition, he insisted on joining the Athenian "tribute" of chosen young men and women sent to Knossos; with the help of the Cretan princess Ariadne, he killed the Minotaur in the labyrinth and freed Athens from her subjugation

Thetis   a sea nymph; wife of Peleus and mother of Achilles

tholos (plural: *tholoi*)   the term is used by Homer to designate a round building; it is applied in modern times to the great round royal tombs scattered throughout Mycenaean Greece in the LH period; usually the dromos is cut into a side hill and the circular tomb chamber is lined with stone in the shape of a dome that protrudes above ground; the dome was covered with a mound, or tumulus, on the apex of which there may have been a stela or marker (Fig. 38)

Thucydides   the most "scientific" of Greek historians; he lived at Athens in the fifth century B.C. and introduced his *History of the Peloponnesian War* with a reconstruction (often called the "archaeology") of conditions in Greece in earlier times *treasury*   the term applied by Pausanias (and often since) to the tholos tombs; no doubt originated from the discovery of one from which robbers had not carried off the precious grave goods

triglyph-metope frieze   the characteristic band of decoration above the columns and architrave of a classical temple of the Doric order; its origin is probably to be seen as a decorative design used in monumental buildings of the Mycenaean period (Fig. 32)

tumulus   an artificial mound heaped up over a tomb or other revered monument

typology   (see *sequence dating*)

Ulysses   (see *Odysseus*)

Warrior Vase   a LHIIIC krater preserving perhaps the most important example of Mycenaean painting; most of the fragments were found by Schliemann in a house near the Grave Circle, although additional pieces have since been recovered (Fig. 20)

Warrior Graves   found by Evans at Knossos and closely connected with the LMII period just before the "final" destruction

whorl   (see *spindle whorl*)

xoanon   primitive wooden statue (ordinarily of a deity)

yellow Minyan pottery   undecorated MH vessels imitating the shapes of gray Minyan pottery; the fabric is often extremely fine and the surface is covered with an excellent slip of dilute clay; Mycenaean pottery consists essentially of Minoan and native decorative motifs applied in a lustrous paint to this fabric (Fig. 71)

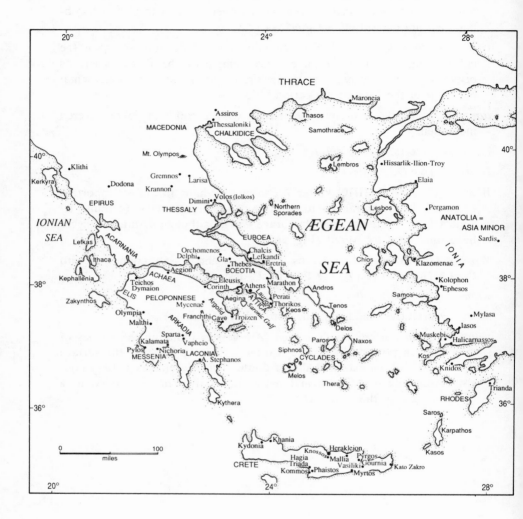

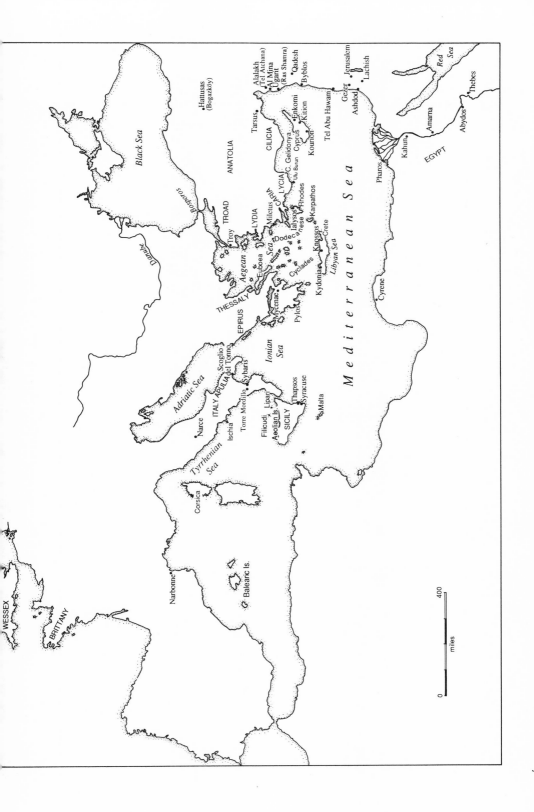

Red Sea

Black Sea

Hattusas
(Bogazköy)

Alalakh
(Tel Achana)
Al Mina
(Ras Shamra)
Ugarit
Qadesh
Byblos
Gezer
Jerusalem
Lachish
Tarsus
CILICIA
Enkomi
Kition
Cyprus
Kourion
Tel Abu Hawam
Ashdod
Amarna
Thebes
Abydos
Kahun
EGYPT
Pharos

ANATOLIA

Bosphorus

Danube

Troy
TROAD
LYDIA
Miletus
CARIA
LYCIA
C. Gelidonya
Ulu Burun
Rhodes
Ialysos
Dodeca
nese
Karpathos
Knossos
Crete
Kydonia
Libyan Sea
Cyrene

Aegean Sea
Euboea
Cyclades
THESSALY
Mycenae
Pylos
EPIRUS

Mediterranean Sea

Ionian Sea

Adriatic Sea

Scoglio
del Tonno
ITALY
APULIA
Sybaris
Thapsos
Syracuse
Malta
Torre Mordillo
Filicudi
Lipari
Aeolian Is.
SICILY
Ischia
Narce
Tyrrhenian Sea

Corsica

Balearic Is.

Narbonne

WESSEX

BRITTANY

0   400
miles

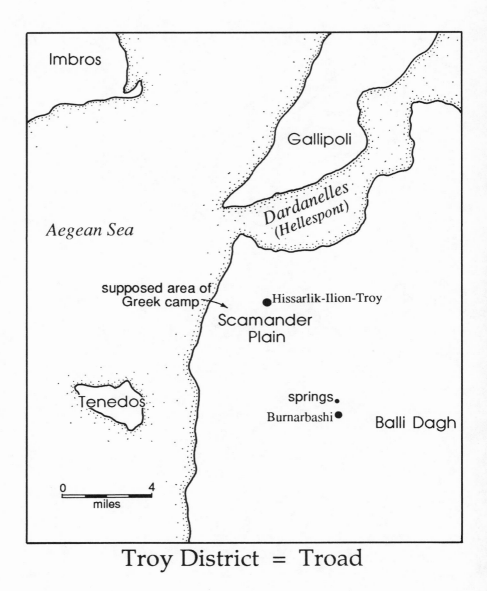

Imbros

Gallipoli

Aegean Sea

Dardanelles
(Hellespont)

supposed area of
Greek camp

●Hissarlik-Ilion-Troy

Scamander
Plain

springs●

Burnarbashi●

Balli Dagh

Tenedos

0   4

miles

Troy District = Troad

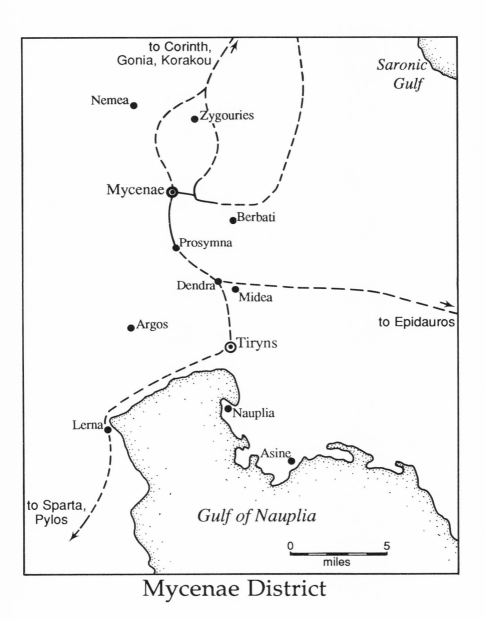

to Corinth,
Gonia, Korakou

Saronic
Gulf

Nemea

Zygouries

Mycenae

Berbati

Prosymna

Dendra

Midea

Argos

Tiryns

to Epidauros

Lerna

Nauplia

Asine

to Sparta,
Pylos

Gulf of Nauplia

0   5
miles

Mycenae District

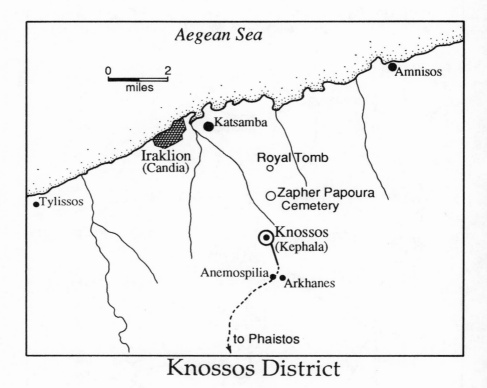

Aegean Sea

0 — 2
miles

• Amnisos

• Katsamba

Iraklion
(Candia)

Royal Tomb
○

○ Zapher Papoura
Cemetery

• Tylissos

◉ Knossos
(Kephala)

Anemospilia • • Arkhanes

to Phaistos

Knossos District

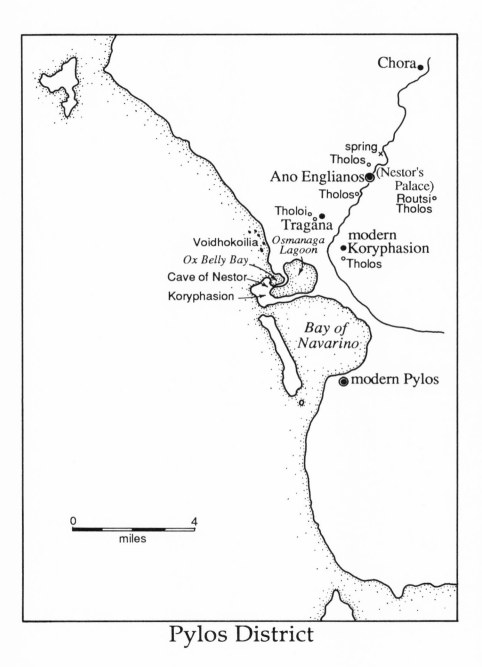

Chora

spring
Tholos
Ano Englianos (Nestor's
Palace)
Tholos
Routsi
Tholos

Tholoi
Tragana

Voidhokoilia

*Osmanaga
Lagoon*

modern
Koryphasion
°Tholos

Ox Belly Bay
Cave of Nestor
Koryphasion

*Bay of
Navarino*

modern Pylos

0   4
miles

Pylos District

INDEX

new chronological table   376

handmade pottery 451

Qadesh 1275 - 443